Capital and Countryside in Japan, 300–1180

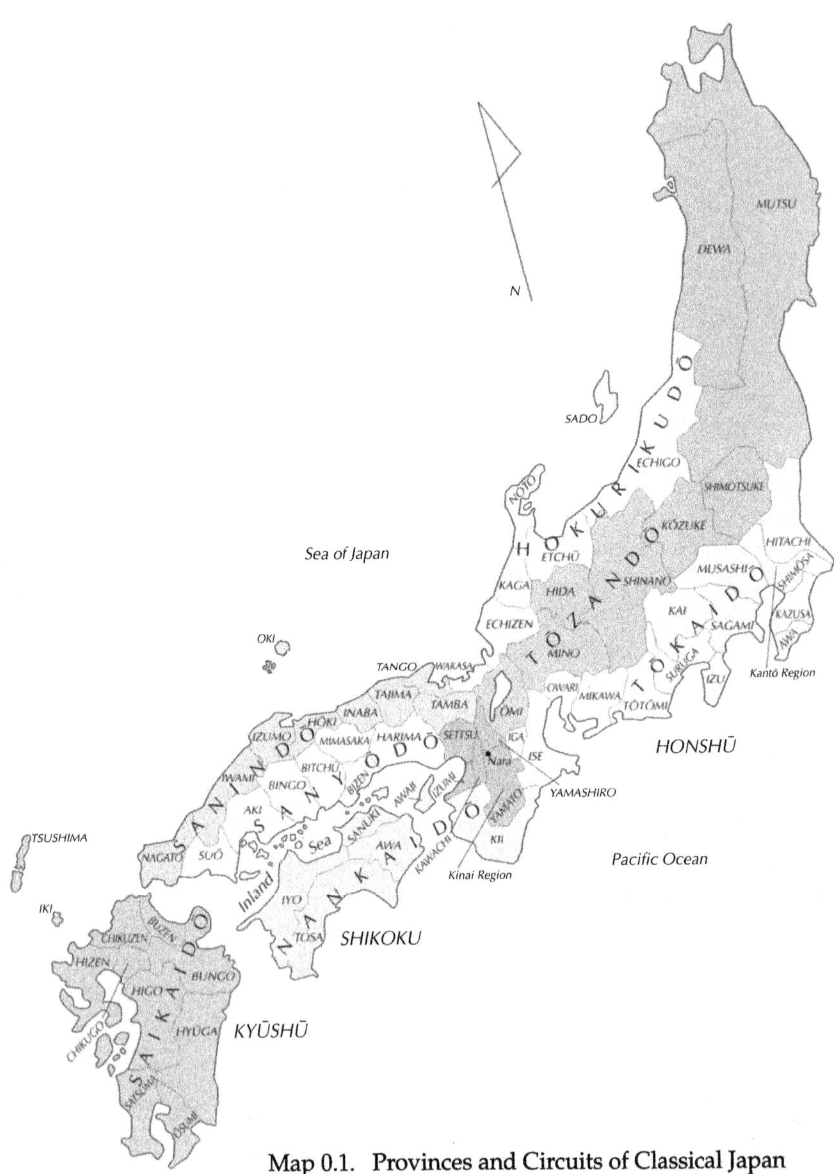

Map 0.1. Provinces and Circuits of Classical Japan

Capital and Countryside in Japan, 300–1180

Japanese Historians in English

EDITED BY JOAN R. PIGGOTT

The Cornell East Asia Series is published by the Cornell University East Asia Program (distinct from Cornell University Press). We publish affordably priced books on a variety of scholarly topics relating to East Asia as a service to the academic community and the general public. Standing orders, which provide for automatic notification and invoicing of each title in the series upon publication, are accepted.

If after review by internal and external readers a manuscript is accepted for publication, it is published on the basis of camera-ready copy provided by the volume author. Each author is thus responsible for any necessary copy-editing and for manuscript formatting. Address submission inquiries to CEAS Editorial Board, East Asia Program, Cornell University, Ithaca, New York 14853-7601.

Number 129 in the Cornell East Asia Series

ISSN 1050-2955
ISBN-13: 978-1-885445-39-1 hc / ISBN-10: 1-885445-39-3 hc
ISBN-13: 978-1-885445-29-2 pb / ISBN-10: 1-885445-29-6 pb
Library of Congress Control Number: 2005936920

24 23 22 21 20 19 18 17 16 15 14 13 12 11 10 09 06 9 8 7 6 5 4 3 2 1

Contents

Illustrations

Figures

Maps

TABLES

Introduction

JOAN R. PIGGOTT

AN IMPORTANT CONCERN for historians is the changing nature of relations between capital and countryside, and the impact of such changes on political, social, cultural, and economic integration over time. Geographically speaking, the topography of the Japanese archipelago is profoundly segmenting—80 percent of the land is mountainous, and its coastal plains, focal points for agrarian developments and population growth, are widely dispersed. And yet historians generally argue that from protohistory onward, the realm of Wa, which came to be known as Nihon toward the end of the seventh century, became increasingly integrated under the leadership of the Heavenly Sovereign's (*tennō*'s) court in mid-Honshū during Nara and Heian times. This collection of fourteen essays, each one rendered from the Japanese by an American researcher who particularly admires its historiographical contribution, focuses on the nature of bonds and relationships that linked capital and countryside from approximately 300 to 1180.

The field of premodern Japanese history—the history of Japan before the founding of the Tokugawa shogunate—is still young in the West. It was only in 1966 that John Whitney Hall's *Government and Local Power in Japan, 500 to 1700* made it possible for English readers to begin to think in significant detail about the myriad ways the *tennō*'s court presided over its realm, how capital and provinces were bonded by practices of law and administration, clientage relations, land tenurial practices, and a host of other means. A series of conference volumes subsequently opened the field to English readers more broadly, but the number of researchers and publications exploring Japan's early history has remained few. Although an increasing number of literary treasures dating from the Nara (710–784) and Heian (794–1180) periods have been translated into English, the historical research needed to contextualize that body of literature remains thin. That is one reason why many of us have hoped to supplement this literature with translations of Japanese scholarship.

With this in mind, some years ago I asked colleagues to prepare annotated translations of particularly useful essays on center-periphery relations between 300 and 1200. The researchers were to select essays to which they frequently returned, and which are still cited frequently in contemporary scholarship. The project excited significant interest and expanded somewhat beyond the original plan, and it has taken rather too long to reach publication. I am nevertheless pleased with the outcome. The essays that appear in this volume represent a half-century of important historical research. Each study opens up abundant new perspectives in terms of issues, approaches, styles, and sources. I am particularly pleased that work by masters such as Ishimoda Shō and Toda Yoshimi, both deceased, appears here in English for the first time. My expectation is that this collection represents just a beginning, and that in future much more research by Japanese scholars concerning premodern Japan will be become available in English and other foreign languages, thereby bringing the history of the archipelago into world history.

We chose our theme—relations between center and periphery, capital and countryside—with the conscious desire to "decenter" classical Japan, to move away from royal metropoles and shine more light on conditions in the countryside. When John Whitney Hall moved his story back and forth between the royal capitals of middle Honshū and Bizen Province on the Inland Sea in his *Government and Local Power,* he successfully demonstrated the critical importance of both ends of the geographical spectrum for comprehending the development of political institutions and their social environment. Here we expand on Hall's example to explore how other factors besides administrative and tenurial practices, including cultural diffusion, colonization, travel, transport, patronage, acculturation, and religious developments all contributed to integrating capital and countryside more closely through late Heian times.

Why focus on the particular time span between 300 and 1180? Aside from the fact that this time frame has been neglected by historians outside Japan, another reason is that these years represent key turning points in the history of state formation and realm integration. In that regard, we begin the volume with archaeologist-historian Tsude Hiroshi's radical hypothesis that the "round keyhole hierarchy" of the third through sixth centuries—not Chinese-style capitals and provincial headquarters of the late seventh and eighth centuries—should be considered visible evidence of Japan's earliest state formation process. Later in the volume comes Ishimoda Shō's famous argument that Japan's distinct transition from classical to medieval was based on a synthesis of divergent urban and rural structures fashioned by local land openers, who subsequently became prime movers in medieval society. Other essays in the volume demonstrate how Japanese researchers have utilized the evidence of bronze mirrors, remains of circuit highways and provincial headquarters, local legends and placenames, handbooks of correspondence, and a huge archive of records and documents brushed on paper and wood to tease out clues to official and unofficial networks of patronage and communication that organized and integrated the *tennō*'s realm up to the 1180s, when civil war led to the establishment of the first warrior government, Minamoto Yoritomo's Kamakura Bakufu. The rise of what recent historians in the West have called a "dual polity"—a power-sharing arrangement between the *tennō*'s court and that *bakufu*—altered radically the circumstances of the *tennō*-centered past.[1]

In a very real sense these essays have been not translated—rather, they have been "interpreted" from the Japanese. Producing the English interpretations here has necessitated intense encounters between scholar-interpreters and the original Japanese texts. The results have convinced us all that only those well versed in the historical subject matter can do such work, which frequently necessitates additional research and, whenever possible, consultation with the original author. The interpreters' primary objective has been to communicate meaning. In some cases, an interpreter has chosen to abridge the original, to abstract it, or to transpose parts of an argument. To maximize readability and comprehensibility for nonspecialist readers, each interpreter has added contextualizing and annotative commentary in the introduction or in accompanying notes, maps, illustrations, and charts. The original essays show a variation in citation styles used by the authors, as prevailing citation styles have changed appreciably over time. Scholar-interpreters have endeavored to fill in the resulting gaps, although some remain.

In a recently published essay somewhat playfully titled "Troubles with Naming," I reflected on the difficulties one encounters when rendering given Japanese historical terms or concepts into English.[2] Such "naming" is of maximum importance, because it deeply structures the reader's comprehension of the Japanese referent. To give one example, in my own work I have had to wrestle with how best to translate the monarch's title, *tennō*, into English. I could have retained the traditional English translation, "emperor," or I could have used a literal translation of the Chinese characters, "heavenly sovereign." In the end, however, I decided to use the original Japanese, *tennō*, because I find "emperor" to be fully at odds with the sacerdotal and ritual character of Japanese kingship, and other alternatives, including "heavenly sovereign," clumsy.[3]

In this volume we have encountered many such troubles with naming. A prime example is the glossing of the Japanese periodizing concept, *kodai* (literally, "old epoch"). To a Japanese historian, *kodai* denotes the period before the medieval age (*chūsei*), and it is typically associated with the polity and society of the Chinese-style *ritsuryō* codes promulgated at the turn of the eighth century. In English the term *kodai* has often been glossed either as "ancient age" or as "antiquity." In this volume, however, we translate it as the "classical age," because it was the epoch when the basic structures of Japanese civilization—courtly culture and society, Chinese-style codes, the *tennō*, a bureaucratic officialdom, the provincial structure, and the acculturation of other Chinese forms—were set in place.[4] Emerging from a protohistoric past for which archaeology and myth-history provide the best evidence, our "classical age" includes the Nara and Heian periods, during which, however much they changed, *kodai* structures continued to wield significant influence. As for other troubles with naming encountered by contributors to this essay collection, the extensive glossary at the end of the volume and the annotated list of sources attests to battles fought and at least tentatively resolved.

Since the objective here has been to expand the discussion concerning relations between capital and countryside from 300 to 1180, a sketch of the current wisdom in the English historiography provides the best framework for reading and reflecting on the fourteen essays that follow. So in a brief overview below I turn to the work of six scholars—Gina Barnes, Bruce Batten, Cornelius Kiley, Thomas Keirstead, Mikael Adolphson, and myself—who have laid the groundwork to which the essays here contribute.

In her pioneering study *Protohistoric Yamato*, Gina Barnes describes how peripheral societies on the Korean Peninsula and on the Japanese archipelago constituted "peer polities" that developed in response to supraregional trade

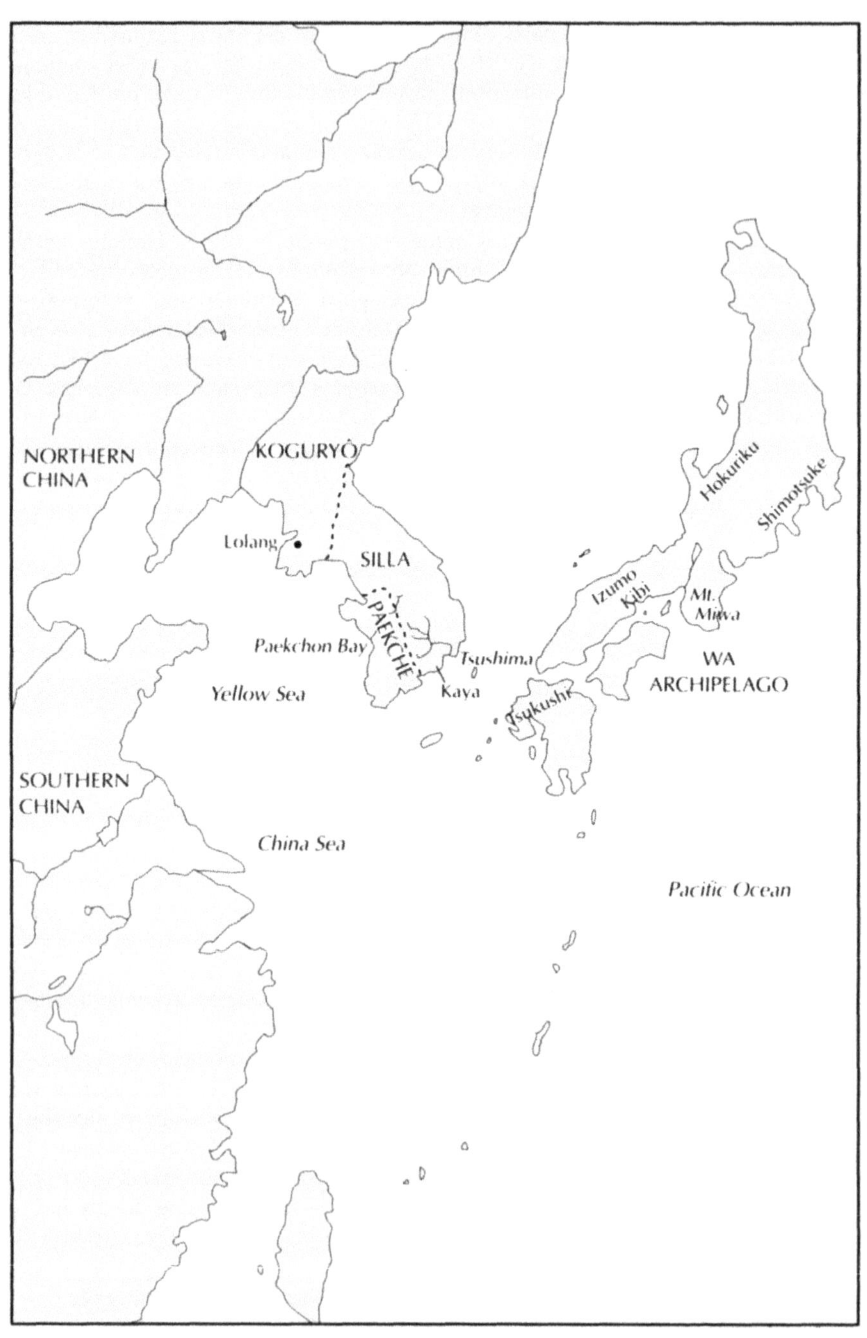

Map 0.2. Wa, in the China Sea Sphere

between points on a complex map of chiefly and confederate relations within the China Sea sphere. In the later third and fourth centuries C.E., the earliest round keyhole tombs in the vicinity of Mount Miwa (near present-day Sakurai City, Nara Prefecture) marked a supraregional paramount's center, the cultural development of which influenced formation of other chiefdoms on its periphery, in regions such as Kibi, Tsukushi, Izumo, Shimotsuke, and Hokuriku (see Map 0.2):

> A domestic and international trading network contributed to the homogenisation of Yayoi elite material culture, creating a pan-regional chiefly culture manifested by keyhole tombs, stone bracelets, bronze mirrors, cylindrical beads, curved comma jewels, ceramic funerary jars and stands.[5]

Barnes therefore emphasizes the importance of trade and cultural diffusion that linked multiple tiers of centers and peripheries at different levels of cultural development.

Moving ahead to the eighth century, in my own work I have identified a "*ritsuryō* process" by which three hierarchies codified by *ritsuryō* law progressively integrated the early eighth-century *tennō*-centered polity. The hierarchy of officialdom incorporated all chiefly elites in the realm; the hierarchy of central places administered the *tennō*'s realm; and a tiered network of ritual centers saw realm-protecting liturgies performed in accord with the *tennō*'s command. Since Chinese-style *ritsuryō* codified preexisting relationships between chiefly elites across the realm, the codes can be seen to have represented a negotiated settlement among those elites, both in the capital and in districts across the archipelago. And although by T'ang times (late sixth through ninth centuries) in China the bureaucracy of the Son of Heaven ruled over a more radial (i.e., centralized) polity, the eighth-century *tennō* of Nihon ruled over a more segmented polity as apical ordinator, ritual coordinator, and prime diplomat. Nonetheless, systems of communication and exchange between the *tennō*'s court and chieftains in the hinterland were working to increase the preeminence of the *tennō* as civilizer, lawgiver, realm-protector, and Buddhist savior-king:

> While the early eighth-century polity remained distinctly segmentary and discontinuous in administrative hierarchy, written codes and the hierarchical networks routinized by the codes opened an increasing number of channels of communication between center and periphery and fostered the development of new cooperative procedures of administration, in which central appointees and hereditary local officials worked side-by-side. A reasonably centered command structure —albeit not fully centralized—and a reasonably unified culture resulted.[6]

However, by the tenth century, Bruce Batten has diagnosed a process of administrative decentralization at work. Specifically, he sees a major retreat of state authority at the local level as the *tennō*'s court led by Northern Fujiwara regents restricted its purview to the level of provincial governorship in every province.[7] One can see this as a new segmentary structure, with provincial governors replacing district chiefs as the main bridging officials linking center and periphery. Some scholars in Japan term the result a "court-centered polity" (*ōchō kokka*), because power at the center was shared by regents, entrenched bureaucratic lineages, elite religious establishments, and retired monarchs. Clients of these powerful authorities, including provincial governors and military elites who served as the court's "claws and fangs," were organized into vertical factions, the members and interests of which served to link capital and provinces. At the same time, provincial headquarters came to be administered in tandem with the households of provincial governors. New connections between capital and countryside developed as staffers at provincial headquarters included retainers (*rōtō*) from the capital who went out to the province with the governor, who was also served by provincial officers resident in the province (*zaichō kanjin*). Meanwhile provincial governors' sons went back and forth between the provinces and the capital, where they served in patrons' households and in guards' postings. Official and unofficial overlapped, as posts and perquisites became hereditary within certain lineages, a trend that some Western historians have called "privatization." While governors rotated every few years, hereditary lineages of provincial officials transmitted specialized knowledge and skills from generation to generation. Aided by such provincials, governors became more entrepreneurial and aggressive; and by the early tenth century they were drafting their own plans for reform to which the court acceded.[8] One such reform was the *myō* system, a new localized system of tax administration negotiated between provincial authorities and wealthy elites, local and otherwise.

Batten argues too that new policies regarding foreign affairs and trade resulted from the court's inability to control the distant Kyūshū border zone. Archaeological finds and scattered records indicate that by the mid-ninth century traffic between the continent and northern Kyūshū had increased to unprecedented proportions. Such "internationalization" was destabilizing because it gave those distant from the capital new advantages and wealth. Faced with such developments and their own limitations, tenth-century regents and their colleagues, the senior nobles (*kugyō*), adopted an isolationist foreign policy. They no longer sent embassies abroad or negotiated new diplomatic ties. The reason they could make such decisions, Batten concludes, lay in the changing nature of the polity:

> During the *ritsuryō* period, diplomacy was pursued for many reasons, but most fundamentally for the prestige it conferred on the *tennō* and his government. By the tenth century, however, the *tennō* had become a figurehead and his government, at least as defined in the *ritsuryō* codes, was beginning to lose its control over the country at large. These changes eroded the active state-oriented ideology of the earlier period and made national prestige less of an issue for policy makers at court.[9]

In Batten's view, this distance from diplomacy and control of trade rendered the court ineffectual in the critical state-maintaining process of boundary formation. While terms such as "inner lands" (*kenai*), "outer lands" (*kegai*), and "province" (*kuni*) corresponded to vaguely defined frontier zones in the eighth century, by mid-Heian times the court had developed a more closed and inward-looking worldview legitimated by fears of pollution.[10] Nevertheless, actual conditions contradicted that worldview—we know from archaeological finds that elites in the capital continued to obtain significant amounts of luxury goods, such as Yue ware and medicine and Buddhist goods, from China and elsewhere. According to Batten, inactivity in such spheres as provincial administration, diplomacy, control of trade, and boundary formation contributed to the fading sense of public authority in the Heian realm, although the greater flexibility enabled by the court's decision to leave most provincial affairs to provincial governors extended the life of the *tennō*-centered polity for several centuries.

Cornelius Kiley has also discussed new types of relations linking center and periphery in later Heian times. He argues that Heian society's privileging of status promoted consociation in the form of vertical faction formation between persons of disparate status: each party was encouraged to aid someone above to obtain rewards for which he himself was ineligible.[11] In such an environment, factional loyalties overrode familial ties while shaping new bonds between capital and countryside. These could take the form of hierarchical bonds between estate administrators and managers, or the chain of command over military specialists, or main and branch temples or shrines. Whatever form the vertical faction—or "patronage pyramid," as Batten terms it—might take, the landed estate system with its shared proprietary relations was critical for stabilizing relations between participants.[12] As Kiley puts it: "The property system of the late Heian period was an important constituent of the estate system as a whole and . . . was totally nonfamilial in content. Indeed, it was the principal means of affiliation (other than the simple faction) between persons of unrelated groups."[13]

Kiley sees the late Heian polity as a "judicial state" that framed competition over vital assets.[14] He agrees with Batten that the polity gained endurance from its flexibility and tolerance, a condition that changed only when Taira Kiyomori's military power strengthened the court's administrative power and impaired its legitimating function after 1159.[15] Subsequently the judicial state that had drawn its legitimacy from deciding suits could continue functioning, but only by utilizing a new structure organized around dual centers of judgment for both courtier and warrior interests.[16]

Looking at estates from the perspective of resident cultivators as well as patrons and managers, Thomas Keirstead sees the commended estate (*kishin shōen*) as a cultural formation, "a constellation of discursive practices that attempted to elide the gap between the proprietary gaze and peasant practices in order to effect coherence."[17] Each estate comprised a hierarchy of guarantors, proprietors, and peasant-cultivators of varying statuses whose daily practices and exchanges reflected a "complex interaction between material conditions and ways estate residents and others experienced, defined, and explained them."[18] The earlier *ritsuryō* polity had as its ideal a unitary realm under the *tennō* wherein officials oversaw the land and tax systems according to Chinese-style law written and interpreted at the capital by court and officialdom. But as such systems became attenuated and commended estates developed in the tenth and eleventh centuries, multiple centers of control and parallel hierarchies of interest and patronage redefined affiliation and competition for resources.[19] In the mature commended estate of the later Heian Period, relations between proprietors (*ryōke*) and upper peasants (*hyakushō*) represented a new negotiated settlement that replaced that between the *tennō*-centered court and district chieftains of the *tennō*-centered *ritsuryō* process, and that between court and provincial governors in the court-centered system.

Mikael Adolphson adds church-state relations to this picture and points out how vertical faction building climaxed in the rival political blocs of late Heian times that included great court-patronized Buddhist monasteries such as Mount Hiei and Kōfukuji. The retired Shirakawa Tennō succeeded in constructing such a political bloc by asserting his preeminence as court leader from 1086 to 1129. A generation later, however, the retired *tennō*'s hold loosened, and competition for land and offices both in the capital and in the countryside escalated. Adolphson argues that two slow-moving processes made it increasingly difficult for a single bloc headed by the retired monarch to govern: in the provinces, local warriors employed military power to expand their influence at the expense of estate proprietors; and in the capital, rival factions competed for leadership and supremacy at court.[20] Elite religious institutions that were staffed by high-ranking scholar-monks from rival factions and which were deeply engaged in competition for resources inevitably became embroiled in the disorder. So it was that elite religious establishments which had historically functioned as realm-protecting ritual centers morphed into enemies of the court, and their members were villified by court authorities as "evil monks" (*akusō*).[21] In Adolphson's story, the Gempei War of 1180 to 1185 was the direct result of the failure of the retired monarch to maintain the integrity of his political bloc.

To move now to our essays and how they contribute to the foregoing discussions of changing relations between capital and countryside, we begin with archaeologist Tsude Hiroshi (1942–), who describes Yamato's emergence in central Honshū as the leading peer polity of late third-century Wa. Tsude argues that the round keyhole hierarchical order of the fourth and fifth centuries provides a visble sign of Japan's earliest stage of state formation. Tsude's radical proposal, reevaluating the importance of the *kofun*, is followed by Walter Edwards' abstracted version of a classic essay written by the late Kobayashi Yukio (1911–1989), also an archaeologist, who anticipated Tsude's ideas by arguing that duplicate sets of bronze mirrors found in widely dispersed tomb mounds provide even earlier evidence of political integration in Yayoi and Kofun Japan.

In his essay analyzing the nature and progress of increasing social complexity in protohistoric Shizuoka Prefecture, Hara Hidesaburō (1934-) employs methods developed by local historians combined with archaeological evidence and written records. Hara thinks that the old province of Tōtōmi, whose name means "distant sea," once formed the frontier of the Great King's realm, and that Yamato culture—visible in the keyhole tombs built in the region during the fourth and fifth centuries—was carried eastward by armed colonists loyal to the Great King. These westerners colonized the eastern marches and set the scene for later unification of the archipelago under the *tennō*'s governance in the late seventh and eighth centuries. Inoue Tatsuo (1928–) explores how a particular noble kin group (*uji*), the priestly Nakatomi, accumulated increasing status and influence both at court and on the eastern frontier as Yamato's Great Kings were becoming *tennō* and one Nakatomi lineage led by Kamatari was being granted the name Fujiwara. He focuses on clues from myth-history found in eighth-century texts such as the *Kojiki*, *Nihon shoki*, and *Hitachi fudoki*.

Moving into the historical era, when the *ritsuryō* process worked to integrate the realm, an essay by Takahashi Tomio (1921–) explores a particular facet of this integrative process, that of boundary formation in northeastern and southwestern Japan. Takahashi describes how the process proceeded in similar fashion but more slowly in the northeast. And in her essay, Takeda Sachiko (1948–) focuses her lens on official circuit roads that symbolized the *tennō*'s preeminence in the eighth-century countryside. Great highways, like the court itself, were considered ritual spaces where "Japanese-style *li*" was observed. Although such protocols did not fully replicate Chinese *li*, they assured a culture gap between the court, where *li* was practiced, and countryside, where *li* remained largely unknown. Highways effectively made the segmentary nature of Japanese polity an ongoing reality. Hotate Michihisa (1948–) then transfers the focus from roads to traffic and transport during Nara and Heian times. He demonstrates how movement and exchange of goods and labor shifted the balance between center and periphery while transforming the character of both; and how the *ritsuryō* tribute system increased interdependence between capital and countryside by increasing traffic between them.

Indeed, by the tenth century the *ritsuryō* centering process had stalled and administration of the *tennō*'s realm needed reorganization. The regent-led court then made provincial governors primarily responsible for center-periphery relations. An essay by Morita Tei (1941–) explores the causes and character of the Northern Fujiwara regency, which he argues strengthened the institution of the monarchy. At base the regency derived from the long-term affinal strategy of Yamato Great Kings and *tennō*: minister-affines had long been strongly bonded to a particular prince, who could employ and enrich them when he reached the throne. Functionally, regents aided the throne's efforts to dominate the aristocratic Council of State, whose members otherwise enjoyed considerable autonomy. According to Morita, it was Fujiwara Tadahira's "mature regency" of the late 930s and 940s that saw greater pragmatism applied to provincial administration, by relying on provincial governors as the bridging figures between capital and province.

Sasaki Muneo (1948–) argues the need for concurrent research on both capital and countryside, and the evolving links between them. In the past, laments Sasaki, classical and medieval historians have diverged in their tendency to concentrate on one end of the geographic spectrum or the other, ending up with an incomplete image of the structures that held the polity together. In Sasaki's view, during the regental era a court-centered state formation replaced the earlier *tennō*-centered polity. It reflected the interests of powerful households (*kenmon seika*) whose clientage networks forged extra-official linkages between capital and provinces. By the late eleventh to twelfth centuries, these powerful households developed into more routinized power centers supported by the public land (*kokugaryō*) and estate (*shōen*) landholding systems.

It was under such conditions that the court of the late Heian judicial state came to function fully as the locus of conflict resolution. In his essay Toda Yoshimi (1929–1991) portrays the urban world of eleventh-century Kyoto with lively images culled from an unusual set of historical sources. He shows, for instance, how provincial elites were less interested in official connections and more involved in unofficial networks affiliating them with the *tennō*'s palace, great religious institutions, or retired monarchs. Toda also describes what he calls "estate-like relations"—vertical factions distributing all sorts of shared property rights in the capital as well as in the countryside during the eleventh and twelfth centuries.

The chains of command that organized this society of competing vertical factions shaped new discursive practices linking capital and countryside by late Heian times. Miyazaki Yasumitsu (1950–) turns his attention to the Genji lineage of Mino Province headed by Minamoto Kunifusa. He explores how a warrior chieftain carved out landholdings and created an armed following to serve his interests in Mino, in the capital, or in distant postings such as in Mutsu Province. Miyazaki demonstrates how their relations with noble and royal patrons allowed Mino Genji patriarchs to aggrandize their budding proprietary interests at the expense of both estate proprietors and provincial authorities, even as they managed to retain significant independence from court and religious patrons.

How did major religious institutions react to the growing instability and competition for influence at court and land in the countryside? In exploring the reasons for increasing protests (*gōso*) by Kōfukuji monks against court authorities during the reign of the retired Shirakawa Tennō, Motoki Yasuo (1954–) argues persuasively that the key issue for Kōfukuji's "evil monks" was not enmity between the senior retired monarch and the regents' line. Rather, Shirakawa's strategies to assure his own dominance over the court-centered polity threatened Kōfukuji's autonomous influence and clientage apparatus, that is, its very status as a "gate of power."

In a frequently cited and magisterial essay that reflects the author's broad interests in political, cultural, and intellectual history, Ishimoda Shō (1912–1986) reflects on the special nature of the transition from "classical" to "medieval" that, in his view, began during the later Heian age. Ishimoda discusses changing conceptions of law, religious beliefs, and literary production that signaled that transition, at the root of which was a progressing synthesis between urban and rural elements. According to his formulation, which continues to influence scholars in Japan today, that synthesis is reflected in tales of war, such as *Shōmonki* and *Mutsuwaki*, which were produced in the tenth and eleventh centuries, as well as by the religious practices of Amidism. A key force driving such developments was the deepening angst of an alienated middling nobility with no future but what they could seize for themselves in the provinces rather than in the capital. Their progeny were resident, land-opening landlords, most of whom had come to think of themselves as professional men-of-war (*bushi*) by the end of the Heian period.

In the final essay of the volume, Koyama Yasunori (1941–) takes up the issue of increasing regional consciousness by examining the emergent sense of an "east country" (Tōgoku) and "west country" (Saigoku) from classical into medieval times. By distinguishing the distinct character of warriors, frontier relations, and estate structures in east and west, Koyama finds a keener consciousness of autonomy among those residing in the east in classical times. In contrast, he argues that it was not until Kamakura times when a real "west country" consciousness emerged in response to the heightened sense of eastern identity associated with the Kamakura Bakufu.

Notes

1. For a clear statement of a new periodizing schema that ends the classical age with the fall of the Kamakura warrior government, see the introduction to Mass 1997, 1-16.

2. Piggott 2001.

3. For a full discussion see Piggott 1997, 8-9.

4. For a good discussion on alternative meanings of "classical," and one that comes to a different conclusion than we have, see Aung-thwin 1995.

5. Barnes 1988, 190.

6. Piggott 1997, 168.

7. Batten 1993 and Batten 1999. See also Batten 1989, 84-87, his dissertation completed at Stanford University.

8. On such household structures see Hurst 1974.

9. Batten 1989, 217-18.

10. According to Murai Shōsuke, such ideas constructed the worldview of court elites from 900 until 1600. See Murai Shōsuke 1995, where Murai observes that from the ninth century on Japan had no formal external relations. "In the minds of Heian court aristocrats, people outside the boundaries had become objects of fear, not objects of royal virtue or civilizing arts [as they were in the eighth century]. By the ninth century there had been a real change in elite attitudes toward foreign parts and peoples."

11. Kiley 1974.

12. See Batten 1989, 33-43. Batten has since published his new *To the Ends of Japan* (Honolulu: University of Hawaii Press, 2003).

13. Kiley 1974, 124.

14. Kiley 1974, 114.

15. "The turbulence of the 1180s, which resulted in the founding of the Kamakura Bakufu, was in a sense a revolt against centralized power. It was not, however, aimed at destroying the noble caste, but rather at preserving it from the depredations of Kiyomori's clique." See Kiley 1974, 124.

16. While it extends beyond the chronology on which this volume focuses, Jeffrey P. Mass' last volume prior to his death does an excellent job in articulating this argument. See Mass 1999.

17. See Keirstead 1992, esp. 98-112.

18. Keirstead 1992, 108.

19. Keirstead 1992, 21.

20. Adolphson 2000, 142. Also see Hurst 1976, esp. 125-53.

21. Adolphson 2000, 182 and 240. It was Go-Shirakawa's edict of 1156 that made such charges most clearly.

1

Early State Formation in Japan

TSUDE HIROSHI

Introduction by Walter Edwards

TSUDE HIROSHI is professor of archaeology in the Faculty of Letters, Osaka University. An Osaka native, he studied under Kobayashi Yukio at Kyoto University. He is best known for his monograph on the formation of Japanese agrarian society, published in 1989, which asserts that society on the Japanese archipelago during the Yayoi (400 B.C.E.–250 C.E.) and Kofun (250–600 C.E.) Periods was far more advanced than has been previously recognized.[1] Most of Tsude's career has been devoted to clarifying the specific mechanisms through which such social complexity developed. In his monograph, he argues forcefully that the cultural achievements of the eighth-century Nara Period were built on an economic base established over the preceding millennium through the importation of advanced agricultural technology from Korea and the development of regional networks of trade and political relations.

The current article, which appeared in 1991, continues this approach by focusing more closely on the foundations of the earliest state-level polity to emerge in the Japanese archipelago. Tsude begins with an examination of theoretical approaches to state formation in Western literature, in which the chiefdom is the social evolutionary stage typically posed as preceding the state.[2] While the line between these two forms of social organization has proven difficult to draw, Tsude notes the consensus that has emerged since the 1970s—that a phase or substage known as the "early state" can be distinguished from chiefdoms by such criteria as social stratification, the use of force to maintain internal order, and a regular economic surplus. In addition, he stresses the role of the state as an integrator of society, an agent whose existence is necessary because it performs a function or functions vital to society itself. In classic Western theory the maintenance of large-scale irrigation systems has been suggested as one such integrative mechanism; Tsude notes this is not applicable to the Japanese case, however, and suggests rather that controlled distribution of vital resources such as iron may have served this integrative function instead.

Tsude turns next to Japanese treatments of the state, which have been strongly influenced by Marxist historical perspectives and thus incorporate many of the assumptions about social evolution held by Frederick Engels. Engels' primary interest was in drawing a broad contrast between civilized society and its precursors, however, and his treatment of social evolution collapsed a wide range of development into a simple, two-stage sequence. Accordingly, factors Engels took as defining the state—the emergence of the family from the communal solidarity of clan society, the development of private property, territorial divisions, taxes, and the military—appear in this simplified paradigm to emerge simultaneously with state organization itself. When this perspective is applied to Japanese history, and if the state is moreover recognized only when all these factors are in place, its emergence comes at a very late date, typically with the establishment of what is commonly termed the "*ritsuryō* order" at the turn of the eighth century.[3]

By using the distinguishing criteria defined above for the early state, however, Tsude asserts that state-level organization developed during the late third to fifth centuries—a span representing the first two-thirds of the Kofun Age, when great mounded tombs in the round keyhole shape (*zenpōkōenfun*) were built as the most visible symbols of the ruling elite's authority. Utilizing the results of recent archaeological research, Tsude presents evidence suggesting the emergence of class distinctions from the third century on. Whereas differences in status are visible in both mortuary treatment and in the size of residences during the preceding Yayoi Period, in comparable materials for the third to fifth centuries the gap between the elite and commoners is seen to widen dramatically, and the rise of a separate, intermediary class can also be discerned. Next, a system of taxes is inferred from the remains of large warehouse complexes, built according to regular plans, and whose capacities in some cases exceed those of government storehouses known from the Nara Period. As another burden imposed by the ruling class on the commoners, a system of corvée labor is induced from the sheer size of the keyhole tombs. The largest of these structures is estimated to have taken 6.8 million man-days of labor to build; other labor-intensive projects include the construction of waterways, sometimes of massive proportions, widely visible by the fifth century. From these materials Tsude asserts that throughout most of the archipelago at this time the ruling elite was organizing the labor of commoners to open new fields and increase production, while appropriating the fruits of that labor through the construction of elaborate residences and burial facilities.

The keyhole tombs, moreover, point to the existence of a centralized hierarchy based in the Kinai region. They are first of all highly standardized in shape compared with the regional diversity in elite Yayoi graves that preceded them, and they also exhibit clear differences in status. Tsude points out that keyhole tombs having squared outlines are subordinate to rounded ones, for example, and further notes that even when tombs in distant regions share the exact shape with ones in the center, differences in rank can be inferred from the smaller scale on which regional examples were built. Other links between center and periphery are visible in correlations between changes in power among central factions. These are indicated by shifts in the locations where the largest tombs are concentrated and by fluctuations in the fortunes of regional chiefly lineages, evidenced by disruptions in the positions of dominance of local groups of tombs. These facts suggest a somewhat fluid political structure, in which occasional struggles for control at the center triggered nationwide changes in local power relations at the periphery. That the central authority nevertheless had a militia, with which it could maintain order even in distant regions, is inferred from discoveries in relatively small regional tombs, thought to be those of warriors, of items obtainable only through close ties to the central elite.

Tsude infers the mechanism that gave rise to the power of this central authority from a variety of sources and proposes the following scenario. A dependence on external sources of iron developed toward the end of the second century, as suggested by the disappearance from archaeological contexts of stone tools, and presumably their widespread replacement with iron.[4] Prior to that time northern Kyūshū had closer ties to Han China than did the Kinai region, as shown by the greater number of Chinese mirrors discovered there, and it probably had better access to Chinese sources of iron at least through the first century. But a general decline in Han influence over East Asia during the second century undermined northern Kyūshū's dominance, leading to a period of strife within the Japanese archipelago at the end of that century and in the first part of the next, as recorded in Chinese records. This ended when the Kinai-based hegemony led by Queen Himiko gained control over sources of iron in the southern Korean Peninsula, which by the third century had become strategically significant.[5] As suggested by standardization in the sizes of iron ingots recovered in fifth-century archaeological contexts, control over this supply of iron continued to be an important mechanism for breaking down the regional autonomy of the former political order and securing thereby the integration of society under centralized authority.

Taking a hint from the term "*ritsuryō* order," which is frequently applied to the Nara-period system of government, Tsude proposes a parallel label, "round keyhole order," for the system of governance achieved by the early state during the third to fifth centuries. While this term has yet to gain widespread acceptance among Japanese scholars, the utility of the early state as a notion for understanding Kofun-period society, and for assessing its differences with the preceding Yayoi Period, has been generally recognized. Tsude's contribution can thus be seen as a development of Kobayashi Yukio's assertion—seen elsewhere in the volume—that the emergence of keyhole tombs marked a significant change in the nature of political authority from the Yayoi to the Kofun Periods. It stands, moreover, as culmination of the general trend of post-World War II archaeological research, which has recognized Kofun-period society as an evolutionary advance over its Yayoi predecessor while seeking to document the nature of that advance.

TSUDE HIROSHI

Early State Formation in Japan

Interpreted by Walter Edwards

Through what manner of process does a state come into being? This paper is an attempt to elucidate the formation of the Japanese state from an archaeological perspective. I begin with the disclaimer, however, that the current work is no more than a rough sketch, limited to a skeletal treatment of the multiple facets presented by the process of state formation.[6]

There is widespread support for the view that traces the foundation of the ancient state in Japan to the establishment of the *ritsuryō* system during the latter part of the seventh century C.E. But the date for the beginning of the process of state formation that led to this result varies widely from scholar to scholar. This variety of opinion includes views taking the "country" of Yamatai as the kernel of the state; views stressing the fifth century, in which the five kings of Wa were active; and views focusing on the reign of Suiko in the early part of the seventh century. Accordingly, descriptions of historical development from the third through seventh centuries diverge strikingly from researcher to researcher, and it would require a book-length treatment just to introduce the major works of relevance.[7] For example, the following two views show highly different approaches to an evaluation of the stage prior to the establishment of the *ritsuryō* system.

Ishimoda Shō discerned the seeds of state organs in the third-century country of Yamatai in the presence of social status differences between kings, greater and lesser free men, and slaves; in such offices as the prefect (*ichidaisotsu*) and the border guards (*hinamori*); and in the existence of taxes, warehouses, and laws.[8] At the end of the fifth century, against the background of conquests by King Bu, a hierarchy incorporating selected provincial chieftains (*kuni no miyatsuko*) was established which was expanded in the sixth century to include provincial chieftains heading coalitions of lesser chieftains. In the reign of Suiko, at the end of the sixth and the beginning of the seventh centuries, these relations were superseded by the establishment of direct hierarchical relations between the court and localized elites through the granting of noble titles (*kabane*) and the establishment of a system of centralized government offices. These developments, Ishimoda argued, became the foundation of the system of direct administrative control over economic production and taxation that was established from the mid-seventh-century Taika Reform on. In making these considerations, Ishimoda stressed the importance of the broader East Asian perspective, placing particular emphasis on the political tensions prevailing from the reigns of Suiko to Temmu as an international stimulus for the maturation of a state structure.[9]

In contrast, Hara Hidesaburō asserts that the half century from 649 to 701 was the period of full-scale development of the state; prior to that time was a stage of a confederacy of tribes. Although Hara recognizes the offices of the third-century country of Wa reported in Chinese Wei Dynasty records as the seeds of a bureaucratic system, he regards the generals named in the Liu Sung records, together with offices named in fifth-century sword inscriptions, as comprising "a simple bureaucratic structure under military rule." Hara characterizes the latter a tribal confederation ruled by a warrior king.[10]

Behind this difference in opinion stand two larger problems. The first involves theoretical frameworks used for defining what the state is. For whether one takes the position, like Hara, of attaching importance to a stage of tribal confederacy, or even if one acknowledges the utility of such a concept, whether or not one recognizes it as applying to Wa society of the third to fifth centuries is a matter of significant theoretical difference.[11] The second problem is a debate at the level of verification. Even scholars who do not place much emphasis on a systematic theoretical view of state development, or who do not indicate their views on the matter, appear to share the general understanding that class differentiation, taxation, household registration, military organization, governmental bureaucracy, and so forth, are important to discussions of the state and of political control. But when it comes to questions of how fully developed any of these indicators were at the time of Wa society—in other words, issues of verification—opinions vary widely because of differences in interpretations of textual materials such as the *Record of Ancient Things* (*Kojiki*) and the *Chronicles of Japan* (*Nihongi*). In this case, among those who maintain a rigidly critical attitude toward historic materials and seek a cautious interpretation that excises portions of the chronicles even slightly suspect of embellishment at the hands of their compilers, there is a general tendency to view each of the indicators just mentioned as being established relatively late. This leads, in my opinion, to an inclination to see the establishment of the state as approaching the time of the founding of the *ritsuryō* order. In addition, while some excellent research has been done examining the period up through the Taika Reform using historical materials, researchers working in this area have decreased in number. As one participating in archaeological research, it is my sense that the boom of the 1960s and 1970s is no longer visible.

Starting from a recognition of problems like these, I first conduct a brief examination of the process in ancient Japan. Next, on the basis of that examination, I approach the problem from a consideration of the results of recent archaeological research.

Theories of State Formation

Disregarding simplistic theories on the process of state formation, such as those invoking conquest, classic theories that have remained influential among views relating the state to frameworks of social structure or historical process are those of Frederick Engels and Max Weber.[12] The former's contribution made it clear that the state is not a necessary component of human society, but is formed through particular historic processes, and that societies exist in which a state did not take shape. Engels' work has provided a theoretical basis for many researchers involved in the study of ancient Japan, including Ishimoda Shō. Weber's work has demonstrated the hypothetical approach of positing ideal types for the purpose of typological comparison in conducting an analysis of state societies throughout world history. He argued that after the two successive stages of "agrarian communism" and "seignorial proprietorship," the paths followed in the classical West and in the Orient differed, with the city as a unitary community (the *polis*) developing in the former, and an urban-based monarchy having a bureaucracy in the latter. Weber's views are characterized by the use of a typology based on the shape of political control, and his concepts of the state based on *Leiturgie* (the duty of service to the state) and of a stage of "world empire" are still worthy of consideration. One example of Weber's influence is seen in the work of Inoue Mitsusada, who has published systematic research on the ancient Japanese state and who claims to have taken a number of hints from Weber's work.[13]

On Chiefdoms

From the 1950s on, neo-evolutionary theories of anthropologists like Elman Service and Marshall Sahlins have provided many suggestions regarding the process of state formation.[14] Although points of emphasis differ among authors, they commonly regard social evolution as following the four stages of band societies, tribes, chiefdoms, and primitive states. In particular, these writers place a strong emphasis on chiefdoms as a social evolutionary stage, pointing out the following characteristics of chiefdoms as compared with those of previous and subsequent stages: (1) although kin relationships are important, they are not based on egalitarian principles as in bands and tribes; (2) although governmental offices of the state are lacking, there is authority concentrated at the center; (3) public authority is strongly personal in character (the heroic or "Big Man" aspects are salient) in comparison with the state; and (4) inequality is seen in status and rank, but political classes have not yet developed.[15]

Furthermore, these writers have made clear the significant point that conical clans are known to exist in many chiefdoms.[16] Lewis Henry Morgan argued that clans are characterized by exogamy, unilineal descent, and egalitarian principles, but in conical clans the ranking of status is prominent, exogamy is not followed, and descent is not unilineal. As demonstrated by the simple expressions of "aristocratic clan" and "commoner clan," descent divides society on the principle of genealogy into ranked strata. In short, the existence of societies based on the principle of kinship (including its extension to fictive kin) but lacking egalitarian principles has been made clear through the structural examination of chiefdoms.

Theories Regarding the Early State

In the 1970s, the issue of the early state was raised by an international research symposium convened by Henri Claessen and Peter Skalnik.[17] The conference brought together scholars from the fields of anthropology, archaeology, and history, who conducted sustained discussions as researchers with a variety of differing theoretical perspectives akin to the views of Marx, Weber, and Sahlins. Using numerous case studies of early societies such as the Maya, Inca, Shang and Chou China, Ur, Egypt, and Germanic tribes, the symposium was a unique experiment in debate on the common theme of state formation.[18]

Based on this joint debate, Claessen and Skalnik have proposed the notion of the "early state." Using data from archaeology, history, and ethnology from twenty-one cases of formative states worldwide for which documentation is sufficient, they conducted a comparison using fifty-one indexes (counting major and subsidiary items) of the characteristics of social structure. These included population size and density, the degree of social stratification, the existence of private ownership of property, the existence and stability of an economic surplus, the existence of cooperative irrigation and water control projects, the degree of specialization of craft production, the existence and shape of trade and merchants, the existence and strength of centralized government, and so on. Claessen and Skalnik have also summarized attributes of the early state as follows: (1) a population large enough to permit social stratification and specialization; (2) citizenship determined on the basis of territory; (3) a centralized government able to maintain order through its authority and the use or threat of force; (4) the ability to maintain society's independence from external threats, and to prevent internal fission; (5) ability to produce a regular economic surplus to support the state; (6) stratification of society into emergent classes, the rulers and the ruled; and (7) a common ideology supporting the legitimacy of rulers.[19]

Comparing these characteristics with the concepts presented by Sahlins and others, the early state may be regarded as close to the stage of the primitive state, posited as following the chiefdom. But an examination of the individual cases in the sample of early states shows that societies considered by Sahlins and others as chiefdoms are included, hence the boundary between chiefdoms and early states is not always clear. In actuality, there were differences of opinion in this regard among the scholars who participated in the conference organized by Claessen and Skalnik. At the same time, the proposal to divide the early state into three phases of "inchoate," "typical," and "transitional" can be said to show that the cases subsumed under the concept of early state include a wide degree of variation. As for differences between chiefdoms and early states, it would appear that the early state as a social evolutionary stage is distinguished from chiefdoms through development of four criteria: social classes, a regular economic surplus, territorial-based social organization, and coercive force.

A Consideration of Engels' Theory

From this examination of recent research on state formation, it would appear that a number of problems are in need of review regarding the traditionally influential classic theories of the emergence of the ancient Japanese state, including an evaluation of those theories and their relevance to ancient Japanese society. Whereas Weber's concept of the state, and particularly his notion of a comparative typology of patterns of authority, has been employed by scholars such as Inoue Mitsusada, Engels' formulation is both more historicist and more comprehensive as an explanatory model of state formation, and for these reasons it has had greater influence in research on Japanese history. Furthermore, because Watanabe Yoshimichi, Ishimoda Shō, Tōma Seita, and others have not simply introduced Engels' theories, but have also attempted historical description through an expansion of those theories using the case of ancient Japan, even scholars who oppose Marxist views or who do not place importance on theoretical concepts have come to utilize elements of Engels' perspective or employ modified versions of it.[20] Indeed, such modification includes the use of such theoretical expressions as "from kinship society to territorial society" or "from village to state," which are often seen in textbooks and general works.

Engels' view of state formation, as seen in *The Origin of the Family, Private Property, and the State,* is characterized by a gross contrast between the state on one hand and the clan-based organization that preceded it on the other. Namely, Engels divided early human history into two evolutionary stages, based on changes from kin to territorial relations, from matrilineal to patrilineal family organization, and from communal to private ownership of property. He then regarded the political organization that accompanied the latter stage as the state. To simplify this formulation, Engels' theory holds that the state is a product of the division into social classes, that private ownership of property was necessary for a division into social classes to occur, and that private property was not possible without the breakup of the communal solidarity of clan society and the establishment of the patrilineal family. In that Engels did not regard the emergence of the family, private property, and the state as discrete phenomena, but rather as inseparably linked together, the title of his work serves as a shorthand expression of his views.

For this reason in particular, Engels emphasized in connection with the establishment of the state the emergence of territorial divisions in place of reliance on the principle of kinship under clan-based organization. Moreover, after class division rendered clan organization incapable of serving as the bond for achieving social integration, the state replaced clan organization as the new integrative principle for preventing internal social division. Engels accordingly stressed the significance of taxes, the military, and other governmental functions as concrete indicators of the authority supporting the state.

In evaluating Engels' theory, I believe attention must be given to the following two items. First, even if the historical data and the logic on which Engels relied are provisionally assumed to be correct, the evolutionary movement in two stages—from kinship to territory, from matrilineal to patrilineal organization, from communal to private ownership, from classless to class society—should be seen as a contrastive logical construct for dividing human history into the two broad stages of civilization and its precursors. But especially in terms of the level of academic research at the time of this theory's publication in the late nineteenth century, it is difficult to declare that these evolutionary criteria would necessarily emerge together in such coordinated fashion from an analysis of the historical processes as then known in every region of the world. This is readily illustrated by the single example of Engels' own logical inconsistency in seeing clan organization surviving strongly in the Germanic nation.[21]

When we make a historical analysis of the formation of the state, however, it is important first of all not simply to employ a logical dichotomy between states and pre-state societies, but rather to illuminate the long course of transition between the two types of society as a historical process. But when deference is given to the outlines of Engels' formulation, and the historical process conflated with this logical dichotomy, then the several criteria he gives for this transition are perceived as emerging in coordinated fashion. The time when such concrete indicators are in full complement is moreover given precedence, and the establishment of the state is necessarily regarded as occurring relatively late. Herein lies the theoretical basis for views that see a late emergence of the Japanese state in the *ritsuryō* period, bringing the detrimental results of devaluing an analysis of the long period of transition prior to the *ritsuryō* order.

The second item to bear in mind is that more than one hundred years have passed since the publication of Engels' theory. During that time a wealth of research has accumulated regarding early human history. In addition, Morgan's theories of kinship, on which Engels relied, have been exposed to criticism. Research on cases of state formation, particularly in East Asia and the Americas, has also made rapid progress in the twentieth century. The contributions of archaeology in this regard have been considerable. As a result, problems and disparities among the evolutionary changes posited above, for instance the assertion of a transition from matrilineal to patrilineal family organization, cannot be supported based on the present body of knowledge of various societies. Even if historical cases of a change from matrilineal to patrilineal kinship exist, matrilineal organization cannot be regarded as universal in the early stage of human history, and the principle that matrilineality came first cannot be upheld.

In the same way, the evolutionary argument forming the basis of the thesis that communal precedes private ownership—that communal labor gives way to individual labor—has to be reconsidered. I have discussed this aspect at length elsewhere.[22] To give only a summary of what is relevant to the current discussion, my views are as follows: in societies with a gathering economy, the basic unit of economic activity is that of the small-scale operator; the same applies in early agricultural societies as well. In the early agriculture of the West Asian plateaus and transalpine Europe, both consisting of husbandry and upland farming that relied on rain water, small-scale management became manifest as the basic unit of economic production. The irrigated cultivation of barley in alluvial areas of West Asia and rice in East Asia began after the onset of upland farming based on rain water. In these cases as well, the unit of cultivation was the small-scale operator. But since the role of communal cooperation was great because of the necessity of large-scale projects for managing irrigation water, small-scale management was suppressed and is not clearly discerned. Despite this difference between agricultural societies in which small-scale management is manifest, as in the former case, and those in which it is suppressed, as in the latter, in the beginnings of human history it nonetheless appears that individualized labor of the small-scale management pattern came first. The community-wide regulations based on communal labor for irrigation and water control appeared later.

If one takes this perspective, a different view of the formation of class relations becomes possible. Namely, in societies within which small-scale management is manifest, class differences may emerge among members of that group. By contrast, in societies that suppress small-scale operations, even if status differences develop among small-scale operators, the basic class relations arise more readily between the chief, who holds strong authority over the management of agricultural lands and products, and the cultivators, who are subject to these regulations.

Moreover, in Morgan's formulation, clan organization was regarded as inseparable from egalitarian principles, but as mentioned above, twentieth-century anthropology has made it clear that even though chiefdoms are based on kinship relations, they exhibit, together with the conical clan organization on which they are based, internal differences in status. In consideration of this fact—and moreover if recognition is given to the difference asserted above regarding the formation of class relations in societies with different patterns of small-scale economic operations—then Engels' theory that private ownership and class differentiation emerge only after the collapse of clan organization on the level of kinship, and after the collapse of communal ownership on the level of economics, requires reexamination. In other words, concerning the assessment of the development of class differentiation, the weight formerly given to kinship principles as expressed through clan organization may be regarded as a secondary factor.

The Concept of a Tribal Confederacy

The next point needing examination is the concept of a tribal confederacy. Theories that place the establishment of the Japanese state in the *ritsuryō* period understand the stage prior to that time as comprising a confederacy of tribes. For example, in a paper that constitutes a comprehensive discussion of the formation of the ancient state, Hara Hidesaburō, whose work is represented in chapter 3 in this volume, spells out this position in the following manner:

> The Taihō Ritsuryō Code was completed in 701, the first year of the Taihō era. At this point the ancient Japanese state should be considered as established in both name and substance. . . . What nature should be prescribed for the ancient Japanese state that emerged in this manner? To use traditional East Asian concepts of state structure, it is possible to regard it as transitional between a "feudal" and a centralized bureaucratic state. But from the perspective of world history, it should perhaps be assessed as transitional between a military monarchy, based on a confederacy of tribes, and "Oriental Despotism."[23]

Hara thus takes the period prior to the *ritsuryō* order as comprising the stage of a confederacy of tribes, which he regards as a pre-state society.

Kitō Kiyoaki, with the intent of producing a theory on East Asian state formation, also applied the notion of a confederacy of tribes to Japanese society, thereby taking a perspective similar to Hara's, yet characterized by an attempt to achieve a new logical formulation.

> The political system in the Kofun Period from the fifth century on corresponds with that of an early premodern stage, such as the militaristic democratic leagues in Europe, but it has a despotic political

> character and is thus closer to a militaristic hierarchic organization than to a democratic league. Rather than regarding it as a confederacy of tribes, it is more appropriately seen as a tribal union formed through a vertical ordering of relations among its component groups. Stretching the point to accentuate the contrast with a militaristic democratic league, it may even be called a "militaristic monarchy."[24]

Yoshida Akira also utilizes the concept of a confederacy of tribes, but in a slightly different manner. Specifically, in his well-known *Establishing the Ancient Japanese State* (*Nihon kodai kokka seiritsushi ron*), he systematically discusses the formation of the early Japanese state as follows:

> Whereas Asian-style communal groups in societies with a primitive social structure (namely, clan society) formed tribal orders such as confederacies, the ancient despotic state did not inherit this type of tribal order *in toto*, because without first demolishing that order, the ancient state could not emerge in despotic form. . . . No matter how a tribal confederacy might have sought to serve as the mechanism for stratified rule, it can only be judged as the final stage of primitive social structure, and from this perspective cannot readily be regarded as representing the emergence of the ancient state. The creation of a system of provincial chieftains in the sixth century was achieved through a thorough revision of the pattern of nationwide rule of the fifth century, and thus holds significance as an indicator of the establishment of the ancient state.[25]

And in his systematic discussion of the process of state formation in the era of keyhole tomb building, archaeologist Kondō Yoshirō also uses the concept of a tribal confederacy to describe the period prior to establishment of the *ritsuryō* state. In an essay entitled "The Discontinuation of Keyhole Tombs and the Formation of a Systematic Status Order," he states:

> And then the tribal confederacies in various regions began to weaken or disband under the supremacy of the Yamato monarchy; and as the rule of the Great King spread over the separate tribes, egalitarian relations were fading in actuality, as had already held in principle. . . . The end of the seventh century and more so the beginning of the eighth . . . comprised the period of the completion of codified and systematic rule—the establishment of the ancient state—as can be discerned from the stabilization of a political center demonstrated by the construction of the Fujiwara and Nara capitals. At this point, the mounded tombs, which had regulated relations within and among various tribes prior to the formation of the ancient state, ended their function.[26]

Hara and Kondō use the term *buzoku rengō*, and Yoshida and Kitō employ *buzoku dōmei*, with the difference stemming from the process of translating "confederacy of tribes" from Morgan's *Ancient Society* into Japanese, but the two terms can be regarded as having the same content.[27] While I feel it makes little difference which term is used, I will herein refer to only *buzoku rengō* to mean "tribal confederacy."

When we use the concept of a confederacy of tribes in an analysis of the history of state formation, attention should be given to the following two points. The first is that both Morgan and Engels basically treated the term as indicating a political organization in societies without class distinctions. The League of the Iroquois and the Aztec Federation were taken as concrete examples, and while the latter was regarded as more politically mature, they were seen as sharing the following characteristics: governance by a council of hereditary chiefs; equality between constituent tribes; a principle of unanimous decision making; and contrapuntal dual leadership by two supreme chiefs who divided military and civil affairs between them. Tribal confederacies were thus seen to be essentially political organizations of a clan system and represented a social order prior to the formation of classes or the state. As will be noted below, however, I regard ancient Japan as a class society at both the third-century Yamatai stage and the fifth-century stage of the five kings of Wa. Accordingly, even if Morgan and Engels' concept of a confederacy of tribes is provisionally regarded as a valid tool for historical analysis, I believe its use in an examination of Japanese society from the third century on is incorrect.

The second point is that the various cases that Engels and others treated together as tribal confederacies, if reconsidered from the present level of academic knowledge, cover a broad range. They include societies that should be regarded as unstratified as well as those with class relations, and reclassification would thus appear necessary. The latter examples probably merit reconsideration as state societies in their formative periods. Also, while there are cases in which fairly mature political organizations developed through lengthy struggles and alliances among tribes within the same region, as with the Aztecs, there are those whose formation was precipitated by external crisis. The various forms of confederacies of Celtic and Germanic tribes in response to aggression by the Roman Empire are good examples of this.

Among confederacies of tribes, the type formed in response to external pressure is generally short-lived. The type of political organization in societies which Sahlins refers to as "segmented tribes" is an example. As he explains, "Certain groups may ally for a time and a purpose, as for a military venture, but the collective spirit is episodic. When the objective for which it was called into being is accomplished, the alliance lapses and the tribe returns to its normal state of disunity."[28] This type of tribal confederacy also existed in the Japanese archipelago. For example, the ethnography of the Ainu of the Saru River Basin, observed by Izumi Seiichi, provides material of great interest in this regard. Each of the more than ten villages in the ninety-kilometer-long basin had its own territory in mountain, river, and coastal areas. When an outside enemy intruded, a leader would appear, and the social unity of the Saru River Basin would become manifest, but there was no regular mechanism for coordinating relations among the villages.[29] Ainu military alliances, such as those known from documentary records of the fifteenth-century Koshamain Revolt and the seventeenth-century Shakushain Revolt, may also be analyzed from the perspective just outlined. Although a temporary alliance was formed in both cases in response to the external aggression from ethnic Japanese, it is worth noting that on neither occasion did a regular political organization mature.

Basic research on confederacies of tribes and similar political alliances will likely be a topic for future examination, using examples that are clearly understood from the current level of research on historical and ethnographic materials. Kitō's observations are an ambitious attempt to approach this problem using the methodology of comparative history.

If labeling societies in which class relations are clearly visible as tribal confederacies is considered inappropriate, then I believe it necessary to posit a new concept of "confederacy of chieftains," as distinct from confederacies in classless societies. Also, by distinguishing between an alliance that is temporary and short-lived from one that is more mature and has sufficient endurance to produce the kernel of state organization—and by considering the historic process through which the latter type is formed—it may finally become possible to recast the classic theories in modern form and create a new theory of state formation.

The State as Integrator of Society

In addition to embodying the authority of the ruling class, the state has the public functions of integrating society and preventing internal divisions. For this reason it is transcendent to society in character. With regard to such functions, emphasis has been placed on the organization of large-scale projects such as irrigation works and road construction. For example, Karl Wittfogel proposed the "hydraulic hypothesis" of society, arguing that social organization and the shape of the state vary with the existence and scale of irrigation works.[30] While Wittfogel's perspective is extremely important, his very direct linkage of the pattern of irrigation with that of society itself produced numerous difficulties in his argument. The weaknesses of Wittfogel's theory are readily discerned, for example, from a consideration of his inability to explain how a unifying authority emerged over such a short period in a place like the Japanese archipelago, where no truly large-scale rivers flow through the entire country.[31]

Along with the public functions of irrigation and other civil engineering projects, another factor that should be stressed is the relationship between authority and the systemization of the circulation of essential materials. While there is already a body of research on this subject in the fields of ancient Chinese and European history, work on early Japan is unfortunately still insufficient.[32] Some advances have been made in the history of transportation and in research on systems of distribution, but it is difficult to regard such work as a key part of any theory regarding the state.[33] When we discuss this problem in relation to the process of state formation, consideration should be made of not only the circulation of economic necessities such as iron and salt but also the distribution of prestige goods such as precious glass ornaments and mirrors received from the Chinese court by Wa chieftains, or other items, such as swords, bestowed domestically by the Great Kings of Wa.[34]

Other important issues that can be clarified through an analysis of distribution systems include the nature of regional economic self-sufficiency and the ways in which political autonomy based on such self-sufficiency is transcended. Whereas agricultural communities and regional political authority stemming from coalitions of chiefs of such communities are rooted in local self-sufficiency, it is worth reconfirming that the state is a political organization founded on a unifying principle of a different order. While it is easy enough to recognize in this regard the special character of classic city-states in ancient Europe—established on an urban nucleus that cast off the economic self-sufficiency of agricultural society, developing instead an internal social division of labor and a dependence on the external economy—in regions like Japan, where residential concentration in urban areas came late, it is difficult to prove the loss of self-sufficiency in agricultural communities using cities as indicators. Accordingly, it may be regarded as more effective to take the regulation of essential materials for which dependence is external, rather than the presence of cities, as a marker for showing whether communal self-sufficiency and social autonomy have disintegrated.

From an analysis of this issue, we may be able to point out the problems involved in Kadowaki Teiji's concept of a regional state (*chiiki kokka*), as well as positive aspects of his work. While granting that the Yamato polity held supremacy in Japan during the third through fifth centuries, Kadowaki advances the notion that regional states existed in Tsukushi, Kibi, and Kenu, and that a unified state emerged from the middle of the sixth century. The regional state is defined in the following manner. (1) Each regional state has a territory centered on a broad alluvial plain, in which a cluster of agricultural communities can be controlled through a network of rivers and roads, and in which the internal contradictions between these local communal units (composed of a number of separate households in which patriarchal control has strengthened) are growing increasingly intense. (2) In each region such groups of communities become unified under the rule of a king who concentrates in himself the authority of the chiefly class of the various communities and who oversees large-scale public works for the region (especially civil engineering and irrigation projects), thus promoting an increase in its productive capacity. Each regional state also develops external diplomacy in an independent fashion. (3) In the course of this process, the king takes command of bureaucratic offices and military troops that have been established in each region while having cultivators fill his central warehouses with taxes paid in goods. (4) In order to maintain this system of control, general laws transcending individual communities are promulgated. Each regional society is thus represented and integrated through the emergence of a state authority having the full complement of these conditions.[35]

The regional-state thesis clarifies the existence of strong regional polities from the third through fifth centuries that were powerful enough to relativize, even if only briefly, the central government based in the Kinai region, thus making it possible to elucidate a historical difference between this period and the sixth century and later. Also, Kadowaki has provided a fresh perspective by questioning the principle on which the state stands, thereby reexamining the tendency to posit the emergence of the state, and particularly the Japanese state, without sufficient scrutiny.

It is indeed true that with regard to the existence of the state, the size of the region that serves as its vessel is not an essential element. City-states existed even in geographically confined societies like ancient Athens. However, in order to recognize a society as a city-state, I believe that not only must there be the "demos"—the authority of a class-based rule grounded in a regional district—but that society must also cast off the narrowly enclosed nature of a self-sufficient communal unit and base itself on an urban-like principle of dependence on the hinterland, taking control of trade and other functions that depend on the outside. In other words, the state is not simply naked authority possessing a means for exercising violence. Rather, I believe that because its authority has public functions that can suppress the self-contained nature of the narrow social units on which it is based, the state is a society in which those lower order units are necessarily drawn inward by that authority. Accordingly, given the relatively late appearance of cities in Wa society, we can proceed by questioning who controlled the circulation of economic necessities. As networks for the distribution of iron and other items were put in place over a wide portion of the Japanese islands as early as the third century, it would appear that the need existed for the public functions of the state to have been established over that portion of the archipelago in rapid fashion. Although in the Mediterranean world and in China during the Warring States Period, wealthy merchants were active in the circulation of economic necessities over a wide area—making it possible for city-states to emerge in restricted geographic regions—in Wa society, merchant activity did not begin until later.[36]

From this perspective it does not appear that the authority characterizing Kadowaki's regional state could have successfully dismantled regional self-sufficiency and established the state, even if we could recognize the existence of political rule uniting chieftains of agricultural communities. Accordingly, rather than positing the existence of the regional state, it is more appropriate to describe such entities as regional polities representing the aggregated powers of a plurality of local chieftains.

Theoretical Problems: A Summary

Key indicators for state formation include the degree of class differentiation and the formation of a system of status differences; exploitative mechanisms such as taxes and corvée duties; and the development of a ruling organization with bureaucratic and military functions. Factors such as the breakup of clan organization, or the weight given to kinship as a basis for social solidarity, should be regarded as secondary. Moreover, in order to distinguish the state clearly from mechanisms for political rule based in local communities, the existence of means to dismantle the isolation of local agricultural communal organizations and the regional spheres of self-sufficiency in which they may be subsumed is critical—specifically, the means of integrating society by controlling the circulation of goods over a wide area is critical.

Fig. 1.1. Mitsudera site

In this regard, based on the results of recent archaeological research, I wish to address various aspects of class relations and a system of status differences, taxes and corvée labor, the organization of government and of the citizenry, and the circulation of goods and political authority. As several separate chapters would be necessary for a full treatment of any one of these factors, I will cite work that has already appeared and ask that readers understand that I will only give an outline of points for debate, leaving full treatment for another occasion.[37]

The Process of State Formation in Ancient Japan

The Formation of Class Relations

I would first like to express my basic views on class relations. These are relations in which differences in ownership of the means of production, and differential positions within the organization of labor, are based on differences in social rank and lead to discrepancies in the division of wealth. To put the matter in different terms, it is a relationship in which, because of status differences between social classes, one party takes as its own the fruits of the other party's labor. Although the task of confirming such an abstract relationship with any accuracy is difficult even with documentary materials, it becomes even more so with archaeological data. But the strength of archaeological data lies in their enabling inferences about the existence and nature of class differences, taking as clues changes in human relations made visible in settlement remains and burial customs. I therefore begin an analysis of class relations with observations on status and other differences between social strata, and then clarify, in the next section, tributary relations as seen in such data as the pattern of warehouse distribution.

Major innovations are discernible both in settlements and in burial customs of the mid-third century, which is called the Shōnai Period in terms of the archaeological ceramic typology, or the era of Yamatai in terms of historical documents. Innovations are indicated in settlement patterns by the breakup of large moated villages and the appearance of elite residential districts. In burial customs, the isolation and growth in scale of chiefly burials, as well as the emergence of communal cemeteries comprised of densely concentrated clusters of pit burials for the lowest stratum of the populace, both show these changes. Developments in residential and burial arrangements thus clearly evidence the growing separation of the chiefly elite from commoners.

Among the elements involved in these changes, the moated village—a defensive settlement surrounded by moats and ramparts—was in existence throughout the Yayoi Period and serves as the characteristic pattern of settlement for that period as a whole. A comparison of the buildings within these villages shows that whereas pit dwellings were the main constituent in eastern Japan, with very little difference visible in class status, within the larger core villages of western Japan a precinct of surface dwellings existed separately from the greater mass of pit dwellings. As these precincts may be inferred to

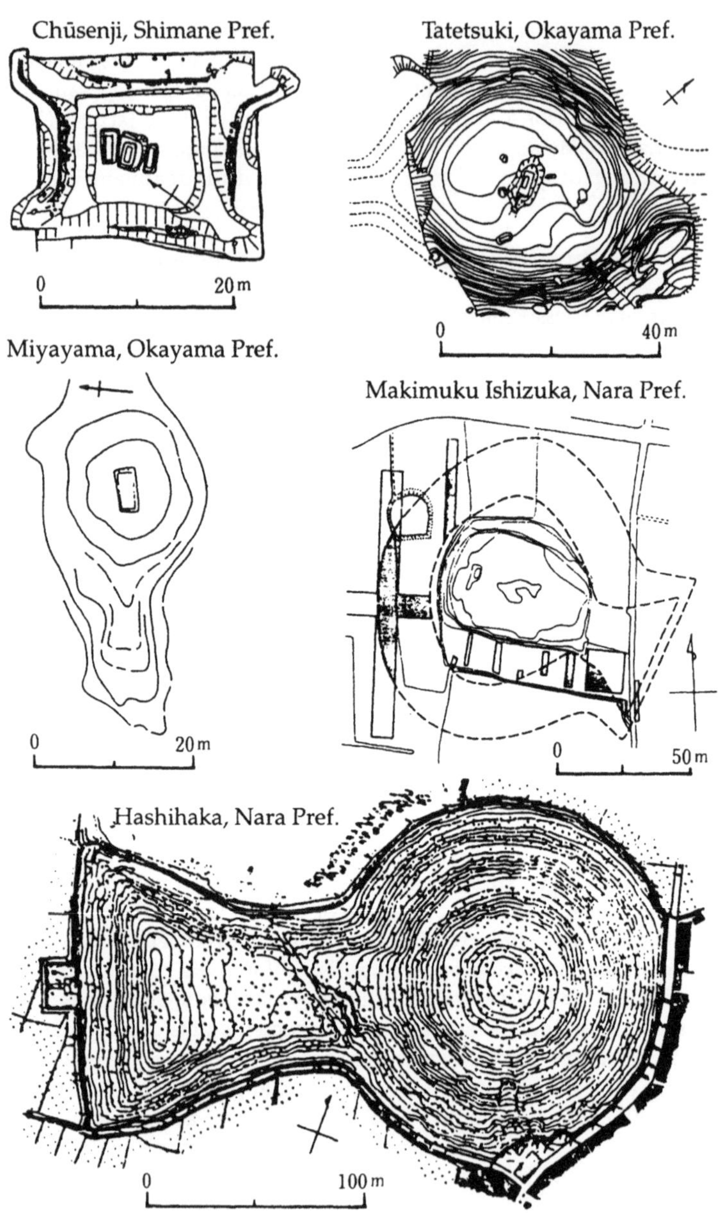

Fig. 1.2. Third-century Mounded Tomb Types, including Tatetsuki

have housed elite residences and workshops for craft production, then status differences conceivably existed within the moated villages of west Japan.

In the Kinai region, as seen at the Karako site in Nara Prefecture, these moated villages were in existence until the very late Yayoi Period (late second century to early third century). But coincident with the period of Shōnai pottery in the middle of the third century, such moated villages disappear and residential precints for the chiefly elite emerge. Whereas late-third-century sites like that at Osako in Ōita Prefecture have been uncovered, the typical form of elite residential precincts is illustrated by the late fifth-century Mitsudera site in Gumma Prefecture[38] (see Figure 1.1). Here a residential tract eighty meters on a side was surrounded by a palisade and a large moat, and was furthermore divided internally with a palisade. The southern portion contained an elite residential compound with a large surface dwelling at the center, while in the northern portion stood a number of pit dwellings. The latter may represent either workshops or residences of personal servants to the chief. Taking into consideration the results of investigations at the Gennojō site in Gumma and elsewhere, a complex of warehouses and other structures probably stood on the unexcavated portions of the Mitsudera site.

The appearance of these chiefly residential precincts is evidence of the elites' move to segregate their living quarters from the rest of society, and thus of their increased social separation from commoners. It is worth noting that the latter also segregated into smaller residential settings surrounded by moats and palisades. A complex comprising four pit dwellings, raised-floor granaries, and a well at the fourth-century site of Kobukada in Shizuoka may be regarded as the residence of the commoner agriculturalist. Also, the fifth-century site of Ōzono in Osaka, comprised mainly of surface dwellings and accompanied by granaries and a well, conceivably represents a higher social stratum than that of Kobukada. It is significant that chiefly, intermediate, and commoner strata can be differentiated in this manner by the size of the residential precincts and the types of buildings they contained. Also noteworthy is the appearance of figures who should perhaps be called shanty-dwellers, as they did not have their own residential land but resided in pit dwellings within the chief's estate, as at the Mitsudera site.[39]

Corresponding to these changes in residence areas are changes in the pattern of burials. Already in the latter half of the second century, large graves with high mounds had moved from the common graveyard and were being built singly on hilltop locations commanding panoramic views. A typical example is the Tatetsuki site in Okayama, which may be regarded as a chiefly tomb because there was only a single individual interred at the center of this forty-plus meter mound (see Figure 1.2). In the third century this type of burial increased in every region.[40] In parallel with the progressive segregation and increase in size of chiefly graves, a different change was taking place in commoner cemeteries. Clusters of densely packed pit burials appeared in the mid-third century and flourished from the fourth through sixth centuries. These represent burial conditions in which small pits with oblong or round outlines are densely concentrated within a confined cemetery.[41] This method of burial

Fig. 1.3. A Fifth-century Storehouse Cluster

was crude even in comparison with the typical communal cemeteries of the Yayoi Period. At the same time, clusters of more sophisticated low-mounded graves were being built on hilltops and ridges. Not only did the number of such graves decrease sharply in comparison with Yayoi Period communal cemeteries, but from the differences in mound size and the amount of grave goods, it can be discerned that status differentiation occurred between persons interred in such graves.

These developments are highly significant. Communal cemeteries, known from the Yayoi Period on, apparently divided in polar fashion: a limited elite stratum had chiefly graves in segregated areas; the greater mass of commoners was buried in clusters of densely packed pit burials; while members of an intermediate stratum were buried in small, individual, low-mounded tombs.[42] The explosive increase in the mid-sixth century of a newer type of tomb cluster, consisting of round mounds with horizontal stone chambers, was formerly interpreted as indicating the breakup of the localized lineage segment and the emergence of the patriarchal family. But given the changes observed in the patterns of settlement and burials, it seems that a major transformation in social strata had already begun in the third century. Furthermore, the mid-sixth century formation of clusters of tombs with horizontal stone chambers should be regarded as the political recruitment of the upper portion of an intermediate stratum that had developed through the process of social stratification from the third century onward.

Taxes and Corvée Labor

By comparing the size and concentration of storehouses and the pattern of their occurrence within settlements, and by thus distinguishing whether those storehouses were used for communal stockpiles of grain or for gathering tributary payments, it is possible to take an archaeological approach to questions concerning the system of taxes and other levies. Regarding corvée labor, I would like to make some observations through estimates of the amounts of labor invested in the construction of monumental tombs, irrigation, and civil engineering works.

In the Kofun Period, groups of raised-floor storehouses of a conspicuously large scale existed in addition to the storehouses of ordinary settlements. Whereas the floor space of the latter type of structure ranged from nine to thirty square meters, fifth-century storehouses at the Hōenzaka site in present-day Osaka or at the Narutaki site in Wakayama were from sixty to ninety square meters (see Figure 1.3).[43] They surpassed the size of Nara-period warehouses as stipulated in the tax registers (*shōzeichō*) as well as those known archaeologically from the sites of provincial headquarters. The estimated storage capacity of the sixteen buildings in the group at Hōenzaka, given in terms of rice, equals approximately 37,000 *koku* (about 189,000 bushels).[44]

The goods stored in these warehouses were by no means limited to rice, however. Cloth, salt, raw iron, or armaments are also imaginable. If such items were indeed included, the total value of the goods held in the storehouses

Fig. 1.4. Daisen Tomb

would probably have exceeded that of rice alone. In evaluating this situation, assuming that the storehouses were piled full with nothing but loose unhulled rice, the expanse of agricultural land necessary to produce 37,000 *koku* of rice is vast in itself.[45]

The storehouse group at Hōenzaka was not only large in scale, but also utilized advanced surveying techniques to obtain a true north-south orientation for the buildings' main axes. It was probably connected with the authority of a Great King who commanded the highest technology of the time, including the use of immigrant artisans. The estimated capacity of the warehouse group at the Narutaki site in Wakayama is also approximately 10,000 *koku* (about 51,000 bushels), and from its high level of architectural technology and location near the mouth of the Ki River, a connection may be inferred with a Great King or with another powerful force such as the Ki clan. If it were only a matter of these two warehouse groups, it would be possible to see them as special facilities for storing military provisions in case of internal strife or external warfare in the fifth century. But as illustrated by warehouse groups in elite residential districts at the Gennojō site in Gumma and elsewhere, the influential chiefly strata in several regions possessed large-scale warehouses for storing grain.[46] Given that ordinary settlements also had granaries, as noted above, larger facilities on the estates of regional chiefs should be regarded as holding accumulations of tributary payments rather than the produce of a local agricultural community. While a number of large raised-floor storehouses attached to the moated village at the Yoshinogari site in Saga during the Yayoi Period may be inferred as holding the collective stores of the entire moated settlement, this does not hold true for later periods.[47] Once the moated settlements dissolved in the third century and elite residences stood alone, a split emerged between the individual granaries in commoners' residences and the "political storehouses" in which taxes paid to the chief were stored.

Next, let us consider the mobilization of labor for the construction of tombs, for water management, and for other civil engineering projects. During the three-hundred-year period following the emergence of keyhole tombs at the end of the third century, it is estimated that 4,000 round and square keyhole tombs were built nationwide. In addition, there were also simple round and square tombs built, whose numbers are estimated to exceed 100,000. By Ishikawa Noboru's calculations, there are still 948 keyhole tombs in the Kinki region, and the combined volume of their mounds is approximately 18 million cubic meters.[48] The largest of these, Daisen (traditionally attributed to Nintoku), has a volume of approximately 1.4 million cubic meters (see Figure 1.4). In calculating the amount of labor involved in the construction of its mound, Umehara Sueji once estimated that if a single worker could dig one cubic meter of earth and transport it for a distance of 250 meters in a day, then with 1,000 workers a day it would require four years to complete.[49] More recently, however, the Ōbayashi construction firm calculated that 6.8 million man-days of labor would be necessary for building the mound and the surrounding moats and for surfacing the mound with stones using traditional methods of construction.[50] They did not, however, calculate labor for the manufacture and placement of ceramic jars

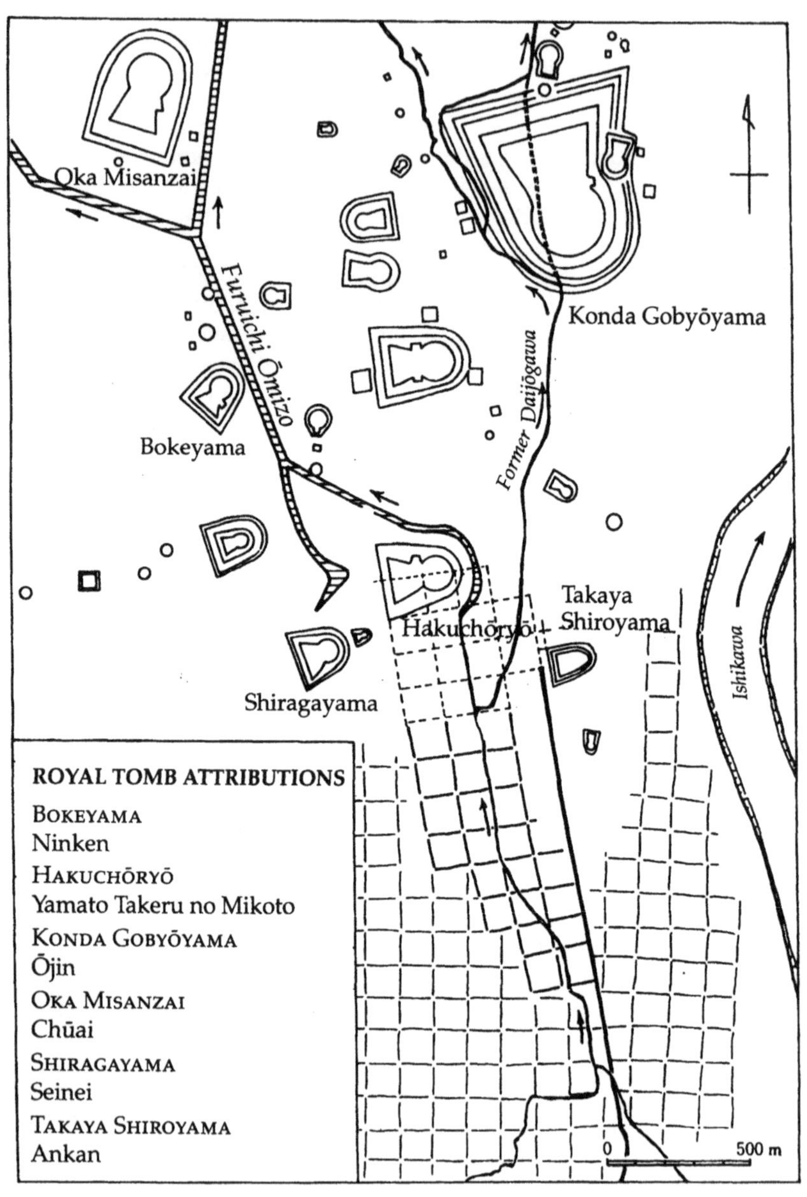

Fig. 1.5. Furuichi Ōmizo and Vicinity

and figures (*haniwa*). The roughly five-fold increase over Umehara's estimate results from a higher assessment for the labor needed per unit volume of the mound, plus considerations for the construction of the moats and the hauling and placement of paving stones, and so on. Larger tomb sizes bring striking increases in the distances that dirt and other materials must be transported. Accordingly, a straightforward calculation based on the figures just given, about 4.8 man-days of labor per cubic meter of mound for the tomb alleged to be Nintoku's, can only be applied with great caution to other tombs in general. But using this as a rough guide for the amount of labor involved in the construction of keyhole tombs in the Kinki region, the total figure exceeds 80 million man-days. Apart from this, round and square tombs are numerous, even though small in scale. If these are included in the calculations, the above figure probably reaches 100 million. The keyhole tombs of the Kinki region alone account for one-fourth of the national total. Because the number of very large-scale mounds in the Kinki is high, the total amount of labor for building all of the tombs nationwide can in no way be taken as four times the figure for Kinki, but some sense can be gained nevertheless of the tremendous size of that total.

Civil engineering projects other than tomb construction included the development of cultivated lands and the associated digging of waterways for irrigation. A large canal, the Furuichi Ōmizo, which spans the cities of Habikino and Fujiidera in Osaka Prefecture, is a massive waterway two kilometers long and up to twenty meters wide (see Figure 1.5). Scholars date its construction to either the fifth or seventh century. By positing an organic link with the large-scale reworking of the natural landscape, including the changing of natural waterways or the digging of man-made ones that accompanied the building of the nearby tomb attributed to the monarch Ōjin, I believe it possible to date the ditch back to the fifth century.[51] It is also clear that major construction of watercourses and large-scale development of agricultural lands took place during the later fifth century in the vicinity of the elite residence at Mitsudera. Among these, at the Ashida Kaiko site, a ten-meter-wide waterway was built over a considerable distance for developing fields on tableland. In addition, Noto Takeshi has inferred from a comparison of the natural settings of the present and former paths of the Karasawa River, and from the results of a partial excavation, that a stretch of several kilometers of the present course of the river results from changes made in the later fifth century.[52]

While it is likely that similar examples of large-scale waterworks from the Kofun Period will be found in every region, it is already possible to make the following two inferences. First, the development of new agricultural lands in the Kofun Period was on a much larger scale than previously believed. The phrase "checkerboard [*jōri*] development" embodies the supposition that the implementation of the grid system used for official land-opening projects in the Nara Period comprised the opening up of new fields, and that it was a time of fundamental change in the development of agricultural lands. Without doubt, implementing the grid system was most likely accompanied by the opening up of many new fields and waterways. However, the true character of *jōrisei* should be regarded as the reorganization of field allotments. Highly significant in this regard is Kishi Toshio's observation, based on a study of *jōri* allotments in Echizen, that "Tōdaiji was only able to establish estates [*shōen*] by selecting an area at the periphery of the region in which the development of *jōri* allotments was already well advanced," suggesting that the distribution of grid allotments in Echizen was the result of field development prior to the mid-eighth century.[53] This indicates the trend in more developed regions, and is evidence of an age of major land development prior to the Nara Period.

The second point is that the widespread building of waterways and the opening up of fields in the vicinity of the Mitsudera site dates to nearly the same period spanned by the elite residence itself, the latter part of the fifth century and the beginning of the sixth. This indicates that the land development project was enacted under the leadership of the chief based at that residence. It may also be inferred that the generations of chiefs who lived there were interred in the three keyhole tombs lying at a point one kilometer to the northwest, the majestic tombs and stately residences serving as monuments glorifying rule over a surrounding area developed at the chiefs' own initiative. The four-part complement of elite residences, watercourse, cultivated land, and tomb comprise a scene that developed not only at Mitsudera, but presumably in every part of the archipelago. The chiefly stratum was constantly mobilizing commoners for the construction of tombs and for the extensive development of agricultural land based on water management projects. This was surely the forerunner of what came to be called *yōeki* (corvée duty) in the eighth century.

Relations between Central and Regional Chiefs

From the discussion thus far it has become clear, based on an analysis of settlements and graves, that a three-tiered hierarchy emerged among chiefs, commoners, and an intermediate stratum. I have also argued that tributary relations involving produce given to local chiefs and to Great Kings can be inferred from the pattern of warehouses at chiefly estates. To summarize this configuration of status differences and tributary relations, the chiefly elite may be recognized as a ruling class that appropriated the fruits of the commoners' labor. Also, it may be inferred that among the "shanty dwellers" on the chief's estate were persons directly subordinate to the chief. Taking as clues the breakup of moated villages, the segregation of the elite residences, and the split of the communal cemetery into polar extremes, the emergence of these status relations can be seen to have progressed rapidly from the mid-third century onward.

Based on such developments, keyhole tombs emerged at the end of the third century. In the preceding Yayoi Period, the upper stratum comprised of the chiefly elite had built large isolated mounds, but regional differences in burial customs were great. In parts of the San'yō region facing the Inland Sea, square mounds (or round mounds, as at the Tatetsuki site) with projections on both ends were utilized during the latter half of the second century and the early third century, whereas in the San'in region on the Japan Sea, mounds were built in a square shape with projections at the four corners (see Fig. 1.2, the Chūsenji tomb). These projections are thought to be ritual sites that were annexed to the central burial facility. By the mid-third century, round mounds with a projection for ritual purposes built on one side only, a shape very close to that of a keyhole mound, appeared in various regions. The standardized keyhole shape that was based on this type of grave is thought to be an indigenous development, incorporating elements inspired by Chinese philosophy such as a three-tiered construction and an orientation of the burial with the head to the north. Given this northern orientation, three-tiered construction, and the ritual use of *haniwa* it may be inferred that the chiefly stratum of the Kinai and Kibi regions formed the nucleus of power that gave rise to the style of ritual associated with the keyhole tombs (see Map 0.2, p. 4).[54]

Keyhole tombs were built on a grand scale from the very onset of their appearance. The mound of Hashihaka in Nara, a classic example of the earliest form of keyhole tomb, is an imposing 276 meters long overall and 28 meters high at the round portion. Its volume, approximately one hundred times that of the Yayoi-period mound of Tatetsuki, vividly displays the amount of energy invested in its construction and the mature level of political authority able to mobilize such energy. Keyhole tombs also followed standard plans for the shape of the mound in both horizontal and vertical outline. A number of plans coexisted at the beginning of the Kofun Period, however, as indicated by differences even within Yamato in the shape of the front portion of the mound for Hashihaka and Sakurai Chausuyama tombs. Also, while the regionally separated tombs of Hashihaka, Tsubai Ōtsukayama in Kyoto, and Urama Chausuyama in Okayama all share the same outline, their relative sizes follow the ratio of 6:4:3, a significant indication that even with the same shape of mound, different ranks existed in terms of size. Further, square keyhole tombs and simple round and square tombs all emerged simultaneously with the round keyhole as the four basic shapes. And while the Kyoto Motoinari and Okayama Kurumazuka tombs are of the square keyhole shape, the proportions of their components are similar in pattern to Hashihaka, while their overall lengths, if that of Hashihaka is given as six, can be expressed as two and one respectively (see Figure 1.6 and Figure 1.2).[55]

From the foregoing we can gain some hints about the relation between round and square keyhole tombs. In mounded graves of the Yayoi Period there were two basic patterns for the shape of the portion of the mound in which the burial was placed, one round and one square.[56] Also, since both round and square tombs (with long narrow projections annexed to them) were constructed at the end of the Yayoi Period, roots of the difference between round and square keyhole shapes can be sought there. Those differences articulate descent and alliance membership. However, as shown by the close relationship in proportion between the standardized round and square keyhole shapes at the end of the third century, a new governing principle was introduced that unified the different mound shapes. For instance, that the earliest Kofun-age tombs in the region bordering the Japan Sea—where in Yayoi times square tombs

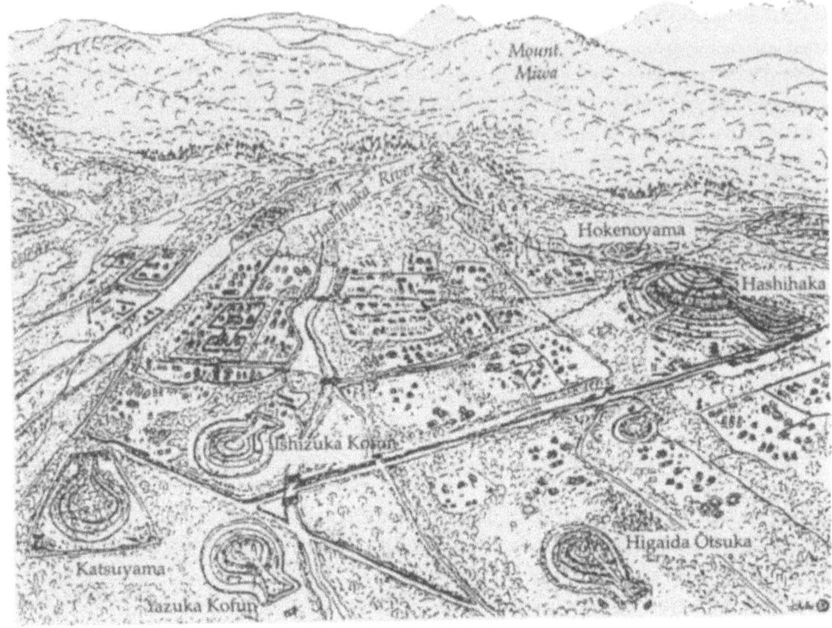

Shapes of the Kofun around Hashihaka

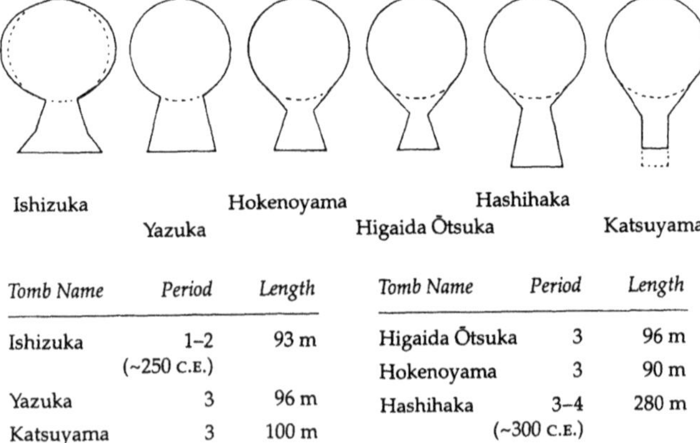

Tomb Name	*Period*	*Length*	*Tomb Name*	*Period*	*Length*
Ishizuka	1–2 (~250 C.E.)	93 m	Higaida Ōtsuka	3	96 m
Yazuka	3	96 m	Hokenoyama	3	90 m
Katsuyama	3	100 m	Hashihaka	3–4 (~300 C.E.)	280 m

Fig. 1.6. The Vicinity of Hashihaka Kofun at the Foot of Mount Miwa in Yamato

with four projecting corners flourished—were square mounds like Tsukuri-yama Kofun, which lacks projecting corners, reflects this new order.

Based upon a study of the distribution of duplicate sets, each made from a single mold, of triangular-rimmed mirrors (*sankakubuchi shinjūkyō*), Kobayashi Yukio established clearly that a close network of political relations existed among chiefs buried in the earliest tombs of the Kofun Period, and that this network operated under the leadership of a powerful chieftain in the Kinai.[57] It is of great interest that of the two tombs holding central positions in the network, Tsubai Ōtsukayama in Kyoto and Kurumazuka in Okayama, the former is a round keyhole and the latter a square keyhole, while the two mounds are also closely related in terms of their proportions.[58] It is also significant that many of the tombs sharing duplicate sets of mirrors with Okayama Kurumazuka are located in eastern Japan, and that square keyhole shapes are common among the earliest tombs of the Kofun Period built in that region.

Taking another look at the relationship between round and square keyhole tombs from the perspective of size, there is a considerable gap in the early Kofun Period between the largest square keyhole mound, Shin'yama in Nara (127 meters), and the 276-meter Hashihaka mound. Moreover, although the square keyhole shape was used for chiefly tombs in every region, including the Kinai, its use for large-scale elite tombs waned in the Kinai area from the middle Kofun Period (fifth century). Also, tombs exceeding 200 meters in size are of the round keyhole shape exclusively throughout the entire Kofun Period, and the continued use of square keyholes during the late Kofun Period was limited to Izumo in western Japan and parts of the Kantō in the east.[59] In other words, the superiority in terms of the difference in size between square and round keyhole tombs, already in place at the beginning of the Kofun Period, developed over time into an absolute gap in their hierarchical relationship. From these considerations it is possible to draw a conclusion regarding the relationship between round and square keyhole tombs. The difference between building round or square graves served in every region to symbolize chiefly pedigrees based on descent and political alliance. However, with the emergence of standardized tomb shapes at the end of the third century, while the old differences in chiefly status continued to be recognized through differences in tomb shape, they were also merged into a unified status hierarchy in which square keyhole shapes were placed one rank below round ones.

How then should it be explained that differences exist in tomb size for both round and square keyhole shapes, and that among round keyhole tombs there are examples only thirty meters long that are far inferior in terms of mound size to some square keyhole tombs? In taking up this problem, I wish to make an analogy to the situation that existed at the formation of the Bakuhan system in the early modern period, when various warlords (*daimyō*) of the later Sengoku Period were designated as blood-related (*shimpan*), traditional (*fudai*), and distant (*tōzama*) based on their relationship with the Tokugawa hegemons. According to this schema, some distant retainers were granted higher rice revenues than were many blood-related warlords. In other words, we can posit that a dual system of status representation was established in the early Kofun Period in which chiefly pedigrees and their status differences were expressed in terms of tomb shape, with tomb size indicating differences in power.[60]

In making the foregoing summary I risk the possibility of being misinterpreted as claiming that at the end of the third century the chiefly elite throughout the Japanese archipelago had already been integrated into an orderly hierarchy, and that the political authority of the Kinai had attained an unshakable position of superiority. In this regard I would like to take up the problem of changes in political relations from the fourth through sixth centuries, in connection with the relationship between the central and peripheral regions. Keyhole tombs seldom exist as single mounds in isolation. It is more common to find them built as a series of tombs forming a local group, attributable to a particular chiefly lineage. Rarely did a single lineage build keyhole tombs spanning the entire Kofun Period in its early, middle, and late phases. A number of different chronologies are known, such as those ending within the early phase, those continuing from the early through the middle phases, those beginning in the middle and continuing into the late phase, and those limited to the late phase. Also, when several chiefly lineages exist in a single region, there are tombs or lineages that stand far superior to the others—in paramount fashion—in terms of mound size and grave goods. But it must be noted that the rank of regional paramount tomb or lineage was not held firmly by a single lineage over time.

By comparing the pattern of continuity or disruption of chiefly lineages and of paramount status in various regions, intervals of exceptional change become evident. These comprise the three periods of the end of the fourth through the early fifth centuries, the end of the fifth century, and the early part of the sixth century. In addition, when this phenomenon is further examined in terms of geographical units based on the ancient provinces or districts, it is seen to have an even more fascinating characteristic.[61] For example, within the Otokuni locale of Kyoto Prefecture, in the fourth century the Mukō family held the paramount status over a number of generations. Then, around the year 400 such status went to the Katakihara lineage; then to the Nagaoka lineage from the early through the mid-fifth century; then to the Yamada lineage at the end of the fifth; then to the Mukō lineage once again in the early sixth; and finally it reverted back to the Nagaoka lineage at the end of the sixth century. Similarly, changes in the locus of the paramount tomb have also been pointed out in various other regions. These have been interpreted as representing either a stage in which chiefly authority was as yet unstable or in which it was shared in rotation, a condition held to characterize the stage of a "tribal confederacy."[62] But considering that the periods of change in chiefly lineages and paramountcy are in agreement in panregional fashion, it is difficult to regard such changes in chiefly lineage fortunes simply as independent developments within any single region.

Of even greater interest are changes within the Kinai region in the location of the tomb cluster producing the largest keyhole tombs, as pointed out by Shiraishi Taichirō. Whereas in the fourth century the locus of the largest tombs was the southeastern portion of Yamato, around the year 400 this moved temporarily to northern Yamato, and in the fifth century it was based in Kawachi and Izumi.[63] As many of these colossal keyhole tombs are traditionally regarded as mausoleums of historical monarchs, two possible interpretations are Shiraishi's view that the actual seat of central authority shifted, and Kondō Yoshirō's assertion that only the locus for constructing chiefly tombs changed.[64] But it is highly significant that the periods of relocation of the sites of these colossal tombs in Kinai often match the points of disruption in the paramount chiefly lineages in various regions. This should probably be interpreted as evidence of nationwide political transformations in which developments at the center and periphery were linked. Specifically, when a change in the balance of power developed among the central chiefly stratum in the Kinai, the struggle grew into a civil war involving not only the middle and lower chiefly strata at the center but also the chiefly lineages in outlying regions. In the new political order that resulted, in addition to shifts in the political power base in the Kinai that gave birth to changes in the center of distribution of colossal keyhole tombs, changes also occurred regionally in relations of dominance among chiefly lineages and in the locus of paramount tombs.

To evaluate this reconstruction historically by employing the results of research with documentary sources, the change at the end of the fourth and beginning of the fifth century may be associated with the emergence of Ōjin and Nintoku's line; that in the latter part of the fifth century coincides with the period in which Yūryaku was active; and that in the early sixth century coincides with political movements attending the emergence of the monarch known as Keitai.[65] It may be noted, moreover, that with the change in the early fifth century, square keyhole tombs were no longer utilized by the chiefly elite in the Kinai region, and with the exception of certain outlying regions, this mound shape entered a state of general decline. The round keyhole remained supreme as the elite tomb shape from this time on. From these facts it appears possible to gain a hint for evaluating political relations in the fourth century. Whereas during the fourth century chiefs buried in round keyhole tombs generally held superior positions, it may be inferred that persons interred in square keyhole mounds had been able to assert a measure of autonomy based on local genealogical claims going back to the Yayoi Period. In other words, in the dual system of status representation posited above and based on the two factors of shape and size, it would appear that autonomy in shape held greater weight in the fourth century than in later times.

The Machinery of Authority and Control of the Populace

Offices such as that of "swordbearer" and "*tensōjin*" (meaning unclear) are known from inscriptions on swords found at the Inariyama tomb in Saitama and at Eta Funayama tomb in Kumamoto.[66] According to Naoki Kōjirō, such inscriptions indicate that a bureaucratic system was established no later than the latter part of the fifth century.[67] Moreover, depending how one evaluates the historicity of the eight-generation genealogy proclaimed in the Inariyama inscription to have "served [the Great Kings] as heads of the swordbearers," there is room to interpret the beginnings of that system of offices as going back further in time.

In the bureaucratic system proposed by Naoki there is also the office of storehouse intendant (*kurahito*), in which the prevalence of persons from immigrant clans is of great significance to a historical evaluation of the warehouse clusters at the Hōenzaka and Narutaki sites discussed above. The overseeing of governmental warehouses for storing tributary payments, which required record-keeping and arithmetic skills, was most likely the specialized duty of these intendants. The Narutaki site is thought to date from the first part of the fifth century; and considering that the technology used in the construction of the warehouses, as well as in the manufacture of the large Sue ware pots used at the site, was strongly influenced by imported techniques, then at this point in time the possibility that immigrant groups were involved as storehouse intendants seems reasonable.

Moreover, Inaridai No. 1 mound in present-day Chiba Prefecture, a mid-fifth century tomb which yielded a double-bladed sword inscribed "bestowed [by] the King," is a small round tomb only twenty-eight meters in diameter, a fact regarded as odd at the time of the discovery but which may turn out to be of great significance.[68] Armor was interred in this tomb along with the inscribed blade. Indeed, for round and scalloped-shaped tombs of the fifth century in general, swords and a set of armor are often found together among the grave goods. This is true for both large-scale round mounds like the seventy-meter Maruyama tomb in Kyoto and small ones like the twenty-five-meter Dōyama No. 1 mound in Osaka. The former tomb also included a gilt bronze quiver, an extremely rare item for the mid-fifth century; and since similar items of approximately the same age have been recovered in Korea from the Pokch'on-dong tomb cluster in Pusan, the quiver can be regarded as an element of imported culture. The grave goods at the Dōyama No. 1 mound included Sue ware as well, produced with technology that had been imported not too long before.

The Inaridai No. 1, Maruyama, and Dōyama No. 1 mounds all share similar sets of military equipment among their grave goods, as well as items that could not have been obtained without a close relationship to the central authority—that is, products obtained through relations with the Korean Peninsula or made with technology imported from that region. Accordingly, it is highly likely that these tombs' occupants were warriors who had close ties with the central political powers in the Kinai, and in the process of combat and other actions against outside forces, were given items rare for the time. The most reasonable interpretation is that the middle and lower members of the chiefly stratum buried in these round tombs were incorporated into a military organization used by the central power in Kinai for domestic and foreign warfare. If a class of swordbearers and swordbearer chiefs was established in the fifth century, then we may infer that the occupants of these round tombs were such middle- and lower-ranking chiefs who formed the outer echelon of the military organization. References in the passage in the *Liu Sung History* (*Sung shu*) concerning the Japanese islands to "troops" and to the

"Commandant Who Subjugates the West" hint that at the center of the Yamato political administration was a Great Chief involved in military affairs.[69] And if it is assumed that additional strata were incorporated beneath this figure, with the middle and lower chiefs of the outer regions included as the rank and file, it is clear that a military organization owing allegiance to a central authority had emerged and was separate from the local militia of various regions.

Having dealt with aspects of administrative structure and military organization, I now take up the question of the organization of the populace based on analysis of settlements. In the fifth century, activities of immigrant groups became prominent everywhere, but until now the location of their settlements could only be inferred indirectly through the existence of tomb clusters having unusual horizontal stone chambers or showing the practice of using oven-shaped funerary items.[70] In recent years, however, it has become increasingly possible to presume the locations of the settlements themselves from residential remains that either yield large amounts of a type of pottery called Kanshiki ware—brought in from Korea—or that have Korean style heating systems with hot air ducts built beneath the floor.[71] From such materials it can be deduced that in the more advanced regions such as Kinai, the admixture of immigrant groups and previously established groups, and the division between them of residential districts, increased from the fifth century on. In conjunction with this, the formulation of regional plans aimed at reallocating residential and agricultural land and cemeteries, or at integrating the populace into the larger social order, conceivably became a political concern.[72]

This is suggested by the planned layouts of settlements and agricultural lands. An ancient grid system covering an area of approximately 46.6 hectares, or 115 acres, in the Ikaruga region in Nara shows the redivision of the local district by Prince Shōtoku's household at the end of the sixth century.[73] But does this not indicate that such planning had been conducted, even if on a limited scale, prior to that time? At the Ōzono site in Osaka discussed earlier, a rectangular residential area was surrounded by a ditch; the principal structures inside were ground-level residences having storehouses and a well; and from the presence of Sue ware jar stands not found in ordinary pit-dwellings, the complex may be regarded as the residence of a petty chieftain or a prominent member of the cultivator stratum. This residential lot did not stand singly, however, but was lined up with others on the northern and eastern sides of the moat.[74] Mizuno Masayoshi further envisions a road regulating the layout of these residential lots.[75] Sekiguchi Kōichi also points out that "ditches and other facilities including tombs and residences were laid out in regular fashion" in the vicinity of the Motojuku-Gōdo site in Tomioka City, Gumma Prefecture.[76] Although verification through further excavation is necessary, these phenomena are worth noting especially in light of the example, seen at Mitsudera, of the development of agricultural lands in the vicinity of a residential precinct.

If only the planned layout of residential areas is taken into consideration, these are of course present in the fourth-century settlements found at the Kobukada and the Ōhira sites in Shizuoka, in which residential precincts share the common size of forty to fifty meters on a side. In these cases the planning probably was not carried out on a scale greater than that of an individual settlement. It may nevertheless be posited that from the fifth century on, because of the need to reorganize residential lands, agricultural lands, and cemeteries, regulations instituted at higher levels with regard to settlement planning were probably enforced across broad areas.

Political Authority and the Organization of the Distribution of Goods

The end of the second century and the beginning of the third (the latter half of the late Yayoi Period) saw the complete disappearance of stone tools and the advent of a full-scale Iron Age. While it is possible that the smelting of iron within the Japanese archipelago, which could guarantee the supply of iron implements, began from this time, at present the oldest material evidence for the production of iron in smelting furnaces is found at the sixth-century sites of Ōzōike Minami in Okayama and Enjo in Kyoto. Even if it is provisionally granted that smelting was known in the archipelago from the third century, the simultaneous dependence on Korean sources of raw iron is suggested by the account of the "eastern barbarians" in the *History of the Wei Dynasty*. This may have been because of a need for high-quality iron for weapons and armor. It is possible that behind the period of "disturbances and warfare" at the end of the second century noted in the Wei records lay competition among the chiefly stratum in western Japan over routes for the importation of iron, particularly between a league of chieftains in northern Kyūshū and another centered in the Kinai region. As archaeological evidence for such warfare, there are hilltop settlements that chould have served as refuges or as sites for communication by smoke signals. Also, interregional exchange of ceramic technology in this period slackened, and the regional differences noted above among chiefly graves may also have been a reflection of interregional rivalry.[77]

Previously, during the first century, the chiefly stratum in northern Kyūshū developed close political connections with the Han Dynasty—as signified by the gold seal inscribed with "The King of Na of Wa [affiliated with] Han," by imported bronze mirrors interred in jar burials, and by the precious glass ornaments found at the Suku and Mikumo sites in present-day Fukuoka Prefecture. Kyūshū chieftains maintained their superiority within Wa society through their contacts with advanced civilizations. Discoveries of iron from settlement sites of this time are relatively greater in northern Kyūshū than in the Kinai region, and it is thus likely that Kyūshū stood in better position for the acquisition of vital resources such as iron, based on the same relationships. But in the second century, perhaps in connection with the decline in the Han Dynasty's political authority in China and East Asia in general, the superiority of the chiefly league in northern Kyūshū presumably weakened, leading to the outbreak of "disturbances and warfare" against a background of imbalance in the power relationships within Wa society. Also, from the first part of the third century to the middle of that century (the period of Shōnai-style pottery), when the strife is thought to have been drawing toward a conclusion, the low-mounded square-precinct style of burial that had developed continuously through the Middle and Late Yayoi Periods in the Kinai region spread into Kyūshū, while Shōnai ceramic technology, which had also developed in the Kinai, began to exert influence on pottery manufacture in every region, including northern Kyūshū. Judging from these developments, it may be surmised that the strife concluded with the chiefly league of the Kinai gaining preeminence.[78]

Shortly afterward, the keyhole tomb also emerged. As previously noted, the establishment of the ritual complex incorporating these tombs and the mechanism for the distribution of triangular-rimmed mirrors were both centered in the zone linking the Kinai and Kibi. If importance is given to this geographic pattern, then we should regard the chiefly alliance of Kinai and Kibi as having played a significant role in concluding the strife mentioned above. When we thus consider, on the basis of archaeological materials, that this same alliance of Kinai and Kibi constituted the paramount political authority from the early to the middle parts of the third century, then it most likely follows that the country of Yamatai, where the *History of the Wei Dynasty* says Himiko resided, was located in the Kinai region.

If we attach significance to the concurrence of the disappearance of stone tools and the conclusion of the conflict, then during the third century, which witnessed Himiko's emergence, it is reasonable to suppose that a major change occurred in the mechanism of distributing raw iron. It is likely that the political center where Himiko reigned was established through its superior control over the distribution of raw iron from the southern part of Korea, especially the Pyonghan region. Using that control as a powerful lever, the center likely extended its hegemony over the various powers in the archipelago. A passage in the *History of the Wei Dynasty* notes, "There are . . . markets in each province where necessities are exchanged under the supervision of the Wa officials," indicating that control over the distribution of goods was important for maintaining authority. It should be recognized that the bestowal of prestige goods, represented by the triangular-rimmed mirrors, was but an alternate expression of control over the mechanism of distribution used for necessary goods such as raw iron.

This relationship concerning the distribution of iron continued in later periods as well. Ingots of raw iron are found in fifth-century tombs. There are larger and smaller standards for the shape and weight of these ingots, and from statistical investigations of these materials found in various regions, it is clear that one-tenth of the ancient Chinese unit of one *kin*, or approximately twenty-two grams, was the basic unit of measure. This finding is of significance for considerations of the nature of the distribution of these ingots, and as an indicator of their use as a form of currency in kind.[79] Furthermore, chemical analysis of raw iron ingots suggest the possibility that they were not produced in Japan.[80] Based on these facts, it may be considered that in addition to political rights and interests, the motivation of securing the supply of raw iron lay behind the claims to supremacy over Korea made with such persistence by the five kings of Wa. The last mission to the southern dynasty was sent by King Bu of Wa, who is presumed to be Great King Yūryaku, and the smelting of iron began on a large scale from the sixth century. It may thus be said that the establishment of a system for the stable procurement of iron in Japan was intimately linked with the political situation in East Asia.[81]

Now even though the making of salt is possible anywhere there is seawater, salt-making in the Kofun Period was carried out only in certain places such as Amakusa; the Inland Sea coastal regions; the regions lining the straits between the Ki Peninsula, Awaji Island, Wakasa, and Noto; and the vicinities of present-day Chita and Atsumi in Aichi Prefecture.[82] This indicates a division of labor, perhaps by political means, among regions in the formation of production sites. The production of Sue ware also began in the first part of the fifth century, and during the initial stage it was limited to manufacturing sites like the Sue Mura kilns in Osaka. But in the sixth century Sue production started up in various regions, and local distribution spheres emerged.[83] Examining the shape of distribution networks of the Kofun Period just enumerated, it is seen that for some items like salt and Sue ware, both production and distribution developed along regional lines. For items like iron, however, the dependence on sources external to Japan through the fifth century is of significance for considering the means by which political authority developed in Japan.

For the distribution of items like iron it is probably necessary to posit, if only for a temporary period, the activity of merchants who operated on the broader East Asian stage. Among the axes, chisels, and so forth recovered from sites of the early and middle Yayoi Period are items made by casting. These were not only technologically beyond the means of Wa society at the time, but were also clearly products of northeastern China on morphological grounds.[84] While it is commonly thought that these iron objects were brought from overseas merely for their rarity, if we attribute significance to the fact that wealthy merchants during the Warring States Period in China conducted large-scale iron manufacturing and extended their marketing routes widely throughout East Asia, then regardless of which of the two conceivable routes was involved (the merchants coming directly, or trading through mediating groups in Korea), this may be regarded as an important source of iron during the first half of the Yayoi Period.[85] The introduction of monopolies on the sale of salt and iron by the Han dynasty, however, would have brought changes to this system of distribution, conceivably resulting in an increase in the relative importance of iron from southern Korea. This made control of the distribution of iron all the more important for political groups in Japan and on the Korean Peninsula from the third century onward.

It is possible to verify the close links thus posited between the development and maintenance of political authority and control over the distribution of economic necessities. In this light, we must consider the later system of taxes in kind under the *ritsuryō* order, and the circulation of goods through markets in the Nara capital and in central government headquarters in the various regions.[86] Even if the later tax system was in essence a method of tribute, it was a politically organized system for the circulation of goods, and may be regarded as state intervention in economic relations. Similarily, in the sixth century the production of iron in Kibi and Tango can be verified, and considering the circulation of salt and Sue ware as well, a mechanism for the distribution of goods that could be called the kernel of the tax-in-kind system can be discerned in the Kofun Period.

Conclusion: A Proposed "Round Keyhole Order"

We have now made an examination of various facets of Japanese society, based on archaeological materials, from the time of the emergence of keyhole tombs at the end of the third century. We have been able to discern, first, the existence of stratification among chiefs, commoners, and persons of intermediate rank from an analysis of settlements and funerary practices; and, moreover, the existence of an order of status rankings visible in the form of differences in the shape and scale of mounded tombs. In addition, we may conclude from the existence of warehouses for tributary payments—separate from those for common stores of grain—that a system of taxes had emerged; and from the colossal tombs and the existence of large-scale facilities for water management, that a corvée system had developed. Accordingly, it may be judged that the stratification was a system of class relations involving economic exploitation. Also, through observations of the organization of administrative officials and military forces, we can recognize the establishment of an organized authority possessing a means of coercion standing distinct from the various local militia of the component regions. Finally, in the mid-third century, the central authority of Wa, grasping control of the means for the distribution of iron and other economic necessities, extended its hegemony over chiefs in the principal regions of the archipelago. Through its control of this vital function, it dismantled the older organizations of society which had been comprised of independent units based on economically self-sufficient communities.

From the foregoing it seems reasonable to say that from the end of the third century, Japanese society had reached the level of a state in its organization. Archaeologically, this social system is symbolized by the emergence of a politicized hierarchy of burial practices with the keyhole tomb at the apex. As a term for this state-level political system that preceded the subsequent *ritsuryō* order, I would like to propose the term "round keyhole order" to reflect the symbolism of the tombs for the political system of this period. There will surely be objections, of course, to the subsumption of these three hundred years under the concept of a single order. In merely comparing the ideal forms of the tombs themselves, a difference in the political nature of the square keyhole shape was noted between the fourth and fifth centuries, while in the sixth century changes took place in the ritual complex of the keyhole tombs as symbolized by the incorporation of horizontal stone chambers, and differences in mound size also became less pronounced.[87] But I would like to stress the common use of keyhole tombs as the means for expressing the political status of chiefs in the various regions until the adoption of square mounds as the shape for Great Kings at the end of the sixth century.

Whereas dating the emergence of the ancient Japanese state coincident with establishment of the *ritsuryō* order is standard, if the round keyhole order can be regarded as a state organization, then it would represent the first half of the earliest Japanese state formation, with the *ritsuryō* order occupying the latter half. Earlier in this essay, I stressed the importance of analyzing state formation as a process of long-term change. In the Yayoi Period, when agricultural society developed in Japan, stratified relations were present from the very early stages; and in the first century C.E. there were already confederacies of tribes in areas such as northern Kyūshū and the Kinai region. If such confederacies are to be taken as the kernels of state formation, the emergence of keyhole tombs at the end of the third century may be considered the beginning of the full-scale process of state formation. Here I wish to conclude by noting our growing recognition of the Kofun Period as a time of tremendous change within a long-term process of development, over a span of approximately one thousand years, from the start of the Yayoi Period to the establishment of the *ritsuryō* order at the turn of the eighth century.[88]

Notes

1. Tsude Hiroshi 1989c.

2. This evolutionary spectrum, along which egalitarian societies, chiefdoms, and states range, is articulated in Service 1975.

3. For an English discussion of this *ritsuryō* order, the system of government based on formalized legal codes that developed in the late seventh and eighth centuries, see Piggott 1997, chapter 6.

4. Due to the acidity of Japan's soils, iron survives poorly under ordinary circumstances, and hence its use must often be inferred circumstantially.

5. For background discussion on Himiko, see Edwards 1996. And for a still more recent synthesis of Tsude's ideas in English, see Tsude 1996.

6. Interpreter's note: The article was originally published as Tsude Hiroshi 1991. Although another translation was previously published (Tsude Hiroshi 1992), the author was enthusiastic when we proposed retranslation for this volume.

7. See Suzuki Yasutami rev. ed. 1983 for a multi-faceted synopsis of the research up to the early 1980s. Also see Kitō Kiyoaki 1985, where Kitō makes an ambitious endeavor to compare issues in postwar Japanese research with those of European and other foreign countries concerning state formation. Interpreter's note: For Kitō's work in English see Kitō Kiyoaki 1990; Kitō Kiyoaki 1995; and Kitō Kiyoaki n. d. Kitō also reviewed Tsude's monograph on agricultural society and state formation in Kitō Kiyoaki 1990. In addition, the essays in *Acta Asiatica* 63 (1992) and *Acta Asiatica* 69 (1995) by Ishigami Eiichi, Tōno Haruyuki, Wada Atsumu, and Satō Makoto concerning Japanese archaeology and early Japanese history are very helpful.

8. Interpreter's note: For references and useful explanatory notes to *ichidaisotsu* in the *Chinese History of the Wei Dynasty* (*Wei chih*) report on Wa in the section entitled Wajinden, see the index and appropriate pages in Mizuno Yū 1987. There is also a reference to border guards (*hinamori*) posted in Tsushima in the Wajinden. See *Nihon kokugo daijiten* (Tokyo: Shōgakukan, 1975, vol. 9, 77). For an English translation of the relevant passages of the Chinese histories, see Goodrich 1951, 8-20.

9. Ishimoda Shō 1971.

10. Hara Hidesaburō 1984. Interpreter's note: For translations of these Chinese records, see de Bary 2001, 6–10.

11. Interpreter's note: See the article by Hara Hidesaburō in chapter 3 of this volume.

12. See Engels 1965; and Weber 1909. In Japanese, see Masuda Yoshirō 1969.

13. Inoue Mitsusada 1965, 532–5.

14. See for instance Service 1971; Service 1975, 303–8; and Sahlins 1968, 20–7.

15. An early introduction in Japanese of the concept of the chiefdom is contained in Masuda Yoshirō 1969.

16. See Kirchoff 1959 and Morgan 1877.

17. Claessen 1978 and Claessen and Skalnik 1981.

18. Claessen and Skalnik reconvene their international conference once every several years. I attended the session held in the summer of 1983 in Montreal, and was greatly stimulated by the three days of vigorous and often humor-filled debate. I am grateful to Professor Ikawa-Smith of McGill University for inviting me to join in that session.

19. Claessen 1978, 21.

20. See Watanabe Yoshimichi 1948, Tōma Seita 1947, and Ishimoda Shō 1971.

21. Interpreter's note: See Engels 1972 ed., 224.

22. Tsude Hiroshi 1989c, 401–93.

23. Hara Hidesaburō 1984, 35.

24. Kitō Kiyoaki 1985, 21.

25. Yoshida Akira 1973, 36 and 148.

26. Kondō Yoshirō 1983, 366 and 377.

27. Morgan 1877, 120–50.

28. Sahlins 1968, 21.

29. Izumi Seiichi 1952.

30. Wittfogel 1939 and Wittfogel 1961.

31. See Tsude Hiroshi 1989c, 421–5.

32. See for instance Childe 1950, Nishijima Sadao 1981, Kageyama Tsuyoshi 1984, and Watanabe Shin'ichirō 1989.

33. Sakaehara Towao 1972 and Matsubara Hironobu 1985.

34. Concerning such mirrors, see chapter 2 by Kobayashi Yukio in this volume.

35. Kadowaki Teiji 1975, esp. 350–1.

36. Nagayama Yasutaka argues, "In Greece . . . territorial rule was not achieved even in such a comparatively small area as the Grecian mainland, which was constantly under a state of warfare . . . society failed to develop the state." See Nagayama Yasutaka 1981, 3. But I disagree. The establishment of the state on the one hand, and its long-term stability and imperialistic expansion on the other, are problems of different orders. I do however agree with Nagayama when he says that "while the early Yamato polity appears to have been no more than a local power essentially in control of an extremely limited territory, the reason it was able to become a unifying power" must be sought in its ability to "secure higher culture from Korea on the authority of its Great King." See Nagayama Yasutaka 1984, esp. 31. The different conditions of Wa and Greece, determined by the degree to which commercial distributive networks had developed, are indeed important points for consideration.

37. Among the images of the Kofun Period to be discussed below, detailed discussions of agriculture, residence, settlement, kinship, and trade have already been undertaken in Tsude Hiroshi 1989c. See also Tsude Hiroshi 1989b, which is amply illustrated with photographs and figures.

38. Inoue Tadao et al. 1988.

39. Tsude Hiroshi 1989c, 232–8.

40. For a comprehensive summary of Yayoi-period mounded graves, see Kondō Yoshirō et al. 1986.

41. Fukunaga Shin'ya 1989.

42. The latter type of clustered burial for the intermediate stratum has been called either "older-style tomb cluster" or "incipient tomb cluster." See Ishibe Masashi 1975, 57.

43. Regarding the Hōenzaka site, see Minami Hideo 1989, Ueki Hisashi 1989, and Sekiyama Hiroshi 1989. For the Narutaki site, see Takeuchi Masato and Doi Takayuki 1983.

44. This is the result of calculating each structure as having 93 square meters of floor space and a vertical capacity of 4.5 meters. Interpreter's note: A *koku* represented the approximate amount of grain to be consumed by a person during one year.

45. If the average yield for the fifth century is assumed to be approximately 7.5 *to* per *tan* (13.6 hectoliters per hectare, or about 15.6 U.S. bushels per acre), then this amount represents the annual yield of about 4,900 *chōbu* (4,860 hectares, or 12,000 acres) of paddy. Accordingly, if the tax level is assumed to be from three to ten percent of the yield, then 49,000 to 160,000 *chōbu* of agricultural land are necessary. Even if the tax rate is regarded as the highest level in the range just given, the amount of land represents four times the entire area listed in a tenth-century tax register, the Settsu-no-kuni *yusōchō*, which records 12,500 *chōbu*. This calculation is based only on the upper limit of payment for a single year, however; in actuality, the amount stored should be regarded as the accumulation of several years. See Izumiya Yasuo 1970, 320.

46. Nakazawa Teiji et al. 1988.

47. Saga-ken kyōiku iinkai 1990, 61–6.

48. Ishikawa Noboru 1989, 148.

49. Umehara Sueji 1955.

50. Ōbayashigumi purojekuto chi-mu 1985.

51. Arguments for a fifth-century date appear in Mizuno Masayoshi 1973, Nogami Jōsuke 1970, and Tsude Hiroshi 1989c, 68–75. For the argument for the seventh century, see Hirose Kazuo 1983.

52. Noto Takeshi 1990.

53. Kishi Toshio 1985.

54. Tsude Hiroshi 1989d.

55. See the following: Wada Seigo 1981, Hōjō Yoshitaka 1986, Okamura Hidenori 1989, Kishimoto Naofumi 1989, and Maezawa Terumasa 1989.

56. Terasawa Kaoru regards round mounds as existing from very early times. See Terasawa Kaoru 1990.

57. Interpreter's note: See chapter 2 by Kobayashi in this volume.

58. Kobayashi Yukio 1961.

59. For basic research on square keyhole tombs, see Ōtsuka Hatsushige 1962 and Mogi Masahiro 1974. For recent developments, see Akatsuka Jirō 1988.

60. The suggestion made by Nishijima Sadao of a link between tomb shapes and *kabane* titles has influenced subsequent research. See Nishijima Sadao 1961. While the criticism was raised that the establishment of noble titles cannot be dated back as early as the beginning of the Kofun Period, Amakasu Ken posits fictive kin relations between central chiefs and those in the outlying regions who share tombs built on the same plan. See Amakasu Ken 1964.

61. Tsude Hiroshi 1988 and Tsude Hiroshi 1990.

62. Yoshida Akira 1973, 114 and Kondō Yoshirō 1983, 217.

63. Shiraishi Taichirō 1969 and Shiraishi Taichirō 1984.

64. Kondō Yoshirō 1983, 218–9.

65. Ueda Masaaki 1967, 131–53 and Okada Seishi 1970, 271–320. Interpreter's note: In English see Piggott 1997, especially chapters 2 and 3, for details.

66. Interpreter's note: On these inscriptions in English see Anazawa Wakou and Manome Jun'ichi 1986. The nature of the *tensōjin* post remains unclear and so the term is not translated here.

67. Naoki Kōjirō calls this bureaucratic system of offices *hitosei,* a proto-bureaucratic "human posting system." See Naoki Kōjirō 1958, 146–245. Hirano Kunio looks to the time of Yūryaku at the end of the fifth century for the reorganization of the *tomo*—a system of offices comprising service roles connected directly with the court, like the *kurahito*—into the hereditary groups of subservient status (*be*). The latter owed a variety of services to the court, to branches of the imperial family, and to other centrally powerful families. See Hirano Kunio 1975, 264–66. Interpreter's note: In English see Hirano Kunio 1977.

68. See Ichihara-shi kyōiku iinkai 1988.

69. Interpreter's note: For an English translation see de Bary 2001, 9–10.

70. Mizuno Masayoshi 1969.

71. Tanaka Kiyomi 1989.

72. Naoki Kōjirō 1965 and Takahashi Kazuo 1979.

73. Iwamoto Jirō 1983.

74. Hirose Kazuo et al. 1976 and Tsude Hiroshi 1989a.

75. Mizuno Masayoshi 1985.

76. Sekiguchi Kōichi 1986.

77. Tsude Hiroshi 1974.

78. I have benefited here from the ideas presented in Yamao Yukihisa 1983, esp. 64–75.

79. Murakami Einosuke 1977 and Azuma Ushio 1987.

80. Kubota Kurao 1973.

81. Hanada Katsuhiro places the period of increased activity in metalworking, including the production of weapons, in the later fifth century. See Hanada Katsuhiro 1989. It is indeed possible that the beginning of iron production goes back before the sixth century.

82. Kondō Yoshirō 1984.

83. Tanabe Shōzō 1981.

84. Murakami Hiromichi 1988.

85. Kageyama Tsuyoshi 1984, 4–12.

86. Sakaehara Towao 1972.

87. Tsude Hiroshi 1989d.

88. Interpreter's note: For insightful reactions to Tsude's proposals, especially the idea that the round-keyhole order evidences the existence of an "early state formation," see Ishigami Eiichi's comments from the forum that followed Tsude's original presentation: Ishigami Eiichi 1991. Yoshida Akira has written a rejoinder to Tsude in Yoshida Akira 1998. See also Tonegawa Akihiko 1999 and Suzuki Yasutami 1996. Tsude has further elaborated his views in Tsude Hiroshi 1996 and Tsude Hiroshi 1998.

2

Treatise on Duplicate Mirrors

Kobayashi Yukio

Introduction by Walter Edwards

THE MOST influential Japanese archaeologist of the twentieth century, Kobayashi Yukio (1911–1989), grew up in Kobe under difficult financial and family circumstances. While developing an avid interest in archaeology as a youth, he was unable to pursue his education at the university level, instead entering a vocational program in architecture.[1] Kobayashi, however, maintained his interest in archaeology, undertaking a comprehensive study of the pottery of the Yayoi Period (400 B.C.E.–250 C.E.) while still a student. His publication of that work, and the assistance he rendered Kyoto University archaeologists in connection with the preparation of site reports, earned him an appointment as assistant in the Archaeology Department of that prestigious institution in 1935.

For much of his professional career Kobayashi remained subordinate in status to senior colleagues, who boasted better academic qualifications but who were outshone by their junior in terms of archaeological achievements. This precarious situation no doubt contributed to the inordinate degree of precaution that characterizes Kobayashi's written work, with the result that his prose is often stilted and difficult to follow. He nevertheless produced a series of influential publications, especially from 1950 to 1965, which are largely responsible for our basic understanding of Kofun Period (250–600) society, and of the qualitative differences separating it from that of the preceding Yayoi era.

The term "Yayoi," taken from a style of pottery first recognized at a site of the same name, is applied generally to the way of life centered around rice cultivation that entered Japan from the Korean Peninsula around 400 B.C.E. It also refers to the period that saw both the spread of this culture throughout most of the archipelago and the increasing maturation of a society based on wet rice production. "Kofun" means literally "old barrow," and denotes the large Japanese mounded burial tombs that were first built, according to current consensus, in the latter part of the third century C.E. Assuming a characteristic keyhole shape, these mounds emerged in the ancient central province of Yamato (essentially coterminous with the present-day Nara Prefecture as depicted in Figure 2.3) and spread outward over most of the archipelago by the end of the fourth century, suggesting a process of political unification under the earliest state-level polity. The society that produced these monuments is now understood as the evolutionary outgrowth of the society of the Yayoi Period (see the chapter 1 by Tsude Hiroshi in this volume). It is not automatically clear, however, that the two were chronologically distinct, and in the early post-World War II years some archaeologists still clung to an older view that the great tombs' construction began during the latter part of the period when Yayoi pottery was still in use.

In an article published in 1952, Kobayashi asserted unequivocally that (1) Yayoi society antedated the Kofun Period; (2) Yayoi society was basically nonstratified, although the spread of iron tools and the increase in productivity in the latter part of the period saw the emergence of status differences; and (3) these differences formed the basis for the stratification later seen with the appearance of the mounded tombs, the graves of a true aristocratic elite.[2] In later publications Kobayashi elaborated on the critical difference he saw between the two periods in the political realm, a difference he traced out through the treatment of bronze mirrors.[3] Chinese mirrors produced during the Han Dynasty (202 B.C.E.–220 C.E.) have emerged from burials of the Yayoi Period, and are especially plentiful in the northern Kyūshū region, where Yayoi culture first flourished. By contrast, Han Dynasty mirrors are generally not seen in the Kinki region, home of the ancient Japanese state, until the Kofun Period, when they were buried together with newer Chinese mirrors of the Wei Dynasty (220–265) and later. Moreover, some of the older items showed signs of extensive wear, suggesting they had received a considerable amount of handling prior to being deposited as grave goods.

Taking a hint from one of his colleagues at Kyoto, who had previously asserted that such mirrors were passed from one generation to the next, Kobayashi also thought their treatment until the Kofun Period demonstrated their role as heirlooms, and further interpreted their deposition in the mounded tombs as indicating a change in the nature of political authority. Namely, the mirrors had been necessary during the Yayoi Period as religious symbols kept by local chiefs, whose role was sacerdotal in nature, and hence the mirrors were passed from each officeholder to his successor. But the mounded tombs, made in the keyhole shape characteristic of elite tombs built by leaders of the central Yamato polity, were symbols of a secular authority backed by alliance with that polity. The older mirrors, having lost their function, were accordingly buried together with newer ones obtained through ties to the central alliance. The deposition of the mirrors and the construction of the mounded tombs thus signaled a change from religious to secular authority as well as the emergence of a political structure that was panregional in nature.

In the paper translated here, Kobayashi demonstrated the latter assertion through an analysis of relations between sets of duplicate mirrors.[4] As for Chinese mirrors produced from the end of the Han and especially during the Wei Dynasty period, it had long been recognized that mirrors made from the same mold, or from identical molds made from the same model, were often deposited in tombs in widely separated regions. Rejecting interpretations of this phenomenon as a matter of chance, Kobayashi meticulously traced out the relationships defined by the sharing of a single set of duplicates, thereby demonstrating the existence of a large network of such relations centering on Tsubai Ōtsukayama, a tomb in the southern part of Kyoto Prefecture, just north of Yamato itself. The figure buried in this tomb, Kobayashi argued, acted as Yamato's representative in the process of alliance building, which process

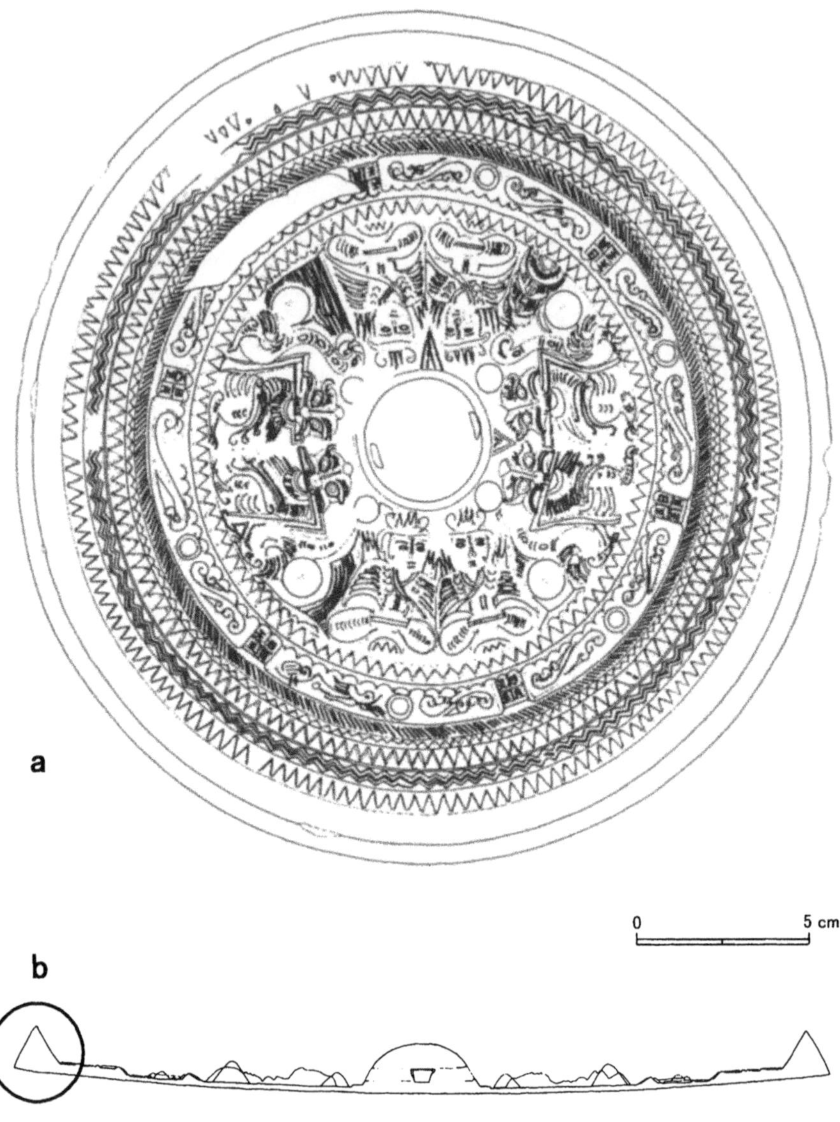

Fig. 2.1. Triangular-Rimmed Mirror (a) decoration on back, (b) cross-section

Source: Yukinoyama kofun hakkutsu chōsadan, *Yukinoyama kofun no kenkyū, Hōkokuhen* (Shiga: Yōkaichi-shi kyōiku iinkai, 1996), 99.

saw mirrors conferred on local chiefs from Kyūshū in the west to the Kantō region in the east to secure their political allegiance.

In addition to being a path-breaking study of mirror distribution, Kobayashi's paper also made a novel attempt at estimating the chronological age of the tombs in which the mirrors were buried, and thereby of the emergence of the Yamato polity itself. His approach was based on assumptions that tie the mirrors to events known from the Chinese *History of the Wei Dynasty*. The section of this work dealing with Wa, the ancient Chinese name for Japan, tells of diplomatic exchanges between the Wei court and a "country" named Yamatai, ruled by an enigmatic Queen Himiko, said to have gained suzerainty over some thirty other countries within Wa after a long period of strife. Around the year 240, Himiko sent envoys to Wei, who returned with gifts from the Chinese ruler to the queen, including one hundred bronze mirrors. Further exchanges are recorded, with the account ending in the mid-260s, after Himiko's death and the initiation of her successor, following a brief period of disorder. Although Chinese envoys also appear to have visited Yamatai, the directions recorded for how to reach that country are hopelessly confused, and its exact location within Japan has remained a mystery.[5]

Kobayashi followed the lead of earlier Kyoto archaeologists like Umehara Sueji, who argued from the prewar period that Yamatai was none other than Yamato, and that the polity centered on that region was the one Himiko had ruled. Umehara's argument had been based on similar evidence: the standardization seen in the form of the keyhole tombs, and the greater concentration of Wei Period mirrors in the Kinki region. But while Umehara was far more knowledgeable than Kobayashi on the subject of Chinese mirrors in general, these items never held much more than intrinsic interest for him. Umehara did not attempt Kobayashi's bold interpretive ploys—suggesting on the one hand that the mirrors themselves were key items in the process of alliance building, and seeking on the other to date the start of tomb construction from the relationships defined by the sharing of duplicate sets.

In extremely rare instances a mirror may bear an inscription indicating the exact year in which it was made. Usually, however, the age can only be estimated on stylistic grounds to the period when it was in common use, such as "Later Han" or "Wei." In either case, the date attributed to the mirror gives only a *terminus post quem* ("date after which") for the context in which it is found: a burial in which a third-century mirror was placed could only have been made in the third century or later, but how much later is not clear from the presence of the mirror alone. Kobayashi sought a more precise answer for the date of the Tsubai Ōtsukayama tomb, which may be placed stylistically among the earliest keyhole tombs known. He assumed that (1) all of the mirrors it contained were obtained through the diplomatic exchanges with Wei and were centrally held by 250 C.E.; and (2) all of the duplicates of those mirrors found in other tombs had passed through the hands of the Tsubai Ōtsukayama chief as part of the distribution process. Since these tombs as a group can be estimated to date no later than the end of the fourth century, he argued, this enables placing parameters on the death of the Tsubai Ōtsukayama chief and on the construction of his tomb, in terms of the series of events into which his role can be hypothetically placed. How long might a person have served in the role of chief? Were the mirrors deposited in every tomb with the initial recipient, or might some have been handed down one generation? And how late must the Tsubai Ōtsukayama chief have lived in order to distribute all of the known mirrors, given various assumptions made in response to the above questions?

Kobayashi's answer, couched in typically guarded language, is of less import than the framework in which he posed his queries. I will return in an afterward to the issue of the long-term value of his thesis, which entails a sorting out of the durable aspects of his thinking from the more transient ones. But first I will take a direct look at Kobayashi's paper translated in abridged form below. I will intersperse my explanatory comments in a distinctive typeface elaborating the argument in more readable form.

KOBAYASHI YUKIO

Treatise on Duplicate Mirrors

Interpreted by Walter Edwards

Among Chinese mirrors unearthed from Japanese mounded tombs (*kofun*), it is by no means rare that two or more specimens cast from a single mold, or cast with molds made from the same model, found their way into Japan in similar fashion and yet were discovered as grave goods in tombs in different regions. This is shown by well-known examples such as the pair of mirrors inscribed with a Chinese dynastic date of 240 C.E. and discovered at Shibazaki Kanizawa in Gumma and at Morio in Hyōgo.[6] Regarding a similar phenomenon involving domestic mirrors, duplicates were often owned by a single individual, and thus buried in the same tomb, as witnessed at Kanagawa Yagami and Fukuoka Ikisan Chōshizuka. This phenomenon was pointed out as early as 1921 by Umehara Sueji, for example, and is mentioned by two or three other scholars each time a new example is discovered.[7] But archaeologists' interest in duplicate mirrors has been limited to technical aspects only: the existence of two or more specimens made from a single model, or from the same mold; and that the casting process made this result possible. While examining some duplicate domestic mirrors in the process of writing the site report for Fukuoka Ikisan Chōshizuka, it occurred to me that an analysis of the distribution of these items in tombs throughout the country might yield new insights on the age of the tombs, an issue on which research has long been stagnant.

Distribution of Duplicate Mirrors

Before explaining how one might use data concerning duplicate mirrors to investigate the chronology of the tombs, data on the mirrors themselves and relationships among the tombs in which they have been found must be presented.

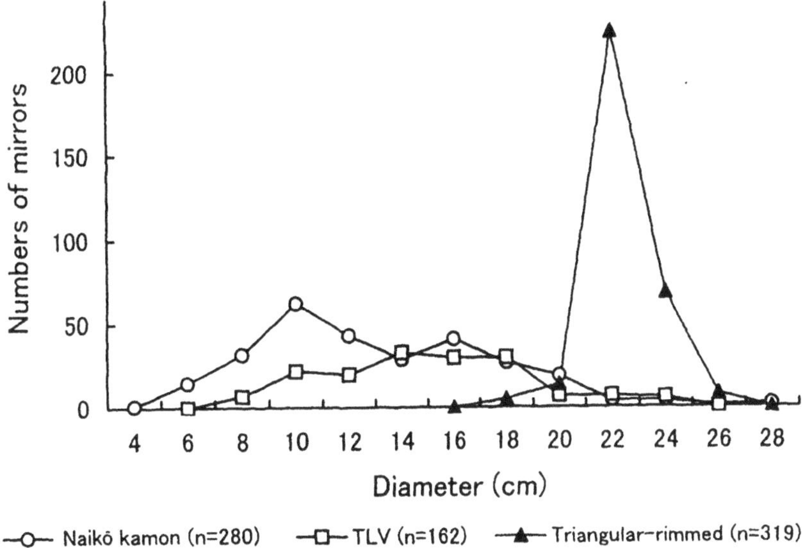

Fig. 2.2. Diameters of Imported Mirrors

At this point Kobayashi included a list of all duplicate mirrors known to him at the time of writing. These totaled 199 examples—51 sets of mirrors thought to have been of Chinese manufacture and 16 sets of domestic imitations—with each set having between two and ten members. These sets can be grouped into several distinct styles on the basis of the designs on the mirrors' backs, or non-reflecting surfaces.

By far the most numerous among these, in terms of both the number of duplicate sets and of total examples, is a style known as triangular-rimmed deity-and-beast mirror (*sankakubuchi shinjūkyō*), hereafter referred to as the " triangular-rimmed mirror." (See Figure 2.1) For Chinese mirrors, these accounted for 42 of the 51 sets, totaling 117 of the 150 imported mirrors listed in Kobayashi's article. Named after its distinctive rim, triangular in cross-section, this style is further distinguished from other imported mirrors in two ways. First, the proportion of duplicates among all examples known for this style is unusually high. At the time of Kobayashi's writing, some two hundred examples of imported triangular-rimmed mirrors had been recovered nationwide, hence the 117 belonging to duplicate sets represent more than half the total—a ratio far higher than for any other style. And notably, by the end of the 1990s further discoveries of these mirrors had swelled the number of imported examples to over 360. As more duplicate relations came to light, the portion known to belong to duplicate sets has risen to over 85 percent.

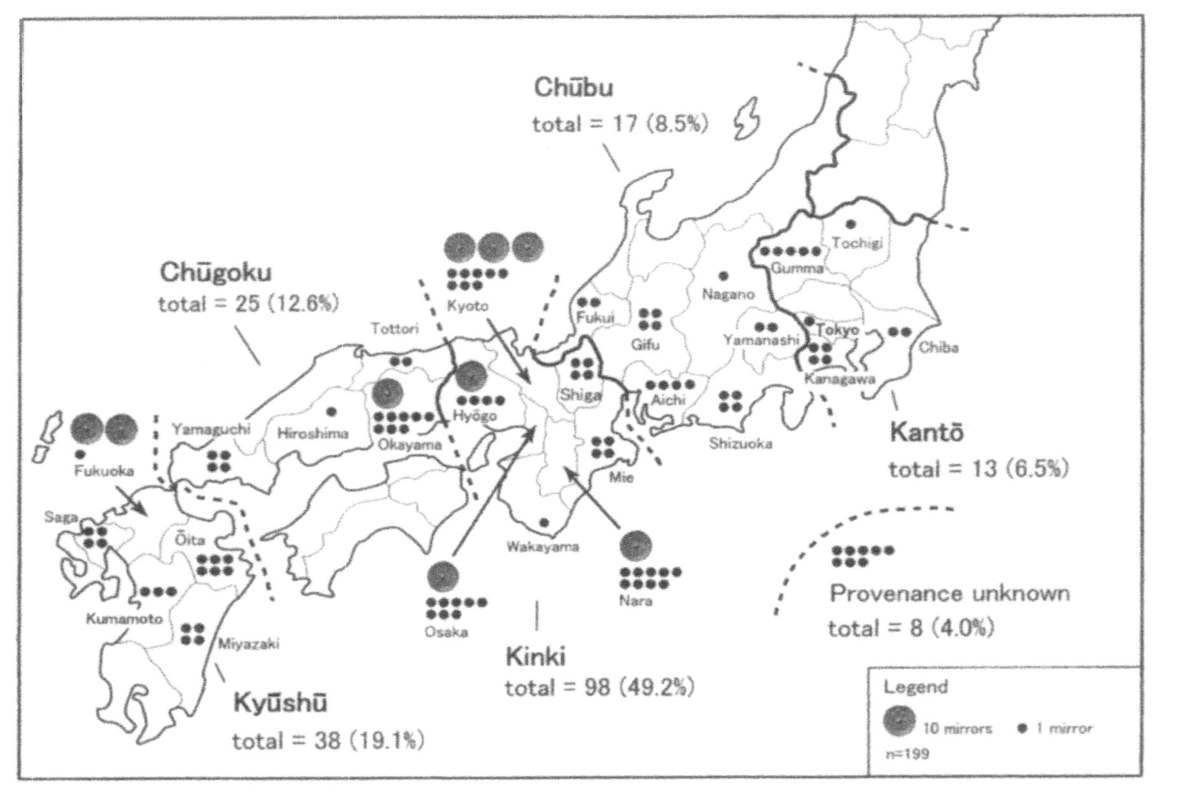

Map 2.1. Distribution by Region and Prefecture of Duplicate Mirrors Listed by Kobayashi

Accordingly, it appears that making these items in multiples was the rule. A second distinctive feature of this style of mirror is its highly standardized size. Figure 2.2 shows a comparison of the distribution of examples by size for triangular-rimmed mirrors and for the next most numerous styles.[8] These two factors—standardized size and the high percentage of duplicates—combine to give the impression that triangular-rimmed mirrors were mass-produced, and for a highly specific purpose.

In Map 2.1 we see the geographical distribution of all duplicate mirrors listed by Kobayashi. Mirrors concentrate in the Kinki region, where the largest keyhole tombs are found. Mirrors belonging to a particular set of duplicates are in some cases found within a single region such as Kinki or Kyūshū. Or rarely, the entire set as known to Kobayashi may have been limited to two or three mirrors found in the same tomb.

More often, however, a set of duplicates was distributed over a wide area, linking tombs in two or three different regions. Focusing on such relationships between tombs, Kobayashi traced out two networks of tombs interconnected by multiple links and accordingly, in his view, comprised of roughly contemporaneous tombs. One such group consisted of tombs he regarded as dating to the first part of the Kofun Period, or roughly the fourth century C.E.; and the other could be dated to the later fifth century. It is the first group, the larger of the two, that is of interest here, and to which Kobayashi turns his attention in the following discussion. The core of this group, shown in Figure 2.3, centers on Tsubai Ōtsukayama tomb in Kyoto Prefecture, and has a secondary focus at Bizen Kurumazuka tomb in Okayama.[9]

Relations Based on Shared Sets of Mirrors

Let us first consider the general significance of members of a single set of mirrors found as grave goods in two or more tombs. One possible interpretation is that of sheer coincidence: that mirrors imported independently by two chiefs were by chance identical; or alternatively, that they may have been brought into Japan together but that in the process of distribution—and with no element of necessity whatsoever—the mirrors came into the possession of the occupants of tombs in different regions. But as already pointed out, instances of two or more specimens from the same set of mirrors being buried in a single tomb are not rare, making it impossible to claim that the possession of such mirrors was in no way influenced by their being identical.

In cases where the possession of duplicate mirrors cannot be attributed to chance, what motivating factors are possible? It should be pointed out in particular that two tombs may share two or three sets of duplicate mirrors between them, as is the case for Tsubai Ōtsukayama, which shares three sets (9, 16, 56) with Bizen Kurumazuka and two sets each with Nara Samida Takarazuka (28, 44), Fukuoka Ishizukayama (35, 105), and Ōita Akatsuka (80, 105).[10] Rather than being the result of mere circumstance, this sharing may be taken to show that the mirrors were regarded as identical and distributed in

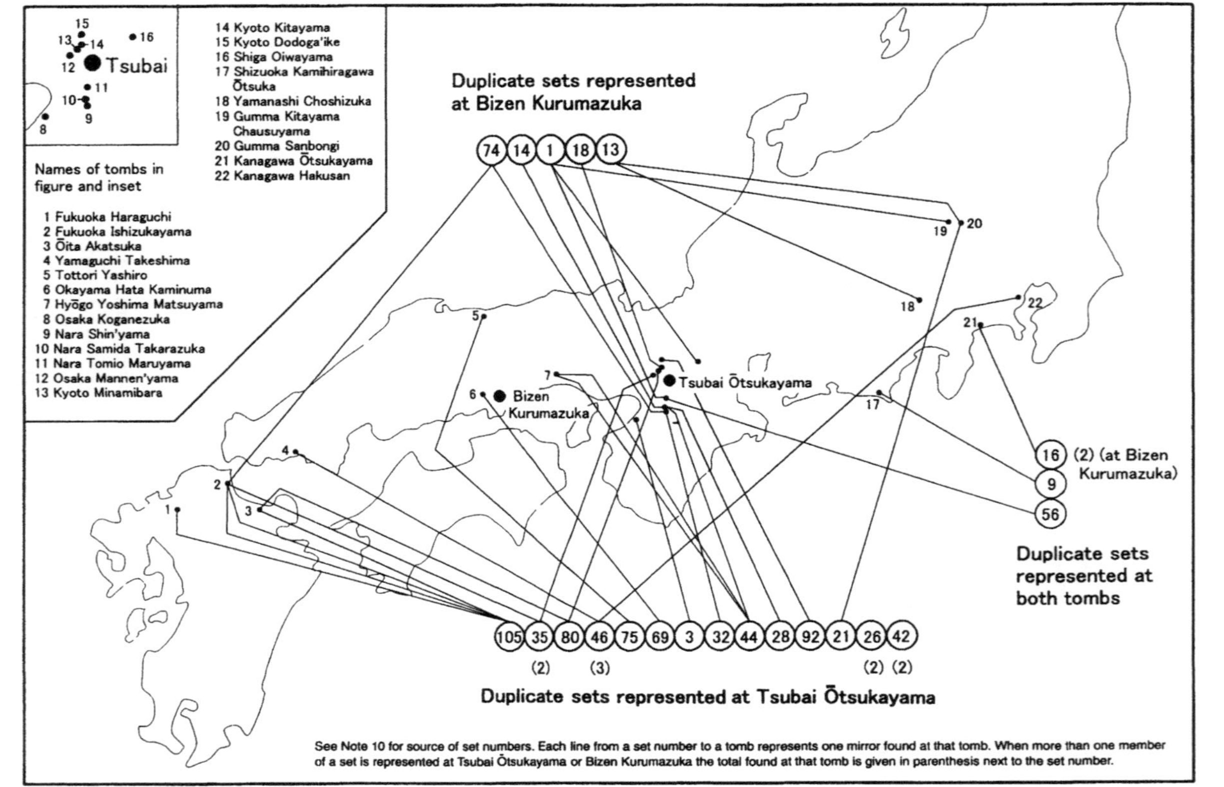

Fig. 2.3. Distribution of Duplicate Mirror Sets Represented at the Tsubai Ōtsukayama and Kurumazuka Tombs

light of that knowledge. Furthermore, the sharing of two or three sets of duplicate mirrors among two tombs did not result from independent events that linked, again by chance, the same two individuals two or three times in the same fashion. Rather the distribution of those sets can be assumed to have taken place on a single occasion.

What interpretation could explain the more common sharing of a single set of mirrors? In this instance as well let us hypothesize a very special circumstance: one tomb having a complex network of sharing with a large number of other tombs. Such a network of distribution centers on two tombs, Tsubai Ōtsukayama and Bizen Kurumazuka, and links a total of twenty-four other tombs (Figure 2.3).

To begin with the gist of what is shown by Figure 2.3, Tsubai Ōtsukayama shares forty-nine mirrors comprising seventeen sets with Bizen Kurumazuka and eighteen other tombs. Bizen Kurumazuka likewise shares a total of twenty-four mirrors comprising eight sets with Tsubai Ōtsukayama and eleven others. An explanation of duplicate mirror distribution resulting from pure circumstance is clearly insufficient here. Were it simply posited that a third party imported a set of mirrors and gave them out to the chief of Tsubai Ōtsukayama and to various chiefs buried in other tombs, an explanation of why such an opportunity was repeatedly given more than a dozen times to the Tsubai Ōtsukayama chief cannot be made by relying on mere chance.

To explain the data for both Tsubai Ōtsukayama and Bizen Kurumazuka while reducing reliance on chance, it is desirable to keep the number of occasions needed to obtain so many duplicate mirrors to a minimum. And if it is assumed that a third party or parties had control over the supply of duplicate sets, it moreover follows that the number of such third parties must also be held to a minimum. In other words, if chiefs possessing large numbers of duplicates, like those buried at Tsubai Ōtsukayama and Bizen Kurumazuka, obtained these mirrors on only two or three occasions, then the possibility of positing only one individual as the source of the mirrors increases.

As noted above, the sharing of two or three sets of duplicate mirrors between two tombs indicates that their distribution took place on a single occasion. To restate this specifically in terms of the data in Figure 2.3, on various occasions when the chiefs buried in Bizen Kurumazuka, Nara Samida Takarazuka (tomb 10 in the figure), Fukuoka Ishizukayama (tomb 2), and Ōita Akatsuka (tomb 3) obtained their mirrors, the Tsubai Ōtsukayama chief also acquired mirrors from the same sets. It therefore must be considered that the Tsubai Ōtsukayama chief obtained duplicate mirrors on at least four separate occasions. Since one of the sets (no. 105) is also shared between Fukuoka Ishizukayama and Ōita Akatsuka, if the duplicate mirrors of these two tombs were acquired simultaneously, then it is possible to adjust the above number to three. However, assuming that of the nineteen tombs sharing duplicate mirrors with Tsubai Ōtsukayama, for just four of those tombs the number of occasions on which mirrors were obtained by the latter was at least three, then the total number of such occasions represented by all nineteen tombs would have to be well above ten. In other words, as long as the distributor of duplicate mirrors is taken to be a third party, the number of times needed for the Tsubai Ōtsukayama chief to obtain so many mirrors cannot be reduced by any appreciable degree. This accordingly involves interpreting these data as the result of accumulated occasions of chance.

If interpretations involving distribution by a third party are therefore seen to rely too greatly on chance, then the remaining possibilities are limited. Namely, the sharing of duplicate mirrors between Tsubai Ōtsukayama and the other tombs must be explained in terms of direct relations between the Tsubai Ōtsukayama chief and the other chiefs. Here again, two interpretations are possible. One is that mirrors were given by regional chiefs to the Tsubai Ōtsukayama chief, or perhaps to a central paramount, and included directly among the grave goods of the Tsubai Ōtsukayama tomb. The remaining members of the various duplicate sets were of course kept by the regional chiefs and buried in their tombs. But to assume that such an interpretation is possible requires a rather unreasonable assumption: that mirrors worthy of being given in tribute were initially distributed across a very broad area, ranging from northern Kyūshū to Kantō as shown by the distribution of the nineteen tombs. The same point can be made for the data involving Bizen Kurumazuka Kofun.

Accordingly, the only way for it to make sense is to posit that the chiefs of Tsubai Ōtsukayama and Bizen Kurumazuka had direct relations with the other chiefs, while assuming that one of the chiefs was both the original owner of the duplicate sets and the distributing agent. As already seen in Figure 2.3, however, Tsubai Ōtsukayama and Bizen Kurumazuka also share three sets of mirrors—specifically, both tombs share set 9 with Shizuoka Kamihiragawa Ōtsuka (tomb 17), set 16 with Kanagawa Ōtsukayama (tomb 21), and set 56 with Nara Tomio Maruyama (tomb 11). Since it is not feasible to see the occupants of these latter tombs as receiving the same mirror from both chiefs together, it must be regarded that a direct relationship of sharing also existed between the chiefs of Tsubai Ōtsukayama and Bizen Kurumazuka. If that is indeed the case, then for tombs like Fukuoka Ishizukayama, Nara Shin'yama (tomb 9), Nara Samida Takarazuka, and Gumma Sanbongi (tomb 20), each of which shares mirrors—but of different types—with both Tsubai Ōtsukayama and Bizen Kurumazuka, it is no longer necessary to think that the mirrors were distributed by the chiefs of the latter two tombs on separate occasions. Rather, it may be supposed that the different mirrors were received together from one or the other, and on one occasion only.[11]

This latter view goes beyond seeing the sharing of mirrors between two tombs as indicating a direct, reciprocal relationship between those tombs only. It opens the way to interpretations in which sets of mirrors were given out to two or more recipients by someone, without retaining a copy, as a unilateral act of distribution by the original owner as third party. . . .

Kobayashi points to Kyoto Minamibara (tomb 13) as a specific example of a tomb sharing one set of mirrors with Tsubai Ōtsukayama, and other sets with three tombs not directly linked to either Tsubai Ōtsukayama or Bizen Kurumazuka. Hence they are not included among the twenty-four tombs shown in Figure 2.3. The Tsubai Ōtsukayama chief may have been the source of the mirrors distributed to the latter three tombs as well, as the third party who gave the Minamibara chief mirrors of at least four sets, while retaining a member from only one of the sets for himself. In similar fashion, the Minamibara chief may have received mirrors of additional sets from the Tsubai Ōtsukayama chief and passed these on to others without retaining any for his own possession. In this manner, Kobayashi asserts, the total number of imported triangular-rimmed mirrors which possibly passed through the hands of the Tsubai Ōtsukayama chief should include those in fourteen additional sets that may have been given to ten intermediary figures like the Minamibara chief, and the total number of tombs which possibly received such mirrors from the Tsubai Ōtsukayama chief increases to thirty-nine.

To summarize, these thirty-nine tombs share some thirty-six sets of triangular-rimmed mirrors between them, and are linked in direct or indirect fashion in a network centering on Tsubai Ōtsukayama Kofun. The most likely explanation for this development is to see the Tsubai Ōtsukayama chief as the distributing agent. No doubt some will hesitate to attribute such an important role to a chief outside the Yamato region. But even if in most cases the distribution of duplicate mirrors was conducted by the Tsubai Ōtsukayama chief, it is quite possible that an unknown third party supplied him with mirrors in large numbers, allowing him to retain some of each set in his own possession.

No tomb attributable to a chief of such status has been identified in the region near Tsubai Ōtsukayama Kofun or in Yamato itself. Nevertheless it is conceivable that the third party in question, even though acting as keeper and supplier of duplicate mirrors, was not considered their owner in any sense of private ownership. So the act of dispensing mirrors would not have entailed retaining mirrors. Accordingly, Tsubai Ōtsukayama Kofun alone appears to have held a prominent place in the distributional networks of duplicate mirrors.[12]

Determining the Chronology of the Tomb Age from Duplicate Mirrors

Assuming that some agent supervising the large group of mirrors represented by those of Tsubai Ōtsukayama Kofun distributed duplicate mirrors to chiefs over a wide area stretching from northern Kyūshū to a portion of the Kantō region, to what time in Japanese history can this be attributed? Given that the problem involves the remarkable phenomenon of duplicate mirror distribution, it may be possible to find an answer by exploiting that evidence.

There are at least two ways in which members of a set of duplicate mirrors can be deposited in different tombs: (1) the mirrors come into the possession of two or more individuals at the same time, and are subsequently buried in their tombs; or (2) the mirrors are held by some person or agent and divided at different times among the individuals who become their final owners, and in whose tombs the mirrors are interred. In the first case, the chronological gap which separates two tombs sharing duplicate mirrors would be equivalent to

TABLE 2.1

Chronological Gap between Tombs Containing Duplicate Mirrors as a function of Length of Chiefly Office (n)

Timing of interment of mirrors as grave goods	Period of distribution of mirrors		
	Takes place simultaneously	Continues through life of original holder	Continued by original holder's successor
Buried with original recipients	*n*	2*n*	3*n*
Transmitted one generation	2*n*	3*n*	4*n*
Transmitted two generations	3*n*	4*n*	5*n*

TABLE 2.2

Dates for Tsubai Ōtsukayama Kofun Estimated under Various Conditions

Chronological gap possible between any two tombs	Period when interment possible			Maximum length of office, *n*
	250–400	250–390	250–380	
Case 1 (2*n*)	320–330	310–330	300–330	80*
Case 2 (3*n*)	280–310	270–310	260–310	60*
	300	290–300	280–300	50
Case 3 (3*n*)	340–370	330–370	320–370	60*
	350	340–350	330–350	50
Case 4 (4*n*)	300–350	290–350	280–350	50
	320–330	310–330	300–330	40

the number of years between the deaths of two persons who were once living at the same time. This number is limited by necessity to the length of the human life span. Moreover, in the case of a chief who leaves the world late in life but who also had to be old enough to achieve a position from which to obtain the mirrors in the first place, the number is further reduced to the length of time he held office. Accordingly, the greatest possible difference in time between two such tombs is equal to the maximum length of chiefly office. If a chief's length of office is given as n, and the mirrors are always interred in the tomb of the first person who receives them, the potential difference in age between two tombs sharing duplicate mirrors can be expressed as n.

However, if we consider the possibility that all of the mirrors in question came first into the possession of one person and were then distributed at later times to others, then it is theoretically possible to see the first person's term of office as the period during which such distribution could occur. Accordingly, it is possible that when an early recipient dies, and his tomb is built, the recipients of the other mirrors would not all be selected. In other words, the chronological gap between tombs containing mirrors received from an initial holder may reach a value as high as $2n$ if the period of continued distribution by that person is included. If it is further assumed that the initial holder is merely an agent entrusted with the mirrors, and that distribution is continued by subsequent occupants of that role, it would result in the potential gap increasing to $3n$ and higher.

Until now we have proceeded on the assumption that mirrors received by individuals were placed in their tombs as grave goods. But as a theoretical consideration we should also examine the possibility that mirrors could be transmitted to the next generation. In such a case, for each generation of transmission, it is necessary to add a value of n years to the potential gap between tombs. The resulting values are indicated in Table 2.1. The values given are the greatest possible values; the smallest possible value can always be taken as n.[13] It goes without saying that the numerical value of n may be zero.[14]

It will hasten a solution if we attempt to clarify the situations that actually occurred rather than examining all the theoretical possibilities. This will be done by focusing on Tsubai Ōtsukayama and the possible gaps between it and the nineteen tombs with which it shares duplicate mirrors. Among the latter are Nara Samida Takarazuka, Osaka Koganezuka (tomb 8), and many others conventionally dated as late as the latter part of the fourth century, but none for which a fifth-century date must be assigned. For the twenty tombs in question, then, we may infer the latter half of the fourth century as the latest date for interment of a duplicate mirror.

By contrast, the task of estimating the earliest date for interment is less simple. The difficulty lies not only in determining which tomb is the oldest, for even if that is made clear, academic opinion on its date would range from the mid-third to the early fourth century. Accordingly, I would base consideration on the date for the importation of the duplicate mirrors found at Tsubai Ōtsukayama and the other tombs. The preponderance of these duplicate mirrors are of the triangular-rimmed style. We may regard these mirrors as belonging

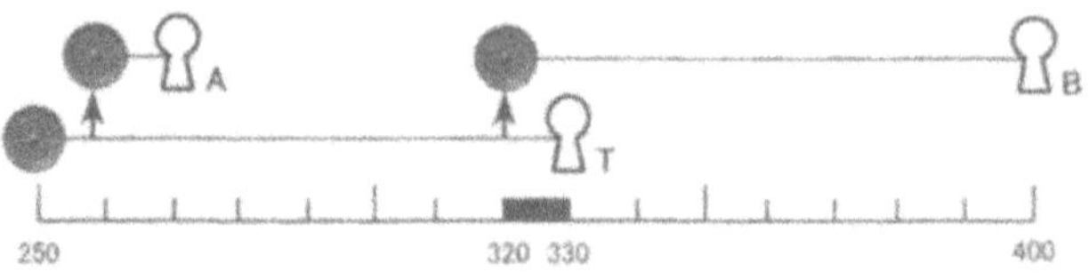

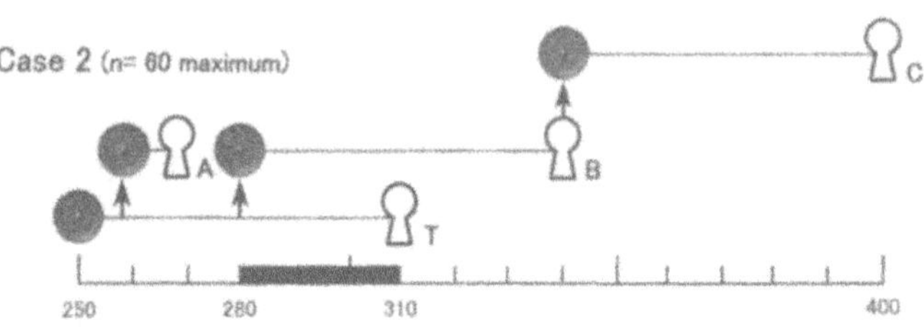

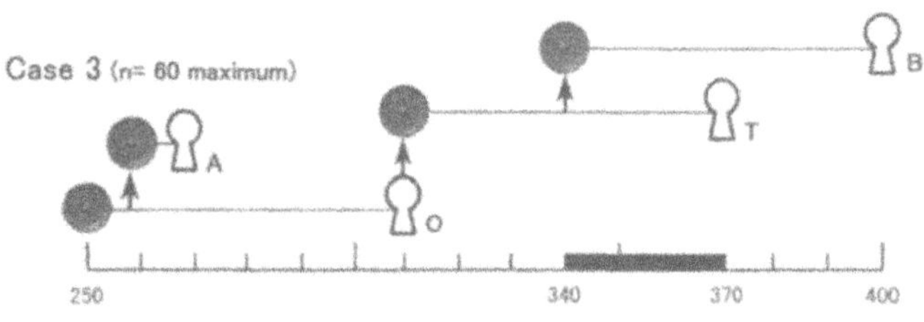

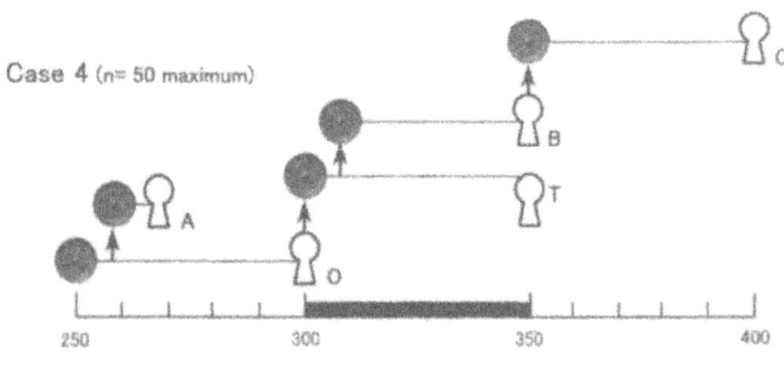

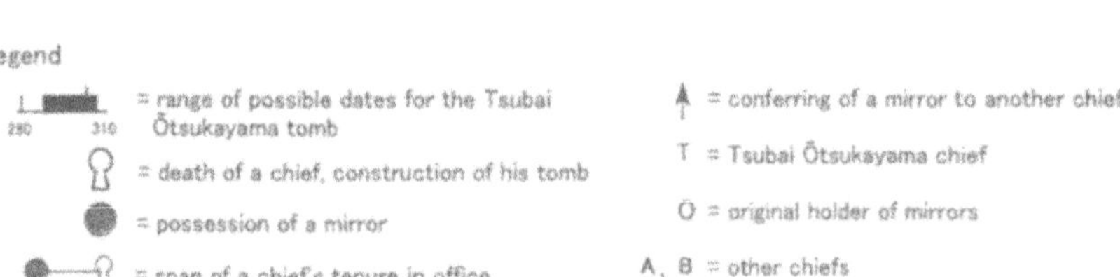

Fig. 2.4. Four Cases of Conditions for Estimating the Age of Tsubai Ōtsukayama

provisionally to the Wei period and date their importation to a time immediately after the envoy from Yamatai to Wei was dispatched by Queen Himiko in 239 C.E.[15] If we suppose that by around 250 C.E. the mirrors were being held somewhere within Japan, we can provisionally use this date as the earliest one possible for their interment.[16] This specifically means we must attempt to solve the problem of the chronological gap between Tsubai Ōtsukayama and the other tombs using the two dates of approximately 250 and the latter part of the fourth century. This period, from the time of importation to the final interment, is the span in which there was opportunity for a single set of mirrors to be split up and buried in separate tombs. A date for Tsubai Ōtsukayama can then be calculated as shown in Table 2.2, for different values of *n* and by varying the value of the span with other tombs from 2*n* to 4*n*. . . .

The explanation Kobayashi provides to accompany his table is extremely terse, and needs supplementary explication to be readily understandable. This is provided here in pictorial form in Figure 2.4, and by the following reworkings of the textual explanations Kobayashi gives for the four cases illustrated. In Figure 2.4, the range of possible dates for the Tsubai Ōtsukayama tomb is indicated on the time line by a solid bar. The keyhole mark represents the death of a chief and the construction of his tomb. Possession of mirrors is shown by a mirror image, and the span of a chief's tenure in office is indicated by the line connecting these two symbols. An arrow pointing to a mirror image indicates the conferring of mirrors to another chief.

In Case 1, it is assumed that the Tsubai Ōtsukayama chief (marked with a *T*) was in possession of the mirrors in 250, and that chiefs who received mirrors from him were buried together with the mirrors as late as 400. The maximum value of any chief's term of office (*n*) is taken to be eighty years, a figure Kobayashi admits is unrealistic, but is used here in heuristic fashion. The Tsubai Ōtsukayama chief could have lived eighty years from 250, or to the year 330, and would have to have lived to at least 320 in order to have passed mirrors to chiefs buried as late as 400. The construction of the Tsubai Ōtsukayama tomb can thus be put in the interval 320–30. The difference between its age and that of any other tomb containing triangular-rimmed mirrors is *n* (up to eighty years), and the greatest difference between any two such tombs, 2*n*, could range up to the span between the burial of an early recipient (Chief *A*) close to 250. C.E., and the interment of the last surviving recipient (Chief *B*) nearly 150 years later.

Case 2 also assumes that the occupant of Tsubai Ōtsukayama was in possession of the mirrors in 250, but persons buried as late as 400 inherited the mirrors from their predecessors, the original recipients. Alternately, the same calculations would apply to instances where the original recipient gave the mirror to another chief, rather than to a successor. Assuming sixty years as the maximum value of *n*, 280 is the earliest date at which the Tsubai Ōtsukayama chief may have passed on a mirror to a predecessor of a chief buried with that mirror in 400, and 310 is the latest date to which the Tsubai

> Ōtsukayama chief himself may have lived. The difference between Tsubai Ōtsukayama and any other tomb may be 2*n*, and the greatest difference between any two tombs may range to 3*n*, up to 150 years in possible absolute value.
>
> In Case 3, it is assumed that the occupant of Tsubai Ōtsukayama received mirrors from an original holder (marked *O*) who had possession of them in 250. The Tsubai Ōtsukayama occupant then gave mirrors in turn to chiefs buried with them as late as 400. Again taking sixty years as the maximum value of *n*, the death of the Tsubai Ōtsukayama chief can be placed no earlier than 340, and no later than 120 years from 250, or 370. The difference between Tsubai Ōtsukayama and any other tomb may reach 2*n*, and the greatest difference between any two tombs 3*n*.
>
> Case 4 assumes the same conditions as Case 3, except that chiefs buried as late as 400 inherited the mirrors from the original recipients. Assuming the maximum value of any chief's term of office (*n*) to be 50 years, the Tsubai Ōtsukayama chief's death can be placed to the range from 300 to 350. The maximum difference between Tsubai Ōtsukayama and any other tomb remains the span of two chiefly terms, 2*n*, but the greatest difference between any two tombs can reach 4*n*.
>
> In addition to the data for the four cases described above, Kobayashi included in Table 2.2 sets of calculations in which the latest date for the interment of a triangular-rimmed mirror is taken to be the years 380 and 390, rather than 400. He also gives calculations in Cases 2–4 using different values for *n*, and places asterisks next to the values of 60 and 80 years for *n* to indicate his opinion that these figures are unreasonably high. Now let us turn to his analysis of the meaning of these results.

According to the figures in Table 2.2, the date for Tsubai Ōtsukayama Kofun can vary broadly from 260 to 370. From the perspective of typological studies of the tombs and other considerations, however, is it realistic to use these calculations for the upper and lower limits of this tomb's age? As already observed in the explanation of Table 2.2, the span between Tsubai Ōtsukayama and any other tomb never exceeds 2*n*, even though the potential difference between two other tombs sharing duplicate mirrors may be considered to reach values of 3*n* or 4*n*. These latter values depend on the possibility that the distribution of duplicate mirrors began before the involvement of the Tsubai Ōtsukayama chief, and also on the assumption that tombs containing them as grave goods were being built in 250. As noted, however, the emergence of the Tsubai Ōtsukayama chief may be considered a highly significant event in terms of the distribution of duplicate mirrors, and in the absence of compelling evidence for the start of distribution prior to his appearance, it is a simple matter to adjust these figures. The gap between two tombs sharing mirrors may therefore be reduced from 3*n* to 2*n*, or from 4*n* to 3*n*. It goes without saying, then, that for Case 3 the gap between Tsubai Ōtsukayama Kofun and any other tomb accordingly diminishes from 2*n* to *n*.

The meaning of such a reduction in the chronological difference between two tombs can be stated in other terms. Namely, if the earliest mounded tombs in Japan are considered to form a single, contemporaneous group, with Tsubai Ōtsukayama Kofun included, then the difference between Tsubai Ōtsukayama and any other tomb in the group will not exceed *n*. In order to make such an assertion, however, it is necessary to limit definition of the earliest tombs to those which share duplicate mirrors with Tsubai Ōtsukayama Kofun. In actuality, it is indeed the case that no other tombs have been discovered that may be considered as old. In this regard, even though the *History of the Wei Dynasty* describes Himiko's grave in terms appropriate for a large tomb, my opinion is that the beginning of the Kofun Period does not extend that far back in time.[17]

It should be reemphasized that this determination of the age of Tsubai Ōtsukayama utilizes only those duplicate mirrors thought to have passed through the hands of the Tsubai Ōtsukayama chief, out of all of the relations of sharing known for such mirrors, and by determining first the date of the completion of their distribution. In other words, it is a matter of determining the age for which political relations had already been established at a certain level between the Kinai polity, which regarded the Tsubai Ōtsukayama chief as an important representative, and the regional chiefs who shared duplicate mirrors.[18] Moreover, there appears to have been a difference in the nature of the political relations forged with regions from the Kinai to the west and from the Kinai to the east.[19]

Namely, of the nineteen tombs sharing duplicate mirrors with Tsubai Ōtsukayama, when the sixteen for which there are sufficient data on their grave goods are divided into eastern and western groups, there are no tombs in the western group with domestic mirrors, Chinese mirrors postdating the Wei Period, or jasper arm ornaments among their grave goods.[20] By contrast, many tombs in the eastern group contain these items, and thus appear to represent a newer cultural phase. Tsubai Ōtsukayama itself is similar to the western group in terms of its artifacts, and thus belongs to the older phase. . . .

An attempted interpretation of these facts is as follows. The first efforts to establish a network of political relations made by the Tsubai Ōtsukayama chief, or by the authority standing behind him, were directed toward chiefs in the western group and involved the distribution of relatively large numbers of duplicate mirrors, with two or more duplicates from the same set often given to a single chief. As relations with the western region were firmed up, operations began toward the east as well. Political relations with chiefs to the east were accompanied by a supply of artifacts from a newer cultural phase; it would therefore appear that these operations continued even after the Tsubai Ōtsukayama chief withdrew from active involvement. Of course, the region to the west was not neglected, but relations were evidently conducted with chiefs of a new generation.

It is difficult to imagine that such dual operations towards the east and west could have been completed by around 260, when problems were reported concerning the internal unification of the country.[21] Let us accordingly reconsider the earliest possible age for Tsubai Ōtsukayama Kofun as the year 280, which appears frequently in Table 2.2. For the latest possible age, since the shape of the mound and the architectural characteristics of the burial chamber render a date of 370 unfeasible, and also taking into consideration the frequency of dates in the table, let us fix this at 350. The earliest and latest ranges of dates in the table should be readjusted accordingly. Both occur for a value of sixty years for *n*: the earliest range under Case 2, and the latest under Case 3. But while a value of sixty years may be within the realm of possibility, it is probably too high for practical considerations. In this regard, the value of eighty years found in Case 1 is also highly improbable; these instances are accordingly marked in the table with asterisks. Removing these from consideration, the possible ranges of dates for Tsubai Ōtsukayama can be given in summary fashion as falling within the two broad categories of early (280–300) and late (300–50).

While the differences among the inferred dates for Tsubai Ōtsukayama stem understandably from the variation in the parameters used for the calculations, the question remains whether any of those parameters may be regarded as decisive. A reexamination of Table 2.2 shows that a third-century date for the tomb is calculated under Case 2 and in some instances under Case 4, whereas dates limited to the fourth century are calculated for Cases 1 and 3. Accordingly, it is clear that the question of whether the person buried at Tsubai Ōtsukayama was in possession of the mirrors by 250 (Cases 1 and 2) or not (Cases 3 and 4) has little effect on the outcome. Rather, the difference appears to stem from whether or not the various chiefs who received mirrors transmitted them to the next generation. Namely, if the other chiefs transmitted the mirrors, as in Cases 2 and 4, then a third-century date for Tsubai Ōtsukayama is possible. But if there was no transmission, its dating is limited to the fourth century. That this relationship is not absolute is shown, however, by the data for Case 4. But it is clear that recognizing the possibility of transmission of the mirrors —recognizing that in some cases duplicate mirrors obtained from the Tsubai Ōtsukayama chief were not buried with their original recipients—yields a date for Tsubai Ōtsukayama that possibly goes back to the third century.

. . . By means of these observations, in addition to the traditional kind of typological arguments made solely on the basis of tomb shape and similarities between burial facilities, it is possible to use links denoted by shared duplicate mirrors as a means for selecting tombs related with each other chronologically. And moreover, by acknowledging the special position of the Tsubai Ōtsukayama chief, we can obtain clues to help discover the earliest tombs among all those in Japan.

Interpreter's Afterword

In this manner, Kobayashi placed the construction of Tsubai Ōtsukayama, and the start of the Kofun Period itself, somewhere within the range of 280–350 C.E. Accordingly, since the duplicate mirrors are thought to date from the end of the

Late Han to the Wei periods, there was in Kobayashi's estimate a gap of one or two generations between the time of manufacture and the time when they were first deposited in the mounded tombs. Kobayashi felt this could be explained by regarding their treatment as that of heirlooms, an extension of the practice he suggested more generally for the Yayoi in the Kinki region, where mirrors are not found in burials of that period. But this particular notion, based as it is on negative evidence, has not been well received by Japanese archaeologists, in part because it is difficult either to prove or disprove.

Another assumption on which Kobayashi grounded his assessment that has come under scrutiny in recent years is that the newest of the tombs sharing duplicate mirror sets with Tsubai Ōtsukayama date to the end of the fourth century, conventionally taken as the border separating the early and middle Kofun Period. But the chronological framework used for defining the middle Kofun Period is based on tombs designated as mausoleums of certain members of the royal line, and the accuracy of such designations prior to the sixth century is open to doubt. A call for pushing the start of the middle Kofun back to the mid-fourth century, based on archaeological considerations alone, was first raised in the 1980s and has been gaining in acceptance in recent years.[22] A 1996 dendrochronological finding has moreover established that pottery used to define the middle Yayoi Period is a century older than previously thought.[23] Accordingly, the dates assigned to the late Yayoi Period are also liable to downward revision, which would make the Kofun Period as a whole older than previously regarded. The result of these chronological adjustments will surely place the start of tomb construction much nearer the time of Himiko and her dealings with the Wei court, reducing thereby the troublesome gap with the deposition of duplicate mirrors in the tombs as a whole. It will also pull the age assigned to the newest of the tombs sharing a duplicate set with Tsubai Ōtsukayama closer to the time when such items are seen as having been imported from China.

None of these revisions will diminish the value of Kobayashi Yukio's seminal work on duplicate mirrors and their role in Japanese history. Upon his retirement from Kyoto University in 1975, after finally gaining the rank of professor, he was immediately granted emeritus status in recognition of his many contributions, which include more than thirty books and site reports which he authored, coauthored, or edited, in addition to his numerous scholarly articles. More significant, his synthesis of the views held by a series of Kyoto University archaeologists on the location of Yamatai and the origins of the early Yamato polity, to which he added his own perspective through his distributional analysis of duplicate mirrors, had by his retirement become the generally accepted outline for viewing archaeological evidence on both the historic events known for the third century and their connection with the emergence of the ancient Japanese state.

Notes

1. Background material on Kobayashi's career is drawn primarily from two sources: Anazawa Wakō 1994; and Harunari Hideji 1997.

2. Kobayashi Yukio 1952.

3. These include Kobayashi Yukio 1961b, first published in 1955; Kobayashi Yukio 1961d, first published in 1956; and Kobayashi Yukio 1961c, first published in 1957.

4. Kobayashi Yukio 1961a. As noted, Kobayashi was an extremely cautious and meticulous scholar, leading to a degree of redundancy in his argument, and a somewhat tedious style that often obscures his intent. An abridged translation of this particular paper, eliminating some of the redundancy of the original, has already been published elsewhere: see Edwards 1995. The current contribution is an attempt to render Kobayashi's work more accessible, presenting excerpts from the earlier translation, paraphrasing the omitted portions, and adding some necessary background information while remaining faithful to the original line of argument.

5. For more detailed discussion of the Yamatai issue, and postwar archaeological approaches to it, see Edwards 1996; Edwards 1999; Farris 1998, chapter 1; and Piggott 1997, chapter 1.

6. Interpreter's note: Because many tombs bear common descriptive names such as Ōtsuka ("big mound"), Kobayashi referred to a tomb by first giving the prefecture in which it is located, followed by a local place name when necessary to distinguish two tombs within the same prefecture, then by the name given the mound in its local region. This practice is adopted here, following the names and readings given in Ōtsuka Hatsushige et al. 1989. The two tombs Tsubai Ōtsukayama and Bizen Kurumazuka are named so frequently in the article, however, that the prefecture names (Kyoto, Okayama) have been omitted.

7. Umehara Sueji, in noting that a mirror found at Nara Samida Takarazuka Kofun was identical with two others known from Hyōgo Yoshima Matsuyama Kofun, wrote "The diameters are equal, and as the patterns moreover replicate each other, they may be considered to have come from the same mold. As the same phenomenon is occasionally seen for other types of mirror as well, it is probable that such mirrors were imported together but then came into the separate possession of men of rank, and were buried with them." See Umehara Sueji 1922.

8. Interpreter's note: Data for Figure 2.2 are drawn from Maizō bunkazai kenkyūkai 1994; and from Kokuritsu rekishi minzoku hakubutsukan 1994. *Naikō kamon* mirrors bear a star-shaped pattern formed by a series of inward-facing arcs transecting the perimeter of a circle. TLV mirrors are so named for their images of a draftsman's tools: a T-shaped ruler, and a compass appearing alternately as an "L" or a "V," depending on its orientation.

9. Interpreter's note: Figure 2.3 shows only tombs sharing at least one Chinese duplicate set with Tsubai Ōtsukayama or Bizen Kurumazuka. By including tombs connected through links of shared duplicate sets with any tomb in this core group, Kobayashi counted thirty-nine tombs in this network for relations involving Chinese mirrors only, and forty-seven tombs for those linked with either Chinese or domestic mirrors.

10. Interpreter's note: The set numbers used in the text and in Figure 2.3 are taken from an inventory of triangular-rimmed mirrors appearing in Kyōto daigaku bungakubu

kōkogaku kenkyūshitsu 1992.

11. Interpreter's note: For example, Nara Shin'yama shares set 12 with Tsubai Ōtsukayama Kofun, and set 22 with Bizen Kurumazuka, but does not share mirrors from a single set with both tombs in the manner of Nara Tomio Maruyama Kofun. Kobayashi's conjecture here is that perhaps the Tsubai Ōtsukayama chief once held both sets, but later gave the Nara Shin'yama chief members of sets 12 and 22, and gave the Bizen Kurumazuka chief a member of set 22, while retaining only one member of set 12 for himself.

12. See Kobayashi Yukio 1961c, 195–99 for detailed discussion.

13. Interpreter's note: This simply means that the conditions given in the table are possible, but not necessary. Where transmission for one generation is allowable, for example, then the value may reach $2n$, but will be only n in cases where transmission does not occur.

14. Interpreter's note: In other words, in any particular instance the phenomenon represented by n may be a short-lived one: a chief may leave office within a year of taking it, passing on a mirror to a successor who rules twenty years. The numerical value of $2n$ in this case would be 0 + 20 = 20.

15. See Kobayashi Yukio 1961d, 166–7 for a detailed discussion of the mirrors' age.

16. Although it would be appropriate to extend the range of possible dates for Wei mirrors to around 260, if we accept the passage in the *History of the Wei Dynasty* stating that Himiko died during the Seishi era (240–248), then her death would be around 248; a rough date of 250 was thus selected for the time after Himiko's death, as it also should be well prior to the date for the envoy dispatched by Iyo (Himiko's successor) to Jin (in China) in 266.

17. Interpreter's note: The *History of the Wei Dynasty* states that Himiko was buried in a large tomb whose size is given with a phrase rendered in the standard English translation as "more than a hundred paces in diameter." See Goodrich 1951, 16. Japanese scholars accept the character rendered "pace(s)" as noting a Chinese unit of measurement, however, which at the time of the Wei Dynasty equaled approximately 1.45 meters. This makes it possible to read the passage as describing a mound of approximately 150 meters. Although the designation "diameter" weights the interpretation toward a mound that is round in shape (see, for instance, Yamao Yukihisa 1972, 137), some writers have nevertheless identified certain keyhole tombs as Himiko's grave by claiming the description applied to the more important round part of the mound, where the main burial facility is located. See, for example, Kasai Shin'ya 1981, 435-36.

Burial mounds of various shapes, and on the order of about fifty meters in length, were built during the middle and late Yayoi Periods prior to the sudden appearance of larger keyhole tombs like Tsubai Ōtsukayama. Accordingly, the possibility remains open that the *History of the Wei Dynasty* account is an exaggerated description of a Yayoi mounded grave. At the time Kobayashi wrote, however, the existence of these Yayoi mounds was unknown. His assertion therefore is simply that the *History of the Wei Dynasty* account should not be taken as describing a keyhole tomb, because he did not think those tombs could be dated back to the mid-third century.

18. Interpreter's note: The Kinai is equivalent to modern Nara and Osaka prefectures, plus portions of Kyoto and Hyōgo prefectures. This area forms the heartland of the modern Kinki, a region made up of Hyōgo, Kyoto, Nara, Mie, Osaka, Wakayama, and Shiga prefectures.

19. See Kobayashi Yukio 1961c for a detailed discussion.

20. Interpreter's note: Kobayashi is utilizing the results of work he had already published. See the article cited in the previous note and also Kobayashi Yukio 1961d. The terms "eastern" and "western" are a bit misleading, as the two groups of tombs so labeled actually overlap in the Kinki region. The distinction is more a chronological one, between tombs containing triangular-rimmed mirrors mixed with items judged to be slightly newer in age, such as the jasper arm ornaments mentioned here, and those lacking these newer elements.

21. Interpreter's note: This refers to a passage from the *History of the Wei Dynasty*, which Tsunoda and Goodrich render as follows: "When Himiko passed away . . . a king was placed on the throne, but the people would not obey him. Assassination and murder followed; more than one thousand were thus slain." See Goodrich 1951, 16. Peace was restored when a relative of Himiko, a girl of thirteen named Iyo, was made queen.

22. Interpreter's note: See for instance Shiraishi Taichirō 1985. Also see the discussion of this issue in Edwards 1996, 74–77.

23. Interpreter's note: This finding is discussed briefly in Edwards 1999, 106.

3

Suruga and Tōtōmi in the Kofun Age

HARA HIDESABURŌ

Introduction by Joan R. Piggott

HARA HIDESABURŌ IS A WELL-KNOWN HISTORIAN of early Japan who spent many years teaching at Shizuoka University, where he had ample opportunity to study the archaeology and history of Shizuoka Prefecture.[1] Hara served as editor for the classical volumes of *Shizuoka-ken shi*, the official history of the prefecture covering the classical age. He wrote the essay that follows for presentation to a local audience in 1986, when Japan was in the midst of a dynamic period of archaeological advances. Like Tsude Hiroshi and Inoue Tatsuo, whose work is also represented in this volume, Hara is particularly interested in the protohistory of Japan's regions and center-periphery relations underlying regional development. He argues that historians must pay close attention to both the Yamato center and to the various regions of the archipelago. They should also compare materials from the earliest written sources such as the eighth-century *Record of Ancient Things* (*Kojiki*) and *Chronicles of Japan* (*Nihongi*) with new knowledge based on regional archaeological finds and developments in linguistics and folklore studies. According to Hara, only painstaking assembly and evaluation of a collage of evidence will result in a better composite image of early history. And of course, it is such a foundation on which our understanding of later history is based. Hara clearly agrees with Marc Bloch, who once chided historians of his generation: "If the best-known theorists of our methods had not shown such an astonishing and arrogant indifference toward the techniques of archaeology, if they had not been as obsessed with narrative in the category of documents as they were with incident in the category of actions, they would doubtless have been less ready to throw us back upon an eternally dependent method of observation [i.e., reading written documents]."[2]

In the following essay, Hara focuses on the vicinity traversed by the Eastern Sea Route, or Tōkai region, that later comprised the provinces of Suruga and Tōtōmi in present-day Shizuoka Prefecture. He sets out to evaluate the significance of clusters of tomb mounds built there in the fifth and sixth centuries, against the background of Yamato monarchy depicted in the early chronicles and that of archaeological finds such as the inscribed Inariyama and Eta-Funayama swords. As was common for Japanese historians of his generation, Hara utilizes Engels' five-stage process of social evolution.[3] But he also considers other clues from local history, such as legends, place-names, and the genealogies of local families.

Most notably, Hara argues against the idea that early *kofun* in the Tōkai region were erected by local chieftains who ruled autonomous regional polities (*chiiki kokka*), a contemporary theory propounded by Kadowaki Teiji.[4] Rather, he affirms the story as narrated in the eighth-century chronicles, the *Kojiki* and *Nihongi*, that parts of eastern Japan were conquered by commanders loyal to Yamato kings and that those commanders subsequently built keyhole tombs as funerary monuments.[5] Following Ishimoda Shō, Hara sees the mid-to-late Kofun Period, the fourth and fifth centuries, as a "heroic age" (*eiyū jidai*) when generals wielding battle-axes carved out domains across the archipelago and on the Korean Peninsula, just as King Bu of Wa boasted in a fifth-century missive to the Chinese Liu Sung court.[6] After their victories such military leaders and their descendents—whose names and genealogies identify them as members of the Abe, Mononobe, and Ōtomo kin—prospered as local chieftains who oversaw expanding wet-rice agriculture throughout the Tōkai region. Acknowledging and supporting the preeminence of Yamato's Great Kings, they were pillars of what Hara terms a "Chou-like feudal [*hōkenteki*] polity" comparable to that of Chou China in the two millennia before the common era. Hara also surmises that in the later seventh century some of these elites chose to return to Yamato, where the Great Kings were strengthening their hold over their island realm. Such is the reasoning underlying Hara's view that the *ritsuryō* political formation at the turn of the eighth century was more fully integrated than many other researchers think.[7]

Of particular interest is Hara's discussion of shrine legends, place-names, local traditions and genealogies, and archaeological finds, which he uses to shed light on Yamato's myth-historical accounts in the *Kojiki*, *Nihongi*, and *Kokuzō hongi*. These are difficult materials for historians, but Hara urges that historians incorporate insights from the early chronicles and local history when internal and external consistencies evidence considerable potential for historicity.

According to Hara, the geography, structure, and size of *kofun* provide important clues to elite family distribution. His objective is to connect particular tomb groups and tombs to a given local family at a particular historical moment. Another method is to work backward—some eighth-century records list prominent local elites whose names reveal proximate relations with prominent courtier families. Hara argues that Lake Hamana in old Tōtōmi Province once represented the eastern border of Yamato royal influence, given that the female monarch Jitō traveled only as far as Tōtōmi during her various royal progresses. Place-names and names inscribed on excavated wooden slips (*mokkan*) and inscribed pottery (*bokushodoki*) likewise reveal linkages between local places and the Yamato court. In terms of folklore, Hara finds clues of Kibi's involvement in Yamato's penetration of the Tōkai region during the mid-Kofun Period in the legends of the princely brave, Yamato Takeru.

The methodologies of regional and local history upon which Hara draws have deep roots in Japan. One could argue that they date back to the eighth-century *fudoki*, which were prepared by provincial officials for their superiors at the *tennō*'s court to familiarize the latter with details of regional geography and culture needed to rule the realm. Local history remained a strong interest of National Studies scholars (*kokugakusha*) in Tokugawa times, and remains popular today. Unfortunately, studies of local history, and the resulting interplay between center and periphery that they consider, have been largely inaccessible to English readers, with a few exceptions. John Whitney Hall's work on Bizen in *Government and Local Power in Japan, 500 to 1700*, is surely a book that any interested reader should consult; Gina Barnes has focused on the archaeology of Kinai's "coalescent core"; and I have discussed early regional development in the northern region of Izumo. Readers of my own work will recognize that my views of the formation of Yamato state and kingship differ strikingly from Hara's—I do not see conquest as the major vehicle of Yamato influence across the archipelago. In particular, Hara has not persuaded me that the early keyholes must have been built by outsiders rather than "indigenous" elites. Nonetheless, I find Hara's demonstration of the tools of local history of great interest—we need such treatments for every region of the archipelago if we are to advance our understanding of Japan's early history, both at the center and in the countryside as well.

HARA HIDESABURŌ

Suruga and Tōtōmi in the Kofun Age

Interpreted by Joan R. Piggott

Clusters of Japanese mounded tombs (*kofun*) have been identified and excavated in Shizuoka Prefecture in recent decades.[8] As evidence from those excavations is considered in light of written historical sources, new historical issues have arisen for both historians and archaeologists. Shizuoka has long been my home—I was educated there and over the last several years I have edited the early documentary volumes of the Shizuoka Prefectural History (*Shizuoka-ken shi*), containing sources that span the fifth through the twelfth centuries. At Shizuoka University's Japan Historiographical Research Center, my colleagues and I have also compiled the *History of Fukuroi City* (*Fukuroi-shi shi*). In the course of work on these projects, we have considered a number of regional historical issues.

I am particularly interested in employing regional historical studies to better understand the process of evolution by which the early polity (*kodai kokka*) took form, and the various phases through which society passed from prehistory into classical times. In this essay I want to explore such issues in the context of regional history in Suruga and Tōtōmi during the fifth and sixth centuries. Young people these days seem to prefer quite detailed studies; but having reached the age of fifty myself, I want to reflect on broader issues. In particular, I want to ponder the larger historical significance of *kofun* in the Shizuoka region and how the tomb mounds can shed light on the history of one of Japan's famous highways and regional circuits, the Eastern Sea Route (Tōkaidō). After situating the tomb age historically, I will proceed with a precis of fifth- and sixth-century history. Then I will turn to particulars of tomb-age history in Suruga and Tōtōmi.

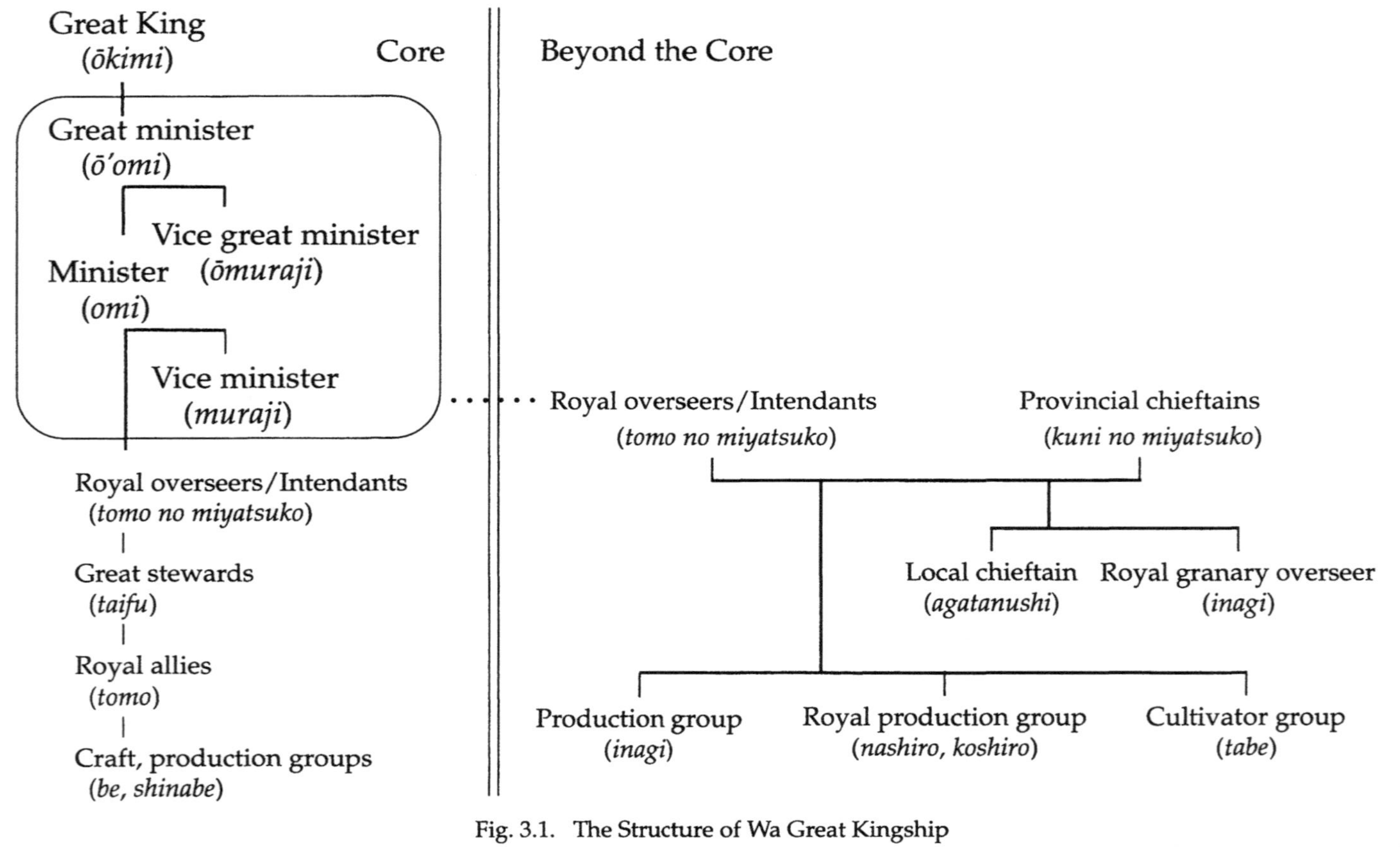

Fig. 3.1. The Structure of Wa Great Kingship

Accepting the evolutionism of Morgan and Engels as I do, I posit that society in Japan evolved from barbarism to civilization through five stages.[9] The first stage saw the dawn of civilization and began around the first century C.E. During this first stage, the chieftain of a regional polity known as Na in Kyūshū received a gold seal inscribed with the characters, "King of Na in Wa of Han" from a Later Han emperor in China. Once parts of Japan like Na joined the Chinese tributary system, the civilizing process was under way. This first stage continued through Himiko's lifetime in the later third century.

During the second stage, between the late third and late fourth centuries, Wa disappeared from the Chinese historical record. We know little about this period, although hints are found in the inscription on the famous seven-branched Isonokami sword, which dates from this time.[10]

The third stage spans the reigns of Wa's five kings during the fifth century.[11] Then in the fourth stage, after the death of the last of the five kings, Japan cut its tributary ties with China and from the late fifth through the late sixth centuries became increasingly independent. Finally, completing the process in the fifth stage, emissaries were sent to China during the reign of Great King Suiko (592–628 C.E.). The *tennō*-centered *ritsuryō* polity took form with the promulgation of the Taihō Code in the early eighth century.

The third and fourth stages, which coincided with the mid-to-late Kofun Period, are the focus of this essay. We must of course consider the complex issue of regional variation as we attempt to describe the process by which *kofun* were constructed in distinct regions of the Japanese archipelago. And starting from the epoch of Wa's five kings, we must consider what sort of age they ruled over: what sort of political institutions had been or were being developed during the late fourth through the late fifth centuries? As a reference for the reader, I have charted the hierarchy of Yamato kingship in Figure 3.1

Since the historicity of the eighth-century *Nihongi* cannot be accepted for this early epoch, scholars have frequently turned to Chinese records archived in the *Liu Sung History* (*Sung shu*) that concern those kings and the realm of Wa. There, we find this entry dating from the 420s or 430s about one of the five kings named Ch'en:[12]

> Ch'en also requested that the title, "Commandant Who Subjugates Barbarians in the West and General Who Serves His Country," be conferred on Wa, Sui, [ ] and others, altogether thirteen men. An edict was issued granting this request.[13]

King Ch'en and other generals were major figures in Wa's ruling structure, the so-called Yamato kingship.

From the perspective of Yamato at this time, its domain extended westward. The title, "General Who Subjugates the West," could well have designated local chieftains whose exploits served Yamato's interests. The fifth century was an epoch characterized by the bestowal of such titles. The paramount King Ch'en referred to here was both commandant and a tribal chieftain (*buzoku no shuchō*) who resided in the region of central Honshū known as Yamato. His kingship embraced the people of his tribe. After King Ch'en's time, during what was probably the reign of the third of the five Wa kings, the number of confederate chieftains increased to twenty-three:

> In the twentieth year [443], Sai, King of Wa, sent an envoy with tribute and was again confirmed as "King of Wa and General Who Maintains Peace." In the twenty-eighth year [451], the additional title of "General Who Maintains Peace in the East Commanding with Battle-Ax all Military Affairs in the Six Countries of Wa, Silla, Imna, Kala, Chin-han, and Mok-han" was granted. Twenty-three designated men were also confirmed in either civil or military titles.[14]

By this time, domains known as *gun* were identified with particular commanders; and rulership over such domains went to those charged with organizing and commanding fighting forces called *gun* as well. Such a correlation is suggested linguistically by the homophones meaning respectively "jurisdiction" and "armed force." The fifth century also saw conquests beyond the archipelago, as the quote about the increase in chieftains indicates. So our image of Wa rulership in that century is one of generals wielding battle-axes to carve out domains at home and abroad.[15]

Providing more substance for this image of fifth-century rulership is the well-known inscription on the Saitama-Inariyama sword excavated from a fifth-century tomb in old Musashi Province, today's Chiba Prefecture:

> Inscribed in July, in the year of Shingai [471 C.E.?]. The ancestor of Ohowake-no-omi was Ohohiko. His son was Takari-no-sukune. His son was Teyokari-wake. His son was Takahahishi-wake. His son was Tasaki-wake. His son was Hatehi. His son was Kasahahiyo. His son was Ohowake-no-omi. From generation to generation they served as heads of the swordbearers. When the court of Great King Wakatakeru was at Shiki, I aided in ruling the realm and had this hundred-[times]-wrought sword made to record the origins of my service.[16]

It is my view that this Inariyama blade belonged to the chieftain (*shuchō*) buried in the Inariyama tomb. At this stage of the development of Yamato kingship, some regional commanders with their armed forces were royal confederates, while others were not. The leader interred at Inariyama was a royal confederate general.

Professor Kishi's theory concerning the inscription on the sword excavated from Eta-Funayama Kofun in Kyūshū is also of interest:

> Under the reign of the Great King Wakatakeru, who ruled the nation, a *tensōjin*, Murite by name, who served [the Great King], in August used a large caldron and a four-*shaku*-long court sword, eighty times wrought, and sixty iron pieces to make a sword overhardened by three-*sun* from the tip. The person who bears this sword shall live long, and his

> descendants shall continue to enjoy the three benefits and shall never lose what they rule. The swordsmith was Itaka, and the inscriber was Chōan.[17]

Most scholars view this *tensōjin* as some sort of civil official. I think that *sō* meant "one charged with a duty." The duties of such an official might well have been connected with the administration of justice because the graph read "ten" suggests a court of judgment. We need more evidence before we can elaborate further about this *tensōjin*, one of the various civil and military functionaries who served in eastern and western Japan. They gave institutional structure to Yamato kingship during the fifth and early sixth centuries, before the provincial chieftain (*kuni no miyatsuko*) and special worker group (*be*) systems were initiated.

It is to this latter epoch that we now turn. While there are few written documents for regional history at this time, we can rely on case studies of particular regions, like those I have undertaken for Suruga and Tōtōmi.

Suruga

Our story begins with an ancient realm (*kuni*) known as "Abe-no-Ihohara," ruled by the Ihohara-no-kimi family and located on the alluvial plain occupied by the present-day cities of Shizuoka and Shimizu[18] (see Map 3.1). Important clues to its history can be gleaned from place-names as well as from legends of the heroic warrior, Yamato Takeru, that are still remembered in the area. We will look at the legends first.

Yamato Takeru is the enshrined deity at Yaizu Shrine in Yaizu City. There is also a place in Shimizu City named Kusanagi, after Yamato Takeru's famous sword.[19] Nearby is Hisagozuka Kofun, and just inland stands Kusanagi Shrine. Moreover, at the foot of the mountains in Shimizu City sits Higashi Kusanagi Shrine, just to the east of a defunct temple known as Obane Haiji (*haiji* means "disestablished temple") and Miikedaira Kofun. The *Nihongi* reports that Yamato Takeru actually came to Suruga, while the *Kojiki* describes his visit to neighboring Sagami, where he appointed a provincial chieftain.[20]

Stories of Yamato Takeru also provide clues to the histories of local families in Suruga, especially that of the Ihohara provincial chieftain. Concerning Suruga's provincial chieftains, the *Original Record of Old Things in Previous Ages* (*Sendai kuji hongi*) reports: "In the reign of the monarch Seimu the ancestor of Lord Ikeda-Sakanai, son of Kibi Takehiko no Mikoto, who was also called Ikabehiko no Mikoto, was appointed provincial chieftain." [21] The *New Register of Aristocratic Kindreds* (*Shinsen shōjiroku*) compiled in the early Heian Period adds:

> His ancestor was the same as that of Kasa-no-omi, that is, Kibi-wake Takehiko no Mikoto. . . . Kibi Takehiko no Mikoto was sent east during Keikō's reign, where he subjugated hairy people and turbulent deities. He reached the province [*kuni*] called Abe-Ihohara. And when he reported his exploits, the place was granted to him.

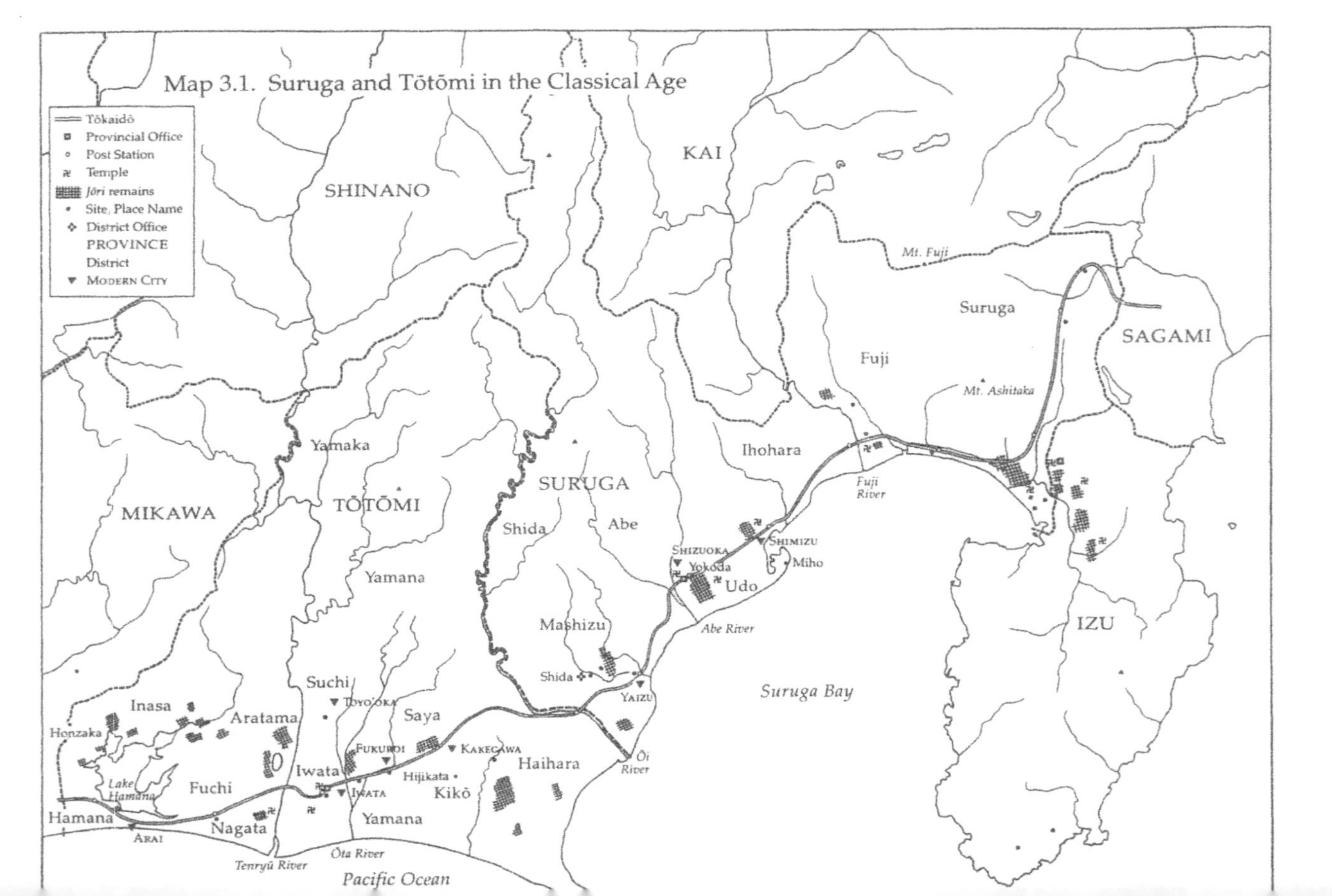

Map 3.1. Suruga and Tōtōmi in the Classical Age

We see here that the provincial chieftain of Suruga was considered a descendant of Kibi Takehiko in early Heian times. Genealogies indicate that he shared this ancestry with other provincial elites from Kibi, including the Kasa-no-omi, Kibi-no-omi, and the Shimotsumichi-no-omi families. And according to the *Nihongi*, "The ruler [Keikō] ordered Kibi Takehiko and Ōtomo-no-muraji Takehi to accompany and serve Yamato Takeru."[22]

After completing the eastern conquest, Yamato Takeru and his company reportedly proceeded to Suzuka in Ise, where Yamato Takeru died. Before the end, however, he sent a message to the Yamato Great King via Kibi no Takehiko, who was rewarded with the domain of Ihohara. The *Original Record* notes that Kibi no Takehiko's son, Okabehiko, inherited the provincial chieftaincy.[23] In terms of evidence from place-names, Okabe was once a lodging place (*shuku*) in Shita District along the Eastern Sea Route, and it could have been named for this Okabehiko. Meanwhile the *Kojiki* records a variant tradition concerning the origins of the Ihohara—it says that Lord Ihohara was a descendant of a Prince Takehiko, son of the monarch Kōrei.[24]

The genealogy of the Ihohara-no-kimi family was originally archived in Shizuoka Prefecture, but it is now kept at Doshisha University in Kyoto. Professor Tatsumi Kazuhiro has studied it and concluded that the Yamato king Kōrei, and his consort, Princess Ōyamato no Kuni Are, were shown therein to be progenitors of the Tonami family of Koshi; of the Kunimae-no-omi of Toyo, who was himself an ancestor of the Ihohara-no-kimi family; of the Ama-no-atai family in Echizen's Tsuruga; and of the Ihohara-no-kimi family. In other words, all these families engaged in marine travel across the archipelago were given a common ancestry.

Moreover, Ihohara involvement in shipbuilding is confirmed in a *Nihongi* entry concerning the fateful battle between the Kudara-Wa allied forces and those of the T'ang-Silla coalition at Paekchon Bay in 663 C.E.:

> Kudara, knowing the strategy of the rebels, instructed its generals, "We hear that General Ihohara of Great Nippon has marshaled 10,000 soldiers to aid us and plans to cross the sea with them. What we ask is that you draw up plans in advance. We will go directly to Paekchon Bay to await and entertain them."[25]

Whether the Ihohara provincial chieftain actually took part in the Paekchon Bay battle is a matter for debate, but we can guess that Shimizu Bay would have been the Ihohara home port, that the provincial chieftain assembled a great armada there, and that he was a regional ruler of significant power and wealth. Ihohara still survives as a place-name in Shimizu City, and the two keyhole tomb mounds there, Miikedaira Kofun and Gōdōyama Kofun, confirm that it was indeed the center of the provincial chieftain's domain (see Map 3.1).

As a university student I participated in the excavation of Miikedaira Kofun.[26] At that time the oldest tomb mound in the region was thought to be Yatsuyama Kofun in Abe District, which dates from the early to mid-Kofun Period.[27] But that was before a third burial crypt at Gōdōyama Kofun was uncovered. Gōdōyama is a square keyhole approximately eighty meters long.[28] The burial in crypt no. 3 utilized a wooden casket laid on a bed of clay. Since a triangular-rimmed mirror decorated with images of immortals and beasts (*sankakubuchi shinjūkyō*) was also discovered therein, many scholars think the Gōdōyama square keyhole predates the Miikedaira round keyhole tomb.[29] But whichever may be actually older, both have small top-opening interment chambers formed of layered rocks. One or both of these tombs were likely the burial places of Ihohara chieftains.

Current thinking is that the Ihohara manufactured a genealogy that linked them with Yamato's monarchs and that these early *kofun* were erected by indigenous local chieftains who gradually expanded their authority from Yayoi times onward. My own view, however, is that we should accept King Wakatake's claims, as archived in his missive in the *Liu Sung History*, that his ancestors conquered fifty-five countries of "hairy" men. And if we accept the proposition that early Kofun-period tomb mounds such as Miikedaira and Gōdōyama entombed the remains of Ihohara provincial chieftains, I think we must recognize that the Ihohara-no-kimi were not descendants of indigenous chiefly lineages dating back to the Yayoi period. Rather, just as their genealogies indicate, the Ihohara were descendants of Kibi no Takehiko, who subjugated this land in the course of an eastward conquest. Taking Ihohara as their domain, his descendants ruled it. And since Ihohara-no-kimi descendants appear in the eighth-century Suruga tax registers as local agents of the royal court, we know that his descendants continued to serve as local royal officials into Nara times. Moreover, appearance of the family name in the Heian-period *Shinsen shōji roku* means that some members of the family returned to the Kinai at some point. We can assume that they did so to serve the court during the formative period of the *tennō*-centered state, even as other kinsmen stayed behind to rule Ihohara.

Discovery of the Saitama-Inariyama inscribed sword, mentioned earlier, has greatly aided the search for connections between *kofun* and specific elite families. How should future investigation proceed? As I have argued above, my view is that we must not ignore the traditions of local families as we consider who built which tombs. In the Ihohara region of Suruga, the lords of Ihohara and their role in legends related to Yamato Takeru provide us with a particularly interesting case study that parallels those of ruling families in the regions of Kibi, Musashi, and Kōzuke. And while I have not yet completed my analysis of the distribution of elite families in Shizuoka relative to the location of various *kofun* groups, I have a general sense of the situation on the alluvial plain around Shimizu City.

To begin, it is notable that the family of the eighth-century district chieftain (*gunji*) known as Udo-no-kimi lacks a noble genealogy. Udo District borders the Pacific coast from Miho to Shizuoka City and includes Shimizu City extending south from the Eastern Sea Route (see Map 3.1). Mount Udo rises at its center, and the vicinity—historically called the Udo District—includes the Yayoi-period Toro site, suggesting the antiquity of rice cultivation there.[30] The defunct Katayama Temple is also located nearby. I would argue that its chieftains were indigenous elites, in contrast with the Ihohara-no-kimi provincial chieftains who came from the west as conquerors. Furthermore, eighth-century tax rolls show other local elites serving as Udo District chieftains, including the Kawabe-no-omi family. Their participation in tax collection indicates their association with the provincial office (*kokufu*). Other local families included the Kusakabe, the Hasetsukabe, the Hanyu-no-omi, and the Yokoda-no-omi kin groups—the latter were based at the post station (*umaya*) whose name they assumed. The Inari-no-omi and Toko-no-omi were probably related to royal cultivator communities called *nashiro* and *koshiro*. And the Hekibe likely once served rulers in distant Yamato as ritualists of a shrine cult they themselves brought to Udo.[31] An issue for future study is to determine if tombs of these families are appropriately distributed throughout Udo District, as I hypothesize they are.

As for Abe District to the west of Ihohara, there is a question about its relationship with the courtier Abe family. The latter held high ministerial posts, participated in royal banquets, and took a major role in diplomacy and foreign affairs in the late sixth through seventh centuries. My theory is that at one time this noble Abe family ruled over not only Abe District in Suruga but also Abe District in Iga. Scattered clues support this proposition. A noble called Abe-no-omi Osada lived in the late seventh and early eighth centuries, and even today there is a place called Osada in Shizuoka City. The place known as Shino'o in Shizuoka City may have been named for Abe-Shihi-no-muraji. And a final clue comes from *New Register of Aristicratic Kindreds*, which contains a reference to the "Abe-Ihohara." My interpretation, for which I hope to gather more evidence in future, is that the Abe-Ihohara initially served as provincial chieftains in Suruga. But then early in the sixth century some of their kin left to reside at the Great King's court in mid-Honshū, where they became influential courtiers. As time passed, however, these courtier Abe retained relatively little power in Ihohara.

In seeking connections between courtier elites and elites active in Kofun-age Suruga, the Sengen Shrine in Shizuoka City offers interesting clues. The Sengen Shrine long served as the premier shrine of the province (*ichi no miya*), but historically the Sengen and Kambe shrines were distinct establishments. Prior to the eleventh century, when the Sengen deity was brought from Sengen Shrine on Mount Fuji, the Kambe Shrine occupied the site alone. This Kambe Shrine probably originated as a local installation of distant Yamato's Miwa Shrine.[32] Scattered clues point to these origins. For instance, Abe District has a township (*gō*) named Miwa. One would expect a connection between this Miwa Township and Yamato's Miwa Shrine. Moreover, the shrine priest at Kambe bore the family name of Shiki. According to a family tradition, they are descended from a branch of the Shiki family from Yamato's Shiki District. They lack a written genealogy, but the potential historicity of their claim should be taken seriously. The Shiki of Kambe Shrine presumably immigrated to Suruga as priests at the time when forces loyal to Yamato kings subjugated the area and introduced worship of the Miwa royal deity in the newly conquered territory. This was not unlike the occasion in the seventh century when Great King Tenji beckoned the Miwa deity to his new capital in Ōmi and called it Hiyoshi.[33] This process of moving a deity with its priestly family to a subjugated land is difficult to trace, but place-names and local traditions cannot be easily ignored.

How might a family serving at the Yamato court and residing in mid-Honshū have administered its holdings in distant Suruga? The genealogy of another family of shrine priests, those of the Fuji Ōmiya Shrine, provides ideas. Their original family name was Wani. The Wani claimed descent from Koshō, the fifth ruler of Yamato recorded in the *Nihongi;* and Koshō's descendent, Waka-Oshihiko no Mikoto, resided in Yamato's Wani township.[34] Further down the Wani genealogy is Takunawa, who served at Shiki no Kanazashi, the palace of Great King Kimmei. The fourth of Kimmei's consorts was reportedly a daughter of the Kasuga-no-omi family that derived from the Wani as well.[35] Meanwhile, in Suruga District to the east, the senior district official (*tairyō*) in eighth-century records came from a family called the Kanazashi-no-toneri, "attendants at the Kanazashi Palace."[36] Based on this sort of evidence it is reasonable to argue that the Wani helped subjugate eastern Suruga and that some of them subsequently settled there. Much later their descendants ruled there as the "Kanazashi-no-toneri" family.

While focusing on clues concerning the local history of Suruga during the fifth and sixth centuries, I have tried to demonstrate here how we can investigate the genealogies of local families in the context of the broader history of the archipelago. Surely some unlikely elements remain, but such evidence needs to be considered along with traditions recorded in the *Nihongi.*

Tōtōmi

Now let me turn to Tōtōmi Province, Suruga's neighbor to the west. Beginning with the old orthography for the province's name, the characters mean "distant faint sea," a clear contrast with Ōmi's name, which means "nearby faint sea."[37] Although there were other such bodies of water—Lake Suwa, Lake Ashi, and Kasumigaura, the contrast between near and far must have denoted a special significance to Yamato rulers: Tōtōmi's distant faint sea was Lake Hamana, which represented a boundary for Yamato paramounts. The world beyond it was one beyond their rule.

The songs of the Kume—*Kumeuta*—some of which are recorded in the *Nihongi* and the *Kojiki*, are of interest here.[38] In the *Kojiki* we find, "On the large rocks of the sea of Ise, of the divine wind, shellfish are crawling around. Like these, we will crawl around and smite them relentlessly." Then again when attacking Yesiki and Otosiki, the Kume troops were exhausted and sang, "Watching the enemy, while going through the woods of Mount Inasa of the lined-up shields, we fought, but now we are starving. Oh Ukai—you keepers of the cormorants of the isles—come quickly to our aid!"[39]

Commentaries suggest that this "Mount Inasa of the lined-up shields" refers to Mount Inasa in Yamato's Uda District, and that since this was a song from the monarch Jimmu's eastern campaign, it must have been sung during the battles for Yamato.[40] While I agree that the *Kumeuta* were most likely genuine war songs, my own view is that where they were sung and under what historical conditions they were actually composed are not necessarily as the

Nihongi and *Kojiki* record. The issue must be considered in broader historical perspective. Initially I had no idea where this Mount Inasa might have been located. But one version of a ritual calendar for Ise Shrine makes reference to songs and dances of the Torina youths: "Tōtōmi, the mallets of Mount Minasa, break the branches, take them, crawl all around. . . . "[41] There are interesting parallels between this song and the *Kumeuta* quoted above, suggesting a link between Mount Minasa of the song and Mount Inasa in Tōtōmi. References to crawling around and "large rocks of the sea of Ise of the divine wind" confirm the link with Ise. The original name of "Ise" was probably "Iso," meaning "seashore." Previously named Iso-no-kuni—Land of Rocks—over time it came to be called Ise. Adjacent to it was Shima-no-kuni, later known as Shima District, which continued to send special royal offerings—food to grace the royal table—throughout Nara times.

The three provinces of Ise, Mikawa, and Tōtōmi have historically been closely connected, and a glance at a map shows why. Ise and Mikawa face each other across a bay. During the Tokugawa and Meiji periods, people who went to Mikawa to manufacture miso and soy sauce came originally from Ise. In the Nara Period, taxes from Tōtōmi were carried straight across to Ise by ship. It has been made clear by research into the origins of Ise Shrine that Ise was the base from which the eastward thrust by forces allied with Yamato Great Kings began. From Ise they proceeded into Mikawa; and crossing the pass at Honzaka, they would have entered Tōtōmi's Inasa District (see Map 3.1). I have concluded therefore that the Mount Inasa of the Kume song was probably Tōtōmi's Mount Inasa.

As further confirmation of this argument, we can observe the origin of the place-name Honzaka Pass on the border between old Tōtōmi and Mikawa provinces (see Map 3.1). *Ho* means "ears of grain" and *saka* means "hill." *Kojiki* and *Nihongi* mention the Ho-no-kuni provincial chieftain, and Ho-no-saka would have been the pass leading into his domain, Ho-no-kuni (Land of Ears of Grain).[42] Crossing Honzaka Pass and proceeding eastward one arrived at Hibizawa and a post station called Itatsuki, probably in present-day Fukuroi City. Then came Inasa Pass. Having crossed it, one would have been able to see Kitaoka-ōtsuka Kofun in the Ii Valley. The fourth largest *kofun* in Shizuoka Prefecture, it is a square keyhole measuring 50 meters in length and dates from the early Kofun Period.

I would therefore argue that the war song about Mount Inasa actually memorializes a strategic battle in the vicinity of Tōtōmi's Inasa Pass which took place during the eastward campaign of forces representing Yamato. "Watching the enemy while going through the woods" recalls the danger of keeping watch for the enemy while on the move. "We fought, but now we are starving" records hunger in battle. "You keepers of the cormorants of the isles" may refer to the people of Amabe District in Ise and the Atsuta area of Owari who made their living by fishing with cormorants. Some of them may have served as cormorant keepers for Yamato forces, and here they were called upon to send reinforcements and nourishment to tired and hungry warriors. Despite its simplicity, the verse pulsates with the real dangers of warfare.

The Eastern Sea Route, originally the route of this eastern conquest, was officially named only in the second half of the seventh century, just before *tennō*-centered *ritsuryō* government was promulgated. In early times it evidently followed a northerly route that skirted the northern shore of Lake Hamana over to Kakegawa (see Map 3.1), as confirmed by the distribution of tomb mounds north of Lake Hamana. The Kōzanji manuscript of the Heian-period encyclopedia *Wamyōshō* lists such townships as Miyakoda, Osakabe, Ii, and Ifuku in Tōtōmi's Inasa District. In Aratama District further east was Miyake Township, probably the site of a royal estate (*miyake*), as well as Akaza Township. And continuing over to Hamana District—now due west of the lake but originally located in the vicinity of present-day Mikkabi—were Sakamoto Township just below Honzaka Pass, and Ōmiwa Township, probably named after the Miwa deity. A post station known as Nieshiro Township, as well as Agata Township, presumably the home of a client chieftain (*agatanushi*) that once served Yamato kings, were also located there.[43] Even today, people in the vicinity bear the surname "Agata." After a period of warfare, all of this conquered land was brought under Yamato authority; and those who gradually brought it under expanded rice cultivation were linked to the Yamato court. Former rulers were incorporated into the new authority structure. Under this new regime the most powerful titled family would have been the Miwa-no-atai, whose name appears in the eighth-century *Hamana District Tax Roll*.[44] They would have entered Hamana as Yamato agents. Over time, they sent out colonists to various locations across the region.

To understand Yamato kingship, it is important to establish the realm's eastern frontier, and scholars have debated whether "the east country" (Tōgoku) began at the eastern border of Owari or at the border between Mikawa and Tōtōmi.[45] Aside from the fact that its name means "distant faint sea," there is other evidence that Tōtōmi was Yamato's eastern frontier. During the reign of Great King Jōmei, "men of the west raised the palace; men of the east made the temple" in 639.[46] And in 642, "The *tennō* ordered the Grand Minister, 'Let a palace be built before the twelfth month. Let the myriad provinces proffer materials for the palace halls. And from Tōtōmi in the east to Aki in the west, let workers be conscripted.'"[47] Then, if we examine the list of "provinces at middling distance from the capital" (*chūgoku*) that provided support for prestigious Daijōe rites celebrating a new reign after Great King Temmu's time through the eighth century, there were only two: Tōtōmi sent offerings in 708 and again in 716; and Echizen sent offerings in 766 and 781.[48] Echizen is known to have had a special relationship with the Yamato throne through its Fujiwara governors. I would argue that Tōtōmi had its own special relationship with the Yamato royal family as the eastern frontier of Yamato's realm during the epoch of Yamato kingship.

Still another clue to this special relationship between Yamato and Tōtōmi comes from the *Nihongi* chapter on the reign of Temmu's consort and successor, the female monarch Jitō (r. 690–697). She loved to travel, and when she made a royal progress to Mikawa between the eleventh and twelfth months of 702, a song celebrating the event mentioned a meadow at a place called Hikuma.[49]

Hisamatsu Sen'ichi argued that Hikuma was in Mikawa, but I think he is mistaken. Another contemporary song mentions Arainosaki, Cape Arai, probably at present-day Arai (see Map 3.1). In later medieval times the area was known as Imagire, because during an earthquake in the 1490s the land caved in. Before that, however, there was but a narrow outlet to the sea. The "distant faint sea" was a fresh-water lake, Lake Hamana, attached by a stream to the sea. When Great King Jitō traveled eastward she would first have arrived in Mikawa, and then she would have embarked and arrived by boat in the vicinity of Imagire. The "shelfless" boat in the song would have been a simple dugout, the simplest sort of craft used in the ancient period. Further up the Eastern Sea Route were Hikuma and Haihara. The monarch must have visited these distant climes because in her day the area was subject to her rule. Soon after, according to *ritsuryō* law, Tōtōmi came to be known as a "province of middling distance" in contrast with Mikawa, which was a "province near the capital" (*kinkoku*).

Of further interest is the fact that Tōtōmi was clearly part of the region where members of the Mononobe family established a strong hold. By looking at the *Original Record of Provincial Chieftains* (*Kuni no miyatsuko hongi*) and *Thoughts on the Record of the Provincial Chieftains* (*Kuni no miyatsuko hongi kō*), we can reconstruct the distribution of Mononobe provincial chieftains.[50] There were six in the Tōkaidō provinces, one in the Tōsandō provinces, three in the Nankaidō region, and two in the Saikaidō area, making a total of twelve. Of those, eight were in the provinces of Mikawa, Tōtōmi, Suruga, and Izu. In other words, Mononobe provincial chiefs were most numerous along the eastern seaboard. Besides the Ho-no-kuni provincial chieftain of Mikawa and the Soga and Ihohara chieftains in Tōtōmi, the five remaining provincial chieftains all claimed to be Mononobe kin; and some scholars also regard the Soga as Mononobe family members. This leads to the question, why were so many of the provincial chieftains along the eastern Pacific coast Mononobe kin? While I have not yet completed my research on Owari and Mikawa, I can report concerning the Kudo chieftains in the Fukuroi vicinity and the Soga chieftains of Saya and Yamana districts.

The Mononobe genealogy offers a wealth of clues. In the *Original Records of Heavenly Grandchildren* (*Tenson hongi*) section of the *Original Record of Old Things in Previous Ages,* two lineages are shown descending from Nigihayahi no Mikoto. One is that of Amanokaguyama no Mikoto of the Owari, and one is that of Umashimaji no Mikoto, the founding ancestor of the Mononobe.[51] Further down the genealogy, Ikashikio no Mikoto was born of Tōchine no Mikoto; then came Katagatashi-no-muraji, ancestor of the Suruga provincial chieftains, and Ikimi-no-muraji, from whom derived the Shiki local chieftain, the Tōtōmi provincial chieftain, and the ancestors of both the Kudo-no-atai and the Saya-no-atai kin. There are alternative traditions, but they too indicate that the Tōtōmi provincial chieftain and the Kudo provincial chieftain were Mononobe kin.

As for the Soga provincial chieftain, "when the realm was at Kashiwara and Jimmu first reigned, one of his courtiers, Mishiini no Mikoto, was appointed provincial chieftain." There has long been a theory that this Soga provincial chieftain was related in some way to the courtly Soga family, but it may be that "Mishiini" should be read "Umashiini," recalling the name of the Mononobe founder, Umashimaji no Mikoto.[52] Meanwhile, the ancestor of the Kudo provincial chieftain is thought to have been Inabani no Sukune, another name that recalls the Mononobe amalgam of "umashi" and "ini." The Soga may well have linked themselves with the monarch Jimmu of Kashiwara to give their new ruling lineage the greatest possible patina of venerable age.

If one follows the Eastern Sea Route west of Kakegawa, there is still a place called "Soga" in the Kudo vicinity of Fukuroi City, between the two old districts of Saya and Yamana. The division creating the two districts took place in 722, when eight townships from Saya were carved out to create the new Yamana District.[53] Six of those townships were listed in the Heian-period *Wamyōshō*, and inscribed pottery fragments from the Sakajiri excavation provide clues to others, including Soga and Kutsube townships.[54] Located within the city limits of Fukuroi, the excavation at Sakajiri revealed continuous human use of the area since late Yayoi times, but Kofun-age residences form the core of the finds.[55] One theory concerning Soga's origins proposes that at the end of the sixth century, to secure a footing in Mononobe-dominated territory, the courtier Soga allied themselves with a branch of the Mononobe Kudo lineage and established this Soga provincial chieftaincy.[56] Pottery fragments from Sakajiri also display the name "Kutsube," probably the last of the eight townships that formed Yamana District. Meanwhile, Kudo chieftains are worshipped at Gumbe Shrine—presently called Kutsube Shrine—and the side-opening Udogaya-ōketsu tomb nearby may well be the resting place of Soga provincial chieftains.[57] Shibata Minoru dated this tomb to the later sixth century, but I think it was probably constructed in the mid-sixth century. Grave goods include a round mirror decorated with a square and images of metamorphosized guardian deities and beasts, a ring-pommeled sword, a sword with a rounded pommel, horse-trappings, halberds, and iron arrowheads. In Kakegawa there is also the seventh-century Jūnigaya-ōketsu Kofun, another side-opening mound the stone chamber of which was found to contain two very unusual coffin rests.

Another Mononobe kinsman active in Tōtōmi was the Shiki chieftain who once served as an *agatanushi*. Tokugawa-period National Studies scholars made a connection between this chieftain and Shiki Township in Yamana, in the vicinity of present-day Shikiji. If one proceeds inland from the foot of Shinboinyama to where the Iwatabara plateau narrows, one ends up at Shikiji. There the Shikiji River also memorializes the Mononobe Shiki chieftain.

There was probably another *agatanushi* named Yamanashi who went unmentioned in the *Nihongi* and *Kojiki*. North of Fukuroi City is a place called Yamanashi, which is written with the characters meaning "mountain" and "pear." Historically it was called Yamana Township. According to the Tokugawa-period gazeteer *Kakegawa shikō* (*Thoughts on Kakegawa History*) and other sources, the place-name "Yamana" came about when the last syllable *shi* was dropped from Yamanashi. Originally the name may have been written with characters for "mountain" and "null" (*nashi*) despite its being called "Yamana."

Another bit of evidence links Yamanashi with the Mononobe. There is a Mononobe Shrine in Kai Province's old Yamanashi District. A gazeteer notes, "According to the *Original Records*, the tenth-generation descendant of Nigihayahi no Mikoto was Mononobe-Inaba-no-muraji. His older sister was Mononobe Yamanashihime, who was born in Tōtōmi's Yamana District. There is also a district named Inaba."[58] Inaba District is in Shimōsa Province to the east. All this suggests a link between Tōtōmi's Yamana District and Shimōsa's Inaba District. Moreover, according to the *Wamyōshō* there was a Yamanashi Township in Inaba District of Shimōsa Province. The Tokugawa gazetteer also made the connection between this Inaba District and two members of the Mononobe-Inaba family, Inaba no Sukune and Inaba-no-muraji, who were closely related to Yamanashihime, Ōjin's consort. Considering all this, I agree that Yamanashihime was probably born in Tōtōmi's Yamanashi. Proceeding in an easterly direction up the Pacific seaboard, one passes through Tōtōmi on the way to Kai Province. It is reasonable that the first Yamanashi place-name should occur in Tōtōmi. Continuing eastward, there is Kai Yamanashi, a new settlement made as the Mononobe moved further east. And finally they pushed into the Kantō plain to settle at Inabanuma in Shimōsa's Inaba District. Places named Yamanashi and Inaba aid us in tracing Mononobe movement in eastern Japan.

How did the place-name "Yamanashi" come to be? Its probable meaning—"without mountains"—is clear when one visits the Wadaoka tomb cluster in Yamana District. A place there, Tsukimisato ("Moon-viewing Village"), was named for its landscape: "Nothing to obscure the moon, Moon-viewing village," says an old verse. Having settled there, the Mononobe subsequently expanded their hold to points eastward, building new communities for which they sometimes used old and familiar names. It seems likely that the Kudo provincial chieftains and the Saya-no-atai followed this same pattern.

What was the time-frame for Mononobe activity in Tōtōmi, and when did they take up residence in Yamana District? Based on a variety of evidence, I think they must have arrived sometime in the mid-fifth century. The early Heian *Shinsen shōji roku* mentions the Sayabe-no-obito family of Settsu. The Sayabe, along with two other lineages, the Karakuni-no-muraji and the Yatabe-no-miyatsuko, claimed descent from the Mononobe. Appearance of the Sayabe signifies the heightened prestige of the Saya-no-atai line relative to their country cousins, the Kudo-no-atai, who were not mentioned in *Shinsen shōji roku*.

How did some members of the Saya-no-atai family come to dwell in the Kinai and become prominent servants of the Yamato court? Clues can be found at a place named Saya in the Naniwa region of Settsu Province. We know that early in 646 the Yamato monarch Kōtoku moved his palace to the royal estate known as Koshiro in Settsu's Sayabe region.[59] Naoki Kōjirō has suggested that managers of such royal estates were often granted the title of *obito* by the Yamato court, making it likely that the Sayabe-no-obito family served as managers of the Koshiro estate. The earliest record of this holding is dated 531, the first year of the monarch Ankan's reign. Ankan reportedly had four consorts but no children, and after his death in 535, four royal estates were divided among his four consorts. Yakahime, a daughter of Mononobe-Itabi-no-ōmuraji, received the Koshiro property. It was probably from this time that the Mononobe kinsman Sayabe-no-obito was recruited to manage the land to provide support for Yakahime. Both the Sayabe-no-obito and Saya-no-atai families were Mononobe kin, but those charged with administering the Sayabe estate recieved the title of *obito* while their kinsmen who served as provincial chieftains in Tōtōmi bore the title *atai*. Chronologically speaking, all this suggests that the Saya family's existence in Tōtōmi must have significantly predated 530.

Therefore, sometime before the early sixth century the Saya-no-atai family branched off from the Kudo-no-atai provincial chieftain lineage. Some of its members migrated to the Kinai to manage the royal estate, whence they received the new family title of Sayabe-no-obito. That is how a Mononobe family from distant Tōtōmi became active serving the Yamato court in the Kinai. The Mononobe must have sunk their roots deeply into the eastern seaboard during the fifth century.[60]

The genealogy of the Hijikata family helps to confirm a mid-fifth-century date for Mononobe activity in the Tōtōmi. The Hijikata base was south of the Ogasa Plain—the place-name still exists there. Their genealogy records that a Prince Tsuburako was a son of Great King Ōjin's Prince Ōyamamori.[61] Tsuburako's mother was Manurahime, a daughter of Tōtōmi's provincial chieftain from Hijikata. We already know that Tōtōmi's provincial chieftain was a Mononobe. Further down the genealogy we find Mane-no-kimi Shōninkan, district chieftain of Tōtōmi's Kikau District. He reportedly served at the court of Great King Kōgyoku (r. 642–645), during which time he received the Hijikata family name. In the mid-seventh century Mane-no-kimi represented the fifth generation of the Hijikata line. If we allow a generous thirty years per generation and figure back one-hundred-fifty years, that would date Prince Tsuburako to the late fifth or early sixth century and confirm a mid-fifth-century date for the Mononobe in Tōtōmi.

The chronology of tomb mounds in Tōtōmi offers further clues to Mononobe history in the province.[62] Hirata Ōtsuka has studied early middle-period *kofun* on the Kikugawa Plain of old Kikau District, and he estimates that some of the round keyholes there date from the early fifth century. Other tombs date from the mid-to-late fifth century. Furthermore, place-names, including those of townships named in the *Wamyōshō*, suggest that the Heki-no-kimi and Haihara-no-kimi kin expanded throughout what became Haihara and Kikau districts in eastern Tōtōmi.[63] Scholars are currently attempting to determine which family built which tombs, a problem that can only be solved by careful study of the various *kofun* and coordinated analysis of family traditions.[64]

The greatest density of Kofun-age tomb building in the Shizuoka region occurred in Tōtōmi east of the lower flows of the Tenryū River in present-day Iwata City. Among the tombs there, Iwata District's Chōshizuka Kofun is a fifth-century round keyhole in the Teradani group that can be associated with the Niu-no-atai family.[65] It is a round keyhole tomb 112 meters long that was found to contain a wealth of burial goods, including a beast and deity mirror and metal goods of copper and bronze. The ruler interred there would have dominated the Iwata plateau east of the Tenryū River. A member of the same Niu-no-atai family is actually mentioned in the eighth-century *Miraculous Stories from Japan* (*Nihon ryōiki*): they were patrons of Iwata Temple, at the suspected site of which eave-end tiles have recently been discovered. According to a tale in the late-Heian tale collection known as *Konjaku monogatarishū*, Iwatadera was built during the reign of Shōmu Tennō (724–749); but tiles from the late seventh and early eighth centuries that suggest earlier construction have been unearthed at the site. Also noteworthy is that there was a Niu Township in Iwata District—glossed as "Nifu" Township in two *Wamyōshō* texts.

Ōmibube Ō—Prince Ōmibube—was another historical personage in Kofun-age Suruga. He was reportedly a worshiper of snakes and a practitioner of Taoism in the Fuji River vicinity.[66] His kin, the Mibube, are known to have managed royal cultivator communities (*nashiro* and *koshiro*); and we know that such groups were widely distributed west of Lake Hamana, where the Miwa-no-atai resided and a number of place-names recall their settlements. As local magnates, the Mibube began to erect Buddhist pagodas in the early eighth century, and one such tower was in fact built at the base of Chōshizuka Kofun. Eave-end tiles uncovered there exhibit excellent workmanship, again raising the important question of whether its patrons were descendants of Yayoi-age chieftains from the area or settlers from outside. In my view Chōshizuka Kofun was certainly built by people sent to Tōtōmi to subdue and rule the area for Yamato Great Kings, including the Haihara-no-kimi, the Heki-no-kimi, the Niu-no-atai, and the Mibube.

Conclusion

In recent years it has been argued that autonomous regional polities developed in various locales and that a confederacy of such polities comprised Kofun-period Wa under Yamato kingship. I argue, however, that the unified state of the late seventh and eighth centuries—*ritsuryō* "Nihon"—was in fact the outcome of a process of conquest. Forces from the Kinai subdued "the four directions," whereupon ensued a period of "feudalism" (*hōken*) not unlike that of Chou China. Conquering generals were rewarded with domains which they opened to cultivation and ruled. It was from such a history that the later *tennō*-centered *ritsuryō* state with its province and district system emerged. I therefore doubt that the well-known Saitama-Inariyama Kofun in Musashi Province was erected by an indigenous chieftain. In my view the Takahashi, a collateral lineage of the Abe kin, went out to rule the area and built the Saitama-Inariyama round keyhole tomb.[67]

In my studies of Kofun-age Tōtōmi and Suruga I have concluded that the argument for construction of *kofun* by descendants of indigenous Yayoi rulers is unpersuasive. Our written sources—and indeed archaeological remains as well—suggest that invaders from the west conquered the land and settled there. Kofun-age culture in eastern Japan does not make sense without such a process. Whether this is true in western Japan I cannot say. There may be areas further east where indigenous rulers held sway—for example, in Suruga's Udo District where the Udo-no-kimi ruled.[68] But the historian should focus on outsiders like the Mononobe, who arrived as settlers from the west. Chronology is admittedly difficult to trace. The Mononobe may have arrived prior to the fifth century. But it is critical to recognize the process by which eastern Japan came to be ruled by the Yamato court through the conquest of "fifty-five countries of hairy men." Some indigenous groups may have developed on their own, but in most cases the leading families of the east were originally sent out from the Kinai as conquerors. In that role they appropriated land and people, settled down, and shaped Kofun-period culture in eastern Japan.

Early in this essay I drew attention to the homophonic *gun*—meaning a military band—and *gun*—meaning a unit of land to be ruled. We saw that the Chinese *Liu Sung History* recorded grants of titles to twenty-three generals in 451, which I interpret as meaning that twenty-three Wa generals received domains to be settled by their followers. That was the process of history in fifth-century eastern Honshū, and it was by such a process that the opening of the country progressed. Over time, descendants of these generals became fully localized and developed a degree of autonomous power. Still later, as the process of state formation quickened during the seventh century, some of their descendants moved back to the Kinai to serve the Yamato court as bureaucratized elites. Others remained at home, where they served as district chieftains or in other local posts. It was by such a historical process that the *tennō*-centered polity came into being: the old "feudal domains" were welded together in a forge of external threat occasioned by fear of invasion by T'ang and Silla forces after the 663 Wa-Paekche defeat at Paekchon Bay. At such a time of shared danger, regional autonomy could be successfully denied, and a state apparatus intended to provide centrally managed security was created.

Notes

1. Shizuoka Prefecture includes three old provinces: Tōtōmi, Suruga, and Izu.

2. Hara reminds us of Marc Bloch in some ways. Joseph Strayer, writing about Marc Bloch in his introduction to *The Historian's Craft*, says "Bloch, in what was probably his greatest book, *Les caractères originaux de l'histoire rurale française*, gave a perfect demonstration of how the job should be done. Old maps, place-names, ancient tools, aerial surveys, folklore—all contributed to his brilliant description of French society during the long centuries when agriculture was the predominant occupation." See Bloch 1953, 53.

3. For Hara's reading of Engels, see Hara Hidesaburō 1971. As seen in Tsude Hiroshi's essay in chapter 1 of this volume, scholars in Japan have begun to move away from this reliance on Marx and Engels.

4. For insights into this "regional polity (*chiiki kokka*) concept," see Kadowaki Teiji 2000.

5. When Hara wrote this paper in the 1980s, his thinking contradicted that of many researchers. But recent work is again favoring the role of conquest as the means by which Yamato influenced regional history. See for instance Kobayashi Shōji's research report on Yamato penetration into the Niigata region: Kobayashi Shōji 2001.

6. See Piggott 1997, 44.

7. See Shizuoka-ken hensan senmon iinkai 1994, esp. 576–648. Also useful are the classical sections in the general history (*tsūshi*) volumes of the histories of Shizuoka and Fukuroi cities: *Shizuoka-shi shi* and *Fukuroi-shi shi*.

8. Interpreter's note: The article translated here was originally published as Hara Hidesaburō 1986. I have worked closely with Professor Hara to adapt this piece, which was originally presented orally to a local audience in Shizuoka, for reading by non-specialists. Material has either been added to the text to facilitate reading, or it has been placed in the notes. Throughout the essay Hara refers the reader to other work he has published in the histories of Shizuoka and Fukuroi cities.

9. Interpreter's note: Here Hara refers to the evolutionary process defined by Henry Morgan and Frederick Engels. For details on Hara's views see Hara Hidesaburō 1984. For Tsude Hiroshi's critique of this use of models propounded by Morgan and Engels, see chapter 1 by Tsude in this volume.

10. Interpreter's note: This famous *Nanasayatachi*—the Seven-branched Sword—is one of the treasures of the Isonokami Shrine in Yamato. It was discovered in 1873 and was quickly associated with an entry in the *Nihongi* reporting that Kudara, a kingdom in southern Korea, presented such a sword to the Japanese monarch as tribute in 372. Inoue Mitsusada, whose interpretation of its inscription is widely accepted, argued that it was forged in 369, probably in Kudara. Thereafter, it was sent as a gift to the king of Wa. See Inoue Mitsusada et al. 1984, 282–83. There is a scholarly debate concerning whether the sword was cast in southern China or Korea. A particularly good discussion of the inscription, with photographs, can be found in Nara kokuritsu hakubutsukan 1989, 36–38. Suzuki Yasutami has reviewed the evidence and supports Inoue's conclusions. The sword demonstrates close connections between Wa (Japan) and Kudara, which were both tributaries of the Chinese Eastern Chin court at the time. As a subset of that relationship, Kudara and Wa were also allies. The sword also demonstrates the importance of the Mononobe clan and its shrine at Isonokami to the Yamato Great King and his polity at that time. See Suzuki Yasutami rev. ed. 1983.

11. Interpreter's note: The names of five "great kings of Wa" appear in Chinese sources. There are various theories as to which Yamato kings described in Japanese sources might correspond to these appellations. In Japanese see Inoue Mitsusada et al. 1984, 287–89. In English see Piggott 1997, chapter 2.

12. Interpreter's note: An English translation can be found in Goodrich 1951, 22–27.

13. Interpreter's note: For a translation of the entire text see Goodrich 1951, 22.

14. Interpreter's note: See Goodrich 1951, 22–23.

15. Interpreter's note: On key developments in the fifth century, see Kiley 1973. Kiley and Hara agree on many points.

16. Interpreter's note: The translation here is based on a reading of the inscription by Inaoka Kōji. He believes that the inscription was probably written by a Korean scribe. The sword was excavated from a relatively small round keyhole-shaped tomb in old Musashi Province. There is some scholarly debate as to the "Shingai" date on the sword, whether it represents 471 or 531. But most scholars now accept the 471 date. The King Wakatakeru named therein is thought to have been Yūryaku. For a discussion in English see Anazawa Wakou and Manome Jun'ichi 1986. Anazawa and Manome note that the sword was made of iron ore available only in South China, which was imported to Japan. They conclude, "The results suggest that Kofun Japan depended heavily on China for the high-quality iron that was so vital as a material for arms and armour."

17. Interpreter's note: The Eta-Funayama tomb, in Kyūshū's Kumamoto Prefecture, was excavated in 1873. A modest moated barrow some forty-seven meters long, it contained many rich gifts including a variety of objects imported from south China. The sword is now thought to have been made in the late fifth or early sixth century. See Anazawa Wakou and Manome Jun'ichi 1986, 390–93.

18. Interpreter's note: The *kimi* element in Ihohara's name is a noble title, or *kabane*, bestowed on the family by the Yamato ruler. It seems to have been widely conferred on local chieftains who claimed descent from a princely ancestor. The name Ihohara is currently pronounced "Iohara."

19. Interpreter's note: See Philippi 1968, 238–39.

20. Interpreter's note: However, according to the *Nihongi*, after he finished the conquest of Suruga Yamato Takeru proceeded to Sagami, beyond Tōtōmi and Suruga: "Next he marched on to Sagami, whence he wanted to proceed to Kadzusa." For an English translation see Aston 1972. For the story in the *Kojiki*, see Philippi 1968, 240. For a map of Yamato Takeru's exploits in eastern Japan from Ōmi to Mutsu, see Shizuoka-ken hensan senmon iinkai 1994, Tsūshihen vol. 1, 346.

21. Interpreter's note: Contemporary historians mostly agree that provincial chieftains were appointed by the Yamato court as regional officials in the sixth and seventh centuries. The largest of the *kofun* tombs in a given region are usually thought to be their tombs. The *Sendai kuji hongi* was compiled in the early Heian period. One section is entitled, "Kuni no miyatsuko no hongi" (Records of the Kuni no Miyatsuko), from which the quote here is taken.

22. Interpreter's note: See the monarch Keikō's fortieth year, seventh month in the *Nihongi*. In English, see Aston 1972, vol. 1, 202–203.

23. Interpreter's note: See the discussion in Hara's essay in *Shizuoka-shi shi* (Kodai-chūsei hen), 594.

24. Interpreter's note: See the reference in Hall 1966, 24–25.

25. Interpreter's note: See Aston 1972, Book 2, 279.

26. Interpreter's note: Miikedaira Kofun is a round keyhole measuring 70 meters in length and located in the environs of present-day Shimizu City. It is thought to date from the fifth century. See Heibonsha chihō shiryō senta- 2000, 522.

27. Interpreter's note: Yatsuyama is a round keyhole tomb measuring 110 meters in length. It is the largest of the early tombs in what became Suruga Province and it is located in the environs of what is now Shizuoka City. See Heibonsha chihō shiryō senta- 2000, 629. A useful list of *kofun* in Shizuoka can be found in Shizuoka-ken hensan senmon iinkai 1994, Shiryōhen 2 Kōkogaku 2, 710–32.

28. Interpreter's note: Concerning square keyhole tombs see Piggott 1989. Square keyholes have often been associated with Kibi, where square tomb mounds were common in the fourth century. When a reception area was added, a square keyhole resulted, just as adding an elongated reception zone to round tombs may have resulted in round keyholes.

29. On the significance of such mirrors, see chapter 2 by Kobayashi Yukio in this volume.

30. Interpreter's note: Toro is an important Yayoi site where traces of wet-rice agriculture and residences were excavated. In English, see Barnes 1982 and Edwards 1991. For the bibliography of Yayoi in general see Barnes 1990.

31. Interpreter's note: *Nashiro* and *koshiro* were specialized worker groups serving the royal family. *Koshiro* have been linked to cultivation of royal estates and they were supervised by court-appointed officials. See Seki Akira 1989, 699–700. The Kusakabe (alt. Kasugabe) were a *nashiro* group widely distributed throughout the Kinai and east Japan

according to Inoue Tatsuo 1989. He thinks the Kusakabe were constituted in Great King Wakatake's era and "sent to cultivate the lands donated to the royal house by regional elites, under the charge of Mononobe and Abe clans." See also Ueda Masaaki 1964. Ueda discusses the emergence of the Nakatomi as court ritualists in the sixth century. Under them served the Heki. Ueda thinks the Heki were particularly charged with worship of the sun. Inoue Tatsuo thinks the Heki were widely distributed throughout Japan from Yūryaku's era onward and he suggests a link between the Heki and the Katsuragi family. See Ueda's discussion in Inoue Tatsuo 1978.

32. Interpreter's note: Miwa Shrine is an important shrine on Mount Miwa in Yamato, near which early tomb builders constructed *kofun*, including the later third-century Hashihaka Kofun. In English, on Miwa Shrine and its connection with Ise Shrine see Wada Atsumu 1995.

33. Interpreter's note: Great King Tenji opened a new capital in Ōmi at Ōtsu in the 660s, after the defeat of the Yamato fleet by Chinese and Sillan forces at Hakusuki'e on the Korean peninsula, and amid concern that the T'ang fleet might soon invade Japan. See Piggott 1997, 117–23.

34. The Wani were an important family in Yamato and they are thought to have originated in the vicinity of present-day Tenri City. Later the Wani took the name Kasuga, but there were other important branches of the family including the Kurita, Kakimoto, Yamanoue, Ono, and Oyaku. The Nara Saki tomb cluster is thought to be their tombs. From the late fifth century on, women from the Wani occasionally served as royal consorts. Interpreter's note: See Koshō's chapter in Aston 1972, 144–45.

35. Interpreter's note: See Aston 1972, 38–41; and Philippi 1968, 388. Great King Kimmei's traditional reign dates are 539–571 C.E. An overview of the Kimmei chapter in both of the eighth-century chronicles (*Kojiki, Nihongi*) indicates overwhelming concern with peninsular affairs—there was ongoing warfare between Paekche and Silla at this time. And according to the *Nihongi*, it was also during Kimmei's reign that the King of Paekche sent many Buddhist images and sutras to the Yamato ruler. Buddhism was supposedly adopted by the Yamato court in 552 C.E. For details see Piggott 1997, 66–79.

36. If one proceeds due north from Numazu City to the eastern foot of Mount Fuji, one is crossing old Suruga District. As the site of Fuji Shrine and Fuji Asama Shrine, this area could also be called Fuji District. Interpreter's note: *Toneri* denotes a court retainer or attendant. Jean and Robert Reischauer's glossary lists four types: those who served the throne; those who served royal princes; those who served high-ranking nobles; and those who served in the provinces. Reischauer and Reischauer 1967. Hara notes that this Kanezashi-toneri family also appears in records from Suruga's Shida District, bordering Tōtōmi Province. But the roots of the family are in Suruga District in east Suruga Province.

37. Interpreter's note: The early tenth-century *Engi shiki* (*Protocols of the Engi Era*) provides a schedule of the number of days required to move between the provincial headquarters in a given province and the Kyoto capital during early Heian times. To reach Tōtōmi from Heiankyō (today's Kyoto) required eight days, and to reach Suruga required nine days. Ōmi, quite close to Heiankyō, required half a day's travel. Before the establishment of the Eastern Sea Route (Tōkaidō) in the late seventh century, the required time would have been longer.

38. Interpreter's note: Hara calls attention to the concept of a heroic era (*eiyū jidai ron*)—he notes that after the death of Ishimoda Shō, who propounded the idea of an heroic age, debate concerning the issue lapsed. He urges study of the *Kumeuta* from that standpoint. *Kumeuta* are folksongs recorded in the *Nihongi* and *Kojiki*. Philippi describes

them as "songs handed down by the Kume clan, perhaps related to the Kumaso of Kyūshū." Jun'ichi Konishi provides an alternative translation for this song as well as translations for others in Konishi Jin'ichi 1984, 46, 113–116, and 133–34. He thinks the Kume may have been natives of Yamato's Uda District. *Kumeuta* were passed down within the court's Bureau of Music (Gagakuryō). On the idea of a heroic age and heroic literature for Japan, see Konishi, 194–200. Nonetheless Konishi rejects the idea of heroic literature in early Japan.

39. Interpreter's note: See Philippi 1968, 176–77.

40. Interpreter's note: See Aston 1972, Book 1, 126.

41. Interpreter's note: The source is Ise Shrine's *Kōtai jingū nenjūgyōji.*

42. Interpreter's note: The *kuni no miyatsuko,* provincial chieftain, was alternatively called *kokuzō.*

43. Interpreter's note: According to Ueda Masaaki, *agatanushi* were allies or subordinates of the Yamato court throughout Japan during the fourth and fifth centuries. The post appears mostly in western Japan; Tōtōmi is the point furthest east where such appointments were made. As areas allied themselves with Yamato, the court dubbed local chieftains *"agatanushi." Agatanushi* were later given the noble title of *inagi.* See Ueda Masaaki 1979. Jean and Robert Reischauer translate *agata* as district and *agatanushi* as district chieftain in their glossary (see Reischauer and Reischauer 1967, part B). However this fails to differentiate them from later district chieftains of *kōri* and *gun.* Up to the mid-seventh century the *agatanushi* is thought to have been the main ally of the Yamato court in a given local area.

44. Interpreter's note: The text, dated Tempyō 12 (740), can be found in Shizuoka-ken hensan senmon iinkai 1994, Shiryōhen 4, 109–20.

45. Interpreter's note: Here Hara refers specifically to Inoue Mitsusada.

46. Interpreter's note: See Aston 1972, vol. 2, 169.

47. Interpreter's note: See the English text in Aston 1972, vol. 2, 176.

48. Interpreter's note: The rites celebrating enthronment for Yamato monarchs were called Daijōe.

49. Interpreter's note: Hara cites Kitayama Shigeo as the source of this information.

50. *Sendai kuji hongi* (Kuni no miyatsuko hongi).

51. Interpreter's note: In English on Nigihayahi no Mikoto, see Aston 1972, vol. 1, 128.

52. This was proposed by Ōta Akira (1884–1956), a native of Osaka Prefecture and a graduate of the Jingū kōgakkan. He worked for the Ministry of Home Affairs (Naimushō) and later became a professor, first at Ritsumeikan University and later at Kinki University. His specialty was the early history of Japan, on which subject he wrote numerous volumes pertaining to the *uji* system, genealogical studies, and local history.

53. Interpreter's note: See *Shoku nihongi,* Yōrō 6 (722) 02/16.

54. Interpreter's note: See Kyōto daigaku bungakubu to kokugogaku gokugungaku kengyūkai 1968. For the names of districts, townships, and villages that appear in the encyclopedia see Ikebe Wataru 1981.

55. Other finds at Sakajiri, excavated in 1980, include remains of a Nara-period post station, and other facilities from the Nara and Heian periods including wells, a moat, Nara-age coins from the Wado era, inscribed pottery, and various ritual objects.

56. Yoshida Akira has researched this problem as well, and arrived at the same conclusion.

57. *Ōketsu* denotes a side-opening tomb mound, or *yokoana kofun.*

58. The gazeteer is *Nihon chiri shiryō* (*Documents of Japanese Geography*) by Muraoka Yoshisuke (1845–1917). Muraoka was a legal scholar and local historian who annotated the six official court annals (known as the "six histories," *rikkokushi*) from the Nara and Heian periods.

59. The Koshiro property was alternatively referred to as Naniwa Miyake—the royal estate of Naniwa. Over time the place-name changed to Sayabe. Still later Sayabe village came to be known as Saya township in Nishinari District, Settsu Province, in present-day Takatsu of Osaka. Interpreter's note: See Aston 1972, Book 2, 209. On the Naniwa palace see Piggott 1997, 107.

60. Interpreter's note: Gina Barnes suggests that the homeplace of the Mononobe was in the vicinity of Furu in eastern Yamato, and she has tentatively dated their cooperation—as military specialists—with the expanding Yamato state from the second half of the fifth century. Thus her chronology and that proposed by Hara agree. She also presents an extremely cogent discussion of *be*, *uji* and *miyake*. See Barnes 1988, 267–77. Also of interest are Hirano Kunio 1983b; Hirano Kunio 1977; Hirano Kunio 1983a; and Vargo 1979, 10–15.

61. Interpreter's note: For Ōjin's offspring see Aston 1972, vol. 2, 255.

62. Interpreter's note: For a list of *kofun* groups in Tōtōmi by location see Shizuoka-ken hensan senmon iinkai 1994, Tsūshihen vol. 1, 244.

63. Interpreter's note: Regarding the Heki family's role as ritualists serving the Yamato Great Kings see note 31 above.

64. See Shizuoka-ken hensan senmon iinkai 1994, Tsūshihen vol. 1, 242–43.

65. For a good discussion see Shizuoka-ken hensan senmon iinkai 1994, Tsūshihen vol. 1, 212–13.

66. Interpreter's note: According to an entry dated 644 07/ in the *Nihongi*, Ōmibube Ō was preaching the new cult of the "God of the Everlasting World" in the Suruga area during the reign of Great King Kōgyoku. See Aston 1972, vol. 2, 188–89.

67. This tomb is famous for the inscribed sword found therein. It was discussed earlier in the essay.

68. Interpreter's note: The Udo-no-kimi family appears in eighth-century tax rolls from Suruga, and Udobe Ushimaro appears in the Nara-period poetry anthology, the *Man'yōshū*, as well. The Suruga provincial headquarters and provincial temple are thought to have been built within the Udo family holdings in the vicinity of Shimizu City to utilize the local authority and influence of the Udo family.

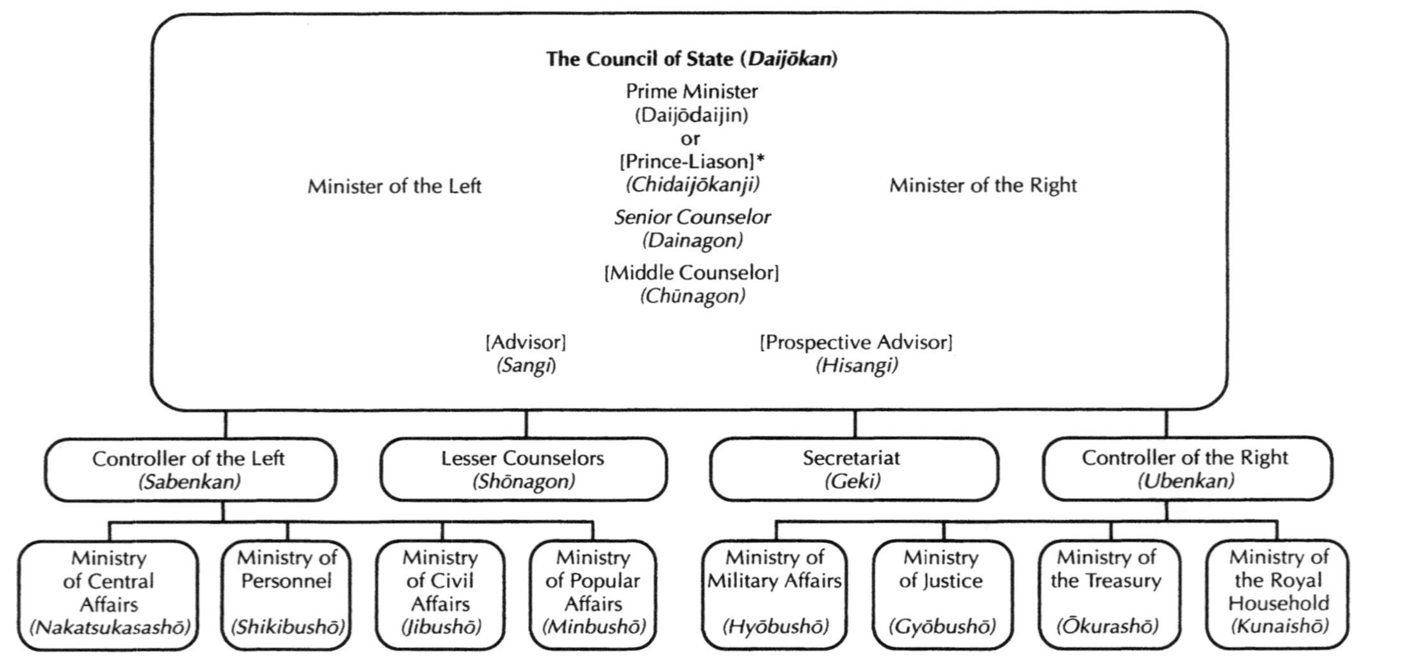

* Posts in brackets were not provided for in the Codes

Fig. 4.1. The Council of State and Its Subordinate Offices

4

The *Hitachi Fudoki* and the Fujiwara

INOUE TATSUO

Introduction by Michiko Aoki

INOUE TATSUO'S *The Classical Age Seen through the Hitachi Gazetteer* (*Hitachi fudoki ni miru kodai*) is a volume that was prepared and published for the general reader—ordinary citizens who have taken great interest in new discoveries concerning early history and archaeology in recent decades. It provides rich insights into how the old eighth-century local gazetteers (*fudoki*) in general and the *Hitachi fudoki* specifically contribute to our understanding of relations between center and periphery in early Japan. What follows is an interpretive abstract of Inoue Tatsuo's views on the compilation and objectives of the *Hitachi fudoki* as articulated in that volume.[1]

First, Inoue answers a key question, what are the *fudoki*? In a broad sense the term *fudoki* refers to any documents dealing with local matters—climate, specialty products, festivals, performing arts, and local traditions. The first two syllables of the word, *fudo*, literally mean "wind and earth," or in an extended sense, "climate."[2] The term does not necessarily refer to classical documents, since there are *fudoki* that were produced during the Tokugawa period, and there are even some modern *fudoki*. The word *fudoki* came into the Japanese vocabulary as a generic term that was sparsely used until the tenth century.[3] A record from 914 demonstrates our first extant use of it. In that year, a court scholar, Miyoshi Kiyoyuki (847–930), advised the reigning monarch Daigo Tennō (r. 897–930) in a written memorial that the government should gather old gazetteers from Bizen Province to utilize the information for improving central administration.[4] In that written recommendation, Miyoshi used the word *fudoki* to refer to those gazetteers.

Whether or not Daigo Tennō was influenced by Miyoshi's advice, the Council of State issued an order using the same term in 925. It mandated that all local officials should seek out and submit *fudoki* records to the court; and if such records could not be easily found, officials were to extend the search within their jurisdictions, asking elders for historical information so that new compilations could be submitted with dispatch.[5] From evidence of this kind, modern scholars such as Origuchi Shinobu have suggested that in 925 there were many provinces that produced the requested information for the first time. In any case, *fudoki* were thus long considered products of the Heian Period (794–1185). It took nearly eight centuries for the Japanese scholarly world to realize that the information in certain extant old reports in fact corresponded to information sought by the *tennō*'s court much earlier than the Heian Period. According to the official annals of the Nara-period (710-784) court, the *Shoku nihongi*, just one year after compilation of the *Record of Ancient Things* (*Kojiki*) in

713, the court ordered provincial governors to collect specific information concerning their provinces. A royal edict directed local officials to adopt auspicious Chinese graphs to designate places under their authority and to make reports about products, local geography, and unusual tales preserved by the elders. The resulting information was to be submitted to the center through reports (*ge*) from lower officials to higher ones. We do not know exactly how many provinces responded or when the information was submitted, but today there are only five such documents in existence—those from the provinces of Hitachi, Izumo, Harima, Bungo, and Hizen. They are known as *kofudoki*—old *fudoki*—because they date back to the eighth century. The old *fudoki* from Hitachi Province is therefore referred to as the *Hitachi no kuni fudoki*, or simply the *Hitachi fudoki*.[6]

Curiously, these eighth-century gazetteers escaped serious scholarly attention until the late twelfth and early thirteenth centuries. Compared with scholarship concerning the *Record of Ancient Things*, *Chronicles of Japan* (*Nihongi*), and *Anthology of Ten Thousand Leaves* (*Man'yōshū*), interest in the *fudoki* was minimal even then. Urabe Kanekata did refer in passing to the old *fudoki* documents when he wrote *Shaku nihongi*, his commentary on the *Nihongi*, in the Kamakura period; and Prince Sengaku mentioned them in his annotated *Man'yōshū* around that same time. Serious study of the *fudoki*, however, did not begin until the eighteenth century, when collecting scattered fragments and copying old *fudoki* became somewhat popular. But even then, research on the *fudoki* was limited to textual criticism, annotation, and study by those seeking geographical information.

Substantial studies of the *fudoki* began to appear only in the late nineteenth century. One such work was published in 1887 by Shikita Toshiharu under the title, *Hyōchū Harima fudoki*. In 1893 Suga Masatomo (1824–1897) wrote an article arguing that it was Fujiwara Umakai (694-737) who provided the finishing touches to the assembled materials that later came to be called the *Hitachi fudoki*.[7] Suga's argument triggered national interest, and the study of *fudoki* became increasingly popular. In 1898 fragments of the *fudoki* were assembled and published by Kurita Hiroshi (1835–1899), one of the editors of the *Dai nihonshi*. Kurita followed up by publishing *Hyōchū kofudoki* in 1903, thereby establishing the basis for further research on the old *fudoki*.

As *fudoki* study got under way, researchers found in them extensive details concerning practices and beliefs of *kami*-worship, or Shintō (literally, "way of the gods"). Such discoveries came contemporaneously with the advent of state sponsorship of major shrines. As the center stage of Japanese politics became an arena for jingoistic hyperbole, myths and old tales included in the *fudoki* were seen as reflections of historical fact. While such developments certainly had undesirable facets, there were positive results as well. For instance, study of the *Izumo fudoki* was firmly launched, an important development because the Izumo gazetteer contained myths contradicting accepted interpretations of early Japan's quasi-mythological era. At this time a Shintō scholar, Hiraizumi Kiyoshi (1895–1984), was appointed professor at Tokyo University; and with Professor Hiraizumi at the helm, an exhaustive study of the *Izumo fudoki* was conducted, culminating in the publication of the *Izumo no kuni fudoki no kenkyū* in 1953. This brought to light much factual information on early Japan and new theories concerning the historical development of the archipelago.

Compared to China, the history of which can be traced back to the second millenium B.C.E, Japan developed later. By the late second century C.E, when Marcus Aurelius was ruling his empire from Rome, Japanese chieftains formed a confederate polity under a sacerdotal paramount. By the third century C.E, warring chieftains came to terms with each other by accepting a theurgist as their leader. She reportedly secluded herself from all mundane affairs and concentrated on communicating with the *kami*.[8]

As the great dynasty of Han China declined and north China succumbed to nomad invaders in the third century, chieftains on the archipelago gained the opportunity to consolidate power. At the same time, a substantial number of refugees from troubled China and its periphery crossed the water, each group bringing new lifeways and notions of social organization. Marital relations between the native chiefly stratum and that of leaders of the newly arrived communities was common. Those who study the old *fudoki* think that legends preserved therein shed light on what actually was happening in Japanese prehistory at this time.

There is no doubt that in the eighth-century *Kojiki*, tales about the forebears of the powerful were skillfully woven into mythology. The *Kojiki* excludes mention of the forebears of less important families who surely must have clamored for recognition of their own ancestors' contributions to Yamato court history. That may be why the *Nihongi*, the official court annal finished about 720, includes information left out of the *Kojiki* and conflicting interpretations of some events.

Most historians agree that by the mid-fifth century the Yamato court had extended its authority into eastern Honshū and the region that came to be known in the eighth century as the province of Hitachi.[9] Evidence of this eastward expansion can be seen in the number of Japanese mounded tombs (*kofun*) that have recently been identified and excavated there. Not only the shapes of these tombs but also their funerary goods evidence links with the culture of the Yamato court based in mid-Honshū. Studies of those funerary items suggest that those buried in the tombs were chiefs whose sacerdotal efficacy was assumed by their followers.[10] Hitachi, part of what was then known as Michinoku (literally, "the end of the road"), was the easternmost base for campaigns to pacify the marches north of the Tone River Valley—during the fifth century, keyhole tombs spread into the vicinity of the present-day city of Sendai.[11] The Yamato court dubbed colonists of the area with such names as the Hekibe and the Himatsuribe—both were groups dedicated to the worship of sun and fire deities—and Urabe, who were diviners.[12] Their names indicate that leaders of these groups claimed priestly ability to communicate with supernatural beings and interpret oracles while their workers provided the Yamato court with various services and provisions, including specialty goods.[13]

But as the fertile valleys were put under rice cultivation and more settlers arrived, a power struggle ensued among groups. Inoue Tatsuo, whose research is introduced here, thinks Nakatomi forebears of eighth-century Fujiwara court leaders had vested interests in the Tone River Valley in what became the province of Hitachi. Inoue argues various connections between the text of the *Hitachi fudoki* and Nakatomi family history. According to Inoue it was the Nakatomi kin that finally managed to draw other local chieftains under their control by the sixth century. He also proposes that Fujiwara Kamatari was a native of Hitachi, which circumstance gave his grandson Umakai a special interest in compiling and presenting the *Hitachi fudoki* to the throne in the mid-720s.[14]

As is well known, early eighth-century chronicles compiled at court celebrate the Nakatomi, the family from which Fujiwara court leaders ultimately derived. In its tales of the mythological court of High Heaven, the *Kojiki* identifies the ancestral deity of the Nakatomi as a close adviser and diviner for the Yamato leader while confirming the priestly role of the Nakatomi at times of realm-wide crisis. For instance, we are told that when an eclipse of the sun plunged the earth into dark chaos, a Nakatomi ancestor (Ame no Koyane) provided the solution by divination, intercessory prayers, and offerings. Through his priestly performance he was able to restore the sunlight, and thereby, order.[15] And in legends of the Queen-consort Jingū (*kōgō*), when the island realm confronted overseas enemies from Silla, a Nakatomi reportedly worked as interpreter of the deities' oracle.[16]

While this episode is missing from the *Kojiki*, it is narrated at length in the *Nihongi*. And yet in the latter it is generally not the Nakatomi who dominate the Jingū legend. Rather it was Takeuchi no Sukune, a mythological forebear of the Soga family, who is said to have served at Jingū's side.[17] This suggests two possibilities to Inoue. First, by the time prototypes of the *Kojiki* tales were being assembled, the Nakatomi were positioning themselves to become exclusive diviners to the throne and priestly intermediaries between ruler and court. Second, it seems likely that ancestors of the Soga once played the role of royal ritualists and that memory of that fact was strong enough to force compilers of the *Nihongi* to honor it. Inoue cautions us not to forget that a Soga played a key role in the palace coup of 645. And after the coup, Soga Ishikawamaro served the new monarch as minister of the right (*udaijin*). So the Soga decline after 645 was not abrupt—it was gradual, and members of the family remained influential leaders through Tenji's era (r. 662-671), when they were prominent in the army supporting his chosen heir, Prince Ōtomo.[18]

Nevertheless, Inoue suggests that the Nakatomi established themselves as priests of the *kami* early on in the history of the Yamato court. He also thinks that, like the Katsuragi and Soga, Nakatomi ancestors may have emigrated from the continent, perhaps from the Korean Peninsula. Certainly, early generations of their kin were skilled in the arts of divination. Since it was customary for the Yamato court to appoint noble managers (*tomo no miyatsuko*) to oversee newly opened rice land, early generations of the Nakatomi probably had such experience. According to Inoue's thesis, the Nakatomi were active in the eastern marches of the Yamato monarch's realm by the late fifth century.

What were Yamato's objectives in the east? Evidence suggests that by the late fourth century Yamato was aware of the potentially fertile land in the lower Tone River Valley. The *Harima fudoki,* which contains numerous episodes relating to the monarch Ōjin—a legendary ruler associated with the early fourth century—speaks of a royal attendant named Manahiko from Upper Keno.[19] The *Hitachi fudoki* testifies to the fact that this Keno was the source of the Keno River, which is an old name for the present Kinu River, a major tributary of the Tone River.[20] Exactly when the Nakatomi established a base in the lower Tone Valley, or how they managed to recruit lesser chieftains into their following, is unclear. But one thing is certain: the Nakatomi used their position as high priests of sun worship to persuade potential followers of the benefits of relations with the Nakatomi rather than with the Soga.

Perhaps the Nakatomi began amassing power in the lower Tone Valley early in the sixth century, just when the Soga were aspiring to power as affines and ministers of Yamato's Great Kings.[21] At court the Nakatomi were lesser aristocrats holding the noble title *(kabane)* of *muraji.* Their offspring, even those sired by a reigning monarch, were not qualified candidates for the throne. But in the latter half of the sixth century, shifts in the political situation on the Korean Peninsula affected the court and its relations with chieftains across the archipelago. Before the sixth century there were only a few aristocratic lineages—the Katsuragi, Heguri, and Wani—qualified to produce royal consorts. In uxorilocal fashion, the locus of the throne seems to have shifted among them, and attendant power struggles often involved bloodshed.

Inoue and other scholars theorize that while such conflicts were taking place at court, deputies of Yamato royal authority in the countryside had ample opportunity to develop as local leaders. The Nakatomi of the lower Tone Valley were such local elites. In addition, they had kinsmen close to the seat of power at court.[22] As more settlers crossed the sea, the court itself underwent significant power struggles until, in the mid-sixth century, the Soga emerged as the leading authority. It was at this juncture that some Nakatomi succeeded in establishing themselves as chiefs of *kami* affairs at the Yamato court.

Things changed for the Nakatomi when in 562 troops of the rising Silla kingdom drove Wa forces from their tiny foothold at Mimana on the Korean Peninsula. A number of refugees followed the retreating troops to settle on the archipelago, and a tide of settlers in search of new land also entered simultaneously from coastal areas of China. The Yamato court, which until then had held only nominal control over the eastern provinces, took a fresh look at the fast-developing river valleys, especially that of the Tone River. According to Inoue, the needs of the court at the time were twofold. It sought to keep political preeminence over the entire realm while at the same time securing economic resources not only from its base of power in mid-Honshū but from outlying areas as well. As Kita Sadakichi (1871–1939) asserted, it is even possible that there was more than one court claiming paramountcy in the islands at the time.[23] The Nakatomi, therefore, who had been successful in organizing their rule over the lower Tone Valley, became increasingly prominent in Yamato politics because of both their sacerdotal role and their managerial skills in organizing local groups of workers serving them. So did the Nakatomi gain a significant edge in court politics and power.

Inoue places compilation of the *Hitachi fudoki* in a historical context whereby the Nakatomi and their descendants, the Fujiwara, wanted to enhance their position at the eighth-century court by commemorating their ancestors' unfailing loyalty and contributions to Yamato rulership. The *fudoki* served this purpose by emphasizing Nakatomi successes in developing the lower Tone delta. We see therein tales focusing on two quasi-mythological eras: that of the early monarch Sujin of Yamato, and that of Yamato Takeru.[24] The *Kojiki* tells us that Sujin—whose very name means "god-fearing"—dreaded the power of the ancestral deities so much that he removed their sanctuary from the palace precincts to set it up elsewhere.[25] Yamato Takeru, on the other hand, was the archetypal hero who devoted his life to his royal father's pacification campaign. In both legendary cycles, Nakatomi ancestors are numbered among the key mythological figures of the Yamato court, making it clear that the Nakatomi and Fujiwara had every right to their status and power at court.

For example, consider the *fudoki* tale relating how the Nakatomi took over priestly functions at the shrine of a local *kami* revered by seafarers. According to the *fudoki*, the event took place during Yamato Takeru's time; and it was a Nakatomi forebear, Ohosayama,[26] who received the sea god's request to dedicate a boat for the *kami*'s use. The story was clearly told by donors of the new Kashima Shrine, Kashima Jingū, whose priesthood was held by the Nakatomi after 645.[27] Indeed, the number of shrine households reportedly increased significantly during the monarch Kotoku's reign (r. 645–654), although work on the shrine itself was undertaken during Tenji's era.[28] Those behind such stories included two Nakatomi who petitioned the high-ranking courtier Takamuku, a royal emissary to the east, to create the new district of Kashima by appropriating land from the territories of two provincial chieftains (*kuni no miyatsuko*), those of Unakami and Naka. The newly created Kashima District was designated a "divine district" so that its produce could be dedicated to maintaining the Great Shrine of Kashima.[29] If indeed the 713 edict was issued with the forthcoming compilation of the *Nihongi* in mind, by describing their forebears as intimate confidants and ritualists of mythological Yamato monarchs, the Fujiwara used the *Hitachi fudoki* to highlight the legitimacy of their contemporary power at court.

INOUE TATSUO

The *Hitachi Fudoki* and the Fujiwara

Interpreted by Michiko Aoki

In all likelihood the *Hitachi fudoki* was assembled, edited, and polished by the staff at the Hitachi provincial headquarters (*kokufu*) between 715 and 723. Final touches to the manuscript were probably added by Takahashi Mushimaro, who worked closely with Umakai, third son of the then-powerful court minister, Fujiwara Fuhito (659–720). Indeed, initial drafting of the old *fudoki* was preceded by a series of aggressive policies instituted by the *tennō*'s court, and it was followed by intense efforts to improve the existence of the tax-paying population. At the center of such efforts was none other than Fujiwara Fuhito. These include the decision to construct a large-scale capital at Nara in 708; the dispatch of Fujiwara Fusasaki (681–737), another of Fujiwara Fuhito's sons, to the Tōkai and Tōsan circuits to oversee administration in 709 (see Map 0.1, Frontis.); construction of the new capital at Nara in 710; prohibition of princes and influential families from increasing their landholdings and interfering with the productivity of ordinary cultivators in 711; the creation of traveling investigators to increase adherence to the *ritsuryō* codes in 712; the promulgation of new standards of measurement, taxes in kind, and rules for government granaries in 713; injunctions to royal inspectors (*chōshūshi*) to prevent cultivators from abandoning their assigned fields and to practice benevolence in 715; presentation to the throne of the newly completed *Yōrō ritsuryō* code; commissioning of royal inspectors (*azechi*) in 719; and completion of the *Nihongi* in 720.

Who was this Fujiwara Fuhito? It is widely accepted that Fuhito was the son of Nakatomi Kamatari (614–669), who had received the new name Fujiwara late in his life after his significant service to the throne, which began with the assassination of the Soga chieftain in 645. But Kamatari died when Fuhito was only ten years old. The Jinshin War of 672 broke out when Fuhito was thirteen; and the aftermath of the war, by which Prince Ōama (later Great King Temmu, r. 673–686) wrested the throne from his nephew Prince Ōtomo, was unsettling for Nakatomi kinsmen. For one thing, the chieftain of the Nakatomi clan, Kane, was executed for supporting Prince Ōtomo. While the young Fuhito escaped prosecution, his future was far from promising. As a Nakatomi, Fuhito needed to hide from public attention. He took refuge in the household of Tanabe Osumi, a scribe (*fuhito*) in Yamashina. That is thought to have been the reason for his name, "Fuhito." Uncertain days ended in 689, however, when at the age of thirty he was appointed a judge (*kotowari no tsukasa*, or *hanji*).

As the context for Fuhito's promotion, the following factors worked in his favor. At the time, almost all high-ranking offices were occupied by men who, by their military contribution, had helped Great King Temmu gain the throne. They were excellent field officers and brave soldiers. But their talents were

TABLE 4.1. The *Ritsuryō* Post and Rank Systems

Post System	Rank System		
Council of State: Decision-making elites, appointed by royal decree from among eligible elites	First		Senior
			Junior
	Second		Senior
			Junior
	Third		Senior
			Junior
Middle Management: Top managers of most ministries and bureaus (Full-time officials)	Fourth	Senior	Upper
			Lower
		Junior	Upper
			Lower
Provincial Governors	Fifth	Senior	Upper
			Lower
		Junior	Upper
			Lower
Lower Bureaucrats: Staff of ministries, bureaus, provincial headquarters (Full-time officials)	Sixth	Senior	Upper
			Lower
		Junior	Upper
			Lower
	Seventh	Senior	Upper
			Lower
		Junior	Upper
			Lower
District Chieftains	Eighth	Senior	Upper
			Lower
		Junior	Upper
			Lower
Apprentice Bureaucrats: Clerks in ministries, bureaus, provincial headquarters (On-call officials)	Initiate	Senior	Upper
			Lower
		Junior	Upper
			Lower
	No Rank		

Ritsuryō *bureaucrat as sketched on a wooden tablet in Nara, circa 750* limited to matters of horseback strategy rather than administration of a complex government based on law. Temmu's court was thus in dire need of literate personnel. Fuhito, who had grown up in a scribe's household, came to the attention of the monarch Jitō (r. 690–697), Temmu's senior consort and successor. Fuhito was among the six men hand-picked to aid her when, after her husband's death, she became virtual ruler of the Yamato court.[30]

Fuhito was aided by a group of young and able literati who were equally anxious to establish the basic structures of institutionalized government. The far-sighted Jitō also chose Fuhito as guardian of her grandson and heir to the throne, whose posthumous reign name was Mommu Tennō (r. 697–707). It was her plan to secure Mommu's future, and that of his posterity, by devising several safeguards to ensure that real political power would remain intact in their hands. One such measure was to provide Mommu with the daughters of powerful men as consorts. In 698 Jitō selected three women for that purpose, one of whom was Fuhito's daughter, Miyako. The others were a daughter of Ki Kamado and a daughter of Soga-Ishikawa Tone. Among these new royal affines, Fujiwara Fuhito was the most prominent.

Having gained the status of royal in-law, Fuhito's influence at court increased. When Mommu Tennō died young in 707 and his mother took the throne as Gemmei Tennō (r. 707–715), Fuhito's role was further enhanced. In 708 he was named minister of the right (*udaijin*) (see Figure 4.1). In that office he stood at the pinnacle of *ritsuryō* administration, which gave Fuhito an ideal opportunity to enforce the *ritsuryō* code that he himself had helped write.[31] So between 708 and 720 a series of supplementary regulations (*kyaku*) and protocols (*shiki*) empowered enforcement of the Taihō Code and supervision of its new bureaucracy (see Figure 4.1 and Table 4.1).

Fuhito's further achievements can be seen in the court's successful efforts to secure information concerning the provinces that could then be utilized to bring the hinterland under firmer control. One tactic used was to create ever-smaller administrative units at the provincial (*kuni*) and district (*gun*) levels.[32] The objective was to divide existing jurisdictions into more manageable units. For example, in 708 the new district of Dewa was created in Echigo Province. Four years later this Dewa District was upgraded into the new Dewa Province. In 713 Tango Province was created from a section of Tamba Province; a new Mimasaka Province was made from part of Bizen Province; and Ōsumi Province was separated from Hyūga Province. In 716 approximately seventeen hundred Korean settlers from Suruga and six other provinces were relocated to Musashi, establishing the new Koma District.[33] By the time Fuhito died in 720 he had helped create six new provinces and fifteen new districts.

Lower levels of administration were also reorganized under Fuhito's leadership. Townships and household units were regrouped and renamed. For instance, a notice in the *Izumo fudoki* says that according to a regulation issued in 715, the graph denoting a township was changed from one that read *(ko)sato/ri* to one that read *(ko)sato/gō*.[34] According to the Taihō Code, fifty households constituted one administrative township, written with the *(ko)sato/ri* graph. Within each township there were to be three "subtownships" (*kosato*);

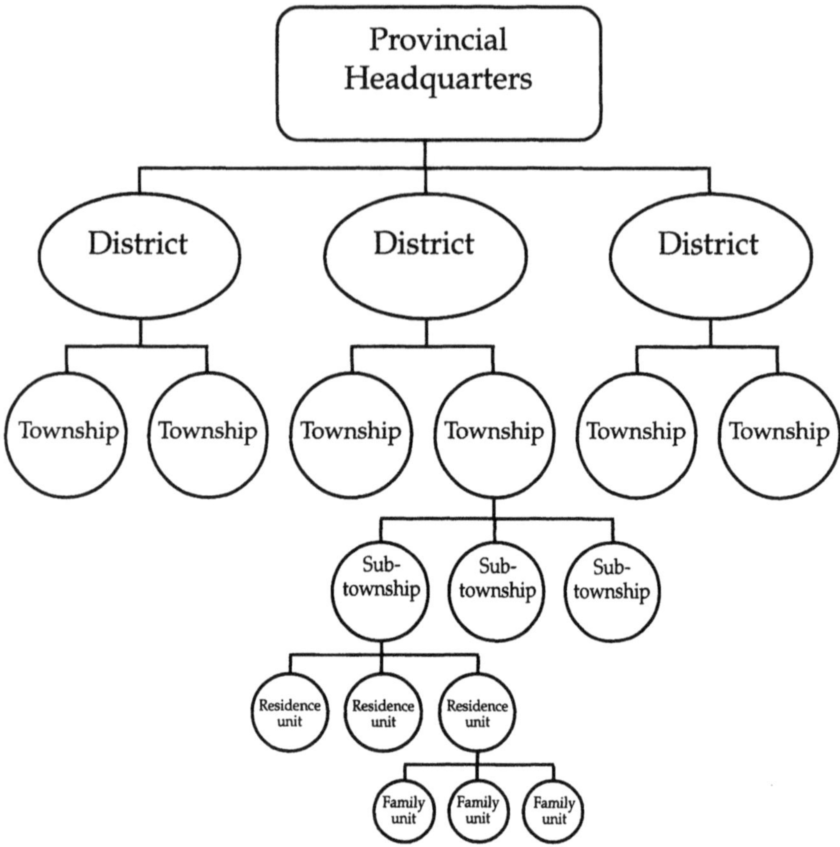

Fig. 4.2. Provincial Administration in the Eighth Century

and each residence unit (*ko*) was further subdivided into what are thought to have been residential family units (*bōko*), the smallest unit of taxation[35] (see Figure 4.2).

As the central government planned and implemented this infrastructure, information concerning local affairs such as history, geography, and production became vital. For this reason the edict of 713 ordered each provincial headquarters to compile and submit reports about its jurisdiction. With this administrative framework in place, the central government gained a better grasp of its tax-paying subjects.[36]

The primary impetus for increasing the number of official posts in provincial and local government came from the actual circumstances in the regions. More local magnates wanted to be recognized by the central government through official appointments than were actually needed; and since most positions in local government, especially the privilege of serving as district chieftain (*gunji*), were hereditary, the problem worsened over time. There were simply not enough positions available for all local chieftains, who, up until the mid-seventh century, had exercised their influence over people in their territories. As centering reforms were put in place across the realm, local leaders suffered a loss of prestige and contending local magnates vied for a limited number of offices at the expense of stability in outlying areas. Fujiwara Fuhito, with his outstanding political acumen, recognized the need to utilize the energy and ambition of local chieftains to the advantage of the central government. It was his astute observation of the local situation that prompted him to persuade all quarters at court to increase the number of administrative units.[37]

Compiling the *Hitachi fudoki*

The talented people staffing the Hitachi provincial headquarters who assembled and edited the *Hitachi fudoki* gave enthusiastic support to Fujiwara Fuhito in his efforts to enforce governmental policies aimed at institutionalizing *tennō*-centered government. Some worked in the Royal Inspector's (*azechi*) Office, an extracodal post created in 719. *Azechi* were temporary investigative officials whose responsibilities included evaluating local officials' treatment of commoners.[38] They were also charged with presenting evidence of acts worthy of praise or blame from throughout their jurisdiction. As noted earlier, in 719 Fujiwara Umakai, Fuhito's third son, was appointed *azechi* together with Tajihi no Mahito Agatamori. Umakai was also serving in Hitachi Province as governor during the years when the *Hitachi fudoki* was compiled.

Notably, it seems that no *fudoki* was completed immediately after the 713 edict. The extant *fudoki* texts cover the provinces of Hitachi, Harima, Izumo, Bungo, and Hizen. Of these, the oldest is thought to be the *Harima fudoki,* completed around 715. As for *fudoki* from Izumo, Bungo, and Hizen, their compilation took place in or around 733.[39] One issue, therefore, is whether the *Hitachi fudoki* was completed more or less contemporaneously with the *Harima fudoki,* or at a time closer to the compilation of the Izumo, Bungo, and Hizen gazetteers.

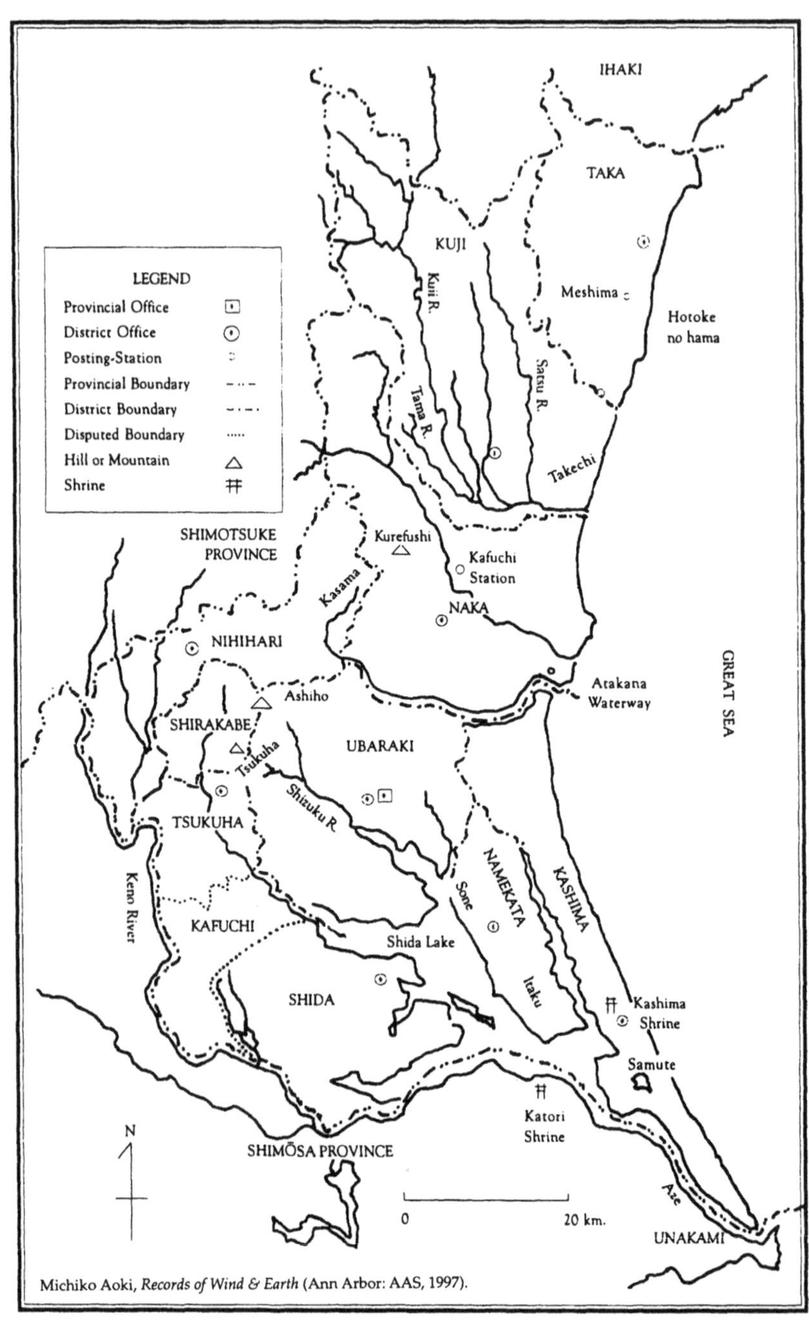

Map 4.1. Hitachi Province in the Eighth Century

My best guess is that the *Hitachi fudoki* was first assembled around 715, coeval with the *Harima fudoki*, but that it underwent several revisions before it took the form we have today. I propose the period between 715 and 723 as the final stage of revision. Let me explain how I arrived at this conclusion.

First, usage of various Chinese graphs to designate a township provides a clue. Some passages in the *Hitachi fudoki* employ the Chinese character read *sato/gō*, which was adopted after 715 to designate a township. For instance, in the section concerning the Namekata District the gazetteer states, "The township [using the *sato/gō* graph] of Tagima is northeast of the district office."[40] This same character is used for the township of Ohota in Kuji District.[41] Both passages were compiled, or at least edited, after the new character usage was mandated in 715.

The controversy over Ihaki (later pronounced "Iwaki") District provides another clue supporting compilation after 715. In the section devoted to Taka District the *fudoki* says, "[The petition was a request to] divide the territory [delineated by Take Misahi] into two separate jurisdictions, the districts of Taka and Ihaki" (see Map 4.1).[42] In small graphs we see, "The district of Ihaki is now within Michinoku [later pronounced "Mutsu"] Province."[43] According to the *Shoku nihongi*, Ihaki Province was created in 718 out of five districts from Michinoku Province.[44] So the above passage was written prior to 718. Around the year 721, however, Ihaki Province was reabsorbed into Michinoku Province. It seems likely that the note inscribed in small graphs was added later and that the *Hitachi fudoki* was therefore edited after 721.[45]

Finally, an entry in the *Shoku nihongi* records construction of ten post stations (*umaya*) in Ihaki Province during 719.[46] The *Hitachi fudoki* states that three stations were located north of the Hitachi provincial office in Ubaraki District, at Kafuchi, Sukegawa, and Meshima. Needless to say, the new stations in Ihaki and those in Hitachi were integral components in the same highway system. Researchers thus assume that stations in Hitachi were refurbished when new ones were built in Ihaki, because the highway connecting Hitachi and Michinoku was vital for sending needed supplies east.[47]

Given this admittedly circumstantial evidence, I think it reasonable to date the compilation of the *Hitachi fudoki* between 715 and 723. We can therefore assume that at least one of Fujiwara Umakai's two predecessors—Ishikawa Naniwamaro or Abe Koma Akimaro—was the principal assembler of the information in the *Hitachi fudoki*.[48] Of the two, Ishikawa Naniwamaro is known to have been an extremely able provincial governor.[49] He was a talented literatus of the time, and one of his kinsmen was known as an "elegant courtier" (*furyū jijū*) during the Jingi era (724–728). While Fujiwara Umakai likely added refinement to the assembled contents of the Hitachi gazetteer, we cannot easily ignore Ishikawa's potential contribution.[50]

Another question concerns the connection between the Fujiwara family and Hitachi Province. Ancestors of the Fujiwara seem to have had close connections with Hitachi before the mid-seventh century. For instance, a tutelary deity of the Fujiwara is thought to have originated in Hitachi. Of four deities enshrined at the Great Shrine of Kasuga, Takemikazuchi seems to have derived from Hitachi.

The Takemikazuchi *kami* is still revered as the presiding deity of the Kashima Shrine (see Map 4.1), making it likely that Kashima District in Hitachi Province played an important role in the Fujiwara family's rise to power.

According to the *Hitachi fudoki*, Kashima District was established along the Hitachi coastline in 649 in response to a petition submitted to Councillor Takamuku, a royal commissioner. The petition was submitted by two men, one named Nakatomi (given name unknown) and another named Nakatomibe Unoko.[51] Since the Nakatomi were a priestly kin group that had originated within the Urabe family, the three families—Fujiwara, Nakatomi, and Urabe—were all related. Nakatomibe kin, like the Nakatomi, attended to ritual and religious matters at Kashima. Given this, Kashima District was considered divine. A later historical compilation, the mid-Heian-period *Great Mirror* (*Ōkagami*), in fact insists that Nakatomi Kamatari, founder of the Fujiwara family, was born in Hitachi, even though traditional scholarship maintains that Kamatari was born at Fujiwara in the district of Takechi in Yamato. What seems most likely is that Kamatari's forebears came from Hitachi.

In earlier times we know that the Nakatomi served as noble managers and handled religious affairs for Yamato kings. According to the *Nihongi*, when Buddhism was introduced, they joined the Mononobe in staging a fierce fight to stop the encroachment of foreign beliefs. But this alliance lost the struggle, and those in the Nakatomi family who had joined it disappeared from center stage of Yamato politics. In their place another branch of the Nakatomi, those who were serving as noble managers of Kashima Shrine in Kashima District of Hitachi, came to the Yamato court to assume posts left vacant by their disgraced kin. From this branch came the famed Kamatari, the man who planned and participated in the coup of 645.[52] All this explains why the section devoted to Kashima District is filled with descriptions attesting to Nakatomi glory in superlatively refined language.

In compiling the *Hitachi fudoki*, Umakai was aided by a subordinate, Takahashi Mushimaro. Supporting documents testify that the relationship between Umakai and Mushimaro was close—they were not only senior official and subordinate, they were also fellow literati. Takahashi is known as a major contributor to the *Man'yōshū* and there is a strong affinity in flavor, setting, and nature between the tales and verses of the *Hitachi fudoki* and pieces bearing Takahashi's name in the *Man'yōshū*. Such topics as Mount Tsukuha and songfests appear in Takahashi's *Man'yōshū* poems, and the same items are discussed with a blend of enthusiasm and refinement in the *Hitachi fudoki*.[53] This is good evidence that Takahashi had significant influence over the ideas and actual writing of the *Hitachi fudoki*. Still, there is little doubt that Umakai supervised compilation of the *Hitachi fudoki*. The gazetteer represented the culmination of Umakai's efforts as provincial governor, in compliance with his father's orders. Like his father, Fujiwara Fuhito, Umakai was a man devoted to bringing about the success of the *ritsuryō* government conceived by his forebears.[54]

The Nakatomi and the Himatsuribe

As we have seen, a new district was created in 649 by severing portions of the territories of two provincial chieftains, and it was then dedicated to the Great God of Kashima. In this reallocation of territory, the chieftain of Naka lost five times as much land as did the chieftain of Unakami. Most important, though, it appears that the Himatsuribe, a group under the tutelage of the Nakatomi, played a crucial role in this maneuver.

Another divine district, that of Ise, was also established during the reign of Great King Kōtoku (r. 645–654). It was administered by a family known as the Nakatomi Kasumi-no-muraji. There, ten townships corporately dubbed *miyake* —"royal granary lands"—were allocated as a "divine district" to serve the needs of the Ise deity. Similar arrangements were made to create two other "granary lands" for the same deity.[55] It is safe to say that it was after the 645 assassination of the Soga chieftain, during the so-called Great Reform (Taika) era, when such divine districts were set up. Notably, in the cases of both Ise and Kashima, members of the Nakatomi were assigned to oversee these divine districts. My view is that it was the Nakatomi themselves who were instrumental in creating such districts.

How did the Nakatomi become so influential that they could alter the territories of local chieftains? Kamatari was certainly highly appreciated and rewarded as the successful planner and strategist of the 645 coup.[56] But this fact alone would not have justified his relatives' appointments as ritualists unless their hereditary status already qualified them for such posts. Clues to this status can be found by looking at a group under Nakatomi control, the previously mentioned Himatsuribe, whose name literally makes them "servants of sun worship."

According to a report presented to the court in 748, a family known as the Osada Himatsuribe-no-atahi held the hereditary privilege of serving in the district chieftain's office of Shimōsa Province's Unakami District.[57] A man named Shinobu, grandfather of Jingo, was granted court rank during the reign of Great King Kōtoku and served in Unakami District as a junior district official (*shōryō*). Then, during the tenure of Jingo's father, the family's post was elevated from junior district official to district official (*tairyō*) of Unakami. Jingo's elder brother, who was given the junior sixth rank, inherited his father's position and served as senior district official. Jingo himself served as a court attendant (*toneri*) for more than three decades before he finally became the full-fledged senior district official of Unakami District.[58] (See Table 4.1 for an outline of the *ritsuryō* post and rank systems.)

The mandate of the Himatsuribe was to promote the authority of Yamato's rulers, who worshiped and used the mystical power of the sun to govern their subjects. During the pre-645 era, the Nakatomi brought the Himatsuribe under their sway and increased their power, since the Yamato royal line revered the Sun Goddess, Amaterasu, as their ancestral deity. Later, as the initial reforms of the post-645 period turned out well, it was time for the Nakatomi to increase their political and economic power in terms of fertile rice fields. Creation of the divine district of Kashima can be viewed as a brilliant strategy to achieve this goal, for income from the divine district was assigned to the Great Kami of Kashima, and the post of high-priest was held by the Nakatomi themselves. Meanwhile the district chieftain of Unakami, who was asked to dedicate one village to the sustenance of the Great Kami, was in turn rewarded with the prerogative of sending offspring to the Yamato court as attendants. In contrast, the former *kuni no miyatsuko* of Naka and his descendents, whose five townships were lost, saw their prerogatives diminish as the borders of old chieftains' territories shifted.

A tale in the *Hitachi fudoki* titled "Pine Grove of the Deity" echoes such political changes in mythical fashion. In this tale the union of the young man of the deity (*kami no wotoko*) and the young woman of the deity (*kami no wotome*) represents the union of the two different areas, Samuta of Naka District and Aze of Unakami District.

> Long ago lived a boy and a girl known to locals as the "Young Man of the Deity" [*kami no wotoko*] and the "Young Woman of the Deity" [*kami no wotome*]. The boy was Samuta no Iratsuko of Naka and the girl was Aze no Iratsume of Unakami. As they were both exceedingly handsome, all the villagers admired them. The boy and the girl themselves, however, knew about each other only through village rumors—they never had a chance to see one another. They had long yearned to meet, a wish that was finally fulfilled on the night of the songfest. And having finally met, the pair left the celebration hand-in-hand to find shelter under the pine trees, where they sat knee to knee, talking about love and oblivious to the passage of time. They were awakened only by the cockcrow at daybreak. Flustered by the thought of being seen together, the loving couple did not know what to do. They only wished to become pine trees on the spot. So were they transformed into a pair of pine trees.[59]

I think the tale constituted an element of the songfest repertory in Kashima District and would have been dramatized with accompanying choruses and dances to justify creation of the new divine district of Kashima.[60]

The *Hitachi fudoki* also includes two verses apparently taken from lyrics used in palace singing and dancing, called *kagura*, that celebrated the union of the two pine trees. One goes, "To the twigs of the little pine of Aze, having tied strips of paper mulberry . . ."[61] Charms made of strips of mulberry were used in propitiatory rituals, and so these two lines may well describe a wand used by a *kagura* performer. The pine branches represent a tall pine tree, to the top of which a god might descend.[62] A response says, "Though obscured I be, in the waves of the crowd at Yasoshima, you have spied me, have you not? Lo, how fast you run, in my direction!" The girl from Aze was among the throng at the songfest but her lover soon found her. A multitude of islands or sandbars (*yasoshima*) and undulating waves (*ushio*) comprise the seascape. Evergreens wave here and there atop the islands. Such an image may have provided the inspiration for the celebration of the Yasoshima Festival at court.[63] In any event, there is no doubt that the tale of the two lovers grew out of the political reality by which the new Kashima District was established in the name of the Great God of Kashima, and led to the establishment of the deity's great shrines.

How was the Kashima deity viewed in contemporary minds? As with deities from lands surrounding the Mediterranean Sea, the genealogies of Japanese deities are complex and reflect various political and historical circumstances.[64] The *Hitachi fudoki* does not specify what sort of deity the Kashima *kami* was. It simply says, "the god who descended from the plain of High Heaven, this is the Heavenly Great God of Kashima." But the *Kogo shūi* history of the Imube compiled in the early Heian period states, "Takemikazuchi, now the Kashima deity . . ." This Takemikazuchi was a thunder god, and since a thunder bolt can cause fire, a thunder deity was seen by the ancients as a violent fire god.[65] At the same time, however, a thunder god was a water deity, because thunder accompanies rainfall. This dual nature of the Kashima *kami* was convenient for myth-makers who could merge therein functions of preexisting shrines revered by locals before the mid-seventh century.[66]

In all likelihood the Nakatomi themselves orchestrated the request by the thunder deity Takemikazuchi to be installed as the guardian deity of the land of Kashima. Their motives are not difficult to understand. Rising to power after the 645 coup, the Nakatomi recognized the need to strengthen themselves as ritualists, not only for their own benefit but also for defense of the Yamato ruler. Customs of the time required that only kin groups so engaged for generations could serve the deities. If the Nakatomi wanted to play the role of ritual defenders of the royal house, they needed legitimate qualifications. Therefore the thunder god, a violent and brave *kami* who could kill humans by his bolts and, at the same time a benevolent deity who could bring rain to the rice paddies, thereby killing insects when the rice stalks were heavy with ears, was beckoned to the land of Hitachi. Installing such a god as tutelary deity of the land and serving as his priests strengthened the Nakatomi as ritual defenders of the heavenly court. In this way, mythmakers in Hitachi took great pains to make the Nakatomi acceptable as ritualists to all in the Great Eight Island Realm.[67]

The *Hitachi fudoki* also takes pains to recount Nakatomi relations with an ancestor of the Yamato monarchs, Prince Mimaki, also known as Sujin. There is, for instance, a tale explaining the annual boat festival of the seventh month during which several boats were dedicated to the Kashima *kami*. The festival was celebrated at the harbor shrine, Tsunomiya, a branch shrine of the Kashima deity. Protagonists of the tale were the quasi-mythological Mimaki and Nakatomi Kikikatsu, whose name means "great listener of the Nakatomi." The following explanation appears in an editorial note entered in small graphs:

> According to local tradition, long ago the Great God of Kashima appeared to Prince Mimaki. While in Yamato Province Prince Mimaki saw a figure in white. . . . It said, "Worship me properly and I will stand by your side. I will have you rule over all the lands, large and small."[68]

Since offerings to the god consisted of arms—ten long swords, two halberds, a pair of metal bows, and two quivers full of arrows—as well as a horse, a set of saddlery equipment, two metal mirrors, and a banner of five-colored coarse silk cloth, we know that the Great God of Kashima was also a war god. In this regard the *Hitachi fudoki* explains that the donor who first proffered these offerings was Prince Mimaki, after receiving advice to do so from his confidant, Kikikatsu.[69] Moreover, in a discussion of the shrine's dedication ritual, it says,

> According to the elders the custom of dedicating boats started during the reign of Prince Yamato Takeru. One day the Heavenly Great God of Kashima said to Sayama of the Nakatomi-no-omi family, "You shall hereafter be charged with my divine boats."[70]

Mythmakers gave the impression that the Nakatomi had long been in the area serving the Kashima deity as ritualists.

Such were strategies by which the Nakatomi amassed influence as one of the foremost kin groups of the time, with significant potential for becoming virtual rulers of Japan within a few centuries. A question remains as to why they were so interested in amalgamating power in Hitachi, an area remote from the Yamato court. As I have argued, one reason is that their forebears were from that region, but this is only part of the answer.[71] My own view is that there were three reasons for the Nakatomi, as well as for the Yamato court, to establish themselves in Hitachi. The first was the fertile delta forming at the mouth of the lower Keno River (the present-day Tone River). Second was the Yamato court's desire to expand its influence in the east. And third, Hitachi was and remained a source of strong soldiers and good horses.[72]

Hitachi's Residents in the *Hitachi fudoki*

Under the system instituted by the post-645 reforms, a cultivator was assigned a portion of land to farm and ordered to pay taxes from the yield. Men were also expected to serve as conscript laborers when the government needed service.[73] The minimum age of a recipient of fields was six.[74] On average, a cultivator paid three percent of his yield as the tax on his fields. By itself this was not too exacting. But other taxes, in kind and corvée, were heavy burdens. For example, if a cultivator from Hitachi was assigned to transport tax goods such as silk cloth and salt to the capital, it took about a month to finish the job. These responsibilities were assigned to cultivators by township officials—each township was a tax-paying unit and cultivators took turns fulfilling this responsibility. Every year some of them traveled to the capital escorted by officials from the provincial headquarters.

If the ruler of any political entity wants to have subjects pay taxes without rancor, he needs devices to convince taxpayers to do so. Festivals were such a means in ancient Japan. As mentioned earlier, the boat festival was devised to justify the role of the Nakatomi as the priests of Kashima Shrine, to which other local shrines were annexed. At each shrine a festival was staged. Food and drink were sometimes provided by officials, but in many cases cultivators themselves brought provisions to enjoy. The *Hitachi fudoki* includes several descriptions of such festival sites and the reasons behind the festivities.

The *fudoki* also contains legends about two peaks, Mount Tsukuha and Mount Fuji, that dominate a vast alluvial plain. One says, "Mount Tsukuha stands only about 800 meters high. However, this mountain is easily distinguishable from others because of two distinct peaks, one male and one female." With its two peaks Mount Tsukuha in Tsukuha District was revered by people who lived nearby. In contrast, the *fudoki* includes a derogatory tale about snow-capped Mount Fuji to the west.

> In ancient times, a Japanese ancestral deity was touring about visiting his descendants. As he came around Mt. Fuji in Suruga region . . . the sun was setting. So the deity asked the goddess of Mt. Fuji for overnight shelter. . . . The goddess of Mt. Fuji, however, was reluctant to extend hospitality to the visiting deity. "We are now observing a period of abstinence for the new crops," she said. "During this time, custom forbids entertaining outsiders in our households. Please try to understand our religious practices." The ancestral deity resented this. Disappointed and angered, he denounced the goddess and all her household: "What do I hear? How could you not let me stay? I am your father. . . . May my curse fall upon you hereafter. May the snow fall and cover you always . . . may you suffer from bitterest cold . . . may no one ever climb to visit you. May no offerings be given to you, forever and ever." Having thus been turned away, the ancestral deity went to Mount Tsukuha and asked for overnight shelter. The goddess of Tsukuha was polite and cordial. She said, "Right now, we are observing a ritual period for the new crops. Nonetheless, we shall comply with your wish because you are our father." The goddess of Mount Tsukuha ordered the food to be served and respectfully attended the deity. The ancestral deity was pleased and sang: "How lovable is my descendant, how lofty stands her shrine! As heaven and earth prosper forever, and as sun and moon shine on forever, may her domain prosper, may her people gather together here, to celebrate good harvests every year."[75]

The *Hitachi fudoki* goes on to say that because of the ancestral god's curse, Mount Fuji has always been capped by snow and difficult to climb. In contrast, Mount Tsukuha has always been free of snow and approachable. People have continually gathered there to eat, drink, sing, and dance. Needless to say this particular tale can be considered a didactic one. It explains rewarding the good and punishing the wicked. Those who treat strangers with respect were to be rewarded while those who did not would suffer retaliation.[76]

There are also tales in the *Hitachi fudoki* articulating victors' boasts after subjugating the region. Consider a passage describing a military campaign staged by the quasi-mythological general Take Kashima (Brave Kashima) against hostile locals.[77]

> According to the elders, the prince [Mimaki/Sujin] who governed Ōyashima from Mizukaki Palace in Shiki, sent Take Kashima, a forebear of the provincial chieftain of Naka, to subjugate the recalcitrant Tsuchigumo on the eastern border. Take Kashima and his soldiers destroyed a large number of rebels and subsequently arrived at Aba no Shima [Aba Island], where they were to take overnight shelter. While making a security check from surrounding vistas, Take Kashima noticed smoke rising in the east. Suspecting that it might be an enemy, he looked up to the sky and prayed to the heavenly deities, "If the smoke be that of friends, may it drift toward us. If it be the smoke of enemies, may it disappear over the sea." The smoke floated toward the sea, revealing the presence of an enemy. In fact there were two Tsuchigumo chieftains in that area, Yasakashi and Yatsukushi. Their base was an underground bunker in which they remained secure. The next morning Take Kashima had his troops eat an early meal and then charge the bunker. The Tsuchigumo were very strong, again and again they came out to counterattack. Once when charged by Take Kashima's soldiers they fled back to their fortress, shut the gate, and resisted successfully for some time. Take Kashima then devised a scheme to destroy the Tsuchigumo. He selected the bravest from among his troops and had them lie in ambush at the foot of the hills. Weapons were lined up on the beach as if on exhibit. Boats were tied up side by side, and a makeshift stage was set up for dancing. Canopies overhung the stage like floating clouds, their colors waving with dazzling hue. The tunes of flutes and zithers harmonized with the sound of the waves, and soldiers danced the Kishima dance for seven days and nights.[78] Seeing such an unusual performance of music and dancing, all the Tsuchigumo came down to the shore. While the enemy was thus engaged by the merrymaking on the beach, Take Kashima had his men close the gates of the Tsuchigumo stronghold and then attacked from the rear. All the Tsuchigumo were taken prisoner and tortured to death. Some were burned to death and others were slain with swords.[79]

Not a trace of the relaxed atmosphere of a songfest exists in this passage. Rather, it relates how Yamato relentlessly imposed its authority over people in the fertile river valley between Mount Fuji and Mount Tsukuha. Indeed the entire corpus of the old *fudoki* contains numerous tales of subjugation, the protagonists of which can be identified as those identified in the early Heian-period *New Register of Aristocratic Kindreds* (*Shinsen shōji roku*) as descendants of deities who came down from the plain of High Heaven.[80] So compilation of the *Hitachi fudoki* was made possible by the efforts of Nakatomi kinsmen, especially Fujiwara Umakai, who was eager to glorify his family's achievements and transmit tales of his ancestors to later generations.

Notes

1. Inoue Tatsuo's monograph entitled *Hitachi fudoki ni miru kodai*, which is abstracted and discussed here, was published by Gakuseisha in 1989. The reader will note that in romanizing the old names found in the *Hitachi fudoki*, I have used the so-called historical *kana* orthography, or *rekishiteki kanazukai* because it retains sound values closer to those of eighth-century Japan. For example, the name of the famous mountain in the present Ibaraki prefecture, Tsukuba, is transcribed as Tsukuha.

2. The first use of the compound word, *feng-t'u* in Chinese (*fudo* in Japanese), appears in the "Kuoyu" chapter of the Chinese classic, *Spring and Autumn Annals* (*Ch'un ch'iu*). See Aoki 1971, 25, n. 5.

3. For that matter, the *Man'yōshū*, whose historicity was once taken for granted, is now the subject of controversy—for example, it was not called the *Man'yōshū* before the Heian period. See Origuchi Shinobu 1955, 184 (an essay that was originally published in 1932).

4. Miyoshi is known to have been a scholar who raised himself from rather humble origins to the status of advisor to the sovereign through the examination system instituted by the *ritsuryō* codes. He was the disciple of Sugawara Michizane (845–903), who tried to check Fujiwara power at court but was accused of malfeasance and exiled in 901.

5. Miyoshi's memorial is known historically as the "Iken fuji jūnikajō," literally, a sealed letter of opinion in twelve items. It was allegedly submitted directly to Daigo Tennō without being read first by officials, hence it was "sealed." The memorial was written in flowery classical Chinese, a model style for literati of that time. For the text see Tokyo daigaku shiryō hensanjo ed., *Dai nihon shiryō*, series l, vol. 5, 769.

6. During the Tokugawa Period it was Kurita Hiroshi, a member of the editorial board for the Mitō domain's *Dai nihonshi* compilation project who began using the term *kofudoki* to designate eighth-century local gazetteers.

7. Suga Masatomo 1907, 629–32.

8. For an assessment of Japanese scholarship on the subject, see Inoue Mitsusada 1965.

9. Kanaizuka Yoshikazu et al. 1982, 12–17, 23–24, 91–92, 106; Shida Jun'ichi 1974, 47–60.

10. Shida Jun'ichi 1974, 28–29.

11. Saitō Tadashi 1966, 140.

12. Inoue Mitsusada 1965, 42–45.

13. It is generally accepted that the Yamato court had a substantial amount of directly controlled rice land in the eastern provinces. See Inoue Mitsusada 1949; Tsuda Sōkichi 1930a; and Tsuda Sōkichi 1930b.

14. Inoue Mitsusada 1965, 40.

15. Kurano Kenji and Takeda Yukichi 1958, 79–81. For a more interpretive paraphrase, see Aoki 1991, 27–28.

16. See Aoki 1974, 6–7.

17. The *Kojiki* does not mention Takeuchi no Sukune in relation to Jingū's expeditionary campaign against Silla.

18. At the turn of the seventh century, many members of the royal family were closely related to the Soga, including the female ruler Suiko (r. 593–628) and her co-ruler, Prince Shōtoku.

19. Akimoto Kichirō 1958, 276–77. For English translations of the *fudoki* see Aoki 1997.

20. Akimoto Kichirō 1958, 36–37.

21. See Aoki 1974, 72.

22. Yamashina, part of present–day Kyoto, was one such power base for the Nakatomi.

23. Kita Sadakichi 1928, 30.

24. For an English translation of the *Hitachi fudoki,* see Aoki 1997. Another English translation can be found in Akashi Mariko 1976-1977.

25. Kurano Kenji and Takeda Yukichi 1958, 178–181.

26. Some commentators read the name as "Omi Sayama."

27. Inoue Tatsuo 1980a, 191–211.

28. Akimoto Kichirō 1958, 68–69.

29. Akimoto Kichirō 1958, 64–65. On shrine households (*kambe*), see Aoki 1971, 18.

30. Interpreter's note: Jitō did not officially take the throne until 690 but the real powers of government were firmly in her hands before that. For more detail see Aoki 1991 and Piggott 1999.

31. For more detail, see Ueda Masaaki 1967 and Takashima Masato 1997.

32. Earlier, the term used for a "district" was *kohori;* even later, when a different character usually pronounced *gun* came to be used, the original term, *kohori,* continued to be its reading. For example, even in the fourth decade of the eighth century, the term for district office was *kohori no ya.* See Katō Yoshinari 1987, 52.

33. For more detailed information on the creation of new administrative units, see Sakamoto Tarō 1960, 157–158.

34. Interpreter's note: *Kosato* is the Japanese pronunciation, and *ri* is the Chinese pronunciation of the graph. The change resulting from this ordinance has been known by Japanese scholars as *gōrisei,* the Sino-Japanese reading. Note that both graphs may be read as *sato* or alternatively *kosato.* As in the case of the change of the graphs to denote the word "district," the pronunciation of the newly adopted graph remained the same.

35. Interpreter's note: It is my assumption that this last unit was comparable to today's "nuclear family."

36. For more information, see Kishi Toshio 1966.

37. Interpreter's note: Another reason for the increase in administrative units was conflict between native local leaders and centrally appointed officials, some of whom were recruited from communities of continental immigrants. For example, the Commissioner of the Eastern Provinces appointed after 645 was known to be a Korean. See Aoki 1974, 96.

38. Local officials were expected to facilitate population increase in order to enhance tax revenues. Their mandate also included exhortation to hard work and increase in quality taxes in kind. For instance, see the rubric establishing the post in Yōrō 3 (719) 7th month, in the *Ruijū sandai kyaku,* an early tenth-century compendium of early Japanese post-*ritsuryō* code ad hoc legislation. See Shintei zōho kokushi taikei *Ruijū sandai kyaku,* vol. 1, 285–86.

39. For instance, the *Izumo fudoki* was completed in 733, while Tajihi Agatamori was regional commander (*setsudoshi*) of the San'in Circuit. See Murao Jirō 1953.

40. Akimoto Kichirō 1958, 65.

41. Akimoto Kichirō 1958, 85.

42. The first reads in full, "Take Misahi was appointed provincial chieftain of Taka. . . . He was . . . entrusted with the area covering the present Taka District and Ihaki District in Michinoku Province." The second quotation reads, "In the year of Mizunoto-ushi [653 C.E.], . . . the magistrate of this territory, together with his kinsman, petitioned

Councillor Takamuku, the royal agent (*subeosa, sōryō*) of Azuma. The petition was a request to divide the territory delineated by Take Misahi into separate jurisdictions, the districts of Taka and Ihaki. The reason was that the original territory was too large, making communication and administration difficult. Those presenting the petition were Miyabe of the Ihaki-no-atahi family and Shikoaka of the Miyatsukobe family." A third quotation is from a note inscribed in small graphs immediately after the above passage. It reads, "The district of Ihaki is now within the jurisdiction of Michinoku Province." See Akimoto Kichirō 1958, 88–89. The district of Taka was located on the eastern border of Hitachi.

43. This note, written in small graphs, must have been a later addition. The district of Ihaki was established in 718, but it was soon absorbed into Michinoku Province.

44. The districts of Michinoku comprising Ihaki were Ihaki, Shimeha, Namekata, Uda, and Watari, all of which were joined to the district of Kikuta from Hitachi Province. See Saeki Ariyoshi 1940, vol. 1, 135.

45. That is the approximate time when Ihaki Province was abolished and all its former territories were absorbed into Michinoku Province.

46. Saeki Ariyoshi 1940, vol. 1, 136.

47. Interpreter's note: The land of Ihaki occupied a strategic position in the development of the east. The *Hitachi fudoki* notes the wreckage of a ship believed to have been used during a campaign conducted during the reign of Tenji (r. 668–671): "The wreckage of a large boat is washed ashore on the beach east of the village of Karuno. The beach is on the Great Sea. The boat is about forty-seven yards long and thirty yards wide. It is decayed and buried in the sand. It is said to be the hulk of a ship built by the order of the ruler [Tenji] . . . he had the shipwrights at Ihaki of Michinoku build a large boat to be used for a survey of the frontier. . . . " See Akimoto Kichirō 1958, 72–73.

48. Nemoto Akira 1974, 22ff.

49. He devised a measure to ease the burden of Hitachi taxpayers. It was called *gun hatsu to* (*gunhatto*), which was a lending program (*suiko*). It should be noted here that under the code, the expense of transporting tax-goods to the capital was the responsiblity of the cultivators who were assigned to the task. Because Hitachi Province was located far away from the capital, the burden of fulfilling such a responsibility was enormous. Ishikawa Naniwamaro devised a method by which the district government set aside five hundred bundles of rice stalks for each cultivator assigned to the task. These were to be loaned at interest, with the interest used to defray the cost of transportation. The idea of loaning rice stalks for interest was not his invention, but to use the interest to aid the cost of tax transportation was new. On *suiko* see Tanami Hiroshi 1960 and Mizuno Ryūtarō 1964.

50. Interpreter's note: Inoue cites research by various scholars to support the argument that Fujiwara Umakai was deeply involved in compiling the *Hitachi fudoki*. His main sources are Suga Masatomo 1907, 63ff; Kojima Noriyuki 1962, 1314–17; and Akimoto Kichirō 1963, esp. 86–89, 94, 98–99, 112, and 115–18.

51. Interpreter's note: The first graph of the Nakatomi petitioner's name is missing. His court rank was equivalent to the junior 6th rank, lower grade. Nakatomibe Unoko's rank was equivalent to the senior 7th rank, upper grade.

52. Interpreter's note: To prove his point, that a branch of the Nakatomi family which produced the forebears of the Fujiwara family was established at the Yamato court by the sixth century, Inoue has undertaken exhaustive studies of extant documents. See Inoue Tatsuo 1980b.

53. Other topics shared by these works are the "Breaching Well" (Sarashiwi) in the township of Naka in Naka District; Tema Beach in Taga Township; Toba Inlet (Toba no Ye), and Karuno in the Kashima District. See Morimoto Jikichi 1942.

54. Interpreter's note: Although Inoue does not emphasize it, the compilation of the *Hitachi fudoki* was the culmination of joint efforts by many dedicated literati officials working under the provincial governor. One should remember that the basic mentality of the time emphasized conformity. As often as not, selecting topics for poetry or storytelling was not an individual's choice. Countless poems and stories were written on similar topics. Even though Takahashi Mushimaro's famous poem on the songfest of Mount Tsukuha is very close to that written in the *Hitachi fudoki,* this alone does not prove that Takahashi wrote the portion included in the *Hitachi fudoki.* By the same token, even if the date of the compilation of the *Hitachi fudoki* is established, and the date coincided with Fujiwara Umakai's stay in Hitachi Province, that fact alone cannot prove Umakai's authorship of the *Hitachi fudoki.*

55. See *Kōtai jingū gishikichō* in *Zoku gunsho ruijū,*.

56. Interpreter's note: See Piggott 1997, 102–17.

57. The source is *Osada no Himatsuribe Jingo ge* (A report from Jingo of the Himatsuribe clan of Osada). See Tōkyō daigaku shiryō hensanjo 1902, 150.

58. This man, Jingo, is known to have served as a servant (*shijin*) of Fujiwara Maro. Later, he was promoted to the position of court attendant at the palace of Queen-consort Kōmyō, Shōmu Tennō's senior consort. He remained in that post for thirty-one years. It is notable that both persons whom Jingo served as attendant were children of Fujiwara Fuhito.

59. Interpreter's note: See the *Hitachi fudoki* section on Kashima District. In English see Aoki 1997, 62–63.

60. Interpreter's note: This tale is included in the *fudoki* section on Kashima District. See Akimoto Kichirō 1958, 72–75. Given the existence of performing arts in ancient Japan, especially court performances of "divine song and dance" (*kagura*), this interpretation is a good one and Inoue is one of a few Japanese historians who interprets them this way.

61. Interpreter's note: An approximate translation of the entire verse reads: "Having tied charm strips of mulberry firm / to the twigs of lovely pines of Aze / You must be pining for me, / Lovely girl of Aze, / How I want to dance with you!" Many Japanese scholars regard this song, and the one after this, as prototypes of later *waka* verse. The original word for "the charm strips of mulberry" is *yufu* (*yū* in modern Japanese). The ancient Japanese used the strips of mulberry bark to hang on the tree branches for magical effects. This item later came to be called *nusa*. See Sansom 1931, 59.

62. Interpreter's note: Such a site was deemed a *yorishiro*: the ancient Japanese believed that something that stood tall had the ability to bring down a divine spirit from above (heaven). This is one of the reasons why the Japanese regard tall mountains as divine. In this connection, it is extremely important to note that a thunder god, Takemikazuchi, was believed to be one of the tutelary deities of the Fujiwara family, and thus a presiding deity of both Kashima Jingū and Kasuga Taisha. For more of Inoue's discussion, see Inoue Tatsuo 1989, 38 and 156–64.

63. Interpreter's note: Inoue reports that there is such a festival in existence in the district of Kashima.

64. Interpreter's note: One of the reliable sources concerning the location of Japanese deities is the *Shinmeichō* (alt. *Jinmyōchō*) in the *Engi shiki*. There is a partial English translation of the relevant section of the latter: Bock 1972, see esp. 9 and 58ff.

65. Hence the prefix *take* of Takemikazuchi, which means "violent, brave, valorous."

66. Interpreter's note: Shrines revered by earlier residents were those at Sakato and Numao. In honor of the seafaring lifestyles of these residents, sea gods were worshiped at both. See Aoki 1974, 140.

67. The "Great Eight Island Realm" is another name for the Japanese islands. The word *ya*, meaning "eight" or "many" is also used in *yasoshima* (many islands) and *yaoyorozu* (myriads), etc.

68. Akimoto Kichirō 1958, 67–68.

69. Akimoto Kichirō 1958, 66–67. Note that the relationship between Prince Mimaki (Sujin) and Kikikatsu in the excerpts closely resembles that between Prince Naka (Great King Tenji) and Nakatomi Kamatari, the principal planners and executors of the palace coup of 645. It is obvious that this tale was concocted in order to justify the Nakatomi position close to the throne.

70. Akimoto Kichirō 1958, 66–67.

71. Interpreter's note: Concerning Nakatomi (Fujiwara) Kamatari's contribution to the 645 coup, see references in the *Nihongi* (in English, see Aston 1972, vol. 2, 184–85 and 191–92); Aoki 1974, 143; and Piggott 1997, esp. 102–22.

72. Hitachi, especially Namekata District, was known to produce fine horses. See Akimoto Kichirō 1958, 56–59.

73. For more information, see Aoki 1971, 10–12.

74. Each female member of a household was also assigned land to cultivate. The amount of land a woman was allotted was two-thirds that allotted to a man. However, females were exempted from corvée labor and taxes in kind.

75. Akimoto Kichirō 1958, 38–40. Interpreter's note: For an alternative interpretation see Aoki 1974, 128–30. Also see Aoki 1997, 40–41.

76. One reading of the tale is that it reflects the struggle between various groups of settlers. Customs such as new crop-tasting rituals were elements of wet-rice culture.

77. According to the *Kojiki*, Take was descended from a son of the monarch Jimmu. Although the claim is mythological, what is important here is that a man who allegedly served as *kuni no miyatsuko* in the area called Naka was included in the Yamato royal genealogy as Jimmu's close kin. If Hitachi Province, especially the fertile land centered around the district of Kashima, was indeed the home of the Nakatomi (Fujiwara) family, the appearance of the name Brave Kashima as a meritorious military captain is not coincidental.

78. "Kishimaburi" is a native dance music known to have been preserved by Kyūshū residents. The fragmentary version of the *Hizen fudoki* records a site where local residents allegedly set a stage for the Kishima dance. See Akimoto Kichirō 1958, 515.

79. Akimoto Kichirō 1958, 58–61.

80. See Saeki Arikiyo 1962.

5

The Classical Polity and Its Frontier

TAKAHASHI TOMIO

Introduction by Karl Friday

AT THE CLOSE OF THE NINETEENTH CENTURY, Frederick Jackson Turner lamented the passing of the American frontier; for it was, as he saw it, the presence of untamed territory—the ever-continuing diffusion of pioneers into lands beyond the pale of both the government and conventional society—that had hitherto molded and shaped American civilization:

> The peculiarity of American institutions is, the fact that they have been compelled to adapt themselves to the changes of an expanding people. . . . This expansion westward with its new opportunities, its continuous touch with the simplicity of primitive society, furnished the forces dominating American character.[1]

Turner's enthusiasm for the role of the frontier as a determining force in American history may have been excessive, but it would be difficult to imagine an account of the development of this region that did not address the expansion of the societies and states created by European settlers at the expense of the continent's indigenous peoples.

Historians of Japan, by contrast, often seem to lose sight of the fact that the country ever had a frontier at all. We tend to focus on developments internal to the Japanese polity—the rise of the *ritsuryō* polity, the shifting locus of power within the court, and the growth of warrior power and warrior institutions—or on the interplay between Japan and states beyond the archipelago, such as China, Korea, and the Ryūkyū Islands. Many textbooks and survey histories have traditionally made little mention of Japanese peoples and cultures on the archipelago outside those of the Yamato polity. Those that do mention them only in passing.

And yet, although the frontier was a major factor in North American history for just over two centuries, the Yamato Japanese were occupied with the assimilation of the lands and peoples of Honshū, Shikoku, and Kyūshū for at least four hundred years (and Hokkaido remained frontier territory for another nine hundred years). The history of the fifth- to ninth-century Japanese is the story of the continuing expansion of the *ritsuryō* polity.

By the late fifth century, much of the Japanese archipelago, from central Honshū to northern Kyūshū, was organized into a loose confederation, presided over by a "royal" house based in Yamato, south of the present-day city of Nara. Over the course of the next two and a half centuries, Yamato kings and their supporters succeeded in reorganizing their polity bit by bit into a centralized regime. The most dramatic phase of this changeover began in the sixth month of 645, when a radical clique led by the future Great King Tenji seized power by hacking their chief political opponents to pieces with swords and spears during a court ceremony. In the wake of this spectacular coup d'etat, Tenji and his supporters introduced a series of Chinese-inspired centralizing measures collectively known as the "Taika Reforms," after the era name in which they were launched.[2] By the early 700s, the Yamato confederation was transformed into the *ritsuryō* state; the Yamato sovereign became the "Heavenly Sovereign" (*tennō*) of Japan, the transcendent repository of all political authority.

Throughout this period, at the same time as the Yamato sovereigns expanded their power over the other great houses of the confederation, they gradually extended their territorial control into the northeast and the southwest. Oddly, while the former process has been studied assiduously for some time by historians both in and outside Japan, the latter has received scant attention in the West.

Takahashi Tomio was one of the first scholars to take up the subject of Japan's early frontiers and their development. The article that follows is adapted from his landmark essay, "Kodai kokka to henkyō," published in 1962, and it introduces many of his most important ideas on the topic.[3]

In the essay, Takahashi describes the incorporation of the northeastern and southwestern frontier regions as a continuation of the process of the formation and unification of the Yamato state itself, arguing that the key issue was not simply the annexation of land but also the assimilation of the peoples that lived on it. In this respect, he observes, the process was similar in both the northeast and the southwest, although it occurred at different times in the two regions. The southwestern frontier and its inhabitants had virtually been absorbed by the Yamato state by the end of the seventh century. In the northeast, the frontier and its indigenous people, the Emishi, remained an important problem for the Japanese court well into the 800s.

Takahashi divides the assimilation of the southwest into an initial phase, during which independent tribes in the southwest clashed with the expanding Japanese state; a middle phase, during which tribes in this region remained formally outside the Yamato polity, but were subordinated to it; and a final phase, during which these hitherto foreign people and their homelands were integrated into the Yamato state. But he argues that the same process in the northeast went through five stages: a period of cultural imperialism; a period in which the territory was formally claimed and organized into provinces and territories; a period of armed colonization; a period of military subjugation; and a period of administration of the territory through indigenous tribal leaders. This model has since become the paradigm adopted by most of the subsequent scholarship on the topic.

Takahashi Tomio

The Classical Polity and Its Frontier

Interpreted by Karl Friday

As applied to early Japan, the term, "frontier" refers to the provinces of Mutsu and Dewa in the northeast and the islands of Kyūshū, Iki and Tsushima in the southwest. These regions were zones of contact between Japanese settlers and other peoples not yet integrated into the Yamato polity. In the initial stages of this contact, the Yamato settlers remained behind the walls of protective fortifications. The lands surrounding these outposts were viewed as something quite apart from the interior provinces of the polity. They were frontiers in the purest sense of the concept, buffer regions fortified against foreign peoples. Legal codes promulgated in the early eighth century refer to these frontier regions as being *kyōgai* ("outside the capital") or, more descriptively, as *kegai* ("outside the transformed"). *Kegai* is contrasted here with *kanai* ("within the transformed"); that is, the area brought within—transformed by—Yamato governance.[4] Thus the frontiers of ancient Japan represented a concept defined largely in the negative—those lands which were as yet outside Yamato control. It was this negative conceptualization of the frontier regions that determined the character of their historical development.

Japanese historical sources not only refer to the frontiers as lands "outside the transformed," they also describe the people living there as barbarians, comparing them to birds and wolves.[5] Modern archaeological studies indicate that such characterizations badly underestimate the level of civilization that existed in the northeast, but it is unlikely that the written sources erred out of ignorance of true conditions in the frontiers.[6] Descriptions like "uncivilized" and "savages" were never meant to be objective; they were recorded by men who viewed their subjects through candidly prejudiced and contemptuous eyes. This is significant, for it reveals an important truth about the relationship between the ancient Yamato court and the frontiers. To those who wrote the sources, the inhabitants of the lands "outside the transformed" formed a world entirely different from their own. It was a world outside the realm of the Yamato polity, but one that needed to be dissolved and absorbed by the Yamato polity.

What, exactly, did the frontiers mean to the ancient polity? What sorts of factors—and what sort of history—shaped the central government's handling of them? Early court chronicles discuss the quiddity of the frontier regions only in idealized, formulaic terms. If we are to understand what actually transpired, we must first disassemble and analyze our sources—reconstruct the raw materials from which the idealizations and formulas were concocted. Even then, we will not be able to view the frontiers from exactly the same perspective as did those in early Japan. That is because the Japanese of the time disesteemed the frontier regions and found them unworthy of study or comment because of their dissimilarity from the center. But we value and strive to understand them for precisely the same reason.

The *Nihongi* relates that during the reign of a monarch known as Keikō, an emissary named Takechi no Sukune reported back to the Yamato ruler that "in the eastern wilderness . . . the land is fertile and wide; we should attack [the inhabitants there] and take it."[7] This, and a number of similar passages in the chronicle, tempt us to conceptualize the subsequent administration of the frontier regions as the management of territories under colonization. But such a conceptualization founders when one considers the sheer size of these regions. In the northeast, the province of Mutsu alone eventually comprised thirty-five districts (*gun*), while Dewa included eleven, for a total of forty-six.[8] This is on the order of eight or more ordinary provinces. The annexation of so large a territory involved a more complex problem than simply filling the area with Japanese settlers. Colonization is really little more than a political form of land reclamation: in Japan, the polity established provinces and districts as it systematically transplanted villages and people to the new territories. However, of far more interest and importance to the course of history on the frontier was the manner in which Yamato absorbed the indigenous inhabitants of these lands and used them in its administration. Yamato's incorporation of the frontiers can, in fact, be better understood as a replay of an older problem: the formation and unification of the Yamato polity itself.

Hairy Men, Bear Killers, Quail Barbarians, and Falcon Men: Peoples of the Eastern and Western Frontiers

The non-Yamato inhabitants of the northeastern frontier are called Emishi in the historical records. This term was initially written with characters meaning "hairy men," but that orthography was later replaced with a new pair of characters pronounced the same but meaning "quail barbarians." In similar fashion the indigenous peoples of the west were known as Kumaso ("bear killers") in very early times and later as Hayato ("falcon men" or "swift ones") (see Map 5.1).[9] There were then corresponding changes in nomenclature applied to the inhabitants of northeastern and southwestern Japan. These changes can be correlated with two stages of development in the regions—that is, to prehistoric and historical times. By analyzing these changes, we can learn a great deal about the early history of the frontier regions.

The character compounds that translate as "hairy men" and "quail barbarians" are both read as "Emishi"—or, alternatively, "Ebisu" or "Ezō," and are synonymous. Chinese historical records originally used the "hairy men" orthography, which they derived from an old appellation for the "eastern barbarians" of their own legends. The "quail barbarians" orthography was created on the archipelago, becoming standard from about the time of the Taika coup d'etat of 645. This new usage was then carried to China by diplomatic and trade missions, probably sometime during the T'ang Dynasty (618–907).[10] Prior to the mid-seventh century, references to Emishi in Japanese sources tended to be vague and general, on the order of "malignant spirits" or "unsubmissive

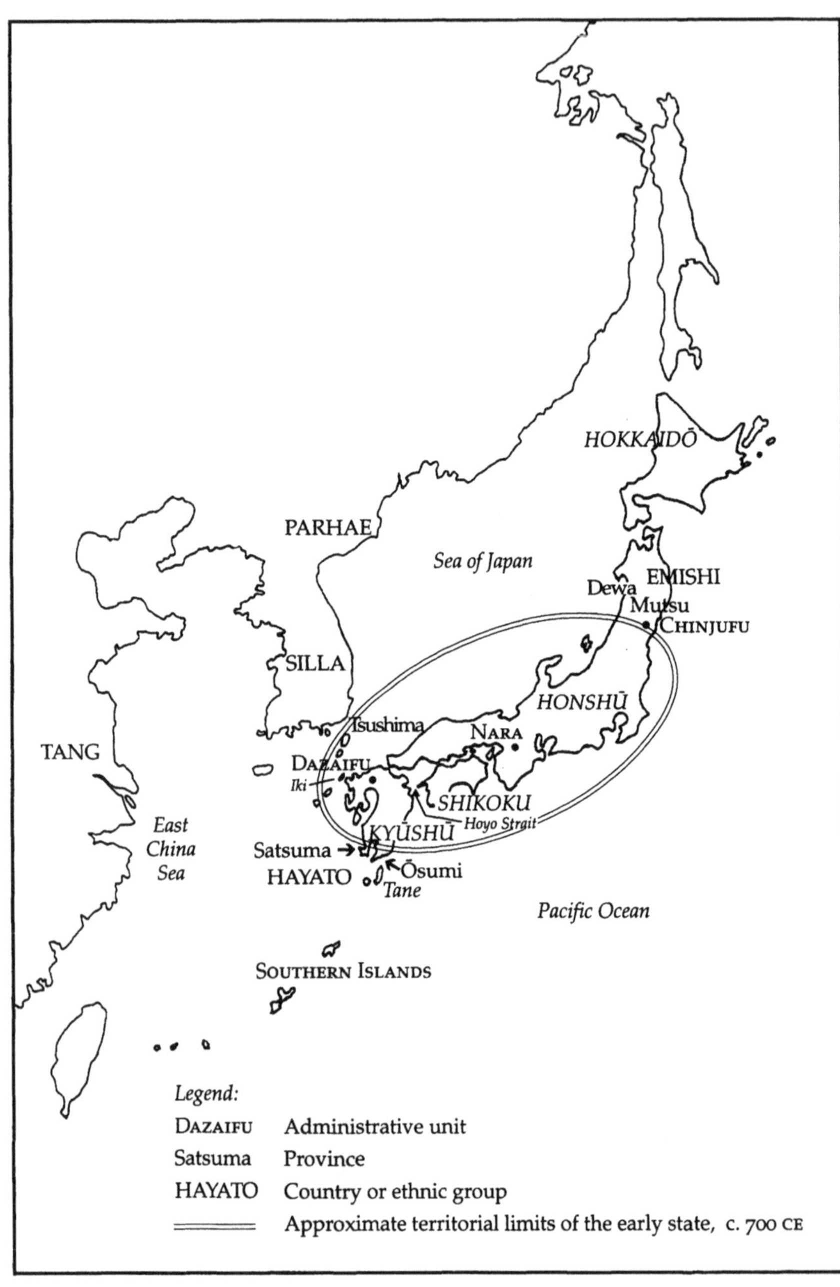

Map 5.1. Japanese Frontiers and Boundaries

peoples," while later passages seem to speak more clearly of a specific foreign people.[11] Thus the new orthography adopted in the mid-seventh century would appear to coincide with a new perspective on the northeastern frontier and the people living there.

A similar kind of relationship probably held between the terms "Kumaso" and "Hayato." Kita Sadakichi (1871-1939) believed that the Kumaso ought to be considered a people of legend, along with the Tsuchigumo, or "earth-spider people," who also appear in the *Chronicles of Japan* (*Nihongi*). The actual people of historical times, says Kita, were the Hayato, who emerged from among these earlier, legendary tribes. Tsuda Sōkichi has further developed Kita's thesis, arguing that the submission of the Kumaso to the Yamato polity seems to have taken place in the early 400s. It was from about this period that this people became confined to a small portion of the southwestern frontier region, and they came to be referred to as Hayato.[12] If this is correct, it suggests that the borderline between legendary prehistory and substantive history in the southwest can be drawn in the early fifth century.

Yamato's interest in incorporating its two ancient frontiers was marked by a change in nomenclature for the peoples living there. The symmetry of the subsequent histories of the two regions is striking. Although the process of incorporation in the northeast lagged as much as three centuries behind that in the southwest, the pattern of development in both areas was remarkably similar. Even legends, such as Prince Yamato Takeru's conquest and pacification of the Hayato, for example, are paralleled by stories of a similar campaign that he conducted against the Emishi a decade later.[13]

The most important differences in the histories of the two frontiers stemmed from the fact that the Hayato had been effectively absorbed into the Yamato polity by the early 700s, while this process was just beginning for the Emishi at that time. By the end of the seventh century, the Hayato homelands had lost most of their "uncivilized" character. When Yamato first laid claim to this area, they dubbed it "Hayato Country." However by 702 the name had been changed to Satsuma Province, completely erasing its nominal designation as barbarian territory. By contrast, the northeast never lost its association with lands beyond the pale of Yamato control, remaining "Michinoku"—often slurred to "Mutsu" Province, "the province at the end of the land"—until modern times.[14] In other words the southwest was a true frontier only in prehistoric times, while the northeast was a frontier during historical times.

Absorption into Yamato and Rule of the Hayato

Efforts to absorb the Hayato and their homelands into the Yamato polity can be divided into three or four stages. The first stage, when the independent Kumaso clashed with the expanding Yamato polity, is obscured by legend. In 478 the Yamato Great King Yūryaku sent an envoy to the Chinese court bearing a message, which read:

> From of old our forebears have clad themselves in armor and helmet and gone across the hills and waters, sparing no time for rest. In the east, they

> conquered fifty-five countries of hairy men; in the west, they brought to their knees sixty-six countries of various barbarians.[15]

The "sixty-six countries of various barbarians" in the west probably refers to the numerous tribes of Kumaso, although the number should not be taken literally.[16] The term "various barbarians," however, is puzzling, as it is even more vague than "hairy men." This suggests that the appellation "Kumaso" did not come into use until after Great King Yūryaku's time. If this is the case, it might have been created as a generalized term for the various unassimilated peoples from all over Kyūshū who, by the late fifth century, had been pushed to the southwest corner of the island.[17] As noted earlier, it was from about this time that these frontier peoples began to be known as Hayato. "Kumaso," in other words, was a manufactured anachronism—the Kumaso legends were formulated to account for the prehistory of the Hayato.

During the second stage, lasting from about the middle of the fifth century to the middle of the seventh, the Hayato remained a foreign people, outsiders to the Yamato polity. At the same time, Hayato rulers subordinated themselves to the authority of the Yamato monarch, and Hayato served the court as artisans, ceremonial singers and dancers, and military guards for the gates of the royal palace and members of the royal house.[18]

The mythical origins of the relationship between the Hayato and the Yamato Great King are given in a story recounted in the *Nihongi* in which the grandfather of the future monarch known as Jimmu (the founder of the royal house) forces his elder brother to agree to become his servant: "On this account the various Hayato descended from [the elder brother] to the present time do not leave the vicinity of the enclosure of the Imperial Palace, and they render service instead of barking dogs."[19] This last phrase, "instead of barking dogs," is curious, but probably reflects the roles of the Hayato at court as singers, dancers, and military guards. Another tale from the same text relates that, following the death of the Great King Yūryaku, a number of Hayato mourned and wailed at his tomb until they eventually starved to death and were buried near the departed monarch. The military function of the Hayato is hinted at more directly in a third story, which tells how the Great King Ritchū (traditional reign dates c. 400–405 C.E.) resolved a succession dispute with his younger brother by bribing a Hayato servant of the brother to murder him.[20]

In the second half of the seventh century, the Yamato polity entered a new phase of evolution, converting itself from a confederation of semiautonomous regional nobles gathered around the Yamato royal house to a more centralized, bureaucratic state modeled after T'ang China. These developments also marked the beginning of a third stage in the polity's relationship with the Hayato, during which this hitherto foreign people and their homelands were integrated into Yamato.

The *ritsuryō* legal codes, which provided the framework for the new political formation, defined an official post, the *Hayato no tsukasa*—chief of the Hayato—whose function it was to supervise Hayato in service to the court. He was "to maintain records, to instruct [them] in song and dance, and to [supervise their] making of bamboo umbrellas." Although the post carried no military responsibilities, it is listed in the *ritsuryō* codes between sections describing the Headquarters of the Royal Gate Guards (Emonfu) and the Headquarters of the Royal Palace Guards (Ejifu), suggesting that it was actually formulated before the *ritsuryō* era, during the second stage of Yamato-Hayato relations, when Hayato were used to guard the palace of the Yamato ruler and other royals. The new law codes transferred this military-protective function to the five royal guard units, but the order of the clauses echoes the earlier arrangement.[21]

The continued existence of the *Hayato no tsukasa* post indicates that a few of the artistic and ceremonial aspects of the service relationship between the Hayato and the court survived into the *ritsuryō* era. Nevertheless, under the new political organization, the Hayato were, for the most part, to be viewed as ordinary subjects, and they were treated in the same manner as the rest of the commoner population. This is made clear by a ninth-century commentary on the *ritsuryō* law codes, which states that Hayato not serving at court, "were assessed taxes and conscripted as soldiers, just like ordinary persons."[22] The advent of the new political formation radically revised the character of the Hayato, eliminating their foreign status. Henceforth they were pushed in the same fundamental direction as the Yamato commoner population, converted from subjects of semiautonomous local powers to tax-paying, direct subjects of the *tennō*.

This process entailed a conversion not only of the Hayato themselves, but also of their homelands. As in the rest of the country, the southwest frontier region was organized into districts (*gun*) and provinces (*kuni*) by central government emissaries called *kunimagi no tsukai*. It appears that initially the whole island of Kyūshū was designated as the single province of Tsukushi. By the 690s this had been divided into the seven provinces of Chikuzen, Chikugo, Buzen, Bungo, Hizen, Higo and Hyūga, the last of which included what had been Hayato territory. In 702 the southwest corner of Hyūga was broken off to form the province of Satsuma; and in 712 this process was repeated to form Ōsumi Province.[23]

Yamato's assimilation of Hayato homelands was not entirely accomplished by peaceful means. Scattered rebellions and resistance efforts necessitated large-scale military pacification campaigns on at least five occasions between 700 and 720.[24] This period of military pacification, then, could be viewed as a fourth—and final—stage in the court's relationship with the Hayato. But we must be careful not to mistake the significance of these military actions. They were conducted in territory already absorbed into the Yamato realm, against pockets of Hayato that had not yet been fully assimilated, or against malcontents that resented their new status. They were, in other words, exceptional incidents, not part of a general pattern of political activity in the southwest. By the early eighth century, when the incidents occurred, the majority of the Hayato needed no military suppression. For the most part they had already been converted into subjects of the *tennō* and their homelands had been reorganized into provinces and districts according to the *ritsuryō* administrative pattern.[25]

The Pacification of the Emishi

Yamato's expansion into the northeast began in the age of legends and continued through the Nara Period (710–784), culminating in a series of enormous pacification campaigns between 774 and 811. The center considered its task formally completed after 811, but efforts to assimilate the Emishi and to establish order in the northeast persisted until the late Heian Period, making the period of Emishi pacification concurrent with the entire premedieval epoch.

To correctly understand this long process, we need to divide it into several developmental stages. In so doing, we must consider the changes that took place in Yamato policies and activities; but we must also consider the changes that took place in the reactions and resistance of the Emishi, the objects of these policies. The manner in which Emishi society and political structure confronted subjugation by Yamato had a decisive effect on the nature of the pacification efforts.

Accordingly, annexation of the northeast and assimilation of the Emishi that occupied it can be broken into five stages: (1) a period of what might be termed "cultural imperialism"; (2) a period in which the territory was formally claimed and organized into provinces and districts; (3) a period of armed colonization; (4) a period of military subjugation; and (5) a period of administration of the territory through Emishi tribal leaders.

The first stage, the period of cultural imperialism, lasted until the mid-seventh century. We have only myths and legends concerning the Emishi of this period. Most of these do not differentiate between the Emishi and other peoples living in eastern Japan, indicating that this was not yet a matter of concern to the Yamato court. The story of Yamato Takeru's campaigns in the east, for example, speaks in only the most general terms about the unsubjugated peoples of the east, and it tells nothing about Emishi society or political organization. Great King Yūryaku's missive to the Chinese emperor telling of his conquest of "fifty-five countries of hairy men" is similarly vague. Some passages in the *Nihongi* do distinguish the Emishi from other inhabitants of the east, but most such entries are simply anachronistic applications of late seventh-century conceptualizations to earlier times.

During this period the Yamato polity existed side by side with the Emishi. But to the Yamato court, Emishi lands represented undifferentiated eastern frontier territory to be opened to cultivation. The Yamato presence in this region was established subtly, and without overt court intervention, as Yamato confederates resident in the east diffused their mode of living to the "barbarian" peoples around them. This sort of uncontrived assimilation of territory through the spread of the culture and lifestyles of the people at the center of the polity can be termed "cultural imperialism." Archaeological studies suggest that its beginnings go back a long way. Wet rice agriculture, which spread from west to east, had already reached the southern parts of the northeast during the Yayoi age (approx. 300 B.C.E. to 250 C.E.). In like manner, the cultural trappings of the

Japanese mounded tomb (*kofun*) culture had found their way into eastern Japan by the middle of that epoch, and from there they penetrated northeast within a century or two of their appearance in central Japan.[26]

Such diffusion of culture was accompanied, to one extent or another, by the spread of political influence. By the sixth century the Yamato court had begun to focus more directly on extending its political power to this region, marking the start of the era of Emishi pacification. Yamato political intrusion into the northeast initially took a loose hegemonic form that gave full rein to Emishi autonomy. It did not provoke violent confrontation and drew little comment in the written sources of the time.

However, after the coup of 645, court policy toward the northeastern frontier shifted in the direction of closer central government supervision of both the lands and people living there. The court's focus during this period was not on the conquest of new territory but on the institutional restructuring of territory already under Yamato authority. In the northeast, as in the rest of the realm, this institutional restructuring took the form of establishing provinces and districts. The second half of the seventh century saw the beginning of the second major stage in the state's assimilation of the Emishi—the organization of their homelands into provinces and districts.

The fact that provinces and districts were established in the northeast during the same period as in the rest of the country should not distract us from the essential point that this process exhibited a fundamentally different character on the frontier from what it was in the interior, since on the frontier it entailed the annexation of hitherto foreign territory. Even the name "Mutsu Province" is meaningful in this regard. As explained earlier, "Mutsu" is a contraction of "Michinoku," which is in turn a contraction of *michi no oku*, or "the end of the land/road," a term that signified the marches outside the pale of Yamato court authority (see Map 5.1). "Mutsu Province" thus literally meant "the province beyond the realm," a paradoxical concept at best, for no province could be established in lands that were truly "beyond the realm." The creation of Mutsu Province, then, amounted to nothing less than a declaration of sovereignty over lands still seen to be outside the grasp of the royal center.

At the same time it entailed a formal equation of these as-yet-untamed lands with those of the country's interior. In 718 two pieces of the southeastern part of Mutsu were broken off and combined with parts of Hitachi Province to form two new provinces called Iwaki and Iwashiro. A few years later these new provinces were abolished and the lands returned to Mutsu.[27] At the time of the division, the territory that had been brought under effective Yamato control probably extended only as far as the present-day Sendai plain—that is, only a short distance north of the ceded districts. Beyond this, however, lay nearly twice as much land that remained "outside the realm." The decision to form the new provinces must have stemmed from the greater degree to which these lands had been colonized and opened to rice culture, thereby gradually becoming incorporated into the Yamato political organization. But it is the decision to restore the ceded lands to Mutsu that is of real interest to us, since it indicates the government's willingness to combine territory under firm control and territory still "outside the realm" into a single administrative unit. The entire northeast, an expanse that elsewhere in the country would have been broken into half a dozen or more provinces, was now organized into only two: Mutsu and Dewa. That the central authorities chose to administer such an enormous territory—which included both Yamato-controlled and Emishi-controlled lands—in this manner indicates that it viewed the region and its Emishi inhabitants as a very special sort of problem.[28]

Around the turn of the eighth century, the new government of the *tennō* stepped up its efforts to absorb the northeastern frontier, shifting to a policy of armed colonization, the third of the five stages outlined above. At the core of the new policy was the establishment of stockade residence units (*kinohe*) throughout the frontier region. Cultivators from further west were transplanted into Emishi territory and settled around a series of stockades, which served both as places of protection and as general administrative headquarters. The first such outposts were established in what would later be called Echigo Province in 647–648, and stockades were discussed in the *ritsuryō* codes. But it was not until the early Nara Period that this institution played a major role in Yamato frontier policy.[29]

Stockade residence units were based near fortifications into which residents could retreat during times of danger, and they were defended by government troops.[30] Thus they represented a military as well as an agricultural presence in the frontier, but their principal character and function was agricultural. The essence of the stockade-and-residence-unit strategy lay in the armed but peaceful establishment of settlements, not in the aggressive suppression of the Emishi.

Even so, this mostly nonbelligerent intrusion into Emishi lands facilitated the spread of the Yamato institutions of governance to the furthest northern limits reached prior to modern times. These institutions were aimed predominantly at Yamato-associated settlers in the region, but in the long run they served to reorganize Emishi society as well. For while the stockade outposts sought only harmonious coexistence with the Emishi around them, their very presence played an essential role in transforming Emishi groups into political units.

This, in turn, precipitated the fourth phase of Japanese expansion into the northeast, the military subjugation of the Emishi that began during the Hōki era (770–780) and continued until 811. The court had conducted earlier military "pacification" expeditions against the Emishi—in 709, 720, 724, and 737—but these were really just shows of force, not suppression campaigns.[31] The fighting that began in the 770s initiated a sustained war of subjugation that, as the commander of the last expeditionary army observed when he demobilized his troops in 811, "lasted these thirty-eight years, from 774 to the present."[32]

These were enormous campaigns, involving armies of as many as 100,000 troops, and conducted at tremendous cost. A contemporary observer ranked the Emishi pacification efforts with the building of the new capital at Heiankyō as one of "the two great burdens" of Kammu Tennō's reign (781–806). But the court, which followed an overall policy of rationalizing and downsizing its military during this period, did not enter into this long, expensive conflict by choice. It was, rather, forced into it by changes in Emishi society that gave birth to a qualitatively new level of resistance to Yamato intrusion into Emishi homelands. This new resistance was the result of a combination of factors.[33]

To begin with, the frontier was filling up. Buffer areas between the Japanese settlers and the Emishi were becoming thinner, putting the two sides into closer confrontation and making the old pattern of peaceful coexistence more difficult to sustain. At the same time, Emishi society itself was becoming more politically organized, as tribal leaders claimed more extensive and specific forms of jurisdiction. The latter development was stimulated in part by the court's policy of "using barbarians to control barbarians," through which Emishi leaders were drawn into the Yamato court's administrative framework as district officials and the like, while maintaining their status and authority as tribal leaders intact. The intent of this policy was to subsume and absorb this tribal-based authority within the authority structure of the Yamato polity, but its effect was to create an independent base of power within the system for Emishi leaders. All of these factors were interrelated and their conflux facilitated the rise of a new and increasingly troublesome form of Emishi resistance to central government authority in the northeast. The court responded with a series of military campaigns aimed at eradicating this resistance.

The pacification wars began in 774, when Emishi attacked Momou Stockade in Mutsu. This outpost was located along the southern flow of the Kitakami River, just northeast of the modern city of Sendai, an area where Emishi political organization was particularly well developed. The government reacted to this attack with the dispatch of a relief force under Ōtomo Surugamaro. After first destroying the enemy's base near Momou, Ōtomo moved his army north, into what is now Iwate Prefecture, to cut off reinforcing Emishi troops that were moving south along the Kitakami River. At this point a riot by construction workers building a new stockade forced the campaign to a halt.[34]

Then in 780 a district official named Iji-no-kimi Atamaro began the largest Emishi revolt up to that time with an attack on the newly established Iji Stockade.[35] Atamaro's initial objective was to kill two local government officials, Michishima Ōtate and Ki Hirozumi; but having accomplished this, he went on to overwhelm Taga Stockade to the south. Atamaro was an Emishi chieftain who had been made a senior district chief (*tairyō*) to oversee his former base area. His original authority as an Emishi tribal leader having been thus repackaged, he and his followers formed the nucleus of royal administrative apparatus in the district. His grudge against Ōtate, a district official of nearby Oshika District and a scion of an elite local family that had long played a key role in the government's supervision of the Emishi, appears to have come about as a result of Ōtate's having called Atamaro a "tamed barbarian." He killed Ki too when the latter supported Ōtate. The roots of Atamaro's rebellion can thus be traced to the court's policy of entrusting responsibility for on-site supervision and control of the Emishi entirely to "former" Emishi chieftains.[36]

The revolt by Iji-no-kimi Atamaro became a catalyst for generalized local uprisings, a spark that spread quickly within the Emishi community. From Atamaro the leadership of Emishi resistance passed to Tamo-no-kimi Aterui, a chieftain from Isawa District in the southeastern part of present-day Iwate Prefecture. In 789 Aterui inflicted an ignoble defeat on a much larger government force at the battle of Kitakami River. Aterui then ran rampant until 801, when he was finally brought to heel by the famous Sakanoue Tamuramaro. After accepting Aterui's surrender, Tamuramaro established stockades in Isawa and Shiba and went on to eliminate organized Emishi resistance throughout the central Kitakami River area.[37]

Following this, the aggressive military policies of the Nara court yielded once more to the spirit of compromise that had traditionally characterized Yamato relations with the Emishi. In 805 the court ordered a halt to the fighting in the north, ostensibly to spare the *tennō*'s subjects further suffering caused by the heavy tax burdens imposed to finance the war and the building of the capital. In 811 one last campaign was conducted against the Emishi after which a royal decree was issued declaring their pacification to be complete. From this point forward the government's view of problems in the northeast shifted from one of controlling a foreign people to one of internal administration and maintenance of order. This had the effect of internalizing and redirecting the expression of Emishi antagonism to Yamato rule. From the straightforward tactics of armed defiance, the Emishi moved on to a more subtle—and ultimately far more effective—political form of resistance.[38]

When the pacification wars ended, the court stepped up its efforts to incorporate the ruling strata of Emishi society—now formally styled "surrendered barbarians" (*fushū*)—into the structure of *ritsuryō* rule. During this fifth stage of Japanese assimilation of the northeast, the apparatus of local rule was given over almost entirely to the Emishi leadership. The central government appointed "surrendered barbarian" tribal chieftains to serve as district officials—a post which, as it did elsewhere in the country, tended to become hereditary. In addition the court created a special post, the *fushūchō*, meaning "chief of surrendered barbarians." This new post is probably best understood as a kind of supra-district official overseeing six districts in Mutsu under the authority of the provincial governor.[39]

From the ninth century onward, Emishi leaders became increasingly adept at exploiting the powers delegated them, to the detriment of court control. By 873 the provincial governor of Mutsu was complaining to the court that control of the finances of provincial administration had fallen into the hands of Emishi leaders and other local elites: "officials in charge are seduced by district officials and tax collectors into accepting straw instead of rice; or they are bribed by the wealthy and powerful into accepting emptiness as reality."[40] Emishi leadership, organized within the *ritsuryō* framework, thus gradually came to circumvent central rule. The power and authority of tribal leadership, in other words, supplanted the power and authority of centralized officialdom from within the very structure of *ritsuryō* rule.

The *Ritsuryō* Polity and the Emishi Polity

The Emishi have a special significance in Japanese frontier history, for they were able to develop a political structure of their own, a distinct polity within the *ritsuryō* system. They did not, however, accomplish this entirely on their own initiative—the Yamato court played a vital causal role. As it advanced into the northeast, the polity attempted to absorb and assimilate the Emishi, positing the ideal of a consolidated, universal realm. At the same time, by delimiting a frontier zone and setting policies for dealing with the indigenous peoples therein, the *ritsuryō* polity defined both itself and the Emishi polity. The conflux of political developments within Emishi society with the policies and actions of the Yamato court gave rise to what should properly be termed an Emishi polity in the northeast.

Emishi resistance leaders of the late eighth and early ninth centuries appear to have achieved a considerable degree of political organization. Reports from the pacification campaigns indicate that rebel lands were arranged in villages and townships. In the northern parts of the frontier, villages and townships were aligned in leagues, similar to the political organization of the late sixth-century Yamato polity. But the Emishi were not able to continue their independent political evolution as the Yamato Japanese had been. The Emishi polity reached its highest development only after it was folded into the local administrative structure of the Yamato court, after the pacification wars had ended and the Emishi were formally declared assimilated.

Subsequently, during the middle and late Heian Period, successive houses of Emishi descent—the Abe, the Kiyowara, and the Fujiwara—were able to establish nearly autonomous satrapies in the northeast.[41] The geographical bases of all three families were six districts in Mutsu, the heartland of "pacified" Emishi territory. But the legal basis of their power was the authority derived from the office of *fushūchō*. He was a tribal head exercising authority buttressed by the power of the Yamato court. The structure of the *ritsuryō* polity's system of local rule was therefore integral to the structure of the Emishi polity that was eventually ruled by the Abe, Kiyowara, and Fujiwara.[42] The Emishi polity, in other words, was built upon, as well as within, the framework of the *ritsuryō tennō*-centered Nara polity.

It was for precisely this reason that Emishi political development should be seen as having peaked during the middle to late Heian Period and not before. For while the advance of the Yamato state into the northeast helped to give shape to Emishi political ambitions, it also checked them. The level of organization that turned a loose collection of tribal villages into a consolidated Emishi polity did not come about until after the intervention of the *ritsuryō* polity. But the autonomy that made possible an Emishi polity had to wait until the grip of the central government on local administration began to loosen, in the late ninth century.[43]

Notes

1. Turner 1921, 2–3, reprint of a paper read at the meeting of the American Historical Association, July 12, 1893.

2. There are debates over the chronology of these reforms. Traditionally, they were thought to have begun shortly after the coup, but more recent thinking has them taking place gradually, during the 650 to 670 period. And a recent wooden document casts significant doubt on the use of the era name "Taika" in the 640s as well. See Piggott 1997, chapter 4.

3. Takahashi Tomio 1962a.

4. *Ryō no gige*, in Shintei zōho kokushi taikei, 105–6.

5. Interpreter's note: The *Nihongi* entry for Keikō 40/7/16 states (here in Aston's English translation): "We hear that the Eastern savages are of a violent disposition, and are much given to oppression: their hamlets have no chiefs, their villages no leaders, each is greedy of territory, and they plunder one another. Moreover, there are in the mountains malignant Deities, on the moors there are malicious demons, who beset the highways and bar the roads, causing men much annoyance. Amongst these Eastern savages the Yemishi are the most powerful, their men and women live together promiscuously, there is no distinction of father and child. In winter they dwell in holes, in summer they live in nests. Their clothing consists of furs, and they drink blood. Brothers are suspicious of one another. In ascending mountains they are like flying birds; in going through the grass they are like fleet wolves. When they receive a favor, they forget it, but if an injury is done them they never fail to revenge it. Therefore they keep arrows in their top-knots and carry swords within their clothing. Sometimes they draw together their fellows and make inroads on the frontier. At other times they take the opportunity of the harvest to plunder the people. If attacked, they conceal themselves in the herbage; if pursued, they flee into the mountains. Therefore ever since antiquity they have not been steeped in the kingly civilizing influences." See Aston 1972, vol. 1, 203. In the following, *Nihongi* entries that cannot be cited by date are cited by page number Shintei zōho kokushi taikei version, unless otherwise noted.

6. Interpreter's note: Rice agriculture was already being practiced in the northeast by the Yayoi age (c. 300 B.C.E. to 300 C.E.) and was widely diffused by the fifth or sixth century. For recent studies of peoples of the northeast see Kudō Keiichi 1960; and Itō Hiroyuki 1987.

7. *Nihongi* Keikō 27/2/12.

8. *Engi shiki*, vol. 22 (Minbu 1), in Shintei zōho kokushi taikei *Engi shiki*, vol. 2, 562.

9. Interpreter's note: The new orthography for Emishi might have been a reference to the quail-like topknots worn by this people. Also, the terms Kumaso and "land of the Kumaso" appear in the creation myths of the *Kojiki* and *Nihongi*. Such texts identify these people as occupying only the southern part of Kyūshū, but this is probably an error on the part of the chroniclers, who wrote long after the fact. The stories related in the texts depict the Kumaso as a people in rebellion across the whole of the island, and their homeland is sometimes treated as an independent country. With regard to the Hayato, the *Hsin T'ang shu* (*New History of the T'ang Dynasty*, an eleventh-century Chinese text) lists three places called Yaku, Haya, and Tane, suggesting that Haya might also have been a country. The name of the people might have been derived from this, or visa versa.

10. On at least one occasion a Japanese diplomatic mission to the T'ang court included an Emishi man and woman among the items brought as tribute to the Chinese emperor. See *Nihongi*, Saimei 5/7/3. Chinese accounts of Wa (the Chinese name for Japan) in the *Sung shu* (*History of the Liu Sung Dynasty*, compiled c. 513), the *Chu T'ang shu* (*Old History of the T'ang Dynasty*, compiled in the early tenth century), and other old records use the "hairy men" orthography exclusively. The *Hsin T'ang shu* and all subsequent works use the "quail barbarians" compound in all instances other than direct quotations from earlier sources. Interpreter's note: English translations can be found in Goodrich 1951.

11. The *Nihongi* contains references to Emishi using the quail barbarian orthography from as early as the Keikō chapter (traditionally dated 71–131 C.E.), but the wording of such passages is strongly suspect. Careful textual analysis and reconstruction has demonstrated that many references to Emishi in the *Nihongi* and the *Kojiki* that purport to date from before the mid-seventh century are not in their original order and were probably tampered with at the time the chronicles were compiled. See Tsuda Sōkichi 1948b, vol. 1, pt. 2, chap. 3; and Sakamoto Taro 1956. It is reasonable to assume that this tampering would have included changing the characters with which the term "Emishi" itself was written.

12. Kita Sadakichi 1929–1930, 331–39; and Tsuda Sōkichi 1948a, vol. 1, sec. 2, chapter 2, especially 174–75. Interpreter's note: The Tsuchigumo are mentioned in several passages of the *Nihongi* and the *Kojiki*. They appear to have been of the same racial stock as the Yamato Japanese, had Japanese names, and inhabited territories within the boundaries of Yamato, although they themselves had not been incorporated into the Yamato polity.

13. See *Nihongi* Keikō 27/10/13 and Keikō 40/7/16.

14. See the entry for Taihō 2 (703)/10/3 in *Shoku nihongi*, the court annal for the eighth century (in the Shintei zōho kokushi taikei version, 15). "Michinoku" is a contraction of "Michi no oku," originally written with characters meaning "at the end of the road." But by the time the *Nihongi* was compiled, a compound meaning "at the end of the land" (or "in the depths of the land") was used. See *Nihongi* Jitō 11 (697)/10/19; Suiko 35 (627)/2/ .

15. The quotation comes from the Chinese *Sung shu*, Weikuotsuan. Interpreter's note: The English translation is taken from Goodrich 1951, 23.

16. The passage continues, "Crossing the sea to the north, they subjugated ninety-five countries." The "95" is probably a mistake for 99, which would leave a very neat lineup of 55, 66 and 99 countries in the various directions. Almost certainly these numbers were invented.

17. "Kumaso" was probably synthesized from place names: the Kuma District of Higo Province and the Sō District of Ōsumi.

18. Interpreter's note: The services rendered to the Yamato court by the Hayato during the sixth and seventh centuries are discussed in some detail in Naoki Kōjirō 1968, 158–71. The Hayato as a source of private military forces for the Yamato king are also given brief treatment in Sasayama Haruo 1975, 74–76.

19. *Nihongi*, Age of the Gods, Sakamoto Tarō et al. 1967, vol. 1, 93. For the English translation see Aston 1972, vol. 1, 100. The story is recounted in several alternative versions in *Nihongi*. In Aston's English version, for instance, see vol. 1, 91–108.

20. *Nihongi* Seinei 1 (480)/1/15; Ritchū, prologue.

21. Shintei zōho kokushi taikei *Ryō no gige*, 56. Interpreter's note: Naoki Kōjirō observes that the manufacture of bamboo umbrellas was a well-known speciality of the

Hayato, who came from an area in which sturdy bamboo was plentiful. See Naoki Kōjirō 1968, 162. In English the structure and evolution of the court's military forces are discussed in detail in Friday 1992, chapters 2–3; and in Farris 1992, chapters 2–4.

22. Shintei zōho kokushi taikei *Ryō no gige*, 56.

23. Kita Sadakichi 1929–1930, 448–50. *Shoku nihongi* Taihō 2 (702)/10/3 and Wadō 6 (713)/4/3. Interpreter's note: Bruce L. Batten provides a detailed treatment of the *ritsuryō* provincial system and the process by which it was established in Batten 1993 and Batten 1989, 46–65.

24. *Shoku nihongi* Mommu Tennō 4 (700)/6/3; Taihō 2 (702)/8/1; Wadō 6 (713)/7/5; Yōrō 4 (720)/2/29, 3/4; and Yōrō 5 (721)/7/7.

25. This assertion must be qualified slightly, for it appears that assimilation of the Hayato and their lands was mainly political during the sixth and seventh centuries. Older patterns of life persisted in the economic and social spheres. The state's system of registration and redistribution of paddy lands (*handen*), for example, was not implemented in Satsuma and Ōsumi until 800. See *Shoku nihongi* Tempyō 2 (730)/3/7 and the topical compendium of the six official histories known as *Ruijū kokushi*, in the *Shintei zōho kokushi taikei*, vol. 3, 112.

26. Itō Nobuo 1955. The historian Tsuda Sōkichi asserted that the court left the problem of managing the Emishi to the residents of the east. See Tsuda Sōkichi 1948b, vol. 1, 222–23. Interpreter's note: A rather extensive literature exists in both Japanese and English on the spread of *kofun* culture and its historical significance. A recent work in English is Barnes 1988. See also Edwards 1983; and Piggott 1997, chapter 2.

27. Interpreter's note: Inoue Tastuo also describes this event in chapter 4 of this volume.

28. *Shoku nihongi* Yōrō 2 (718)/5/2. The date of the re-merger of the two provinces into Mutsu is traditionally believed to have been 724, but this cannot be confirmed by any extant source from that period. *Shoku nihongi* Wadō 5 (712)/10/1 shows two districts in western Mutsu being combined with an area known since 708 as Dewa District to form Dewa Province.

29. *Nihongi* Kōtoku 3 (647)/12/30 and Kōtoku 4 (648)/4/1; *Ryō no gige*, 197–98, 200. Interpreter's note: An excellent study of the stockades and the stockade household system aimed at the general reader is Kudō Masaki 1989.

30. Interpreter's note: According to the *Ryō no gige*, the *ritsuryō* codes dictated that the troops to defend the stockade be drawn from local regiments, supplemented when necessary by local residents called for corvée service. From the 720s the regiments were supplemented with a new type of frontier guard force called *chimpei*, or "pacification soldiers." See *Ryō no gige*, 198 and 200. Further information on *chimpei* can be found in Takahashi Takashi 1972; Takahashi Tomio 1962b; and Kudō Masaki 1973. In English see Friday 1992, 24–25.

31. *Shoku nihongi* Wadō 2 (709)/3/5, 7/1, 7/13, and 8/25; Yōrō 4 (720)/9/28 and 9/29; Yōrō 5 (721)/4/9; Jinki 1 (724)/3/25, 4/7, and 11/29; and Tempyō 9 (737)/1/24 and 4/14. Interpreter's note: Concerning the 709, 720, and 724 campaigns, the text records only the appointment of an officer in charge of the operation and his return to the capital. Greater detail is given for the 737 campaign, which probably indicates that nothing noteworthy occurred in the earlier actions. Even the 737 campaign was conducted without bloodshed. The Emishi pacification campaigns are discussed extensively in Friday 1997; and in Farris 1992, 82–104.

32. *Nihon kōki* Kōnin 2 (811)/intercalary 12/11. Interpreter's note: The third of the official court annals, the *Nihon kōki* covers the period 792–833.

33. *Nihon kōki* Kōnin 2 (811)/6/19 and Enryaku 24 (805)/12/7. Interpreter's note: For more on the state's reorganization and streamlining of its military during the late eighth century, see Friday 1992, chap. 2 and Farris 1992, 104–19.

34. *Shoku nihongi* Hōki 5 (774)/7/23 and 10/4. Interpreter's note: The location of the new stockade, called Kakubetsu, is unknown. It is not even clear whether the fort was ever completed.

35. Interpreter's note: "Atamaro" is read by some scholars as "Azamaro." Similarly, "Iji" can also be read as "Ihari."

36. *Shoku nihongi* Hōki 11 (780)/3/22. The character of Atamaro's rebellion receives extensive treatment in Kadowaki Teiji 1953. Valuable information on Michishima Ōtate and his family is given in Inoue Mitsusada 1956.

37. *Shoku nihongi* Enryaku 8 (789)/6/3 and Enryaku 9 (790)/9/19. Interpreter's note: An excellent capsule history of Sakanoue Tamuramaro's campaigns appears in Yasuda Motohisa 1984, 22–23.

38. *Nihon kōki* Enryaku 24 (805)/12/7 and Kōnin 2 (811)/7/14.

39. See *Ruijū kokushi*, Shintei zōho kokushi taikei , vol. 4, 336. The designation of Emishi leaders as district officials was not unusual. The Yamato court had followed a practice of appointing local magnates to serve in this capacity since the seventh century. Interpreter's note: The *Ruijū kokushi* is a collection of abstracts of the *rikkokushi* (*six national histories*), arranged topically.

40. *Nihon sandai jitsuroku* Jōgan 15 (873)/12/23, in Shintei zōho kokushi taikei. Interpreter's note: *Nihon sandai jitsuroku* is the last of the official court annals.

41. Interpreter's note: Two excellent introductory studies of the Abe, Kiyowara, and the Northern Fujiwara are Shōji Hiroshi 1977 and Takahashi Tomio 1984.

42. Interpreter's note: For later developments in the northeast, see Yiengpruksawan 1999.

43. Interpreter's note: The trend toward decentralization in local administration is discussed in Morris 1980, Batten 1989, and Farris 1985.

6

Roads in the *Tennō*-centered Polity

TAKEDA SACHIKO

Introduction by Joan R. Piggott

STUDY OF JAPAN'S CLASSICAL TRANSPORTATION SYSTEM has expanded exponentially in recent decades. During the archaeological boom of the 1970s and 1980s, historians and archaeologists hypothesized the existence in pre-Nara times of at least four great roads in the Kinai that made Asuka their hub.[1] Research by the late Kishi Toshio (1920-1987) was especially central to that endeavor.[2] A sampling of press releases from the monthly *Bunkazai hakkutsu shutsudo jōhō* further evidences discovery of numerous segments of the seven circuit highways, the *shichidō,* since 1990. Those circuit highways were built to link the Nara capital with its provinces during the eighth century. In 1990 Kinoshita Ryō published his report entitled *Studies Reconstructing the Planned Straight Highways of Japan's Classical Age* (*Nihon kodai ritsuryōki ni fusetsu sareta chokusenteki keikakudō fukugenteki kenkyū*). The Society for the Study of Classical Transportation (Kodai Kōtsū Kenkyūkai) was founded in the early 1990s as well.[3] Meanwhile, archaeologists have described and analyzed new finds identified as provincial offices (*kokufu*), district offices (*gunga*), post stations (*umaya*), bridges (*hashi*), barriers (*seki*), ports (*tsu*), and vehicular roads (*kuruma no michi*) for use by carts. Reconsideration of the written record in light of the newly excavated physical evidence has significantly expanded understanding of society and polity in classical times.

In her essay that follows, Takeda Sachiko argues that official highways laid down in the Nara Period had a symbolic significance far beyond their physical reality as splendid man-made arteries built with straight edges and paved with pebbles to conduct travelers from one point to another. The circuit highways of the *ritsuryō* polity that were overseen by the Ministry of Popular Affairs (Minbushō) integrated the classical realm in symbolic as well as geographic terms. The *tennō*-centered polity (*ritsuryō kokka*) of classical Japan incorporated the region immediately surrounding the capital, called the "Kinai" after classical Chinese usage, and the seven circuits comprising the various provinces. Both the circuits and the circuit highways serving them were known by the same names: Tōkaidō, Tōsandō, etc. At 30-*ri* intervals (approx. 16 kilometers) along the circuit highways, post stations (*umaya*) were constructed. The seven circuit highways were prioritized according to the traffic they bore, which determined how many horses were required to be stabled at the post stations along them. For instance the San'yōdō was the sole "great road" (*dairo*) with 20 horses to be stabled at its post station stables; the Tōkai and Tōsan circuits were "medium roads" (*chūro*) with 10 horses at each post station; and other circuits were "lesser roads" (*shōro*) with only 5 horses at each station (see Maps 0.1, Frontis. and 6.1).

Map 6.1. The Circuit Highways of Classical Japan

Highways provided a means whereby the courtly center's integrative functions —as apical ordinator, culture source, and information coordinator—penetrated the countryside. Roads also facilitated the diffusion of courtly etiquette, written language, and other practices while serving to distinguish the *tennō*-centered official sphere from local, unofficial spheres. And in addition to metaphorically representing the *tennō*'s courtly world, the circuit highways carried foreign emissaries and agents of the royal center whose dress, behavior, and literacy demonstrated the *tennō*'s authority and preeminence. Official highways served thus to produce a worldview, a *mentalité*, that confirmed the *tennō*'s capital as the center of civilization.

Taking inspiration from work by Ishimoda Shō (whose work also appears in the volume), Takeda notes that the *tennō*-centered government considered the circuit highways to be spaces where Chinese-style decorum (*li*) should function just as it did at court. That is why rubrics concerning official conduct on highways were inserted into the Law on Decorum and Governmental Procedures (Giseiryō), a chapter of the *ritsuryō* codes. In the last half of her essay, to further illustrate her argument, Takeda provides a short case study of one of the circuit highways, the San'yōdō, that passed along the Inland Sea region of western Japan.

We gain quite a different view of the nature of Japan's early *ritsuryō* polity from Takeda's essay than we might take away from a narrative focused on legal prescriptions and administrative practices. According to Takeda the operative concept that shaped the eighth-century official view of highways was *li*—variously translatable as decorum, etiquette, protocol, or ritual—which in China and throughout China-influenced polities of classical East Asia provided a basis for official prescriptions concerning hierarchy and associated dress and conduct. Takeda nonetheless finds important variations in Chinese and Japanese expectations with regard to the practice of *li*—there was, she argues, a Japanese-style *li*. While the Chinese stressed dress as a key element differentiating the civilized from the barbarous, Japanese gazetteers (*fudoki*) describing the people of the provinces disregarded clothing. They focused instead on livelihoods, local products, place-names, and legends. Even more striking is that in contrast with the Japanese view of *li*, travel routes were not treated as public space in Chinese law of the T'ang Period (618-907).

Takeda posits that the reason underlying such differences is to be found in the character of the Japanese *ritsuryō* polity and society. On the archipelago the gap between local customs and capital usages was wide, making it important for the *tennō*-center to ignore what could not be changed while focusing on what was transformable. In addition, the Chinese system of *li* as adopted and adapted by the *tennō*'s court mainly functioned within the elite strata allied with the Heavenly Sovereign, that is, in the world of officialdom. Takeda argues that unlike the realm of continental Sons of Heaven that it sometimes took as its model, the *tennō*-centered polity on the archipelago was distinctly segmentary. Standards of dress and behavior in the Kinai and beyond, and distinctions between rulers and ruled, were various. Although in China *li* was to be observed in both official and unofficial matters, in Japan only the sphere of official matters was covered by *li*. The status differentiations of the Law on Decorum and Government Procedures did not apply to commoners in Japan.

In this regard Takeda explores the curious paradox that despite Japan's insular geography, the *tennō*-centered polity mandated travel to the capital by land rather than by sea. Unlike in T'ang China where taxes could be transported by any available means, Japan's *ritsuryō* ordered overland transport by tax payers. Similarly, in the early Heian Period accommodations at post stations, provincial offices, Buddhist temples, and even commoner residences along the San'yō Road (San'yōdō) were spruced up to impress embassies from the Manchurian kingdom of Parhae, who were ordered to use it to travel to the new capital at Heian. As Takeda puts it, "As long as foreign ambassadors came and went by sea, the dignity and affluence of the *tennō*-centered polity could not be adequately displayed." Just as kings of Yamato are described in *Man'yōshū* poems surveying their domain from high vantage points in realm-viewing (*kunimi*) rites, *tennō* and their ministers wanted all to appreciate the land of the "all under Heaven" where the Heavenly Sovereigns reigned. Dynamic construction of roads and associated structures was therefore a critical element in establishing the idea as well as the reality of the *tennō*-centered realm, seen from inside and out, or from center and periphery.

TAKEDA SACHIKO

Roads in the *Tennō*-centered Polity

Interpreted by Joan R. Piggott

The *tennō*-centered polity (*ritsuryō kokka*) of classical Japan incorporated the region immediately surrounding the capital, called the "Kinai" after classical Chinese usage, and seven circuits comprising the various provinces. Both the circuits and the circuit highways serving them were known by the same names: Tōkaidō, Tōsandō, and such (see Map 6.1). At 30-*ri* (approx. 16 kilometers) intervals along the circuit highways, post stations were constructed. The seven circuit highways were prioritized according to the traffic they bore, which determined how many horses were required to be stabled at the post stations along them. For instance the San'yōdō was the sole "great road" (*dairo*) with 20 horses to be stabled at its post stations; the Tōkai and Tōsan circuits were "medium roads" (*chūro*) with 10 horses at each post station; and other circuits were "lesser roads" (*shōro*) with only 5 horses at each station.

These official highways helped shape the relationship between local communities and the *tennō*-centered polity, which assigned a variety of functions to roads in addition to transporting goods, official correspondence, or travelers.[4] Moreover, transport as a historical issue encompasses far more than economic activities like trade in merchandise, flow of currency, business transactions, and the sharing of agrarian technology. Transport facilities influence activities in the political sphere, such as war and diplomacy, as well as concerns of the intellectual sphere, in which writing and law are of critical importance.[5] By my reading, this intellectual sphere should not be limited to the transmission of information and administrative procedures through writing and law. We must also explore the new worldview of eighth-century Japan that resulted from the inception of a network of roads tying the realm together. In this essay, I propose to examine transportation in the eighth and ninth centuries through an analysis of the official network of highways and the advent of a new worldview nurtured by that network. The roads discussed here lay outside established local communities, and so were separate from the daily lives of inhabitants of those communities. As man-made arteries constructed by an authority transcending the local community, such highways directly linked locals with the political center.

The distinction between the political center and localities, as well as greater control of the periphery by the royal capital, emerged concurrently with the establishment of the *ritsuryō* polity in the late seventh and early eighth centuries. Both developments were significantly influenced by the effects of transportation. The section describing the Ministry of Popular Affairs in the *ritsuryō* code's Law on Personnel (Shikiinryō) defined the responsibilities of the Minister of Popular Affairs as "monitoring roads and bridges, ferries and fords, canals and ponds, mountains and rivers, bushes and marshes." An early Heian-period legal commentary, the *Commentary on the Administrative Code* (*Ryō no gige*), interpreted the law as, "Simply know the boundaries of territories as outlined in the map. Do not interfere when surveying land."[6] The later *Collected Commentaries on the Administrative Code* (*Ryō no shūge*) confirms this. It cites the *Ana* commentary, which states, "As for all the land under Heaven, it shall all be known."[7] Use of maps by the Ministry of Popular Affairs demonstrated the principle of territorial control through knowledge of geography. The ultimate goal was full comprehension of the territory.

An earlier order from the eighth month of 646 reportedly mandated provincial governors and other officials to "oversee the boundaries of your territory, record them in documents or draw maps, and submit them for presentation."[8] While this earlier decree considered the locale and boundaries of territories merely as elements to be included in maps, in *ritsuryō* law it was the means of transportation across those regions—"bridges and roads, ferries and fords"—that were mentioned first. This is significant in considering the meaning of roads in Japan's classical age. The government was well aware that territorial supervision had an essential precondition, the construction of an infrastructure for transportation.

The character of official highways in classical times has gradually been clarified thanks to dynamic progress in the discipline of historical geography in recent decades. We know now that official roads were far wider than those of the medieval and early modern periods, that they were on the whole well planned and ideally connected in straight lines, and that they were sometimes even paved with stones. Recent revelations that their construction was so well engineered have had a profound impact on reseachers and provoked calls for a revision of the current assessment of the classical polity. Here I would like to focus on the roads themselves as man-made objects, to better understand their role in the *ritsuryō* system. I also hope to suggest some of the effects their actual form and circumstance had on the collective psyche of people in classical times. First we will look at the differing views of central administrators in Japan and China regarding people distant from the center.

Dress and Propriety in Japan and China

A comparison of Chinese and Japanese gazetteers demonstrates contrasting views about outlying domains held by central authorities. Official Chinese historical writings contain full details concerning the clothing worn in every region under every dynasty, whether that of indigenous peoples in peripheral areas or that of inhabitants of interior regions under direct rule. This was because evaluations of such phenomena determined whether or not given groups conformed with teachings about propriety and decorum (*li*). The categories "Chinese" and "barbarian" were determined by conversance with ideals typically termed "Confucian." In essence, knowledge of the canonical classics was to lead to compliance with various behavioral patterns and daily rituals advocated by the classics. "Barbarians" who did not fit the model were distinguished as ethnically foreign or different.

What phenomena were the foci of these behavioral patterns and customary rites? Provisions in the military section of the "Record of Court Officials" in the *New T'ang History* (*Hsin T'ang shu*) concerning senior local officials responsible for tribute payment and geographic intelligence direct, "If different people enter the domain, sketch their appearance and clothing and submit a report." Here the most important items to be reported when "different people" appeared were such external characteristics as deportment, ritual, and clothing. Furthermore, the first roll of the *Annotated Water Classic* (*Shuijing zhu*, c. 510 C.E.) contains the following entry: "Hsintou River – West of the river are the countries of T'ienchu [India], and to the south all belongs to China. The people are prosperous. Their food and clothes are the same as in central China. Therefore this area has been called China." Behind this observation lies the belief that commonality in clothing and cuisine denotes common ethnicity. Variance in garb, on the other hand, indicates foreignness.

In contrast, clothing was not regarded as a means of distinguishing ethnicity in classical Japan. Japanese gazetteers from the eighth century contain descriptions of various foreign peoples, but as one glances through those concerning the Tsuchigumo, Kuzu, and Hakusuirō peoples, it is apparent that differences in garb were ignored.[9] For instance, in the report of the Hitachi gazetteer (*Hitachi fudoki*) concerning the Kuzu of the Ibaragi area, the Kuzu are said to have dwelt in holes in the ground. "Their customs are somewhat removed from ours," it observes. The term "customs" here does not include clothing. We know this because the provision on foreigners in the *ritsuryō* era's Law on Official Communications and Practices (Kushikiryō) mandates submission of illustrations describing appearance and clothing. Customs, by contrast, were to be described in writing. Clothing and customs were clearly separate categories. "Customs" meant occupations and daily practices, as distinguished from clothing and eating characteristics. In the Hizen gazetteer (*Hizen fudoki*), the entry for the Matsura area describing the Hakusuirō of Chikashima notes the appearance, etiquette, and linguistic characteristics of the Hakusuirō but makes no mention of distinctive fashion: "Their features are similar to the Hayato, they enjoy hunting from horseback, and their language differs from other local people." And in the royal edict ordering compilation of the gazetteers by provincial officials, the focus was on products from the land, origins of place-names and geographical landmarks, and legends and myths handed down in each territory. The *ritsuryō* polity was not conscious of clothing as a concern of rulership.

Why should this have been the case? One possibility is that, prior to the compilation of the gazetteers, habits of dress by inhabitants throughout the archipelago had already been standardized. Or perhaps the opposite was true—perhaps people in the archipelago, including subjects such as the Kuzu and Tsuchigumo, did not outfit themselves in a single fashion that visually reflected the influence of the *tennō*-centered polity. Were such the case, clothing style could not have differentiated between "us" and "others" in eighth-century Japan as it did in China.

In fact I believe the latter was the case. In my monograph *Fashion and the Development of the Classical Japanese Polity*, I argued that although the *ritsuryō* polity adopted the Chinese dress code, it was forced to restrict its use to official functions because there was a gap between the local customs and usage in the capital.[10] Satake Akira has noted how both bureaucrats and commoners participated in rituals held before the main gate of the imperial palace during China's T'ang Dynasty (617–907).[11] The objective of governmental mandating of such participation was to imprint on the people's minds the greatness of the Son of Heaven. The Japanese court, however, never prepared the space necessary for such ceremonies. According to Satake, the only concern in Japan was where rankholders fit within the hierarchy of society. Therefore, rankholders alone gathered in the capital, with the *tennō* at their head. There they ruled over the people as a body and exercised overwhelming power and authority.[12]

In terms of the official dress code, commoners and even slaves were compelled to wear formal clothing in official spaces. A hierarchical order from *tennō* down to slaves was rigidly systematized as the basis for the Japanese organization of *li*, but it operated only in the special space of officialdom.[13] Moreover, its proponents displayed no desire to proclaim the rightfulness of the system to outsiders. Was it perhaps because the power of the Japanese *tennō* and the rank-holding class of courtiers around the throne was more autocratic than that of China?

The Chinese imperial capital system, including its rituals and uniform dress code at such events, was a product of domestic politics and society. The world of the capital had the sovereign as its supreme master, while the relationship between the monarch and commoners during rituals at the main palace gate directly demonstrated the legitimacy of imperial rule. That is the reason such rituals were open to the public.[14] People who participated in such rites accepted thereby the status order of *li* by their very presence, and they aided development of imperial autocracy by their acceptance of the ritual hierarchy with the emperor at its apex.

In contrast, the rank system in Japan could not be in accord with domestic circumstances as long as it was defined—because of international circumstances—by the Chinese order of *li*. Thus Japan had no choice but to develop its own *li* hierarchy within a limited space. Regardless of whether an inhabitant was listed as a registered commoner or as a payer of tribute, as long as island society followed its own customary practices, including those of fashion and cuisine, any space that was not an official one was essentially categorized as barbarian space. The Chinese value system was applied only to the world of officialdom.

An important reason was that eighth-century society was based on what has been called "the Asian chieftain system." Ishimoda Shō argued that the domination of transport by the chiefly class affected class stratification, administrative style, and political organization. He even claimed that the gulf between the chieftain class, which appropriated Chinese characters and Chinese literature for its own use, and their subjects, who had no writing system, contributed decisively to the division of labor in society.[15] Between Nara-period elites—who read historical documents and classical texts in Chinese, wrote royal edicts in Chinese, owned Chinese classics, and had become sinicized even in their personal thought patterns—and commoners, there was not a single shared practice, despite their common residence in the islands and their shared language.

This situation suggests not only the gulf between ruler and people. It also points to the lack of a common cultural denominator between the Nara-period ruling class—comprised of the *tennō* and his officials—and commoners. Furthermore, we must assume that the lack of external commonality would have influenced internal consciousness as well. That the exterior defines the interior is a basic tenet of *li*. So long as the Chinese principal of *li*—that "the character of a person is determined wholly by his or her outer appearance and behavioral acts"—served as the nucleus of the official order in Japan, rulers and ruled could not manifest an ethnic commonality.

There are two final reasons why the gazetteers may have been silent concerning variant clothing styles. After all, those who ruled throughout the archipelago, and perhaps even in parts of the Kinai, were designated "outer officials" because they resided outside the capital. Such elites necessarily had diminished consciousness of what constituted "inside standards" of dress at court. Moreover, gazetteers may well have been intended for display by ambassadors sent to T'ang China, in which case descriptions of variant styles of clothing in the archipelago would have been avoided. Officials in eighth- and ninth-century Japan—diplomats especially—were very eager to present images of their realm that conformed to Chinese classical values, thereby demonstrating Japan's successful development into a polity that had mastered *li*.

Court and Highways—Japan and China Compared

Beyond the court and its various adminstrative offices in the capital, provincial headquarters, district offices, and tax-storage compounds were all considered official spaces as well. An entry for 669/01/14 in the *Chronicles of Japan* (*Nihongi*) records: "[The *tennō*] proclaimed standards for etiquette at court as well as what to avoid along the road." Thus, both court and roads were designated as spaces where *li*, propriety, should be practiced. Judging from the fact that distinct graphs (*koku*) were used to denote rural pathways, the term for "road" used here referred to the circuit highways under the supervision of the Ministry of Popular Affairs. Such travel routes were considered official spaces where *li* functioned just as at court precisely because these highways connected provincial government offices with the court in the capital.

Now in fact the provision concerning travel routes in the *ritsuryō* Law on Decorum and Government Procedures enjoins observance of formal etiquette during journeys: "On all travel routes and local paths, the lowly make way for the noble. The young move aside for the old. The inferior yield to the superior." Spaces affected by these directives were not just major routes. They included local paths as well. According to various interpretations of the law compiled in the *Ryō no shūge*, etiquette to be practiced on both types of roads applied to commoner and official, to the "good taxpayer" and to "the lowly." Instead of operating according to complicated gradations of rank and office, the Law on Decorum employed a more general concept of hierarchy that set up binary oppositions between humble and noble, young and aged, inferior and superior. These rules covered a wide range of human relationships in eighth-century society and would have had broad effects on popular etiquette.

For these rules to actually function, however, there had to be ways a traveler on the roads could evaluate the difference between his own status and that of a traveler approaching him. An account of the Wa people—that is the Japanese—in the *History of the Wei Dynasty* (*Wei chih*) records, "inferior persons, on encountering great ones on the road, hesitate and step into the grass."[16] This is evidence that by the third century *li* was already practiced in Japanese society. Such respectful behavior was only possible, however, between noble and humble, as demonstrated by the phrase "venerable and lowly each observe order," because status differentiation had already developed to that extent. We can assume that tattoos and other visible signifiers of status existed because the *History of the Wei Dynasty* also says, "Tattoos in the various provinces differ; some are on the right, some on the left; there is distinction between venerable and lowly." The behavior described in the *History of the Wei Dynasty* required such markers by which the hierarchical relationship between high and low could be recognized.

What happened then between persons of equal status? Obeying provisions in the Law on Decorum and Government Procedures was not totally impossible in encounters between groups of bureaucrats or titleholders, or when one met the provincial governor. Officials wore court clothing appropriate to their ranks and posts, and as long as their use of the roads was for bureaucratic purposes, they were required to travel in those clothes.[17] It must have been comparatively easy for each side to ascertain status by a glance at the colors of robes and other markers. As we have seen, however, court clothes were reserved for use inside bureaucratic space. Without uniform standards of fashion for private costume, it must have been impossible for officials in ordinary clothes and for commoners to determine one another's relative social position unless they belonged to the same local community or had some other relationship.[18]

On the side of the *ritsuryō* polity, it seems that there was no expectation that relevant rules would be observed by commoners. During China's Northern Sung Dynasty (960–1127), there was an imperial edict urging rigorous attention to the rules of *li*. Specifically, in 984 Kung Ch'eng-gung demanded that informative tablets bearing such orders be erected at post stations and mounds to mark distances in both capitals (Ch'ang-an and Loyang) and in the provinces. The emperor's proclamation was inscribed to urge attitudes appropriate to *li* and thereby improve manners and customs. If this was happening even in China—the country where *li* functioned throughout society as the norm—then we can conclude that the effectiveness of the law governing etiquette on official roads in Japan would have been quite limited. It is even harder to imagine that such etiquette was habitually practiced across the archipelago, where *li* functioned only within the restricted domain of officialdom. Indeed, since there is no trace of a royal edict commanding obedience to such laws, protocols mandated by the Law on Decorum and Government Procedures were not meant for commoners. Directives proclaimed in 670 concerning "ceremonial observances on the road" were aimed at officials and were associated with rules for court etiquette promulgated at the same time. The two sets of protocols were thus meant to denote court and travel routes as a single arena for the practice of *li*.

That the Japanese Law on Decorum and Government Procedures placed provisions on travel routes after the rubric barring entry to the court by those wearing inauspicious apparel provides further evidence that in Japan travel routes were considered official space. Not only does this arrangement differ from the order of relevant provisions in Chinese law; moreover, by placing the provision on roads and paths after that prohibiting inauspicious clothing (such as mourning apparel and priestly robes), the Law on Decorum brought those journeying on official business into the category of those for whom court clothing was prescribed. In contrast, according to the mandate against court entry for those garbed inauspiciously, *zaika* ("at home") was defined as traveling on personal business to and from one's home place. Donning court clothing was not required on such occasions. In other words, *zaika* was the opposite of "official" and covered passage on both "travel routes" and "local paths." There was thus a clear distinction between personal affairs and public duties; and those on official business were to wear court clothing that evidenced their rank and promoted decorum by prompting proper hierarchical deference among travelers. Such hierarchy was the very core of *li*.

Dress for Monks and Nuns in the Sōniryō

Clothing restrictions described in the Yōrō Code Law for Monks and Nuns (Sōniryō) also illustrate the relationship between dress, official space, travel, and formal etiquette.[19] When monks and nuns attended to private affairs in an official setting, they were temporarily to adopt secular fashion. One such occasion might be when they visited government offices to lodge personal suits. Robes of monks and nuns were limited to such colors as *mokuran* (a blend of yellow, crimson and red), turquoise, black, yellow, and earth color. Wearing secular garb, including court robes, was usually forbidden. But when clerics entered official space for legal proceedings, they were subject to provisions barring entry by those wearing "inauspicious" clothing. An explicating note from the eighth-century *Ana* commentary in the *Collected Commentaries on the Administrative Code* noted that monks and nuns were expected to wear colors indicative of their rank—as official personnel they were to don court robes in official space.

This provision on dress for monks and nuns pertained not only to clothing worn inside official buildings but also to what was worn enroute to official spaces. The oldest commentary on the Taihō Code, the *Koki*, cites this passage from the Law for Monks and Nuns: "If visiting a bureaucrat, go in secular guise," which interprets the original protocol to mean, "When approaching the court, wear secular clothing. When returning to the temple, wear monastic robes."[20] A later commentary in the *Collected Commentaries on the Administrative Code* states, "Approaching in 'secular guise' means that one should use one's secular name since one is already in secular form." In other words, the commentator takes it for granted that those filing private lawsuits should wear secular clothes. Depending on their motives for utilizing travel routes, the qualifications of travelers differed. The point where one's status came into question was, needless to say, in the definition of one's obligations in the realm of *li*. When encountering officials of the third rank or higher, monks and nuns on the road were to retire from sight. When meeting those of the fifth rank or above on foot, they were to retreat. On horseback, they were to dismount and deferentially allow their superior to pass. However, when travel was for personal reasons and conducted as a layperson, the guidelines of the Law on Decorum applied. At such times, monks had to defer to all superiors, including those higher in position due merely to advanced age.

The fact that status ultimately was determined not by the position of the person traveling but rather by what was to occur at the destination consistently posed a problem with regard to status on travel routes. Clerics wore holy robes on travel routes when they approached bureaucrats on matters of religious duty; but on private business they dressed as laypeople. Status was thus determined not by a person's actual position in society but by the responsibilities carried out in official space. What is clear is that "travel routes" were connected to "official space."

However, in the preface of the Chinese *Proper Usages of the Great T'ang K'ai-yuan Era* (*Ta T'ang K'aiyuan li*), compiled between 713 and 742, stipulations concerning rites for private mausolea come before those concerning travel routes and local paths. Therein, travel routes were not treated as public space. Does this not mean that in China *li* was observed even in private matters; therefore "travel routes" and "local paths" linked both private and public spheres—that is, all of society? If so, differing conceptions of "travel routes" in Japan and China can be confirmed.

On the Japanese archipelago, court and highway merged on one plane, where *li* functioned. Highways were fashioned to demonstrate characteristics shared with other official spaces—they were to be built as straight as possible, their branches were to be ten meters wide, and their surfaces were often paved with pebbles. Provincial headquarters and district offices linked by official roads were sites of regular rituals and festivals while their official-looking architecture made them replications of miniature walled cities, like the palace in the Kinai capital (see Map 0.1).[21] The existence of "travel routes" as bridges over the spatial gulf from the center to the periphery, from court to provincial office, was indispensable.

The Circuit System and Post Stations on the San'yōdō

Japan's geopolitical cosmos—with its five-province hub in the capital region and its seven circuit highways—was modeled on T'ang China's ten-circuit system (see Map 6.1). It differed, however, in the circumstances of its creation. Japan's system was created as an extremely functional grouping of regions along official roads pointing outward from the Kinai metropole. In contrast to China, where a powerful polity built roads to link itself with neighboring states, Japanese roads radiated out from the Kinai in long and narrow routes to aggregate adjacent provinces into circuits and thereby constitute the *tennō*-centered realm.[22] This method of geosymbolic territorial aggregation was chosen for the convenience of central authorities, who were insensitive to the self-consciousness of various regions. It was a simple matter for them to view these circuits, each defined by its highway, as similar to the Kinai hub with which they were well acquainted. We have seen how the highways linked the central court and government offices in the provinces as unified space where a Japanese-style *li* operated. Since the nation was linked by the circuit highways, the *tennō*'s government was attempting to merge the entire archipelago into one geocultural entity wherein a single value system of Japanese *li* held sway.

Turning now to the functionality of official highways, I want to look at the relationship between highways and the government as expressed by the architecture of post stations on the roads. Official roads were inseparably tied to these post stations, and the role of the latter as architectural monuments provides additional evidence as to how courtly rulers regarded travel routes in *ritsuryō* times.

Glosses on the Law on Decorum and Government Procedures in the *Collected Commentaries on the Administrative Code* support the premise that post station houses were not considered official spaces. Like storehouses and kitchens, which were official facilities but not ritual spaces, post stations were considered facilities of convenience. We know this is so because the provision concerning officials stationed outside the capital as well as messengers in the Yōrō Code's Law on Official Leave (Kenyōryō) reads, "Upon receiving news of a relative's death, locally posted officials as well as messengers are permitted to remain in their official residences (*kansha*), but they must not grieve in the official spaces of the provincial headquarters or district office."[23] Mourning was prohibited in such buildings because inauspicious clothing—including that worn during mourning—was forbidden there. The characters used to express "residence" were those used for "mansion" (*teisha*) in the Taihō Code. And according to the *Koki* commentary on that code, *teisha* referred to a provincial governor's residence as well as post stations. Post stations, then, were different from "official buildings in the provinces." Like the residences in which governors resided, they were simply considered as shelters in which people could spend the night or reside for longer periods.

During the latter half of the seventh century tributary relations between Japan and Silla were strengthened. During the late 720s an ambassador from the Manchurian kingdom of Parhae had even visited the Japanese court. To further actualize the "mini-empire" conception of the island *ritsuryō* polity, and in the belief that the foreign guests could be encouraged to travel up the highway linking Kyūshū with the capital, post stations along the San'yō route were ordered beautified by the addition of "tile roofs and white-wall huts."[24] Ambassadors from Silla on the Korean Peninsula traditionally traveled by sea to the Japanese court, but in 806 fifty thousand sheaves of rice were allotted to improve post stations along the San'yōdō. Protocols emphasized that embassies were to be led by ship from the northern coast, where they arrived, to the Kyūshū headquarters at the Dazaifu. Then they were to proceed up the San'yōdō to the Nara capital. This circuitous route was most certainly designated to assure the visual effect of scenery along the highway. According to the royal edict of 806, the exteriors of the station houses were to be transformed solely in expectation of the appreciative gaze of foreign guests.[25]

Judging from stipulations in the *ritsuryō* codes, visitors from abroad were to stay in post stations while enroute to the capital. The Law on Official Communications and Practices orders, "Foreigners who surrender to the royal virtue shall be provided with official quarters. They must not come and go as they please."[26] The *Shu* commentary cited in the *Collected Commentaries on the Administrative Code* observed that "*banjin kika*" were foreigners, "whether ambassadors or naturalized people." So were ambassadors "foreigners"; and they were mandated by the *ritsuryō* to lodge at post stations, according to the *Koki* commentary for the Law on Official Leave.

The provision concerning mounts and pack horses in the Law on Stables and Pastures (Kyūbokuryō) indicates that providing for foreigners included "offering a place to spend the night." This is further proof that foreign ambassadors were to be domiciled at post stations. The sole aim of such kindness was to provide relief from the evening dew—there is no mention of banquets such as those held when new governors arrived in their bailiwicks to take over from their predecessors. The Law on Official Communications and Practices cited earlier insists that foreigners "must not come and go as they please," an interpretation supported by the *Shu* commentary. The intention here must have been to prevent interaction with provincial officials—indeed, the section concerning the Bureau for Alien and Buddhist Affairs (Gembaryō) in the early tenth-century *Engi shiki* forbids provincial officials from speaking to foreign guests on the road when the latter pass through the provinces.[27] It also forbids interviews between foreigners and provincial officials. The *tennō*-centered polity clearly disapproved of such mingling and tried its best to prevent it. We can thus conclude that post stations on the San'yōdō were not refurbished for the purpose of carrying out rituals in which diplomatic decorum was displayed toward foreign ambassadors.

However, the homes of bureaucrats of fifth rank and above, and those of wealthy commoners, were not improved only for the safe housing of foreigners. Even if foreign dignitaries did stay in these post stations, they were not really built for such a purpose. A hint comes from an earlier order of the eleventh month of 724. It commanded that, "Persons of the fifth rank or above and commoners who are able should erect homes with tile roofs and paint the walls red and white" in the capital. It continued, "The capital is the domicile of the *tennō,* the place of governance for all under Heaven. Without its splendor, what would express the virtue of the sovereign?"[28] In other words, to prepare for the advent of foreign emissaries, it was necessary to beautify the capital. Homes with tile roofs, white walls, and red pillars were deployed as objects displaying the capital's splendor. Refurbishing of these residences, then, was decreed to create an impressive image of the capital for foreigners. Traditional "huts of board and grass" were rejected in favor of more complex structures that were difficult to build and which collapsed easily. In making these, the Japanese government clearly tried to display Chinese-like architecture in an effort to amaze foreign visitors.

The reason for erecting the post stations and homes with tile roofs and white walls along the San'yōdō was to impress upon transiting foreigners that Japan had developed cultural standards competitive with those of the great T'ang Dynasty. Given such an objective, building interiors did not matter; nor were post stations of the San'yōdō judged for their functionality. Whatever would remain unseen by ambassadors could take any form, whether thatched or boarded. In that, these buildings resembled a movie set.

Unfortunately, however, it seems that these stage sets were hardly given a chance to serve their assigned purpose. Although the *ritsuryō* codes dictated that foreigners should use the land route from the Dazaifu to the capital, Hirano Takuji has concluded that Sillan embassies never ceased following the traditional water route through the Inland Sea; and visitors from Parhae arrived on the Japan Sea coast in the Northern Territories despite repeated requests that they utilitze the Dazaifu route. This explains why construction of an "official" guest house in Noto Province was urged in 804 as the court finally abandoned the idea of having ambassadors from Parhae travel along the San'yōdō. Sources confirm as well that T'ang ambassadors continued to sail the sea route to Naniwa. So, during the entire eighth century, not one embassy approached the capital by traveling up the San'yō highway.[29]

An important issue is why the *ritsuryō* government, once it finally succeeded in creating a tributary relationship with Parhae, put so much effort into preparing the San'yōdō for envoys. Ambassadors from Parhae were requested to enter the capital through the Dazaifu to make the headquarters into a diplomatic focal point. But why did the court attempt to make them travel along the land route instead of letting them take the traditional sea route from the Dazaifu up the Inland Sea?

Land Routes and Sea Routes

Before the *ritsuryō* polity conceived of a network of official roads, Japan, surrounded by the sea, had an efficient system of water travel that included boat transport in the Inland Sea.[30] According to the *Nihongi*, the legendary Yamato Takeru "killed the evil deities and opened up sea and land routes" when he subjugated the barbarian Kumaso people in the twenty-eighth year of the sovereign Keikō's reign.[31] The juxtaposition of "opening up water and land routes" and the subjugation process indicates that both sea travel and land travel were important for early state formation in the archipelago. Indeed, a *Man'yōshū* poem reads, "Under the heavens, roads in four directions extend as far as would wear out a horse's shoes or the prow of a boat."[32] The *Engi shiki* quotes a celebratory prayer offered at the harvest festival: "The nations of the four directions are . . . in the blue sea, punts and oars never dry. As far as a ship's helm can go, ships continue to fill up the great ocean. On the land routes, they tighten packing ropes and plod over rocks and tree roots until the horses' hooves wear out, continuing to travel the long road without rest." Such passages indicate that both water and land routes connected center and periphery under Yamato's rulers before the promulgation of the Chinese-style *ritsuryō* codes in the late seventh century.

Nonetheless, *ritsuryō* law emphasized land routes as the primary means of communication, and transport by land was the reason the post station system was initiated. As we have seen, the codes presupposed use of land routes by foreign envoys, even if Sillan and T'ang ambassadors entered the capital via sea.[33] Codal provisions mandating ambassadors to use land routes also occur in the Law on Miscellaneous Matters (Zōryō), in the Law on Military Defense (Gumbōryō), in the Law on Official Communications and Practices, in provisions concerning the utilization of oxcarts and manpower in the Law on Corvée (Buyakuryō), and in provisions concerning utensils such as pots and hoes in the Law on Decorum and Government Procedures. The refurbishing of post stations on the San'yō Road seems to have been an attempt to enforce this *ritsuryō* principle emphasizing land transport.

In this regard Katō Tomoyasu has noted that the provision concerning transport of tax goods in the Japanese Law on Taxes deletes stipulations for dispatch by cart and boat that are found in T'ang law. This does not mean that Japan's transport system by land and sea was deficient. Rather it means that tax goods were habitually sent via land and carried by porters paid by the taxpayers themselves.

Katō's observation on the forbidding of tax transport via third parties is an important one.[34] The government had several reasons for establishing the fundamental principle that taxpayers should take full responsibility for getting tax goods to the capital by land. First, there must have been fears that the safety of marine transport could not be ensured. If the arrival of tax goods in the capital was the economic foundation on which the polity rested, it was better to have taxpayers take responsibility for land transport rather than risk losing goods at sea. Moreover, in the case of transport by foot, arrival time in the capital could be more accurately predicted. We can conclude that the government mandated land transport in order to guarantee reliable deposits into the official storehouses.

An unanswered question still remains: Why did the government prohibit the use of carts for transporting tax goods to the capital? The reason is that commoners in the eighth century did not own carts, meaning that use of a cart would have necessitated third-party involvement. The prohibition was likely intended to provide peasants with direct experience in dispatching their tax goods to the capital. Indeed, transport of tax goods to the capital was, in principle, the duty of all commoner males. By carrying goods on their backs or on their horses, they bore the weight of the goods while actually experiencing the trip to the *tennō*'s capital. That experience, engraved in commoners' minds, would have strengthened their self-consciousness as subjects who owed tribute to the *tennō*'s government. Such self-consciousness evoked awareness of the government itself.

Following this same line of thought Matsubara Hironobu has suggested that the reason subjects were held responsible for transporting their own tax goods, however inefficiently, was that by such means the *tennō*'s subjects were made aware that they owed taxes to the *tennō*, not to provincial chieftains (*kuni no miyatsuko*). Matsubara has also observed that it was this transport system, centered around tax goods, which caused the synthesis and development of culture.[35] It seems incontrovertible that the dispatch of goods by land was a result of *ritsuryō* emphasis on the direct relationship between the government and its taxpaying subjects. Roads conjoined the *ritsuryō* government and its people rather than merely linking the center with regional localities. The route by which people could reach the capital by laboriously plodding over the entire distance was the land route. It is not difficult to conclude that the government was more interested in highlighting relations between itself and each subject—between the *tennō*'s government and regional cultivators—than in efficient dispatch of tax goods to the capital.

The road traveled was the mode by which people learned this new view of their world. The continuity of these highways as well as their construction by human hands made people conscious of the unity between capital and localities. Road porters and travelers took step after step along circuit highways heading more or less in a straight line to the capital. The roads led those who used them to acknowledge their irreducible ties to the *tennō*'s center as well as their inescapable fate as bearers of tribute. Only land routes could achieve such objectives—water routes obviously could not produce a concrete sense of continuity. The court's emphasis on land routes made the bonds unifying capital and provinces visible.

Official highways should be distinguished from footpaths used by the inhabitants of local communities or passing animals. The *History of the Wei Dynasty* observed the following about roads in Wa: "The roads are like wild animal trails," and "grass and trees grow abundantly; wherever one goes, one meets not a soul."[36] Lawmakers of the *tennō*-centered polity understood that man-made highways constructed by higher authority and removed from the daily life of the neighborhood helped to make the nature of the polity clearer by linking local communities to the capital.

The roads were first laid out and constructed for the purpose of unifying the land, just as the legendary four generals had been dispatched by Suijin Tennō to the four regions through which circuit roads would eventually pass—Hokuriku, Tōhoku, San'in, and San'yō.[37] Ultimately, of course, the government's regional governing and military control had the aim of enabling the exploitation of surplus goods by the center. The roads became visible reminders of the military and economic unity of the center and its provinces. The classical *tennō*-centered polity relied on the irrefutable reality of the highway that traversed the realm and bound center and periphery in unified space. Indeed, Aritomi Yukiko has pointed out that in the classical period temples in the provinces were scattered along official roads and main travel routes, at key nodes for communication with the Kinai.[38] Not only post stations but also the tile-roof temples that bordered them architectonically bore witness to the homogeneous culture of the Kinai and its network of highway circuits.

When the highways are seen in this light, the refurbishing of post stations makes excellent sense. For foreign ambassadors the sea route was more convenient and its use had been customary since ancient times. However, the San'yō Road was designated for envoys, and its post stations were to be restyled with sinicized architecture. The road from the Dazaifu in Kyūshū to the capital was viewed as the great highway symbolizing the *tennō*'s rule over the realm. Its very characteristics—straight, broad, far-reaching—replicated the virtues of the royal polity which it in turn helped to define.

As long as foreign ambassadors came by sea—an unadorned passageway that lacked architectural accoutrements—the dignity and affluence of the royal realm could not be displayed. That was why the *ritsuryō* court proclaimed the San'yō Road the official route by which foreigners were to approach the capital, even at considerable expense to the throne's coffers. The arrival of ambassadors by land, however, never became reality.

Conclusion

The unification of capital and countryside through the *ritsuryō* process meant the extension of central hierarchy and its values to localities throughout the realm. The road was a concrete object by which the *ritsuryō* center attempted to universalize itself. Using the highways to connect regional territories and provinces, rulers in the capitals at Nara or Heian expanded the enclosed space of the court to unite the center with its hinterland as a much broader public space—the official realm.

Some time ago, Ishimoda Shō urged us to study transport by reflecting on its economic, political, and intellectual aspects. What I hoped to emphasize in this essay, however, was that in considering the realm of the intellect, we must not be limited to the domains of literacy and law, or in other words, the movement of information and administrative technology. We must also examine the new worldview that took form out of a society newly connected by roads. Just as the identity of the officials of the archipelago as members of a single ethnic group was to be articulated by the wearing of standardized court robes, so did the concrete form of man-made highways and circuits evoke increasing consciousness of the unification of the archipelago.[39] The great official highways were not just physical surfaces linking center and regions. With its thoroughfares, the government connected a quantity of autarkic spaces into a single entity bound by a single system of values. Indispensable for this strategy was the network of official roads—the visually discernible sign of the man-made constructedness of the realm—which made the provinces acutely conscious of the existence of the *tennō*'s court.

Notes

1. Useful overviews include Takahashi Mikuni 1991, Kinoshita Ryō 1996, and Hirose Kazuo 1994. For new finds on the circuit highways see special issues of the journal *Kodai bunka* 47.4 (1995) and 49.8 (1997). On recent overviews of our understanding of the classical transportation system, see Tateno Kazumi 1998, and *Shigaku zasshi* 105.3 (1996).

2. Kishi Toshio was a specialist in classical history and taught at Kyoto University. For a short bibliography of his work, see Nihon rekishi gakkai 1999, 111-12.

3. Presently based at Kokugakuin University, the Society publishes an annual journal entitled *Kodai kōtsū kenkyū*, of which the first issue appeared in 1992. See also their new dictionary of historical roads, Kodai kōtsū kenkyū 2004.

4. For the original article see Takeda Sachiko 1989.

5. See Ishimoda Shō 1971.

6. Interpreter's note: The *Ryō no gige* is a commentary on the Yōrō Code (compiled about 718 and promulgated in the 750s) composed in 838 by Kakuda Imatari.

7. Interpreter's note: *Collected Commentaries on the Administrative Code* (*Ryō no shūge*) is a compilation of various commentaries on administrative law completed during the early Heian period, between 859 and 868. One of those commentaries was the *Anaki*. Takikawa Masajirō dates its compilation to the period from 797 to 812. Inoue Mitsusada thinks some parts were earlier in provenance and others later. An accessible text of the *Ryō no shūge* is in the Shintei zōhō kokushi taikei series of historical sources. For this citation see vol. 1, 95.

8. *Nihongi* 646 03/19. Interpreter's note: In English see Aston 1972, vol. 2, 225.

9. Interpreter's note: The *fudoki*—records of customs and topography, or gazetteers—were compiled after 713 by royal order. See chapter 4 in this volume.

10. See Takeda Sachiko 1984, 283–303.

11. Interpreter's note: Called the Heaven-receiving Gate (*Ch'engt'ien men*), it was the south central gate of the imperial palace.

12. Satake Akira 1988.

13. Takeda Sachiko 1984.

14. Interpreter's note: On this point see Wechsler 1985.

15. Ishimoda Shō 1971.

16. The *Wei chih*, the official history of the Wei Dynasty, was compiled before 297.

17. This comes from the *ritsuryō* Law on Decorum (Giseiryō). For this and all other references to the code, see the reconstructed Yōrō Code in Inoue Mitsusada et al. 1976.

18. Takeda Sachiko 1984, 57–98.

19. Interpreter's note: For a translation of the Law for Monks and Nuns, see Piggott 1987, 267–73.

20. Interpreter's note: The *Koki* commentary, citations from which appear in the *Collected Commentaries on the Administrative Code*, was probably compiled between 737 and 740. It seems to reflect usages closer to T'ang models, and may have been compiled by scholars who returned from the continent, some of whom were Korean.

21. Wada Atsumu 1985.

22. Takeda Sachiko 1988b.

23. See Inoue Mitsusada et al. 1976, 423.

24. Ishimoda Shō 1971 and Sakamoto Tarō 1928. The latter has been republished in volume 8 of Sakamoto Tarō's collected works (*chōsakushū*) by Yoshikawa kōbunkan. Interpreter's note: The San'yō Road ran inland from the coastline of the Inland Sea and traversed the provinces of Nagato, Suō, Aki, Bingo, Bitchū, Bizen, Mimasaka, and Harima.

25. Interpreter's note: This edict, dated 840 05/08, is recorded in the *Nihon kōki*, the third of the royal annals, which covers the years from 792 to 833.

26. Interpreter's note: See Inoue Mitsusada et al. 1976, 401–2.

27. Interpreter's note: The *Gemba shiki* is a section of the *Engi shiki* pertaining to the Gembaryō, or Bureau for Alien and Buddhist Affairs. The *Engi shiki* is a massive compilation of protocols compiled in 927.

28. *Shoku nihongi* 724 11/08. See Aoki Kazuo et al. 1989-, vol. 2, 157.

29. Hirano Takuji 1988.

30. See, for instance, Matsubara Hironobu 1985, esp. 15–49.

31. Using the dating system of the *Nihongi*, this event took place in the year 98 C.E. However, these early dates in the *Nihongi* are not considered reliable. Traditionally the epoch of Yamato Takeru's legendary exploits, by which the influence of Yamato was extended eastward and northward, are dated to the fourth and fifth centuries.

32. *Man'yōshū*, vol. 18, poem no. 4122. Interpreter's note: An accessible text of the *Man'yōshū* in Japanese is Kojima Noriyuki et al. 1971-75; in English see Nihon gakujutsu shinkōkai 1965.

33. Hirano Takuji 1988.

34. Katō Tomoyasu 1979.

35. Matsubara Hironobu 1985, 166–90.

36. Interpreter's note: For an English translation see Goodrich 1951, 8–16.

37. Interpreter's note: In chapter 3 of this volume, Hara Hidesaburō discusses aspects of the early history of sections of the Tōkaidō circuit, that is the region through which the highway passsed, in the provinces of Tōtōmi and Suruga.

38. Aritomi Yukiko 1989. Interpreter's note: For recent archaeological finds and analysis concerning roads in the classical epoch see Kimoto Masayasu 2000 and the annual issue of *Kodai kōtsū kenkyū* published by the Kodai kōtsū kenkyūkai.

39. See Takeda Sachiko 1988a.

7

Traffic between Capital and Countryside in *Ritsuryō* Japan

HOTATE MICHIHISA

Introduction by Janet R. Goodwin

THE JAPANESE TERM *kōtsū* has a wide range of meanings, from "traffic" in the narrow sense to "relations" in a broad sense. Perhaps we may say that Hotate Michihisa has made "traffic" between city and countryside a synecdoche for relations between the two in the *ritsuryō* age, roughly the eighth through the early tenth centuries. The article that follows shifts back and forth between *kōtsū* defined as traffic and as relations, demonstrating the close connections between them. Hotate demonstrates the ways in which traffic, exchange, and migration shifted the balance between center and periphery and altered the nature of both.

The underlying theme here is the expansion and decline of the relatively centralized polity in the classical *ritsuryō* age, the epoch in which Chinese-style institutions were adopted, an urban capital was established, and resources from across the archipelago were sucked into the hands of an elite living in the royal capital.[1] Conversely, however, it was also a period in which private interests in both city and countryside expanded their wealth and power at the eventual expense of the official system. The *ōchō*, or "court-centered," polity that followed, although still firmly based in the capital, rested in large part on patron-client ties with the provinces. The political formation that Hotate describes as a "despotic" system of tribute extraction eventually gave way to one of increasing interdependence between center and periphery.

Hotate's arguments take place within a Marxist analytical framework. The *ritsuryō* system is defined as an "Asiatic" social system characterized by a despotic central authority based in an urban capital surrounded by economically self-sufficient rural communities from which the center extracted wealth. At the center was an elite bloc with common interests; and the rest of the society, although organized hierarchically, lacked the complex stratification and occupational differentiation of later social class arrangements. The capital is characterized as a superstructural entity that lacked a permanent urban population other than those of the elite bloc. Use of the term "tribute" rather than "taxes" suggests a fiscal system wholly oriented toward the welfare of the center, rather than one that benefited the periphery at least in part. In addition, the tribute system is described as having religious and ideological underpinnings that glorified the center as it was enriched.

Hotate's task in this article is to demonstrate how the tribute system and other elements of the transportation network altered the *ritsuryō* polity and eventually led to its collapse. Throughout the article he is continually mindful of what replaced the old system: the historiographical question of the origin of medieval society underlies Hotate's analysis and helps to shape the questions he asks of his sources. Hotate does not define the term "medieval" in this article, but like other contemporaries in Japan he does not equate the medieval age with an age of warriors. Rather, he sees it as the age of complex relationships between center and periphery based on the estate (*shōen*) system and a social hierarchy centered around patron-client ties. Of particular importance in studying the process by which Japan became medieval, then, is the identification of "seeds" of later developments, such as the "lodgings, storehouses, day labor, an urban underclass, and special transportation privileges" that developed within the *ritsuryō* transport system.[2]

Hotate demonstrates how various elements of that transportation system initially supported the dominance of a central urban elite over the periphery. The goods extracted as tribute from the provinces were hauled to the capital by provincial commoners impressed into corvée service—they were even required to furnish their own provisions while they were on the road. Government officials at all levels supervised the tribute caravans and managed the storehouses where tribute goods were warehoused. Transportation activities, however, were not limited to those under official auspices; acting in more unofficial—that is to say, private—capacities, members and families of the elite bloc promoted commerce and exploited privileges derived from their public authority. Hotate also discusses public works projects—the development of highways and maritime transport systems that enabled goods to be transported more efficiently from countryside to city.

In Hotate's formulation, the *ritsuryō* polity was eventually undermined by its own mechanisms and its own elites' self-interest. We see how the tribute transport system was manipulated by officials, overseers, and even corvée porters. The system provided opportunities for some people to establish clientage ties with wealthy families in the capital and even to settle in the capital themselves, which contributed to the transformation of the city from a top-heavy political center into a complex urban society, and eventually into the nucleus of a distinct economic region. As private interests worked around a cumbersome official system, new forms of labor for hire began to replace the old conscript arrangement.

A related phenomenon detailed by Hotate was the split within the ruling elite itself. Some elites remained in the capital, where they became the courtiers and officials of the later court-centered polity. Others emigrated to the countryside, where they became provincial elites, undermining the old powerful families, the *uji*, that once had supported the *ritsuryō* system. In both cases Hotate excavates seeds of class stratification, which he considers to be the prerequisite for the development of medieval society.

The final section of the article treats the overt misuse of and resistance to the official transport system that contributed to the final breakdown of the *ritsuryō* polity. The process accelerated after the capital was moved to Kyoto at the end of the eighth century. The system was disrupted when private

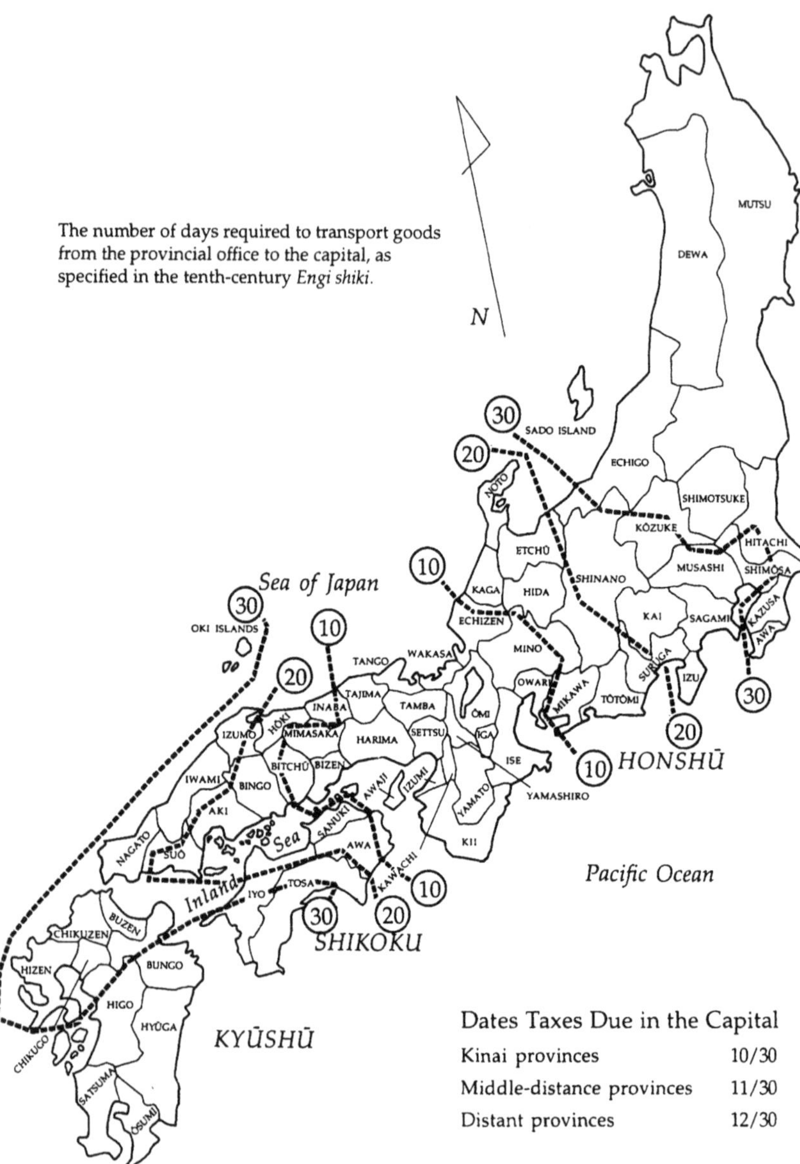

Map 7.1. Transport Days to the Capital

individuals appropriated transport facilities for their own use and plundered tribute caravans, often with the support of high-placed patrons. Rather than concentrating solely on the disruptive potential of such developments, however, Hotate sees them producing a new set of economic relationships between powerful households and their dependents. He also describes how popular resistance to corvée service, sometimes taking violent forms, contributed to the breakdown of the *ritsuryō* system.

Hotate bases his analysis in large part on legal sources, many of them derived from standard sources, such as the eighth-century court annal, the *Shoku nihongi*, and the tenth-century compendium of court protocol, the *Engi shiki* (*Protocols of the Engi Era*). His most frequently used source, however, is the *Ruijū sandai kyaku* (*Compendium of Legislation of Three Reigns*), a compilation of Council of State directives and royal decrees dating from the eighth through the early tenth centuries. This text demonstrates the way in which the legal system actually worked, including the extent to which laws were violated or manipulated. Although almost all materials from the period were compiled by authorities, Hotate has successfully mined them for evidence of popular activities. Rather than providing us with a top-down analysis of a failed experiment in adopting Chinese institutions, Hotate's article provides a dynamic view of complex relationships between center and province and the changes worked on both.[3]

HOTATE MICHIHISA

Traffic between Capital and Countryside in *Ritsuryō* Japan

Interpreted by Janet R. Goodwin and Gustav Heldt

In an influential account of relations between center and periphery in early classical (*ritsuryō*) society, Ishimoda Shō proposed that "under the *ritsuryō* system, links between city and countryside were effected by the organs of the polity that subordinated agricultural communities to the capital."[4] In addition to Ishimoda's work, there have been several other groundbreaking interpretations of such relations, focusing on such topics as the connection between the development of harbors and the management of estate storehouses, and the early post station system.[5] This essay expands on such work through research based on primary sources. How was the general populace affected by center-periphery relations, particularly by traffic and transportation between capital and countryside? The lives of people in the *ritsuryō* polity—which used a class-based system of control to accomplish the initial unification of the realm—were affected by the harsh conditions imposed by treks to the capital for delivering tribute demanded by the government. In this essay I reevaluate the historical nature of the *ritsuryō* system while examining two key issues: how did the polity extend its control to distant regions, and why did its considerable power begin to unravel after less than a century?

Transport of Tribute under the *Ritsuryō* System

Rulers of the *ritsuryō* polity—the sovereign, members of the royal family, and the court nobility—formed an elite bloc concentrated in the capital that cast a long shadow over provincial society. As the rulers proceeded to amass the realm's wealth, people set out from the provinces each tax season to deliver their tribute to the capital. Tribute goods (*chō*) and labor service (*yō*, usually commuted to payments in cloth) were due between the tenth and the twelfth month; and crop taxes (*so*) were due by the end of the eighth month (see Map 7.1).[6] The seasonal cycles of these tributary flows led to dramatic but regular shifts in the urban population as it expanded or contracted according to the flow of people bearing goods. The arteries that linked city and countryside pulsed according to this same rhythm, and the urban population had not yet crystallized into a permanent body. Thus the capital manifested characteristics of what has been termed an "Asiatic" social organization—it resembled a superstructure built atop the original economic structure of rural society.[7]

Most of the people who lived in the provinces had neither reason nor opportunity to travel to the capital except when mobilized for government labor service. Such journeys were full of hardship, and conscript workers might even have lacked the resources to return home. Some sustained themselves as dependents of powerful households, but if they fell ill they were abandoned in the street to beg, or starve.[8] One source refers to them as "tormented demons."[9] Other conscripts collapsed on the way home, their corpses abandoned by the roadside. We must consider the conditions that made it possible for the realm's wealth and labor power to be absorbed by the capital in such a manner.

It is commonly acknowledged that transport of tribute goods was accomplished through harsh corvée service. Conscripts worked in many capacities to deliver the tribute goods prescribed by the legal codes. The codes list the following conscript services: general corvée laborers, provincial regiment soldiers, palace guards, border guards, and laborers to repair ports, bridges, and roads.[10] Other categories of workers are found in ad hoc legislation dating from 822, which lists those exempted from corvée levies.[11] Many such workers provided "miscellaneous labor services deemed necessary by the central government."[12] They include aides to messengers to the court, tribute caravan overseers, laborers at post stations, stablemasters, overseers and porters transporting official goods, various types of runners, post station kitchen staff, and temporary laborers at post stations and stables. According to the *Koki* (*Ancient Records*) commentary on the Taihō Code cited in the Heian-period *Collected Commentaries on the Administrative Code* (*Ryō no shūge*), conscript workers were also required to repair government ships, build roads and bridges, and provide offerings of local products for the court.[13] In other words, the place of transport-related labor within the *ritsuryō* corvée system is large enough to merit a full-scale reevaluation. The sheer variety and quantity of such labor in and of itself attests to the vital role the system played in the circulation of tributary goods within the classical transportation network.

In general, conscripts furnished their own provisions while they were on the job,[14] essentially paying a surtax in addition to their labor. Labor service was a collective responsibility: designated "tribute households" (*yōchō no ie*) provided workers or their equivalent in provisions.[15] The communal nature of labor service is demonstrated in the use of such terms as "companion" and "older and younger brother" that were used to refer to one another by members of the same labor group.[16]

There were also religious dimensions to this corvée system. According to a commentary on the *ritsuryō* Giseiryō (Law on Decorum) regarding springtime village rituals for *kami* (deities) of the fields, "When the villagers commute to other provinces on public or private business, they must carry prayer-slips along with them" to present at shrines along the way.[17] A poem in the eighth-century *Man'yōshū* verifies this practice:

Within the courtyard
of the *kami* of Asuwa
do we offer branches;
I'll keep my sacred vows
until I return home.[18]

Prior research has outlined the role played by small village shrines on the margins of the *ritsuryō* religious system.[19] Local shrines performed a crucial ideological role in mobilizing villagers for labor service. One facet of this ideology was encouraging veneration for the ruler on the part of conscript laborers and soldiers, as expressed in many *Man'yōshū* poems such as this one, attributed to frontier guards from Kazusa:

For our Great Lord,
before whose will we tremble,
have we come here,
in longing for our loved ones
who clutched our garb at parting.[20]

Such were verses of praise that accompanied the goods and labor that commoners offered up to their ruler, the *tennō*. They give us a glimpse of the ideology that mobilized residents of far-flung provinces to labor on various projects for the realm, an ideology that is a special feature of this so-called tribute system.

The basic principles of *ritsuryō* society have been analyzed in various ways. In my view, the *ritsuryō* system was an advanced form of an Asiatic social structure in which the ruling class was composed of a despotic monarch, the royal family, and an aristocracy supported by ideological reinforcements such as those we have been discussing here. Members of the ruling bloc concentrated in the capital equated the polity with their own interests. With the force of government institutions and structures supporting them, they transformed existing relations between subordinate groups of people in the countryside and titular leaders at court into a set of hierarchical class relations that cut across regional identities.

The realm-wide organization of tribute labor, which brought the surplus value of provincial labor and products to the capital, occupied an important place within this new form of society.[21] This was accomplished by the administrative structures of the province, district, and township. For example, the provincial government carefully inspected goods under its jurisdiction prior to transport, and issued appropriate documents for shipment, as indicated in the *ritsuryō* Law on Granaries (Sōkoryō):

> Precise lists of the amount and kinds of tax goods and labor service payments to be sent to the capital must be drawn up for inspection. Provincial officials shall clearly record the details and hand documents over to the porters' overseers [*kōchō*], to be forwarded to the appropriate officials. These documents shall be called *kadobumi* [bills of lading]. Once recorded, the goods should all be sent to the capital.[22]

Names of overseers were appended to a single sheet listing those in charge of transporting the goods, while porters under their supervision were to be listed separately.[23] According to the Law on Barriers and Markets (Kanshiryō), similar registers were also prepared for inspection of goods at barrier stations along the road:

> When workmen, their supervisors, or porters carrying tax goods approach a barrier, they shall submit a document from their home province listing their names, and they will be permitted to pass the barrier along with supervising officials.[24]

Provincial headquarters also took charge of transporting provisions for laborers, which were carried in provincial cargo ships built especially for that purpose.[25] Lists of provisions were included in tribute records. Two laws recorded in the *Ruijū sandai kyaku* clearly indicate the ultimate responsibility of provincial officials for inspecting tribute shipments and preparing appropriate documents to be forwarded to the capital.[26]

District officials were also involved in the transport of tribute goods, as shown by a side note to the Law on Labor Taxes (Buyakuryō).[27] In fact, district chieftains (*gunji*) played an important role not only in the shipment of goods but also in their storage and the general management of storage facilities, including the purchase and sale of land for such purposes. For example, a bill of sale dated 756 indicates that land belonging to a "tribute warehouse" maintained in the capital by the Sagami provincial government was sold to officials of the Tōdaiji Construction Agency (*Zō-Tōdaijishi*), and it contains signatures for several proxies of officials from Sagami districts.[28]

This document raises two important issues. First, what were tribute warehouses? It seems that provincial governments maintained them in the capital as temporary storehouses for tax goods, gathering places for porters, and holding centers where some goods were sent off for sale at the eastern and western markets where items in short supply could be purchased.[29] Since the early tenth-century *Engi shiki* contains regulations concerning the management of tribute warehouses, such were probably standard facilities used by provincial authorities.[30]

Agents who collected tribute payments on the township level probably also had a role in transporting them to the capital. There is no clear historical material about township heads (*gōchō*) in this regard, but many organizations of lower officials from the second half of the eighth century include people involved in the transportation of tribute goods. For example, *Veritable Records of Three Reigns in Japan* (*Nihon sandai jitsuroku*) includes the story of an overseer (*fukuchō*) who accompanied district officials in charge of tribute to the capital: because delivery was not smoothly accomplished, he was denied provisions and starved to death.[31] Since the term *fuku* indicates a porterage function, the man was probably the overseer of porters carrying tribute.[32] An overseer who appears in *Miraculous Stories from Japan* (*Nihon ryōiki*) "unlawfully seized the goods of cultivators." The maritime equivalents of such overseers were *tsuchō* (harbor masters), one of whom is known to have conducted official business in a township of Harima Province.[33] By employing such officials, the *ritsuryō* government mobilized the entire administrative structure comprising provinces, districts, and townships to extract wealth and labor from the countryside and draw it to the capital.

However, relations between the capital and farming communities were not confined to the official framework of provincial, district, and township administration. Private commerce developed by the royal family, the nobility, central and provincial officials, and regional elites facilitated the division of labor and cohesion of social relationships between capital and countryside. In this regard, Ishimoda Shō argued that the *ritsuryō* system took shape by incorporating pre-existing household production units: private traffic within these organizations was subsumed by public traffic and received protection from the government.[34]

The activities of the royal family, the greatest property holders of all, provide a prime example of this process. Harvests from the sovereign's fields in the Kinai and elsewhere were transported as "offerings," using porters, post stations, and vessels supervised by provincial and district government transport chiefs.[35] Bearers were authorized to use horses to carry the goods to the palace in the capital.[36] In fact, it seems likely that the post station system was established to transport "exotic and flavorful products" as offerings from the provinces sent to the court via the system prior to 730.[37]

Later, new methods of transport were established. In 807 horses to be maintained at post stations along the San'yōdō and other highways were reduced by one-fifth, a policy enacted because sea routes were being utilized.[38] By the early tenth century, 197 seafarers were serving on vessels sailing from the

Dazaifu, the government's headquarters in northern Kyūshū, and they were being supported by tribute from 396 residence units.[39] Such vessels transported silk, cotton, and other tribute offerings and received special treatment per the following stipulation: "When ships from Dazaifu bearing official tribute pass by, officials in maritime provinces shall inform them of navigable channels and places to harbor."[40]

The royal family and aristocratic families also dispatched retainers and slaves to trade goods and engage in rice-seed lending (*suiko*). Although such retainers were forbidden to set up stalls at markets, the Yōrō Code states, "It is not forbidden for them to engage in lending of rice seedlings at the market or to send representatives far afield to conduct trade."[41] However, only those of the fifth rank and above—the court nobility—were authorized to operate private transport in the Hōyo Strait, at the southwestern entrance to the Inland Sea (see Map 6.1, p. 148). For instance, a communiqué from the Dazaifu dated 716 reads: "Distinctions between high and low, noble and base, must be made without fail. It should not be prohibited for those of the fifth rank and above to send retainers back and forth."[42] According to tribute records from Tajima, moreover, provincial government authorities furnished provisions for "a collector of rice for the Queen-consort's Agency."[43] Thus, the functionaries of royal and noble households received special support from the government.

Moreover, according to legislation promulgated in 748, authorities at the provincial headquarters were to take charge of the transport of tax goods from all prebendal residential units (*fuko*), and provisions for bearers were to be taken from tax stores.[44] Aristocratic establishments also received special transportation privileges. For example, provincial authority was required to guarantee that shipments from the fields and gardens of the Fujiwara family academy, the Kangakuin, and the rents and trade profits of the Kokusōin emergency stores were forwarded to their proper destinations.[45] Such special aristocratic prerogatives in the area of transportation were probably established quite early. In sum, various establishments beyond those provided for in the *ritsuryō* codes received privileges related to transportation from an early date.

It is important to note that royal and noble households participated in the transportation system under the cloak of public authority. A passage in the *Kojiki* preface, completed around 712, expresses in idealized fashion the monarch's supreme rights over the transportation network: "Ruling in the Purple Pavilion, [Gemmei Tennō's] virtue extends as far as do horses' hoof-prints. Dwelling in the concealed palace, her influence illumines as far as our ships sail."[46]

Royal and noble households also expanded their productivity by incorporating dependents from various strata in the provinces. Two passages from the eighth-century court annal, the *Shoku nihongi*, indicate the way in which cultivators shifting their residence or, seeking to avoid tax obligations, joined powerful households as low-ranking official staffers (*shijin*):

> Cultivators flee to the four corners of the realm, avoid taxes and labor service, and become dependents of princely and ministerial households.

> There are those who hope to become someone's personal retainer, while others seek to enter Buddhist orders.
>
> Many cultivators in the realm abandon their official place of residence and wander as they please, avoiding taxes and labor service. Those drifters who lodge in a [new] place for more than three months will thereby be considered to have settled there and will be subject to taxes and corvée labor according to the regulations of that province.[47]

The government recognized two categories of itinerants: drifters who went back and forth from one province to another, but who continued to pay all their taxes; and out-and-out absconders, who fled to another province to avoid taxes altogether.[48] According to the second of the two passages above, regulations for leaving one's province stipulated that someone who had settled in a new province for three months was considered a permanent resident and should be eliminated from the original local family register.[49] Later, however, this regulation was criticized as being too strict, and it seems that people continued to travel back and forth between their original domiciles and places where they had made new homes with the aid of patrons. For example, there were people from Mutsu and Dewa Provinces "hired as dependents of princely or aristocratic households [who] moved to the capital" but who also returned home periodically.[50] A *Shoku nihongi* entry dated 780 indicates that even the wishes of drifters themselves were considered when deciding where to register them as residents.[51] Such evidence suggests the ways in which the "unofficial" activities of royal and noble households influenced the lives of drifters.

Provincial governors and lesser provincial officials also contributed to the development of unofficial traffic between capital and countryside. Yoshida Takashi has noted the brisk trade carried out by lower-ranking Tōdaiji officials.[52] Legislation dated 736 stipulates, "There is no ban on provincial governors conducting trade and transporting goods within their jurisdictions."[53] Using evidence such as this, Sawada Goichi and Sakaehara Towao have demonstrated that provincial governors, as well as princely and noble households, were involved in private trade activities.[54] It is clear that the power base of government officials was often rooted in forms of unofficial commercial intercourse that was beyond the purview of *ritsuryō* legal structures.

Kinship groups based in the provinces also developed forms of center-periphery traffic under their own control. Under the *ritsuryō* system, kin groups with royal titles, known as *uji*, began to fissure into powerful federations of patriarchal families. Despite the acceleration of this trend, the *uji* did not completely lose their earlier functions.[55] Hereditary titles (*kabane*) that the throne awarded to *uji* leaders incorporated them into a hierarchical ruler-subject relationship. As Ishimoda Shō noted, "The economic and kinship relations that linked the nobility to the local elite in fact joined them together in a system external to the polity."[56] Members of the *uji* served the central political structure in both official and unofficial (and therefore private) capacities: as district officials in provincial government and as attendants (*toneri*) at princely and noble houses. From the viewpoint of *uji* members, however, they were subject to the same authority in either case. For instance, heirs of powerful regional families came to the capital as palace retainers or university students, while lesser members of the same kin might pursue careers as princes' retainers or government clerks. Personnel sometimes moved from the center back to the provinces: those who served with merit might return to their townships as district officials, while former palace guardsmen might become lieutenants in provincial military units.[57]

In addition to this "transfer route" connecting the center and the provinces, local priests who traveled back and forth to the capital to perform religious duties under the auspices of the government's system of official shrines also created important linkages.[58] For instance, *uji* ritualists went to the capital every year to receive prayer slips from the Council of Deity Affairs. These were later offered up at local shrines, for example, at the spring and autumn festivals of the Ono *uji* deity (*ujigami*) in Ōmi Province's Shiga District.[59] As late as the end of the ninth century, *uji* members who had moved to the capital still maintained their religious bonds with their kin's native places and were welcomed back home at ancestral rites during the second, fourth, and eleventh months.[60]

While provincial residents' involvement in relations between city and countryside was shaped by the hierarchical relationship between court and regional *uji*, we can also discern complex developments beyond that framework. Indeed it is probable that one function of the district government proxies at the Sagami Province tribute warehouse mentioned earlier was to maintain the role of their kin in the official tribute transportation system. Furthermore, as Sakaehara Towao has demonstrated, powerful provincial clans often entrusted dependents with local products to sell in the capital.[61]

Even corvée laborers and porters were involved in such commercial activities. When they arrived in the capital as members of tribute caravans, such workers bargained for goods to take home or to use along the road. Eighth-century sources provide glimpses of their activities. A *Nihongi* entry from the third month of 646 (Taika 2) notes:

> There are cases in which cultivators on their way to the capital fear that their horses will become too worn out to continue. They pay men from Mikawa or Owari a couple of lengths of cloth or a couple of bundles of hemp to care for the horses. On their return from the capital they add a spade in payment, [but then find that the horses have not been fed properly and have starved to death].[62]

A *Shoku nihongi* entry of 714 tells of cloth peddlers who crossed the three barriers along their journey to the capital.[63] The *Nihongi* passage quoted above suggests that these "peddlers" may have been cultivators from the eastern provinces on corvée service who traveled to the capital carrying cloth and hemp to exchange for spade tips that they carried back home. Cloth and hemp were means of payment for those who cared for the cultivators' horses along the way—actually, the cultivators used such goods to trade for the iron goods such as spades needed for use in land reclamation projects in the eastern provinces. In Sawada Goichi's words, "It would be hard to imagine that these healthy young men would return home empty-handed."[64]

Establishment of a unified realm thus entailed opportunities for unofficial traffic between city and countryside involving a variety of groups and social strata to develop on an unprecedented scale. As long as this functioned as a mechanism for ensuring the dominance of the *ritsuryō* system, the cyclical flows of tributary traffic were reproduced exponentially.

Public works projects provided another form of support for the unified polity's tribute transportation system, while also stimulating class stratification.[65] Such projects could not be accomplished through private efforts; they required the overwhelming power of the *ritsuryō tennō*-centered infrastructure. While such projects certainly supported the tribute traffic system, they also produced the opportunities for the sorts of private exchange discussed above.

Government highways radiated outward from the capital to headquarters and offices in the country's provinces and districts. Constructing these highways, an enterprise that included the establishment of post stations and barrier gates as well as the provincial and district government offices themselves, was an important facet of the public works program and involved numerous carpenters and specialists from across the archipelago. We hear, for example, of a construction specialist, Ihokibe Aramasa, who worked on the Kiso Road, a segment of the Tōsandō; and of workmen who were sent to drain flooded roads in Owari Province.[66] Under these technicians labored even greater numbers of government-drafted workers. The annual upkeep and repair of this transportation infrastructure was carried out by menial laborers forced into service by provincial government officials.[67] While the care of horses at relay stations severely burdened laborers drafted from households designated to support the post station system, it also expanded the use of horses in rural society. We know that by 756 many powerful cultivators had begun to supply horses for transportation in lieu of payment of the rice tax.[68]

Meanwhile, a full-fledged maritime transportation system was being inaugurated. In 684 many government tribute vessels set anchor in the harbors of Tosa Province.[69] References to shipwrights, sailors, and levies for shipbuilding appear frequently in both the *Nihongi* and the *Shoku nihongi*. From Lord Kawabe, who built ships from timbers blessed by the deity of lightning, to the famed carpenter Arata Ihirafu, who dug out the Horie Canal in Naniwa, these pioneering engineers and builders labored on the court's behalf in a variety of forms that rivaled those of their inland counterparts.[70] Such infrastructural projects were the primary engine behind the development of realm-wide occupational specialization in the field of transportation.

The far-flung network of roads and shipping routes gave rise to another aspect of economic development as well, namely establishment of currencies of exchange. The passage cited above about corvée laborer-cultivators bartering for spade tips in the capital makes it clear that hemp and cloth functioned in that way. And a record from 712 notes that the rate of exchange between cloth and coinage was set by the central government to establish a basis for the use of cloth to pay expenses along the road.[71] The government announced a plan to reward those who turned in hoarded coins with promotions in rank, probably to assure the availability of coins for use by tribute caravan porters. Consider the following account:

> Porters endure long ordeals while on the road. If they carry enough provisions for the journey, they will not be able to bear all their tribute goods. But if we lighten their burdens [by reducing their provisions], we fear that many will die of starvation. To help with expenses, porters should each carry a sack of coins as well as a fire-making stick; and they should be provided with what they need for the return trip. Also, let provincial and district officials organize local wealthy households to see that rice stores are placed along the road.[72]

Moreover, *Ruijū sandai kyaku* records that people who lived along the road sometimes loaned money to "strangers," perhaps including porters.[73] For the tribute system which supported the *ritsuryō tennō*-centered government to work, porters had to be able to exchange goods and obtain lodging along the road.

The establishment of these land and maritime transportation networks qualitatively changed the nature of relations between travelers and the rural dwellers whose hamlets they passed by. In one account dating from 646 we see that travel at that time was still mired in a variety of communal taboos involving everything from dealing with corpses to borrowing cooking implements.[74] When taboos were violated, the travelers were held responsible for purification rites, which led to the abandonment of fallen comrades:

> By the paddy-fields were people bearing their official burdens. When they had finished their duties and set out for home, they suddenly fell prey to illness and many fell dead by the road. Whereupon those who lived by the road said, "Why are there so many dead bodies lying along the road? The cause must lie with their comrades—a ritual cleansing must be carried out." Although there were "elder brother" overseers who had died, their "younger brother" followers did not gather them up. There were also many farmers who drowned in the river. Those encountering their corpses said, "Why are we encountering so many drowned bodies here? The cause must lie with their comrades—a ritual cleansing must be carried out." And so they made the comrades of the dead carry out a purifying rite. Even though there were "elder brothers" among the drowned, the bulk of their "younger brothers" did nothing on their behalf. There were still other corvée laborers who cooked their rice by the road. Whereupon those with houses along the road said, "Why are there so many corvée laborers cooking their rice by the road—a ritual cleansing must be carried out." There were still other farmers who lent out steamers to cook rice. But when their steamers touched other objects they were overturned, and the owners forced the users to carry out a purification

> rite. [The countryside] is awash with such foolish practices. They have now been dispensed with and should not be allowed to revive![75]

This account reflects the culture gap between local communities that made tribute payments or lived along the tribute caravan route and the porters who often came from elsewhere bearing tribute to the capital. The government hoped to ban the "foolish practices" of the former to enable its authority.

As the centralizing authority struggled to form a unified polity, legends of the pacification of "raging deities" may reflect clashes with such communal taboos. Provincial foes of authority are described by such formulas as "[It] spit poisonous vapors, bringing agony to travelers."[76] Other legends hint at actual conditions, such as the tale of Ayashi Omaro of Harima Province, who "was powerful and ferocious. He wantonly committed violent acts such as robbing travelers along the highway and obstructing the passage of messengers. He also detained and plundered merchant ships, violating every law of the province, and he refused to pay taxes or render labor service." When the monarch Yūryaku's soldiers torched his house, Ayashi transformed himself into a white dog.[77] Tales such as this suggest the ways in which provincial *uji*, personified in the first passage as "raging deities," resisted the extension of central authority. They also suggest that military pacification of such groups was an important precondition for realm-wide expansion of the transportation network.

Another legend recalls successful imposition of royal authority on provincial transportation systems. According to the *Harima fudoki*, when the monarch Keikō went out incognito to seek a wife, the ferryman at Takase crossing in Settsu Province asked him, "Are you in the ruler's service or not?" Since Keikō was trying to hide his status, he could not answer and had to pay the boat fare.[78] In other words, ferrymen held sway at ports and fords and demanded fares for crossing, but they routinely submitted to the ruler's authority and gave his retainers free passage.

In sum, our picture of relations between capital and countryside under the *ritsuryō* system includes both the administrative powers of the central government, based on the mass mobilization of corvée labor, and the unofficial networks of trade and commerce linking the ruling classes of the capital and the provinces. The social conditions for this arrangement were in part structured by public works projects in the transportation field. Under *ritsuryō* governance, relations between the center and the regions developed rapidly and enabled an exponential expansion of *ritsuryō* control of the realm. At the same time, however, this process intensified contradictions inherent to the *ritsuryō* transportation system.

Relations between City and Countryside and Social Specialization

According to Ishimoda Shō, "The formation of centralized authority took as its premise the lack of class stratification in the provinces. Increasing stratification in peripheral areas could not help but challenge central control."[79] Ishimoda correctly pointed out the problem: when the corporate body of central elites used the tribute system to facilitate their control of the provinces, the resulting relations of exchange gave rise to social stratification in those various provinces. In this section I examine three aspects of this problem: (1) conditions along major trade routes; (2) the role of provincial residents in developing links between center and provinces; and (3) conditions in the vicinity of the capital.

Their expansion stimulated by public works projects, highways were soon crowded with envoys of noble families, porters and packhorse drivers, peddlers, and provincial inhabitants, all participants in the transport system. Here I examine their activities along three of the great circuit highways, the Tōkaidō, San'yōdō, and Saikaidō (see Map 6.1).

The Tōkaidō route connecting the capital with Pacific coast provinces to the east was transformed by the transportation activities of various groups. The latter included the Kōyō band[80] and "envoys of powerful nobles"[81] who traded in horses from the northern frontier as well as captives to be sold as slaves. There were also "bands of traveling peddlers," who would pass through the Shirakawa and Kikuta barriers, having bought special products from Mutsu originally destined for government use,[82] and packhorse drivers who contracted to transport weapons between the Tōkaidō and the Tōsandō regions.[83] Such bands (*tō*) were often unruly and threatened travelers. One revealing account tells of Kudaranokonishiki Keichū, a former governor of Musashi, who returned to the capital in 841 after completing his term. According to his obituary, when he reached a ferry crossing, a rogue leading such a band approached the boat anchorage, drove off bystanders, and took possession of the boat, although the governor tried to defend himself with a whip.[84]

Facilities such as pontoon bridges, ferries, and emergency lodgings were to be established at river crossings along the Tōkaidō in the provinces of Owari, Mino, Mikawa, Tōtōmi, Suruga, Sagami, Shimōsa, and Musashi, according to a Council of State directive dated 835.[85] These facilities were set up to accommodate tribute porters, who sometimes were stranded for many days and quarreled among themselves. From the viewpoint of *ritsuryō* officials, these were probably mere scuffles among coarse and witless corvée laborers, but many of the fights seem to have been provoked by "crafty rogues" such as packhorse drivers. The deficiency of the transport infrastructure along the Tōkaidō from the early half of the ninth century led to the regular outbreak of such conflicts, and eventually prompted construction of many facilities at river fords and ports.[86] There gathered day laborers who worked in transportation, such as the "harbor folk" who operated small craft at Umazu station on the eastern bank of the Sunomata River in Owari (see Map 6.1), or those who unloaded cargo at Kusatsu crossing in the same province.[87]

The development of estates (*shōen*) along the Tōkaidō enabled the activities of specialized transportation networks and contributed substantially to development of the transport system. For example, estates in Kazusa Province were managed by the family of the former assistant provincial governor, Fujiwara Yoshinao, who settled in Kazusa after his retirement. These holdings, known as Mohara no shō and Tashiro no shō, were typical of early estates in the eastern provinces. Tashiro comprised thirty *chō* of newly opened land, part in Nakara District in the eastern part of the province and part in Amaha District in the west.[88] The Amaha sector was located near the sea crossing at Miura Peninsula, which linked Kazusa to the Tōkaidō, and it had a post station nearby.[89] While both estates were located mainly in Nakara District,[90] the Amaha holding served as harbor for both properties and included warehouse facilities for harvests bound for the capital. As a route that linked capital and periphery, the Tōkaidō included such relay stations that directly connected estates like Tashiro and Mohara to the capital.

The Tōkaidō region witnessed development of maritime routes as well. According to the *Engi shiki,* sea routes developed between Ise and Owari Provinces and between Tōtōmi and Suruga.[91] Another source mentions that 10,000 *koku* of grain was "rowed" from Sagami, Musashi, Awa, Kazusa, and Shimōsa to military outposts in Mutsu Province.[92] Thus there were probably sea routes between Mutsu and the harbor at the mouth of the Naka River in present day Ibaraki Prefecture (see Map 6.1).

A tally of references to barrier checkpoints on the San'yōdō and Saikaidō circuit highways reveals considerable activity, such as that of traders who led thousands of horses from Kyūshū through the Nagato barrier every year,[93] and the royal tribute envoys from the Dazaifu who made use of public post stations to ship private goods.[94] Maritime traffic on the Inland Sea is especially worthy of note. As mentioned earlier, by 716 envoys of noble families of the fifth rank and above were traversing the Hōyo Strait.[95] And in 746 "bands of officials, cultivators, and itinerant peddlers" were shipping provincial specialties to Naniwa from harbors in Buzen and Bungo Provinces.[96] The following passage indicates the variety of such traffic up to the turn of the tenth century, and some of the problems that ensued: "Ships belonging to royal and noble families, as well as merchant ships, are permitted to enter and sail from the Dazaifu. However, their staff must not cause commotion among laborers and cultivators, auction rice, or buy horses."[97] In addition to such improper activities by merchant seamen, district officials sometimes took advantage of their jurisdiction over tribute shipments to purloin some of the cargo and sell it for their own profit.[98]

We catch glimpses how maritime traffic was organized by reviewing the types of passes issued to transport workers' groups. For example, in 844 some three thousand fishermen reportedly massed on the beaches of Awaji Province, bearing passes from royal and noble households.[99] Far from being simple fisherfolk, these people seem to have been acting as household retainers for the aristocracy in Awaji Province. They gathered to make sure that Awaji would continue to be used as a stopover on the way to the main government port at Naniwa, thus guaranteeing the continued importance of the island as a focal point for Inland Sea traffic. Like officials from the Office of the Royal Table (Naizenshi) and others from the royal household who traveled throughout Ōmi Province, these fishermen wore pennant-like badges at their waists that authorized them to carry out their business.[100] No doubt these badges functioned as a sort of pass (*kasho*) issued by royal and aristocratic households to their porters.

Such barrier passes appear in other guises as well. In 796 the Dazaifu proposed an increase in restrictions governing maritime routes: ships without permits from both the Dazaifu and Buzen provincial officials were to be boarded and penalized at Naniwa, their final destination. But the Council of State rejected this idea and instead decided to allow "government or private vessels" with only a pass from the Dazaifu to proceed freely to Naniwa from Kyūshū ports.[101] In 823, moreover, the Council of State abolished Dazaifu's official ships and the properties that produced food for the royal table, as well as the levies on certain households formerly used to support these operations. Instead, the government used stores of tribute rice to charter private ships that carried silk floss and other tribute goods.[102] The chartered ships were to accommodate between 250 and 300 *koku* of goods, indicating that the private mariners' organizations operating them had enough manpower to propel large vessels.[103] They must have included seafolk from wealthy local families.

At the same time that such powerful mariners' groups were forming, impoverished "boatmen for hire" began to crowd Inland Sea ports.[104] These groups neither farmed nor engaged in commerce—they lived solely by hiring out their labor. It is difficult to imagine how over three thousand people might be involved in maritime commerce in a single province such as Awaji without the participation of these laborers. Such seafarers may have joined the pirate gangs that inspired the government to set up spies who exposed "hidden crimes" in return for a bounty along main highways and in commercial ports "full of unruly crowds."[105] The need for such measures suggests the extent to which pirate bands had already organized themselves and expanded their activities even in the eighth century.

Port facilities such as market towns and highways where hired laborers gathered began to spring up all along the Inland Sea. For example, by 845—the year after the incident in which the Awaji seafolk gathered—cargo vessels and ferries began to ply the waters between Akashihama in Harima Province and Iwayahama in Awaji (see Map 6.1). This latter was the locus of activity for sailors called "Iwayabune" some centuries later. In sum, bases for seafaring commerce of diverse types were set up at various locations during the *ritsuryō* age.

As the above evidence suggests, the Tōkaidō, San'yōdō, and Saikaidō circuits all witnessed the formation of lively interprovincial traffic supported by a substantial concentration of both hired labor and transport facilities at the various stopover points along the major routes. Such facilities also foreshadow inns for medieval travelers that developed as the post station system evolved, including lodgings near government storehouses at the Dazaifu and the inn in Aki Province where a local farmer furnished provisions for travelers who had lost their baggage in the wind and rain.[106]

What was the "commercial geography" of goods transported along these routes? An abbreviated list would include rice and silk floss from Kyūshū; agricultural byproducts and handicraft items such as cloth and dyes from the eastern provinces; seafood and salt from the Inland Sea; marine products such as pearls from Tsushima and sea-mammal hides from Watarishima in present-day Hokkaidō;[107] livestock such as wild horses and riding horses from Mutsu, Dewa, and Kyūshū; minerals such as gold dust from the far north; imported goods from T'ang China and elsewhere; and finally, human beings captured in war or otherwise taken as slaves.

Goods were exchanged all over the archipelago. For example, wild horses were acquired from the Emishi of northern Japan in exchange for cloth and iron, and the latter was then used to make farming tools.[108] If we include those trade items listed in the *Engi shiki* stipulations for market officials, the array of goods in the transport system proves even more diverse. Similar items appear in the mid-eleventh century *Shinsarugakuki* as goods bought and sold by a "merchant prince." Most likely these were finished goods and regional specialties introduced to markets in the capital as tribute goods from the provinces. Their appearance in the *Shinsarugakuki* suggests that the active trade in specialty products in the *ritsuryō* age contained seeds of the far-flung exchange of such items that later characterized medieval commerce.[109]

Previous research has established that wealthy local elites (*fugō no tomogara*) of the *ritsuryō* period—whose land reclamation projects foreshadowed similar projects in the medieval age—accumulated considerable wealth in movable goods.[110] The specialties mentioned above played a role in this process, reflecting the flourishing of regional society throughout the archipelago. Local elites prompted the development of spheres of regional trade and production that introduced local specialties to the trade routes.[111]

As shipping centers grew up along highways and maritime routes, transportation activities came to depend on movable goods and means of transportation—oxen and horses—possessed by local elites. These same elites made conspicuous efforts to open new roads, as noted in the official court histories.[112] Local residents of various strata were also involved in the salt production industry that flourished in the Inland Sea region. We know, for example, that even harbor masters and laborers from neighboring districts and provinces held some property rights in mountain lands where one could find the special timber used to make salt kilns, indicating the widespread sphere of production related to the salt industry along the Inland Sea.[113] In the neighboring province of Sanuki, local residents often protested to port officials against pursuit of excess profits by wealthy salt dealers.[114] And in Bizen as well, wealthy local families are known to have engaged in salt making.

Local elites traveled between the capital and the countryside using regional trading spheres and production of local specialties as their foothold in commercial activities. Thus they were liberated from the transportation network dominated by the old *uji* system, a process that led to the eventual destruction of *uji* relationships. The first issue to consider in this regard is the way kinship ties between people of the capital and those in the provinces were formed outside the old *uji* structure. When elites from the capital embarked on tours of duty in provincial government, they sometimes married locally or settled permanently in the countryside. One example was Sagami no Sukune Nimaro,

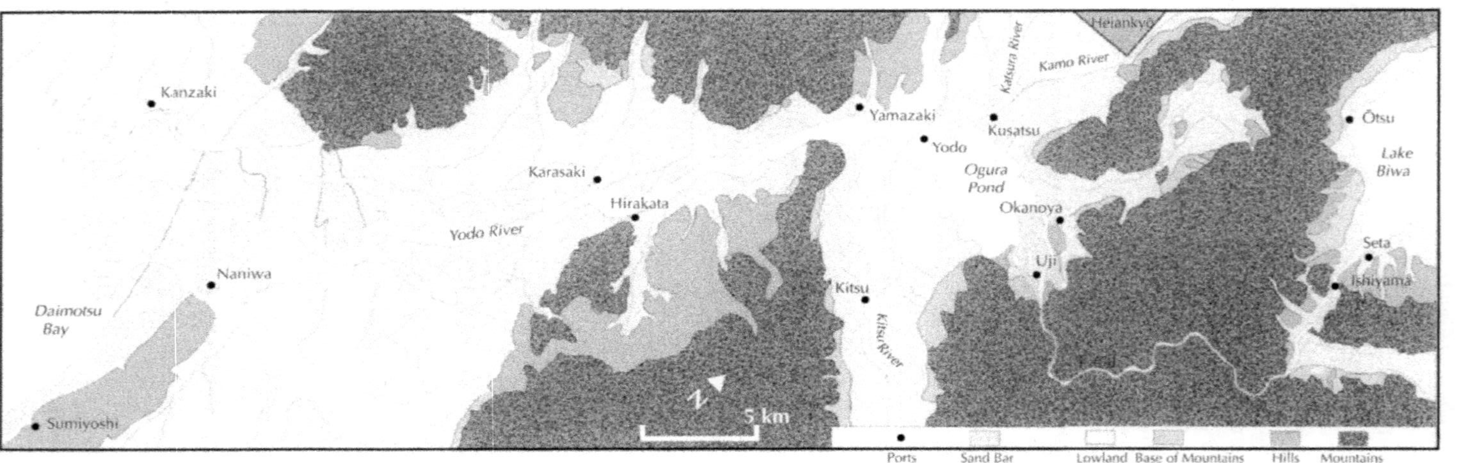

Map 7.2. The Yodo River Basin

originally from Yamato Province, who was appointed to the post of senior fourth-level (*sakan*) governor of Kawachi Province in 814. Taking up residence in Kawachi, he married a local woman, and the couple had many children and grandchildren. In 885, one of his descendants asked "to be removed from the official census registers of his original province and registered in [Kawachi] Province."[115] Another example involves Mohara no shō in Kazusa. As mentioned earlier, the estate was managed by the descendants of a former governor who had settled in the province. One of them, Fujiwara Harutsugu, posted in Hitachi as second-level governor (*suke*), married the daughter of a fourth-level governor in that province, and later returned to Mohara.[116] And in 891 a Council of State directive complained that scions of royal and noble families from the capital were settling in the provinces, marrying local women, and even pursuing farming or a trade in their new homes, working alongside local people.[117]

Kinship relations were sometimes interrupted when people illegally moved to the capital, "hiding in shadows" by using assumed names, and falsely enrolling in another household's register:

> One hears that people from other provinces unlawfully settle in or near the capital, many shirking their tax obligations and neglecting their own province. The minister of the right received a royal order that such was to be firmly forbidden, in accord with an order of the Enryaku era [782–805]. However, if some have had themselves illegally entered into a household register and still remain there, *uji* chieftains shall investigate, add their signatures, and inform the authorities.[118]

Another directive some decades later noted: "In recent years cultivators from other provinces bribe petty officials and then infiltrate the capital or its environs, or bribe household heads and assume false family names."[119]

Another result of the dramatic increase in traffic between capital and countryside was the weakening of religious ties that previously bound *uji* members together. In 958 a man named Kageko Tachibana Motozane, scion of a high-ranking family, donated to Tōdaiji the timber from his clan's ancestral graveyard, presumably protected by the *uji* deity.[120] His reason for doing so, he said, was that various calamities resulting from his refusal to allow Tōdaiji to cut the timber in the Engi era (901–922) had forced him and his family to drift off to other provinces. In reality, however, before making the donation he had already sold a portion of the cemetery plot and had used the proceeds for his travels. This suggests the weakening of his religious ties to his *uji* deity and the site of the family graves.

In fact during the ninth century the entire *ritsuryō* shrine system began to unravel in various ways. Officials and priests increasingly performed shrine rituals and duties not for religious reasons but rather to advance their personal status. For instance, a provincial official would claim that miracles had taken place at a shrine in his province and ask for a promotion of the shrine's official rank. Since sometimes this resulted in a conferral of the third rank or above, provincial functionaries competed for posts as shrine priests, aiming to secure special exemptions from duties imposed on them by the provincial office.[121] In this manner the status of shrine priest was strategically deployed by powerful members of local society to gain secular privileges that ultimately undermined government authority.

Officially appointed priests were supposed to travel to the capital each year to obtain prayer slips from the Council of Deity Affairs to offer up at their shrines, but there were complaints that often "they did not perform this duty, or hired proxies to substitute for them rather than going themselves."[122] There is even a story of a shrine official who, after solemnly receiving prayer slips in the capital and tucking them into his robe, threw away the ceremonial halberds, keeping only their blades; and then after a drunken spree, sold off the shrine's horse at the marketplace.[123] Such behavior was symptomatic of a widespread breakdown in the cyclical system of priests' annual journeys to the capital, a ritual that symbolized *uji* subservience to central government authority.

Through grants of noble titles, the central *ritsuryō* authorities had once used the *uji* organization as a means to dominate the provincial population. For wealthy local elites, however, the *uji* had become an increasingly hollow institution, as had relationships between center and periphery centered on the *uji*. Through relationships based on the early estate system and by providing local specialties to the capital, local elites began to form unofficial and private ties with nobles and officials. The special prerogatives that local elites accrued fundamentally endangered the *ritsuryō* system, as seen in the following complaints voiced in early tenth-century legislation:

> People wander into the capital, wishing to become dependents of wealthy households. They either falsely claim that they have donated their rice fields, or cleverly pretend that they have sold their houses. Working through agents, they obtain enabling documents from noble households.[124]

Even those provincial and district officials who journeyed to the capital to supervise the transportation of tribute goods often chose to further their own private interests. According to the *Engi shiki*, one benefit that accrued to these officials was the opportunity to skim profits from the goods they were in charge of transporting:

> The share of tribute sent to the capital that is allotted to officials in charge of transporting goods is over three hundred *koku* of rice, distributed to clerks in the provincial office as well as senior officials. If there is anything left over, some goes to district officials or their sons and younger brothers, and important people from rich cultivators' households also line up to get their share.[125]

Elsewhere authorities complained, "District officials and cultivators falsely claim [that they are shipping] official goods, get barrier passes through deception, and constantly travel back and forth peddling their merchandise."[126] Moreover, tribute caravan overseers sometimes pilfered the cargo, "seeking commercial profits through selling off stolen goods," often earning enough to buy houses and settle in the capital.[127] Such activities altered both the tribute transport system and the dominance of center over periphery based on *ritsuryō* authority.

The development of relations between city and countryside, spurred on by economic growth in the countryside—including the opening of new fields —benefited the region surrounding the capital and led to changes in the capital itself. These included the formation of new organizations involved in transport, as well as an influx of people into the capital as labor opportunities expanded. For example, repeated references to the maintenance of the Yamazaki Bridge at Ōyamazaki on the Yodo River south of the capital suggests some of the social and demographic changes taking place (see Map 7.2). The following complaint comes from a report (*ge*) dated 857 and issued by the office charged with maintaining the bridge:

> The bridge is presently caked with mud and excrement, and if it is not cleaned promptly, it will completely rot away. Another problem comes during floods. Cargo vessels get stuck beneath the bridge supports and damage them. Yamashiro and Kawachi Provinces, through which the river flows, have been ordered to station guards at the north and south ends of the bridge, and to have prominent local people watch out for trouble as well. If there is a threat of flooding and the river threatens to overflow, boats should be driven downriver [westward] beyond the bridge, and floating timbers should be secured with rope [to prevent them from damaging the bridge].[128]

As this passage makes clear, responsibility for maintaining the Yamazaki Bridge lay primarily with prominent people in the local community. They were to protect the bridge during floods by moving boats and timber floats to the west of the bridge.

Ōyamazaki, a densely populated relay point between the capital and the western provinces, is famous for its sake making and its shops selling fish and salt. But many people there also worked at lumberyards and in water transportation. As Nishioka Toranosuke has pointed out, territorially based organizations of people in such occupations were also found in ports such as Ōi (in Gifu Prefecture, present day Ena City), Ōtsu, Uji, Izumi Kizu, and Naniwa, indicating conspicuous development of ports and cargo facilities especially in the region surrounding the capital (see Map 7.3).[129]

The transfer of the capital to Heiankyō at the beginning of the ninth century—where it remained until modern times— produced structural changes in the region surrounding the new capital.[130] Among the conspicuous differences from the early *ritsuryō* period was the formation of a settled urban population in the central Kinai region. A huge influx of prosperous folk from the provinces contributed to this demographic transformation. References to dependents of noble families who moved to the Heian capital are

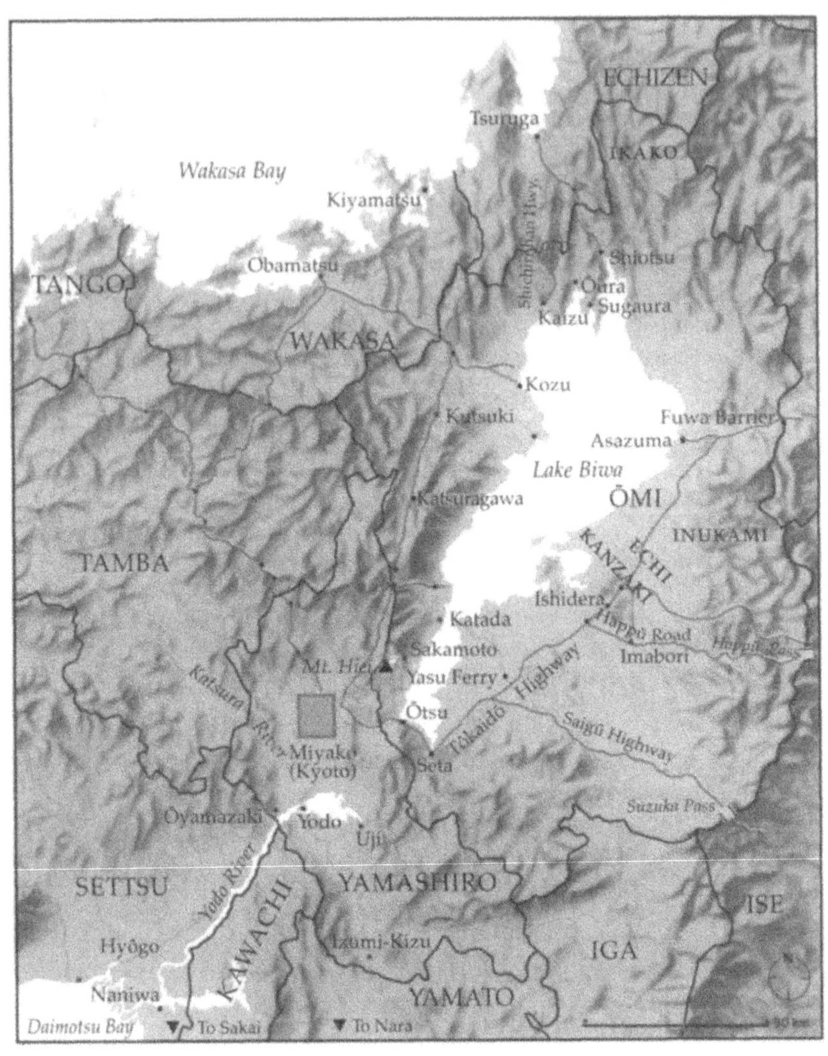

Map 7.3. Transportation in the Kinai

scattered throughout the six official histories and other sources. For instance, legislation from 897 points out that many people who had left their provinces without permission had become dependents of wealthy urban families, suggesting the extent to which drifters were a common fixture in the capital.[131] And as already mentioned, by the late ninth century provincial transport overseers sometimes "bought houses and settled down, remaining in the capital."[132] Taking advantage of their assignment to carry tribute goods, they guaranteed themselves a base in the capital and helped to establish further links between the capital city and the provinces.

Also worthy of note are the urban dwellers who specialized partly in transportation work, such as laborers later known as packhorse drivers (*umakashi*) and carters (*kurumakashi*). Day laborers (*yōchin no tomogara*) who hauled official or unofficial cargo swarmed at the anchorages in Yamazaki or Ōtsu.[133] In every province wagoneer gangs (*chinsha no tō*) transported goods such as lumber to ports from mountain way stations.[134] Certainly the lumber at the Yamazaki Bridge mentioned earlier was on its way to the capital, hauled by such workers. Another category of transport laborers is that of harbor workers, including raftsmen and haulers who collected lumber at the Yamazaki Bridge, warehouse laborers who hauled the timber onshore and stacked it, oarsmen and sailors who rowed the cargo boats, and bridge watchmen. Drifters were absorbed into the labor force of such ports. For example, in the Jōgan era (859–877), when monks and lay believers who lived near Senkyōji at Kizu in Izumi Province joined efforts to purchase two large vessels to transport horses plus one smaller one, the Yamashiro provincial headquarters supplied two drifters to man the boats and guard the bridge nearby. Meanwhile, two local residents and ten drifters were employed as watchmen at the Horie Temple on the Horie River at Naniwa.[135] Their jobs probably included operating a ferry on the river.[136] Both temples mentioned above claimed the famous popular proselytizer Gyōki Bosatsu (668–749) as their founder. The communal spirit at Izumi Kizu, where monks and lay believers "chanted [prayers and scriptures] in unison" and joined efforts to establish a cargo transport service, stemmed from faith in Gyōki.

The provincial office participated in this communal effort by supplying drifters as laborers on the boats. As discussed earlier, both the Yamashiro and Kawachi provincial authorities participated in local notables' management of the Yamazaki Bridge and shipping in its vicinity. In this regard, the term *tone* was probably used to denote local officials supervising transportation activities as well as local notables who served quasi-public functions. *Tone* at sea and river crossings investigated illegal activities on the part of the "wagoneer gangs" who transported lumber.[137] Influential men who lived near the Yamazaki Bridge who participated in public management duties were probably also called *tone*. The first verifiable use of the term to refer to Yamazaki port officials in charge of criminal investigations can be dated to 974, but organizations staffed by ninth-century provincial officials and *tone* were probably prototypes for similar structures in the medieval age.[138]

In addition, low-status people (*senmin*) in the capital had begun to form an urban day-labor force. They included the "rogue monks and butchers," mentioned in the *Engi shiki*, who were forbidden to live in the area immediately south of Kamo Shrine,[139] as well as retainers and slaves of nobles who hunted with falcons and fished in mountains and rivers near the capital,[140] or those tending hawks and hunting hounds for the palace Falconry Office (Takatsukasa).[141] According to Ōyama Kyōhei, the starting point for discrimination against urban low-status people can be found in the ninth century, as ghettos called *shuku* and *sanjo* were established in provincial transportation centers.[142]

Low-status people appear in various guises in ninth-century sources. In legislation promulgated in 844 we find complaints of "gangs of hunters" who polluted the river that ran beside the Kamo Shrine by butchering their meat there.[143] The official *Shoku nihon kōki* annal relates the same incident, but identifies the hunters as "retainers of royal and noble families, and cultivators."[144] In other words, such royal and noble retainers included organizations of slaughterers and butchers who worked on the banks of the Kamo River, perhaps as followers trailing along after skilled hunters traveling between countryside and capital.[145] In later times low-caste people called *sakamono*, who were residents of Kiyomizuzaka in the capital, and *kawaramono*, riverbank people, emerge as porters in urban transportation.[146] In this early period as well, such people must have been employed as day laborers in various transportation operations.

Thus, in the ninth and tenth centuries the capital region transformed itself, through trade and specialized economic relations with the periphery, into a distinct regional society. Ishimoda Shō's proposition that the medieval age has its origins in the agricultural countryside is accurate overall. But since it appears that the capital region developed as an independent entity within the social structure of the *ritsuryō* epoch, it is necessary to examine developments in the urban region itself as well as relationships with provincial regions linked to it.

Popular Resistance to *Ritsuryō* Control and Breakdown of Relations between Center and Provinces

The breakdown of the *ritsuryō* tributary traffic system was not simply a natural outcome of economic growth and development. Rather, it was a complex political process directly tied to the breakdown of the unified *tennō*-centered polity itself. In this section I examine the establishment of new types of relationships that resisted *ritsuryō* control. Kudō Keiichi has argued that early medieval relations between the capital and farming communities were centered on the twin axes of estate and provincial government structures.[147] After examining the pre-medieval roots of such developments, I investigate fissures in the *ritsuryō* ruling class and the popular resistance that contributed to such divisions.

In the late ninth century the households of powerful royals and nobles rapidly developed early estates (*shoki shōen*) based on clientage relations with provincial elites. Such relations resulted in powerful independent households with considerable productive capacity.[148] Estates themselves had been increasing in number and expanding geographically since the end of the previous century. Estates distributed all over the archipelago included those controlled by the royal family, such as *chokushiden* (land for opening rice fields granted by an edict from the throne), *goinden* (land for opening fields to support the retired monarch), and *shinnōshiden* (land for opening fields to support princes).[149] There were also estates held by senior nobles such as Fujiwara Yoshimi (813–867)[150] and Tomo Yoshio (d. 868),[151] and temple and shrine properties such as those that supported Jōganji[152] and Anjōji.[153] Tōma Seita has based his conclusions regarding typical estate distribution patterns on Tōdaiji's holdings, which were centered in the Kinai and its environs, and in the San'yō and Hokuriku circuits.[154] Here I take up the problem of the private commercial and transport mechanisms that linked these far-flung landholdings together.

I have already shown that the central government granted special privileges for the transportation of private goods produced by noble and official families who were also supported by sustenance households and land awarded according to their rank. The question here is: as such private productive power increased, how did these privileges function within the tribute transportation system—and how did they disrupt that system?

To begin, let us examine the problem of private mobilization and misappropriation of government labor services, especially in the post station system. Legislation of 859 accused "unprincipled fellows" who tended falcons for aristocratic households of misappropriating tribute goods and exploiting public transportation facilities for private gain.[155] Apparently the falconers were using official permits to appropriate horses that were supposed to carry tax goods. Another complaint, dated 905, accused "skilled hunters in the service of royal households" of using post station horses to invade and rob people's homes.[156] Also involved in such exploitation were wranglers in the service of the Bureau of Horses who attended equestrian tribute bearers from royal pasture lands. In 869 they were accused of making the lives of post station hands miserable by appropriating tribute goods and misusing station facilities.[157] Such people manipulated the post station system, which had been designed for the transport of official goods.

According to Tanaami Hiroshi, "improper and unauthorized use of transport facilities [was] an important cause of the dissolution of the post station system."[158] Sakamoto Tarō attributes the illegitimate use of transport facilities at the stations to the "shameful characters of lower-class officials."[159] In fact, however, members of royal households and other figures of authority also allied themselves with wealthy local families to abuse the post station system and embezzle from the people. Such actions hastened the dissolution of the post station system.

A report (*ge*) from Harima Province dated 901 demonstrates the spread of the problem beyond the post stations:

> People who pass through the province, including the envoys of officials and royal and noble households, are typically accompanied by three or four palace guards. Some brandish counterfeit permits, while others idle away their time together. They make a point of doing things that are illicit, immoral, and harmful. Reflecting upon such things we can conclude that these envoys have their attendants wear peach-colored robes and carry large swords, passing themselves off as royal guardsmen and making themselves look ferocious. Provincial and district officials, even seeing through the pretense, shrink before these attendants' savagery and cannot apprehend them. There are riots within our jurisdiction and the people lament and suffer greatly. This is intolerable.[160]

The document further complains that envoys who crossed the Harima border on the San'yō highway abused local cultivators by impressing them into service. In the provinces along the main highways, private agents frequently demanded the use of corvée porters and public transport facilities. For example, when sumo wrestlers chosen from guard units passed through Bingo Province, they appropriated goods designated for the royal household, stole horses from the post stations, kidnapped post station hands, and demanded travel provisions from provincial and district offices.[161] Skilled hunters in the services of royal and noble households used documents from their patrons to requisition horses, while those of the fifth rank and above, as well as officials from the Six Guards,[162] committed similar acts.[163] In short, such practices were widespread in the early tenth century.

Authorities' misuse of corvée transport services extended to the provinces as well. A number of ninth-century sources complained of the impressment of packhorses and cargo vessels to carry goods from provincial estates to estate owners' residences in the capital.[164] The term "impressment" (*kyōkō*) first appears in a law of 835, which notes that "retainers of two retired sovereigns, Saga and Junna," as well as "various officials and retainers" had engaged in the practices which by 894 had spread to provinces along the Tōkaidō and Hokurikudō including Kazusa and Echigo.[165] The year 835 was also when the Council of State recognized the relative inadequacy of the Tōkaidō transport infrastructure and the frequent occurrence of scuffles at its ferry crossings. Impressment of the means of transport may have helped produce such conditions, which contributed to the stagnation of tribute traffic.

As noted earlier, aristocratic institutions such as the Kangakuin and Kokusōin possessed special transportation rights, and activities of the retainers of retired sovereigns Saga and Junna point to similar rights exercised by royal households. Unlike other retainers, those attached to royal households maintained powerful personal privileges, such as exemption from corporal punishment. If they committed misdeeds, their names were simply forwarded to their patron's office.[166] Thus, as Nishioka Toranosuke pointed out many years ago, as impressment became a common occurrence, contractors who transported goods on horseback for the retired sovereign's household and other royal households increasingly developed independent coercive power.[167]

Impressment became a customary practice, especially among powerful families active in the eastern provinces. For example, Fujiwara Haruaki of Hitachi took Taira Masakado's uprising in the late 930s as an opportunity to "plunder goods in transit and use them as provisions for his family."[168] We also find a complaint by Fujiwara Ariyuki, governor of Shimōsa Province, that "in all the provinces east of the mountains, evil gangs maraud government facilities, plundering goods and assaulting people along the road."[169] The rebellion launched in 1028 by Taira Tadatsune, who "falsely claimed to be a tribute caravan overseer, and with a heart full of treachery, violated the laws of the court, embezzling official goods and pillaging tax payments," is another example.[170]

The disruption incited by officials and other powerful people in the capital region was another important factor in the dissolution of the tributary traffic system. According to legislation issued in 867, goods were being seized at Ōtsu and Yamazaki, the first mention of such violent activities in the environs of the Heian capital. Raiders also plundered tribute cargo at important harbors near the capital.[171] Such brigands first appeared in the 880s and 890s, waylaying district officials and tribute-bearers entering the city and seizing not only private goods from aristocratic holdings but also official tribute shipments.[172]

Disruptions along tribute caravan routes were not limited to the outskirts of the capital, but occurred in the official markets of the capital as well. We have clearly seen that the eastern and western markets supplemented the *ritsuryō* system by providing the sites for selling off excess tribute goods and purchasing other needed goods.[173] In 834 violence paralyzed the markets:

> Urban commoners in large numbers have been appointed to the Guards Headquarters, and reside permanently near the markets. They continually use strong-arm tactics to force others to buy their goods. The shameless actions of petty officials, runners, hawkers, weavers, and kennel-keepers know no bounds. They slander high officials, disrupting activities at the market stalls and impeding official business.[174]

By the mid-860s merchants at the markets had become dependents of high-ranking authorities and refused to obey the market officials who nominally supervised their activities.[175]

Thus the *ritsuryō* tribute system was disrupted in the ninth century by the special prerogatives of powerful people that enabled misappropriation of tribute goods, impressment of means of transport, obstruction of shipment, and forced sale of goods—all with impunity. The special privileges that grew parasitically and sapped the lifeblood of *ritsuryō* government cannot be explained by the role of envoys and merchants who served those in power or by the activities of wealthy families attached to them. Rather, a new, powerful system of transportation privileges was forged by such independent activities.

The result was the epochal establishment of prerogatives essentially comprising new unofficial—that is to say private—networks of production.

The Harima provincial report cited earlier indicates that when they traveled in the provinces, retainers of royal and noble households were escorted by warriors carrying long swords and wearing the peach-colored clothing of royal guard officers.[176] In other words they displayed symbols of the monarch's supreme authority. And when retainers assumed posts as estate officials, they must have marked their shipments of dues to the capital with flags of a special color reserved for their patrons and forbidden to others. The scarlet banners adorning official tribute or the permits worn on transport workers' belts discussed earlier serve as examples. The envoys mentioned in the Harima report who brandished their permits were doubtless displaying insignia of special transportation rights. Restrictions concerning estate management promulgated in the Engi era indicate the importance of permits: aristocratic households with estates were comprised not only of envoys, overseers, clerks, and custodians, but also of those who issued official documents and permits.[177] In other words the networks that made up the systems of private estates utilized household administrative documents as their means of communication and information.

Perhaps the best indication of the way "colors" and household badges marked special transportation privileges is the example of the waist badges and the insignia worn by people in Ōmi Province who supplied offerings for the royal table and various royal palaces. In the latter case the badges indicated their wearers' right to fish. But the badges were also markers of monopoly fishing rights on certain bodies of water, including the right to ban entry to others while at the same time enjoying the right to violate others' boundaries.[178] These prerogatives presaged the privileges, such as those guaranteeing exclusive rights to supply festival offerings for particular shrines, of guild organizations within the mature estate system.[179]

Such privileges were often legitimated by the ideology of the monarch's supreme rights over transportation as articulated in the *Kojiki* preface cited earlier. The private transportation system established by the powerful in the ninth century adopted this ideology as its own, symbolizing it by "colors" and household permits. In this sense power was derived from the dominance of *ritsuryō* organs, themselves based on the concept of monarchical authority. At the same time, however, their actions attenuated the very system that guaranteed their privileges and paved the way for new networks of traffic and new economic relations in the medieval age.

Ninth-century provincial officials also helped to form a private transportation network outside the government system. As Toda Yoshimi has shown, officials sometimes remained in their provinces after completing their assignments, establishing a base for private power there.[180] Examples include the former Kazusa governor Fujiwara Yoshinao and the former Chikuzen governor, Funya Miyata Maro (active 839–843), who continued to lead bands of followers in Chikuzen. The latter used his Naniwa mansion as a base for trade with merchants from the Korean kingdom of Silla. Such arrangements provided yet another form of commercial activity linking the western provinces to the capital.[181]

Established by eighth-century provincial governors to link the capital and the provinces, unofficial transportation networks had expanded by the end of the century, by which time governors had begun to use government facilities to carry goods from their own privately managed holdings. Such efforts were probably led by such people as Funya's followers, who formed a typical governor's retinue. As indicated by law codes and legal commentaries, traveling elites or newly appointed provincial officials were usually accompanied by retainers, servants, and relatives—for example, a governor could take his children and brothers under the age of twenty out to his post.[182] The system of transporting the private goods of provincial governors also depended on many other types of organizations, some headed by government bureaucrats and others staffed by drifters hired nominally for public transport duty.[183] Other unofficial transport workers were given special rights to use post stations, such as the envoys who carried offerings of *hijiki* (a variety of seaweed), medicine made from bear tallow, and *kombu* (kelp), as well as gold dust and medicinal plants for the governor of Mutsu. In reality, vagabond gangs who transported "countless loads of private cargo" swelled the ranks of such official envoys.[184]

Amid such practices, the methods of transportation administered by provincial, district, and township authorities underwent large-scale change. In the first place, local elites rather than village communities as a whole began to supply corvée labor for the transportation of tribute. Mobilization of local elites for such duties in the late ninth century has been explained as a strategy to reorganize a stratum that had opposed provincial control.[185] Under such policies, men of importance selected during a governor's tenure carried out their duties in turn, in a system developed to transport official goods as a communal public obligation.[186] This system contained the seeds of later developments in the age of the Fujiwara regents, when the provincial transportation network was upheld by frequent travel between city and countryside on the part of provincial magnates (*kokunai meishi*).[187]

In the early *ritsuryō* period, tax goods had been borne to the capital by essentially uncompensated corvée labor; but the official transport system later began to rely heavily on hired workers and organizations that were paid with provisions and fees. As mentioned, in 823 the Council of State abolished official ships and estates overseen by the Dazaifu that had produced food for the royal table, as well as the sustenance households supporting these operations. In their place private vessels were hired to ship tax rice.[188] This decision was doubtless one facet of the famous policy initiated in 822 to "exempt the cultivators in the realm from corvée labor; and if this cannot be done, those laborers who must perform service shall be given provisions."[189] Indeed, the following course of events suggests that the two policies were related: in the seventh month of 822 Ono Minemori (778–830)—elevated in court rank and appointed administrator (*daini*) at the Dazaifu four months earlier—put exemptions from corvée service into effect.[190] Ono also recommended the establishment of public contract fields (*kueiden*) under his jurisdiction. In the first month of 823, a royal edict ordered the Council of State to investigate the proposal.[191] It was just two days later when the Council sent its memorial to the throne recommending abolition of the Dazaifu ships and their support households.

The objective of instituting public contract fields was to alleviate the burdens of corvée service by supplying provisions to laborers, a policy that became pivotal in the Kōnin era (810–824). Various types of transportation laborers were to be provided with "a daily rice portion of one *shō* [about 1.8 liter] per person" from tax stores.[192] This was a policy that had resulted from frequent protests against the corvée system. Needless to say, the policy played an important role in the so-called exhaustion of tax resources that bankrupted provincial governments.[193] The new policy also led to further changes in the ways that tax goods were transported to the capital.

As Sakamoto Tarō has pointed out, the *Engi shiki* clause regulating the transportation of tax goods from the provinces stipulated compensation for packtrain drivers and oarsmen carrying tribute goods, distinguishing such payments from the ordinary provision for corvée laborers consisting of "two *shō* of rice and two *shaku* [.0018 liter] of salt for adults."[194] In other words, professional packtrain and boatsmen's crews transported tax goods at set times in return for payment. Note, moreover, that the payment for ordinary laborers in the Engi era—at the turn of the tenth century—was double that designated in 822. As taxes extracted from the people circulated back to specialized transport workers in the form of provisions and compensation, traffic between capital and countryside accelerated even more. On the other hand, while neglecting their duty to supervise the transportation of tax goods, provincial governors also developed private transportation networks for their own gain. It is clear that the system of transporting official goods mentioned in the *Engi shiki* did not operate solely through the mobilization of corvée labor under the government's authority and administrative apparatus.

Thus did official and unofficial forms of transportation develop rapidly in competition with one another, contributing to the eventual dissolution of the official system. Two factors proved decisive in this regard: the breakdown of the concentration of elite residences in the capital, and the pressure of popular protests against the government.

I have dealt elsewhere with the first issue, changes in the residence patterns of elites as provincial appointees settled in the countryside after their tenure was over.[195] Since others have also raised this issue, I will not discuss it further.[196] Briefly, I have argued that as the tribute system dissolved and *ritsuryō* aristocrats worked against their own class interests in the transportation arena, some settled permanently in the provinces, encouraged by the development of private commerce and transport. This resulted in factional splits in the core of the ruling class. Powerful retainers of royal households—including officials on royal estates—allied with aristocratic emigrants to the provinces. One source complains that these retainers "abused trust" by committing misdeeds while in official service.[197] Aristocratic migration to the provinces was linked to problems of the late ninth-century estate system that eventually resulted in grave political crises.

Popular challenges to the government in the same period have considerable historical significance. As mentioned earlier, aristocratic migrants sometimes married locally and pursued trade or farming in the provinces where they settled. A Council of State directive dated 891 complains that "they form wicked bands that invade farming communities, kidnap provincial officials, and menace the lower classes."[198] Thus the outbound migration issue is linked to armed aggression against central authority. For the *ritsuryō* polity, the migration problem was so serious that reforms to check it were initiated in the Kampyō era (889–898).[199]

Armed bands (*tō*) led by migrants from the capital were new organizations that developed outside the old *uji*. They were rooted in leagues of wealthy local families active in agriculture and commerce who were probably involved in regional trade as well. Armed bands may also be viewed as a form of resistance to government power by provincial residents, who sometimes protested against injustices to the central government and sometimes incited violent insurrections along transportation routes.

Complaints known as "accusations and indictments" might claim, as did one in 853, that a provincial governor had "shamelessly piled up [wealth] at his home."[200] In 834 representatives of cultivators from the distant province of Sado were sent to the capital to protest the governor's investigative and judicial authority. In the process they scuffled with retainers of the crown prince.[201] As has been made clear elsewhere, such activities were harbingers of "suits and protests against the harsh administration of provincial governors" that emerged in the tenth and eleventh centuries.[202] Protests of this type are evidence of the development of independent political action by provincial residents who traveled between capital and countryside.

Raids on tribute caravans by leagues of armed men who prowled highways and maritime routes represented a second form of resistance to government authority. These included the well-known series of insurrections in the eastern provinces by marauders called "packtrain bands." Since I have discussed them earlier, I will turn here to the pirates who terrorized the western provinces in the 860s and 870s, during the Jōgan era.

Pirates roamed the peninsulas and islands of the Inland Sea, plundering maritime traffic from a base at Miyazaki in Iyo Province (see Map 6.1), where as noted in an 883 text, "envoys of those of fifth rank and above" had traveled back and forth to conduct private trade since the eighth century.[203] Pirates also based their operations at the inlet on the south side of the tip of Sata Cape (at the present town of Misaki). That location overlooked the Hōyo Strait, where bands of officials, cultivators, and itinerant peddlers had conducted illicit marine transport since the mid-eighth century.[204] The same inlet also overlooked the island where the pirate Fujiwara Sumitomo (d. 941) based his predatory activities. The commercial traffic along Inland Sea routes described earlier provided ample opportunities for piracy, and it was not easy to suppress the murder of travelers and plunder of public and private shipments of goods.[205] In the ninth century, and in both eastern and western provinces, attacks by armed leagues on central tribute routes increased, eventually paralyzing tribute traffic.

Resistance to and violation of government authority thus disrupted tribute traffic routes and weakened *ritsuryō* control of relations between capital and countryside. Such phenomena, along with fissures in the ruling elite exemplified by migration to the provinces, menaced central dominance over the periphery. Needless to say, these forms of resistance did not always benefit the populace; but at the base of such destructive power lay the accumulated effects of popular opposition to the corvée system, including evasion of tribute transport duties, pillaging of tribute goods, and the everyday resistance to unpaid labor that eventually won compensation for corvée service.[206]

All these phenomena were adaptations accompanying development of social class stratification and the growing traffic between capital and countryside. They can also be seen as forms of popular solidarity and resistance to the severe conditions of corvée service. Resistance also liberated people from regional biases and primitive taboos surrounding travel that were common in the early *ritsuryō* period. As early as 722 it was "difficult to prevent guardsmen in corvée battalions from plotting together to escape."[207] Such resistance on the part of ordinary people often appeared in the guise of satiric verses that mocked elites, or as rumors of angry spirits, that attacked their persecutors. In such forms, popular protest was introduced into the capital by popular shamans or holy men who built the groundwork for a broad consciousness by which authority could be resisted.[208] In this we can glimpse figures of ordinary people in the embryonic stages of the medieval age, the world of the "folk" unfolding.[209]

Notes

1. As discussed in the Introduction, we use "classical" in the volume to denote the period when the foundations of Japanese civilization took form. Although we are aware of the debate as to the appropriateness of the term, nonetheless "early" and "ancient" seem too vague. On that debate, see Aung-thwin 1995.

2. Hotate Michihisa 1978, 52–54.

3. Professor Hotate has informed the translators that since this article was published, a number of related works have appeared. In particular, he recommends Kushiki Yoshinori 1996, which presents a number of new issues and views.

4. Ishimoda Shō 1957, especially 255, 199, 220, and 247. Interpreter's note: "Traffic between Capital and Countryside in *Ritsuryō* Japan," by Hotate Michihisa was originally published as Hotate Michihisa 1979. On Ishimoda's theories of "medieval" in Japan, see chapter 13 of this volume.

5. See Nishioka Toranosuke 1953 and Sakamoto Tarō 1928.

6. See the following sections in the Yōrō Ritsuryō Code: Law on Labor Tribute (Buyakuryō), clause 3; and Law on Rice Fields (Denryō), clause 2. Interpreter's note: The Yōrō Code was compiled in the 720s but was not promulgated until the 750s. For the reconstructed code, see Inoue Mitsusada et al. 1976 and Aida Hanji 1964 (cited hereafter as Aida). For this section see Aida's commentary on 542 and 492.

7. Interpreter's note: According to Marxist theory, the "Asiatic mode of production" is characterized by a society (i.e., Asiatic social organization) in which there is no private property and cultivator communities are self-sufficient, basing their economies on

agriculture and handicrafts. A "despotic state authority" is based in an urban center, rural areas are forced to pay tribute to the urban center, and geographical or climatic conditions make the rural sector dependent on the capital for large-scale projects such as irrigation and hydraulic works. See Gorman 1986, 43-44. Karl Marx discusses the Asiatic mode in comparison with other modes in Marx 1964, 69-70, 79-83. Hotate, in agreement with many other Japanese historians, portrays *ritsuryō* society in Japan as largely fitting this description.

8. *Shoku nihongi* Tempyō Hōji 1 (757)/10/6.

9. *Ruijū sandai kyaku* Kōnin 4 (813)/6/1.

10. See the Yōrō Code Law on Corvée (Buyakuryō), clause 3, 38; Law on Fields (Denryō), clause 2; Law on Defense (Gumbōryō), clauses 54, 12; Law on Construction and Repairs (Eizenryō), clause 12. Interpreter's note: See Aida 542, 492, 582, 863, and 815.

11. *Ruijū sandai kyaku* Kōnin 13 (822)/9/20.

12. Nagayama Yasutaka 1970.

13. Interpreter's note: The *Koki* is a lost commentary on the Taihō Code, but citations from it are found in the *Ryō no shūge*, Buyakuryō section.

14. See the commentary on the Buyakuryō, clause 3, and on the Denryō, clause 2 in the *Ryō no shūge*. See also Kitayama Shigeo 1976, esp. 205.

15. See Yōrō Code, Buyakuryō, clause 3 (Aida 542).

16. *Nihongi* Taika 2 (646)/3/22. Regarding these points, see Yoneda Yūsuke 1970, 245. Interpreter's note: For an English translation see Aston 1972.

17. See Yōrō Code, Giseiryō, Clause 19 (Aida 915). The note is in the *Ryō no shūge*.

18. *Man'yōshū*, vol. 20, poem no. 4350. Interpreter's note: This oldest extant official anthology of court poetry in Japanese was compiled in the eighth century. For an English translation of 1000 selected poems, see Nihon gakujutsu shinkōkai 1965. Ian Levy has translated the first five books into English in Levy 1981. Unfortunately, neither version contains an English translation for poem no. 4350.

19. Okada Shōji 1970. Interpreter's note: For an English translation of an essay by Okada, see Okada Shōji 1987.

20. *Man'yōshū*, vol. 20, poem no 4358. Interpreter's note: For an alternate translation, see Nihon gakujutsu shinkōkai 1965, 253, no. 779.

21. Interpreter's note: "Surplus value of labor" is a Marxist concept indicating the value of a product or service beyond the cost of compensating the workers who produce it.

22. Yōrō Code Law on Official Stores (Sōkoryō), clause 10. Interpreter's note: Aida's rendering differs slightly from Hotate's. See Aida 1092.

23. Takeuchi Rizō 1962, vol. 1, 327–8, (*Izumo no kuni keikaichō*). Interpreter's note: *Nara ibun*, in which this document is archived, is a compendium of Nara-period documents in three volumes. Hereafter it will be cited as *NI*.

24. Yōrō Code Law on Barriers and Markets, Kanshiryō, clause 5 (Aida 1199).

25. *Ryō no shūge*, *Koki* commentary on the Law on Construction and Repairs (Eizenryō), clause 13 (Aida 967).

26. *Ruijū sandai kyaku* legislation dated Jōwa 9 (842)/1/27, which interprets legislation dated Hōki 6 (775)/6/27; and legislation dated Jōgan 4 (862)/9/22, which interprets legislation dated Hōki 1 (770)/5/15.

27. Yōrō Code, Buyakuryō, clause 3 (see Aida 542–43).

28. *NI*, vol. 2, 642.

29. Sakaehara Towao 1972, and Hayashi Rokurō 1969.

30. *Engi shiki,* Board of Censors (Danjōdai) section. While Sakaehara (see preceding note) argues that such warehouses were not common in the capital, the *Engi shiki* material suggests otherwise. Furthermore, signatories of the above bill of sale notably include three proxies for district officials, one of whom also figures in a document from the previous year concerning exchanges of land with the Tōdaiji Construction Agency (*Zō-Tōdaijishi*). This individual, identified in the 756 document as proxy for the Ashinokami district clerk, had resided in the capital for about three months and had taken charge of duties at the tribute warehouse such as buying and selling goods. The record from 755 indicates that such officials as well as cultivators determined prices of land and bought or sold it. In lengthy negotiations with the Tōdaiji Construction Agency, the district officials pressed their demands that the temple buy the storehouse land outright. Research on the document suggests the extent to which district officials were required to help maintain and manage the warehouses, and thus the key roles they played in the transportation of tribute goods. See *NI*, vol. 2, 641–42.

31. *Nihon sandai jitsuroku* Gangyō 7 (883)/11/2.

32. Morohashi Tetsuji 1955. There are two opinions concerning the derivation of *fukuchō*. One explains the term as a derivative of *ifuku* (clothing). See Asaka Toshiki 1971, 107; and Morita Tei 1973. The other explanation views *fukuchō* as the person responsible for the transportation of tribute goods. See Izumiya Yasuo 1972, 109. The latter seems the logical one. As for the term *kōchō*, since its initial character means "to bundle up and carry," it too probably refers to the portage of goods. The term *fukuchō* also appears in a list of lower officials from districts and townships who served in each province in 822. This list includes *kōchō* as overseers in charge of delivering miscellaneous official goods—see the legislation in *Ruijū sandai kyaku* and dated Kōnin 13 (822)/intercalary 9/20.

33. Katsuura Noriko 1976, concerning document no. 9 in *Heian ibun*. See Takeuchi Rizō 1973-1980, vol. 1, 4-5; and in the unpublished *Tōdaiji monjo* (vol. 3, 6) in the archives of the Tokyo University Historiographical Institute. Interpreter's note: The *Heian ibun* is a compendium of Heian Period documents. Hereafter, it will be cited as *HI*.

34. Ishimoda Shō 1973, part 1, chapter 1, sec. 2.

35. *Ruijū sandai kyaku* Jogan 2 (860)/4/19. Murai Yasuhiko argues that the harvest from royal fields in various provinces was to be transported by provincial authorities. Confirming that, undated tax records submitted by an unnamed provincial governor recorded in the protocols for the Bureau of Taxation (Shuzeiryō) section of the *Engi shiki* include an entry for the "sovereign's edict rice." See Murai Yasuhiko 1968, 228. The same term is identified in an entry of 1086/12/29 in *Chōya gunsai* as payment to the Bureau of the Palace Kitchen (Ōiryō). The latter was an office that managed land rent payments from the sovereign's "edict rice fields" (*chokushiden*), per the courtier journal *Shunki,* in its entry dated 1038/10/8. It is possible that the "sovereign's edict rice" noted in the provincial governor's report was the harvest from such fields.

36. See the *Koki* commentary on the Law on Official Communications (Kushikiryō), clause 49 (regarding officials in the capital) in *Ryō no shūge*.

37. Yōrō Code on Personnel (Shikiinryō), clause 39 (Aida 219); *Shoku nihongi* Tempyō 2 (730)/4/10. Katsuura Noriko has come to the same conclusion: see Katsuura Noriko 1977. This means that views of Sakamoto Tarō and others which limit the role of post stations to communications functions need reexamination.

38. *Ruijū sandai kyaku* Daidō 2 (807)/10/25.

39. *Engi shiki,* Popular Affairs (Minbu), section 2.

40. *Ruijū sandai kyaku* Jōwa 7 (840)/9/23; and *Engi shiki*, Miscellaneous Procedures (Zasshiki) section.

41. Yōrō Code, Zōryō (Miscellaneous Laws), clause 24 (Aida 1359).

42. *Shoku nihongi* Reiki 2 (716)/5/16.

43. *NI*, vol. 1, 246.

44. *Ryō no shūge*, Buyakuryō, clause 8; see also Aida 549.

45. *Ruijū sandai kyaku* Jōgan 14 (872)/12/17; and *Nihon sandai jitsuroku* Jōgan 12 (870)/2/22. Interpreter's note: The Kangakuin was a dormitory for Fujiwara *uji* members attending the Royal University (Daigaku). It was established by Fujiwara Fuyutsugu in 821. The Kokusōin was a storehouse filled with supplies for emergency use in the capital. It was established between 806 and 810. Its director was generally a senior noble (*kugyō*). A Kokusōin merchant-envoy appears in a document dated 864 that is cited in *Seiji yōryaku*, vol. 95.

46. Similar phrasing appears in other sources as well: for instance, in the *Shoku nihongi* Tempyō 8 (736)/11/11; and in festival prayers (*norito*) from the monthly festival of the sixth month in the *Engi shiki*, Jingi (deities), section 8. Interpreter's note: For an English version of the festival prayer, see Philippi 1990, 38. For an English translation of the *Kojiki* preface, see Philippi 1968, 42.

47. *Shoku nihongi* Yōrō 1 (717)/5/17, and Reiki 1 (715)/5/1.

48. Ōmachi Ken 1978. Ōmachi quotes a commentary on regulations regarding the abandonment of one's official residence.

49. There are two different definitions of the criterion that differentiated drifters from absconders. Kawakami Tasuke argues that the difference depended on whether or not the individual paid taxes and rendered labor service. See Kawakami Tasuke 1946. But Yoshimura Takehiko and Ōmachi Ken (in the work cited above) maintain that it depended on whether or not the individual had settled illegally in another province. For Yoshimura, see Yoshimura Takehiko 1973. In this essay, rather than focusing on the legal definitions debated by these scholars, I concentrate on the way the differences played out in actual practice. Moreover, as Yoshimura's work indicates, there are differing interpretations of the term *dodan* (translated here as "leaving one's province"). My definition of the term is based on the meaning of *do* as *kuni* (as defined in Morohashi Tetsuji's *Dai kanwa jiten*). Moreover, the expression "staying in the province" (using the "earth" character to mean "native province") is found in *Nihon ryōiki*, middle scroll, tale 20. Interpreter's note: See Nakada Norio 1975; and in English, see Kyōkai 1972.

50. *Ruijū sandai kyaku* entry dated Kampyō 5 (893)/7/19, with a quote of former legislation dated Ten'ō 2 (782)/intercalary 1/26.

51. *Shoku nihongi* Hōki 11 (780)/10/26 (see Aoki, vol. 5, 157).

52. Yoshida Takashi 1983, 378.

53. This legislation is recorded in a *Shoku nihongi* entry dated Tempyō Shōhō 6 (744)/9/15.

54. Sawada Goichi 1972, 561; Sakaehara Towao 1976.

55. Tōma Seita 1947a, chapter 2; and Yoshida Takashi 1976, 155.

56. See Ishimoda Shō 1971, 396 and 127.

57. *Ruijū sandai kyaku* Jinki 5 (728)/3/28 and *Ruijū sandai kyaku* Engi 14 (914)/5/9. Regarding such transfers, see Nishiyama Ryōhei 1978.

58. *Ruijū sandai kyaku* Kampyō 5 (893)/3/2; Okada Shōji 1970.

59. *Shoku nihon kōki* Jōwa 1 (834)/2/20.

60. *Ruijū sandai kyaku* Kampyō 7 (895)/12/3.

61. *Ruijū sandai kyaku* Jingi 5/3/28; Sakaehara Towao 1976.

62. *Nihongi*. Interpreter's note: An accessible edition is Sakamoto Tarō et al. 1967. For this section in English see Aston 1972, vol. 2, 222.

63. *Shoku nihongi* Wadō 7 (714)/02/.

64. Sawada Goichi 1972, 561.

65. Regarding the place of public works projects in the sphere of transportation in Asiatic social structures, see Marx's *Precapitalist Economic Formations and Capital*, vol 5; and vol. 3 (for an account of the Inca empire).

66. *Shoku nihongi* Wadō 7 (714)/intercalary 2/1; and Jingo-keiun 3 (769)/9/8. Also see Sasaki Ken'ichi 1975.

67. Yōrō Code, Eizenryō (Law on Construction and Repair), clause 12 (Aida, 966).

68. Regarding conditions in 756, see *Ruijū sandai kyaku* Daidō 5 (810)/2/17.

69. *Nihongi* Temmu 13 (684)/11/3 (Aston, pt. 2, 366).

70. Concerning Kawabe, see *Nihongi* Suiko 6 (618). Concerning Arata see *Nihongi* Taika 3 (647) and Hakuchi 1 (650)/10. Interpreter's note: See Aston 1972, vol. 2, 147, and vol. 2, 228 and 240, respectively.

71. *Shoku nihongi* Wadō 5(712)/12/7; Sakaehara Towao 1975.

72. *Shoku nihongi* Wadō 6 (713)/3/19.

73. *Ruijū sandai kyaku* Jōwa 2 (835)/12/3.

74. *Nihongi* Taika 2 (646) 3/22.

75. *Nihongi* Taika 2 (646)/3/22. Interpreter's note: For a somewhat different English rendering of this passage, see Aston 1972, vol. 2, 221–22.

76. Matsubara Hironobu 1976, 502 (note).

77. *Nihongi* Yūryaku 13 (469)/8. Interpreter's note: A slightly different English rendering is found in Aston 1972, vol. 1, 361. It should also be noted that assignment of dates for reigns before Suiko's era are debated by historians. The most recent chronologies do not provide dates for these early reigns.

78. Interpreter's note: *Harima fudoki* is one of the provincial gazetteers compiled in the early eighth century by order of the court. On the gazeteers and especially that from Hitachi, see chapter 4 by Inoue Tatsuo in this volume.

79. Ishimoda Shō 1957, 199.

80. *Ruijū sandai kyaku* Enryaku 6 (787)/1/21. Interpreter's note: "Kōyō" refers to a Chinese Han-dynasty figure named Sō Kōyō (in Chinese, Sang Hong-yang), who managed salt and iron production and earned the trust of the emperor, but eventually fomented a rebellion and was put to death. See Morohashi Tetsuji 1955, vol. 6, 338.

81. *Ruijū sandai kyaku* Kōnin 6 (813)/3/20.

82. *Ruijū sandai kyaku* Jōwa 2 (835)/12/13.

83. *Ruijū sandai kyaku* Shōtai 2 (899)/9/19.

84. *Shoku nihon kōki* Jōwa 8 (841)/4/20.

85. *Ruijū sandai kyaku* Jōwa 2/6/29. A similar item concerning the Hirose (Tenryū) River in Tōtōmi Province is recorded in an entry dated Ninju 3 (853)/10/22 in *Nihon Montoku Tennō jitsuroku* (*The Records of Japan's Montoku Tennō*).

86. Interpreter's note: Hotate discusses these conflicts in a Marxist context, using the term "contradiction" to denote a class-based conflict.

87. Concerning Umazu, see *HI*, vol. 2, p. 480, doc. 339: clause 19 of the well-known Owari *gebumi*, a petition by the cultivators of Owari Province protesting illegal acts by the governor in 988. Concerning Kusatsu, see the Nara-period tale collection, *Nihon ryōiki*, middle scroll, tale 27. Umazu station was an extensive operation with four ferryboats and a lodging house nearby. As the final stop on the river route from Enatsu station in Ise Province, Umazu was a major port used by various sorts of water craft.

88. See *Chōya gunsai* Kampyō 2 (890)/8/5, a *shōen* register signed by Fujiwara Sugane and others. Regarding this estate, see Toda Yoshimi 1975a.

89. See Yoshida Tōgo 1922–23.

90. Shimizu Masatake 1965. Interpreter's note: To locate these estates, see Takeuchi Rizō 1975, vol. 1, 83. The Nakara District location of Tashiro estate is marked, but the Amaha location is not.

91. *Engi shiki*, Shūzeiryō (Bureau of Taxation), section 1, concerning transporting tax goods from the provinces.

92. *Shoku nihongi* Ten'ō 1 (781)/2/30. Interpreter's note: One *koku* is the equivalent of 4.895 bushels or 350 pounds. A *koku* is said to be the amount of rice consumed by an individual during a year.

93. *Nihon sandai jitsuroku* Jōgan 12 (870)/2/22.

94. *Engi shiki*, Zatsushiki.

95. *Shoku nihongi* Reiki 2 (716)/5/1 6.

96. *Ruijū sandai kyaku* Tempyō 18 (746)/7/21.

97. *Engi shiki*, Zatsushiki.

98. *Ruijū sandai kyaku* Daidō 4 (809)/1/26. Interpreter's note: See the discussion of Inland Sea traffic in Matsubara Hironobu 1994. *Kodai kōtsū kenkyū*, published by the Kodai kōtsū kenkyūkai, appears annually and provides the best new information concerning transportation, by land and by sea.

99. *Shoku nihongi* Jōwa 11 (844)/5/19.

100. *Ruijū sandai kyaku* Gangyō 7 (883)/10/26. Regarding such badges, see Aida Nirō 1962, vol. 1, 550. Materials on badges that served as passes are described in an entry dated Bun'ei 9 (1272)/2 in Fukui kenritsu toshokan 1963, *Hata monjo* 19. Another example of people who wore banner-type badges appears in the *Azuma kagami* entry for Jishō 4 (1180)/8/23.

101. *Ruiju sandai kyaku* Enryaku 15 (796)/11/21.

102. *Ruiju sandai kyaku*, legislation dated Jōwa 7 (840) /9/23 interpreting a Council of State memorial to the throne in Kōnin 14 (823)/1/29.

103. *Engi shiki*, Zatsushiki.

104. *Kanke bunsō*, "Ten Verses on Winter Grasses." Interpreter's note: This is a collection of Chinese verse by Sugawara Michizane (845-903).

105. *Nihon sandai jitsuroku* Jōgan 9 (867)/3/27.

106. See *Ruiju sandai kyaku* Jōwa 2 (835)/12/3; and *Shoku nihon kōki* Tenchō 10 (833)/10/9.

107. *Ruiju sandai kyaku* Enryaku 21 (802)/6/24. Hides, especially yellow sealskin, are mentioned as tribute goods from Mutsu and Dewa in the Minbu section of the *Engi shiki*. According to a *Nihon kōki* entry dated Kōnin 1 (810)/9/28, the hides were used chiefly for ornamentation.

108. *Ruiju sandai kyaku* Enryaku 6 (787)/1/21.

109. Tōma Seita 1966, 161–62.

110. See Toda Yoshimi 1967b, 33–34. Toda's remarks are part of a historiographical debate on the origins of medieval society. Disagreeing with Toda's interpretation, Nagahara Keiji (Nagahara Keiji 1968, 52) argues that the importance placed on movable property indicates the immaturity of the concept of land ownership. In a critique of Kadowaki Teiji 1971, Sakaguchi Tsutomu points out the adherence to communal mechanisms for collecting wealth and the household slave system that lay at the heart of the tax and labor service system (Sakaguchi Tsutomu 1963). However, the key issue in this discussion is whether or not the movement toward social stratification and the opening of

land in agricultural villages were the sorts of processes that led to medieval society. Interpreter's note: In English Nagahara's views on medieval society can be read in the two chapters he contributed to Yamamura 1990, 260–343.

111. See Kadowaki Teiji 1971.

112. Konishi Toru cites sources such as *Ruiju sandai kyaku* Tenchō 5 (828)/7, in Konishi Toru 1970, 52.

113. See Katsuura Noriko 1976.

114. See the *Kanke bunsō*, "Ten Verses on Winter Grasses," poem no. 10; and *Nihon kōki* Enryaku 18 (799) 11/14.

115. *Nihon sandai jitsuroku* Ninna 1 (885)/9/21.

116. *Chōya gunsai* Kampyō 2 (890)/8/5; and *Sonpi bun'myaku*, vol. 2, 419.

117. *Ruiju sandai kyaku* Kampyō 3 (891)/9/11. Interpreter's note: In fact the directive prohibited such behavior, as had another directive seven years earlier, in 884. See Friday 1992, 96.

118. *Ruiju sandai kyaku* Saikō 2 (855)/3/13.

119. *Ruiju sandai kyaku* Kampyō 3 (891)/9/11.

120. *HI*, vol. 1, 398–99, doc. 271.

121. *Ruiju sandai kyaku* Jōgan 10 (868)/6/28.

122. *Ruiju sandai kyaku* Kampyō 5 (893)/3/2.

123. Miyoshi Kiyoyuki (847-914), "Iken jūnikajō" (Twelve observations), from a memorial of 914 archived in *Honchō monzui*. Interpreter's note: *Honchō monzui* is an anthology of Sino-Japanese materials compiled by Fujiwara Akihira between 1037 and 1045. Miyoshi's memorial to the throne containing these twelve points is analyzed in Tokoro Isao 1970.

124. *Ruiju sandai kyaku* Engi 2 (902)/3/13.

125. *Engi shiki*, Minbu section, part 2.

126. *Ruiju sandai kyaku* Daidō 4 (809)/1/26.

127. *Ruiju sandai kyaku* Kampyō 8 (896)/intercalary 1/1, and *Ruiju sandai kyaku* Kampyō 3 (891)/9/11.

128. *Ruiju sandai kyaku* Ten'an 1 (857)/4/11.

129. Nishioka Toranosuke 1953. Interpreter's note: In English on a slightly later period see Wakita Haruko 1983.

130. Interpreter's note: For a schematic representation of changes in Kinai transit between Nara and Heian times, see Matsubara Hironobu 1985, 276.

131. *Ruiju sandai kyaku* Kampyō 9 (897)/4/10. There has been little research on the special significance of drifters in the central area of the capital, and detailed investigation remains to be done. *Ruijū sandai kyaku* notes the presence of drifters in capital environs in legislation dated Ten'an 1 (857)/4/11; Hōki 11 (781)/10/26; Saikō 2 (855)/3/13; and Kampyō 8 (896)/4/2.

132. *Ruiju sandai kyaku* Kampyō 3 (891)/9/11.

133. *Ruiju sandai kyaku* Jōgan 9 (867)/12/20.

134. *Ruiju sandai kyaku* Jōgan 10 (868)/3/10.

135. *Ruiju sandai kyaku* Jōgan 18 (876)/3/1; and *Nihon sandai jitsuroku* Jōgan 18/3/3.

136. *Engi shiki*, Minbu section, part 1; and *Nihon Montoku Tennō jitsuroku* Ninju 3 (853)/10/11.

137. *Ruiju sandai kyaku* Jōgan 10 (868)/3/10.

138. *Ten'en ninenki* 974/intercalary 10/25. Interpreter's note: This is a fragment from a journal kept by the courtier Taira Chikanobu (946-1017), grandson of the beloved

Tokimochi (877-938) who served the earlier monarchs, Uda, Daigo and Suzaku. Chikanobu was essentially a houseman (*keshi*) of the regent Fujiwara Koremasa.

139. *Engi shiki*, Jingi section, part 3.

140. *Nihon ryōiki*, middle scroll, tale 40; *Shoku nihon kōki* Jōwa 11/4/30.

141. *Ruiju sandai kyaku* Jōwa 1 (834)/12/22.

142. Ōyama Kyōhei 1976.

143. *Ruiju sandai kyaku* Jōwa 11 (844)/11/4.

144. *Shoku nihon kōki* Jōwa 11 (844)/11/4.

145. Toda Yoshimi 1970, 43.

146. Ōyama Kyōhei 1976.

147. Kudō Keiichi 1960. Interpreter's note: For a translation of Kudō's work in English see Kudō Keiichi 1983.

148. Toda Yoshimi 1968, 20–21. Interpreter's note: For a translation of one of Toda's essays, see chapter 10 in the current volume.

149. Miyamoto Tasuku 1973.

150. Prior to his death in Jōgan 9 (867), Minister of the Right Fujiwara Yoshimi (one of Fuyutsugu's five sons, and brother to both Yoshifusa and Montoku Tennō's mother, Junshi) donated a total of 400 *chō* (1 *chō* = 2.94 acres) from eight holdings in Mino, Shinano, Musashi, Shimotsuke, Bingo, and Iyo to the temple known as Jōganji, along with an additional property called Okada in Yamashiro. See *HI*, vol. 1, 160–64, doc. 165. Jōganji was originally one part of Kajōji, Nimmyō Tennō's memorial temple, situated in the Fushimi area. But Jōganji became independent in 862, and numerous properties were donated to it. The Bingo estate donated by Yoshimi was called Fukatsu, probably including the market place referred to in the *Nihon ryōiki* (final scroll, tale 27). The holding in Iyo was Utsu no shō. In addition, Yoshimi managed Hakata no shō in Chikuzen Province as director (*bettō*) of the household of the royal princess Takako to whom the property had once belonged (*HI*, vol. 1, 136–37, doc. 158). It appears then that Yoshimi's holdings gave him significant control of key points along Inland Sea transportation routes. Interpreter's note: Hotate's text reads "Kusatsu no shō," but the editors of Kokuritsu rekishi minzoku hakubutsukan 1997 list Utsu no shō in Iyo (p. 795).

151. *Nihon sandai jitsuroku* Jōgan 8 (866)/9/25. According to entries dated Jōgan 17 (875)/11/15 and 866/12/5, Yoshio held forest land, rice fields, and salt-making facilities in Ise and other provinces. See Toda Yoshimi 1967b, 138.

152. *HI*, vol. 1, 160–64, doc. 165; and Kudō Keiichi 1960.

153. *HI*, vol. 1, 140–60, doc. 164. The temple had holdings in Yamashiro, Ōmi, Awa, Shimotsuke, and Suō.

154. Tōma Seita 1947b. However, there may be need to reevaluate Tōma's findings.

155. *Ruijū sandai kyaku* Jōgan 1/8/13. The falcon-tenders later became *kugonin* (official purveyors) of fowl for the court.

156. *Ruijū sandai kyaku* Engi 5 (905)/11/3.

157. *Ruijū sandai kyaku* Jōgan 11 (869)/6/13. This very interesting historical material indicates the internal structure of specially privileged wranglers' organizations in the eastern provinces.

158. Tanaami Hiroshi 1969, 197–201.

159. Sakamoto Tarō 1928, 138–39.

160. *Ruijū sandai kyaku* Engi 1 (901)/12/21.

161. *Ruijū sandai kyaku* Engi 6 (906)/7/28.

162. Interpreter's note: The Rokuefu ("Six Guards") were the six guard units that patrolled the royal residence, the greater palace precincts, the palace gates, and the streets of the capital in Nara and Heian times. See Friday 1992, 224.

163. *Ruijū sandai kyaku* Engi 5 (905)/11/3.

164. The phenomenon of impressment is analyzed by Shinjō Tsunezō 1970 and by Toda Yoshimi 1968.

165. *Ruijū sandai kyaku,* commentary dated Jōgan 9 (867)/12/20 on earlier legislation dated Jōwa 2 (835)/10/18; and *Ruijū sandai kyaku* Kampyō 6 (894)/7/16.

166. Toda Yoshimi 1968.

167. Nishioka Toranosuke 1956–1957, vol. 1.

168. Koten isan no kai 1963, vol. 1, 211. Interpreter's note: *Shōmonki,* completed in 940 by an unknown author, chronicles the rebellion of the warrior Taira Masakado against the court in the mid-tenth century. It is available in several versions, including the one cited by Hotate, and another in Kajihara Masaaki 1976. According to Kajihara, Fujiwara Haruaki was probably appointed second-ranking governor of Hitachi Province by Masakado. Kajihara does not give birth or death dates for Haruaki, and says that his lineage is uncertain. See vol. 2, 3–4.

169. *Chōya gunsai,* vol. 22, report to the Council of State dated Tenryaku 4 (950)/2/20.

170. *HI,* vol. 3, 775–78, doc. 640. Interpreter's note: On Taira Tadatsune see Takeuchi Rizō 1999. An English translation of the tale in *Konjaku monogatarishū* describing this revolt can be found in Wilson 1979, 13–15. An account is also found in another tale collection, the *Uji shūi,* tale 128. For an English translation of the *Uji shūi,* see Mills 1970. There is a discussion of Tadatsune's resistance in the context of Heian warrior history in Farris 1992, 192–200.

171. *Ruijū sandai kyaku* Jōgan 9/12/20.

172. *Nihon sandai jitsuroku* Gangyō 5 (881) /12/7; and *Ruijū sandai kyaku* Kampyō 3 (893)/5/29. See also Takahashi Takahiro 1972.

173. Sakaehara Towao 1972.

174. *Ruijū sandai kyaku* Jōwa 1 (834)/12/22.

175. *Ruijū sandai kyaku* Jōgan 6(866)/9/4.

176. For clothing regulations see the Yōrō Code, Ifukuryō (Law on Dress), clause 14 (Aida, 951-52).

177. *Ruijū sandai kyaku* Engi 2 (902)/3/13 (*Kokushi taikei* version, page 605); and *Ruijū sandai kyaku* Engi 2 (902)/3/13 (*Kokushi taikei* version, page 608). The *ryō* of *ryōshū* is the same term that appears in bills of sale denoting a "buyer's deed" or "shareholder's deed." For instance see *HI,* vol. 1, 337, doc. 232, and *Ruijū sandai kyaku* Jōwa 11 (844)/intercalary 7/7. The term reflects possession of paper documents. The *Kokushi taikei* version of *Ruijū sandai kyaku* renders this term incorrectly.

178. *Ruijū sandai kyaku* Kampyō 4 (892) /5/15 and Enryaku 19 (800)/2/3. See Araki Toshio 1974. Araki approaches the problem from the perspective of the breakdown of the system of geographical specialization of local society. In addition, see *Nihon kiryaku* Kōnin 10 (819)/12/6.

179. See *Ichō Hidefumi monjo,* copied materials regarding Kamo Shrine proprietary holdings archived at the Historiographical Institute of Tokyo University. Also see Amino Yoshihiko 1972. In this article and in other works, Amino argues that special client groups of purveyors called *kugonin* managed to appropriate as their own the rights to mountains, meadows, rivers, and seas held by cultivators according to the *ritsuryō* codes. However, the right to use such natural resources was fundamentally different from the right to use roads because the highway system had been developed for commerce and

delivery of tribute, both created by the rulers to extract wealth from the populace. The fundamental historical issue is the way transportation facilities changed and labor became increasingly specialized as contradictions among strata and classes intensified in the wake of exploitative tax collecting. As the *ritsuryō* ruling stratum disintegrated and popular resistance grew, transportation rights changed accordingly and favored groups such as the *kugonin* purveyors who lay claim to privileges that had already existed in the abstract under the *ritsuryō* control system.

180. Toda Yoshimi 1967c and Toda Yoshimi 1975a.

181. *Shoku nihon kōki* Jōwa 10 (843)/12/24, and Jōwa 9 (842)/1/10. Also see Yoshie Akio 1970, 36. Interpreter's note: On Funya and others like him, see Batten 1989.

182. Attendance on one's patron during his travels, including carrying baggage, was part of a dependent's duties, a tradition that can be found in the *Kojiki*: When the deity Ōkuninushi was forced to serve his brothers, he had to lug their baggage (*Kojiki*, book 1, chapter 1). "Sack-bearers" were generally despised. For instance, in a *Nihongi* account from the later fifth-century Yūryaku's reign (Yūryaku 14 /4/1), the descendants of an enemy of the sovereign were made into sack-bearers as punishment. Interpreter's note: For an English-language version of the *Nihongi* passage, see Aston 1972, vol. 1, 364.

183. *Ruijū sandai kyaku* Jōgan 8 (866)/10/8.

184. *Shoku nihon kōki* Jōwa 12 (845)/1/25.

185. See Toda Yoshimi 1967b, chapter 1. Also see Takahashi Takahiro 1972, and Izumiya Yasuo 1972, chapter 4.

186. *Ruijū sandai kyaku* Engi 2 (902)/4/11.

187. Toda Yoshimi 1976, 161–65. Interpreter's note: See the English translation of this article in chapter 10 of this volume. The pertinent material appears in section 1.

188. Ishimoda Shō 1973, part 1, chapter 1, sec. 2.

189. *Ruijū sandai kyaku*, legislation dated Kōnin 13 (822)/intercalary 9/20, citing a royal edict dated 822/7/28.

190. See the *Kugyō bunin* entry for 822 (Kōnin 13), vol. 1, 92.

191. See the *Ruijū sandai kyaku*, Council of State memorial to the throne dated Kōnin 14 (823)/1/27.

192. See *Ruijū sandai kyaku* Kōnin 13 (822)/intercalary 9/20.

193. Murai Yasuhiko 1968, 97.

194. Sakamoto Tarō 1928, 97. Interpreter's note: The *Engi shiki* provision can be found at the very end of volume 26.

195. Hotate Michihisa 1978, 52–54.

196. See Toda Yoshimi 1967c and Niunoya Tetsuichi 1975.

197. *Ruijū sandai kyaku* Kampyō 6 (894)/2/23. The term *koshū*, which is translated here as "abused their trust," indicates someone who commits a crime while in a position of official service. See Morohashi Tetsuji 1955, vol. 4, 4395. Interpreter's note: The legislation cited in *Ruijū sandai kyaku* was issued in response to a petition from Kii Province (*Kii no kuni ge*). For a discussion of conditions in Kii at the time, see Niunoya Tetsuichi 1976.

198. *Ruijū sandai kyaku* Kampyō 3 (891)/9/11.

199. See Hotate Michihisa 1978.

200. *Nihon Montoku Tennō jitsuroku* Ninju 3 (853)/3/22.

201. Charges of slander against the crown prince's retainers can be found in *Seiji yōryaku*, vol. 84, in a petition submitted by cultivators from the three districts of Sado Province dated Jōwa 1 (834)/11/5. Interpreter's note: The *Seiji yōryaku* is a mid-Heian compendium of legislation, compiled in 1008.

202. Toda Yoshimi 1967a; Toda Yoshimi 1975b, vol. 2, 29–31, 82. Such complaints are recorded from as early as the Taika era: an entry in the *Nihongi* dated 646/2/15 records that people sent to the capital for corvée labor were detained by government officials and forced to labor on other projects. The entry further notes that people had made many protests. In short, forwarding complaints to the central government and traveling from the provinces to the capital for political purposes were earlier traditions that re-emerged under the *ritsuryō* system. Interpreter's note: For the Taika event, in English see Aston 1972, vol. 2, 211–12. The earliest of the tenth-century complaints was issued in 974, and the last was dated in the mid-eleventh century (1052). In total nineteen petitions are recorded in historical sources, the best known of which is the *Owari gebumi* of 988.

203. *Nihon sandai jitsuroku* Gangyō 7 (883)/10/17; and *Shoku nihongi* Reiki 2 (716)/5/16.

204. *Ruijū sandai kyaku* Tempyō 18 (746)/7/21. Also see Naganuma Kenkai 1956; and Tōma Seita 1966, 146–76.

205. *Nihon sandai jitsuroku* Jōgan 4 (862)/5/20.

206. This viewpoint has already been advanced by Takahashi Takahiro in Takahashi Takahiro 1972.

207. *Shoku nihongi,* entry dated Yōrō 6 (726)/2/23. Interpreter's note: For the term translated here as "plotting," see Morohashi Tetsuji 1955, vol. 1, 877.

208. Sekiguchi Hiroko 1972.

209. Kawane Yoshiyasu 1971, 337–65. Interpreter's note: Hotate agrees with Ishimoda Shō's view, that the medieval age can be termed one of "the people" or "the folk." See chapter 13 by Ishimoda in this volume.

8

Toward Regency Leadership at Court

Morita Tei

Introduction by Joan R. Piggott

Readers of Japanese history in English have long known that regents from the Northern lineage (Hokke) of the Fujiwara family presided at court during the mid-Heian period, but how they came to do so and the actual nature of regental power beyond the general rubric of "marriage politics" has remained unclear. As the art historian Mimi Yiengpruksawan has observed, we surely need to dig deeper into the so-called Fujiwara Period to better understand the courtly world that produced Murasaki Shikibu and Sei Shōnagon, whose writings are loved but too-little illuminated by historical analysis.[1] The following essay explains something about why and how *sesshō* and *kampaku*—translated here as regents and viceroys—came to power.[2] Morita's story begins with what he considers "the seeds" of the regency in Fujiwara Fuyutsugu's day (775–826), continues through an era of "early regency" under Yoshifusa (716–777) and Mototsune (836–891), and ends with a sketch of the "mature regency" under Tadahira (880–949) in the first half of the tenth century. Other scholars recommend other periodization schemes, but Morita provides a sense of the issues and contextualizes them in court politics.

Morita argues that regental authority was the result of the long-term alliance, what I call an affinal strategy, that bound Fujiwara minister-affines and the throne in the effort to maximize royal control of *tennō*-centered government in the ninth century. While the eighth-century *ritsuryō* codes made the *tennō* the ultimate decision-maker who was to respond to memorials and requests for decisions from the ministerial Council of State (Daijōkan), by the early ninth century senior nobles (*kugyō*) on the Council came to take an increasingly important role in both policy making and promulgation of royal commands (see Figure 4.1).[3] Furthermore, although the *ritsuryō* codes called for the preeminent member of the Council, usually either the minister of the left or the minister of the right, to preside over the Council, and for all members of the Council to co-sign formal memorials resulting from Council discussions, by the Kōnin era (810–824) in practice any Council member from middle counselors and up could memorialize the throne, solicit a royal command, and have the royal command written out and executed by the Office of the Board of Controllers (Benkankyoku).

Making relations between throne and Council yet more complex, the Heian Council of State came to be mixed in membership—in addition to aristocrats it included scholar-officials appointed by early Heian monarchs as buttresses against oligarchy. Monarchs such as Kammu, Heizei, and Saga promoted men of talent—including literati and good provincial administrators—who supported the exercise of royal power. But Saga Tennō (r. 809–823) also needed high-powered political help to fight against his elder brother and predecessor on the throne, the retired *tennō* Heizei. So he turned to a scion of the aristocratic Northern Fujiwara lineage, Fuyutsugu.[4] Fuyutsugu served loyally as head of Saga's newly created Royal Secretariat (Kurōdodokoro) and in the Council of State during the reigns of two of Saga's heirs, Junna and Nimmyō. As court leader, Fuyutsugu defended his power on various flanks: in response to new circumstances in the provinces he was a pragmatic statesman who integrated the new wealthy in the countryside as the basis of provincial administration; he won the admiration of the court with his literary talents; and he relied on his daughter, Fujiwara Nobuko, to manage the back palace.[5] Nobuko (809–871) served as consort to the crown prince during the reign of Junna Tennō, and gave birth to the prince who became Montoku Tennō (r. 850–858). In other words, Fuyutsugu maximized his influence over the Council of State, the back palace, and the throne, all of which was possible because of his close affinal relations with Saga Tennō and his successors. According to Morita, this was also the nature of the power enjoyed by later regents and viceroys. In short, Morita argues that the powers of the regency derive from the throne.[6]

Coups and plots served to strengthen such power for Fuyutsugu's descendents. The Jōwa Coup of 842 led to the enthronement of the first child *tennō*, Seiwa (r. 858–876), for whom Fuyutsugu's son, Yoshifusa, was named prime minister and regent. In 866 the burning of the Great Heavenly Gate (Ōtenmon) along with allegations of plotting by middling members of the Council of State led to Yoshifusa's appointment as viceroy, even if the prerogatives of that post were not yet fully elaborated. Notes Morita, "One key prerogative of the regency would be to preside over and unify the senior nobles" at just such moments of crisis. According to Morita unified control of the Council of State was the purpose for which the regency was established. Some twenty years later, in 884, Kōkō Tennō took the throne after the reportedly mad Yōzei was forced to abdicate. An older man little prepared to govern, Kōkō (r. 884–887) relied heavily on Yoshifusa's help, as his own words indicate: "Coming in he aids me, going out he oversees officialdom. . . . Whatever he memorializes and commands, let it be so." According to Kōkō's edict, which contains the first extant use of the term *kampaku*, Yoshifusa was to control memorials to the throne as well as the transmission of royal commands. Such duties came to be termed the "inner (i.e. royal) inspectorate" (*nairan*), which meant reviewing all documents going to or coming from the throne, and both the post and its occupant came to be referred to by this term, *nairan*.[7] The same powers were proffered to Yoshifusa's heir, Mototsune, when Uda Tennō (r. 887–897) proved unable to conduct court business without his aid. Morita terms the eras of Yoshifusa and Mototsune "the early regency."

After Mototsune's death in 891, Uda Tennō ruled alone; and after his son's accession as Daigo Tennō (r. 897–930), he sought to guard his royal power by making Mototsune's son, Tokihira, share court leadership with a scholar-official, Sugawara Michizane. But Uda's efforts failed when his heir was persuaded by Tokihira to exile Sugawara in 901, after which Tokihira stayed on as court leader. Tokihira's brother, Tadahira, later inherited that leadership. For Morita, Tadahira's promotion to minister of the left in 924 marks the beginning of the "mature regency." Especially after the accession of his nephew, seven-year-old Suzaku Tennō (r. 930–946), Tadahira's regental power embraced the same three bases utilized by his great great grandfather, Fuyutsugu: control of throne, Council of State, and back palace. In 936 Tadahira was promoted to the post of prime minister (*daijōdaijin*), and in 941 he became viceroy. By this time, the sense of differentiation between regency for a child monarch and the viceroy post to aid an adult monarch had become clearer, as had the distinction between the posts of *daijōdaijin* and *kampaku*.

In terms of initiatives in provincial administration under the Northern Fujiwara regency, Morita contrasts its "court-centered polity" (*ōchō kokka*) with earlier *tennō*-centered *ritsuryō* polity. The essay by Sasaki Muneo translated in chapter 9 of this volume is more explicit on the subject, but Morita associates the beginning of a new style of center-periphery relations with the pragmatic statesman Fujiwara Fuyutsugu, and notes as well that "the mature regency occurred more or less contemporaneously with what historians term 'court-centered polity.'"

Morita Tei

Toward Regency Leadership at Court

Interpreted by Joan R. Piggott

From the time the capital was moved to Heian in 794, government administration over the capital and the provinces followed lines defined by the eighth-century Chinese-style law codes. These penal and administrative codes, known as *ritsuryo*, gave leadership over the system to the Council of State, composed of the *tennō*'s leading advisers. In Heian times these royal lieutenants—including the prime minister, ministers (*daijin*) of the left and right, senior and middle counselors (*nagon*), and advisors (*sangi*)—were called *kugyō*, or "senior nobles."

According to the codes, policies for governing the realm were to be debated in discussions by the Council of State followed by a royal decision based on such discussions. Following the Law on Official Communications and Practices (Kushikiryō) in the eighth-century codes, written drafts of royal commands were called either *shōsho* or *chokushi*.[8] Such drafts, as well as reports of *kugyō* discussions in the form of formal memorials (*ronsō* or *sōji*)—were to be submitted to the throne. But since such formal memorials required painstaking procedures, informal reports and requests for royal decisions known as *gebumi* (reports) were also submitted by central and provincial officials to the Council of State and later sent on to the monarch for a decision. Such informal reports were categorized as "general documents for consideration and judgment" and constituted a more convenient manner of memorializing the throne. Together with formal memorials, they came to be called *kansō*, Council of State memorials to the throne. Over time the more formal memorials were used only on special occasions, such as enthronements or new year's celebrations. Preparation and submission of *kansō* became an important activity for daily government administration (*seimu*).

In terms of actual execution, when the *tennō*'s commands or reports of the senior nobles' discussions were prepared in writing, or when a royal decision in response to an informal memorial was handed down, the Board of Controllers (Benkan) wrote the draft as well as subsequent directives that were dispatched to government offices in the capital and provinces as either orders (*senji*) or missives (*chō*) from the Council of State. Formal memorials were to be signed by all members of the Council of State before being presented to the throne, and royal proclamations (*shōsho*) were also to be signed by all the senior nobles before promulgation. Royal edicts known as *chokushi,* however, did not necessitate senior nobles' signatures and could be issued by the autonomous order of the *tennō*. Nonetheless, early Heian-period ritual handbooks such as the *Shingishiki* (*New Ceremonial Protocols*) directed that senior nobles ascertain the royal will and have it prepared in written form.[9] So by early Heian times *kugyō* involvment in the preparation of royal edicts became customary.

And as we have seen, the most important administrative procedures at the court were handled by the *kugyō*. The *kugyō* responsible for dealing with a given matter was termed the *shōkei,* or "senior-noble-in-charge." Among the senior nobles, the prime minister was preeminent in rank. But since that post was often left vacant, the minister of the left (*sadaijin*), or in his absence the minister of the right (*udaijin*), acted as presiding minister (*ichinokami*) of the Council. For everyday matters this presiding minister functioned as senior-noble-in-charge.

Still there were occasions when the ranking minister did not preside. A Daijōkan protocol (*shiki*) of the Kōnin era (810–824) read, "In general, report affairs to the Council of State. Should a senior minister not be available, relay matters to a middle counselor or higher [official]. In the case of very important matters [that minister should then] memorialize the throne for a decision. Otherwise, follow usual procedures." The same practice is noted in a Daijōkan protocol of the Engi era (901–923). Such rules make it clear that a middle counselor or counselor of higher rank could receive reports or requests from agencies and provinces, decide how to respond, inform the throne, await the royal decision, and then order the *tennō*'s decision promulgated. In fact, a scan of the early tenth-century compendium of supplementary legislation *Ruijū sandai kyaku* indicates that more than half of such regulations were Council directives resulting from a Council member soliciting a royal command. In such cases the royal command was conveyed to the Board of Controllers to be put into writing. On his own initiative a couselor or minister could memorialize the throne—there was no need to discuss the matter with fellow members of the Council. By way of contrast, senior nobles below the position of middle counselor had to discuss their concerns with other *kugyō*—they could not approach the throne on their own. Procedurally, it was the prerogative of top-ranking senior nobles to come up with plans, present them to the throne, wait for a royal decision, and then direct the controllers to draw up promulgating orders.

This meant that the highest-ranking minister of the Council could not restrain his counselor and ministerial colleagues who were middle counselors or higher. Any one of them could approach the throne and request a royal command that could then be drafted into law by the controllers. Actual leadership of the Council by the highest ranker, the presiding minister, was therefore quite uncertain—there was always danger that rival views could be taken to the *tennō* and become law.

Such uncertainty played a key role in prompting emergence of the Northern Fujiwara regents in Heian times. In the eighth century, members of the Northern Fujiwara lineage had allied themselves with the throne to strengthen the authority of the presiding minister of the Council of State. But at the ninth-century court, middling and lower officials like Tomo Yoshio (809–868) emerged as royal intimates and rose to powerful posts on the Council of State, from which they challenged even higher-rankers.[10] Establishment of the new offices of *sesshō* and *kampaku* was a response to the danger posed by such rivals to the preeminent minister. A *sesshō* came to be appointed when the monarch was a minor, and he was charged with actually rendering royal decisions as the monarch's leading minister. The *kampaku* serving an adult *tennō* was to oversee officialdom while exercising plenary royal powers (*banki*). Prime ministers concurrently serving as *kampaku* oversaw the dual responsibilities of memorializing the throne and receiving royal commands. They transmitted the royal will through orders called *senji*, while they also headed up the deliberative activities of the Council of State preceeding submission of a memorial to the throne.

So, as we shall see, while any senior noble holding the post of middle counselor or above could memorialize the throne, establishment of the *sesshō* and *kampaku* posts enabled members of the Northern Fujiwara lineage to assert leadership over the Council from a position possessing prerogatives beyond those of other *kugyō*. The historical trajectory over which regental authority emerged was a long one with many twists and turns. Chronologically speaking, regency leadership emerged during the reign of Seiwa Tennō (r. 858–876) when Fujiwara Yoshifusa functioned as leader of the court. However, since the monarchs Uda and Daigo did not appoint regents, I use the term "early regency" to refer to the era of Fujiwara Mototsune (836–891), which was one of formation. I consider the tenth-century era of Tadahira, who presided during Suzaku Tennō's reign (930–946), to have witnessed emergence of the mature regency.

A High Point of Royal Authority: The Early Ninth Century

We begin by considering the early ninth-century era of Saga Tennō (r. 809–823) and conditions that led to Fujiwara Yoshifusa's regency. The most visible characteristic of Saga's reign and that of his successors Junna Tennō (r. 823–833) and Nimmyō Tennō (r. 833–850) was continuation of policies from the earlier reigns of Kammu (r. 781–806) and Heizei (r. 806–809). The authority of the *tennō*

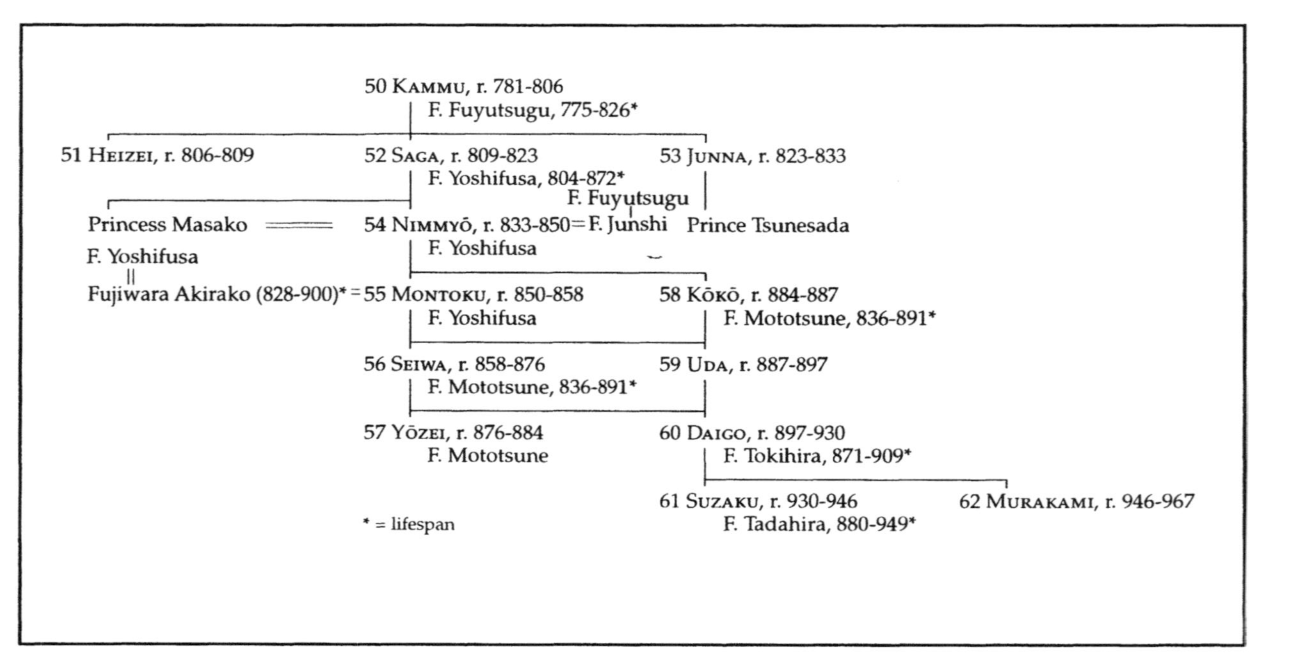

Fig. 8.1. Early Heian *Tennō* and Northern Fujiwara Ministers, Regents, and Consorts

increased and the sphere of *tennō*-centered politics expanded. Kammu Tennō had functioned very much as leader of his own court—he left the headship of the Council of State vacant. There was but a twelve-month period from the sixth month of 781 to the sixth month of 782 when Fujiwara Uona served as minister of the left. Kammu Tennō consciously kept the *kugyō* stratum in check, a policy that was continued during Heizei Tennō's reign. Only toward the end of Junna's reign, in 832, was Kammu's loyal adviser Fujiwara Ōtsugu appointed minister of the left. During this period when there were few high rankers on the Council, middling members became more prominent. They gained the favor of the throne based on their individual talents, and those who rose to prominence within the household of the crown prince were particularly notable. In short, from the eighth century onward, because of the gradual penetration of *ritsuryō* policies and the coincident decline of the status order founded on great titled families (*uji*), those backing more autocratic monarchy held sway and the preeminent role of the *tennō* was strengthened.

The monarchs Saga, Junna, and Nimmyō were energetic supporters of T'ang court culture and they worked to advance literati officials as court leaders (see Figure 8.1). All three *tennō* admired Chinese poetry and since they themselves composed and enjoyed both prose and poetry in Chinese, their intimates were talented poets or others who emerged from studies at the Royal University (Daigaku). There were frequent banquets and hunting parties during which the *tennō* sponsored poetry reading, writing, and discussion. It was an age when the *tennō* and courtiers shared a profound sense of mutuality, when even those of middling status possessing scholarly talents could rise to *kugyō* posts and receive appointments in the Royal Secretariat and the Office of the Board of Controllers.

While historians have sometimes referred to the reigns of these monarchs as an era of "governance by nurturing literature," royal intimates were not simply poets and literary scholars. "Virtuous provincial governors" (*ryōri*) were also royal intimates. For Kammu Tennō and his successors, a major concern was reforming *ritsuryō* administration linking capital and countryside.

An examplary official who distinguished himself in this regard was Ono Minemori (778–830), whose father Nagami had served as second-in-command at the provincial headquarters in Mutsu and as an assistant commander (*sei-i-fuku-shōgun*) in the military on the eastern frontier. Ono served on the crown prince's staff prior to Saga's accession and thereafter oversaw operation of the Inner Palace Storehouse (Uchikura). In 822 he was promoted to the post of advisor on the Council of State and also served as senior administrator (*daini*) at the Dazaifu. It is not clear whether he ever studied at the Royal University, but like many other contemporaries with literary talent he was made junior second-in-command in the Ministry of Personnel, and his poems were selected for official collections of verse in Chinese such as the *Cloud-borne Anthology* (*Ryōunshū*), the *Collection of Literary Masterpieces* (*Bunka shūreishū*), and the *Anthology Ordering the State* (*Keikokushū*).[11] His literary talents clearly gained him close relations with the *tennō* and a seat on the Council of State. In fact, many of his poems were written in response to verses by Saga Tenno himself.

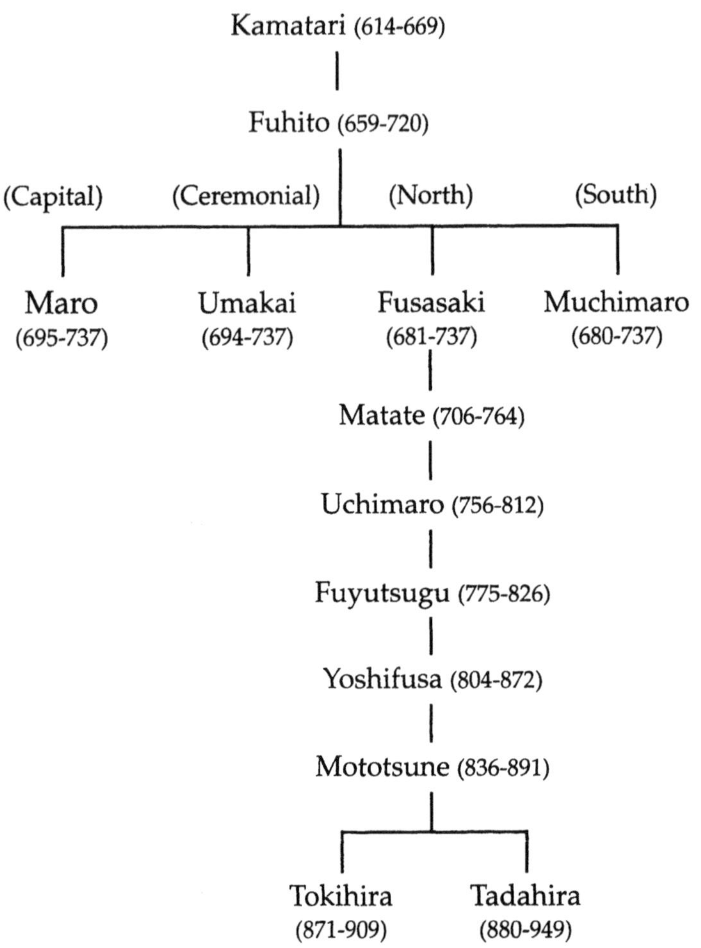

Fig. 8.2. Selected Genealogy of the Early Northern Fujiwara Regents' Line

However, Ono was more than a poet. As overseer of affairs at the Dazaifu he memorialized the throne to recommend implementation of a new policy of state-managed fields (*kueiden*) in Kyūshū—the idea was to contract out cultivation of some 12,000 *chō* (1 *chō*=2.94 acres) of public fields. In responding to the initiatives and wishes of provincial governors and officials in his jurisdiction—the various provinces of Kyūshū were overseen by the Dazaifu—Ono demonstrated unusual ability and effort as a public administrator. In addition to Ono, there were other men of letters who had fathers of fourth or fifth rank and who were eventually promoted to seats on the Council of State, including Asano Shikatori, Prince Naoyo, Tachibana Tsunenushi, Kiyohara Natsuno, and Minabuchi Hirosada. All were courtiers during the reigns of Saga, Junna, and Nimmyō.

Although a number of middle-ranking men of letters emerged around the throne, hereditary aristocrats did not lose their influence. The Fujiwara, who had been accumulating wealth and influence since the eighth century, gave up some 15,000 prebendal residential units (*fuko*) in 820 in exchange for tax-free status over five generations. And while their members did not hold the exalted post of minister of the left in Saga's time, members of the Northern Lineage such as Uchimaro (756–812) and Sonohito (756–818) nonetheless served as influential members on the Council of State. Fujiwara Fuyutsugu (775–826) played a particularly important role in the emergence of the Northern Fujiwara regency.

Fuyutsugu, a son of Uchimaro, was born in 775 (see Figure 8.2). He served as a third- and then second-level manager in the household of Crown Prince Kamino before the latter took the throne as Saga Tennō. According to his posthumous biography, Fuyutsugu was a man of great ability and energy who excelled in performing official tasks. His talents included both the civilian and martial arts, and he was considered someone who planned well for all eventualities. In character he was reportedly benevolent, sociable, and empathetic. But it was his self-confidence and skill in letters that attracted his royal patron's favor. Fuyutsugu served as one of the compilers of the *Collection of Literary Masterpieces* and more than a few of his poems are extant, many of them written in response to Saga's command. Although Fuyutsugu was the scion of a hereditary lineage of nobles, he cultivated the mien of a literatus (*bunkajin*). When the Royal Secretariat was established in 810, he and Kose Notari became its directors; and during the following year, Fuyutsugu was granted a seat on the Council of State as an advisor. And when Fujiwara Sonohito died in 818, Fuyutsugu was promoted to senior counselor and later served as minister of the right, which made him the leader of the Council of State. Thus, Saga Tennō demonstrated abiding confidence in Fuyutsugu. Meanwhile, Fuyutsugu's daughter Nobuko became the senior consort of Saga's Prince Masanaga; and Saga's daughter, Minamoto Kiyōhime, became a consort of Fuyutsugu's son, Yoshifusa. Because of his ancestors' leading roles at earlier courts, Fuyutsugu was able to cultivate the talents needed to gain a place close to the throne while deepening affinal ties with the royal line. So did his lineage prosper. After Fuyutsugu's death Nobuko's son assumed the throne as Montoku Tennō (850–858), and Fuyutsugu was posthumously honored by promotion to the supreme office of prime minister. His role in laying the foundation for the Northern Fujiwara regency is unquestionable.

An Era of Political Reform

In Fuyutsugu's day political reform was an important topic of discussion. The *tennō*-centered *ritsuryō* polity was by then a century old, and various problems had become apparent. The efficacy of census registers (*koseki*), tax registers (*keichō*) based on them, and officially distributed fields (*handen*) had steadily declined and the need for corrective measures was apparent. There were two options: a more conservative one stressing reform and a more pragmatic and innovative one responding to contemporary conditions.

From the reign of Kammu Tennō onward, policymakers had decided that dealing with the increasing poverty of ordinary cultivators was pivotal. Their approach, based on *ritsuryō* concepts and structures, was fundamentally conservative—they hoped to "restore" *ritsuryō*-based governance. But when no measures to deal directly with the problem were proposed during the reigns of Kammu, Heizei, and Saga, cultivators grew more impoverished and a new group of local elites gained power. Although Fujiwara Sonohito (756–818), Uchimaro's successor as leader of the Council of State, had made repeated memorials stressing the importance of rescuing impoverished cultivators, Fuyutsugu gave up restoring the past. Instead he recognized the existence of the new wealthy (*fugōsō*) in the countryside and proposed making them the new base of provincial administration. When Fuyutsugu replaced Sonohito as ranking member of the Council of State in 818, there were visible changes in policy. For instance, by the early 820s official rice loans (*kusuiko*) were no longer levied on individuals but were based on the area of land under cultivation. At the same time, Ono Minemori's new strategy of contracting out cultivation of public fields also called for taxes computed on cultivated land area. This new reliance on contracted fields was an attempt to integrate wealthy elites in the countryside by putting elites themselves in charge. *Ritsuryō* methods such as census-taking and field distribution were never formally cancelled, but new methods replaced them, and Fuyutsugu led in developing such policies. He was not merely a court politician—he played a key role as policymaker, and in that respect can be considered initiator of the Northern Fujiwara regency.

Yoshifusa's "Early Regency"

After fourteen years of rule, in 823 Saga Tennō retired and passed his throne to his younger brother, Prince Ōtomo, who reigned as Junna Tennō. Junna's crown prince was his nephew, Saga's Prince Masanaga, born of Saga's queen-consort, Tachibana Kachiko (786–850). Masanaga took the throne to rule as Nimmyō Tennō in 833. In turn, his crown prince was Junna's son, Prince Tsunesada, born of Junna's queen-consort, Princess Masako, one of Saga's daughters. During these years relations within the royal family were harmonious, and Fuyutsugu was successful in expanding his influence at successive courts. Meanwhile, royal finances depended on royal grant fields (*chokushiden*).[12] During this time the retired monarch Saga functioned as patriarch of the royal house and controlled both the court and the larger polity.

But when Saga In died in 842 there were rumors about a planned coup by supporters of Prince Tsunesada. The royal guards were mobilized, the crown prince's guards were disarmed, and those accused were exiled. Historians call this the Jōwa Coup, after the era name, and at the time the mischief was blamed principally on men serving in Crown Prince Tsunesada's household, including Tomo Kowamine and Tachibana Hayanari. When we examine the matter closely, however, there seems to have been no reason for Tsunesada's supporters to remove Nimmyō Tennō from the throne. The end result was that Nimmyō Tennō's Prince Michiyasu, the grandson of Fujiwara Fuyutsugu through his daughter Nobuko, became crown prince in Tsunesada's place. Undoubtedly a key supporter of Prince Michiyasu's candidacy for the throne was none other than his uncle, Fuyutsugu's son and heir, Fujiwara Yoshifusa (804–872); and Princess Masako, Tsunesada's mother, reportedly blamed her own mother, Queen-mother Tachibana Kachiko, for the affair. All this suggests that the plot may well have been hatched by Kachiko and Yoshifusa acting together—indeed, Yoshifusa's sister, Nobuko, was Nimmyō's queen-consort (*kisaki*), while the new crown prince was Kachiko's grandson and Yoshifusa's nephew. Making this scenario still more likely is the fact that as a result of the incident all those senior to Yoshifusa on the Council of State were removed from power, enhancing Yoshifusa's power significantly. Meanwhile, the party of men of letters that had been so prominent at the early ninth-century court was significantly weakened by the events of 842.[13]

Nimmyō Tennō died in 850 and was succeeded by Michiyasu as Montoku Tennō. Meanwhile Yoshifusa's daughter, Akirakeiko, became queen-consort, assuring that Yoshifusa's influence over the throne would increase.[14] When Yoshifusa had become minister of the right in 848, Minamoto Tokiwa was minister of the left; but Yoshifusa now began to function as leader of the Council of State even before he was named prime minister in 857. The latter appointment signaled the high point of Yoshifusa's power and made him the first minister-regent.[15] At the time, Montoku Tennō was 31 years old, obviating the need for a regent, but Yoshifusa nevertheless functioned much as did later *kampaku*. Then in 858 when Montoku died and was succeeded by the nine-year-old Prince Korehito as Seiwa Tennō (r. 858–876), Yoshifusa was once again charged with overseeing royal affairs as "aid and guide" to the child monarch.[16] The term *sesshō* was not yet in use but the office was already functioning. Yoshifusa's era clearly witnessed the beginning of the regency.

The Ōtenmon Affair and Fujiwara Yoshifusa

On the tenth evening of the third intercalary month of 866—less than a decade after Yoshifusa's appointment as prime minister, the Great Heavenly Gate (Ōtenmon) that opened on the precincts of the Throne Hall burned down. Reports suggested arson, and rumors implicated a senior counselor named Tomo Yoshio, possibly acting together with one of Yoshifusa's younger brothers, Minister of the Right Fujiwara Yoshimi. Days later a judgment to the effect that Minister of the Left Minamoto Makoto was complicit was also issued, and royal agents were sent to arrest Minamoto at his mansion without Yoshifusa's knowledge. When the matter was subsequently reported to him, Yoshifusa entered the royal presence, found that such arrests had not been made by royal command, and freed Tomo, Minamoto, and others. But on the third day of the eighth month, another accusation was made against Tomo Yoshio and his son, Nakatsune. This time the residences and property of both men were confiscated, and they were sent into distant exile. This affair has long been known as the Ōtenmon Coup (*Ōtenmon no hen*).[17]

On the day when Yoshio was questioned, a royal edict was issued that ordered Yoshifusa to "carry out governance of the realm."[18] Since the *tennō* had undergone his coming-of-age ceremony in 864, technically Yoshifusa's role as regent should have been terminated then. But in the crisis following the ominous burning of the palace gate, and given the charges against a leading member of the Council of State, the young *tennō* depended heavily on Yoshifusa. As a result, the latter wielded extraordinary authority.

One prerogative of the regental post—presiding over and unifying the Council of State—was precisely what Yoshifusa needed to assert authority over his brother, Minister of the Right Fujiwara Yoshimi, and Senior Counselor Tomo Yoshio. It is likely that Yoshimi and Tomo Yoshio had actually sent agents to Minamoto Makoto's mansion without a royal order, and despite Yoshifusa's post as the *tennō*'s leading minister, these two lower-ranking members of the Council could not be easily stopped.

As a result of these events of 866, Yoshifusa's authority was significantly increased over that of lower-ranking members of the Council. It is also notable that Tomo Yoshio was not a literatus—he came out of the ranks of "virtuous provincial governors."[19] In his conduct throughout the incident Yoshifusa anticipated the strategy of later viceroys who aimed at restraining literati and middling royal advisers who engaged in willful behavior. Although the offices of *sesshō* and *kampaku* were not yet fully institutionalized, Yoshifusa succeeded in exerting power over independent minded senior nobles, just as would later viceroys.

Fujiwara Mototsune (836–891) as Viceroy

Yoshifusa died in 872, and for a time Seiwa Tennō reigned unaided. But when he retired in 876 he passed the throne to a son, the nine-year-old Prince Sadaakira, who ruled as Yōzei Tennō (r. 877–884). Yōzei's mother was Takaiko, sister to Fujiwara Mototsune, Yoshifusa's adopted son and heir.[20] When Yōzei took the throne, a royal edict ordered Mototsune to "protect and aid the young lord, and oversee affairs of the throne as did Yoshifusa in past."[21] Mototsune was minister of the right, but when he thus was named regent—which by precedent now included leadership of the Council of State—he surpassed Minister of the Left Minamoto Tōru as head of the Council. Yoshifusa had served as the first regent for a child monarch but now the office was becoming institutionalized. Four years later, in 880, Mototsune was named prime minister; and the *Kugyō bunin*, a register of appointments to the Council of State, terms

Mototsune *kampaku* from that time on. In fact, however, the distinction between the *sesshō* as a regent for a young monarch and the *kampaku* as royal aide or viceroy for an adult monarch had not yet been clearly articulated.

In 884 Yōzei Tennō was removed from the throne, reportedly because of violent behavior, and Kōkō Tennō succeeded him. Kōkō and Mototsune had no affinal ties, but Mototsune aided the new ruler greatly. On the fifth day of the sixth month of 884, an edict stated that "coming in he aids me, going out he oversees officialdom. Let whatever he memorializes and commands be so." From this we know that Mototsune was empowered to control the memorializing process (*sōsei*), as did subsequent viceroys.[22] When Kōkō died in 887, Uda Tennō took the throne and commanded that Prime Minister Mototsune continue to oversee officialdom and exercise all the plenary powers of the throne, including oversight of memorials and written orders as in the past. His edict indicates that Mototsune was actually to function as viceroy without formal appointment to that office. It was at this point that the so-called Akō Incident divided the court: when Mototsune refused the royal command because of unworthiness, the scholar Tachibana Hiromi, who was extremely close to Uda, wrote in response, "Yoshifusa should be named *akō* [most trusted minister]."[23] This memorial initiated debate over the nature of the *akō* office and its prerogatives. Tachibana subsequently lost the battle and was forced to admit to a scholarly error, while Mototsune's authority over other members of the Council, as *kampaku* rather than *akō*, became clearer.

Regency Politics Regularized

Yoshifusa used the Jōwa and Ōtenmon crises to expand his power as aide to the throne. Literati and other senior nobles from mid-ranking families who had increased their influence dynamitically in the early decades of the ninth century were forced into retreat by this leading aristocrat at the helm of the *tennō*-centered court and polity. By the time Mototsune came to lead the court during the reigns of Kōkō and Uda, the trajectory of Northern Fujiwara power was clear and unremitting. Domination of top posts by royal collaterals (especially the Saga Genji, scions of Saga who were given the Minamoto surname) and the Northern Fujiwara in the Royal Secretariat, the Office of the Board of Controllers, and the eight ministries was also pronounced. So from the later ninth century onward the tendency for the Regents' Line to dominate leading court posts increased.[24] One official reportedly lamented, "If one is not backed by the [Northern] Fujiwara, one's lineage cannot succeed."[25] Opportunities for literati and middling nobles significantly decreased as aristocrats came to dominate the hierarchy of officialdom.

Fujiwara Mototsune died in 891, after having built up the power of the regency to an unprecedented degree. Uda Tennō, bitter over his defeat in the Akō crisis, used the opportunity to promote his beloved adviser, Sugawara Michizane (845–903), while initiating his own independent reign (*shinsei*). Then, after Uda's retirement, Daigo Tennō continued to rule without a regent; but by this time *ritsuryō* governance was in its final days—provincial governors were making more and more policy decisions on their own.[26] Various Council of State directives (*kampu*) were issued seeking to stem wrongdoing by powerful aristocratic houses and to strengthen the unity and organization of provincial government along *ritsuryō* lines. But it was too little too late to overcome the crisis in provincial administration.

The presiding senior noble at that time was Fujiwara Tokihira, Mototsune's eldest son (see Figure 8.1); and although Tokihira demonstrated himself to be an able political strategist, Uda Tennō treated him coldly, choosing to rely instead on commoner princes like Minamoto Sadami and other mid-rankers. In particular, Minister of the Right Sugawara Michizane represented the hopes of mid-rankers because he had opposed Tokihira. Friction between the two increased steadily until 901, when Michizane was finally exiled to the Dazaifu in Kyūshū. Thereafter, Tokihira tightened his hold over the court; but he too died at the young age of thirty-nine in 909, at a historical moment when provincial governors were enjoying a heyday.

Thereafter, Uda's strategy of making Fujiwara Tokihira and Sugawara Michizane joint overseers of the memorial process [from 898 onward] shaped the special circumstances of Daigo Tennō's reign.[27] Specifically, they had oversight of memorials submitted upward, of royal commands handed down, and approval of Council directives.[28] Tokihira and Michizane were not given the specific post of *kampaku*; but their mandate was the same as that exercised by later holders of that office. And after Michizane's exile, Tokihira exercised the full powers of the *kampaku* post although that title had not yet been coined.

Fujiwara Tadahira as Regent

Following Tokihira's death, Minister of the Right Minamoto Hikaru became presiding minister of the Council of State until his death in 913.[29] Thereupon Tokihira's younger brother, Tadahira, became the leading member of the Council of State. Although Tokihira and Tadahira were brothers, their political careers were notably different: Tokihira had built his power as minister of the left gradually but Tadahira rose at court during Uda Tennō's reign and was even friendly with his brother's rival, Sugawara. And while Tokihira was a firm adherent of *ritsuryō*-based reform, Tadahira believed that such reforms would not prove sufficient. Tadahira had served a long tenure in the Board of Controllers' Office in relatively low-level posts and had come to the conclusion that more flexible policies were needed to administer the realm.

Moreover, although Tokihira had become friendly with Daigo Tennō, Tadahira had rather distant relations with that monarch. Indeed, after Tadahira became minister of the right, even without any other senior member on the Council it took him ten years to be promoted to minister of the left in early 924. Frosty relations between Tadahira and the ruler contributed to political stagnation during the second decade of the Engi era (901–923), and it was only in the subsequent Enchō era (923–931), when sickness spread and royal princes and grandsons were dying of plague, that Daigo's leadership flagged and Tadahira became increasingly prominent. After Tadahira was finally named minister of the left in 924, an epoch of administrative reforms ensued. It was at this time that poll taxes were discontinued in favor of land-based taxes.

Although some changes had already taken place at the provincial and district levels, they were formally accepted by the Council of State only during Tadahira's tenure as court leader. In other words, what some historians have called the "court-centered-polity" system was finally ratified at the top as a result of Tadahira's leadership.[30]

Tadahira gained the office of regent at a particularly dramatic juncture —when lightning struck the royal residence, the Seiryōden, and Daigo Tennō fell ill in 930. It was then that the three-year-old Suzaku Tennō (r. 930–946) was enthroned. Six years later, in 936, Tadahira was named prime minister. It was some years after Suzaku's adult initiation in 936 that Tadahira was allowed to resign as regent and only then was he named *kampaku*. At that point, Tadahira's son, Fujiwara Saneyori, was serving on the Council of State, and Tadahira's elder sister, Fujiwara Onshi, oversaw the back palace as queen-mother (*taikō*). Such arrangements allowed Tadahira and his supporters to enjoy preeminent power at court in this era of what can be termed "the fully mature regency."[31] Although after Tadahira's death, during Murakami Tennō's reign (946–967) no regent was named, from Reizei's reign (967–969) on, regental appointments became common practice, with Tadahira's sons and grandsons occupying these posts.

To conclude, from the era of Fujiwara Fuyutsugu to that of Tadahira, Northern Fujiwara regents asserted their authority over literati and middle ranking officials who had gained prominence during the early decades of the Heian period. The regency was thus fashioned by Fujiwara Fuyutsugu's heirs, scions of his lineage of the Northern Fujiwara. Also worthy of further study is the fact that the "mature regency" emerged more or less contemporaneously with the "court-centered polity." The relationship between these two historical developments needs further research and articulation.

Notes

1. Yiengpruksawan 1994.

2. This essay originally appeared as Morita Tei, "Sekkan seiji e no michi." See Morita Tei 1991. On "court-centered polity," see chapters 9 and 10 by Sasaki and Toda respectively in this volume.

3. The Council of State was composed of ministers (*daijin*), counselors (*nagon*), and advisors (*sangi*) appointed by the *tennō* to advise him and carry out his orders. There might be anywhere from ten to twenty members, with advisors generally holding the fourth or third rank, counselors holding the third or second rank, and ministers generally holding the first rank. By Heian times Council members were collectively known as *kugyō*; and besides participating in various activities of the Council, individual members managed key ministries, the Royal Police (Kebiishichō), the Six Guards' Headquarters (Rokuefu), the Board of Controllers Office (Benkankyoku), as well as households of queen-consorts (Chūgūshiki, Kōgōgūshiki) and the crown prince (Tōgūshiki). Such concurrent postings greatly facilitated communication between components of court government. By the tenth century individual members who were middle counselors

(*chūnagon*) or higher were charged with superintending specific activities or responsibilities, in which capacity they were called the "senior-noble-in-charge" (*shōkei*). Over time such specialization led to fewer meetings, and less influence, for the Council as a corporate group.

4. The attempted coup is sometimes termed "the Kusuko Coup" (*Kusuko no hen*), after one of its participants. But there is little doubt that the organizer was the retired monarch Heizei himself.

5. Morita's chronology for governmental pragmatism in dealing with the countryside begins earlier than that in Batten 1993. Batten dates pragmatism in countryside administration from the tenth century.

6. In his recent overview of scholarship on the regency, Sasaki Muneo notes that some scholars see the regent's powers deriving from the throne while others see them deriving from the Council of State. See Sasaki Muneo 1999.

7. As Sasaki points out, the term *kampaku* can be found in the *History of the Former Han Dynasty* (*Ch'en Han shu*), which text was popular at the Japanese court from at least the late seventh century. According to Sasaki's reading, the *kampaku* was "the preeminent minister who was to take care of all things and then report to the throne." See Sasaki Muneo 1999, 4.

8. Interpreter's note: According to the Heian-period legal commentary, the *Ryō no gige*, *shōsho* were to be used in the case of very important matters while *chokushi* were to be used for everyday affairs. See Satō Shin'ichi 1997, 55–56.

9. Interpreter's note: The *Shingishiki* is a handbook of court ritual drafted between 947 and 957, with additional notes added through the 960s. It was compiled by order of Murakami Tennō (r. 946–967). For the text, see *Gunsho ruijū* (Kujibu 1), 219–57. A recent discussion is that by Furuse Natsuko 1998, 321-22 and elsewhere.

10. Interpreter's note: Tomo (alt. Ban) was a descendent of the ancient noble (*uji*) family, the Ōtomo. His rise within the palace indicates his strengths as a scholar and writer. First, he spent a decade or so in the palace Kyōshoden, a library administered by the Royal Secretariat (Kurōdodokoro). By 842 he was a senior residential palace secretary (*dainaiki*) with concurrent responsibilities in the monarch's private Royal Secretariat and in the Ministry of Personnel as third-in-command (*jō*). In 847 Tomo was head of the Royal Secretariat as well as middle right controller. In 848 he was seated on the Council of State as an advisor (*sangi*) with junior 4th lower rank, and he functioned as both senior right controller and head of the Right Palace Guards. By 864, when the Ōtenmon burned and he was implicated, Tomo had risen to the high post of major counselor (*dainagon*).

11. Interpreter's note: These compilations date from 814 to 827 and attest the classical Chinese principle to the effect that "literary arts make the realm." They continued the tradition begun by Nara-period poetry anthologies of both Japanese and Chinese poetry. For instance, the mid-Nara *Kaifūsō* anthology contains Chinese poems written by courtiers from the late seventh century up to the 750s. See Borgen 1986, 41-43. For a meticulous discussion of the idea of *keikoku*—"a realm founded on the classics"—in T'ang China, see Bol 1992, 76–98, esp. 84.

12. Interpreter's note: In the early Heian period, *chokushiden* were unopened tracts of public land to be opened by the grantee so that rent from the fields could be used for the grantee's support. Those who opened such fields included retired monarchs, members of the royal family, and temples and shrines. The term first appears in a document of 806. Proprietors, eager to establish rent-yielding estates (*shōen*), reportedly enticed farmers away from officially distributed fields (*kubunden* or *handen*) to work these newly opened estates. Historians assume that rent on such estates together with other conditions of

cultivation (such as exemption from provincial labor conscription) must have been attractive to cultivators. Naturally such estates impacted the original tax structure envisioned by the *ritsuryō* codes. Over time estates gradually became the single most important source of support for Heian royals and aristocrats.

13. Interpreter's note: Satō Makoto has noted that the Jōwa Coup reimposed the Chinese ideal of patrilineal stem succession of the throne; it also distanced Northern Fujiwara rivals in the Ceremonial Branch (Shikike), as well as a leading Tachibana minister, from power. Junna's royal line, which lost out in the affair, had as its founding mother a woman from the Ceremonial Branch, Fujiwara Tabiko. See Satō Makoto 1991 and Endō Keita 2000.

14. There were opponents of this disposition of the succession: supporters of Prince Kunitaka, born of a daughter of Ki Natora, strongly opposed Akirakeiko's appointment.

15. During the Nara Period there had been powerful ministers such as Fujiwara Nakamaro and Dōkyō, but both perished after having been accused of rebellious activities. Their tenures should not be considered precedents for Yoshifusa's conduct of his office.

16. See the note in the register of *kugyō*, which paraphrases the edict to this effect, in Shintei zōhō kokushi taikei *Kugyō bunin,* vol. 1, 121 (Ten'an 2, 858).

17. Interpreter's note: Aside from being the subject of a tale in the *Uji shūi monogatari* collection, the Ōtenmon affair is the subject of a well-known illustrated scroll from the late Heian period, *Ban Dainagon emaki.*

18. Interpreter's note: A compilation of documents concerning the regency is Kūnaichō shoryōbu 1981–82. For the appointment of Yoshifusa, see that compilation's vol. 1, 4.

19. Interpreter's note: Morita cites a verse by Sugawara Michizane from around 867 which "betrays the sadness of literati and middle-rankers who felt the pressure exerted by leading aristocrats." But Robert Borgen disagrees that regental power was set that early. See Borgen 1986, esp. 154.

20. Interpreter's note: Kurihara Hiromu has recently described the relationship between Yoshifusa and Mototsune (Kurihara Hiromu 1999). He argues that Mototsune was likely adopted by Yoshifusa prior to 851, when Mototsune was given the high and rare honor of receiving his cap in the crown prince's residence, the Tōgū, or Eastern Palace. Yoshifusa may have intended to unite the Northern Fujiwara by adopting a particularly talented son of his elder brother as heir. Also demonstrating Yoshifusa's influence, Mototsune was appointed to serve in the Royal Secretariat from the age of seventeen, and his advance quickened after the Ōtenmon affair as Yoshifusa's power increased. Kurihara also makes the strong argument, against such historians as Hashimoto Yoshihiko and others, that regents from Yoshifusa's time on were extremely willful in their control of the succession process.

21. Interpreter's note: See Kūnaichō shoryōbu 1981–82, vol. 1, 4-5 for documents concerning Mototsune's appointment.

22. The official responsible for overseeing officialdom was the *hyakkan sōki,* an alternative title for *kampaku.*

23. Interpreter's note: The first extant use of the term *kampaku* appears in 887. In the discussion of what powers were included in the office, the scholar Tachibana Hiromi compared the post of *kampaku* to that of the *akō*—the most trusted minister—in China. Mototsune was dissatisfied with this comparison, considering the *akō* post to be more honorary than substantial. As it says here, Tachibana was ultimately forced to withdraw

his opinion, and his position at court—as advisor, royal affine, and scholar—suffered greatly in the process. For a discussion in English see Borgen 1986, 169–81.

24. Interpreter's note: Here Morita cites two texts as evidence. They are the *Kanshoku hishō* and the *Shokugenshō*. The first is a Heian-period text describing the *ritsuryō* post system, including extralegal posts added during Heian times. The *Shokugenshō* was a similar compendium compiled in 1340.

25. The complaint was supposedly occasioned by the fact that Mototsune's candidate, Fujiwara Sukeyo, was named special scholar of letters (*monjo tokugyōsei*).

26. Interpreter's note: The best discussion in English is Batten 1993. See also Kiley 1999.

27. Interpreter's note: According to the *Kugyō bunin*, this strategy was in place by 898. See *Kugyō bunin*, vol. 1, 155.

28. Interpreter's note: See *Kugyō bunin*, vol. 1, 153 and 155.

29. Interpreter's note: There is at least one historian that believes Tokihira's sucessor, Tadahira, was responsible for that suspicious death. See Tsunoda Bun'ei 1966.

30. Interpreter's note: In English, see Batten 1993.

31. Interpreter's note: A recent essay by Yoshikawa Shinji agrees with much of Morita's argument but argues that since Tadahira based his authority on the legacies of Yoshifusa and Mototsune, they should be considered founders of the regency. See Yoshikawa Shinji 1998.

9

The Court-centered Polity

SASAKI MUNEO

Introduction by Joan R. Piggott

IN HIS book-length study, *Nihon ōchō kokka ron* (*Debates on Court-centered Polity*), Sasaki Muneo outlines a new periodization schema for classical and early medieval Japan. Sasaki is particularly interested in elaborating the character of the "court-centered polity"—both at the court in the capital and in the provinces—which, according to him, bridged the classical *tennō*-centered polity and the early medieval polity that revolved around the retired monarch. We need, he argues, a new and more detailed vision of the government system comprising monarchy, court, and provincial government that operated for two centuries during the tenth and eleventh centuries. Since there has been little written in English on this court-centered polity of mid-Heian times, and because Sasaki's formulation is revisionist in its coverage of both court and provincial administration, his discussion is of great interest. I have translated sections of his introduction and the conclusion from his book.[1]

Sasaki provides a context for his study with an overview of periodizing schemes for premodern political formations in Japan. He notes that while the classical polity has often been described as "aristocratic," the medieval polity has been termed "feudal." Bringing these together, the historian Ishimoda Shō (1912–1986) saw the tenth century as an important transitional epoch in the countryside, when a new system of contractual cultivation (*ukesaku*) began and a new stratum of wealthy cultivators came to wield power. Building on Ishimoda's work, other historians have seen the tenth and eleventh centuries as the epoch when a post-*ritsuryō* political formation—a "court-centered polity" —replaced the earlier *tennō*-centered polity. But in Sasaki's view classical and medieval historians have concentrated too exclusively either on the center (the *tennō* and court) or the periphery (the provinces). His project is to draw the two together by investigating the "court-centered polity" that linked throne, court, and provincial administration together; and to investigate the organization, process, and interactions that characterized each of the three elements.

Sasaki begins by considering monarchical decision-making, aristocratic policy deliberation and formation, and the resulting memorials to the throne to see how monarch, regent, retired monarch, senior nobles (*kugyō*), and controllers (*benkan*) carried out governance at court. He spotlights the age of Regent Fujiwara Tadahira in the 940s, because it witnessed a new system of deliberations by the senior nobles known as *jin no sadame*, which resulted in advisory memorials (*kansō*) to the throne submitted by the regent (*sesshō*) or viceroy (*kampaku*). In the court-centered political formation as reconstructed by Sasaki, the throne, senior nobles, and other court authorities shared supreme policymaking, and executive and judiciary authority. The latter became increasingly important because it provided adjudication for disputes between factions or institutions, quarrels that were becoming increasingly system-threatening. Military needs were jointly managed by provincial governors or, in cases of *extremis*, by the throne acting with the Council of State to issue royal orders to military specialists who pursued and destroyed court enemies.

Out in the provinces governors were given increasing discretion in exchange for meeting annual tax payment quotas. The main objective behind this strategy, according to Sasaki, was to discourage capital elites and religious institutions from forming patron-client relationships with elites in the countryside, thereby weakening provincial administration. Nonetheless, at the same time, a correlate system of oversight was also emerging by which the court kept governors under control. It included the checking of provincial and district records, a process of praise and blame evaluations, and development of protocols for the appointment and tenure of provincial governors. By Regent Fujiwara Tadahira's era the center was able to manipulate these elements to better assure receipt of taxes from provincial governors.

To flesh out details of his proposed periodization scheme, Sasaki points to differences between court-centered polity and the ensuing early medieval polity (*chūsei kokka*), which was centered around retired *tennō* from the late eleventh century onward. One such change was that great noble households (*ōshinke*) of the court-centered polity era, especially those of retired monarchs and the Northern Fujiwara regental lineage, the Sekkanke, developed into official power centers of the medieval polity. The change can be traced, Sasaki argues, by looking at support for Buddhist rites. While Buddhist rites sponsored by the earlier great noble households were generally supported by private wealth, those of later medieval times were supported by provincial taxes. Additional changes characterizing the early medieval retired-*tennō* centered political formation include loosened controls over provincial governors, many of whom were important clients of retired monarchs; accumulation of large territorial estates (*chiiki shōen*) by the royal family and the regents from the late eleventh century onward; a routinized and unified provincial taxation system; and the appearance of powerful military lineages, especially the Ise Taira, which by the second half of the twelfth century had been given a supraprovincial police mandate over much of the realm. Since the hierarchical structures of both estates and military lineages were characterized by unofficial dependent relations—cliency—such relations came to predominate in early medieval society.

These excerpts from Sasaki's book provide a good outline of debates currently engaging both classical and medieval historians who study Heian Japan. To aid the reader I have fashioned the appended Table 9.1 that traces aspects of the changing political formation from classical to medieval times, at the center and at the periphery, and considers provincial administration, military, and judicial elements.

Sasaki's paradigm of court-centered polity as the bridging political formation between the classical *ritsuryō* and medieval polities is by no means the only way of looking at the tenth- and eleventh-century politics. Nonetheless his work provides a good discussion of many of the key issues researchers are attempting to resolve.

SASAKI MUNEO

The Court-centered Polity

Interpreted by Joan R. Piggott

Since the publication of Ishimoda Shō's famous essay, "The Tenth Century as the Transition from Classical to Medieval" in the 1950s, researchers have viewed the tenth century as a key epoch politically and socially, a time of departure from *ritsuryō* structures toward those characterizing the subsequent medieval age.[2] Following Ishimoda's essay, approaches to the political and social history of the tenth century and beyond can be divided into two groups. While researchers specializing in classical history have used such terms as "aristocratic monarchy" (*kizoku ōsei*) and "aristocratic polity" (*kizoku seiken*), those specializing in medieval history have posited the existence of a transitional political system that they call *ōchō kokka*, or "court-centered polity."

Ishimoda Shō based his discussion of the transition from classical to medieval times on what he called "the paradigm of landlordship [*ryōshusei*]." He saw a developmental trajectory away from a conscript-based labor system in *ritsuryō* times toward a distinctive contractual cultivation system in the tenth through twelfth centuries. He acknowledged that the medieval landlord system remained undeveloped in the tenth century and that courtier-aristocrats continued to depend on a polity shaped by classical structures. The monarchy remained aristocratic, which meant that the *tennō* was relatively passive and advised by aristocratic ministers. In Ishimoda's formulation, the actuality of regental governance by Northern Fujiwara regents remained important.[3]

Kitayama Shigeo (1909-1984) also used the concept of "aristocratic monarchy." According to Kitayama, *ritsuryō* structures and "aristocratic despotism" were in decline by the tenth and eleventh centuries. But in his mind tenth-century government and earlier *ritsuryō* governance of the eighth and ninth centuries were not very different—control of the court by Northern Fujiwara regents simply represented a form of classical aristocratic monarchy.[4] On the other hand, Satō Sōjun has argued that the regents succeeded in grasping control of the court after the fighting of the Shōhei and Tengyō eras (931–947) and only thereafter did they rely increasingly on provincial governors (*zuryō*) to administer the provinces. According to Satō, it is at that point that we can see the emergence of a new and distinct "aristocratic polity" out of the earlier *ritsuryō* bureaucratic organization.[5]

Concepts such as "aristocratic monarchy" and "aristocratic polity," as elaborated by Ishimoda, Kitayama, and Satō, all focus on political leadership by the Northern Fujiwara regental lineage, the Sekkanke. Nonetheless, detailed research concerning the actual political organization remained sketchy until Hashimoto Yoshihiko contributed his detailed analysis. He denied the prominent political role of the administrative offices (*mandokoro*) of the Northern Fujiwara regents (*sesshō*) and viceroys (*kampaku*) and of retired monarchs (*in*), pointing out that leadership of the Council of State (Daijōkan) continued through the eras of both the regents and the retired monarchs.[6] For that reason he termed the political organization of both the regents and the retired monarchs "aristocratic." According to Hashimoto's chronology, the first stage of regental aristocratic polity dates from Fujiwara Tadahira's era (930s–940s). Its markers included the regularized regency structure, including its rituals and associated protocols, and the aristocratic alliance system that supported regental leadership. In the actual administration of political affairs under the regents, government led by the *tennō* declined and was replaced by deliberation and proposals for policy by the Council of State ministers in assembly, known as the *jin no za*. Memorials resulted from their deliberations, termed *jin no sadame*.[7] Later, when the influence of powerful retired monarchs predominated, memorials (*sōji*) and deliberations at the retired monarch's palace replaced the *jin no za* meetings at the royal palace.

Hashimoto's research has been extremely useful, but questions remain. One concerns the role of the monarch. Even at the height of regental leadership the *tennō* could still make decisions.[8] So to clarify the political process we must examine the role of the *tennō* and consider relations between regent and throne in greater detail. Also of concern is Hashimoto's view that the Council of State remained the nexus of politics. If he is right, then from the *ritsuryō* era through the eras when regents and retired *tennō* led the court, political organization remained essentially unchanged. Before we accept this continuity however, we need a clearer image of political organization and processes through time, especially as concerns leadership by the senior nobles. Third, we must consider not only chronological development but shifts in the modes of monarchical decision-making and aristocratic policy formation by means of deliberation and memorializing the throne. Specifically, how did monarch, regent, retired monarch, senior nobles, and controllers called *shikiji benkan*, who were concurrent members of the Royal Secretariat, carry out tasks of governance?[9]

Research by Furuse Natsuko and Yoshikawa Shinji has helped to clarify important aspects of political organization and process. Furuse has described how from the ninth century onward new extracodal political structures formed around the throne, including the Northern Fujiwara regental line, the royal secretariat (*kurōdo*), and the body of royal intimates known as *tenjōbito*. According to Furuse's formulation, appointees to such extracodal offices enjoyed essentially unofficial and personal relations with the throne. Over time their influence transcended that of regular *ritsuryō* officials. The result was an aristocratic society essentially founded on unofficial, private relations.[10] On the other hand, Yoshikawa Shinji argues that during the ninth and tenth centuries the *ritsuryō* bureaucracy was reorganized and that monarch-subject relations contracted such that in the new configuration only a few individuals functioned as royal intimates and officials.[11]

While helpful, there are points on which these researchers disagree, and the body of their research is overly focused on limited facets of political organization. Furuse's theory about unofficial private relations ignores official relations during these centuries; and although Yoshikawa's theory regarding the establishment of Heian aristocratic society is generally persuasive, it lacks detailed analysis of political organization after the ninth century. Furthermore, if we exclude Kitayama, all the scholars discussed here see the tenth century as an epochal time of transition, and yet they agree with the contradictory assertion that classical polity and society continued to function after the tenth century. Finally, I am concerned that Ishimoda's argument concerning the actual substance of the transition from classical monarchy to a more locally organized society, and his attempt to trace the emergence of new structures therein, have disappeared from discussion. While it has become clear that the political and social organization from the tenth century onward was different from that of the earlier *ritsuryō* polity, the substance of the resulting political formation has not been sufficiently articulated.

In contrast to the focus on the center by classical historians, medieval historians Toda Yoshimi and Sakamoto Shōzō have investigated links between the Heian capital and the provinces by focusing on the countryside. Toda argued that from the tenth through twelfth centuries a distinct transitional polity could be characterized as "court-centered polity" (*ōchō kokka*). This political formation had three important characteristics: its basic mode of social-economic organization was that of a serf system with small production units; the polity incorporated competition between aristocrats, local land openers (*zaichi ryōshu*), and cultivators; and the fundamental administrative role of provincial headquarters (*kokufu*) therein was to promote "feudal" relations in what Toda considered an "early-stage feudal polity."[12] Toda also described how the political formation began to change in the tenth century as new policies entrusted wealthy cultivators with oversight of cultivation and collection of taxes in the countryside.[13]

Sakamoto Shōzō has also analyzed aspects of provincial administration in the court-centered polity in considerable detail. From the early tenth century onward, newly opened fields within licensed estates (*kanshōfu shōen*) were confiscated by provincial authorities. That was the pivot of a new system of provincial administration in the post-*ritsuryō* court-centered polity. Sakamoto concluded that the court turned over the proprietor's right to conduct field surveys (*kendenken*) to provincial governors. Provincial maps (*kokuzu*) became critical records as governors were entrusted with collection and submission of taxes to the court. Taxes were levied on "named units" (*myō*) throughout the realm, and governors set their own tax rates in various commodities as they wished. The result was popular resistance, to which the court responded with reforms by the 1040s. At that point court-centered provincial administration entered a second stage. Collection of taxes in the provinces was regulated by new protocols, "special tax units" (*betsumyō*) were established, and the district and township system (*gungōsei*) was reorganized. Such reforms led in the direction of the medieval land-tenure system.[14]

Those who employ the concept of a transitional court-centered political formation, including Toda and Sakamoto, argue that such a polity advanced "feudal relations."[15] But significant disagreements remain. Satō Shin'ichi has stressed the increasing "contracting out" of official posts (*kanshi ukeou*) to specific families and lineages, which passed them down hereditarily by the mid-twelfth century.[16] Courtier families took over key agencies such as the Office of the Board of Controllers, the Secretariat of the Council of State (Gekikyoku), and the Royal Police Office (Kebiishichō) and passed official posts down to family members from generation to generation. Since this practice continued into medieval times, Satō did not differentiate the court-centered polity from the later medieval polity. For Toda, however, the court-centered polity represented a bridge between the *ritsuryō* polity and the medieval polity. I agree with Toda—it is important not to confound the two.

Researchers of the medieval age also disagree on how and when this court-centered polity ended. Both Toda and Sakamoto argue that the court-centered polity disappeared with the establishment of the Kamakura warrior government. But for Toda, political changes made during Go-Sanjō's Enkyū era (1069–1074) divide court-centered polity into early and late stages. Sakamoto, on the other hand, views the 1040s—when estate (*shōen*) regulating laws were issued—as epochal.[17] The medieval historian Kawane Yasuhira also stresses the importance of estate regulations, followed by the retirement of Shirakawa Tennō in 1086, as the beginning of government dominated by retired monarchs. Under the latter, Kawane sees powerful warrior lineages emerging as resident landlords as a particularly telling indicator of change.[18] While everyone agrees that the tenth century represents the debut of the court-centered polity, there is no consensus as yet on its denoument and periodization.

Another debate concerns the vectors of historical change. Neither Toda nor Sakamoto, who see court-centered polity continuing until the founding of the Kamakura warrior regime, have explained the transition from court-centered polity to what they term "medieval polity." Meanwhile Kawane's theory that emerging military lineages were critical lacks clear evidence that the late eleventh century actually saw martial figures functioning at the highest levels of government.[19] As for periodization, Toda simply argues that control of homesteads (*zaike*) in townships of the public domain by provincial authorities strengthened provincial governance. Only Sakamoto argues persuasively that the 1040s saw real changes, including reform of district and township administration and emergence of special tax units as evidenced by later provincial field registers (*ōtabumi*). But such registers were compiled later and fail to constitute adequate proof of change in the eleventh century. Nor can it be proven that a realm-wide law regulating taxation of public fields was actually promulgated in the 1040s.[20] In other words, Sakamoto's arguments concerning the late stage of court-centered provincial administration remain inadequately substantiated.

Other issues needing further study include relations between the court and the provinces as well as the actual organization of court governance. Researchers propounding the concept of court-centered polity have not concerned themselves adequately with the details of provincial administration, while investigation of relations between the capital and the provinces has been overly concerned with how the posts of provincial staffers (*zaichō kanjin*) became hereditary. A fundamental problem contributing to these gaps derives from Ishimoda Shō's original formulation, which is taken as the starting point by researchers of both the classical and medieval periods. For Ishimoda, the polity itself was aristocratic—governed by courtier aristocrats—but he considered both provincial administration and local organization as "feudal" elements. The rubric of court-centered polity has further strengthened this notion. For Sakamoto, early court-centered governance assumed the gulf between central politics and provincial governance. Meanwhile, scholars who concentrate on aristocratic affairs and the monarchy put aside the concerns of local governance, assuming that local and court organizations are distinct and founded on variant logics. But the fact is that we have not adequately investigated whether or not relations between the central government, provincial headquarters, and local tax-collecting elites (*fumyō*) were actually based on varying modes of authority, and we cannot seriously argue that the court-centered polity was a distinct political formation until we resolve that issue.

What is clear is that from the tenth century onward the discretionary powers of provincial officials increased substantially. Still, that is no basis for arguing that there was a significant gap between structures of authority at the central and provincial levels. We must consider the two—the political organization and administrative systems of center and periphery from the tenth century and beyond—in tandem. That is why I have focused my research on relationships between the central government and provincial headquarters, and on the character of provincial administration. I am particularly interested in changes in government structures and their character at given moments to see how long such structures were operative.[21]

It is well known that the provincial administration of *ritsuryō* was segmentary—it depended on local elites governing their own bailiwicks.[22] But that system decayed as those elites faced decline and were replaced by newly wealthy cultivators. Bonds between noble households and these wealthy cultivators soon formed. In response, the court developed strategies to inhibit such alliances, concentrating the various powers of the polity in the hands of provincial governors. The result was a new provincial administrative system. This reorganization proceeded dynamically through written directives of the Council of State (*kampu*) from 891 through the early Engi era (901–923) at the turn of the tenth century.

It is now widely acknowledged that during the tenth century head taxes were discontinued. Tax levies came to be based on the area of land cultivated by the taxpayer. At the same time, local elites acted as tax farmers and were free to organize cultivators as they wished.[23] A new land tenure system emerged that was based on provincial charts, land survey registers (*kendenchō*), and land-holding certificates. Elements included tax levies, tax-exempt fields, and land proprietorship. I refer to this system as one of "cultivation of tax-exempt fields by dependents" (*menden yoriudosei*). In this investigation I am most interested in landholding certificates, provincial maps, and field surveys (*kenden*) as well as the relations between the court and provincial headquarters that they demonstrate.

Provincial governors were the key players at such headquarters from the tenth century onward. The common wisdom posits that provincial governors contracted to deliver tax proceeds in return for unfettered jurisdiction over their provinces.[24] Nonetheless it was surely important for the court to oversee provincial governors, whose service was at the core of the system. Indeed, my research has demonstrated that at the same time political power was concentrated in governors' hands, the court developed a system of oversight for these officials. That system matured in the era of Fujiwara Tadahira in the 940s and continued into the twelfth century. Oversight consisted of three elements: first, presentation and checking of records kept by both provincial governors and district chieftains; second, a "praise and blame" process for evaluating service by provincial governors; and third, development of protocols and regulations concerning the appointment and tenure of provincial governors. By manipulating these three elements, the court oversaw provincial governors and assured delivery of tax goods to the capital.[25]

So in the tenth and eleventh centuries a distinct system of governance held sway: provincial administration was concentrated in the hands of provincial governors, and alliances between high-ranking nobles and wealthy cultivators were more effectively blocked. But, oversight of provincial governors was also instituted when an administrative system comprising land management and taxation and based on provincial charts, survey registers, and land deeds was put into effect.

Now, shifting our gaze back to the court in the capital, we need to reconsider whether such paradigms as "aristocratic monarchy," "aristocratic political formation," or "court-centered polity" fit the political organization and processes of governance there. Our point of departure should be the role of the monarchy in policymaking during the tenth and eleventh centuries. When Uda Tennō reigned during the Kampyō era (889–898), new practices for Council of State memorials to the throne and the handling of reports and requests from officialdom (*mōshibumi*) emerged. The result was a new mode of monarchy and court administration.[26] Then from Tadahira's regency during Murakami Tennō's early reign onward, supporters of the monarchy referred key issues for deliberation and decision-making to the senior nobles. The resulting process of deliberation was termed "*jin no sadame*"—literally, "deliberations in the guards' quarters." Important issues continued to be debated and resolved in this way until the late eleventh century, although everyday matters were handled mostly by a senior noble acting as minister-in-charge (*shōkei*) together with a controller (*ben*), who might nevertheless look to the throne and its advisers for input.

Regents aided a young monarch while adult *tennō* were assisted by the viceroy cum royal aide, who oversaw the submission of memorials to the throne, transmission of royal orders, and subsequent issuance of orders by the Council of State. Nonetheless, it is important to remember that the regent still received his mandate from the monarch's father (the retired *tennō*) and from the queen-mother.[27] When the *tennō* was an adult, decisions, administration, and selection of personnel were based on consultation between the *tennō* and the viceroy cum royal aide. When differences of opinion arose between the two, the preeminent authority was that of the *tennō*. If we consider all this, as well as participation of Council of State members in the *jin no sadame* deliberative process, terms such as "regency government," "aristocratic monarchy," and "aristocratic polity" fail to characterize the system. Specifically, we need a new elaboration of "court-centered polity" as the political formation that succeeded the *ritsuryō* polity. It had three key components: the monarchy, the court, and provincial governance, and we must be sensitive to the organization, processes, and interactions of all three.

What were the broad outlines of court operation at this time? The earlier *ritsuryō* polity had been focused on processes involving the seal of the *tennō*, known as the inner seal (*nai'in*), and that of the Council of State, known as the outer seal (*ge'in*). After Northern Fujiwara Yoshifusa (804–872) gained control of both the monarchy and the Council of State, such processes fell into disuse. And after the monarchs Uda (r. 877–897) and Daigo (r. 897–930) took over the powers of the Council of State themselves, the result was a new system of court operation by the mid-tenth century. Therein the *tennō*, his viceroy, and the Council of State, together with other officials including the Royal Secretariat and the Board of Controllers (Benkan), performed the various tasks of governance (*seimu*).[28]

Shimomukai Tatsuhiko and Yoshie Akio have studied the military, judicial, and penal spheres of this new organization of governance. According to Shimomukai, following military reforms in the Engi era (901–923) and the rebellions in the Shōhei (931–938) and Tengyō eras (938–947), "valorous fellows" (*buyū no tomogara*)—provincial military specialists—seized control of military affairs in the provinces.[29] Council of State directives to pursue and destroy court enemies were dispatched by the court to the provinces.[30] According to Yoshie, whereas during the *ritsuryō* era royal decisions articulating such policy were royal responses to memorials by court leaders, from the mid-Heian period onward the throne itself took the lead in decision-making on military issues, which resulted in this new military and penal system of the tenth century.[31]

As noted earlier, the basis for provincial administration in the court-centered polity was a system of exempting taxes on fields held by dependents (i.e. clients of powerful households and religious institutions). Provincial government controlled the land and people of a given province. But those holding a legal grant of tax exemption, or those otherwise specifically permitted by the provincial headquarters, had their fields exempted from ordinary and extraordinary tax levies (*rinji zōyaku*). Under this system the powers exercised by the provincial governor in each province were substantial. But as we have seen, the court maintained a system of oversight to control governors, and by skillful managment they assured delivery of tax goods to the capital. Therefore, the political organization presided over by the *tennō* with his royal aide—*sesshō* or *kampaku*—should not be termed despotic because nobles served as chargé-d'affaires and took part in formal policy-deliberating meetings of the *Kugyō* Council. At the same time, noble houses held prebendal residential units and exempt fields, but these were under the jurisdiction of the court and its provincial governor emissaries rather than under the direct management of prebend holders.

It is also clear that from the late eleventh to the early twelfth centuries the decline of this system of provincial goverance was caused by the weakening of provincial control over both land and people. Specifically, provincial authorities rejected the system of exempt fields held by dependents and moved toward a more unified system of controlling land and persons according to where the latter was actually located or resided, whether on estates (*shōen*) or within the provincial domain (*kokugaryō*). In this way the governance system changed considerably in terms of relations between the court in Kyoto and provincial headquarters. What had been the very core of provincial control over land—the yearly provincial survey—took a new form, that of a single survey of each unit in the province during each governor's tenure. Measures for overseeing governors that had been so important in the tenth and eleventh centuries thus slackened by the beginning of the twelfth.[32]

There was also a great change in how the court operated in the twelfth century. The retired Shirakawa In's grasp of both royal and regental powers, together with the decline of senior nobles' deliberative and memorializing prerogatives, gave way to court leadership by the retired *tennō* through his own housemen, who served concurrently as controllers and royal secretaries. As for ritual activities, from the twelfth century onward the ceremonies of officialdom as well as those performed by the retired *tennō* and the regent were all supported by taxes and rents from various provinces and estates. All such rites shared the same official and public character.

So did noble houses play an increasingly important official role in the early medieval polity. In this regard, I have traced variations in the number and character of official and unofficial Buddhist rituals over time and have concluded that the distinction between official and unofficial Buddhist rites that had characterized the court-centered polity disappeared in the later era of the early medieval polity.[33] As retired monarchs gained control of the court, the number of official Buddhist rites increased dynamically, and Buddhist rites patronized by the retired *tennō* and the regents' house had an official character that they had not enjoyed earlier. At the same time, household offices maintained by retired monarchs, princes, and court leaders, as well as the administrative offices of powerful religious institutions, developed into more autonomous and influential centers, which is why historians refer to them as "gates of power" (*kenmon*). They had a very different status compared with their earlier existence as unofficial household offices in the court-centered polity.[34]

I have sketched changes at court that represented the transition from the court-centered polity to its successor, the retired-*tennō* centered early medieval polity. Out in the provinces changes in how public lands were controlled can be seen in land registers called *jōri tsubotsuke* from the early twelfth century. Mizuno Shōji has investigated registers from Ōyama Estate in Tamba Province, where he found that registers dating from 1061 and 1102 changed significantly. In particular, notations revealing the location of "checkerboard" grid units (*jōri*) of cultivated fields decreased.[35] In other words, one facet of the establishment of the medieval estate and the public land system with its territorially unified *shōen* was this jettisoning of control over cultivated fields in the provinces based on *jōri* registration. As Kinda Akihiro has made clear, the "checkerboard" grid was drawn in accord with legal practice and served as the basis of land management between the tenth and twelfth centuries.[36] It served as the line of defense in disputes between provincial governors and estate proprietors (*ryōshu*). But when we look at records from Tōdaiji's Ōi Estate in Mino Province, after Tōdaiji established unified control over the estate from 1108 onward, *jōri* notations no longer appear in temple documents. At both Tōji's Ōyama Estate and Tōdaiji's Ōi Estate, recording of *jōri* locations ceased and landholdings came to be articulated simply by province and district.

Payments from prebendal residential units (*fuko*) also declined in the twelfth century. For instance in the fourth month of 1108 we find the Kyoto temple Tōji submitting a complaint concerning incomplete payment from its *fuko*. Payment problems become increasingly notable in records between 1099 and 1104. The roots of this development lay in the discontinuation of oversight of provincial governors—governors were thereby liberated from making complete payments of *fuko* tax collections to nobles and offical religious institutions. From the more than twenty provinces from which Nara's Tōdaiji was to receive *fuko* payments in 1147, all provinces were noncompliant except its special jurisdictional unit in Iga Province. It is clear that by this time the *fuko* system had ceased functioning. In the early years when Shirakawa In dominated the court (1086–1129), Fujiwara Munetada observed in his *Chūyūki* journal that proceeds due to shrines and temples from *fuko* were not being paid, thus affecting major religious establishments and noble households. Then in 1162 Prime Minister Fujiwara Koremichi submitted a memorial to Nijō Tennō where he noted that in the 1060s, Inner Minister Fujiwara Morozane had constructed a great mansion, the Kazan'in, using one year of his proceeds from *fuko* tax receipts. But in 1162 the highest-ranking courtiers were receiving no payments from *fuko*, and without estates they had no income. Koremichi asked rhetorically, "Without estates, how can we carry out official responsibilities?"[37] Since leading courtiers of Koremichi's time could not depend on the proceeds from their prebendal *fuko* units, estates and prebendal provinces (*chigyōkoku*) became mainstays of the nobles' economy.[38]

Meanwhile, the windfalls that provincial governors had enjoyed from collecting provincial taxes in the tenth and eleventh centuries had decreased significantly by the early twelfth century. In an account dated the first day of the sixth month in 1127 by Senior Secretary (*Daigeki*) Nakahara Morotō of the Council of State, we see notations for the total amounts of tax goods collected by Nakahara's grandfather, his father, and by Morotō himself during their successive tenures as provincial governors. When Morotō's grandfather was governor of Aki Province between 1048 and 1052, he reportedly collected 10,000 *koku* of rice and 8,000 *koku* of various grains annually. When his father was governor of Awaji from 1067 to 1071, he had collected 6,000 *koku* of rice and 500 *koku* of salt every year; and as governor of Tosa between 1078 and 1084, he collected 30,000 *koku* of rice, 300,000 *hiki* of silk, 100 *koku* of oil, 300 *koku* of a commodity called *kasu*, and 3,000 *tan* of white cloth. Up to the time of his death as governor of Higo, Nakahara Morotō's father had succeeded in collecting 100,000 *hiki* of silk. But Morotō himself complained that as governor of Settsu between 1117 and 1121 he had collected less than 10 *koku* of rice! While he was undoubtedly exaggerating, what could be collected by provincial governors had decreased greatly by the twelfth century.[39] This helps to explain why provincial governors stopped journeying out to their provinces after the turn of the twelfth century.[40] For example Ōe Masafusa (1041–1111), who was made presiding official at the Dazaifu in 1108, was still in the capital in 1111. And when disorder broke out in Masafusa's jurisdiction about that time, Fujiwara Munetada observed in his journal, "It is not good for the realm that Masafusa fails to follow orders."[41]

No doubt provincial governors remained in the capital because court oversight had loosened. But still another reason was that provincial administration was no longer based on a system of exempt fields and dependent individuals over which governors had a say. According to the principle of unified control over an entire province by provincial authorities, the most important principle of taxation was location, whether cultivated fields lay within an estate or in the provincial domain. And as the influence of nobles and religious institutions functioning as "gates of power" increased, provincial governors no longer went out to their provinces. They were better off remaining in the capital where they could see to their ongoing amicable relations with the "gates of power."

By the beginning of the twelfth century, all facets of the court-centered governmental system—relations between court and provinces, and the organization of court and throne—had been rejected. The royal house, the Regents' Line, and other powerful houses were functioning as increasingly autonomous entities. Their economic base had shifted from prebendal residence units and tax-exempt fields to territorial estates and prebendal provinces.[42] This was the background against which the estate and provincial domain system of land tenure emerged, and various elements that would characterize the medieval polity became more pronounced.[43]

Mammoth territorial estates held by the royal house and the Regents' Line were the earliest visible elements of the new system. In 1118 a thousand *chō* (one *chō* = 2.94 acres) of rice paddy land in Awaji Province was incorporated as an estate by the royal temple Ninnaji. Then in 1119 an estate comprising some 5,000 *chō* in Kōzuke Province was incorporated as a holding of the viceroy, Fujiwara Tadazane.[44] Shimazu Estate owned by the Regents' Line and covering the three Kyūshū provinces of Hyūga, Ōsumi, and Satsuma, was created during Fujiwara Tadazane's era (1078–1162), when Shirakawa In led the court.[45] And during the reigns of the retired monarchs Toba and Go-Shirakawa, additional gigantic estates appeared, some of which encompassed an entire district. For example, in 1138 a district-wide estate in Mutsu Province's Iwase District was incorporated as the holding of Minister of the Left Minamoto Arihito (1103–1147).[46] According to an extant copy of a missive dispatched by the Council of State on the nineteenth day of the eighth month in 1143, two additional estates held by the royal cloister Anrakujūin, Tado Estate in Sanuki Province and Kusu Estate in Bungo Province, were incorporated and named for the districts comprising them.[47] And in 1159 the Hōshōgon'in cloister's Minuma Estate in Chikugo Province, as well as the Aso Estate in Higo and the Ashikaga Estate in Shimotsuke Province held by the Anrakujūin, were incorporated as district-size estates.[48] Thus, the royal house—the retired *tennō*, the *tennō*, royal ladies (*nyōin*), and "royal vow temples" (*goganji*)—and the Regents' Line divided up the realm as estate proprietors of the new land tenure system. Transforming themselves into "gates of power," they fashioned the new medieval polity.

Commended estates (*kishin shōen*) also proliferated during the twelfth century. Fukuda Toyohiko has analyzed estate documents from the Kantō region during the era before the Gempei fighting began in 1180. Of some fifty estates there, nine were established in the ninth century, one was established between the tenth and late eleventh centuries, and the others were all created in the twelfth century.[49] So while the system of exempt fields cultivated by dependents in the tenth and eleventh centuries saw the emergence of some "early estates" (*shoki shōen*), the special circumstances of the twelfth century encouraged incorporation of many more *shōen*. Fukuda's conclusions can be extended beyond the Kantō region as well. In analyzing field registers from Noto Province, Ishii Susumu found that estates covered 74 percent of the province during Toba In's day. And in Wakasa Province during Go-Shirakawa In's era (1180–1192), estates covered about half of the province. Using the example of Iga Province, Ishii argues that Shirakawa In's reign was epochal for the *shōen* system in the Kinai and nearby provinces.[50] The key point is that commended estates developed into unified territorial holdings of the "gates of power." Meanwhile, they possessed a special character because of the mediate role therein of local elites as land-opening resident landlords. Under such circumstances, local landlordism advanced dynamically.

Contemporary with the development of the tenure system based on estates and the provincial domain we can also make out signs of an emergent province-wide tax rate (*ikkoku heikinyaku*), which represented a new administrative system for the provinces. From Toba In's day (1129–1156) onward, documents written by "gates of power" administrators and local landlords began to use that term, and by Go-Shirakawa In's era the term was used at court as well.[51]

Another significant change can be seen in the late Heian provincial military. During a debate in the palace quarters of the viceroy concerning pursuit and suppression of Inland Sea pirates in the fourth month of 1135, Viceroy Fujiwara Tadamichi (1097–1164) articulated the issue as follows: "These days, pirates operate in bands obstructing the vessels of high or low. The pirates should be pursued, and royal orders (*senji*) to that effect have been sent out to the provinces, but without effect. What should be done?" In the ensuing discussion Fujiwara Akiyori expressed the view that pirate leaders were in fact estate residents and that estate proprietors should therefore be ordered to deal with them. There were others of like mind, but Fujiwara Munetada countered with the proposal that the Bizen governor Taira Tadamori and the royal police agent (*kebiishi*) Minamoto Tameyoshi be sent to suppress the pirates. As the result of a subsequent memorial to Toba In reporting these deliberations, Taira was so delegated.[52] The key point here is that several discussants thought that estates over which "gates of power" presided could manage the pirate scourge better than could provincial headquarters.

The dispatch of Taira Tadamori as search-and-destroy agent was an extraordinary tactic in 1135, but three decades later the military structure of the realm looked quite different. As Gomi Fumihiko has made clear, the directive of 1167 naming Taira Shigemori search-and-destroy agent against pirate bands in the Tōsan, Tōkai, San'yō, and Nankai circuits gave him ongoing martial authority over many provinces. This directive represents the high point of military development in the age of retired monarchs and is the starting point for the Taira military system.[53] From this point onward, the Taira used their police powers over various provinces to create patronage relations between themselves and provincial warrior clients. The Gempei civil war was the eventual result.

The development of district-wide estates, the emergence of commended estates, the establishment of a unified province-wide tax structure, the birth of warrior lineages as "gates of power" supporting a new military system, and the assigning of prebendal provinces all resulted in the new medieval provincial administration system.[54] Moreover, it is clear that the retired-monarch-led polity advanced medieval relations. With the forming of bonds linking local hamlets, and the appearance of estates into which officials were forbidden entry (*funyū shōen*), the great noble houses became "gates of power." They made possible the dynamic advance of field-opening and local landlords who closely allied themselves with absentee proprietors in the capital.[55] The resulting system made the retired monarch and the Regents' Line estate proprietors of mammoth proportions; it advanced and supported control over the provinces by the power centers we have dubbed "gates of power," one function of which was the resolution of quarrels between those same powerful entities. The advance of local landlordship and the emergence of powerful warrior lineages with their characteristic lordship relations acted as push factors that advanced the transformation of polity, society, and economy. Once the process began, it was self-propelling. The system fostered medieval social-economic relations, and since warrior power was at its very core, the polity was "medieval" in both name and reality.

Excepting its military organization and the role of local landlords, in most respects the resulting medieval polity maintained the character of the retired-monarch-led polity, including the estate and public domain land tenure system and the dependent (feudal) relations inherent in the "gates of power" structure. Therefore I would argue that in essence the twelfth-century polity already had a medieval character. The transition began at the end of the eleventh century and was completed by 1107, when Shirakawa In established his control over the throne. That era thus saw the birth of the early medieval polity.[56]

TABLE 9.1

Sasaki Muneo's View of Changing Political Formation—from Classical to Early Medieval Times

	CLASSICAL POLITY (*Ritsuryō kokka*) 8th c. ->	COURT-CENTERED POLITY (*Ōchō kokka*) 10th c. ->	EARLY MEDIEVAL POLITY (*Chūsei kokka*) later 11th c. ->
AT THE CENTER	*tennō* center	*tennō*-centered monarchy	*tennō*-centered monarchy
court government	*ritsuryō* structures *ritsuryō* process		retired *tennō* as court leader
		regency (regents & viceroys) as court leader Royal Secretariat royal intimates reduced size/role of officialdom	*shikiji benkan* as *In/Kurōdo* link some noble households become "gates of power" (*kenmon*)
	Council of State	senior nobles' consultative discussions (*jin no za*) Senior-noble-in-charge (*shōkei*) system	waning influence of senior nobles
AT THE PERIPHERY provincial administration	provincial headquarters distribution of public fields district chieftains (*gunji*) as tax collectors	provincial governors with significant discretionary power contract field system (*ukesaku*) cliental exempt field system land surveys by prov. governor land-based taxes local elites as tax collectors deeds, provincial charts as records	declining oversight of prov. officials decreasing provincial tax collection prov. governors remain in capital estate- & public-land tenure systems territorial estates replace prebend *fuko* cliental (*shujū*) relations dominant commended estates province-wide unified tax rate
military authority	provincial headquarters	provincial headquarters' hired swords	powerful military lineages with supra-provincial mandates "gates of power" preeminent
judicial/penal authority	provincial governors/ district chieftains	oversight of prov. governors by court throne, regent, senior nobles negotiate to resolve quarrels between noble households (*ōshinke*)	court + "gates of power" negotiate to resolve disputes

Notes

1. See Sasaki Muneo 1994. For a view of court-centered polity in English focused on provincial administration, see Batten 1993.

2. This translated extract combines parts of the introduction and conclusion of Sasaki's monograph, Sasaki Muneo 1994, 3–9 and 345–54. For the Ishimoda essay mentioned here, see Ishimoda Shō 1956b.

3. Ishimoda Shō 1962.

4. Kitayama Shigeo 1970.

5. Satō Sōjun 1977.

6. Interpreter's note: In Japanese these are termed the *Mandokoro seiji ron* and *In no chō seiji ron*. According to these theories, the household offices (*mandokoro*) of the Regents' Line and the retired *tennō*'s office (*in no chō*) dominated government. Hashimoto argues against both propositions in Hashimoto Yoshihiko 1976.

7. Interpreter's note: *Jin no sadame* (alt. *jōgi*) denotes the deliberations of the *Kugyō* Council, when its members met in the Left Guards' chamber (*jin*) adjacent to the main reception pavilion (Shishinden, alt. Naden) of the residential palace (*dairi*), to discuss and debate (*sadame*) matters of policy. Results were subsequently reported to the *tennō* as memorials. First, a controller (*benkan*) was charged with investigating precedents; second, he directed a secretary (*geki*) of the Council of State to write a policy recommendation paper (*kanmon*); third, *kugyō* gave their opinions thereupon, by order of their status; fourth, senior *kugyō* (*shōkei*) made a decision concerning a proposal (*sō*) to the throne; fifth, an adviser (*sangi*) drew up the decision in the form of a written document, and passed it to a royal secretary (*kurōdo*) for presentation to the *tennō* to evoke a royal decision. In some ways this process is seen to be a simplification of earlier *ritsuryō* practices involving the Council of State. Under the leadership of the Northern Fujiwara regents, however, even this process became increasingly formulaic.

8. See, for instance, the discussion in Tsuchida Naoshige 1965.

9. Interpreter's note: Unfortunately there is not yet work in English on this question. I have tried to provide some information to illustrate Sasaki's argument in footnotes below. In Japanese see Hashimoto Yoshinori 1981; Ōsumi Kiyoaki 1991; and Sasaki Muneo 1999. I plan to speak to some of these points in a forthcoming essay that will accompany a translation of entries from one year—939, when the court was threatened by rebellion in the east and the west—from the journal of the early Northern Fujiwara regent Tadahira, to be published in the near future.

10. Furuse Natsuko 1986.

11. Yoshikawa Shinji 1989.

12. See Toda Yoshimi 1972 and Toda Yoshimi 1968.

13. Toda Yoshimi 1958.

14. Sakamoto Shōzō 1972.

15. For examples, see Morita Tei 1980.

16. Satō Shin'ichi 1983.

17. Interpreter's note: In English see Hurst 1976, esp. 110–18 and elsewhere; and Satō 1979.

18. See Kawane Yasuhira 1964 and Kawane Yasuhira 1971.

19. Takada Minoru 1966, 117.

20. According to Morita Tei, for example, institutionalization of the special tax unit system took place in the tenth and eleventh centuries. The problem is not simply one of

much later *ōtabumi* records. In addition, Fukuda Toyohiko has argued that reform of the district and township system in the Kantō region did not occur until the twelfth century. See Fukuda Toyohiko 1974b. Sasaki concludes that the special tax unit system could not have been established before the mid-eleventh century. All instances demonstrating a uniform tax rate for public fields (*kōden kammotsu sotsuhō*) date from the twelfth century, meaning that Sakamoto's view remains unproven.

21. For more detail, see specific chapters of Sasaki Muneo 1994.

22. Ishimoda Shō 1971.

23. Murai Yasuhiko 1958.

24. Interpreter's note: This is a strong emphasis in Batten's discussion of court-centered polity. See Batten 1993.

25. Interpreter's note: Sasaki argues that court and provincial officials allied to suppress exempt fields under proprietary management, and that the rank-perquisite system (*irokusei*) was the correlate reward for provincial officials' assistance. During the regency of Fujiwara Tadahira in 940, provincial governors were charged with limiting tax-exempt fields in order to increase tax proceeds. Then rank perquisites were reorganized to guarantee official incomes by stabilizing tax proceeds for those of the fourth and fifth ranks.

26. Interpreter's note: On changes during Uda Tennō's era, see Morita Tei, chapter 8 of this volume.

27. Kuramoto Kazuhiro takes the *tennō*, with his father the retired sovereign and his mother the dowager, as "the nucleus of royal authority." See Kuramoto Kazuhiro 1987. However, this formulation still fails to expose the locus of power adequately.

28. Interpreter's note: An illustrative process that demonstrates how such corporate efforts worked is the *gekisei*, which consisted of deliberations by the senior nobles of the Council of State on reports, requests, and other documents submitted by officials from agencies and the provinces to the Council via the Board of Controllers. *Gekisei* was to be conducted daily, save for special days when court activities ceased. In *gekisei*, first the Board of Controllers saw to the ordering and categorization of various petitions and reports from agencies and provinces. According to a fixed procedure, controllers assisted by assistants (*shi*) handled all such documents in the preparatory process called *katanashi* in the Katanashi Hall (Katanashidokoro). The documents were then presented for deliberation by the senior nobles in the Geki Office (Gekichō). There the members of the Council of State assembled together with controllers and others. A controller would order an assistant to read out the presented documents. Deliberations by the senior nobles were presided over by the noble-in-charge, who held the post of middle counselor or higher. Reports of these deliberations then made their way to the throne, usually via the regent or royal aide, as memorials, which resulted in a royal decision issued as a royal command (*senji*). Such commands, again usually transmitted by the regent or royal aide, made their way back to the Council staff and controllers for drafting as written orders for promulgation by the agencies of government. See Yoshioka Masayuki 1993 and Ōsumi Kiyoaki 1991.

29. Shimomukai Tatsuhiko 1981; and Shimomukai Tatsuhiko 1987.

30. Interpreter's note: See Friday 1992.

31. Yoshie Akio 1986.

32. Two specific protocols that became perfunctory, indicating weakened control over provincial governors, were *zuryō kōka sadame* and *fukan sadame*.

33. Interpreter's note: Sasaki argues that the relationship between official (*kuji*) and other rites in the court-centered polity, and their transformation during the era of retired

monarchs, needs further study. He suggests that the moment of Horikawa Tennō's death in 1107, when supporters of the throne undertook to have the controller-in-charge direct Buddhist rites, was a particularly significant event.

34. Interpreter's note: How and when "gates of power" developed is a central question for historians of Japan. In English on this issue see Adolphson 2000, esp. 12–13 and chapters 4 and 5; and the special issue of the *Journal of Japanese Religious Studies* 1996 on the work of the late Kuroda Toshio. Kuroda pioneered the concept of the "gates of power."

35. Mizuno Shōji 1988.

36. Kinda Akihiro 1990.

37. The document is known as the *Taikai hisshō*. See it in *Gunsho ruijū*, (Zatsubu).

38. Interpreter's note: A province held as a "proprietorship" by a central noble house was a prebendal province. Prebendal provinces were assigned to retired monarchs, the regent, or royal ladies. See Hall 1988, 20–21.

39. See Kurokawa Harumura 1989–90, vol. 21. This is a seminal Tokugawa-period compilation of 340 journals and other records (*kiroku*) written by courtiers, warriors, and monks.

40. Gomi Fumihiko 1984b.

41. *Chūyūki* Ten'nin 1 (1108) 03/05.

42. Interpreter's note: The possessor of a prebendal province enjoyed the prerogative of appointing its provincial governor, who then supported the patron.

43. Interpreter's note: In English, on the *shōen-kokugaryō* system of medieval land tenure and provincial administration see Ōyama Kyōhei 1990, esp. 89–95.

44. *Chūyūki* Gen'ei 1 (1118) 07/25 and Gen'ei 2 (1119) 03/25.

45. See Ishimoda Shō 1956a.

46. See Takeuchi Rizō 1973-1980, vol. 5, doc. 2395. Interpreter's note: *Heian ibun* is a collection of Heian Period documents. Hereafter it will be cited as *HI*.

47. *HI*, vol. 6, doc. 2519.

48. *HI*, vol. 6, docs. 2986 and 3029. On district-wide estates in Kyūshū see Kudō Keiichi 1974.

49. Fukuda Toyohiko 1974a.

50. Ishii Susumu 1991.

51. Uejima Susumu 1990.

52. *Chūyūki* Hōen 1 (1135) 04/08.

53. Gomi Fumihiko 1979. In English, see Farris 1992, 275.

54. For more on *chigyōkoku*, see Gomi Fumihiko 1984a.

55. Interpreter's note: On this point Sasaki would seem to disagree with William Wayne Farris, who insists that substantial increases in the acreage under cultivation did not occur in Heian times. On alliances between hamlets and *shōen* formation, see Ōyama Kyōhei 1974.

56. Interpreter's note: Both Hurst and Adolphson would agree with Sasaki on the importance of Shirakawa In's era as an epochal moment; but the arguments on which that judgment is based differ. Chapter 13 by Ishimoda in this volume also discusses such issues, including the nature of the transition from classical to medieval.

10

Kyoto and the Estate System in the Heian Period

TODA YOSHIMI

Introduction by Janet R. Goodwin

HISTORIANS OF JAPAN often characterize the medieval age (*chūsei*) as one of warrior dominance. When warriors wrested control of major political, social, and economic institutions from the civilian court aristocracy, the medieval age is said to have begun. While earlier periodization schemes designated the late twelfth century as the onset of medieval times, recently scholars have argued convincingly that the transfer of power from court to military aristocracy, as well as a number of related social changes in other spheres, in fact took place in the early fourteenth century. According to this thinking, the Kamakura Period (1185–1333) represents the waning years of courtier dominance, the Kemmu restoration (1334–1336) ushered in a new age, and the Ashikaga period (1336–1568) saw the achievement of complete warrior dominance and was hence medieval.[1]

While Toda Yoshimi might have agreed that true warrior dominance dates from the fourteenth, not the late twelfth, century, he does not define the medieval age as an age of warriors. Instead, he locates the transformation of Japan from classical (*kodai*) to medieval society in the eleventh and twelfth centuries, earlier than either of the two "warrior-dominance" schemes mentioned above. Toda sees the eleventh and twelfth centuries as a transitional period between the classical and medieval ages marked by the development of new power arrangements and the rise of a new social order that differed sharply from that of classical society. The defining feature of the medieval age is the *shōen-ryōshu* system: a system of privatized estates (*shōen*) distinguished by multiple rights to income from the same holding, in which court nobles and central religious institutions held rights as overlords (*ryōke*) but actual administration was in the hands of local manager-holders (*ryōshu*).[2] According to Toda, such changes proceeded through two eras: the Regency era of the late ninth through early eleventh centuries, when Northern Fujiwara regents led the court; and the subsequent Insei era, when retired monarchs led the court. The transition lasted almost to the end of the twelfth century.

As will be apparent in the translated essay that follows, the key to the operation of this system was exchange and cooperation between absentee overlords and local managers and holders. Except for a few important shrines and temples, most overlords were based in the capital, while the estates themselves were located throughout Japan. The exchange, therefore, bound together center and periphery and contributed to the social and economic development of both. Toda makes it clear that this was a two-way reciprocal process in which those in the capital and those in the provinces obtained and exercised power by manipulating and depending on the other. Rather than focusing on the "rise of the warriors" as an oppositional force which eventually overcame the power of courtiers, Toda concentrates on relationships rooted in the estate system that spilled over into nonagricultural areas such as commerce and transportation. True enough, armed men played a part in this system, since some came from the local holder class and others were provincial government functionaries. But in Toda's scheme they share the stage with functionaries of central institutions who borrowed the power and wealth of their patrons to secure profit in the countryside.

Toda's definition of the medieval age is tightly bound with his concept of the *ōchō kokka,* a term that may be generally translated as "court-centered polity" but which in his view is much more complex and comprehensive than such a simple translation indicates. Toda refers to Kyoto in the middle and late Heian periods as the *ōchō toshi* (*toshi* = city). Elsewhere in the volume that contains the translated essay, Toda defines the *ōchō toshi* as Kyoto in transition from a royal capital centered on government facilities and residences of aristocratic officials to the medieval city that served as the political and economic nucleus of society. In this transformation process the capital reflects the *ōchō* polity, structures and policies which were based on the evolving *shōen-ryōshu* system.[3]

While struggling to find an appropriate English equivalent for *ōchō,* I came to realize that for Toda the term embraces the dynamics of center-periphery relations and the complexities of change in the period. To focus on the court, therefore, is to see only half of the *ōchō* equation, since it was developments in the provinces that shored up courtiers' power. On the one hand, local holders were clients of the powerful nobles at court who could jockey for tax exemptions and defend them against the predations of local enemies. On the other hand, locals comprised a provincial power base on which their noble patrons sometimes needed to depend. The capital was not just a city of court nobles who held title to estates, but also the site of exchange between nobles and their provincial functionaries. Through a variety of means—commerce, lending, travel, appointments and assignments to the provinces, among others—the capital was organically linked to the periphery and could not have existed in its late Heian form without support from the provinces.

Thus in Toda's scheme the term *ōchō* describes a period in transition from the classical to the medieval age. Medieval society, Toda argues, saw the rise of new socioeconomic classes that developed in response to the growth of estates. The period was characterized not only by economic activities such as land reclamation, trade, and lending activities, but also by the rise of new social strata: "local holders [*myōshu*] and cultivators [*hyakushō*], artisans [*shokunin*] organized into guilds [*za*], merchants [*shōnin*], artists [*geinin*], marginals such as vagabonds [*ronin*] and low-status persons [*hinin*], local landlords [*zaichi ryōshu*] and their followers, armed men [*bushi*] and bands of housemen [*kenin*]" who formed a completely different social structure than that of the earlier classical society.[4] In Toda's view, the *ōchō* polity, which spanned the periods when Northern Fujiwara regents and then retired monarchs (*in*) dominated the court apparatus, was the womb of these new strata, along with social and economic arrangements that supplied them with a share of political power. In short, Toda saw the *ōchō* period as a time of dynamic change resulting in a new form of society that he calls "medieval."[5] Toda's emphasis on the provinces and new social strata corrects a viewpoint centered on capital and court that sometimes mistakenly represents Heian society as static and composed only of rulers and ruled.

Toda's foray into the provinces required an adventurous use of source materials. Some of them were preserved only through strokes of luck—correspondence collected in a textbook on how good letters should be written, for example, or documents snatched from the waste heap to be used as writing paper for other purposes. In the translated essay, Toda explains that it is not sufficient to depend on official documents, which by their nature focus on legal and theoretical issues and do not reflect the actual conditions of provincial society. Instead, he has chosen some materials that illuminate these conditions by focusing on the people involved in them. Taken together, the protagonists of the vignettes included throughout this essay represent the variety of positions and activities that characterize the middle level of early medieval society.

The essay is composed of five sections. Like many Japanese scholars, Toda has declined to write an extensive introduction or conclusion; had he written either, they might well have addressed these issues. His first two sections are general overviews of *kokunai meishi*, a term that can be translated as "provincial notables." Most of these notables were both clients and agents of influential courtiers. They extended their own power and that of their patrons through commerce, lending, and the performance of prestigious religious duties.

In his third section Toda focuses on several documents that illuminate the relationship between the capital and the countryside. This section concentrates on local power relationships and the way they were enhanced by connections with the capital. Toda also discusses the "personalization" of official functions that resulted, fortuitously, in document preservation: official materials kept at a director's home were often likely to be used as paper for other purposes. Equally important is the development of patron-client ties, similar to those that characterized the estate system.[6]

In the fourth section Toda turns to the subject of lending. Middle-strata clients of central nobles and religious institutions often profited through lending out their patrons' stores to provincial cultivators. Based on these activities, such patrons inserted themselves into the local power structure. Some of these middlemen were armed, adding the threat of violence to economic muscle. The fifth section returns to the capital, examining the way its land was used by prosperous urban dwellers. The phenomenon of "shared residence," in which several parties used the same site—wealthy provincial governors built storehouses within the compounds of high nobles or temples, for instance—is viewed by Toda as a replication of the estate system with its shared rights to a given plot of land.

As a Japanese scholar addressing a Japanese audience, Toda's writing style differs sharply from that of most Western scholars. Many of the details Toda includes here would not have found their way into a Western scholar's essay based on principles of tight analytical argument. Scholarly Japanese writing packs seemingly unrelated information into dependent clauses of a single sentence; within an essay, the scholar may seem to have wandered far from his or her original points. In this translation, a few of Toda's "digressions" have been placed in footnotes, but to do so consistently would have been to privilege argument over the rich informativeness that makes Japanese scholars' work such treasure troves for extending one's own research. That being said, this is not a literal translation, but an adaptation in which I have occasionally moved sentences around and added explanatory material to clarify Toda's points.

Toda Yoshimi died in 1991 after a productive scholarly career, which culminated in an appointment as distinguished professor at Kobe University. In addition to the themes treated in the essay translated here, his work has embraced such topics as roads and travel, pilgrimages to Kumano Shrine, and relations between Japan and the rest of East Asia. His work continues to be widely cited.[7] As for this essay, his innovative use of source materials and his thorough exploration of complexities of class structure and center-periphery relationships make it especially useful for both scholars and students, and especially appropriate for inclusion in this collection.

TODA YOSHIMI

Kyoto and the Estate System in the Heian Period

Interpreted by Janet R. Goodwin

This essay analyzes two interrelated processes of the late Heian period: the establishment of the medieval estate system and the development of Heiankyō (Kyoto) as a city of estate proprietors—aristocrat-officials who lived in the capital as opposed to local landlords residing in the village.[8] To date, research on individual estates has focused on the agricultural village, but to examine the estate system across Japan we must also understand relations between city and countryside as well as the structure of the capital city. In an earlier essay I suggested that forms of communication between the city and rural villages needed special study.[9] Here I will delve into the world of contacts and communication that spanned city and countryside during the Regency and Insei eras.

Provincial Notables in the Regency Era

Historians who base their research on estate documents face serious limitations. Such documents were regulated in form and content by their legal and political functions and by the ways in which they were selected and preserved.

Moreover, they do not deal directly with the many historical matters outside the legal-political sphere. It is relatively easy to obtain information from extant estate documents on matters related to the formation and structure of estates, such as their establishment and legal status, transmission of land rights, and principles of control over land and populace. It is extremely difficult, however, to use these records to reconstruct actual conditions of local society, including measures to control the populace and popular resistance to such measures. So while research into estate structure and the apparatus of control has progressed, understanding of the dynamics of vertical and horizontal relationships linking individuals and groups in the Regency era—from the late ninth to the late eleventh centuries—lags far behind.

However, important new insights are provided by a noteworthy find: a manuscript from the archives of the Buddhist temple Kōzanji titled the *Old Primer* (*Ko ōrai*), which seems to have been a textbook compiled from personal correspondence about travel during the Regency era.[10] The collection is unusual in that each letter in it is specific and realistic, revealing information about both city and countryside far beyond the requirements of travel records. Village life is portrayed concretely by the correspondents, apparently local provincial officials (*zaichō kanjin*) as well as middling and lesser elites in the provinces.[11] I will refer to all these individuals as "provincial notables" (*kokunai meishi*).

Here are some representative scenes from the *Old Primer* collection:

> —A landholder requested a loan of three hundred bundles of rice for spring planting, but his correspondent refused to provide the loan, claiming that he had already allotted his thousand or so bundles remaining after taxes to "one or two runners" and "servants [*ge'nin*] under his jurisdiction." (Letters 3 and 4)
>
> —A so-called commander [*shōgun*] of warrior lineage was designated to guard tax rice on its way to the capital, his authorization deriving from provincial decrees issued to past generations of his family. (Letters 5 and 6)
>
> —An aristocratic family in Kyoto summoned a man to serve as a retainer at their home, but at the time he was traveling to the provincial government headquarters to deliver tax goods [*kuji*]. He sent a letter to Kyoto agreeing to serve but apologized for not complying immediately with the order. (Letters 7 and 8)
>
> —Without authorization, a young attendant from the stable of a noble's son, dressed in an elegant patterned robe and accompanied by his dependents, trespassed on newly opened fields and harvested every bit of the crop, claiming it as fodder. (Letter 10)
>
> —A man took possession of tax rice, lent it to people in the spring as seed, and received the interest in the fall. However, he was either unable

to collect the principal or he had lost everything gambling, including his wife, children, and riding horses. Unable to submit the twenty-five *koku* with which he had been entrusted, he effectively had embezzled the tax rice. (Letters 14 and 15)

—A district official borrowed a horse and sent it to the provincial governor to satisfy religious obligations, explaining that the district's ruined condition was due to the harsh administration of the former governor. Nonetheless he pledged to work hard to nurture agricultural production in the district. (Letters 16 and 17)

—A correspondent described a performance by famous *sarugaku*, *kugutsu*, and *hikimai* performers at the provincial temple (*kokubunji*) that evening.[12] He suggested arriving early to get good seats near the stage (Letter 22). His correspondent gladly accepted the invitation to see the performance and to hear the accompanying sermon, adding that it would be a shame not to offer congratulatory gifts to the performers. (Letter 23)

—A military man named Kanooka, who worked as a bodyguard for the provincial governor, was ordered to participate in a hunt to be held by his patron. Lacking a good horse, however, Kanooka sent gifts to a horse dealer, the monk Hōsan, proposing to borrow an inferior horse from him. Hōsan replied that he lived his life partially as a monk and partially as a layman, that he traveled a lot, and that he would obtain a horse from the eastern regions (Tōgoku). He would put the word out at a place where people gathered—namely, at banquets held on Kōshin Day at the mansion of the former governor, surnamed Fujiwara—and would supply Kanooka with a horse. (Letters 27 and 28)

The *Old Primer* thus provides vignettes of the lifestyles of provincial notables who figure on its pages. It is difficult to correlate these individuals with the local elites whose names appear in estate records; but in general the letter-writers are large-scale cultivators, private landholders, and tax collectors, as well as district and village officials, attendants (*toneri*) for noble houses, provincial-office scribes, provincial guards, estate officials, and the like. We could say that the text presents a group portrait of the sort of people who might generally be termed "people of the provinces."

Reading between the lines of the *Old Primer*, we can assume that provincial notables included official appointees of central government institutions and powerful shrines and temples, the priests and monks of provincial religious institutions, and the leaders (*chōja*) of various organizations that dealt with the distribution of labor, the circulation of goods, and communication in provincial society.[13] *Kokunai meishi* certainly included local powerholders, local landholders, warriors, and the like—groups linked organically by occupational character, status, power, and prestige in the political and social spheres.

As seen in the *Old Primer*, provincial notables had opportunities to gather together, such as at the Kōshin Day celebration held at the headquarters of a former Fujiwara governor who had remained at his residence in the province after retirement. Kōshin Day occurred once during the Chinese sixty-day cycle, at the conjunction of the seventh and ninth astrological signs. On that occasion the former governor invited people from the area to worship Taishakuten, one of twelve heavenly deities from the Indian pantheon adopted by Buddhism, and Seimen Kongō, a blue-faced deity with healing functions, at an all-night banquet where guests ate, drank, chatted, and played games.[14]

This Kōshin Day gathering was an interesting manifestation of provincial culture. Important issues to examine include the social strata of invitees and the functions that the party served for guests. Among those invited was the representative of the above-mentioned archer and elite guardsman, Kanooka— in this case his son, Masaakira— along with the horse-dealing monk Hōsan. While at the banquet Hōsan sent word to Kanooka that he had three good horses available for the guardsman to use at the governor's hunt[15] The festivities clearly provided an opportunity for the social interaction of provincial notables within a selected circle, and it became a regular occasion for them to exchange information and communicate in other ways. Thus they could elevate their own status and benefit from mutual exchanges such as borrowing seed rice for planting or obtaining fast horses for hunting. They used the resulting contacts to survey the activities of retainers, servants, and cultivators under their control. Complaints against harsh provincial administration characteristic of the Regency era probably could not have been made without relationships such as those formed at the Kōshin Day banquet illuminated here.[16]

This account of the Kōshin Day celebration (Kōshin'e) also indicates that the former governor spent considerable time in Kyoto, demonstrating that residence in the province was closely linked with the capital. Functions of the governor's provincial base included the management of estate holdings that he had obtained during his tenure, oversight of followers and housemen in the province, and management of elite patrons' holdings. The governor used his headquarters in the provinces to provide lodging, receptions, laborers, and horses for aristocrat-officials among his acquaintances who traveled between capital and countryside. In other words, the former governor's residence-office (i.e., headquarters) was a junction for private traffic between city and countryside in tandem with the official provincial government headquarters (*kokufu*). Provincial notables obviously had many different reasons for visiting there.

Close ties between capital and countryside are further evidenced by the direct exchange of letters between provincial notables and middling and lesser aristocrats in the capital. According to the *Old Primer*, an aristocratic household in the capital sent a letter via courier to a former retainer, the well-known and skilled literatus Ono Harumasa, asking him to summon a provincial acquaintance to serve at their Kyoto mansion (Letter 7). Provincial notables certainly required a network for correspondence with the capital. The unofficial letters in the *Old Primer* paint a realistic picture of such political, social, and cultural contacts—including those characterized by opposition and competition—among provincial notables, and between these elites and provincial government officials or middling and lesser aristocrats in the capital. The missives reveal characteristics of both city and countryside. Indeed, exemplary texts of the *Old Primer* were compiled precisely because provincial notables had to learn to write letters transmitting ideas and information to important provincial officials, estate managers, and urban nobles.

It goes without saying that provincial notables were involved in both official and unofficial affairs that took them back and forth between capital and countryside. For example, consider the activities in the household of Minamoto Norisuke, governor of Mikawa Province around 1039.[17] Minamoto died at his mansion in the capital in the tenth month of that year. According to the journal of the royal adviser Fujiwara Sukefusa, the *Shunki*, lodgers and provincial retainers who had come to the capital from Mikawa served as guards for the mansion. And since the wives of Tamesuke and Tomonori, two functionaries in Minamoto's household, resided in Mikawa, the men must also have been from that province. Tomonori's position in the household is clarified by the fact that he drew up detailed records (*ketsuge*) of silk, thread, and other items in Minamoto's storehouses.

Among Minamoto Norisuke's family holdings was Nagayama Estate in Mikawa Province. It was likely located either at Nagayama, below the Tomogawa market near the provincial government headquarters, or at Kaminagayama, near the Ichinomiya shrine. When Minamoto died, supplies in his Kyoto storehouse were so meager that silk collected as the annual land tax levy (*nengu*) was transported from the estate to be used for funeral robes. Minamoto's intimate, the Mikawa monk Kiben Hōshi, was designated to bring the materials to Kyoto, but enroute his attendants were robbed by a fellow provincial who claimed Kiben was guilty of "evil deeds." An attendant named Noriyasu was dispatched as the regent Kujō Yoritsune's messenger, bearing instructions from Minamoto Norisuke's principal wife, a relative of the regent. Noriyasu conducted a survey of Nagayama rice paddies, entrusted the annual levy subsequently harvested to a man named Ichisuke, and returned to the capital. Ichisuke was probably an on-site representative of the governor working at the estate.

Visitors and dependents from the provinces—attendants like Tamesuke and Tomonori, and trusted followers such as the monk Kiben and Ichisuke—performed management functions that supported the governor's provincial administration as well as his household, which oversaw estate holdings. Such men were Mikawa notables who frequently traveled between province and capital to perform their duties. For instance, Noriyasu, the attendant-cum-messenger mentioned above, traveled to Kyoto via "a road traversing Ise." So do we learn that the main route taken by Minamoto Norisuke's retainers began at the provincial port of Mito, crossed the bays of Mikawa and Ise until reaching land at Ise's Ano Port, and then crossed Suzuka Pass to arrive at the capital.

Violent conflicts sometimes occurred in the provinces between those notables who were under direct control of the governor and those who were not. An example is the incident cited earlier in which a provincial notable slandered the governor's intimate associate, the monk Kiben, and robbed his attendants. Results of such tensions included complaints against provincial governor malfeasance by district officials and cultivators. One report observed that armed clashes in the province were frequent, with participants numbering in the thousands. Rival lineages formed and various types of armed clashes, beginning with seizure of land and unlawful foraging of crops on public lands and estates, were widespread in the Regency era. Amidst all this, warrior (*tsuwamono*) households and their bands extended their power through their own violent and menacing methods.

While provincial notables enjoyed an independent system of communication and exchange, they also lived in a violent and tumultuous environment. Fundamental causes of this violence were increased opposition to governors' policies by cultivators, together with competition and disputes among the elites themselves as they were transformed into landholding arms-bearers doubling as government officials and leaders of local society. Violence also resulted as middling and lesser aristocratic officials began to muscle into the sphere of provincial notables. In 1050, for instance, a petition from the Izumi governor asked the court to forbid "violent and wicked fellows" from moving to the province.[18] According to his complaint, many officials from the fifth rank down had taken up residence in the provinces and their dependents were accused of "conspiring with [residents on] other estates to resist government officials or seizing cultivators' fields to add to their own holdings." Such fellows had banded together "to pounce on people and forcibly rob them, committing arson and murder."

Such officials did not begin moving to the provinces in the Regency era. They were carrying on an earlier practice by which emigrants from the capital continually changed places with country dwellers who moved to the city, thereby replenishing the rural population. Aristocrat-officials who emigrated to the provinces during the Regency era carved out niches for themselves by expanding their roles on estates and increasing their private landholdings. The development of the estate system, a landholding network centered in the capital, owed much to the ambitions and activities of people from the city who moved into agricultural communities in these ways. Even though they moved out to the provinces, they maintained their foothold in the capital, which meant that they entered the provincial notable stratum as privileged individuals with official court rank.[19]

Provincial Notables in the Insei Era

During the era when retired monarchs led the court, provincial notables served as functionaries of major religious institutions such as Hie Taisha (Hie Grand Shrine) in Ōmi Province, which was the guardian shrine of the Buddhist temple Enryakuji and a component of the Sanmon monastery-shrine complex on Mount Hiei (see Map 10.1). Documents from 1106 offer a concrete view of the estate system of the Sanmon complex, a major central religious proprietor that combined management of its estate system with control of the Ōmi provincial government. In addition, these documents provide insight into the general situation of provincial notables in the late eleventh and twelfth centuries.

The two pertinent historical records from 1106 are a list, dated the third day of the eighth month, of people associated with Hie Shrine, and a petition from royal provisioners (*kugonin*) of pheasants in Ōmi Province's Echi District.[20] According to three records, Hie Shrine had established a branch shrine in Echi District known as the "new Echi Shrine" (Echi Shingū). An annual festival was held at both shrines on the sixteenth day of the third month, and people were chosen to serve at the festival from among the province's provisioners of various types—dependents (*yoribito*) and cultivators of public land (*kōmin*), who worked on nobles' estates alongside the royal provisioners. Staffing for such festival posts rotated from year to year. In 1106 five individuals designated by Hie authorities included two to serve at the main shrine and three for the new shrine. Personnel chosen for the main shrine included Fumi Sukenori of Ikako District, a falconer and provider of supplies for the royal table; and the assistant administrative chief of the royal falconry grounds, a man of the Kii family who held the fifth rank. The three chosen for the new shrine were Hata Yoshinori, an officer of Kawara Estate in Inukami District as well as local manager (*gesu*) of Shimizu Estate; the assistant administrative chief and attendant (*meshitsugi*) in the retired *tennō*'s office, Nakahara Nariyuki; and the monk Ryōin, a resident of Kanzaki District. Given that Nakahara Nariyuki was a resident of Echi District, Hie Shrine had selected one person from each district in Ōmi east of Lake Biwa.

It is clear from their status and occupations that the appointments of 1106 (and those of previous years as well) went to specially privileged clients of central authorities, or to functionaries of the Ōmi provincial office. In other words, it was not functionaries on Hie estates who were expected to provide service to the shrine.[21] Rather, service at the shrine was an obligation levied on several districts by the provincial government. In fact, in 1106 Hie Shrine forwarded to the provincial governor the list of names of those chosen and requested him to order the performance of duties to the shrine in accord with precedent.[22] In other words, Hie Shrine's right to designate individuals for shrine duties was based on public authority, and approvals or exemptions came under the governor's jurisdiction. Since the provincial authorities prepared a report on conditions of service at the shrine, we know that they supervised such service and kept pertinent records. But unlike ordinary provincial taxes and labor obligations, shrine service was an honor. Those chosen for yearly duties came from the provincial notable stratum, including the retired monarch's administrative chief Nariyuki and various types of royal provisioners.

Other duties at religious establishments within the province, beginning with Takebe Shrine—the preeminent first-shrine (*ichinomiya*) of the province—were also ordered by provincial government proclamation. Conflicts sometimes arose, however, when provincial notables preferred service at the more prestigious Hie Shrine. According to the pheasant provisioners' petition, the guardsman Funya Kanemoto had previously abandoned his provincial religious obligations, falsely claiming to be a shrine associate (*jin'nin*), and he was then chosen to serve at the new Echi Shrine. In other words, he exchanged local shrine duties imposed on him by the provincial government for more prestigious religious duties at Hie. In this case, the workings of a relationship similar to those characterizing the estate system itself are visible: a provincial notable was attempting to establish ties with central powerholders through service at Hie, the province's most prestigious shrine with direct ties to the capital.

Nakahara Nariyuki is another interesting provincial notable. His name is recorded in several documents, including one dated 1122 in which he is identified as the chieftain of Echi District. A record of 1136 identifies him as an Ōtsu resident and associate of Hie Shrine; and the genealogy of the Nakahara family in Ōmi identifies him as a son of the chamberlain (*jijū*) and governor of Tango, Nariyoshi, as well as a younger brother of the Middle Captain of the Left Guards (*chūjō*) Tsunenori.[23] A side note adds that Nariyuki was appointed senior chieftain (*dairyō*) of Echi District around the time when Horikawa Tennō retired.[24] The note adds that when the Nakahara first entered the province, during Suzaku Tennō's reign (930–946), they settled in Echi District's Nagano vicinity. We cannot rely simply on the genealogy, but the document of 1122 verifies Nakahara Nariyuki's status as Echi chieftain. The tradition that his family lived in Echi's Nagano is probably credible as well.

It is unclear whether or not the district chief and "official without post" (*san'i*) named Nakahara who affixed his seal to a petition of 1138 was Nariyuki, but that document indicates that either Nariyuki or a close relative held court rank, probably the fifth.[25] We cannot determine the accuracy of his paternal ancestry as given in the genealogy—neither the third-ranking Provisional Middle Counselor Asayuki, listed as his grandfather, nor the man listed as his great-grandfather, Minister of the Left and General of the Right Yasumichi, appears in the *Kugyō bunin*, a register of appointments to the Council of State.[26] It seems likely that either Nakahara Nariyuki or a paternal ancestor was the last scion of a middling official family to live in the capital, and that the Nakahara family came to live in Echi District just like the officials "from the fifth rank down to miscellanous functionaries" who immigrated to Izumi Province in 1050.[27]

When Nakahara Nariyuki appeared in the document of 1106, he was a lead attendant (*meshitsugi*) in the household of the retired monarch Shirakawa. *Meshitsugi* were low-ranking functionaries in the attendants' office assigned miscellaneous duties such as arranging for the retired monarch's journeys. For instance, in the eighth month of 1103 there were 264 attendants from the capital and 635 rural attendants, all called *meshitsugi*, serving at the ceremony of the first wearing of the robes of Kaya no In, consort of the prince who later became Toba Tennō.[28] Nakahara Nariyuki probably journeyed to the capital at that time as one of the rural attendants, and as their leader he may well have led the entire *meshitsugi* delegation from Echi District. Nearly two decades later in 1122 Nariyuki appears in a document as the Echi chieftain summoned to the capital by the provincial governor Fujiwara Sanemitsu, who charged him with having withheld tax receipts for the previous two years. According to that record, "he dared to muster a threatening force of *meshitsugi* and refused to perform his tax-forwarding duties." It would seem that Nariyuki still had status as Shirakawa's attendant.[29]

As a scion of an urban aristocratic family, a leading attendant of Shirakawa In, Echi District senior chieftain, and designee to serve at the new Echi Shrine, Nakahara Nariyuki is a representative provincial notable. Moreover, because of his position in the entourage of the retired *tennō*, he frequently traveled back and forth between Kyoto and Ōmi and had strong ties with the capital. His frequent trips between Kyoto and the countryside were not only for the purpose of discharging official duties. Such trips must have also improved his own status and economic position, for example as a member of the Hie Shrine associates of Ōtsu, an organization that embraced merchant-lenders in the capital.

In this regard Nakahara Nariyuki's activities are evidenced in a document dated 1136, which provides a good account of usurious lending by associates of Mount Hiei at the time.[30] As a Hie associate resident in Ōtsu, Nakahara contracted for use of rice paid as a surtax (*jōbun*) to the shrine, which he then seems to have lent out to Fujiwara Akiyoshi. I will discuss the full details of such lending activities later, but for the moment I want to focus on Nakahara Nariyuki's service at the new Echi Shrine.

The petition of the Echi pheasant providers dated 1106 says, "Recently the retired *tennō*'s attendant Nariyuki, while appointed chief of those designated to serve at the Shingū festival, also became a follower of the Hie Shrine ritualist and provisional governor."[31] Nakahara Nariyuki's new patron was the shrine's head ritualist (*kannushi*) and also provisional governor of Kaga, Hafuribe Narifusa, one of three shrine officials whose name was affixed to a list of Hie functionaries dated 1106.[32] Apparently Narifusa and Nariyuki had formed patron-client ties that resulted in Nariyuki's selection as head of the Echi Shingū functionaries. In other words patronage bonds underlay selection for desirable shrine service performed as duty to the realm.

It appears that this Narifusa was a central figure in shrine affairs at the time; his name appears in the twelfth-century ritual handbook, the *Shisseishoshō*, as one of those at Hie Shrine responsible for abbreviated readings of the Dai Hannya Sutra in spring and winter on behalf of the regents' house. Provisions for Buddhist monks who conducted the sutra reading came from dues levied on stables maintained by the Regent's house at Ōtsu in Ōmi, and instructions from the regents' household ordering the distribution of provisions were sent to Hafuribe. According to this same *Shisseishoshō*, a representative of the regents' house was to summon Hafuribe to acknowledge receipt of those instructions on the sixth day of the seven-day *sutra* reading. His name also appears in Fujiwara Munetada's journal, the *Chūyūki*. According to this source, when Hie functionaries in Settsu Province were disbanded and problems arose concerning one of them, Munetada suggested summoning the overseer, Hafuribe Narifusa, to deal with the issue.[33] The fact that Hafuribe held such a post indicates his influence. All this indicates that Nakahara Nariyuki's activities as an Ōtsu associate of Hie Shrine had a great deal to do with his relationship with Hafuribe.

The new Hie Shrine in Echi, where the main Hie deity, Sannō Gongen, was venerated, was also the center for Mount Hiei's religious control of Ōmi Province east of Lake Biwa. Thus it was necessary for Hie Shrine to maintain close relations with the Echi district chief. Indeed, according to the petition of the Echi pheasant providers noted earlier, a new shrine-held property called Hie *hō*, or Hie New Township, was established in the environs of the new Hie Shrine and it expanded rapidly. We are told that when one Harunomiya Makoto served as Ōmi governor, fifteen *chō* of land from that property were opened in the neighborhood (*mura*) known as Heru.[34] Since tax-exempt fields were added to the holding every time a new governor was appointed, by 1106 the property had over two hundred *chō* of land and more than two hundred cultivator households, all dependents of Hie's new shrine. At the center of this expanding holding was the old Echi District locale called Himata; perhaps the new shrine itself was located there. Nagano, where Nakahara Nariyuki lived, was nearby. The chief estate official was someone named Tsuneyori, but Nakahara must have had an important role in managing the new township.

Up to this point I have sketched portraits of twelfth-century provincial notables in provinces near the capital, situating them within networks of local relationships and in the nexus of urban-rural relations. Now I want to consider the activities of Ōmi Province's pheasant providers and falconers associated with the royal palace.

Since the eleventh century there had been a royal reserve for pheasant hunting in Ōmi Province.[35] In that regard we know that in 1076 Taira Sukenori, a minor controller (*shōben*) concurrently posted in the Equestrian Bureau's Right Division who had his main residence in Ōmi, applied for appointment as custodian of the pheasant reserve.[36] The duty of pheasant provisioners was to present offerings of fowl for the Hagatame, ceremonial banquets served at the palace to celebrate the new year. The primary method of obtaining the birds for this and other events was falcon hunting—pheasant providers were a service group based in mountain and hunting organizations, not in agricultural communities.[37] Pheasant providers and falconers lived in the Ōmi districts of Ikako, Inukami, and Echi; and they probably also provided fowl as tribute offerings at the main and new Hie shrines.

In the twelfth century, however, the pheasant providers began to refuse to perform services for the new Echi Shrine. Their petition was presented as a deposition to the Ōmi provincial headquarters records office (*kumonjo*), and it pointed out that more than two hundred cultivator families lived on the two-hundred-plus *chō* of the Hie New Township. Service ought to be provided by the cultivators as shrine dependents, alleged the petitioners.[38] The existence of dependents tied to Hie through what can be characterized as "estate-like relations" thus gave rise to a quarrel between the provincial government and residents of public lands. The quarrel weakened, and precipitated collapse of, the system of selecting provincial notables for shrine service as an obligation to

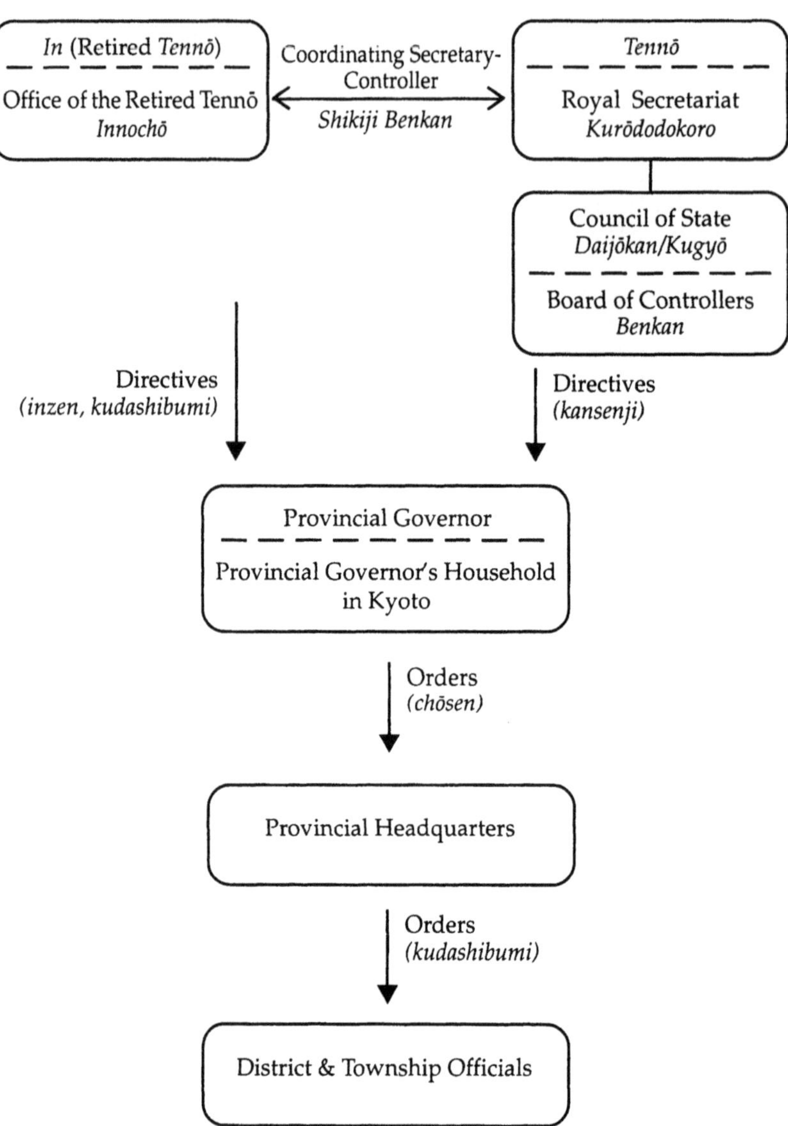

Fig. 10.1. Provincial Governance in the Twelfth Century

the realm. The dispute also led provincial notables to reorganize their affairs—namely, it stimulated the strengthening and expansion of estate-like service relationships that linked provincial notables with central authorities and religious institutions.

Estate Organization and Urban-Rural Bonds in Later Heian Times

In order to exercise absentee control over public lands and estates in the provinces, government officials and other elites in the capital had to develop a relatively sophisticated system of keeping and transmitting official records, in addition to the unofficial correspondence archived in collections such as the *Old Primer*. Knowledge of this system illuminates important aspects of the communications network that linked the capital with the provinces and estates. Here I analyze how two documents were transmitted and preserved. Then, in order to shine light on relations between city and countryside, I explore features of the control over the estates exercised by retired monarchs.

Four documents were discovered on the reverse side of a manuscript of *Ishimpō*, a Heian-period medical text preserved in the Royal Household Agency archives. Two of them, both dated in the eighth month of 1127, were petitions sent to Kyoto from Kaga Province; one was submitted by officials in Enuma District, and the other was from the dependents of Nukata Estate in the same district.[39] Since both documents were used as copy paper for the same volume of *Ishimpō*, they have been transmitted together up to the present day.[40] Nonetheless, while the documents were prepared at the same time and place, there is no direct relationship between their contents: one is a request for permission for district officials to travel to Kyoto, and the other is a petition from Nukata residents to the estate proprietor regarding rules for assessing their dry-field and head taxes. It is no accident, however, that these two seemingly unrelated documents were transmitted as a set. Most probably they were sent at the same time to the same recipient in Kyoto via the same messenger or runner. The petitions were addressed to the provincial governor of Kaga, Fujiwara Ienari (1107–1154). Ienari maintained dual roles, as provincial governor and estate official, which made him an appropriate recipient of both petitions. The Ōe family, prominent among signatories of the two documents, also had corresponding dual functions on the local level.

In the first month of 1127, Fujiwara Ienari, an adviser to the newly retired sovereign Toba, was appointed governor of Toba's proprietary province of Kaga.[41] It was undoubtedly in his capacity as governor that he received the request from village officials in Enuma District for official approval of their planned visit to the capital (see Figure 10.1). Ienari was probably still in Kyoto in the eighth month when the petition was delivered to his office-residence there, since he appears in the courtier journal *Chūyūki* two months later as a member of the entourage of Shirakawa and Toba on a pilgrimage from the capital to Mount Kōya.

The petition from Nukata Estate residents to the proprietor, on the other hand, was probably sent to Fujiwara Ienari in his capacity as estate official. Several items of evidence suggest that Nukata was the holding of Ienari's patron, retired sovereign Toba, and that Ienari served as the estate custodian (*azukaridokoro*). I base this conclusion on three factors: first, another attendant of a retired sovereign, the former governor of Sagami named Fujiwara Morishige, had previously doubled as the custodian of Nukata Estate; second, when Nukata Estate was established, it was decided that "submission of annual rents . . . is to follow the example of the estates of the senior retired monarch [Shirakawa]," indicating that the proprietor of Nukata was a retired sovereign. By 1195 the same estate had become a holding of Go-Toba In, further evidence that Nukata proprietors were retired monarchs. Finally, Ienari, a member of the provincial governor (*zuryō*) class, was appointed governor of Kaga, Toba's proprietary province, as a client of the retired monarch.[42]

To some extent Ienari's career paralleled that of the Sagami governor Morishige, appointed in the twelfth month of 1120. Morishige was also an intimate retainer of a retired monarch: in the fourth month of 1127, in fact, Toba In's second princess attended the governor's housewarming celebration.[43] And according to side notes in the aristocratic genealogical compilation known as the *Sonpi bun'myaku,* Morishige—originally a resident of Suō Province—had become a favorite of Toba's predecessor, Shirakawa, while serving at the retired monarch's palace in his youth. During adulthood he became the retired monarch's attendant and was appointed successively to the governorships of Shinano, Sagami, Higo, and Iwami. Like Morishige a provincial governor and close retainer of a retired monarch, Fujiwara Ienari was a suitable successor to Morishige as custodian for a retired monarch's estate.

Nukata was in all likelihood Toba's holding, as suggested by the petition from Nukata Estate provisioners—the petitioners complained that in assessing taxes, the former custodian (Morishige) had frequently violated the precedent established when the estate was founded, that levies should "follow the example of the senior retired monarch's holdings."[44] Finally, we can assume that in the first month of 1127, Ienari—a son of Fujiwara Ieyasu, an official in the office of the retired monarch, the *In no chō*—was appointed custodian for Toba's holdings in the province of Kaga as well as governor of that province. The significant factor here is that when such custodial provincial governors were appointed, administration of the retired monarch's proprietary province and of his estates in the province were placed under a unified system of control.

Now let us turn our attention to the local power relationships that underlay this system. Officials in Enuma District sought the governor's approval for a "lawsuit with multiple complaints," and they planned to visit the capital to further the suit. The five petitioners included a former provincial official and the heads of four townships (*gō*). Four of the five were surnamed Ōe, indicating that in Enuma District the Ōe were provincial notables who controlled both district and township administration. In that capacity they were responsible for encouraging people "to diligently cultivate crops in the spring and to earn profit from the exchange of goods in the summer." During the interim period before tax payment time at the end of the year, the five petitioners had free time to go to Kyoto to further their lawsuit.

Signers of the other petition sent to Ienari included ten tax collectors (*bantō*) and one record keeper (*anju*). The record keeper, a local estate official, was also surnamed Ōe, and Ōe Kinmasa was among the tax collectors. We may conclude that the Ōe family played a prominent role in Enuma District, both as officials and as local estate managers.[45] Local elites such as the Ōe prepared petitions concerning both public land and the retired monarch's estates, such as the documents of 1127, which may have been sent in the same package to absentee provincial governor cum estate custodian Ienari at his mansion in the capital.[46]

Provincial notables sometimes took advantage of ties with the capital to increase the chances that their petitions would be successful. For example, they would ask Kyoto literati to draft documents to present to central authorities. An episode in the thirteenth-century collection of court reminiscences *Kojidan* (*Talks about Matters Past*) illustrates how this might have worked. According to that story the Council of State secretary (*geki*) Ōe Yasutada drafted a petition for residents of Ikeda Estate in the mid-twelfth century.[47] Ikeda, a proprietary holding of a branch temple of Hōjōji known as Higashitōin, was located in Yamashiro Province's Kii District and had the Regent's house as its preeminent proprietor.[48] The episode narrates how during Konoe's tenure as retired monarch, officials of Ikeda Estate submitted a petition to the regent's administrative office (*mandokoro*) complaining of various transgressions. One phrase in the complaint, "The accused not only made light of the lord's majesty, but also committed wicked deeds in the rafters," drew the attention of Regent Fujiwara Tadamichi. Noting the allusion to the Chinese classic, *History of the Latter Han* (*Hou Han shu*), in which "lord of the rafters" is a euphemism for "thief," Tadamichi declared, "This petition is not the work of country bumpkins but rather of a proper Confucian scholar. We should make inquiries." When estate officials were summoned and questioned, they answered, "We relied on our ties with a man named Secretary Ōe Yasutada, and asked him to write the petition." Tadamichi reportedly acknowledged Yasutada's literary skills and subsequently employed him as an archivist for the regent's household.

In order to further their lawsuit, the residents of Ikeda Estate traveled to Kyoto and convinced an official in the secretariat of the Council of State, the Gekikyoku, to draft their petition. Ikeda Estate was located on the outskirts of Kyoto, but petitions from estates throughout the provinces were also drafted by other than "country bumpkins." When necessary, petitioners relied on long-standing connections and traveled to the capital to make requests of "proper Confucian scholars," thereby obtaining drafts written in elegant and ornate prose. The famous petition from Owari Province submitted by district officials and cultivators in 988 was also composed in an ornate literary style that alternated phrases of four and six characters, indicating that it too could hardly have been the work of "country bumpkins."

If we wish to understand communications between city and countryside that provided the context for the drafting of elegantly worded petitions such as the one that figures in *Kojidan*, we must clarify how the form, literary style, and vocabulary of estate documents were standardized realm-wide, how petitions reached their addressees, and what devices and conditions were involved in the process. Much of that work remains for future research.

Now let me take a brief look at the contents of documents related to central authorities' official posts, family holdings, and household administration. As evidence, I will use the documents found on the reverse side of the *Gumaiki* courtier journal. There are fourteen such "reverse-side documents" (*uramonjo*) in *Heian ibun*, and except for one from 1029, all are dated between 1124 and 1151, during the tenures of Shirakawa and Toba as retired monarchs. This was the era of Sanefusa's grandfather, Prime Minister Saneyuki, and his father, the Inner Minister Kinnori. The Sanjō family filed the documents in their archives and eventually used the discarded paper for the *Gumaiki*, the journal kept by Minister of the Left Sanjō Sanefusa (1147–1225). These fortuitously preserved documents can be divided into three categories according to their contents: documents related to the Royal Police Office (Kebiishichō) of the Outer Palace Guards, documents related to family land holdings, and family registers.

Among documents concerning Sanjō family holdings are duplicate copies of reports dated 1134 and 1135 concerning miscellaneous dues from the Yodo Sagami lowlands on Yodo Estate.[49] This was a property that served as a wharf storehouse in Yodo, the outer port for the capital.[50] The holding was made up of more than seven *tan* of dry fields and twenty-six households. Residents of the latter paid various dues to the Sanjō family, whose head at the time was Provisional Major Counselor Saneyuki. Such dues included more than eight hundred bundles of straw as taxes on dry fields; seasonal dues to support annual rituals—irises in the fifth month, melons and eggplants for seventh-month offerings for the Bon Festival, and firewood for the end of the year; fresh fish and shellfish as special taxes; and labor service on boats passing from Yodo to Kawajiri, Ōtsu, or Toba. Excellent research has already been done on this holding, which was known as a *sanjo*—a place where those of certain occupations resided.[51] The documents informed the Sanjō household office of the various tax items and labor services owed by residents. There is a note of confirmation from the Sanjō house attached to the original 1124 document which says, "Following submission of this report, residents are to send an acknowledgement," and the report was apparently returned to the sender. A draft of this tax memorandum was preserved by the Sanjō family, and it was this draft that was discarded and later used as writing paper. Would that the Sanjō family had kept a copy of the acknowledgment sent by residents in response!

Among the documents written on the back of the *Gumaiki* manuscript is one that was previously published with the identifying title, "Report on a Certain Estate's Thatch Tribute."[52] At first glance this appears to be a document concerning a payment of thatch from a Sanjō family property, but instead it probably concerns the levy of a province-wide flat tax by order of the *tennō* or retired *tennō*. The levy of 100,000 sheaves of thatch was ordered in the first month of 1149 at the recommendation of the Settsu governor, Fujiwara Shigeie, who had been appointed in the eleventh month of the previous year.[53] It seems likely that the 100,000 sheaves were to be collected from estates only in Shigeie's province. The collection was enforced by warrior-officials of Royal Guard units and the Royal Police. According to the document, two military specialists (*bushi*) were charged with overseeing collection of the thatch. One was Minamoto Chikayasu, a member of the retired Toba Tennō's Northern Guards. Chikayasu had been appointed to the Royal Police Office in 1130, and in 1147 he was still serving in the capital as third-in-command of that office. The other, Taira Kinsuke, was reappointed to the Right Palace Guards in the twelfth month of 1149 and was posted to the Royal Police as third-in-command during the following year. Not coincidentally, Fujiwara Kinnori of the Sanjō house was associated with both of these organizations: in the twelfth month of 1147 he resigned his post as director (*bettō*) of the Royal Police, and afterward he served as first-in-command of the Left Palace Guards until the eighth month of 1150.[54] He also accompanied Toba In's party on a pilgrimage to Shitennōji in the twelfth month of 1149 as director of the retired monarch's office.[55]

In another document, Commander Kinnori of the Left Palace Guards denied provincial officials the authority to tax certain exempt properties held by the royal temple, Daigoji.[56] This indicates that Kinnori played a central role in overseeing enforcement of royal orders issued by the *tennō* and the retired *tennō*, and it provides additional evidence that the levy of 100,000 sheaves of straw was a province-wide flat tax (*chokuji inji*) collected through the tax-gathering apparatus of the Palace Guards, the Royal Police, and the *In no chō*.

How did the retired *tennō* use these sheaves of straw from Settsu once they were collected? The thatch was likely utilized as roofing material for mansions and smaller buildings needed by the government, elites, and aristocratic temples. Many such structures were being built, repaired, and rebuilt in the capital and in the Toba and Shirakawa suburbs. The thatch-payment document reads, "The Toba Lord Chikatada has requested 30,000 sheaves," suggesting that a great deal of the straw was utilized for construction projects in Toba.[57]

The very fact that an official document of this sort ended up in the household of Sanjō Kinnori and was used along with family documents as writing paper for his son Sanefusa's diary suggests how courtiers exercised their official duties. The same may be said of the seven "reverse side" documents relating to the Royal Police. For instance, a document dated 1124 and addressed to the Royal Police Office was written while Sanjō Sanefusa's grandfather Saneyuki was the Royal Police director; and the following documents date from Kinnori's tenure in that office: a Royal Police Office letter dated 1142 and four documents dating from 1142 to 1146, including reports and court judgements. It appears that the director stored police documents at his home during his tenure. After his retirement, when a certain time period had elapsed, the family disposed of them as they also disposed of name registers (*kajin myōbō*) and documents related to family holdings.

Since the current director's home was the place where official decisions were made, reports and court decisions were not necessarily preserved in the Royal Police Office archives. On the fifth day of the first month of 1114, for instance, the director of the Royal Police, Provisional Middle Counselor

Fujiwara Munetada, began to oversee official matters from his home at Nakamikado Tomikoji, and police officers reported to him there. New Year congratulations were issued, miscellaneous business was conducted, and reports were sent to the court from Munetada's mansion. A thief was also questioned outside its gate.[58] This was how the first duties of the New Year were carried out. Soon thereafter, police officers began to visit the mansion any time there was a problem, and decisions came to be announced there as well. According to Fujiwara Munetada's *Chūyūki*, official documents were also perused at the mansion: "[The Kebiishi] officer Akikane came yesterday, bringing records of an investigation"; and "Morimichi arrived, and we looked over reports of armed robberies." Thus, public documents were collected at the director's mansion, and after his retirement they became household property. This indicates that in the late Heian capital, posts were exercised much like rights to family property, including proprietary estate holdings.

Lending Operations and Estate Control

Elsewhere I have described how local officials and provincial notables used income payable to nobles to engage in high-interest lending in the early years of the Heian capital.[59] Moreover, district officials who collected produce and labor taxes (*chōyō*) from the provinces and delivered the payments to Kyoto frequently borrowed from officials and families in the capital to make up for deficiencies in payments. As the Heian capital developed, urban merchant-lenders came to form a parasitic relationship with the *tennō*'s government, the nobility, and the official stipend and taxation systems.

Urban merchant-lenders in the capital during the late Heian era were portrayed as rich usurers in an essay in the twelfth-century anthology, *Honchō zoku monzui*. It describes how they "either borrow from the environs of the capital and earn three times the profit in the distant provinces, or invest a small amount in the springtime to reap huge interest in the fall. By expending a few winter coals over and over again, they can build up a trove that will last just about a lifetime. Poor people cannot resist the moneylenders' power, and they abscond, abandoning their homes entirely and selling their wives and children into long periods of servitude, making them into slaves."

Merchant-lenders like those portrayed in this essay probably operated a kind of consignment-sale business in which they collected specialized goods produced in the capital and its environs, such as handmade arts and crafts items; and later they distributed them in the countryside, receiving high profits based on the difference between the value of the goods in the city and in the provinces. To set up such a business, it was necessary to borrow goods on consignment through established relations of trust, and to guarantee packhorse or sea shipment as well as safety on the roads. In addition, merchant-lenders conducted agricultural lending programs in farming villages where they lent out rice seedlings in the springtime and received principal plus interest when the grain was harvested in the fall.

This may have been possible in agricultural villages close to Kyoto, but what about in distant provinces? The system worked best if a percentage of interest earned from lending operations in the provinces were reinvested locally as capital to fund ongoing operations. In addition, lenders had to find a local custodian to invest and secure goods, as well as a place to store them. A base for such activities already existed within the public and estate land systems. In both, the tax collection structure was founded on a system in which powerful cultivators acting as contracting agents (*risō fumyō*) stored tax grain in warehouses (*nassho*).[60] Wealthy Kyoto merchants with capital could wedge themselves into this system and turn a profit in the countryside. If they attached themselves to district and estate officials who exercised local power, they could guarantee even greater profits.

An effective tool for such merchant-lenders was an array of licenses—permissions, exemptions, and guarantees—granted by central officials, powerful religious institutions, provincial governors, and the like. For example, a license from the Royal Secretariat (Kurōdodokoro) could facilitate travel and transport of goods. According to an entry dated the tenth day of the tenth month of 1017 in the *Sakeiki* courtier journal, the Secretariat issued licenses for passage through Harima and Awaji provinces to a messenger headed for Usa in northern Kyūshū. And according to the *Shunki* journal, in the fourth month of 1039 pilgrims to Ise Shrine were advised to "obtain a license from the Royal Secretariat for the journey." The entry continues, moreover, "There are instances of even ordinary folk and people traveling to hot springs and gaining a license from the Royal Secretariat." Such examples indicate the widespread use in the Regency era of a system of licenses from the Royal Secretariat to facilitate travel—including unofficial journeys—between city and countryside.

As noted earlier, the Ōmi Echi District notable Nakahara Nariyuki was an associate of Hie Shrine from Ōtsu, Kyoto's eastern gateway. In the late eleventh and twelfth centuries, such shrine associates conducted commercial lending operations in the Heian capital. The document that best represents such activities at the time is a legal expert's brief (*kanmon*), dated 1136, that lists a number of delinquent borrowers who had not yet paid back their loans from surtax rice stores belonging to Hie Shrine.[61] The lending agents were Hie associates from Ōtsu. The same document includes a deposition from Hie Shrine officials complaining to the court that the delinquents had failed to respond to demands for payment. We learn here too how shrine associates engaged in various efforts supporting Hie Shrine's religious activities: "They either travel through the provinces circulating goods or arrange to lend out surtax rice." In regard to the latter, "they contract for the rice stored [by the shrine], and taking [the borrower's] possessions as collateral, they have promissory notes made out." Thus they lent out Hie Shrine surtax rice to "all people, high and low." Each participating shrine associate took charge of a portion of the surtax rice, with responsibility for "investing" it, traveling from province to province in order to lend it at high interest.

Table 10.1 lists names of the associate-lenders and their debtors, adopting the arrangement and terminology used by the associates themselves. Among the twelve Ōtsu lenders with lay names were eight officials with rank but without posts (*sanmi*). In a later example from the early Kamakura Period, among twelve Ōtsu associates who were signatories of a petition dated 1202, ten were officials without portfolio. We can surmise the status of other associates from this information. We can also see that on occasion a single associate could lend to several borrowers. Individual associates conducted business on a broad geographical basis while borrowers ranged from court nobles (such as the Counselor and Controller of the Left, junior third-ranking Fujiwara Tametaka, who died in 1130); former and current provincial governors; other central government officials; and down to various provincial residents and cultivators, as well as a female peddler from Shijō in the capital.

Although most borrowers were from the capital, some were from the provinces of Ōmi, Echizen, and Etchū. Ōtsu associates traveled to various provinces, especially to those where Mount Hiei possessed estates. Many local residents were caught in the net of agricultural lending: for example, government guarantees of titles for rice fields put up as collateral for Fujiwara Sadasuke's loans by residents of Ōmi Takashima District filled five volumes. And consider how Wakae Kanetsugu traveled great distances to make loans: he went as far as Ashiyatsu at the mouth of the Onga River in Kyūshū's Chikuzen Province in search of borrowers. There, however, his surtax rice was seized by a warrior named Hyōdō Takiguchi, from whom Wakae subsequently demanded repayment.

Around 1112 Hie lenders were also active in Settsu Province. But in the fourth month they were disbanded by order of the *tennō*. According to the *Chūyūki*, one Kunimitsu protested, claiming to be an Ōtsu shrine associate serving as chief offerant to the *kami* at a festival that month. As for the activities of the Ōtsu associate-lenders in Kyoto, an edict issued by the *tennō* in the seventh month of 1163 claims that "Enryakuji monks and Hie Shrine associates have rioted in the capital" to demand the arrest of "those fellows who default on their agricultural loans."[62]

In provinces where Mount Hiei had proprietary holdings, shrine property was stored in the homes of associate-lenders. Evidence of this from a later period comes from records of an incident in 1202 in which a military steward (*jitō*) from Toyoda Estate in Echigo Province arrested a provincial Hie associate, confiscated his house, and seized the shrine property he had in his possession.[63] The document also describes a Hie branch shrine where "portraits of the three saints of Sannō were venerated, served by more than thirty shrine associates." When monks and associates from the central complex came to visit, this was their base.

Moreover, officials from Kumano Shrine in Kii Province handled surtax rice in much the same fashion as did officials from Hie. According to a document from the tenth month of 1144, Kumano officials used their connections with Ise Shrine's Ōpa Estate (*mikuriya*) in Sagami to store rice levied on the province.[64] Kumano Shrine associates often stored annual land tax levies (*nengu*) of rice under the roofs of estate residents and used it for agricultural lending. Moreover, the accumulation of Kumano surplus tax rice in eastern provinces such as Ise was facilitated by the evangelistic activities of Kumano pilgrim guides (*sendatsu*) and shrine associates. In some cases they took advantage of central proprietors' religious devotion to Kumano to divert tax rice from their estates. For instance, in the sixth month of 1111 a messenger from Provisional Middle Counselor Fujiwara Munetada's salary fields in Tōtōmi Province arrived at Munetada's mansion in the capital to report that rice designated as the counselor's income from the fields had not been forwarded to Kyoto. Instead it had been left in place and stored as "a contribution to Kumano Shrine." Munetada explained that the contribution of rice had been his own idea, saying "I had originally allotted it for that purpose."[65] It was invested by Kumano pilgrim guides in an agricultural lending program to support the shrine.

What about lending activities in the capital? Base locations in Kyoto for lending out Hie surtax rice no doubt included Gion Shrine and the temple known as Kyōgokuji, both branches of Mount Hiei; dwellings of monks at the various subtemples on Mount Hiei; and Kyoto residences of Hiei monks and shrine associates. But as we saw in the case of Kumano, rice for lending was also stored at unexpected places. In the seventh month of 1114, Kumano officials informed Fujiwara Munetada, then serving as Director of the Royal Police: "Last year we collected the surtax rice and stored it in the homes of a Kyoto resident. But since they did not send it on to us, we request that you deal with the master of the house." When Munetada inquired who that master might be, he was informed that it was "a disciple of the retired *tennō*'s sutra-copier, [Monk] Jin'i."[66] The fact that a private home of a disciple of an attendant to the retired *tennō* had become a storage place for Kumano surtax rice indicates that the Kyoto organization enabling Kumano lending had inserted itself deeply into the lives of capital residents.

Let me now turn to the politics of monastic lineages as they affected estates and branch temples in the provinces. To illuminate this matter, I examine the activities of the Hiei monk Hōyaku Zenshi, known as the leader of Mount Hiei's "evil monks" (*akusō*).[67] During the era of Shirakawa In, Hōyaku belonged to the Kajii monastic lineage (*monzeki*), headquartered at a cloister known as the Enyūbō in the Eastern Pagoda South Valley and at Entokuin in Higashi Sakamoto.[68] After the death of the Tendai head monk (*zasu*) Ninkaku (1045–1102) of the same lineage, a member of a rival monastic lineage—Kyōchō (1027–1107) of Yokawa—became Mount Hiei's abbot with the support of a monk named Teijin from the Western Pagoda. This gave rise to constant quarreling, and in the tenth month of 1104, Kyōchō was driven off Mount Hiei by forces led by Hōyaku Zenshi.[69]

A *Chūyūki* entry of that month adds information collected by the Royal Police Office concerning this Hōyaku: "Among the monks on the Tendai mountain is one Hōyaku Zenshi. The monks' corporate decision-making body [*taishū*] at the Eastern Pagoda made him monastic superintendent [*tsuina*] of the main temple.[70] But his martial valor exceeds that of ordinary men, and he has a heart that loves fighting. He is always eager to participate in an armed quarrel on the mountain. He has held concurrent posts on various estates belonging to Mount Hiei's branch temples [*matsuji*], and has led troops of dozens of fighting men. He travels back and forth to Kyoto and to other provinces morning and night. He likes to rob people of their goods or cut their heads off. Monks from throughout the realm cannot help but flock to him."

What draws our attention is that Hōyaku held concurrent posts at estates belonging to Hiei branch temples and shrines, and that as an envoy of Mount Hiei, he frequently traveled between Kyoto and the countryside, accompanied by armed monks and laymen. Activities such as these were critical to the operation and expansion of Mount Hiei's estates. Men like Hōyaku supported the activities of the Ōtsu Hie Shrine associates, helping to link capital and provinces.

Hōyaku's efforts to control estates belonging to Hiei's branch temples are illustrated by his seizure of the temple directorship (*bettō shiki*) at Taisanji, an Enryakuji branch temple near the Dazaifu headquarters in Kyūshū's Chikuzen Province. The incident is recorded in detail in a Royal Police report dated the tenth month of 1105 as well as in the *Chūyūki*.[71] In the tenth month of the previous year, Hōyaku's representative, Monk Gen of Enryakuji—also an official at Hie Shrine—journeyed to Taisanji to oversee its administration. During the administration of Hōyaku's foe Kyōchō, however, Hiei authorities had obtained an order from the retired sovereign placing one Kōshō, director of Iwashimizu Hachiman Shrine, in charge of Taisanji. Gen's job was to regain control of the temple and its estates for Hōyaku. To do so, Gen recruited two Taisanji monks as intermediaries and took goods on consignment from Chinese merchants at the Dazaifu and at the nearby port of Hakata. He used these goods to "successfully petition for the Dazaifu's approval" of his appointment as Taisanji's director. In other words, with capital from Chinese merchants, Hōyaku and Gen "made donations" to the Dazaifu—they bribed officials there to obtain an order recognizing Hōyaku's authority over Taisanji's estate holdings.

Just as the Hie Shrine associate Wakae Kanetsugu traveled to Ashiyatsu in Chikuzen Province to carry out lending activities, Hie associate-lenders and Chinese merchants were engaged in business using Northern Kyūshū as a base for networks forged by cooperation and exchange. Indeed, in the early Kamakura Period, the Chinese seaman-merchant Ch'ang Kuang-an appears in the historical record as an affiliate of Kamado Shrine as well as of its affiliated temple (*jingūji*) Taisanji, both branch institutions of Mount Hiei.[72] The interregional activities of Hiei monks and shine associates, who formed the nucleus of the Mount Hiei estate system, thus spanned much of the archipelago. In Northern Kyūshū, that organization embraced even Chinese merchants who carried goods throughout East Asia.

The Estate-Like Structure of the Late Heian Capital

Relations between city and countryside helped to actualize a new system of control within the medieval estate system established when retired monarchs led the court. My primary objective in this article has not been to examine the internal structure of individual estates or dynamics of the legal establishment of estate proprietors' rights and transmission of those rights to others. Rather, I have tried to reassess the estate system as one in which the proprietor class that lived in the Heian capital controlled estates distributed across the archipelago. But there remain a number of topics that have not been adequately studied, especially modes and organization of transportation between city and countryside that developed with the estate system, as well as the structure of the capital itself seen from the perspective of that system. Up to this point I have approached these problems through the activities of various social strata as they functioned within the estate system. In this final section I wish to consider the estate-like structure of the capital city of Heiankyō.

According to Yoshishige Yasutane's *Chiteiki* (*An Account of My Retreat by a Pond*) written in 982, the tenth-century Heian capital had changed in basic ways.[73] Private residences were by then clustered in the eastern areas, known as the "Left Capital" (*sakyō*). The political center—the city's northern sector, which abutted the eastern side of the palace, contained the mansions of various nobles and governmental offices.[74] The Yōmei Gate, the most commonly used entrance to the palace, occupied the pivotal position; and Konoe Avenue (Konoe Ōji), which stretched eastward from the gate, served as the axial thoroughfare. The homes of nobles and officials extended south of Third Ward Avenue (Sanjō), while urban merchants and craftsmen resided in the market district around Seventh Ward Avenue (Shichijō) to the south. Small houses of lower functionaries (*zōnin*), servants, and other city folk were found within both the elite residential and the market districts. Outlying districts such as Kawara on the banks of the Kamo River, Shirakawa, Kitano, and Hanazono developed into suburbs on the edge of the capital. There sprawled the villas of the powerful as well as great shrines and temples. Interspersed among them were the residences of middling and lesser officials (see Map 10.1).

Housing site plans and construction styles in the capital were shaped by status regulations. The standard plan for mansions of royals and nobles occupied a one-*chō* square, with left and right walls equidistant from the central gate. But many high-ranking courtiers found a one-*chō*-square residence insufficient for their needs. Meanwhile, houses of various provincial officials were not to exceed one-fourth of a *chō*, and "those from the sixth rank down were forbidden to have roofed mud walls or cypress bark roofs."[75] Temple construction within the capital was also regulated, and even the chapel at Tsuchimikado [Higashi] Kyōgoku built by the former prime minister Fujiwara Morozane (1042–1101) was not permitted a tiled roof or bell tower, "because it is located right in the capital."[76] Nonetheless, violations of these regulations took place at all social levels. According to the *Kojidan*, when one regent constructed a splendid mansion at Nijō Higashi Tōin, it was two *chō* square in area and built of earth and stone. Meanwhile, the Kaya-no-in precincts enclosed a four-*chō* area and included structures of earth and stone, even though such architecture was forbidden along Kyoto streets.[77] It is also well known that nobles and provincial governors frequently built one-*chō* houses even when they were not entitled to do so.

Although I cannot describe nobles' residences or household operations in detail here, it is clear that such residences included storehouse quarters with lodgings, kitchens, and artisans' workshops that functioned as the adminis-

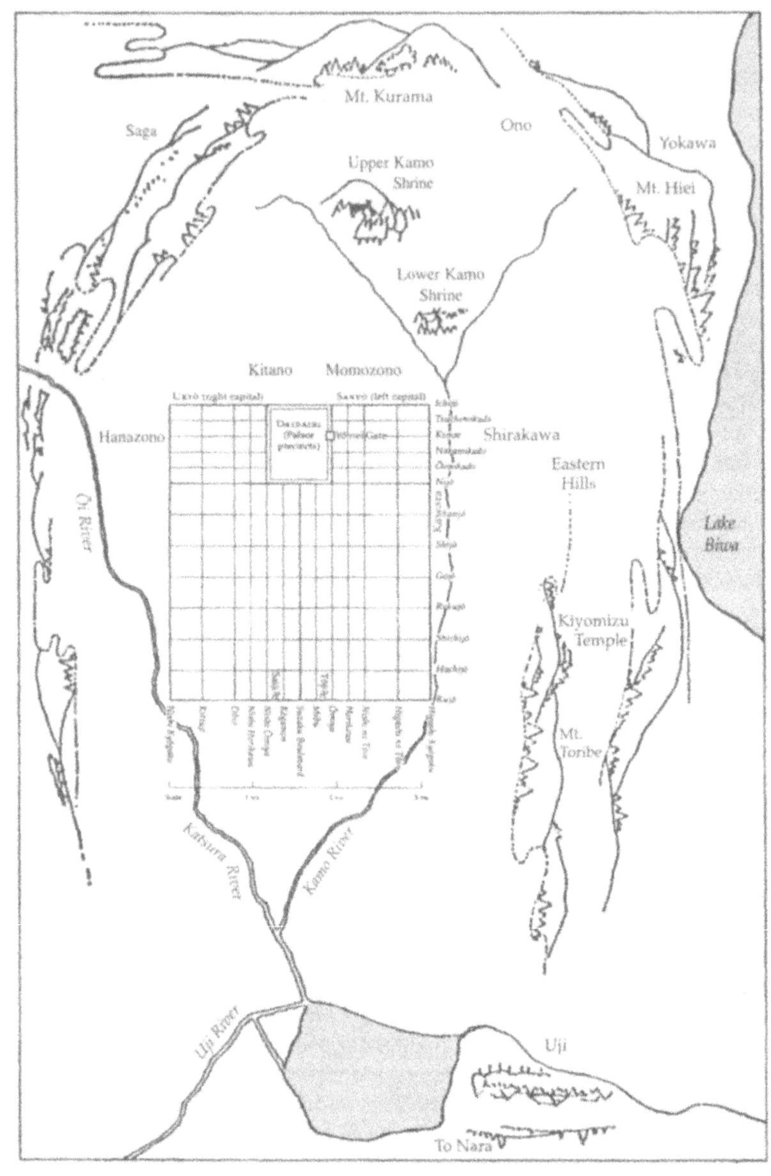

Map 10.1. Heian Capital and Vicinity

trative heart of an aristocratic household economy based on estates.[78] The storehouse quarters provide especially important clues to relations between city and estates. Below I examine the various personal relationships involved in the use of storehouses by middling and lesser aristocrats, especially as shared or temporary arrangements wherein people constructed or used storehouses occupying others' property. Such arrangements amounted to a reproduction of the shared property rights that characterized the estate system.

In 1102 the mansion of Provisional Middle Counselor Fujiwara Suenaka (1046–1119) burned to the ground.[79] At the time, five storehouses belonging to Ōmi provincial governor Fujiwara Takatoki, who shared the residence, were also lost. Along with Takashina Tameaki (1059–1103), Takatoki was a noted retainer of the retired monarch.[80] The complex at Takatoki's Kyoto residence, which symbolized his prosperity, was known to all as the "five storehouses of Ōmi Province."[81] The fact that Takatoki shared the residence with Suenaka meant that large storehouse complexes utilized by provincial governors were not necessarily located on independent residential properties. They could occupy either rented land or space within multiple-tenure holdings. The actual conditions of the "shared residence" arrangement remain hazy, but the *Chūyūki* report of the fire indicates that Suenaka was the master of the house and Takatoki was permitted to live there while maintaining his five storehouses.

Likewise, seven storehouses belonging to the former governor of Chikugo, Nakayoshi, were located within the temple precincts at Ninnaji. It appears that Nakayoshi had established his residence and seven storehouses at Ninnaji to escape the danger of fire.[82] As witnessed by the destruction of Takatoki's storehouses, there was real concern that Kyoto's frequent fires would level such treasure troves. Storehouses safely located on the outskirts of Kyoto often utilized the spacious grounds of monasteries, which were located beyond the capital boundaries where urban construction regulations were not enforced.

As for Nakayoshi's seven storehouses, "five contained clothing, food, and household goods; and the other two contained rare treasures including seven urns full of gold and 70,000 *ryō* [taels] of silver, plus innumerable precious goods from China and Japan." These were extremely luxurious contents indeed. Moreover, it seems that Nakayoshi constructed a subtemple at Ninnaji as a pretext for building his storehouses there. The *Chōshūki* courtier journal also notes that "a wall was built at Ninnaji between certain armed monks' dwellings and the subtemple of the former governor of Chikugo, Nakayoshi, and the latter took up residence there." The subtemple served as Nakayoshi's mansion, but it also included "raw materials, a house, a storehouse, a chapel with a pagoda, and a rear garden with trees," as well as lodgings for attendants and servants. When one observer remarked, "The splendor of homes in the western capital exceeds that of T'ao Chu [a wealthy man of ancient China]," he may have been referring to the residences of wealthy urbanites like Nakayoshi. Documents described as evidentiary papers for proprietary holdings entrusted to Nakayoshi by a former Kamo priestess were also kept at his Ninnaji residence—he may well have managed her holdings as her custodian. We know he had strong connections with the former priestess, since he was expected to participate in an exorcism known as the Karasaki Oharae over which she presided.[83]

The Chinkōji, a Tōji branch temple east of the capital, was another base for rich urban dwellers' capital-accumulating activities.[84] Taira Masamori (1151–1185), governor of Tango Province and a pillar of the rising Ise Taira family, rented two parcels of Chinkōji-held dry fields (covering one *chō* eight *tan*) under the alias Uchikura Yasutomi ("He who keeps his wealth in a storehouse").[85] One could assume such an alias, contract for land, receive a document confirming the allotment from the proprietor, and enjoy sole rights to its use under conditions similar to those regulating the cultivation of fields on either an estate or on public lands. Notably, Taira's contract was dated on the eighth day of the eleventh month, rather than in the spring, prior to planting season. We can thus suppose that his purpose in contracting for Chinkōji-held dry fields was not simply to cultivate them.

An analogous situation sheds light on Taira Masamori's intentions. In 1101 a former governor of Hida Province named Munenori and an unnamed officer of the Left Palace Guards contracted to rent Chinkōji-held land and built temples and residences there.[86] The former governor built a subtemple on a plot measuring twenty-two *jō* east to west and thirty *jō* north to south. He established twelve dwellings on the opposite side of the road south of the chapel, seven outside the west wall and six outside the north wall, and opened paddy and dry fields.[87] On a somewhat smaller scale, the Left Palace Guards officer built a subtemple on a site measuring sixteen *jō* east to west and twenty-eight *jō* north to south. Outside its wall were six residences as well as paddy and dry fields. In each case the rented premises had at their center a Buddhist subtemple enclosed by a wall, with residences and fields beyond.

In 1112, around the time when Taira Masamori appeared on the scene at Chinkōji, there were forty-eight subtemples there.[88] Twenty were within the walls of the temple, but among the twenty-eight outside the wall were subtemples established by a Shimotsuke governor, an assistant governor named Minamoto, a fifth-rank official from Kii, a Yamato governor, and a lay monk from Awa. The layout and function of these subtemples may well have resembled those belonging to Nakayoshi, the Tango governor Masamori, and the former Hida governor Munenori.

In order to establish and maintain these subtemples as private chapels and residences within the Chinkōji precincts, it was necessary to offer the temple monks gifts and official appointments. For instance, when Taira Morimoto, an Officer of the Right Palace Guards appointed to the Royal Police in 1097, rented two *tan* of land west of Chinkōji West Lane in 1101, he donated materials for repair of the temple and three hundred lengths of silk. Declaring that the land would be designated "to provide sake and fish for officials," he also promised to provide laborers for cleanup duty when the temple was repaired.[89] That duty was to be carried out by residents of the homes attached to various subtemples. In documents concerning Chinkōji, the rental arrangements for subtemples within the temple precincts were described by terms indicating a contract between the temple proprietor and the user of the land. The former Chikugo governor Nakayoshi had built seven storehouses and subtemples at Ninnaji under just such a contractual arrangement.

Since the relationship between title to the land and the right to occupy and use it in the capital was the same as that on estates in the provinces, urban land possession reflected what can be called an "estate-like structure." As another example, according to a *Chōshūki* entry dated the twenty-ninth day of the twelfth month of 1130, one Yorinori, a fifth-rank official of the Left Palace Guards, lived in Saemonchō, where offices and residences of his official unit were located.[90] The Royal Police director routinely levied a homestead tax (*zaikefu*) on Saemonchō residences. Not everyone who lived there, however, belonged to the Guards or to the Royal Police. Yorinori's live-in followers, in fact, were assigned to attend the *tennō*'s consort at meals; and when the director of the Royal Police, Fujiwara Saneyuki, enforced the tax on this household, he incurred the censure of Sutoku Tennō (r. 1123–1141). It seems that branch offices and personnel located in the district but serving other patrons were considered exempt from the homestead tax. Relationships involving such households and their dependents were similar to those that characterized the estate system.

Because of urban disasters such as fires, floods, and epidemics—in addition to landlords' changes of residence or death—rebuilding constantly took place at abandoned and empty sites, and residents and residences changed frequently. A story in the *Collection of Tales Old and New* (*Konjaku monogatarishū*) collection of tales describes an abandoned Kyoto residence in this fashion: "Squatters had completely dismantled the sleeping quarters for firewood. . . . One room was full of trash [thrown there by] people who walked by."[91] When urban residences were left vacant for various reasons, the title of a landlord who held verifiable documents was still guaranteed, but it was a problem of a different order to determine who had the right to occupy abandoned land and how it should be used. Since all strata of urban residents spent their resources on and made legitimate use of property that they occupied, their rights could not be eliminated easily. At some point after a mansion was abandoned, people would build small huts on the land and cultivate scallions and other dry field crops in the beds of dried-up ponds. This common urban practice did not constitute illegal occupancy—it was probably publicly sanctioned unless the rightful owner was using the land.[92] The various relationships that developed through contract rental of vacant or abandoned land, and through "temporary residence" or squatting on such land, became a powerful stimulus for urban change.

Storehouse complexes such as those described here had their roots in the estate system. Moreover, when we examine these storehouses and the activities of their managers and functionaries, it is clear that they were organically linked to changes in the urban structure in the eastern capital. It is also clear that regions surrounding the capital were bound to the city by conditions resembling those characterizing the estate system. When we understand these points, we may discern one way the urban landscape of Kyoto developed as Japan's medieval capital.

Table 10.1

Delinquent Borrowers, Hie Shrine, 1136

Names of Hie Ōtsu associate-lenders	Names of debtors
Official without portfolio Fujiwara Kunisada	The late former official of Nōtō province
Official without portfolio Minamoto Kuniyoshi	Same as above
Monk Ryūkai	Same as above
Official without portfolio Fujiwara Sadasuke	Residents of Takashima
Official without portfolio Fujiwara Kunisada	Kamo resident Shirō *taifu* (fifth rank official) Tadatōshi
Official without portfolio Tachibana Narichika	The late former governor of Bingo
Official without portfolio Minamoto Sadamoto	Sanuki governor
Official without portfolio Minamoto Sadamoto's proxy Narimoto	Mikawa governor
Official without portfolio Tachibana Narichika	The late Counselor of State and Major Controller of the Left (Fujiwara Tametaka)
Official without portfolio Tachibana Narichika	The current Nōtō governor
Former official in Etchū governor's office (?)	Cultivators
Official without portfolio Minamoto Munesada	A female peddler from Shijō
Nakahara Nariyuki	The governor of Mimasaka (Fuji[wara]?)
Saeki Tokikuni	The Suō lay monk, a warrior called Eshige
Official without portfolio Fujiwara Sadasuke	Kiyohara Toshitaka and his son Saburō
Official without portfolio Fujiwara Tsunetoki	Secretary of the Office of the Palace Table Hanamitsu
Official without portfolio Fujiwara Tadatsune	An estate official (*kengyō*), resident of Echizen province Kita Estate
Official without portfolio Fujiwara Tsunetoki	Chinu Sadakane
Wakae Kanetsugu	Bingo assistant governor and official without portfolio Lord Ōe
Wakae Kanetsugu	A *taifu* of the Kurōdodokoro
Wakae Kanetsugu	Palace repairs bureau vice chief
Wakae Kanetsugu	Hyōdō Takiguchi
Ōnakatomi Kagemoto and monk Chikei	Ōi Akira

Notes

1. For essays promoting this view, see Mass 1997.

2. See Toda Yoshimi 1991a.

3. See Toda Yoshimi 1976.

4. Toda Yoshimi 1991a, 1.

5. Readers will want to refer to another discussion of this subject in chapter 9 of this volume by Sasaki Muneo.

6. For an analysis of the estate system and the way it bound together different social strata in the capital and provinces, see Kiley 1974.

7. In recent work on the history of the city of Kyoto, for instance, Toda's work is considered the foundation. As an example, see Kitamura 1995.

8. Toda Yoshimi 1976.

9. Toda suggested five topics for further research, one of which is taken up here. The other four are patterns of nobles' residence in the city and geographical distribution of government offices; the characteristic social structure of the urban landholding class, and their methods of controlling people and goods; ways in which ordinary urban residents actually lived; and various urban quarrels and popular movements. For more on these topics, see Toda Yoshimi 1991b. Toda notes that preliminary investigations concerning relations between city and countryside were undertaken by Nishioka Toranosuke and other researchers. As representative of that early work he recommends Nishioka Toranosuke 1953.

10. Kōzanji tenseki monjo sōgō chōsadan 1972. Interpreter's note: Kōzanji is a Shingon temple in Kyoto Prefecture reportedly founded by the monk Son'i in mid-Heian times. Later it was rebuilt by Myōe in 1206, at the order of the retired *tennō*, Go-Toba. The temple has an extensive library of manuscripts, many of which are being published in the 21-volume *Kōzanji shiryō sōsho* by Tokyo Daigaku shuppankai.

11. Okuda Isao 1972.

12. Interpreter's note: *Sarugaku* performances included miscellaneous singing, dancing, and vaudeville-type entertainments. *Kugutsu* performances included puppet shows and magic acts. *Hikimai* was *sarugaku* performed by dwarves.

13. The *Chōshūki* confirms in an entry dated 1119/12 that one hundred armed followers who were led into Kyoto by Taira Masamori included many provincial notables (*meishi*) from western Honshū and Kyūshū.

14. Interpreter's note: The Kōshin Day Banquet was the Japanese version of a Chinese Taoist practice. During such banquets, people were expected to stay up all night or face dire consequences for their longevity if they fell asleep. It became popular in Japan during the Heian period.

15. See Toda Yoshimi 1974–1975.

16. Interpreter's note: Here Toda is referring to numerous complaints submitted to the court concerning the conduct of provincial governors during the tenth and eleventh centuries. One of those complaints was the well-known Owari Petition (*gebumi*) of 988—of at least nineteen such complaints against governors filed, it is the only one extant. The Owari petition lodged thirty-one complaints against the governor, Fujiwara Motonaga, and it was signed by "the district chieftains [*gunji*] and yeoman cultivators of Owari Province."

17. Murai Yasuhiko 1974.

18. Takeuchi Rizō 1973-1980, vol. 3, 814–15, doc. 682 (dated 1050 7/22). *Heian ibun* is henceforth cited as *HI*.

19. Interpreter's note: Ishimoda Shō makes a similar point in chapter 13 of this volume.

20. Interpreter's note: These two records are found on the back of one manuscript of the *Insei*-period tale anthology, *Uchigikishū*. *Uramonjo* were discarded documents on the back side of which other records and literary texts were written. The *Uchigikishū* manuscript referred to here is the "Yamaguchi Mitsumara Manuscript." For the documents discussed, see *HI*, vol. 4, 1508–09, docs. 1652 and 1653.

21. Confirming this view, appointees from previous years included the royal guard Funya Kanemoto, the royal provider Miyamichi Shigenari, and the royal provisioner Echihata Tsuneyasu.

22. The provincial governor at the time was Taira Tokinori, who was concurrently serving as provisional middle controller of the left.

23. *HI*, vol. 5, 1714-15, doc. 1962; and vol. 5, 1990-91, doc. 2350.

24. Interpreter's note: Horikawa Tennō retired in the seventh month of 1107 and died later in the same month.

25. *HI*, vol. 10, 3879, doc. 5007.

26. See Shintei zōhō kokushi taikei *Kugyō bunin*.

27. Interpreter's note: For Nariyuki or his father to have been the immigrant, the notation in the genealogy that immigration occurred in Suzaku's time would have to be in error.

28. Interpreter's note: Toda does not define the Japanese term, *onsōzokushi*, translated here as "ceremony of the first wearing of the robes." It was likely a coming-of-age ceremony of some kind.

29. *HI*, vol. 5, 1714–15, doc. 1962.

30. *HI*, vol. 5, 1990–91, doc. 2350. This document, entitled "Myōhō-hakushi *kanmon*," is dated the ninth month of 1136. The original can be found in the archives of the Mibu family. The document is rendered into a table at the back of the paper.

31. Interpreter's note: There is a difference between the characters in the text used by Toda and those used in *HI*, vol. 5, docs. 1652 and 1653. But Toda notes that a photograph of the original document taken by Japanese literature scholar Ikegami Jun'ichi has characters as in his text.

32. *HI*, vol. 4, 1508, doc. 1652.

33. Interpreter's note: See *Chūyūki* 1112/4/18. *Chūyūki* is the journal of Fujiwara Munetada, and covers the years 1087-1138.

34. Yoshie Akio 1973. Harunomiya Makoto may have been a pseudonym for Fujiwara Tamefusa (1049–1115).

35. Okuno Takahiro 1943.

36. *Chōya gunsai*, 224-25.

37. Other such groups included dog-breeders, falcon-egg gatherers, and tanners.

38. *HI*, vol. 4, 1508-09, doc. 1653.

39. *HI*, vol. 5, 1812, doc. 2106; also vol. 5, 1812–13, doc. 2107.

40. *Ishimpō*, vol. 25. Interpreter's note: Toda refers to the *Ishimpō* manuscript as a *koshahon* (old copy), a term denoting documents predating the Muromachi Period.

41. See *Chūyūki* 1127 01/.

42. Interpreter's note: The term *zuryō* indicates provincial officials who actually assumed their posts in the provinces rather than remaining in Kyoto and delegating their duties to on-site representatives.

43. See *Chūyūki* 1120 12/24. Interpreter's note: It is not entirely clear from Toda's discussion whether Morishige was Shirakawa's attendant only, or whether he also served Toba somewhat later in his life.

44. The assessment was one eight-*jō* length (1 *jō* = 3 meters) of silk per *tan* (.294 acres) of land in exchange for three *tō* (1 *tō* = .49 bushel) of rice. The cloth was to be used as material for making clothing.

45. This contrasts with circumstances on the northern plain districts of Kaga, where members of Fujiwara Toshihito's lineage were provincial notables in Togashi, Hayashi, and Itazu Districts. They also served in the provincial government headquarters of the absentee governor. Interpreter's note: See *Sonpi bun'myaku*, the compendium of elite genealogies, in Shintei zōho kokushi taikei.

46. According to the *Sonpi bun'myaku*, that mansion was located at the crossing of Nakanomikado and Higashi Tōin Streets.

47. See the *Kojidan*, vol. 6, tale 43.

48. See Takeuchi Rizō 1984–1995, vol. 28, 298, doc. 21736. *Kamakura ibun* is hereafter cited as *KI*.

49. *HI*, vol. 5, 1942, doc. 2300; and vol. 5, 1960–61, doc. 2321.

50. See Nishioka Toranosuke 1953.

51. See Hayashiya Tatsusaburō 1955 and Wakita Haruko 1969.

52. *HI*, vol. 6, 2260-62, doc. 2684.

53. He was also on a list of attendants at a special event at Iwashimizu Shrine in the third month of 1149. See *Kugyō bunin* and *Honchō seiki*. Interpreter's note: *Honchō seiki* is a twelfth-century annal. Extant portions cover the years 953–1153.

54. See *Kugyō bunin*, vol. 1, 420.

55. *Honchō seiki* 1149 11/ .

56. This tax exemption covered the estates known as Kashiwabara and Kawachi in Ōmi Province, Suita in Settsu Province, and a smaller holding (*myō*) in Yamashiro Province. See *HI*, vol. 6, 2267, doc. 2704.

57. See *HI*, vol. 6, 2260-61, doc. 2684. "Chikatada" here may refer to the Uona-line Fujiwara Chikatada (1095-1153), an influential provincial governor who was quite close to Bifukumon'in (1117-1160), the beloved consort of Toba Tennō.

58. See *Chūyūki* 1114 01/05.

59. See Toda Yoshimi 1967.

60. See Yoshida Akira 1958; Murai Yasuhiko 1965; and Katsuyama Seiji 1995.

61. See "Myōhō hakushi kanmon," in *HI*, vol. 5, 1990–91, doc. 2350.

62. *Hyakurenshō* 1163 07/10.

63. *KI*, vol. 3, 65–66, doc. 1309.

64. *HI*, vol. 6, 2148–49, doc. 2548.

65. *Chūyūki* 1111 06/07, and 06/08.

66. *Chūyūki* 1114 07/18.

67. Interpreter's note: *Akusō* (evil monks) were armed fighting men who wore monastic robes and were attached to various important temples. They were famous during Heian and Kamakura times for taking up arms to defend temple holdings and interests. Their "evil," of course, was perceived by their opponents and the central authorities with whom they sometimes had hostile relations. See chapter 12 by Motoki Yasuo in this volume as well as Adolphson 2000.

68. Interpreter's note: Traditionally Mount Hiei's Enryakuji was divided into two sectors, the "Eastern Pagoda," and the "Western Pagoda."

69. See Inoue Mitsusada 1985. Interpreter's note: on Hōyaku, also see Adolphson 2000, 113-15.

70. *Chūyūki* 1104 10/07 (in the Shiryō taisei edition see vol. 2, 380). The monastic superintendent was the second ranking member in a temple's administrative cabinet (*sangō*). Such temple administrators were elected by the corporate body of temple monks. In Heian times, however, they were usually confirmed by a royal order.

71. *Chūyūki* 1105 10/30. Taisanji was also affiliated with with Kamado Shrine as a *jingūji*, a shrine-affiliated temple. Interpreter's note: Toda does not supply a source for the full police report.

72. *Azuma kagami* 1218/9/29; and *Hie sanō risshōki*, an illustrated chronicle of Hie Shrine. The character for the seaman's family name is different in the two sources, but one of the two is probably a mistake, and the sources are thought to refer to the same person.

73. Interpreter's note: For a full translation with background information concerning Yoshishige, see Wetzler 1977.

74. The northern sector of the Left Capital included the area from Higashi Kyōgoku to Ōmiya in an east-west direction and from Ichijō to Sanjō (First-Ward Avenue to Third-Ward Avenue) in the north-south direction.

75. See *Chūyūki* 1108/7/26; and *Nihon kiryaku* 1030/4/23. Interpreter's note: *Nihon kiryaku* is a late Heian-period annal.

76. *Hyakurenshō* 1095/6/18.

77. Interpreter's note: The Kaya-no-in was originally built in early Heian times as the mansion of Prince Kaya. It served as the palace for two *tennō*, Go-Reizei (r. 1045–1068) and Go-Sanjō (r. 1068–1072), and eventually came into the possession of Regent Fujiwara Yorimichi (990-–1074).

78. See also Hayashiya Tatsusaburō 1970, vol. 1, 220-67.

79. *Chūyūki* 1102/03/28.

80. *Honchō seiki* 1103/12/20.

81. Takatoki was appointed governor of Ōmi Province in the spring of the year when the fire broke out. Because the fire occurred before he actually assumed office, the storehouses cannot have been built with tribute exacted from Ōmi. The reference to the province signifies only that he held the governor's post at the time.

82. Information about the storehouses comes from *Chōshūki* 1134 05/01, /02, and /03. Interpreter's note: Ninnaji, a temple just northwest of the capital, served as a residence for retired monarchs who had taken the tonsure.

83. *Chōshūki* 1134 05/03. Interpreter's note: In this ceremony, held at Karasaki Shrine in Ōtsu on Lake Biwa, the retiring Kamo priestess underwent ablutions. See Kurahayashi Shōji 1983, 125.

84. Chinkōji was an old temple, the founding of which may have predated the establishment of the Heian capital. It was located east of the Kamo River across from the Fifth and Sixth Ward Avenues in the vicinity called Rokudō and Toribeno. The latter was well known as a burial ground for capital residents, and the theory is that prominent families originally began building their own funerary and memorial chapels within the Chinkōji precincts. See Shimonaka Kunihiko 1979, 229–31.

85. *HI*, vol. 4, 1610, doc. 1781.

86. *HI*, vol. 4, 1401–02, doc. 1444.

87. The total cultivated area was two *tan* 240 *bu* (paddy: 180 *bu*; dry fields: two *tan* sixty *bu*).

88. *HI*, vol. 4, 1601, doc. 1770.

89. *HI*, vol. 4, 1403, doc. 1446.

90. Interpreter's note: Saemonchō was located east of Nishinotōin and extended over to Muromachi; and north to south it covered the area between Tsuchimikado and Konoe Streets.

91. *Konjaku monogatarishū*, vol. 19, tale 5. Interpreter's note: While many of its tales have been translated by Robert Brower, Marian Ury, and Royall Tyler, I know of no translation of this tale.

92. See Toda Yoshimi 1991b.

11

The Mino Genji in the Late Classical Age

MIYAZAKI YASUMITSU

Introduction by Joan R. Piggott

THE IMPORTANCE OF "HIRED SWORDS" to the Heian-period court and polity, as well as how elite families and religious institutions recruited warriors to serve their interests both in the capital and in the provinces, is well known. In Miyazaki Yasumitsu's vivid description of a collateral line of the famous Kawachi Genji that established its base in Mino Province in mid-Heian times, we learn how specific regional circumstances in Mino supported the martial, political, and economic ambitions of the warrior chieftain, Minamoto Kunifusa, and his heirs.[1] Miyazaki describes how Mino Genji chieftains recruited and led a broad-based band of warriors (*bushidan*) whose members resided at estates and in the public domain (*kokugaryō*) all over Mino and in neighboring provinces at the beginning of the twelfth century. Toward the end of his essay, Miyazaki specifically addresses the nature of Mino Genji lordship—how Minamoto Kunifusa and his heirs recruited the horsemen and followers they needed, and how the loyalty of the latter depended on strong linkages between capital and province skillfully utilized by Minamoto Kunifusa.

Minamoto Kunifusa, together with his heir Minamoto Mitsukuni and, in the next generation, grandsons Mitsunobu and Mitsuyasu, is not one of the best known Heian warrior chiefs. But Miyazaki's carefully researched study offers a clear image of how warrior leaders like Kunifusa tacked back and forth between capital and province to serve their own interests, and those of noble patrons at court. It demonstrates how warrior leaders depended upon martial might, political connections, postings in officialdom, landholdings, and wily strategies to gain and maintain followers who would join them in their fights against provincial officials, assorted tax and dues collectors, uninvited patrons' agents, and rival warrior bands.

By means of his careful archival research using a variety of official and unofficial annals and courtier journals, Miyazaki shows us how the members of the Seiwa Genji lineage established influence in Mino Province when Minamoto Kunifusa's grandfather, Yorimitsu (948–1021), served as provincial governor at the turn of the eleventh century; how, while later serving serially as provincial governor in various provinces and as a client of the retired monarch Shirakawa, Kunifusa was able to open or steal landholdings of his own through nefarious dealings as Tōdaiji's overseer (*shōshi*) at Akanabe Estate in Mino and as temple representative at Ōnari Estate in neighboring Owari Province[2]; and how his successes angered temple patrons and local elites even though as a well-connected warrior Kunifusa was well enough protected to ignore court orders to cease and desist his obstreperous activities. We learn how Kunifusa and his progeny fought rivals from the Seiwa and Kawachi Genji lineages to secure his reputation as a canny fighting man; how the court named Kunifusa's son Mitsukuni "pursuit agent" against Minamoto Yoshitsuna when battles between rival branches of the Kawachi Genji threatened the peace in the 1090s; and how Mitsukuni, later acting as governor of distant Dewa Province, served in the Royal Police Office (Kebiishichō) against "evil monks" (*akusō*) at the dawn of the twelfth century.

Although they sometimes served as the court's claws and fangs—enforcers of law and order—these Mino Genji and their followers were not always law-abiding. Even as they were recruited as fighting men for the Royal Police in Kyoto, members of Mitsukuni's band reportedly included brigands who resided at various estates in Mino. Later Mitsukuni's heir, Mitsunobu, also served as a member of the Royal Police who battled armed monks while acting as a "guardian king" for the sitting and retired monarchs, Toba and Shirakawa (see Figure 11.1). And finally, we see how Mitsunobu's younger brother, Mitsuyasu, was able to survive the exile of his elder brother in 1129 because his daughter had entered the palace as a beloved consort to the retired monarch, Toba In. Ultimately this Mitsuyasu attained the senior fourth lower rank and served beside Fujiwara Shinzei as director of Toba In's funerary rites just before the Hōgen Coup of 1156.

Miyazaki's tale of the Mino Genji demonstrates well that Kiyomori's Ise Taira were not the only warriors of the time who enjoyed status in the entourage of a retired monarch, and that such connections could be both affinal and property-based.[3] We also see here that such connections were unstable—Miyazaki explains how Minamoto Mitsuyasu got into difficulties in 1160, leading to his exile and execution. His death left the field of capital politics with fewer obstacles for a rising Taira Kiyomori to overcome.

Written in the late 1970s, Miyazaki's essay may stress the Mino Genji's landed interests more than would a researcher working today. But the control of men through land—sometimes termed "lordship"—was certainly critical to Minamoto Kunifusa and his warrior band. As Miyazaki notes, the latter included a number of tax managers (*myōshu*) for *myō* units, many of whom were deeply involved in the opening of new rice fields at places like Uzura Township (Uzura gō) in Mino and at Ōnari Estate in Owari Province. Such men were willing, under Kunifusa's leadership and with his backing, to fight any and all who threatened their prerogatives and perquisites based on their landholdings, which were confirmed by their postings (*shiki*) in the developing private-public domain (*shōen-kokugaryō*) system. Kunifusa's followers all depended on their lord for support, just as he depended on them. So did they serve him locally, throughout the province, in neighboring provinces, or in the Heian capital, which was located a day or more to the southwest. As Miyazaki concludes here, the resulting network of lord-and-follower relations—what Marc Bloch termed "bonds of dependence"—were finally based on the fact that "the potential for

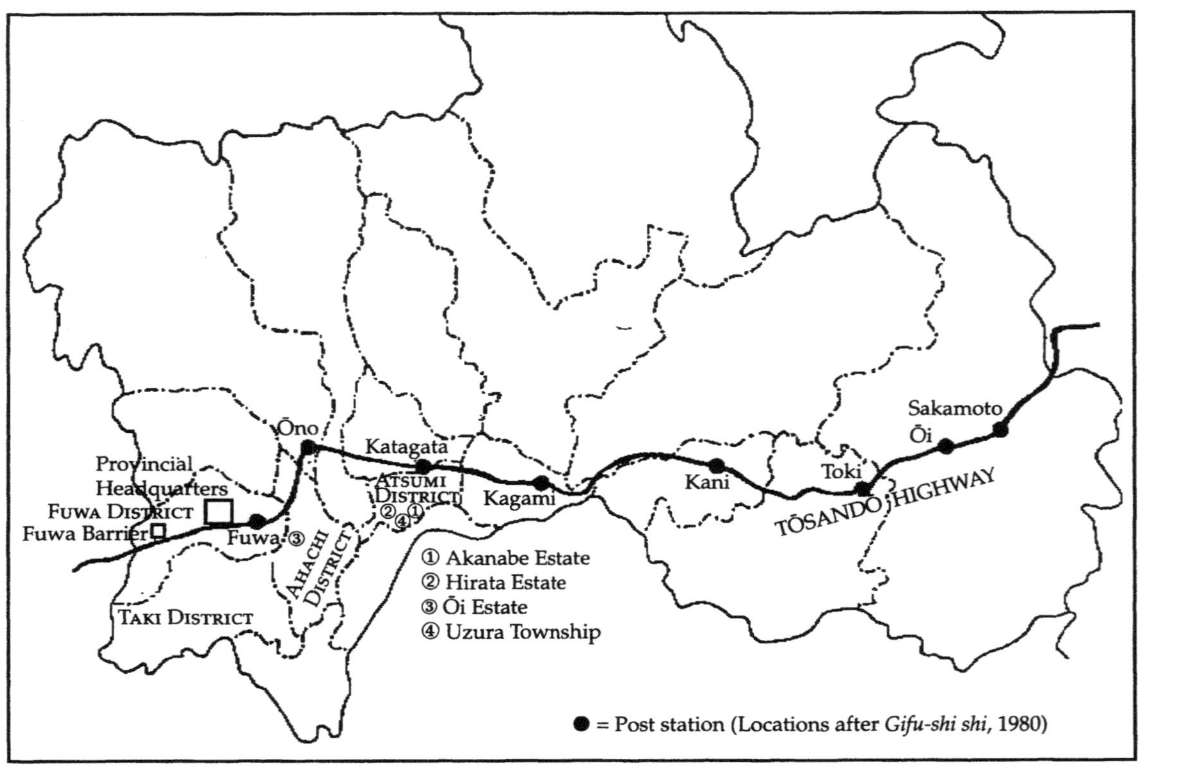

Map 11.1. Mino Province in the Mid-Heian Period

gain as well as the need for protection swelled the body of those who signed on as followers" in the later eleventh and early twelfth centuries.

MIYAZAKI YASUMITSU

The Mino Genji in the Late Classical Age

Interpreted by Joan R. Piggott

The lineage of the Seiwa Genji founded by Minamoto Kunifusa came to be known as the "Mino Genji" because its geographic base was the province of Mino.[4] During the Heian period Kunifusa's son, Mitsukuni, and Mitsukuni's sons—Mitsunobu and Mitsuyasu—all served retired monarchs Shirakawa and Toba as military commanders and courtiers. Here I investigate the Mino Genji in order to shed light on the organization and activities of a leading warrior lineage in the late classical age.

Kunifusa and Mitsukuni

An entry from 1064 in a courtier's journal notes, "There was a battle between the governor of Iyo, Minamoto Yoriyoshi, and the now deceased lay-monk Yorikuni-shichi Kunifusa."[5] Another account in the *Hyakurenshō* notes, "There was a battle between Yoshimune and Kunifusa,"[6] but "Yoshimune" here is thought to be a copying error for "Yoshiie," [referring to Minamoto Yoshiie]. And the *Kojidan* reminiscences describes discord and fighting between the two as well. That there was an armed struggle in the mid-eleventh century between Minamoto Kunifusa of Mino and Yoriyoshi (988–1075) and Yoshiie (1039?–1106) of the Kawachi Genji is confirmed by these reports.[7] According to the *Kojidan*, the root of the feud lay in Kunifusa's insult to a man-in-arms (*rōtō*) in Yoshiie's employ. Having heard about the incident, Yoshiie attacked Kunifusa's residence in Mino Province to regain his honor.

Kunifusa did not earn his reputation as a warrior for battling only rivals from Kawachi. Some years after his fight with the Kawachi Genji, he also engaged Minamoto Shigemune in battle at Kunifusa's residence in Mino's Taki District in 1079 (see Map 11.1). Shigemune resided in nearby Katagata District and his reputation for martial prowess, like that of Kunifusa, developed early.[8] Their confrontation, which earned them both a summons to court for castigation, must have been a battle of some magnitude.[9] Shigemune, however, refused to heed the summons and was terminated from his official post. Later the former provincial governor of Shimotsuke, Minamoto Yoshiie, was sent to apprehend him, and Shigemune petitioned the viceroy, Fujiwara Morozane (1042–1101), to plead for exile rather than more serious punishment. But since his crime was seen to be a serious one, Shigemune was imprisoned. Judged less culpable, Kunifusa was barred from participation in future archery contests at court.[10]

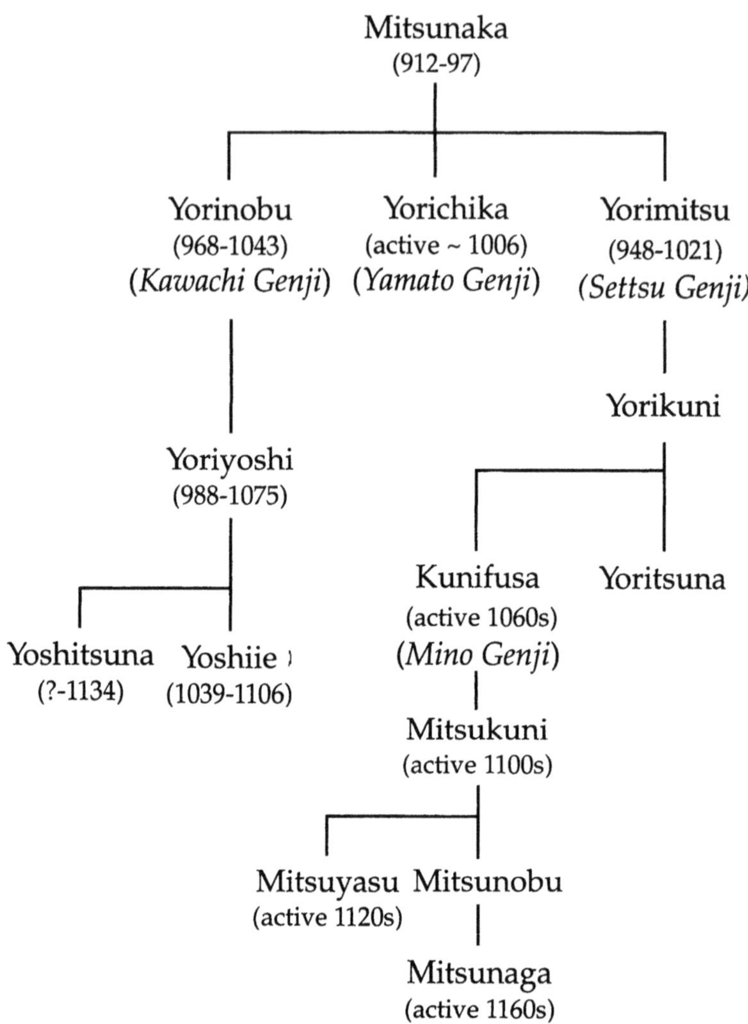

NOTE: The Mino Genji (alt. Minamoto) lineage branched off from the main line of the Minamoto (the Seiwa Genji) sired by Seiwa Tennō in the generation of Kunifusa, son of Yorikuni. Since Yoritsuna was the heir of the main line in Kunifusa's day, he was Kunifusa's bitter rival for posts as an elite warrior in the capital. A collateral line, known as the Kawachi Genji because of their residence in Kawachi, was established by Yorinobu, son of Mitsunaka, two generations before Kunifusa's time. As Miyazaki relates in this essay, the Kawachi Genji, including Yoriyoshi and his son, Yoshiie, occasionally feuded with the Mino Genji. It was into the Kawachi Genji house that the founder of the Kamakura Bakufu was born in the twelfth century.

Fig. 11.1. The Settsu, Yamato, Kawachi, and Mino Genji

According to various genealogies, Minamoto Kunifusa was the sixth son of Yorikuni (see Figure 11.1). Known also as "Mino Shichirō," Kunifusa raised his martial standard early on in Mino.[11] How he came to reside there is not clear—perhaps he established himself there during the lifetime of his grandfather, Yorimitsu. As a retainer of the Regents' household, Yorimitsu had held a variety of provincial governorships and accumulated great wealth—and he served twice as Mino's provincial governor.[12] When Yorimitsu's younger brother, Yorichika, served three terms as Yamato governor, the former acquired numerous private holdings in Yamato. So it is not difficult to imagine that Yorimitsu accomplished the same in Mino.[13] Thereafter, Kunifusa's father also served as governor of Mino in his elder years, so there was ample opportunity for the foundation of Kunifusa's wealth and influence to be established in Mino Province.

After his battle with Shigemune, Kunifusa disappears from the historical record for a time, but he reappears in 1096. In that year he was named Tōdaiji's overseer (*shōshi*) at Akanabe Estate in Mino (see Map 11.1).[14] At the time Tōdaiji was quarreling with provincial officials over complaints concerning "illicit additional fields outside estate boundaries" (*kanōden*) at both Akanabe and Ōi estates.[15] According to a fragment from a Council of State order (*kansenji*) dated the twelfth day of the fifth month of 1096, when provincial agents entered Akanabe Estate to survey fields, Kunifusa, acting as the temple's deputy, "dispatched several brawny men," who attacked both residents and the provincial agents.[16] The same account indicates that Kunifusa was acting as director (*bettō*) at Ōi Estate in neighboring Ahachi District. Why his followers roughed up residents at Akanabe Estate is not clear—perhaps the cultivators provoked Kunifusa's men by permitting authorities to enter the property or by answering their questions. In any event, when damage to the estate resulted, Tōdaiji complained to the court, insisting that all fault lay with the province. But provincial officers claimed that they had merely been doing their duty pursuant to levying and collecting taxes. Of special note here is the province's claim that "the estate manager and governor of Izu, Minamoto Kunifusa, sent several 'brawny warriors' [*yūsha*]."

As this document records, Minamoto Kunifusa was actually serving as the governor of Izu Province when these events transpired.[17] He had been assigned to the Izu post earlier that year. Three years later he became governor of Shinano Province and was promoted to junior fifth upper rank.[18] According to the compilation of courtier lineage genealogies known as the *Sonpi bun'myaku*, besides serving as governor of Shinano and Izu, Kunifusa's resumé included appointments as third-in-command (*jō*) in the Ministry of Civil Affairs (Jibushō), third-in-command and later first-in-command in the Royal Police Office, and as governor of the provinces of Tosa, Iyo, and Mutsu. His governorships doubtless followed his tenures in the Ministry of Civil Affairs and the royal police. Both his father and later his son served in that latter office before they were made provincial governors—such was a common career track.[19] Kunifusa's reputation in the capital would have been firmly established by 1096. He could only have been appointed governor of Izu because of the strong backing of the retired monarch, Shirakawa (tenure as *in*, 1086–1129).[20] And there is little doubt that his appointment as director of two of Tōdaiji's most important estates resulted from this same connection. That Kunifusa was chosen by Tōdaiji from among the retired monarch's various intimates says a great deal about Kunifusa's stature as a warrior chieftain in Mino.

What caused Tōdaiji to appoint a local warrior chieftain to the staff of its estates? The later eleventh century witnessed a raging battle between provincial authorities and proprietors over estate regulation and confiscation of "new estates." It was precisely from 1096 onward that confrontations with provincial authorities attempting to confiscate fields at Ōi and Akanabe began. This was also a time when Ise Shrine was energetically imposing corvée and construction levies on provincial headquarters and estates across the archipelago. Given the location of Ise Shrine due south of Mino, it is no surprise that attempts to collect these levies were particularly aggressive in Mino Province.[21] Documentary archives for Tōdaiji's Akanabe and Ōi Estates demonstrate the friction between agents attempting to make these collections and those asked to pay them.[22]

The precise period during which Minamoto Kunifusa served as Tōdaiji's overseer for Akanabe Estate is not known, but his activities there could not have started much before 1096. According to the statement of an elderly resident in 1142, before Kunifusa's tenure the district chieftain of Mino's Atsumi District had served as local manager (*geshi*) at both Akanabe and neighboring Hirata estates while the district chieftain's younger brother, a lay monk named Jōzō, served as director of the managerial staff (*shōkan*) at Akanabe.[23] We can surmise then that Kunifusa's appointment as estate manager resulted in intense friction with district authorities, which is why Kunifusa chased the district chieftain and his brother off the temple's property. That is also why the district chieftain subsequently testified against Tōdaiji on behalf of the provincial authorities in 1096. Like Kunifusa—himself a provincial notable—the Atsumi district chieftain would have been a man of significant local influence who used his membership in a locally powerful family to manage the estate. But unlike Kunifusa, the local district chieftain would have had no connections with the retired monarch's entourage in the capital. Tōdaiji clearly hired Kunifusa so that his ties to the retired monarch's court as well as his martial following could be utilized to keep provincial agents and collectors at bay.

As it turned out, however, Kunifusa's appointment as estate overseer ultimately proved regrettable from the temple's perspective. It soon became clear that a warrior chieftain's interests and those of the Nara temple were not compatible. Just west of Akanabe Estate was Uzura Township, the site of Kunifusa's residence (see Map 11.1).[24] After his appointment as the temple's overseer at Akanabe, Kunifusa ordered the removal of boundary markers on the western border of Akanabe, "just as he pleased, without rhyme or reason." In the process he added two *chō* of property east to west and ten *chō* north to south, almost sixty acres, to his own holding in Uzura.[25]

The temple retaliated by canceling Kunifusa's mandate concerning the estate and by requesting that agents from the court go to Mino and replace the original boundary markers. But apparently the agents either feared Kunifusa or were bribed by him, because they failed to replace the markers. This remained the situation until 1117, when an order from the retired monarch forbade further interference at Akanabe as well as violent acts by Kunifusa's son, Mitsukuni, and other residents of Uzura Township. The order described conditions at Akanabe Estate as follows:

> They use their martial might without fear of the *tennō*'s interdiction. They have torn out boundary markers, attacked estate cultivators, and they plot murder more and more. . . . They steal cows, horses, and many other goods from the estate, killing residents and burning their homes.[26]

Mitsukuni, however, defended himself by insisting that the temple's complaints were falsehoods; and that as far as accusations of murder and arson were concerned, he had been residing in the capital and had no knowledge of such matters.

In 1124 Tōdaiji complained again.[27] After the Council of State had read testimony filed by both sides, it ordered the provincial government to clearly settle the boundary problem between Akanabe and Uzura, proclaiming, "If Mitsukuni indeed had not ordered it, would there have been such crimes committed by the Uzura Township headman [*gōchō*]?"[28] This township headman and his fellows were none other than local cultivators who had opened Uzura Township to cultivation. They also aided Minamoto Kunifusa in managing Akanabe Estate while Kunifusa served as overseer there. They were followers of Kunifusa and later served his son, Mitsukuni. They did so to maximize their own opportunities, at home and vis-à-vis authorities in the capital.

Not surprisingly the order of 1117 did not stop the violence at Akanabe. Minamoto Mitsukuni's autonomous holding in Uzura Township came to be designated a special jurisdictional unit (*beppu*) under the patronage of a second-rank courtier whose holdings included the nearby Hirata Estate.[29] By gaining the sponsorship of this high-ranking patron, Mitsukuni consolidated his hold over Uzura Township, a process begun by his father Kunifusa four decades earlier. That Tōdaiji proved unable to reverse Mitsukuni's success is clear from a record of 1142, when the situation remained unchanged.[30] Mitsukuni's expansion of his property at the expense of Tōdaiji's Akanabe Estate was a warrior chieftain's success story.

The Mino Genji in Kyoto

Minamoto Kunifusa was active in the capital, but his son Mitsukuni's connections there are even more striking. Specifically, in the fourth month of 1087 Mitsukuni was appointed third-in-command of the Left Guards. Then in the last month of that year he made a lateral move to the Right Guards. Five years later, when Shirakawa In made a pilgrimage to the Kuruma Temple, Mitsukuni had not yet been appointed to the Royal Police Office. But he was promoted to junior fifth lower rank in the first month of 1099 and thereafter would have sought a governorship. Instead, he was appointed to the Royal Police, where he served for the next ten years as third-in-command.[31]

When Prince Munehito—the future Toba Tennō—became crown prince in 1103, Mitsukuni was one of ten archers who flanked the carriage of Shirakawa In on that occasion. These marksmen were all from the elite Northern Guards (Hokumen no bushi), and they held either the fifth or sixth rank. Mitsukuni also served in the retired monarch's retinue during a pilgrimage to Iwashimizu Hachiman Shrine south of Kyoto in 1106. He was probably on hand to help members of the royal police, including Minamoto Yoshiie and Minamoto Yoshitsuna, chase Enryakuji's "evil monks" from the capital in 1104; and he would have manned the barriers in 1105 when the capital was subjected to demonstrating monks from the same temple. At that time, the two Minamoto commanders—Yoshiie and Yoshitsuna—were already preeminent among warriors of high status residing in the captial.[32]

Circumstances were different, however, in 1091, when a quarrel broke out between the same commanders' followers in Kawachi Province. The court was so concerned over this threat to the peace that it ordered the barriers protecting Kyoto to be closed. Two decades later, the feud still raged, and in the course of these ongoing hostilities, Yoshiie's fourth son, Yoshitada, was murdered; and orders to apprehend Yoshitsuna were dispatched. Tameyoshi, from Yoshiie's own line, and Mitsukuni, then serving as governor of Dewa Province, were ordered to apprehend Yoshitsuna. Tameyoshi's appointment is understandable, but we must wonder why Mitsukuni was assigned this duty? Historian Yasuda Motohisa has concluded that Mitsukuni was the retired monarch's choice to deal with Yoshitsuna, whose power had been greatly aided by an alliance with the Northern Fujiwara regent's line.[33] The torch that would ignite the battles of the 1150s—when the enmities of warriors and courtiers would mingle and clash during the Hōgen and Heiji eras—was already beginning to burn.

After dealing with Yoshitsuna, in 1110 Mitsukuni set out for his post in Dewa Province. But in the following year he returned to the capital, and on the way he stopped off in Mino. In 1112 the court inquired as to why he had not yet returned to his Dewa governorship. Mitsukuni responded by urging that someone else be appointed Dewa governor, but the court sent an agent to interview him.[34] Unfortunately, we have no record of that discussion. There is little doubt, however, but that one reason for Mitsukuni's decision to retire from the Dewa governorship was the trouble he was having with the Regents' House over Sagae Estate there.[35] Mitsukuni does not seem to have returned to Kyoto—he seems to have remained on his holdings in Mino. But there may have been other reasons behind Mitsukuni's decision to stay in Mino: he had been outside the province for some years, in the capital and in Dewa; and he had had little opportunity to acquaint himself with local affairs. Furthermore, given the demise of Minamoto Yoshitsuna's whole family at this time, there was a vacuum, and Mitsukuni would have been well placed to expand his influence. That would have been quite impossible to do from Dewa.

In the eleventh month of 1111 the court again reprimanded Mitsukuni for remaining in Mino. According to the official complaint, "He has been the source of disruption in his home province and committed crimes of disloyalty while failing to complete his term of office."[36] Mitsukuni was ordered to return to Dewa to finish his term.

Whether Mitsukuni followed that order is unclear. But when a huge force of two thousand Hiei monks descended on the metropole in 1113, Minamoto Mitsukuni, Taira Masamori, and Minamoto Tameyoshi were all arrayed to defend the capital.[37] Their combined forces consisted of several tens of thousands. Whether that estimate is true or false, Mitsukuni was clearly one of three elite commanders on whom the court depended to protect the capital.

After this, Mitsukuni disappears from the historical record. Around 1113, when he reached fifty, he may well have passed his post to his heir (*chakunan*), Mitsunobu (see Figure 11.1). The ensuing retirement would have left Mitsukuni plenty of time to direct operations in Mino while his son took over duties elsewhere. According to various genealogies, Mitsukuni died at the age of eighty-five in 1147. The *Sonpi bun'myaku* records that Minamoto Mitsunobu served as one of the "guardian kings" who protected Toba In, the senior retired monarch from 1129 to 1156. And according to Jien's *Gukanshō* history compiled in the thirteenth century, after Toba Tennō's accession in 1107, Shirakawa In ordered that three members of the Royal Police—Mitsunobu, Tameyoshi, and Yasukiyo—be posted continuously at the palace. Mitsunobu was clearly an intimate of Shirakawa by that time.

Minamoto Mitsunobu's service as a member of the Royal Police is visible in documents dating from 1119, but the most dynamic phase of his career began in 1129, when he was sent to seek out and apprehend "evil monks" in the old capital of Nara. These events occurred just after Toba Tennō retired, on the eleventh day of the eleventh month. Mitsunobu, Minamoto Tameyoshi, Taira Masahiro, Fujiwara Morishige, and Minamoto Yoshinari were all sent to Kōfukuji, the Fujiwara clan temple in the old Nara capital, to deal with thuggish monks residing there. Arriving in Nara before his fellows, Mitsunobu ordered his soldiers to surround each monastic cloister before proceeding with the search. Other enforcers arrived one after the other and their men aided in the operation. Reports clarify how each warrior leader mobilized and directed his warrior band, and how the "chase and apprehend" function was actually carried out.[38] The raid at Kōfukuji, which occasioned the fiery destruction of the prized Sahodono long used by Fujiwara clan heads, was a serious blow to the head of the Regents' line, Tadazane himself.

Despite his useful service to the retired monarch at Kōfukuji and elsewhere, Mitsunobu was exiled in the eleventh month of 1130 when he was accused of gathering troops and causing a brawl. The affair involved someone named Yoshichika, who had come to the capital from the east in 1129. This Yoshichika had been instructed by Toba In to take up residence at the Kamoin, originally an estate of former chancellor, Fujiwara Tadazane.[39] Then on the twelfth day of the eleventh month this Yoshichika was set upon and killed by some twenty horsemen and forty or fifty foot soldiers.[40] Since Yoshichika had been pursued earlier by Taira Masamori, at first Masamori's son, Tadamori, was the suspected villain. But in the end, Mitsunobu was judged guilty and exiled to Tosa.[41] His lieutenants—Fujiwara Mitsunori, a man named Hironobu, and Kiyowara Chikamune—were exiled to Izu, Awa, and Hitachi respectively.[42] Only in 1143, after some thirteen years, was Mitsunobu finally allowed to return from exile, and he was then awarded the junior fifth upper rank as well as a post in the Left Guards of the Royal Police.[43] But he died two short years later, at the age of fifty-three.

Mitsunobu's younger brother, Mitsuyasu, who was at the time serving in the Right Guards, was also blamed for abetting Mitsunobu's crime, and he too lost his post. Nonetheless, he soon returned to duty and was promoted—he is listed as a member of the Left Guards in 1135 and as a member of the Royal Police in 1137.[44] Mitsuyasu enjoyed a distinct advantage—he was the father of one of the retired monarch Toba's best-loved consorts. In 1151 he was permitted an audience with Toba In; and in 1154, he was named governor of Izumo Province. Then in the third month of 1154 he was further promoted to the junior fourth lower rank; and in the following year, he was raised first to the junior fourth upper and then finally to senior fourth lower. Mitsuyasu's unprecedented rise in rank was mainly due to his affinal ties with the retired monarch.[45]

When Toba In died in 1156, Mitsuyasu joined Fujiwara Nobusuke and the laymonk Shinzei as leaders of the ex-sovereign's funerary activities; and then in the Hōgen Coup of that same year, he carried out Toba's will by supporting the young *tennō*, Go-Shirakawa.[46] He did not, however, distinguish himself during those events. Three years later in the Heiji Disturbance Mitsuyasu seemed to support Minamoto Yoshitomo, but in the end he chose not to involve himself. Nevertheless in the sixth month of 1160 he was accused of treason and exiled to distant Satsuma in Kyūshū, where he was executed.[47] Because of his death, activity by the Mino Genji in the capital was substantially decreased. His son, Mitsunaga, appears in the historical record from time to time; but in this era of Taira glory, no other warrior could match Kiyomori's influence.

Housemen of the Mino Genji

Over several decades in the later eleventh century, the Mino Genji succeeded in wresting land away from Tōdaiji's Akanabe Estate for Uzura Township. They were also able to demonstrate martial might as warrior chieftains in the capital, where they served as members of the Royal Police and received appointments as provincial governors. Such success necessitated the wherewithal to recruit, lead, and maintain substantial military followings. During the eleventh and twelfth centuries, family members must have traveled back and forth between Kyoto and Mino frequently as they energetically expanded their power and influence. Kunifusa's takeover of Ōnari Estate in Owari Province during the first decade of the twelfth century demonstrates one strategy for attracting and supporting followers, known alternatively as housemen (*ke'nin*).

Ōnari Estate was situated in Owari's Ama District, and its proprietor was Tado Jingūji. Tado Jingūji was also considered a branch temple of the capital's Tōji (lit. Eastern Temple). But Tōji complained that in 1075 a cleric at Tado Jingūji conspired with both the warrior chieftain Taira Masahira and a monk named Ryōshin to make Tado Jingūji a detached cloister (*betsuin*) of Mount Hiei's Enryakuji.[48] Rent payments to Tōji subsequently ceased, and Enryakuji claimed Tado Jingūji and its estates (including Ōnari) as possessions. Records also show that in 1089 and 1104 the Hiei temple sent its agent to Ōnari.[49]

Some two decades later, in 1106, another agent accompanied by armed warriors carried an order from an Enryakuji monk named Ninyo, who purported to represent the temple's administration. But in reality it seems that Ninyo was in league with Minamoto Kunifusa, who may well have had discussions with Tōji. We learn from a complaint later lodged by Tōji that Kunifusa chased the Ōnari estate overseer off the property, harvested rice from some ten *chō*, stole possessions from residents, and had a houseman named Taira Yukinaka take over estate management.

Having considered Tōji's complaint, the court ordered Kunifusa to respond to the charges.[50] But neither Kunifusa nor the monk Ninyo bothered to answer, and they continued their illegal activities at Ōnari. Many estate residents were slain in the ongoing violence. So in 1107 Tōji complained anew, this time with an accompanying testament from Taira Morimasa, then the court-appointed director (*zokubettō*) of Tado Jingūji. It seems likely that he was none other than the estate manager whom Kunifusa had chased off Ōnari Estate.[51]

While few documents concerning these events are extant, two things are particularly striking about Minamoto Kunifusa's role in this fight over Ōnari Estate's management. First, we learn from all this that geographically speaking Kunifusa's influence extended from Mino into Ise and Owari Provinces. Specifically, Kunifusa's relationship with Taira Yukinaka may well have been the reason for his interest in Ōnari Estate. Yukinaka, placed in charge of the estate after the raid, must have originally been a man of influence from the area, and Tōji's complaint indicated that Yukinaka was told by Kunifusa to manage the property "according to the order (*senji*) by the Council of State."

Although no such order is extant, Tōji's complaint suggests that such an order confirmed its claims to the property. Kunifusa was not denying Tōji's claim to Tado Jingūji—it was simply that he wanted to appoint his own man to manage the property. Tōji claimed that Kunifusa wrongfully took over the estate, but in reality the Kyoto temple may well have invited him to do so at some point in the interest of restoring its own claims. Kunifusa's intent was to expand his authority by placing his own man at Ōnari—which temple succeeded in gaining proprietorship was of little concern to Kunifusa. From the perspective of Taira Morimasa, however, Kunifusa had taken over the estate without cause. Armed conflict between Kunifusa and Morimasa highlights the existence of at least two factions within the estate itself—one that supported Morimasa and one that supported Yukinaka, or perhaps Kunifusa himself.[52]

Aside from the affair at Akanabe in 1096 when Kunifusa and his followers defied an agent sent to collect corvée duties, a series of events in 1114 contributes additional clues to means used by Mino Genji chieftains to assure their ability to assemble horsemen and footmen as needed.[53] In the third month of 1114, in the course of the questioning of a bandit called Ki Jirō Takakata at Royal Police headquarters in the capital, Takakata signed a confession. Therein he indicated that his fellow gang member, Kunikata, had fled to Minamoto Kunifusa's place in Mino and that Kunikata was Kunifusa's man-in-arms. Both Takakata and Kunikata had been associated with a warrior chief named Motozane, who had been defeated. Thereafter, Kunikata joined up with Minamoto Kunifusa and Mitsukuni.[54] Mitsukuni was subsequently summoned to the capital and ordered to bind up and dispatch to the capital any dangerous criminals from among his following; then he was to report to the director of the Royal Police that he had done so.[55] Whether Mitsukuni did so or not is unclear, but shortly thereafter a shipment of rent dues from an estate in Shinano Province owned by the royal temple Sonshōji was set upon by thieves. A report made to the head of the Royal Police confirmed that Mitsukuni's men were among the criminals. Mitsukuni had already reported the matter to his patron, Shirakawa In, and then he turned the thieves over to the police. There were some eighteen men in the band, including residents from estates belonging to Regent Fujiwara Tadazane, Minister of the Left Minamoto Sukefusa, the director of the Ise Princess's Bureau, and Atsuta Shrine. One of the bandits, Kiyohara Sadamoto, came from an estate of which the regent was proprietor, and Kiyohara was clearly a member of the provincial elite.[56]

In short, this bandit group was broad-based and active over a broad geographic region. Indeed, these estate residents who moonlighted as brigands were little different from Minamoto Kunifusa's followers who vexed tax-collecting officials. In terms of their standing, many were well-to-do tax managers (*myōshu*) who also applied themselves to the opening of new fields. For instance, one of Mitsukuni's followers was Munesato, who hailed from Sagami Province. He was a well-known *sumo* wrestler who held the fifth rank and came from a household with official status, either that of a district chieftain or a township headman. Munesato himself visited the court of the retired monarch Shirakawa, and when he left before a final contest could determine his mastery in *sumo*, he was pursued by order of the retired monarch.[57]

The Nature of Mino Genji Lordship

Minamoto Kunifusa and Mitsukuni, as we have seen, had numerous followers in Mino. How did the Mino Genji organize their relations with such followers? Kunifusa's landholdings in Mino contributed greatly to his local authority. Many retainers serving Kunifusa and Mitsukuni were land openers, and they included residents of their lord's private holding, Uzura Township. But there were also many followers who came from outside Uzura Township. Some held posts within both the public and private domains, within which they had their own "private holdings" (*shiryō*) from which they drew livelihoods. But these holdings were always vulnerable to confiscation or interference by provincial governors. Even those dwelling within an estate might experience attempts by *shōen* proprietors to disappropriate them for the sake of "consolidated control." There were also family feuds to worry about. Such persons clearly needed protection, which is where warrior chieftains such as Kunifusa and Mitsukuni came in. A leader of warriors did his best to support his followers as members of his own military force; in return, the followers supported their lord to receive protection from him. Their followership was quite calculated. Mino residents who supported their Mino Genji warrior lords in the capital did so for just such reasons.

Among the men from Mino who went up to the capital to serve Mino Genji lords were followers of Minamoto Mitsukuni who were chained up in the West Jail in 1128.[58] These included Kunikata and other thieves who had escaped from the capital in 1114. Still earlier, in 1094, when the retired abbot of Mount Hiei had had his residence in the right (west) capital robbed, perpetrators of the crime were members of the Royal Police that included Mitsukuni's men.[59] Men-at-arms serving warrior chieftains in the capital were linked by a variety of bonds, and at times even crime might bring them together.

Yet these linkages between lords and followers were fairly fleeting in late Heian times. When Minamoto Mitsunobu's man committed murder in the first month of 1129 and was given amnesty, there was an argument between Mitsunobu and Tameyoshi over who the man's lord was. In the course of the argument their two armed forces faced each other in the capital and caused great concern at court.[60] In 1114, a retainer of Minamoto Yukitō of the Left Guards was killed by three of his fellow retainers.[61] According to an investigation by the Royal Police, one of the murderers was being harbored by Minamoto Tameyoshi. But Tameyoshi insisted, "His master is another. Ask around, he is not with me."[62] Tameyoshi refused to turn over the accused, and on the face of it he had sufficient military power to withstand demands even from the Royal Police. But a subsequent entry in the *Chūyūki* notes that on the fifteenth day of the fifth month, in the dead of night, the criminal and his henchmen were ultimately turned over—a lord's protection only went so far. A further notice indicated that the criminal was indeed Tameyoshi's man.[63]

Another interesting case is that of Kinmasa, a retainer of the third-in-command of the Royal Police, Minamoto Shigetoki. After borrowing some goods from Shigetoki, Kinmasa sought Minamoto Tameyoshi's protection. Shigetoki complained to the retired monarch, who summoned Tameyoshi several times. When there was no response, the retired monarch ordered the Royal Police to summon Kinmasa. But when the director, Fujiwara Munetada, received that order, he felt it necessary to consult with the retired monarch as to which police agent to charge with the matter. This was one indication of Tameyoshi's fearsome reputation as a warrior. Eventually Kinmasa was turned over, after being hidden by powerful men from Awa and Izu Provinces, men who were in contact with Tameyoshi.[64] According to the police report, when he was finally turned over, all that happened was that Kinmasa apologized and returned the borrowed goods to Shigetoki.[65]

In relationships between a warrior chieftain and his followers, the follower remained reasonably autonomous and allegiance was a fluid thing. A follower might well have two lords, and such vertical relations were inherently unstable. As we saw at the beginning of this chapter, when Minamoto Kunifusa and Yoshiie fought, it was because Kunifusa had demeaned one of Yoshiie's followers. The friction between Yoshiie and Yoshitsuna in 1091 started because of a fight between their followers. In other words, a warrior chieftain had to protect his men—on such protection rested his military might. A warrior chieftain who could not protect his men could not recruit them.[66]

Notes

1. "Minamoto" was one of the special surnames given to princes whose princely names were removed from the royal family register when they became commoners in Heian times. Many of Saga Tennō's princes were given the name Minamoto, as were sons of Nimmyō, Montoku, Seiwa, Yōzei, Kōkō, Uda, Daigo, Murakami, Kazan, and Sanjō. When the graph that is read "Minamoto" in Japanese (*kun'yomi*) is read in Chinese (*on'yomi*), it is read "Gen"; and when the graph meaning aristocratic clan is added, the result is "Genji." Of the various Minamoto lineages that became famed as martial provincial governors, the most famous was the Kawachi Genji. Various progeny from that line became governors of other provinces and established their own lineages with property in those provinces, just as Miyazaki describes the Mino Genji doing in this essay.

2. Tōdaiji is a royal temple founded in the eighth century by Shōmu Tennō in Nara, then the capital. During the Heian Period it remained an important site for realm-protecting rituals which were supported by properties in the countryside called *shōen*.

3. Taira Kiyomori (1118–1181) was the son of Tadamori, and he served as right-hand man and military commander to Go-Shirakawa Tennō. After his victory in the Hōgen Coup of 1156, he steadily rose at court, from advisor in 1160 to Prime Minister in 1167. Due to illness, in 1168 he retired and took lay vows but he continued to be influential at court. In 1171 his daughter Tokuko entered Takakura Tennō's backpalace; but in 1177 Go-Shirakawa conspired to assassinate Kiyomori, and in 1179 the retired monarch was put under house arrest. In 1180, Tokuko's son was enthroned as Antoku Tennō, leading to the outbreak of the Gempei hostilities that same year. After failing to move the capital to Fukuhara, Kiyomori died in 1181.

4. For the original article see Miyazaki Yasumitsu 1978. Interpreter's note: Kunifusa was the grandson of Minamoto Yorimitsu (948–1021), who served two terms as provincial governor of Mino, thereby establishing his heirs' fortune in that province. Yorimitsu also served in Settsu Province, leaving heirs there as well. Yorimitsu is known to have shared the wealth gained from his tours of provincial duty with his patrons in the Regents' line—among his gifts presented to Fujiwara Kaneie were 23 horses, and he gave all the goods needed to furnish a new mansion to the court leader Fujiwara Michinaga. In Japanese, see Yorimitsu's biography: Ayusawa Hisashi 1968. It was from this Mino Genji family that the well known medieval Toki warrior family derived. There were other famed Minamoto lineages based in Settsu, Yamato, and elsewhere.

5. *Suisaki* Kōhei 7 (1064) 10/19.

6. *Hyakurenshō* Kōhei 7 (1064) 12/24.

7. There is also a story about this rivalry in Ōe Masafusa's reminiscences, the *Gōdanshō*, in the passage entitled, "Discord between Yoshiie and Kunifusa."

8. According to the genealogical compendium *Sonpi bun'myaku* and the *Suisaki* journal, Shigemune lived in Katagata District. His father, who had served as provincial governor of Suruga, had resided in Mino before him.

9. *Fusōryakki* Shōryaku 3 (1079) 07/02; *Tamefusakyōki* Jōryaku 3 07/02. Interpreter's note: At the time, Shigemune held a post in the Headquarters of the Right Guards

(Uhyōefu) as third-in-command. There were four ranks of managerial officials—in descending order: *kami, suke, jō,* and *sakan*—in most *ritsuryō* agencies.

10. See the following: *Tamefusakyōki, Fusōryakki,* and *Hyakurenshō* Shōryaku 3 (1079) 08/17; *Suisaki* Shōryaku 3 08/21; and *Tamefusakyōki* Shōryaku 3 08/28 and 09/22. *Keizu san'yō,* a genealogical compilation of royal and elite lineages compiled in the Tokugawa period, notes Kunifusa's exile to Awa in the seventh month of 1079.

11. Interpreter's note: Miyazaki provides a more detailed genealogy than my own. See his note 8.

12. Oboroya Hisashi 1968.

13. Oboroya Hisashi 1968; Izumiya Yasuo 1959; Nagashima Fukutarō 1960.

14. *Tōdaiji monjo* Eiji 2 (1142) 10/, *Dai nihon komonjo Tōdaiji monjo,* vol. 4, doc. 13 (alt. *Heian ibun,* vol. 6, 2072-74, doc. 2469). Interpreter's note: Tōdaiji had two important estates in Mino, Akanabe and Ōi. Both seem to have come into the temple's hands in the late Nara or early Heian period. Akanabe was located in present-day Gifu City while Ōi was in present-day Ōgaki City. The prefectural history, *Gifu-ken shi,* devotes an entire volume to estate records from Ōi and Akanabe estates: Hōgetsu Keigo and Tokoro Mitsuo 1971. For *Dai nihon komonjo Tōdaiji monjo,* see Shiryō hensanjo 1955. For *Heian ibun,* see Takeuchi Rizō 1973-1980. Subsequent citations for *Heian ibun* will use *HI.*

15. Interpreter's note: It was common practice at estates of the time to open new fields and declare them part of previously tax-exempted fields. Provincial authorities called such land *kanōden,* denoting illicit additional fields beyond estate boundaries.

16. Interpreter's note: See *Dai nihon komonjo Tōdaiji monjo,* vol. 5, 211–15, doc. 98, in Shiryō hensanjo 1955; or *HI,* vol. 4, 1312–15, doc. 1353.

17. *Chūyūki* Eichō 1 (1096) 01/23.

18. *Honchō seiki* Kōwa 1 (1099) 01/06; *Chūyūki* Chōshō 1 (1132) 11/04.

19. *Shōyūki* Chōwa 2 (1013) 01/25.

20. *Gonijō Moromichi ki* Eichō 1 (1096) 01/24.

21. Oyamada Yoshio 1967.

22. Interpreter's note: For the collected documents for Ōi and Akanabe Estates, see Hōgetsu Keigo and Tokoro Mitsuo 1971.

23. Interpreter's note: For the document see Hōgetsu Keigo and Tokoro Mitsuo 1971, 107–9, doc. 113.

24. Interpreter's note: Such a township was often the site of newly opened fields recognized by the provincial authorities as an autonomous holding (*betsumyō*). The opening process was probably begun by Kunifusa's grandfather, Yorimitsu. A parallel example is known in Harima Province in 1075. There the Hata chieftain of Akaho District developed Hisatomi Township using 5000 laborers (probably conscripted from the district) to dig new irrigation ditches. He then requested jurisdiction over it from the provincial governor: "A request from the district chieftain of Akaho District to the governor of Harima Province: the chieftain requests that, both for the benefit of the state and as a reward for his services, he be granted direct authority over the irrigation wells and ditches which are in a state of disrepair, and the uncultivated fields of Hisatomi Township in the district of Akaho." See *HI,* vol. 3, 1126, doc. 1113.

25. See *Dai nihon komonjo Tōdaiji monjo,* vol. 4, doc. 13, Eiji 2 (1042). Interpreter's note: One *chō* equals 2.94 acres, therefore 12 *chō* would equal nearly 36 acres.

26. Interpreter's note: *Dai nihon komonjo Tōdaiji monjo,* vol. 2, 367–69, doc. 556.

27. Tenji 1 (1124) 06/20. See *HI,* vol. 5, 1758, doc. 2017.

28. Interpreter's note: Hōgetsu Keigo and Tokoro Mitsuo 1971, 84–5, doc. 104.

29. Interpreter's note: The earliest document for Hirata no Shō situated in the present-day Gifu City area appears in 1053 when it was the proprietary holding of the otherwise unidentified "household of the late minister of the second rank." See Kokuritsu rekishi minzoku hakubutsukan 1997, 447.

30. Tenji 1 (1124) 08/20. See *HI*, vol. 5, 1759, doc. 2021.

31. *Tamefusakyōki* Kanji 1 (1087) 04/13; *Honchō seiki* Kanji 1 12/23; *Chūyūki* Kanji 5 (1091) 09/24; *Chūyūki* Kaho 1 (1094) 09/01; and *Honchō seiki* Kōwa 1 (1099) 01/06. Also see the entries for Kōwa 1 (1094) 12/23 in *Gonijō Moromichi ki, Tokinoriki,* and *Honchō seiki.*

32. *Tamefusakyōki* Kanji 1 (1087) 04/13; *Honchō seiki* Kanji 1 12/13; *Chūyūki* Kanji 5 (1091) 09/24 and Kaho 1 (1094) 09/01; *Honchō seiki* Kōwa 1 (1099) 01/06, as well as the entries in *Gonijō Moromichiki,* and *Tokinoriki;* and *Honchō seiki* Kōwa 1 (1099) 01/23. Interpreter's note: In English see Friday 1992, 88-93 concerning these high ranking warriors (*kyō no musha*).

33. Yasuda Motohisa 1976. This feud has been known as "the Minamoto family feud." Interpreter's note: For the historical context see Hurst 1972 and Hurst 1976. Most recently is Hurst's contribution to *The Cambridge History of Japan,* Hurst 1999.

34. *Chūyūki* Ten'ei 2 (1111) 06/05.

35. *Denryaku* Ten'ei 1 (1110) 03/27. Interpreter's note: Sagae Estate was a holding of Regent Tadazane himself. See Kokuritsu rekishi minzoku hakubutsukan 1997, 488.

36. See the entries for Ten'ei 2 (1111) 11/19 in *Chūyūki* and *Denryaku.*

37. *Chōshūki* Eikyū 1 (1113) 04/01.

38. *Chōshūki* Daiji 4 (1129) 11/11 to 11/18; and *Chūyūki* Daiji 4 (1129) 11/11 to 11/26. Interpreter's note: For context and more detail in English, see Adolphson 2000, 75-124.

39. *Chūyūki* Daiji 4 (1129) 09/05 and 09/19.

40. See the entries for Daiji 5 (1130) 11/13 in *Chūyūki* and *Chōshūki.*

41. *Chūyūki* Daiji 5 (1130) 10/14.

42. See the entries for Daiji 5 (1130) 11/23 in *Chōshūki* and *Chūyūki.*

43. *Honchō seiki* Kōji 2 (1143) 01/27.

44. *Chōshūki* Hōen 3 (1137) 01/30.

45. *Gukanshō,* part four; *Taiki* Nimpyō 1 (1151) 01/23; *Heihanki* Kyūju 1 (1154) 01/23, and 03/28; *Heihanki* and *Sankaiki,* Kyūju 2 (1155) 10/23 and Hōgen 1 (1156) 01/06.

46. *Heihanki* Hōgen 1 (1156) 07/05. Interpreter's note: For more on the Hōgen Coup in English, see Farris 1992; and Wilson 2002.

47. *Hyakurenshō* Eiryaku 1 (1160) 06/14; and *Teiōhennenki* Eiryaku 1 06/14.

48. *Tōji monjo* Shōho 2 (1075) 05/12, *HI,* vol. 3, 1127, doc. 1115. On the relationship between Tado Jingūji and the Ise Taira, see Takahashi Masaaki 1975. Also see Takahashi Masaaki 1984.

49. *Tōji monjo* Chōji 2 (1105) 07/14, *HI,* vol. 4, 1505, doc. 1646.

50. *Tōji monjo* Kaho 1 (1094) 08/14, *HI,* vol. 4, 1520, doc. 1663.

51. *Tōji monjo* Kajō 2 (1107) 12/28, *HI,* vol. 4, 1532-33, doc. 1681; *Tōji monjo* Chōji 3 (1106) 02/07, *HI,* vol. 4, 1507-8, doc. 1651. See also Takeuchi Rizō 1973, 242.

52. Interpreter's note: In this regard, see Cornelius Kiley's comments on the importance of "vertical factions" in Heian society, in Kiley 1974.

53. *Chūyūki* Eichō 1 (1096) 12/01 and Eikyū 2 (1114) 03/04.

54. Interpreter's note: On the subject of *bushidan,* see the translated article by Ishii Susumu entitled, "Formation of Bushi Bands" (Ishii Susumu 1985). Also useful is Helen McCullough's translation of the early military chronicle, *Mutsuwaki* (*Tales of Mutsu*), McCullough 1964–65. See also the discussion in Friday 1992.

55. *Chūyūki* Eikyū 2 (1114) 04/02 and 05/14.

56. *Chūyūki* Eikyū 2 06/18.
57. *Gonijō Moromichi ki* Kanji 6 (1092) 08/21. See also Kometani Toyonosuke 1975.
58. *Chūyūki* Daiji 4 (1129) 01/07.
59. *Chūyūki* Kaho 1 (1094) 09/01.
60. *Chūyūki* Daiji 4 (1129) 01/07.
61. *Chūyūki* Eikyū 2 (1114) 05/03.
62. *Chūyūki* Eikyū 2 (1114) 05/10.
63. *Chūyūki* Eikyū 2 (1114) 05/16.
64. *Chūyūki* Eikyū 2 (1114) 05/17 and 06/28.
65. *Chūyūki* Eikyū 2 (1114) 08/16 and 08/21.
66. Interpreter's note: On this subject in English, albeit for a later period, see Conlan 1997.

12

Kōfukuji in the Late Heian Period

MOTOKI YASUO

Introduction by Mikael S. Adolphson

THE LAST CENTURY OF THE HEIAN AGE is most appropriately characterized as an era of intense factionalism among elites of the Kyoto court, caused by the resurgence of the royal family under the leadership of retired sovereigns and the increasing involvement of warrior leaders in capital politics. This process is well documented in many Japanese and Western works, but a third and equally important component of the ruling establishment, religious institutions, received scant attention until the mid-1960s. The pioneering scholar Kuroda Toshio offered a revolutionary theory that viewed religious institutions as legitimate co-rulers of what he called the medieval state. According to this theory, the highest authority in the state was shared by a number of elite groups known as *kenmon* ("gates of power").[1] These elites were the leaders of three power blocs—the court nobles (*kuge*), the warrior aristocracy (*buke*), and the officials of temples and shrines (*jisha*)—which ruled the realm together by sharing responsibilities of government and supporting each others' privileges and status.[2]

The first signs of such a cooperative ruling system appear, according to Kuroda, late in the eleventh century, when members of the royal family reasserted their influence vis-à-vis the Northern Fujiwara regental lineage (Sekkanke), which had dominated earlier sovereigns through clever marriage politics. Beginning with Shirakawa, who retired from the throne in 1086, the royal house transformed itself into an extragovernmental elite, amassing estates (*shōen*) and attracting retainers of its own. The period from 1086 to 1185 is therefore known as the era of "rule by retired monarchs" (*Insei*), though Kuroda also pointed out that other elites, such as the Fujiwara, were never completely eclipsed. The crucial point at this juncture was that rulership now took place without dependence on high government offices, indicating that the power of government came to rely more and more on nongovernmental (unofficial) assets and support.[3] The *kenmon* style of rule was further expanded in the twelfth century as this "privatization" of power and property continued and other elites came to share the responsibilities and privileges of government. These new elites—from religious institutions and the warrior aristocracy—had performed functions within the state for centuries, but they now acquired enough independence and power to assume the characteristics of *kenmon*.

The *kenmon* performed specific duties (administrative, military, and religious), sharing the responsibilities of rulership while receiving judicial and economic privileges in exchange. The court nobility, consisting of the royal family and the capital aristocracy, held the administrative and ceremonial responsibilities of the state. Supported by their own organizations and assets, nobles maintained their office-holding privileges and remained the formal leaders of the state. The warrior aristocracy was responsible for keeping the peace and physically protecting the state. Beginning in the mid-twelfth century, these duties were entrusted to prominent warrior leaders from the Minamoto and Taira clans. This unofficial division of responsibilities was formalized with Minamoto Yoritomo's (1147–1199) establishment of the warrior government in the east—the Kamakura Bakufu—in the 1180s, which Kuroda saw as a second phase of the *kenmon* system. The Bakufu's main responsibility was confined to maintaining peace and controlling the warrior class. The court and the Bakufu consequently complemented each other in an overlapping rulership, which has been termed "a dual polity" by some historians.[4]

The third component in the ruling triumvirate—the religious establishment—supplied the state and its members with spiritual protection. It also supported a vertical differentiation among the rulers and the ruled through magical and expensive rituals that only the most prestigious courtiers could afford. During the ninth century, the most popular Buddhist schools developed close relations with the most powerful families in the capital. However, after two centuries of patron-client relations, the larger temples became less dependent on direct and voluntary support from the capital nobility. By the eleventh century, these temples had tax-exempt estates of their own, a vast number of monks, lay followers, and branch institutions over which they held exclusive judicial rights. Administrative duties and the management of these assets were handled by the temples' own headquarters. A head abbot, often of noble birth, represented the temple and served as the channel of communication with the other elites. Even though the head abbot was principally a chosen leader, his leadership within the temple community was not unlike that of the Fujiwara chieftain or the retired sovereign. In short, these religious centers had been "*kenmon*-ified."[5] Meanwhile, a doctrine that supported the interdependent relationship between the court and Buddhism developed: "the interdependence of the King's Law and the Buddhist Law" (*ōhō buppō sōgo izon*), representing the idea that the state and Buddhism were interdependent, much like a bird needs two wings or a cart two wheels. This ideological concept, which included the idea that the native gods (*kami*) were vital in protecting the Buddhist deities and institutions, can be found in religious sources and documents of more secular character from the mid-eleventh century. It provided the ideological foundation for the participation of Buddhist institutions in government while linking together the realms of the *kami*, the Buddhas, and the living.[6]

In substance the *kenmon* system was a ruling system in which a number of elites—"gates of power"—ruled through their own assets, and it was the head of the most powerful *kenmon* who typically dominated government. The headquarters of that elite thus assumed a semiofficial character and issued documents to different institutions and government organs within the framework of the Heian polity. The retainers of the *kenmon* leader also came to serve the government and received official titles. At the same time, not even the most dominating *kenmon* chief had enough power to become an absolute ruler.

He was dependent on the support of the other elites, who assumed specific public responsibilities in exchange for confirmation and support of their control of land and their own lineage. *Kenmon* rulership was, in other words, a ruling system in which official and unofficial powers were combined to achieve efficient government over land and people.

Kuroda's *kenmon* concept is especially appealing because it treats religious institutions as political powers both in their own right and as providers of spiritual doctrines and support. Despite some criticism for its failure to acknowledge the structural differences between the more integrated noble and military blocs, on the one hand, and the more diverse religious bloc, on the other, Kuroda's theory has received widespread acceptance both in Japan and in the West. Yet few attempts have been made to address the questions raised by Kuroda's theory. For example, even though many scholars now acknowledge religious institutions as political actors as well as spiritual centers, the interaction among the elites, especially involving temples and shrines, has not been scrutinized until recently.[7]

Western readers first learned about the emergence of retired sovereigns as court leaders in late Heian times from G. Cameron Hurst's important book, *Insei*, in the 1970s; and my study of the symbiotic relationship of political and religious power in the late Heian and Kamakura eras, published in 2000, placed the elite temples close to the center in this process.[8] Motoki's piece offers a refreshing perspective, as he, building on Kuroda's theory of shared rulership, explores the importance of Nara's Kōfukuji, the clan temple of the Fujiwara, during the period when power was reorganized in the twelfth century. It is an illuminating study, bringing to light for the first time in Japanese the close relation between the new religious policies of the retired sovereign and the eruption of more intense and serious disturbances involving one of the leading religious institutions. Motoki specifically refutes the widely accepted idea that demonstrations staged by powerful Buddhist temples in the capital were attacks on the court, causing in the end the decline of the Heian political system. Instead, we now realize that the religious disturbances of the twelfth century were primarily induced directly by policies of the retired monarch or indirectly by land encroachments by his retainers. In response the elite temples attempted to preserve the established balance among the various schools by actively resisting in various ways the retired sovereign's efforts to shift the balance in his own favor. The retired *tennō*'s intent was, in short, to augment his power by controlling important religious ceremonies, monk promotions, appointments, and even the monastic complexes themselves. Motoki even argues that the policies of Shirakawa as retired sovereign were primarily directed at Kōfukuji instead of his Fujiwara opponents. As a result, Kōfukuji's status, both religious and political, was greatly affected by the emergence of the retired monarch as a contender for power, providing further evidence of the tremendous importance of religious institutions in the late Heian age. Readers will find that Map 12.1, Table 12.1 and Figure 12.1 in this chapter will aid their reading of the essay.

MOTOKI YASUO

Kōfukuji in the Late Heian Period

Interpreted by Mikael S. Adolphson

ACCORDING TO THE WELL-KNOWN *Gukanshō* compiled in Kamakura times by the Tendai abbot Jien (1155–1225), warrior rulership began with the Hōgen Coup in 1156.[9] But there were also other armed groups with expectations involved in the battles of the twelfth century. In planning his strike against Go-Shirakawa Tennō, Fujiwara Yorinaga—minister of the left (*sadaijin*) and family chieftain of the Northern Fujiwara—decided against a surprise night attack in favor of sending a plea for armed support to two Kōfukuji monks, Shinjitsu and Genjitsu.[10] The courtier journal *Heihanki* confirms that estates were later confiscated from Shinjitsu after the incident "for having sided with the minister of the left and dispatching 'evil monks' [*akusō*]."[11] The military power of Kōfukuji, one of the *kenmon* temples that were located in Nara and Kyoto, and its "evil monks" made it a significant enough force to be called upon in a major uprising.

In addition, the Hōgen Coup of 1156 was the first time "evil monks" were summoned by the Fujiwara chieftain to become involved in a strictly political dispute. Until then they had only staged demonstrations or confronted other temples to defend their own privileges. The plea to Kōfukuji in 1156 reflects a new development in which Fujiwara Tadazane and his son Yorinaga successfully employed the monk Shinjitsu as ringleader of Kōfukuji's "evil monks."[12] As we shall see, Tadazane managed to control Kōfukuji through Shinjitsu from the 1140s onward, thereby obstructing the clergy's attempts to stage "forceful protests" (*gōso*) in Kyoto during Toba's era (1129–1156), while also weakening the influence of his rival, Fujiwara Tadamichi[13] (see Figure 12.1). Kōfukuji was, in other words, a vital political resource for the Fujiwara chieftain at the time of the Hōgen Coup.

Since Tadazane's alliance with Shinjitsu and successful control of the Nara temple cannot be properly understood if conditions leading Kōfukuji to accept such an arrangement are ignored, in this chapter I analyze Kōfukuji's internal conditions and political stance during the eras of Shirakawa and Toba, when the foundation for Fujiwara Tadazane's control was laid. I also scrutinize the shift of power from the Northern Fujiwara regents to the royal family, headed by retired monarchs. For Kōfukuji, as the most influential Fujiwara family temple, there can be no doubt that this realignment greatly affected the temple's political position. In fact, the clergy's forceful protests in the capital directly reflect the relationships, tensions, and conflicts between elite temples and secular authorities at court. For this reason I also analyze the Kōfukuji *gōso* in the capital—their origins, frequency, and change through time—while comparing them to protests staged by other temples. Finally, I further explore the conditions under which the "evil monk" Shinjitsu took charge at Kōfukuji,

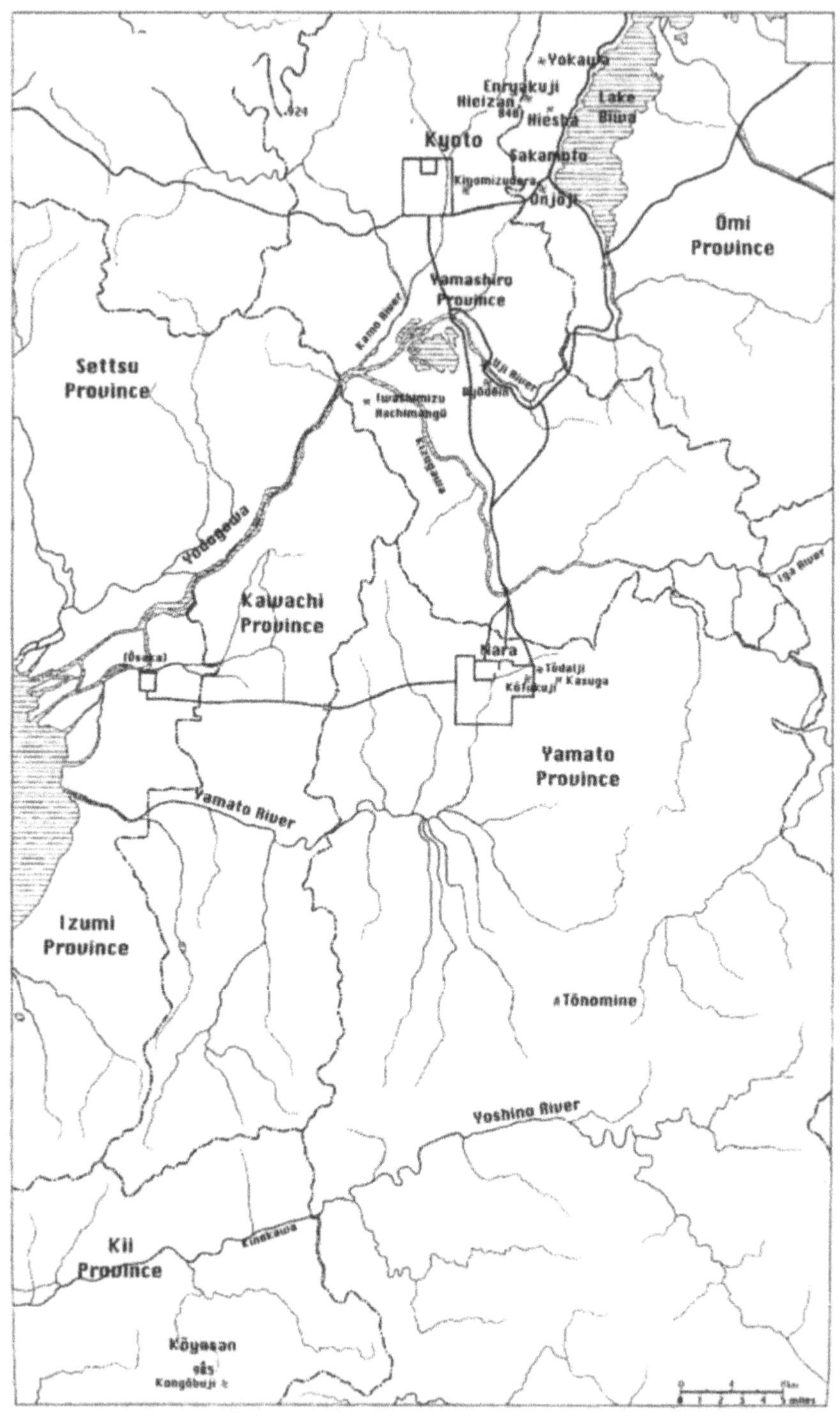

Map 12.1. The Kinai Region and Selected Influential Temples

utilizing changing internal conditions and the temple's more visible position as an important ally of the Fujiwara chieftain during the time when retired *tennō* led the court.

Forceful Protests in the Regency Era

One of the most conspicuous characteristics of medieval Japan is the cycle of confrontation and disputes between various secular powers on the one hand and powerful temples reinforced with military forces on the other.[14] The scale and frequency of such disputes not only reflected the strength of these elite temples, perhaps most adequately termed "gates of power" (*kenmon*), just as did the number of monks from a given temple appointed to the Office of Monastic Affairs (Sōgō), or the number selected to participate in prestigious official Buddhist rites.[15] In this essay it will become clear that Kōfukuji's forceful protests also reflect the changes characterizing the transition from the era when regents presided at court to the age when retired monarchs dominated the court.

Records mention unruly monks in the ninth century, but the first confirmed presence of private monks rampaging in the provinces comes from Miyoshi Kiyoyuki's twelve-article statement to Daigo Tennō in 914 recommending that "the evil acts of monks in various provinces and the atrocities performed by military servants and guards must be prohibited."[16] Thereafter, the Tendai head abbot (*zasu*) Ryōgen noted the tyrannous acts of armed "evil monks" within and beyond the Enryakuji monastic complex in his twenty-six articles of 970.[17] These are the earliest documentary evidence we have of clerics carrying arms within temple confines hitherto reserved for Buddhist studies. Disturbances involving "evil monks" became increasingly frequent as regents and retired sovereigns came to dominate the court; and as demonstrated in Table 12.1 (appended at page 319), monk demonstrations in the capital became still more frequent in the late eleventh century, coinciding with the resurgence of the royal family led by retired monarchs.[18] The vast majority of these demonstrations were staged by the two most influential temples, Enryakuji and Kōfukuji (see Map 12.1). In the following analysis, I compare incidents involving these two temples.[19]

In the era of the Northern Fujiwara regents, forceful protests were rare, and there are also several cases where the historicity of reports is in doubt (Table 12.1, cases 1, 5, and 9). Nonetheless there are important signs of disputes involving Enryakuji and Kōfukuji that must be considered. First, estates held by Kōfukuji were under pressure from members of the provincial governor class, compelling the temple to launch demonstrations and appeals. Notably, the Fujiwara chieftain did not always support his own family temple in such lobbying (Table 12.1, case 4). We can surmise that the regents valued their relations with the provincial governor class highly, perhaps because of their own influence over appointments to such offices. As a result, Kōfukuji was treated with a certain indifference.

In contrast, whereas Kōfukuji's early *gōso* were a response to an intensified competition with provincial governors over estates, Enryakuji's forceful protests

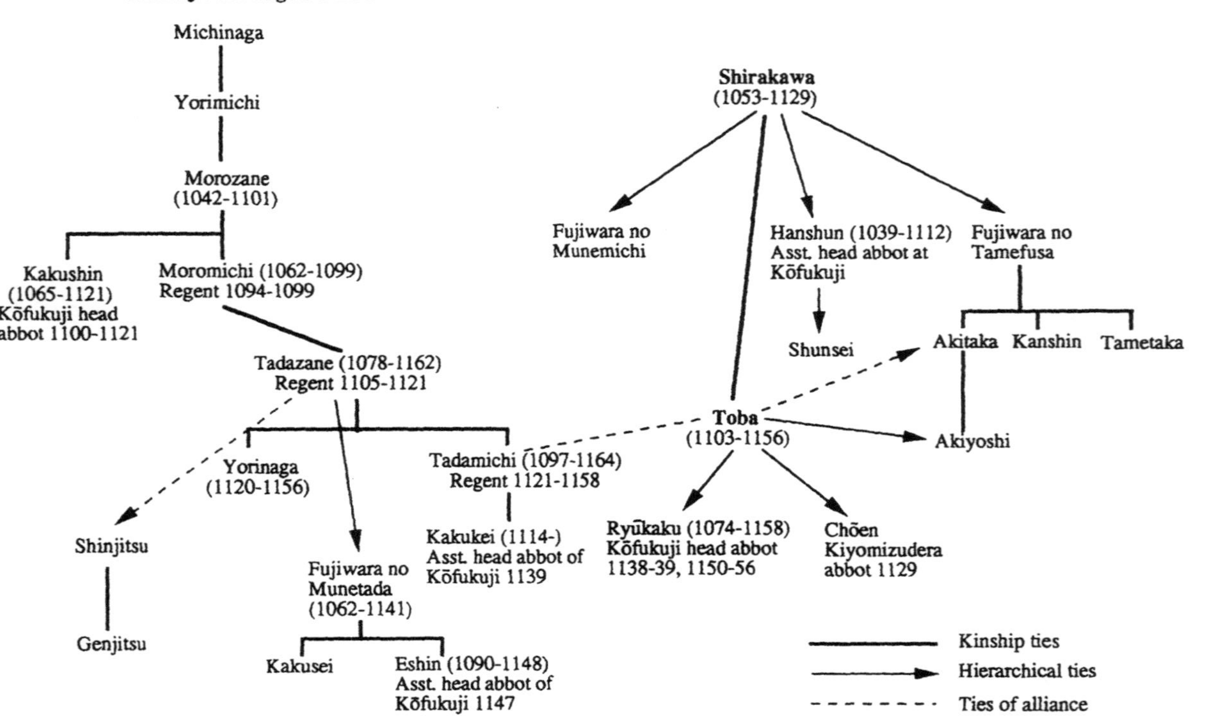

Fig. 12.1. Court Factionalism at Kōfukuji in the Early Twelfth Century

were related to appointments of abbots to superintend important temples. Three incidents (Table 12.1, cases 2, 7 and 8) were reactions to regental favoritism toward monks from Onjōji, the Tendai sibling cloister and rival of Enryakuji. Moreover, the struggle between Enryakuji and Onjōji concerning the abbotship of Hosshōji, built by Fujiwara Tadahira (880–949), provides further proof of close relations between the Tendai school and temples built by the regents.[20] Indeed, as evidenced by the successful career and commanding position of Ryōgen and his disciple Jinzen, himself a scion of the regental lineage (Sekkanke), intimate ties were already being created and maintained between regents and clerics of the most important temples during the Regency era. The lack of conflicts over estates between Enryakuji and provincial governors during the Regency era evidences a notable contrast between Kōfukuji and Enryakuji, one that was made starker by cases when the regent even harbored Tendai estates against governor intrusions.[21] In short, monk protests during the Regency era were related either to conflicts and confrontations over estates or to personnel appointments at the main or branch temples. Both were also key reasons for protests in the subsequent era of retired monarchs as well, but with a few notable distinctions.

Forceful Protests in the Late Heian *Insei* Era

Forceful protests greatly increased during Shirakawa's tenure as retired *tennō*. Shirakawa resigned from the throne in the eleventh month of 1086, but his reign as senior retired monarch did not begin immediately. For a time, in-laws of Horikawa Tennō, Fujiwara Morozane and Moromichi (see Figure 12.1) of the regent's line, continued to wield considerable political power. But the regent Moromichi died suddenly in the sixth month of 1099 at the young age of thirty-seven, causing a considerable decline in the authority of the regent's line. Notably it was widely believed that Moromichi's untimely death was caused by a curse cast by priests at the Hie Shrine, Enryakuji's main shrine affiliate, for Moromichi's role in forcefully quelling an Enryakuji protest in 1095. Such a rumor caused great fear among the capital nobles, and it serves as a marker of the increasing power of temples and shrines. So it is not surprising that we find a dramatic increase in monk protests thereafter—twenty-two out of twenty-six protests during Shirakawa In's era occurred after Moromichi's death. Widespread belief that Hie's curse of Moromichi caused his demise apparently obsessed Kyoto nobles at the very moment when the powers of the retired sovereign were increasing and religious protests were becoming more frequent.

During Shirakawa's era, Enryakuji and the Hie Shrine staged fifteen protests while Kōfukuji and the Kasuga Shrine launched seven. Both religious complexes clearly remained central in the late Heian polity. And as Table 12.1 shows, causes behind most protests were the same as during the regents era: conflicts with provincial officials over local estates and domains of branch temples (hereafter "estate conflicts"), and conflicts concerning rewards, appointments, and punishments of monks and personnel (hereafter "appointment conflicts"). In the case of Enryakuji, where appointment disturbances had been common during the regents era, protests were caused by such problems on seven occasions (Table 12.1, cases 18, 24, 26–29, and 34), compared with five incidents caused by estate-related conflicts (cases 14, 15, 17, 37, and 39).[22] In Kōfukuji's case, there were three estate conflicts (cases 16, 35, and 43) and four appointment conflicts (cases 19, 21, 30, and 32). Accordingly, we find no major differences between the nature of estate conflicts when looking at the two complexes at this time, because both had developed into substantial proprietors of estates. Tensions between governors on the one hand and shrine associates (*jin'nin*) of Hie and Kasuga on the other stand out as the primary cause for estate conflicts at both Kōfukuji and Enryakuji. The most common demand made in the course of these protests was deposition and exile of a provincial governor. But since the latter was often a retainer of the retired monarch, punishments were frequently delayed even if "guilty" judgments were rendered. In fact enforcement of a punishment depended on a number of factors, such as how close protesters came to the palace, the retired monarch's success in suppressing the protests, and general political conditions at the time. Although often effective, the protests hardly show elite temples and their associated shrines as irresistible forces.[23]

On the other hand, when we consider protests over monastic appointments involving Mount Hiei and Kōfukuji during Shirakawa's era, we see significant differences. At Enryakuji we find an incident caused by the appointment of a Tōji liturgist for a ritual at the royally supported Sonshōji (cases 28 and 29), a continuation of the conflicts with Onjōji (cases 18 and 24), and an internal conflict (case 34). None of them indicates any substantial changes from earlier times. But at Kōfukuji we see unprecedented protests over appointments motivated by the retired sovereign's punishment of monks (cases 19 and 32) and by willful appointments (case 30). These protests concerning punishments and monastic appointments distinguished Kōfukuji's experience with the court during Shirakawa's era from that during the preceding regents' age. And in the subsequent tenure of Toba In, the trend became even more obvious.

During Toba's twenty-seven-year reign as retired *tennō*—from Shirakawa's death in the seventh month of 1129 until the seventh month of 1156—there were four protests by Enryakuji/Hie supporters and five by Kōfukuji/Kasuga supporters. Among these, Enryakuji's estate conflicts included cases 44 and 48, while case 43 was occasioned by Kōfukuji's opposition to a land survey by the Yamato provincial governor. In terms of appointment conflicts, there were none involving Enryakuji but three by Kōfukuji (cases 40, 42, and 47). Case 40 specifically demonstrates the continuing opposition over religious appointments between Kōfukuji and the retired *tennō* caused by the latter's willful appointments and refusal to hear a plea from the Hossō clergy in the eleventh month of 1129. That there was a close correlation between royal policies and attempts by Fujiwara Tadazane and Fujiwara Yorinaga to control Kōfukuji more directly is evident.

After the Hōgen Coup of 1156, protests over religious appointments did not occur as frequently, since conditions in the capital became more stable.[24] Nevertheless, new trends characterized religious conflicts. In the case of Enryakuji, protests regarding estates occurred repeatedly during Go-

Shirakawa's era, as more problems with Anrakuji's holdings are evident in cases 49 and 51, mirroring problems of Shirakawa's day (cases 26, 27, and 37). In addition the Tendai center on Mount Hiei experienced serious problems regarding its estates in northern provinces. By contrast, whereas Kōfukuji was involved in severe confrontations with governors in each region during Shirakawa's age, we find no further examples of such conflicts in the subsequent era, excepting a single dispute with the governor of Yamato (case 43) in Kōfukuji's home province.

Based on this analysis, we can conclude that the two monastic complexes of Enryakuji and Kōfukuji moved in different directions as elite temples. Kōfukuji's most extensive and serious problems during the eras of retired monarchs Shirakawa and Toba were intimately related to the retired sovereigns' aggressive meddling in appointments and promotions, as well as their strategy of penalizing monks and other affiliated institutions such as Kiyomizudera.[25]

Kōfukuji and the Establishment of the *In*-led Court

In considering Kōfukuji's political status during the twelfth century, it is helpful to begin with the temple's position during the earlier regency era. Jinzen, the son of Minister of the Right Fujiwara Morosuke (908–960), became the nineteenth Tendai head abbot. His was the first instance of a Sekkanke son to enter and head the Tendai order. By contrast, at Kōfukuji the first Sekkanke scion to lead the Nara monastery was Morozane's son Kakushin in the late eleventh century. Despite its designation as the Fujiwara family temple, Kōfukuji was treated quite differently from Tendai temples in terms of human ties with powerful members of the Northern Fujiwara regental lineage. One reason for this difference is that there were many opportunities for Tendai and Shingon monks of the esoteric lineages to form close relationships with the secular elites through prayers at times of illness and through appointments as attending monks and spiritual protectors (*gojisō*) at court. Even more important were the strict promotion procedures for the six Nara schools, whose monks could only advance through participation in one of the three great official ceremonies (*sandaie*): Kōfukuji's Yuimae, the palace's Misaie (or Gosaie), and Yakushiji's Saishōe. By contrast, monks from the esoteric schools—Tendai and Shingon—could be promoted regardless of their merits as lecturers or masters of ceremonies at important court ceremonies, making advancement more dependent on personal connections. In fact, the esoteric career was occasionally referred to as "a short cut to promotion," indicating that other matters besides religious merit, such as blood ties and patronage, played a role in securing important monastic titles.[26] Whereas the route to promotion among the temples and schools in Nara, including Kōfukuji, depended greatly upon the monastic law, monks of the esoteric schools of Tendai and Shingon gained opportunities for promotion based on recommendations from secular elites. It is this condition, and the uncertainty that followed arbitrary promotions, that caused conflicts between the political elites and powerful Tendai temples over appointments during the Regency era.

The different circumstances characterizing opportunities for monks from the Kyoto and Nara schools were obvious in the Office of Monastic Affairs, where there was a clear correlation between protocols for promotions and the ratio of membership. The Office of Monastic Affairs consisted of monks from the four main schools: the two Tendai lineages represented by Enryakuji and Onjōji, Shingon's Tōji, and Hossō's Kōfukuji. From the middle of the eleventh century, that is in the second half of the Regency era, the two Tendai lineages maintained a clear advantage over the other schools by controlling 70 percent of Sōgō membership. By contrast, although Kōfukuji monks had dominated the Sōgō in the early Heian period, the Hossō center never claimed more than 20 percent of its seats, and it was surpassed even by Tōji in the era of retired monarchs.[27] Kōfukuji's weakening influence within the Office of Monastic Affairs—indicating its declining influence at the court—had already begun during the Regency era.

Kōfukuji also experienced problems in securing income from its estates, over which it came into conflict with provincial governors and the regents. In Table 12.1, case 4, for instance, Michinaga squarely favored his own retainer, who was the governor of Yamato, Minamoto Yorichika, in a dispute with Kōfukuji—he squelched the temple's protest and punished only temple officials.[28] Similar incidents occurred during the era of Fujiwara Yorimichi, Michinaga's son and successor. An entry for 1023 from the courtier journal *Shōyūki* describes how the Kōfukuji head abbot and other ranking Hossō monks declined Yorimichi's order to attend a religious ceremony at the Kayanoin.

> The history underlying this matter is that the present Fujiwara chieftain has not cared for the temple—he has enabled governors of various provinces to collect rents from *shōen* without forwarding the part owed [the temple]. Several appeals have been lodged, but [the crimes against Kōfukuji] have not been acknowledged. Other matters are also deeply resented. In particular there are great losses from estates in Ōmi and Bitchū, whose revenues are earmarked for the sustenance of the temple. As for the present Fujiwara chieftain, it is highly inappropriate that the temple should be ignored, while the resulting lack of loyalty by temple monks is without precedent. In the end, how can the words of the governor be trusted? What sadness, indeed![29]

It is hardly surprising to discover that the provincial governors of Ōmi and Bitchū were long standing housemen (*keishi*) of the Fujiwara chieftain.[30] The regent unquestionably preferred to support the provincial governors, with whom a bond was cemented by reciprocity in benefits gained from rulership in the provinces, rather than relying on less certain benefits from ties with ranking monks at Kōfukuji, regardless of its status as the family temple.

By the end of the eleventh century, however, we find a sharp change in the relationship between the regents and Kōfukuji. The historian Ōyama Kyōhei has previously noted that the aforementioned Kakushin entered Kōfukuji in 1075, the same year his father Morozane was appointed viceroy. This reflected an obvious development in the Sekkanke's policies with respect to Nara.[31] Already under attack by Go-Sanjō's new policies, meaning that its domination was challenged even before Shirakawa's era, and facing conflict among its own collateral lines at the same time, the chieftain of the main line began to make efforts to create a bond with Kōfukuji to benefit from and control its religious power.[32]

Kōfukuji, for its part, struggled to resist the weakening of its influence stemming from the establishment of three new official yearly lectures in Kyoto as well as other Buddhist rituals patronized by Go-Sanjō and Shirakawa.[33] The temple needed the assistance and authority of the Northern Fujiwara regents. By strengthening its tie with the regents, Kōfukuji further managed to complete the process of merging the Buddhas and the *kami*, fully extending the temple's influence over the Fujiwara's Kasuga Shrine. As a result, Kōfukuji came to hold more extensive possessions throughout Yamato, in addition to controlling Kasuga's shrine associates, who themselves maintained considerable influence throughout the region. In this regard we find the first documented proof of a union of the forces of Kōfukuji and Kasuga in 1093 (Table 12.1, case 16), when a branch from Kasuga's "sacred tree" (*shinboku*) was brought to the capital to add spiritual pressure to a forceful protest by Kōfukuji. The sacred branch subsequently became a frequent component of Kōfukuji protests, causing great fear among the Fujiwara nobles in the capital.

While strengthening its ties with the Northern Fujiwara regental lineage, Kōfukuji continued to rely on the celebration of its official Yuima ceremony (Yuimae) for its religious status and as the basis for getting its monks promoted. For his part, Shirakawa In suppressed the regents' line and promoted his own network of temples and monks to establish himself as the dominant leader in the capital. Consequently, he and Kōfukuji came face to face in opposition, as the following section demonstrates.

Kōfukuji during Shirakawa In's Tenure

The outstanding feature in conflicts between Kōfukuji and the retired monarch Shirakawa was the latter's intervention into staffing matters and the levying of unprecedented penalties against monks. The earliest instance of a dispute involving Shirakawa and Kōfukuji occurred in the tenth month of 1100, when the Tōji monk Hanshun was named extranumerary director (*gon no bettō*) of Kōfukuji. This Shingon monk had "served as a spiritual adviser for the retired emperor, and had lived at the Toba Palace for decades"—he was unquestionably an intimate of Shirakawa's.[34] Notably, the *Register of Appointments of Tōji Monastic Directors* (*Tōji chōja bunin*) records that Hanshun was "a rare breed at Tōji, as he had no experience as a master of any of the three lecture ceremonies and became the choice of the clan [as assistant head abbot] only on the recommendation of the retired monarch."[35] Hanshun had been appointed to the Office of Monastic Affairs as a preceptor (*hokkyō*) in the fifth month of 1092 after having served in the esoteric Mishihō liturgy with the retired monarch himself.[36] Since he lacked experience in leading any of the great Buddhist ceremonies, Hanshun's appointment as Kōfukuji abbot was highly unusual. Even more interesting is the fact that the retired sovereign's edict was issued after a Sekkanke "recommendation," an indispensable part of Kōfukuji appointments. But this approval came quite easily, since the young Tadazane, who had become Fujiwara clan chieftain following Moromichi's sudden death in 1099, served Shirakawa as inspector of royal documents (*nairan*). Indeed, Tadazane was not even appointed viceroy until 1105, leaving that office vacant for four years. Together with the appointment of Hanshun, all this reflects a severe decline in the Sekkanke's authority and essentially marked the end of Northern Fujiwara predominance at court. In the process Kōfukuji, which had depended on the Fujiwara chieftain to protect its interests, was forced into a direct and lonely confrontation with the retired sovereign.

The issue of Hanshun's appointment led to a more drastic response by the Kōfukuji clergy as it reacted vehemently against Shirakawa's recommendation of Hanshun as lecturer for the Yuima ceremony in early 1101. They objected that "such a recommendation cannot be accepted without passing through the Office of Monastic Affairs," a point that even the retired monarch was forced to acknowledge.[37] Then, to retaliate for an earlier verdict issued by Shirakawa against Kōfukuji's head abbot Kakushin, and to punish Hanshun's disciple Hansei for rioting within the Kōfukuji precincts, the Hossō clergy attacked and destroyed Hanshun's own dwellings on the sixth day of the eighth month of 1102. Following these incidents, Hanshun appears to have given up on a career as a prestigious prelate to live a quiet life in seclusion.[38] In a similar conflict Shirakawa appointed the monk Ensei, trained at Enryakuji, as abbot of Kiyomizudera in the intercalary third month of 1113 (case 30). Unsurprisingly, the Kōfukuji clergy reacted forcefully with another protest, forcing the retired monarch to cancel the appointment.[39]

Such events demonstrate not only the weakening of the Northern Fujiwara chieftain's influence, but also how Kōfukuji's monastic community successfully resisted Shirakawa's religious initiatives. Shirakawa's ambitions, however, went beyond just influencing appointments of temple officials. He also attempted to control assignments of ranking monks as lecturers at the Yuima ceremony, as evinced by his recommendation of Hanshun in 1102. Moreover, at the time of a meeting to determine lecturers in 1114, the regent Tadazane sent his messenger, Fujiwara Munetada, to Shirakawa's mansion, where he announced that "it would be appropriate to appoint Myōsen and Kakugon because of their public service," in accordance with precedents.[40] Shirakawa sent the following response to Munetada through Fujiwara Munemichi, one of the retired monarch's own ranking retainers:

> I do not know whether these monks are appropriate or not. It is therefore difficult to make a decision. Lord [Fujiwara] Tamefusa recommended Kanshin, but I do not have a strong impression of him. I have heard that your [Munetada's] son Kakusei is extraordinarily gifted, so he should have the honor of being the master of ceremonies. However, he is a little young, so you should discuss it with the viceroy.[41]

In other words, Shirakawa rejected the viceroy's recommendation, ordering instead that Tadazane consider Shirakawa's own nomination of Munetada's son, Kakusei, who indeed became the master of ceremonies that year. Since Shirakawa could so easily reject Tadazane's nominations, we must conclude that the definitive authority to select the Yuima ceremony leader at the time had shifted to the retired monarch. Moreover, the latter was able to ignore established protocols and the wishes of Kōfukuji's own monks in making the selection.

As seen here, one of the retired sovereign's retainers, Fujiwara Tamefusa (see Figure 12.1), suggested his own son Kanshin as master of ceremonies, and Shirakawa selected him for the following year's Yuima ceremony. But such arbitrary appointments were now becoming troublesome to the outspoken Munetada, who objected to the retired monarch's violation of the established order at Kōfukuji and other Nara temples. He specifically noted that Kanshin had not served as examiner of younger monks for the Yuima ceremony. Without such experience or any merit for the great ceremonies, "to honor him with an edict as master of ceremonies is entirely without precedent."[42] Unsurprisingly, the Kōfukuji monks agreed with Munetada, and reacted forcefully when Kanshin eventually approached Nara.

Kanshin initially postponed his participation following the death of his father Tamefusa, and only in the tenth month of 1116 did he finally proceed to Nara. The monks there promptly demonstrated against him, arguing first that he "had not accrued the necessary merit," and second that his elder brother Akitaka had committed "several evil deeds against the temple."[43] Kanshin and another brother, Tametaka (who accompanied him as a royal messenger), were subsequently forced by the angry clergy to return to the capital. Tadazane thereupon suggested that "the appointment should be amended," but Shirakawa reiterated his royal opinion that "the ceremony should be performed as ordered." He then rhetorically inquired if "the Fujiwara now were without the means [to control Kōfukuji]?"[44] The dispute ended in a compromise: Kanshin was allowed to serve as a discussant-commentator (*ikō*) for attendees while Tōdaiji's Kakugon was appointed lecturer.[45] Again, we detect a decline of the Northern Fujiwara chieftain's power, willful meddling in temple matters by Shirakawa, and the effects of forceful opposition by the Kōfukuji clergy, finally resulting in a compromise with the retired sovereign.

Next, let us examine punishments against members of monastic communities by Shirakawa. First, the reason for his unprecedented suspension of the monk Kakushin as abbot of Kōfukuji lay in the clergyman's harassment of messengers sent to Nara from Shirakawa's headquarters in the seventh month of 1102.[46] Tadazane, the Fujiwara chieftain at the time, noted in his journal:

> Kizu in Izumi Province is part of the temple's domain. However, the retired sovereign's retainers, claiming to be conscripting laborers, led several tens of people in evil acts. For that reason, the Kōfukuji clergy assembled, squared off with the retainers, and drove them away. The abbot is my brother.[47] The situation is truly beyond belief. Because of

> crimes like these, it was ordered that the head abbot be suspended, which is truly hard to accept.[48]

As reflected here, the penalty meted out by the *in* on this occasion was quite severe compared with that for other crimes. But, to make matters worse, Shirakawa also rejected a plea to pardon the abbot in time for the Yuima ceremony on the tenth day of the tenth month, even though there was no precedent for performing such a ceremony without the Kōfukuji abbot in attendance. Regardless, the ceremony was performed with the royal messenger Toshinobu directing.[49] Kakushin was only allowed to return to Kōfukuji and resume his duties as temple head in the fifth month of 1103.[50]

Other disturbances confirm Shirakawa's harsh attitude toward Kōfukuji. Consider, for example, the exile of the ranking Hossō monk Jikkaku, partly in response to powerful pressure from Enryakuji in 1113 (Table 12.1, case 32).[51] The Kōfukuji clergy responded by staging a demonstration in the capital, causing Shirakawa to ponder ordering the arrest of some of the temple's demonstrating monks.[52] Shortly thereafter, in the sixth month of 1113, there were rumors that the angry clergy had put curses on the retired monarch, which induced Shirakawa to order punishments without even investigating the truth of the rumors.[53] Shirakawa's verdict may have been a reaction not only to the suspected curse but also to the pent-up frustration that he felt with the Kōfukuji monks, who had also demanded earlier that year that a new abbot should be appointed for Kiyomizudera (case 30). Notably, we do not find such punishments levied against other elite temples—in particular against Enryakuji—when their monks quarreled with the retired monarch and the court. Punishments against Kōfukuji were relatively heavy, and there is no doubt that both the retired sovereign and the *tennō* were attempting to weaken the Nara Hossō center. To put these verdicts in perspective, we need to consider Shirakawa's meddling in other appointment issues and his strict penalties seen within the broader context of his religious policies.

The Religious Policies of Shirakawa's Age

In considering the reasons for Shirakawa's efforts to control Kōfukuji, we must take into account his ambition to suppress the Northern Fujiwara regental lineage. It is not difficult to see that the retired sovereign, in order to dominate capital politics, needed to subdue Kōfukuji, which had augmented its own religious authority by strengthening its relationship with the Sekkanke. It is also evident that the union between the Northern Fujiwara regental lineage and Kōfukuji weakened other Fujiwara lineages, dismaying descendants of minor branches who served as retainers of the retired monarch. These retainers inevitably played a crucial role in the latter's attempts to control Kōfukuji. The recommendation of Kanshin as lecturer for the Yuima ceremony by Fujiwara Tamefusa—the father of Kanshin and a houseman of Shirakawa—is representative of their responses. Notably, the ambitions of Tamefusa's descendants strongly affected the Hossō center, as Tamefusa's eldest son and heir, Akitaka (Figure 12.1), continued to express opposition to the Fujiwara clan temple. Akitaka was the husband of Toba's wet nurse, and his close relationship with that monarch appeared threatening to Kōfukuji, causing Tadazane to complain that Akitaka "spread evil rumors to Shirakawa" about Kōfukuji, and that "it was highly inappropriate to force people of the [Fujiwara] family to appeal such things."[54] Indeed, it was Akitaka, attempting to improve his own position, who influenced Toba Tennō to suspend for a second time the abbot Kakushin, himself a descendant of the Northern Fujiwara regental lineage, in 1117.[55] The person behind this conflict was Akiyoshi, Akitaka's son and the governor of Sanuki Province, who carried out his father's strategy by disputing land rights with Kōfukuji (Table 12.1, case 35).[56] Toba Tennō, who was Akiyoshi's foster brother, was greatly angered over the clergyman's behavior.[57] He refused to punish Akiyoshi, which caused Kakushin to resign as head of Kōfukuji in the fifth month of 1117.[58]

Yet the conflict between Shirakawa and the Northern Fujiwara regents should not be interpreted as the sole cause behind the retired monarch's aggressive policies against Kōfukuji. First, the alliance between the regents and Kōfukuji was not primarily a strategy to resist Shirakawa. Rather, it was an effort to unite and control other Fujiwara branches. Second, the retired monarch's efforts to control and subjugate Kōfukuji did not commence until after the untimely and premature death of Fujiwara Moromichi in 1099, which indicates that Shirakawa used the weakening of the Sekkanke as an opportunity to subjugate Kōfukuji, rather than suppressing the temple in order to get to the Fujiwara chieftain. It was Kōfukuji itself that was foremost in the confrontation between the retired monarch's faction and the temple.

Many disturbances were related to the Yuima ceremony. The appointment of Kanshin in 1114 is an obvious example, but the nomination of Shirakawa's spiritual adviser Hanshun as master of ceremonies fourteen years earlier also stirred up Kōfukuji's hostility. In addition, Kakushin's suspension as abbot during the Yuima ceremony of 1102 intensified the bitter dispute. Conflicts between Kōfukuji and the retired monarch were thus closely related to the Yuima ceremony, which was doubly important—as one of the three great lecture ceremonies, and as one of the main routes for promotions for Hossō monks to and within the Office of Monastic Affairs.

The route for monastic promotion within the esoteric Buddhist (*mikkyō*) schools of Tendai and Shingon was primarily based on performances of initiation ceremonies (*denpō kanjō*), for which the opinions of the secular rulers were particularly influential. As noted, prestigious religious offices for Nara monks were, by contrast, awarded only after participation in the three great lecture ceremonies. As can be expected, the shift of court leadership away from the Northern Fujiwara chieftain as regent to the retired sovereign affected the lives of monks, as well as the balance among powerful temples in the early twelfth century. Monks of the esoteric schools, who served close to the royal family as spiritual advisers, received frequent opportunities for promotion in direct correlation to their loyalty to the retired monarch. Despite the competition between Shingon and Tendai, the retired sovereign managed to expand his control through a consolidation of his influence over initiation rituals at Sonshōji and Tōji, in which monks of the two schools were promoted.[59] Moreover, new religious rituals—the Hokke'e at Enshūji, the Daijōe at Hosshōji, and the Saishōe at Enshūji, collectively known as the three great official ceremonies of the northern capital (Kyoto)—were established as part of the new programs of Go-Sanjō and Shirakawa, opening yet another route for monk promotions. As the importance of Kōfukuji and the Yuima ceremony diminished, monks of the Tendai and Shingon schools and those in the southern capital were further distanced, aiding Go-Sanjō and Shirakawa in suppressing the ties between the Fujiwara Sekkanke and ranking Tendai monks. Most important, religious rituals that decided monk promotions were now all but limited to those held at the specially designated temples of the royal family. The retired monarch also managed to extend his control over appointments to the Office of Monastic Affairs by promoting the new religious ceremonies and favoring schools and lineages of his own preference.[60]

The retired monarch thus held ultimate authority to appoint monks to posts for a majority of the newly instituted Buddhist state rituals, in addition to being able to promote monks for services rendered by constructing temples or accompanying royal pilgrimages.[61] But there were still monks from the Office of Monastic Affairs that the retired monarch could not control completely. The route of promotion to the Office of Monastic Affairs for Nara monks was generally controlled by the Northern Fujiwara chieftain through Kōfukuji's Yuima ceremony. Monks of the esoteric schools from Nara who reached such ranking posts were thus an important group beyond the direct influence of the retired sovereign. And because of the forceful opposition of Kōfukuji, the retired monarch could not simply move the Yuima ceremony away from Nara. To make up for this flaw, he used the weakening of the Fujiwara chieftain as an opportunity to control appointments for the Office of Monastic Affairs while also working to influence the selection of lecturers and appointments for temple offices. For example, according to protocol the Fujiwara chieftain would select the Yuima lecturer, whose appointment was then announced in a royal edict "following the will of the heavenly monarch [*tenki*]" and based on a recommendation from the Office of Monastic Affairs. But as the power of the Fujiwara chieftain declined, "the will of the monarch" (with the retired sovereign behind the throne) became that much more powerful. As can be seen by the selection of Kakusei in 1114, it was Shirakawa who now held the authority to appoint lecturers.

Yet even Shirakawa's authority was in the end limited. He could not bend the entrenched protocols of the communities of Kōfukuji and other Nara schools, as is clearly evident in the repulsion of Kanshin as Yuima lecturer. Notably, it was only threats of demonstrations and the mobilization of holy symbols of the Kasuga deity by the Kōfukuji clergy that managed to stop the retired sovereign's willful promotions of his own clients from the esoteric schools. In other words, as the political clout of the retired monarch grew superior to that of the Sekkanke, and as the former also exercised his control of appointments to monastic offices more effectively, it was only the combined political and spiritual power of the clergy that could protect the traditional independence of Kōfukuji's largest and most important Buddhist ceremony. It is in this context that Shinjitsu and other "evil monks" eventually took control of the temple under the leadership of Fujiwara Tadazane.

In the end it seems inevitable that the clergy's interests and stance put it on a collision course with the retired sovereign in the twelfth century. Shirakawa's strict and one-sided punishment of Kōfukuji's "evil monks" during the protests of the Eikyū years (1113–1118) was one aspect of this confrontation. And Shirakawa's successor, Toba, again faced the Kōfukuji clergy soon after the beginning of his own tenure as retired monarch, beginning in 1129.

Kōfukuji's Clash with Toba In

Toba took over as senior retired monarch in the seventh month of 1129, after the death of Shirakawa. While he continued earlier policies, as the new court leader he also instigated important changes. In particular, his policies against Kōfukuji display a new vigor.[62] The disturbance over the appointment of the monk Chōen as Kiyomizudera abbot is evidence of this trend.[63]

Chōen was a craftsman who made Buddhist images (*busshi*) in Kyoto, and a protégé of Toba's most beloved consort, Lady Sanjō. He was also the son of Ensei, who had been forced to resign from his appointment as Kiyomizudera abbot because of a forceful protest by the Kōfukuji clergy in 1113. Chōen was not a Kōfukuji monk, and it is hardly surprising that he faced an angry Kōfukuji community when it became known that he, like his father, aspired to the abbotship of Kiyomizudera. As a result, he was attacked as he set out to Nara in the eleventh month of 1129.[64] Toba was infuriated when he received reports about the attack, and he decided to dispatch members of the Royal Police to arrest the unruly monks. He did so without consulting the Fujiwara chieftain Tadazane and compounded this breach of protocol by having the police officers violate the prohibition against officers entering temple grounds.[65] By appointing Chōen abbot of Kiyomizudera through a retired monarch's edict (*inzen*), Toba also ignored the normal procedures of going through the Fujiwara chieftain.[66]

In contrast to earlier incidents when the retired sovereign was forced to retreat or compromise because of protests from the clergy, this occasion undoubtedly marks an important departure from Shirakawa's policies against Kōfukuji. But it is also notable that the captain of the Royal Police, Minamoto Tameyoshi (thought to have been a retainer of Fujiwara Tadazane), sheltered Shinjitsu—one of the ringleaders—thereby suggesting a bond between Tadazane and Shinjitsu. This incident marked the beginning of Tadazane's expanded authority over Kōfukuji, which eventually resulted in unprecedented control of the temple and its "evil monks," effectively offsetting Toba's plans.

In an attempt to block Tadazane's strategy and to keep the Fujiwara chieftain in check, Toba had the monk Ryūkaku, a Murakami Genji by descent, appointed director (*bettō*) of Kōfukuji in the seventh month of 1133. Ryūkaku was close to Toba, whose ambitions to extend his control over Kōfukuji were never in doubt in the capital. Fujiwara Munetada noted in his diary that "there is no tradition of members of the Minamoto clan becoming temple officials [*jishi*], and since this secondary prelate [*sōzu*] is a Minamoto, this is an unprecedented appointment."[67] Not satisfied with these measures, Toba continued to promote his own monastic allies. Another incident occurred in the first month of 1137, when the Kōfukuji clergy lodged a "strong protest" to successfully oppose the retired monarch's appointment of the Tōji monk Jōkai as senior prelate (*sōjō*) in the Office of Monastic Affairs, which would have bypassed the more experienced Kōfukuji abbot Genkaku (Table 12.1, case 40).[68] Even the senior nobles thought that "there is much reason in Kōfukuji's appeal," and Toba was unable to mete out punishments.[69] On the other hand, contrary to the proper etiquette and precedent, Genkaku was excluded from the Saishōkō lecture in the fifth month the following year, because "the retired monarch did not approve of him."[70] And when Toba appointed Ryūkaku to succeed Genkaku as abbot in 1138, Shinjitsu and other members of the clergy responded with heated resistance. The resulting forceful protest in the third month of 1139 was subsequently blocked by the retired monarch, who managed to best the clergy by employing the warriors of Taira Tadamori and "the armed forces of various provinces" (Table 12.1, case 42). The clergy was thus prevented from entering the capital, and Shinjitsu and his associates were arrested.[71] Nonetheless, Ryūkaku subsequently suffered a severe blow when he tried to exert revenge on his enemies, and he relinquished the abbotship later in 1139.[72]

The retired sovereign's increased power and aggressive ambitions thus expanded the influence and the opposition of "evil monks," causing changes in the hierarchy within Kōfukuji itself. We see this clearly by the ninth month of 1138 in a directive from the Fujiwara chieftain issued immediately following the death of Genkaku. It ordered that "Extranumerary Head Monk (*Gon no Jōza*) Shinjitsu should manage the administrative duties of the temple."[73] Judging from later events, there can be no doubt that this edict was issued according to the wishes of Tadazane, father of regent Tadamichi. Tadazane attempted, and eventually managed, to strengthen his control of Kōfukuji through the "evil monk" Shinjitsu. Let us now turn to analyzing the context within the temple community that allowed for such a development.

Tadazane and Kōfukuji's "Evil Monks"

If we consider Tadazane's close relationship with Toba In, it becomes apparent that the Fujiwara chieftain's extended control over Kōfukuji's clergy was not directly intended to oppose the retired monarch but rather to organize the monastic community and promote peace between Kōfukuji and the court's leader. The pacification of a Kōfukuji protest in 1148, which was staved off by Tadazane (Table 12.1, case 46), and the willful appointment ten years earlier of Ryūkaku as abbot according to the wishes of the retired monarch, were actually enforced by the Fujiwara chieftain.[74] But why did the clergy, which responded so fiercely against the intervention of the retired monarch, submit to Tadazane, whose attitude toward Toba was quite amenable?

First, it should be noted that Shinjitsu, who managed the affairs of Kōfukuji without holding any rank or office in the official monastic hierarchy, received support from Kōfukuji's clergy. That support reflected the success of a bold but pragmatic leadership policy in opposition to traditional protocol, which dictated temple rulership by the abbot. Shinjitsu's unofficial leadership was a solution to the increasing need to suppress the power of "evil monks" and maintain order within the monastic community at the temple.[75]

Second, it must be pointed out that it was only Tadazane, maintaining a close and friendly relationship with Toba, who defended the retired sovereign's aggressive policies against Kōfukuji. During Toba's era, the retired sovereign's power stabilized and reached a new level of maturity compared to that of Shirakawa's days. As a result, it became more difficult to confront and oppose the retired monarch's authority through forceful protests. Tadazane's intermediary role between Toba and Kōfukuji stands out all the more, considering these circumstances.

Third, we must also pay attention to the clergy's role as local landholders (*zaichi ryōshu*), such as in the case of Shinjitsu. He and his son Genjitsu were scions of the Seiwa Genji clan, and we may assume that their martial might stemmed from their own position as landholders with warrior followers (*bushidan*).[76] There were in fact more than a few members of the monastic communities in Nara, including "evil monks," who based their power on their positions as local landholders.[77] Yet these monk leaders needed the support of a powerful patron in order to protect their holdings. The judicial authority for most estates held by Kōfukuji and Kasuga depended on that of the Northern Fujiwara chieftain—a tie with him was undoubtedly crucial to ranking Kōfukuji monks.[78] Indeed, after gaining the upper hand against Tadamichi, Tadazane and his successor Yorinaga used their authority as clan leaders to intervene in land issues to increase their power through clientage relationships with the clergy. Moreover, the confiscation of estates held by the lineage of Kakukei—Tadamichi's son and thus rival to Tadazane—before 1156 was perhaps related to new donations to Shinjitsu and other "evil monks," indicating the way in which both estates and powerful monks became useful to the Fujiwara chieftains.[79] In other words, the alliance of Tadazane and Yorinaga with Shinjitsu and other influential monks was strong enough to allow Shinjitsu to lead the Kōfukuji clergy during the Hōgen Coup, when he supported Yorinaga's failed *coup d'état* against Go-Shirakawa.

Conclusion

Herein I have traced the preconditions underlying the alliance of Shinjitsu and Kōfukuji with Fujiwara Yorinaga's military forces in the Hōgen Coup of 1156. The reasons lay in the movements of the clergy, the internal conditions of Kōfukuji, and in particular the political stance of the Hossō center in its opposition to the retired sovereign. I have touched on many aspects of capital politics, but the main points can be summarized as follows.

First, the tensions and conflicts between Kōfukuji and secular elites were intimately linked to intrusions into temple estates by provincial governors during the Regency era. But during the subsequent era of retired sovereigns, the main causes for conflict were the retired monarch's meddling with religious appointments and harsh punishments meted out to Kōfukuji's monks. To fully understand the opposition between the retired sovereign and Kōfukuji, we must take into account the ambitions of the latter's retainers, who included members of lesser branches of the Fujiwara clan that opposed the Sekkanke. In response, the Northern Fujiwara chieftain attempted to improve his own position by allying himself more closely with Kōfukuji, thereby expanding factional competition between the retired sovereign and the Sekkanke leaders to include monks as well as military leaders serving as governors. Nevertheless the more serious problem from the Hossō center's point of view was probably the retired monarch's efforts to take control of the Office of Monastic Affairs by intervening in monastic appointments for the Yuima ceremony, the sole route for official advancement of Nara monks. However, Shirakawa's attempts were either defeated or compromised because of the protests and resistance by Kōfukuji's monastic community. And yet the royal family was considerably strengthened during Toba's era, causing Tadazane, the Sekkanke leader, to strive for peaceful cooperation between Kōfukuji and the retired sovereign. In this way the establishment of the retired sovereign as court leader greatly affected the religious world. His constant pressure on Kōfukuji combined with the Sekkanke's political decline not only strengthened the alliance between the temple and the Northern Fujiwara regental lineage but also induced the clergy to augment its own political and military power. Obviously, these developments were closely related to the military trends characterized by the Hōgen Coup and the later Gempei fighting of the 1180s.

The effects of these developments in the religious sphere are perhaps most clearly demonstrated by the change in Kōfukuji's status after the Hōgen Coup. Specifically, Yorinaga's defeat deeply affected conditions within Kōfukuji. After he lost Yorinaga's support, even the bold and successful Shinjitsu was attacked and defeated by his own clergy when he cooperated with the Yamato governor Taira Motomori, who was performing a land survey.[80] Later Eshin (1124–1171), a son of Tadazane's client Munetada who had risen from obscurity to replace Kakukei as abbot, was eventually defeated by the clergy on the battlefield and ended his life in exile and disgrace.[81] The retired sovereign and the Taira clan subsequently increased the pressure on Kōfukuji, resulting in the forceful protest of 1173. It was then that Go-Shirakawa ordered the temple's proprietary holdings confiscated in entirety, a truly unique punishment (Table 12.1 case 58).[82] This was the reason why, in the end, the temple joined with Prince Mochihito's forces against the Taira in the early stages of the Gempei fighting, resulting in the unprecedented destruction of the entire Hossō complex at the hands of Taira troops late in 1180.

TABLE 12.1. *Late Heian-Era Monk Demonstrations in the Capital*

#	Date	Temple	Conflict	Result
1	968/7	Kōfukuji	Dispute with Tōdaiji	Unknown, record's authenticity doubtful
2	981/12	Enryakuji	The appointment of Yōkei as abbot of Hosshōji	Yōkei's resignation
3	986/2	Kōfukuji	The intrusion of an estate by governor of Bizen Province	Unknown
4	1006/7	Kōfukuji	Appeal against Yamato governor Minamoto Yorichika	Hossō monks excluded from public ceremonies
5	1017/6	Kōfukuji	Unknown	Unknown, record's authenticity doubtful
6	1028/10	Kinpusen	Appeal against Yamato governor Fujiwara Yasumasa	Unknown
7	1038/10	Enryakuji	Demands to replace head abbot Myōson	Unknown
8	1039/2	Enryakuji	Demands to replace head abbot Myōson	Myōson driven off Mt. Hiei
9	1066/1	Kōfukuji	Unknown	Unknown, record doubtful
10	1079/6	Enryakuji	Demands replacement of abbot of Gion	Protesters driven away
11	1081/3	Tōnomine	Appeal against Kōfukuji's attack on the Tōnomine monastery	Examination of local conditions
12	1085/10	Kumano	Appeal against officials of Owari Province	Unknown
13	1085/7	Kōfukuji	Appeal against intrusions into temple estates	Unknown
14	1092/9	Hiesha	Appeal against Kaga governor Fujiwara Tamefusa	Tamefusa deposed
15	1092/9	Enryakuji	Demands Tamefusa's exile in conjunction with #14	Tamefusa exiled
16	1093/8	Kōfukuji	Appeal against Ōmi governor Takashina Tameie	Tameie exiled
17	1095/10	Enryakuji	Appeal against Mino governor Minamoto Yoshitsuna	Protesters driven away
18	1102/5	Enryakuji	Demands Ningen appointed Hōjōji abbot	Ningen appointed
19	1102/8	Kōfukuji	Demands to stop retired emperor's verdict against head abbot Kakushin	No protest staged in the capital
20	1102/9	Tōdaiji	Appeal against intrusions by Kōfukuji	Verdict by Shirakawa
21	1103/3	Kōfukuji	Demands to change referees for the Yuima ceremony	Tadazane complies
22	1103/7	Enryakuji	Unknown	Protesters driven away
23	1104/2	Iwashimizu Hachiman	Demands for appointment of a reconstruction manager	No protest in the capital
24	1105/1	Enryakuji	Demands the deposition of manager of Enshūji	Shirakawa complies
25	1105/6	Hie, Gion	Appeal against Royal Police Captain Nakahara Norimasa	Unknown
26	1105/8	Enryakuji	Appeal against Kyūshū official Fujiwara Suenaka	Unknown
27	1105/10	Enryakuji	Appeal against Iwashimizu because of #26	Suenaka exiled
28	1108/3	Enryakuji, Onjōji	Demands to replace performer of initiation ceremony at Sonshōji	Protesters driven away
29	1108/4	Enryakuji, Onjōji	Demands to replace performer of initiation ceremony at Sonshōji	Shirakawa complies
30	1113/int. 3	Kōfukuji	Demands to replace Kiyomizudera abbot	Shirakawa complies

(Continued)

31	1113/4	Enryakuji	Demands to exile Kōfukuji head abbot and other ranking monks	Shirakawa complies
32	1113/4	Kōfukuji	Demands to stop exile of temple officials	Protesters driven away
33	1113/4	Enryakuji	Plans to confront Kōfukuji clergy in battle	Warriors stop rioters
34	1113/9	Enryakuji	Demands the reinstatement of Ningō as head abbot of Tendai	Protesters driven away
35	1116/8	Kōfukuji	Appeals against Sanuki governor Fujiwara Akiyoshi	No protest in the capital
36	1116/10	Onjōji	Appeal to make Kitashirakawa's Hosshōji a branch of Onjōji	Protesters driven away
37	1118/5	Enryakuji	Demands to appoint abbot for Chikuzen's Anrakuji	No protest in the capital
38	1120/8	Kōfukuji	Appeal against Izumi governor Minamoto Masataka	Masataka is deposed
39	1123/7	Enryakuji	Demands the release of "evil monks" apprehended in Echizen	Protesters driven away from capital
40	1137/2	Kōfukuji	Appeal against appointment of Tōji monk Jōkai as "Great Master" over Kōfukuji head abbot Genkaku	Toba In complies
41	1138/4	Enryakuji	Demands to prohibit Kamo Shrine officials to participate in Hie festival	Toba In complies
42	1139/3	Kōfukuji	Demands to stop appointment of Ryūkaku as head abbot	Protesters driven away
43	1144/11	Kōfukuji	Appeal against Yamato governor Minamoto Tadakiyo	Tadakiyo transferred to Iwami
44	1147/4	Enryakuji	Demands to transform Echizen's Hakusan into a branch temple of Enryakuji	Protesters driven out of capital
45	1147/6	Enryakuji	Demands to exile Harima governor Tadamori and son because of confrontation with Gion shrine head	Warriors fend off protesters
46	1148/8	Kōfukuji	Unknown	Protesters return after order from Tadazane
47	1150/8	Kōfukuji	Demands to appoint abbot for Kōfukuji and Iwashimizu	Ryūkaku re-appointed head abbot
48	1154/9	Enryakuji	Demands to cancel pardon of Kaga resident Rinkō	Toba In complies
49	1160/10	Enryakuji	Appeal regarding burning of Echizen's Kamado no miya and Anrakuji	Unknown
50	1162/int. 2	Enryakuji	Demands to replace head abbot Kakuchū	Kakuchū deposed
51	1162/11	Enryakuji	Demands to make Echizen's Anrakuji a branch of Enryakuji	Permission not granted
52	1165/8	Enryakuji	Conflict with Kōfukuji, parts of Kiyomizudera are burned down	Kiyomori refuses to confront monks
53	1165/8	Kōfukuji	Demands to have Tendai head abbot and others exiled	Go-Shirakawa obliges
54	1169/12	Enryakuji	Appeal against Owari provincial proprietor Narichika	Narichika's exile (later pardoned)
55	1170/1	Enryakuji	Demands to have Narichika exiled	Narichika exiled
56	1171/9	Kōfukuji	Demands to establish new branches and estates in Shimotsuke and to exile former governor Nobutō	No protest in the capital
57	1172/12	Kōfukuji	Appeal against retainers of Taira Shigemori	Protesters driven away
58	1173/11	Kōfukuji	Appeal to punish Enryakuji and pardon Kōfukuji monks	Protesters driven away
59	1177/4	Enryakuji	Appeal against Kaga governor Morotaka	Protesters driven away
60	1177/4	Enryakuji	Demands to have Morotaka exiled because of #59	Morotaka exiled

Notes

1. This summary of Kuroda Toshio's "gates of power (*kenmon*) theory" is a condensed version of that in the introduction to Adolphson 2000. Among Kuroda's own essays, particularly helpful are Kuroda Toshio 1980, Kuroda Toshio 1975a, Kuroda Toshio 1976, Kuroda Toshio 1975b, and Kuroda Toshio 1963.

2. Kuroda Toshio 1976, 17–18, 31, and 78; and Kuroda Toshio 1963, 265–79.

3. Kuroda Toshio 1976, 277–80.

4. Kuroda Toshio 1976, 17–18, and 21; and Kuroda Toshio 1963, 275–79. See also Mass 1999, 8.

5. Kuroda Toshio 1980, 255–56; and Kuroda Toshio 1976, 454–55.

6. Kuroda Toshio 1980, 257; and in English, Kuroda Toshio 1996.

7. Besides the various studies by Motoki and Adolphson, also see Taira Masayuki 1992b.

8. See Hurst 1976 and Adolphson 2000.

9. Interpreter's note: The English essay here is an interpretation of chapter 7 in Motoki Yasuo 1996, 241-267. The source referred to here is *Gukanshō*, vol. 4. See Okami Masao and Akamatsu Toshihide 1967, 206. For an English translation, see Brown and Ishida 1979.

10. See *Hōgen monogatari*, vol. 1: "Shin'in gosho kaku monmon katame no koto tsuketaru ikusa hyōjō no koto." Interpreter's note: An accessible text in Japanese is Tochigi Yoshitada 1992. See page 4 for this section, as well as the *Gukanshō*, vol. 4, on Go-Shirakawa (see Okami Masao and Akamatsu Toshihide 1967, 220–21).

11. *Heihanki* Hōgen 1 (1156) /7/11.

12. See Motoki Yasuo 1996, 220–30.

13. Fujiwara Tadamichi remained viceroy and, as such, was opposed by Tadazane and Yorinaga, as well as by other members of less influential Fujiwara lineages who also served the retired *tennō*. Interpreter's note: To clarify some relationships mentioned in the text, see Figure 12.1.

14. Interpreter's note: Although the "medieval age" has been commonly considered to begin with the establishment of the Kamakura Bakufu in 1185, many Japanese scholars have begun to include the epoch of the retired monarchs as court leaders, termed in Japanese the "*Insei* age" (1086–1185), as well. To exacerbate the debate, a recent volume even suggests that the medieval age in Japan has its origins in the fourteenth century. See Mass 1997, 1–14. In either case, the usage of such terms and the general issue of periodization deserve further attention in a joined effort by Japanese and Western scholars.

15. Interpreter's note: Appointments to the court-controlled Office of Monastic Affairs and appointments of monks to preside at official Buddhist ceremonies tended to articulate the balance of power among the eight original schools of Buddhist studies professed by monks in Nara and Kyoto. In this regard, see the *Sōgō bunin* register of prelates' appointments, in *Dai nihon bukkyō zensho*, Kōfukuji sōsho, pt. 1.

16. Interpreter's note: See Tokoro Isao 1970, 160; and Katsuno Ryūshin 1955, 10–11.

17. See "Tendai zasu Ryōgen kishō" in Takeuchi Rizō's *Heian ibun*, vol. 2, doc. 303; and Kuroda Toshio 1980, 28–30. Despite efforts to restrict the usage of arms among the clergy, Ryōgen is often blamed for secularizing Enryakuji, due to his welcoming of Fujiwara Morosuke's son, Jinzen, as disciple and successor. Interpreter's note: The Tendai school was founded by the monk Saichō at the beginning of the Heian Period after his

return from a trip to China and a visit to the leading T'ient'ai monastery there. It became one of the leading schools of Buddhism and had its headquarters at Enryakuji on Mount Hiei, northeast of Kyoto. Saichō emphasized scholarship and what was known as exoteric Buddhism in contrast to Kūkai's esoteric (*mikkyō*) Buddhism. For more on Saichō and his founding of the Tendai school, see Groner 1984. And on Ryōgen, see Groner 2002.

18. On the activities of the "evil monks" of that era see Katsuno Ryūshin 1955, 4; and Kuroda Toshio 1980, 28–38. Interpreter's note: In English see Adolphson 2000.

19. Interpreter's note: Kōfukuji was in Nara and it was closely associated with the Northern Fujiwara regental lineage, the Sekkanke.

20. For a detailed treatment of Hosshōji, the struggle for its abbotship between the Enchin and Ennin lineages of Tendai, and disturbances surrrounding Yōkei's appointment as Tendai head, see Hiraoka Jōkai 1981a, esp. 581–85.

21. Interpreter's note: Although Motoki does not elaborate further concerning the different problems facing Enryakuji and Kōfukuji, it should be noted that the Fujiwara chieftain likely felt compelled to court the Tendai center more actively because of its higher degree of autonomy.

22. One could argue that incidents 26 and 27, concerning the appointment of an abbot for Anrakuji in Chikuzen Province, were problems related to estates and branch temples. But as Mikawa Kei demonstrates, this disturbance was caused by the retired *tennō*'s attempt to appoint his own retainer Kōsei, abbot at Iwashimizu Hachimangū, to lead Anrakuji as well. This incident therefore fits into the category of appointments. See Mikawa Kei 1996 and Uwayokote Masataka et al. 1994, 104–08.

23. For a treatment of conditions during the religious demonstrations of Shirakawa's and Toba's eras, as well as of the political backdrop in general, see Takahashi Masaaki 1984. The enforcement of punishments and protests directed at the retired *tennō*'s mansion are discussed in Motoki Yasuo 1993.

24. Interpreter's note: The new circumstances to which Motoki refers were the result of the victory by the Go-Shirakawa faction over that supporting the junior retired monarch Sutoku. Matters in the capital became more stable as competition within and between powerful noble factions decreased, if only for two decades.

25. Interpreter's note: Kiyomizudera was Kōfukuji's most important branch temple in Kyoto.

26. The *Shakke kampanki*, an exposition of clerical ranks written in the fourteenth century, states that "lecturers do not receive appointments, but are promoted directly in the prelacy hierarchy (*gōi*)" as "a short cut to promotion." Further, "Such promotions are strictly prohibited in the southern capital [Nara], but there are many such precedents since ancient times in the northern capital [Kyoto]." See *Gunsho ruijū* 24 (Shakke bu).

27. Nishiguchi Junko 1986, esp. 248–52.

28. See Fujiwara Michinaga's *Midō kampakuki* Kankō 3 (1006) 7/12 through 7/15.

29. Interpreter's note: At issue was the Hyakuza Ninnōe, a ceremony performed for the realm in times of national crisis. See *Shōyūki* 1023 5/20.

30. The governors of Ōmi and Bitchū, Minamoto Yasumasa and Fujiwara Masaie, were retainers of Michinaga. See the register of governors in Miyazaki Yasumitsu 1990, vol. 4, 135 and 279–280; and Satō Ken'ichi 1964, 335. Interpreter's note: on these household officials and their service as provincial governors, see Hurst 1974, esp. 48-49.

31. Ōyama Kyōhei 1985.

32. See Nishiguchi Junko 1986, 248–52.

33. Interpreter's note: The "three great rituals of the northern capital" (*hokkyō no sandaie*) were established as a counterweight to Kōfukuji's near monopoly of the three great lecture meetings held in Nara and the royal palace.

34. *Chūyūki* Ten'ei 3 (1112) /4/24.

35. See *Tōji chōja bunin*, a register of Tōji abbots (*chōja*), in *Zoku zoku Gunsho ruijū* (Kokusho kangyōkai 1969).

36. See the *Sōgō bunin*, 159. For more on Hanshun, see Takahashi Masaaki 1984, 98–104.

37. *Denryaku* Kōwa 3 (1101) /10/17.

38. *Chūyūki* Kōwa 4 (1102) /8/6 and 21. Interpreter's note: See also Adolphson 2000, 104–107.

39. This incident is described in detail in the twelfth-century journal *Chōshūki*, written by the courtier Minamoto Morotoki. See the entry for Eikyū 1 (1113) /int. 3/20 and 22. It is also described in the *Eikyū Gan'nenki*, in the entry for Eikyū 1/int. 3/20 and 21. Interpreter's note: See also *Dai nihon shiryō* (Tōkyō daigaku shiryō hensanjo 1901-*)*, series 3, vol. 14, 138-40. The latter seems to be a section of the *gekiki*, or records kept by the secretaries of the Council of State. The appointment of an Enryakuji-trained abbot at Kiyomizudera, Kōfukuji's most important branch in the Kyoto capital, was thus perceived as a serious threat to the Kōfukuji-based Hossō school's presence in the capital. For an English account of this conflict, see Adolphson 2000, 115–17. The dispute between Kōfukuji and the retired monarch over Kiyomizudera's abbotship emerged early in Toba's era as well, when Toba In began to pursue his goals more aggressively by arresting monks. This marked another turning point in the relationship between court and temple.

40. *Chūyūki* Eikyū 2 (1114) /5/29.

41. *Chūyūki* Eikyū 2 (1114)/5/29. The regent Tadazane responded to Munetada that "to have Kakusei serve as master of ceremonies is an honor from heaven. His age should not matter, and it should therefore be commanded today." The right to give final and formal approval was thus held by the regent, but he acted according to Shirakawa In's wishes.

42. *Chūyūki* Eikyū 2 (1114) /10/26.

43. *Sanne jōikki*, section 1.

44. *Denryaku* Eikyū 4 (1116) /10/11.

45. *Sanne jōiki*, 22–23; and *Sōgō bunin*, 180.

46. For a thorough record of this incident from its beginning to the retired sovereign's verdict, see *Chūyūki* entries dated Kōwa 4 (1102) /7/11, 12, 16, 18, 19, 20, 27, and 28; and /8/1, 2 7.

47. Kakushin was actually Tadazane's uncle, but the latter was adopted by Kakushin's father (Tadazane's grandfather), Morozane, making the monk and Tadazane stepbrothers. See Figure 12.1.

48. *Denryaku* Kōwa 4 (1102)/7/29.

49. *Chūyūki* Kōwa 4 (1102) /10/9.

50. See the entries in *Chūyūki* and *Denryaku* for Kōwa 5 (1103) /5/11. The pardoning of Kakushin was intended to calm the clergy, which had been rioting since the third month.

51. *Chūyūki* Eikyū 1 (1113) /4/1. See also Takahashi's study, noted earlier. Interpreter's note: Jikkaku's full title was "provisional lesser secondary prelate" (*gon no shōsōzu*) in the Office of Monastic Affairs. The Enryakuji clergy demanded Jikkaku's exile following a Kōfukuji demonstration in the capital in the intercalary third month of 1113, when some of the Hossō protesters were accused of having caused damage to Gionsha

(alt. Yasaka Jinja) in Kyoto, which shrine was closely associated with Enryakuji as a detached cloister (*betsuin*).

52. See *Kōfukuji ryakunendaiki*, in Zoku gunsho ruijū (Zatsubu 2), 144.

53. *Denryaku* Eikyū 1 (1113)/6/8.

54. *Denryaku* Gen'ei 1 (1118) /8/3. See also 9/3.

55. *Denryaku* Eikyū 5 (1117) /5/21.

56. According to the *Kasuga kannushi Suketaka ki*, the sacred Kasuga branch had been moved already in the fifth month of 1116 (Eikyū 4). See *Zōho zoku shiryō taisei* (Zōho shiryō taisei kangyōkai 1955-59). Regarding the origins of this dispute, the same journal states that "the Sanuki governor Akiyoshi, the son of Middle Counselor Akitaka, harassed the temple's servants in this province." Various stages of this incident are also described in the *Denryaku*, in entries dated Eikyū 4 (1116) 7/13, 14, 23, 24, 26, 27, and 28; and 8/3, 13, and 15.

57. *Denryaku* Eikyū 4 (1116) /7/26.

58. According to *Denryaku* Eikyū 4 (1116)/12/17 and Eikyū 5 (1117) /5/21, the deputy was punished but Akiyoshi remained governor until the first year of Hōan (1120). Interpreter's note: Kakushin was immediately reinstated by Shirakawa, who, as retired sovereign, acted contrary to the wishes of his own grandson, the reigning Toba Tennō.

59. Interpreter's note: My own research suggests that Shirakawa In's policies were less consistent towards Tendai than Shingon institutions. As I have argued (Adolphson, 2000), the retired Shirakawa initially promoted Enryakuji monks. Later, however, he shifted his support to Onjōji once he realized that he could not gain the control he wanted of the monastic community on Mt. Hiei. Nonetheless Motoki's point is well taken: Shirakawa was surely trying to shift the balance among the religious establishments by promoting certain temples over established and more independent ones.

60. Regarding establishment of the "three ceremonies of the northern capital," see Hiraoka Jōkai 1981b and Taira Masayuki 1992a.

61. Nishiguchi Junko 1986, 251–52.

62. In general Toba's reign is characterized by the end of Tadazane's seclusion and a hiatus in the confrontation with the Sekkanke. But this also represented the weakened position of the Northern Fujiwara regent and the strengthening of the royal family under the retired sovereign's leadership. In this way, the posture of Toba In reflects a more aggressive policy vis-à-vis Kōfukuji.

63. For a detailed treatment of this incident, see Tsunoda Bun'ei 1977, 341–42. And for an analysis of its historical significance, see Uwayokote Masataka 1981, 165.

64. *Chōshūki* Daiji 4 (1129) /11/11.

65. See the entries in *Chōshūki* and *Chūyūki* for Daiji 4 (1129)/11/11, and 12.

66. *Chūyūki* Daiji 4 (1129)/11/30.

67. *Chūyūki* Chōshō 2 (1133) /7/17.

68. *Chūyūki* Hōen 3 (1137) /1/14, /2/11; see also *Sōgō bunin*, 210.

69. *Chūyūki* Hōen 3/1/24.

70. See *Kōfukuji bettō shidai*, a chronology of the tenures of Kōfukuji abbots, in Dai Nihon Bukkyō Zensho, Kōfukuji sōsho pt. 2, 15.

71. See *Kōfukuji bettō shidai*, 16; and the *Nanto taishu jūrakki* entry dated Hōen 5 (1139) /3/9-29. Regarding this incident, also see Takahashi Masaaki 1984, 198–99.

72. *Nanto taishu jūrakki* Hōen 5/11/10-/12/10; and *Hyakurenshō* Hōen 5/11/16, 12/2. Interpreter's note: Ryūkaku did return to serve as head abbot of Kōfukuji from 1150 to 1156.

73. *Kōfukuji ryakunendaiki*, 147 and *Kōfukuji bettō shidai*, 15.

74. *Taiki* Kyūan 4 (1148) /8/27. Interpreter's note: Motoki explains Tadazane's role in the incident more extensively on page 227 of his book. See also *Nanto taishu jūrakki* Kyūan 6 (1150) 6/16.

75. Interpreter's note: The same trend is evident in the opposition Tadazane's estranged son, Tadamichi, later faced when he attempted, and failed, to control Kōfukuji through his son Kakukei, who had entered the temple as assistant abbot some time before 1139. See Motoki Yasuo 1996, 223-24.

76. For more information regarding Shinjitsu, see Hirata Toshiharu 1986, esp. 282–86.

77. For example, the "evil monk" Kakunin derived his military power from his position as a landholder during his monastic career in Nara. See Hisano Nobuyoshi 1980. The strengthening of Kōfukuji's alliance with the Kasuga Shrine and the temple's absorption of shrine associates, which provided an important foundation for the local land holders and the wealthy cultivator stratum in Yamato, was noted earlier in this essay. According to Takeuchi Rizō, Kōfukuji assembled "secular warriors" in large numbers from Yamato in cases of large-scale forceful protests. See Takeuchi Rizō 1958. Interpreter's note: In the latter essay Takeuchi represented a longstanding assumption, for which there is, in fact, no contemporary evidence. Warriors were never recruited or used in temple protests in the pre-1400 era. See Adolphson 2000, chapter 6. However, Kōfukuji did hold a position of political leadership within the local landholding class in Yamato at the time. It is also possible to discern the employment of warrior bands from nearby during internal disputes between temple leadership and temple monks. For example according to the *Kōfukuji bettō shidai*, head abbot Eshin dispatched Minamoto Yoshimoto and Minamoto Tadakuni during a battle with the clergy.

78. For example, according to an entry dated Nimpyō 3 (1153) /6/6 in the *Heihanki*, Yorinaga exercised his authority as chieftain during an internal dispute over land between monks within Kōfukuji.

79. Regarding the confiscation of the monk Kakukei's estates, see *Heihanki* Hōgen 1 (1156) 7/11.

80. Regarding Shinjitsu's decline and fall, see Tsunoda Bun'ei 1977 and Hirata Toshiharu 1986.

81. *Kōfukuji bettō shidai*, 19. See also Ōyama Kyōhei 1985.

82. For an extensive treatment of this incident, see Tanaka Fumihide 1994, 170–72.

13

Japan's Medieval World

Ishimoda Shō

Introduction by Joan R. Piggott

Born in Sapporo in 1912, Ishimoda Shō is widely regarded as a master historian of premodern Japan. Until 1948, Ishimoda worked as an editor. Then, based on the growing reputation his published research was gaining for him, he was appointed lecturer in the history of law at the prestigious Hōsei University Law School. He later served terms as dean and trustee there before retiring in 1981. Ishimoda's collected works, published in sixteen volumes after his death in 1986, attest to his interest in a broad range of historical issues spanning prehistory through what he himself termed "the second medieval age" during the fourteenth through sixteenth centuries.

In 1946 Ishimoda published what is probably his most frequently read monograph, *Chūseiteki sekai no keisei* (*The Formation of the Medieval World*). Begun in 1944, therein Ishimoda presented his ideas concerning the historical transition from "classical" (*kodai*) to "medieval" (*chūsei*) based on his reading of hundreds of extant documents concerning Kuroda Estate in Iga Province, a proprietary holding (*shōen*) of the royal temple Tōdaiji in Nara. That estate had endured through a long history, from the eleventh through the fifteenth centuries. Ishimoda saw Kuroda as a microcosm within which the broader national transition from classical to medieval could be traced. Tremendously popular, the book was reprinted in many editions, by its original publisher Itō shoten up to 1956; and then, from 1957 onward, by Tokyo University Press. In 1988 it was published yet again by Iwanami Shoten as volume 5 of Ishimoda's collected works.[1] Almost sixty years after its original publication, Ishimoda's story of Kuroda's history as a microcosm of national historical change still strikes readers as deeply insightful and provocative, and specialists read and cite it today.

I chose to render one chapter entitled "The Medieval World" from that book into English because in it Ishimoda elaborates many of his conclusions based on his study of Kuroda Estate, including how the transition from classical to medieval affected relations between capital and countryside. The essay presents a challenging read, however, because of its diffuse style—the Japanese sometimes strikes the reader as stream-of-consciousness—and because the reader needs some background from the book in which the essay is embedded. For that reason an abstract of Ishimoda's reading of Kuroda Estate history —even beyond the chronological parameters of this book—is necessary.

Ishimoda elaborates Kuroda's story in four main sections. In the first he describes early but ultimately unsuccessful efforts by the bureaucrat and land opener, Fujiwara Saneto, to reopen fallow fields in various parts of Nabari

District and elsewhere in Iga, where he functioned as a private landlord (*shiryōshu*) in the mid-eleventh century. The second section describes increasing activity by Tōdaiji's administrative monks, who were developing the temple's landed interests as a state-recognized estate proprietor (*ryōke*) from the mid-tenth century onward. The third section examines the emergence of resident landlords (*zaichi ryōshu*) and their associated warrior bands (*bushidan*) at Kuroda—by the later eleventh century the most successful of these was allying himself with the provincial headquarters against Tōdaiji, initiating a struggle that lasted over three centuries. The fourth section relates how in the thirteenth century estate residents, including resident landlords, grew increasingly hostile to temple management and formed "evil bands" (*akutō*) to resist temple control. Such bands remained active until Kuroda Estate faded from the historical record in the fifteenth century.

Epochal moments in the estate's history include 1033, when Tōdaiji's mountain forest (*soma*), including some twenty-five *chō*—73.5 acres—of fields worked by temple "servants" and exempt from provincial taxes, was established as a proprietary holding of the temple; 1088, when the Iga provincial headquarters recruited the Nabari district chieftain (*gunji*) as its ally against growing temple interests in Nabari, public lands called *dezukuri*, meaning "cultivated land outside the estate"; 1145, when an official hearing in the capital at Kyoto determined that 360 *koku*—enough rice to feed 360 persons for a year—produced on fields cultivated by temple "woodsmen" in Nabari District should go to the temple to replace other revenues owed to the temple by Iga Province; 1157, when the temple made one of its high ranking monks, Kakunin, custodian (*azukaridokoro*), and charged him with responsibility for managing its interests at Kuroda Estate; and 1174, when an order from the retired monarch's office finally made Kuroda an estate completely secure against entry by provincial officials, as a *funyū shōen*. Although Taira authority in the capital and Gempei fighting in the 1180s caused havoc at Kuroda Estate as elsewhere, Minamoto Yoritomo's eagerness to present himself as a champion of the gods and Buddhas, plus his cooperation in rebuilding Tōdaiji, meant that during the era of Kamakura warrior government (1180–1333) temple interests were not adversely impacted. Few Tōdaiji estates had military stewards (*jitō*) assigned to them. In Ishimoda's mind, the result was that temple management at Kuroda no shō during the Kamakura Period remained "classical" in form, even though outside Kuroda's small world the authority of warrior leaders in Kamakura reflected a significant historical advance for the interests of resident landlords who were none other than the *bakufu*'s housemen.

Despite strong temple resistance in the thirteenth centry, small-scale resident landlords at Kuroda made significant advances in opening new fields and establishing dependent relations with less successful cultivators. And these same resident landlords joined other estate residents to resist rent increases imposed by the temple. For Ishimoda, these resident landlords and their warrior bands who resisted temple authority represented a key vector of medieval history, while the temple's proprietary interests represented the waning classical past.

An epochal moment in this struggle between the classical and the medieval at Kuroda came in 1264, when Tōdaiji was forced to call on the *bakufu* and its provincial constable (*shugo*) to fight "evil bands" at Kuroda. Thereafter, outbreaks of violent resistance continued in the 1270s and 1280s, in the early 1300s, and in the 1320s. Only in 1343 did the Ashikaga *shugo* Niki Gikaku finally succeed in defeating the Kuroda "evil bands." But such did not prove to be a victory for the temple. Instead, the constable proceeded to organize the defeated *akutō* into his own band while asserting his authority over temple fields and cultivators.[2] So began what Ishimoda termed "the second medieval age," which was characterized by the "purely feudal" territorial rulership by the *shugo*. Whereas Ishimoda considered the Kamakura Period one of transition, this second medieval age under the Ashikaga Bakufu saw increasingly autonomous *shugo* domains; the dissemination of Shinran's Amidist teachings to commoners; the spread of Kakuichi's *Heike monogatari* (*Tale of the Heike*) as popular literature; diffusion of the spirit of medieval law in the 1232 *Judicial Formulary* (*Goseibai shikimoku*) and through new provincial law codes issued by the *shugo*; and a complete synthesis of "national" (*kokuminteki*) and "commoner" (*shōminteki*) cultures. So did Tōdaiji's Kuroda no shō, an artifact of "the classical" that had survived the first medieval age, finally fade into history. The last extant document from the estate—an oath whereby estate residents pleaded with Tōdaiji to assert its power against the *shugo* in return for their disvowing of *akutō* ways—is dated 1439. But the request and Tōdaiji's help was to prove of no avail. The provincial constable's authority in Nabari District was already substantial, and the Nara temple was weak.

Ishimoda's essay, "The Medieval World," which is taken from the fourth section of the book, comprises six parts. In the first of these, Ishimoda contrasts written law as it functioned in the classical capital with the unwritten custom of agrarian hamlets in the classical countryside. For Ishimoda, Chinese ways, on which the *tennō*-centered court's government was based, represented "the classical world"; while the foundation of medieval law, seen in the 1232 *Judicial Formulary* (*Goseibai shikimoku*), eventually resulted from a synthesis of custom and *ritsuryō*.[3]

The second part of the essay focuses on the changing concept of *dōri* through time. *Dōri* might be alternatively translated as "what is right," "custom," or "law," as it changed from a transcendent "way of the gods," to represent the more pragmatic, man-made practices of resident land openers and warrior bands in the later Heian age, to its final incorporation into the *Judicial Formulary* in Kamakura times. For these two early sections of the essay, Ishimoda the professor of legal history is at the lectern.

In the third section, Ishimoda turns to religion and literature in the later Heian Period to seek evidence of an aristocracy in crisis and a society rent with contradictions: between Fujiwara regents and lesser aristocratic families; between the *tennō* and the regents; between the regents and old religious institutions like Tōdaiji; and between elites in the capital and those in the countryside. In religion, Ishimoda focuses attention on the diffusion of Amidism. Although embraced by aristocrats in Heian times, Ishimoda sees

Amidism presenting a sharp critique of aristocratic values—it insisted on the equality of all beings in terms of their potential for salvation. In literature, Ishimoda explores new genres of fiction, especially romances (*monogatari*) and military narratives (*gunkimono*). These were, he says, intellectual responses to the existential crisis of the aristocracy. The Heian and Kamakura periods marked a time of transition, from the sprouting of seeds in late Heian to their profuse growth in Kamakura times. They provided a solid foundation for what Ishimoda characterizes as "the three pillars of Japan's medieval world": the *Judicial Formulary* of the Kamakura Bakufu dating from 1232; the corpus of war tales recounting fighting between the Taira and the Minamoto between 1180 and 1185 compiled in Kakuichi's *Heike monogatari*; and the primer containing the sayings of the Amidist preacher Shinran (1173-1262) known as the *Tannishō* (*Notes on Lamenting Deviations*).[4] All three, he argues, demonstrate a common determination to educate and enlighten the masses. And all three contributed to a heightened self-consciousness of commoners during Japan's "first medieval age."[5]

In his fourth section, Ishimoda's gaze focuses on Kakuichi's *Heike monogatari*, which Ishimoda saw as a work of "popular literature" that was accessible to and ultimately shaped by commoners. Then a fifth section elaborates Ishimoda's notion of popular culture, which he sees as having rejected Chinese ways long associated with the *tennō*'s court, government, and culture. And finally, in his sixth section, Ishimoda briefly outlines his view of Tōdaiji and Kuroda Estate as representative structures of the waning classical age. In his view, their vulnerability in late Kamakura times presaged the full emergence of Japan's medieval world.

Scholars in Japan today would certainly argue for amending certain of Ishimoda's notions.[6] But at a time when historical study has become narrow and specialized, Ishimoda's broad inquiry into the trajectories of historical change from classical to medieval times seen through the multiple lenses of law, culture, and politics cannot but impress and inspire.[7]

Ishimoda Shō

Japan's Medieval World

Interpreted by Joan R. Piggott

The formation of Japan's medieval world was a more complex and multifaceted process than elsewhere in world history.[8] That complexity was rooted in the slow decline of the classical world. The medieval world did not emerge fully mature out of the destruction of the classical world because the structures of the classical age exhibited great vitality. The maturing process of the new medieval world was extremely gradual and uneven, with elements of both the classical and medieval worlds coexisting throughout.

There was no unified process by which the classical world was transformed into the medieval one. Instead, there were multiple complex historical trajectories. For instance, the proprietary holdings of shrines and temples (*jisharyō*) [like Kuroda no shō] continued as prominent components of the proprietary system from classical into medieval times. In addition, aristocratic society (*kizoku shakai*) persisted throughout classical and medieval times, albeit under quite different circumstances. Nonetheless, classical elements declined in an increasingly broad fashion during Heian times, and we can also trace the emergence of elements opposing these classical structures. In Japan structures of the classical age contained seeds of change—for example, early estates (*shoki shōen*) gave birth to the larger and more autonomous estates held by temples and shrines in later Heian times, while spiritual beliefs of the classical age spawned the antecedents to those of the medieval world. Such are just a few of the reasons for the complexity of the religious culture of Kamakura times.

The process by which the classical world produced forces inimical to itself advanced over the long centuries of the Heian and Kamakura periods both within urban aristocratic society and within agrarian hamlet society. At the same time classical structures were in decline, the various vectors that gave shape to the medieval world advanced and formed the rich if chaotic streams of Kamakura culture. One such vector was the merger of certain classical traces with an evolving system of lordship in rural hamlets. A second vector was the worsening of contradictions within classical structures themselves. As these two vectors conjoined, the basis for reciprocal relations joining the Heian capital and rural hamlets took shape.

Custom and Law

Power relations in hamlet society are said to have been based on custom. Warrior law, which developed out of agrarian society, is termed "customary law" to distinguish it from "courtier law," which was rooted in power relations founded on Chinese-style administrative and penal law (*ritsuryō*). Although there may be a degree of truth in this, it is difficult to discuss customary law with any degree of specificity. It is more informative to investigate the emergence of the landed warrior-proprietor (*ryōshu bushi*) stratum and its historic transformation. That is what I have done through my research into Kuroda Estate (Kuroda no shō) in *The Formation of the Medieval World*.

When cultivation is done by slaves or members of one's own kin, legal thinking is unnecessary. One's possession of the land is guaranteed by residents of the hamlet or neighborhood. The operation of hamlet society follows custom, and custom works best the smaller the area under cultivation. Generally it cannot be separated from a particular locale because the social life of the community depends on the group. The right to use common land, one's place in the order of irrigation, rights to residential land or to small newly opened fields, and the perquisites of landlords vis-à-vis members of the hamlet all depend on the customary law recognized by the community. From classical into medieval times, the social hierarchy of the hamlet depended on such custom.

However, as landed proprietors (*ryōshu*) emerged and had cultivators work the land during the Heian Period, the mode of social organization was significantly transformed from one based on custom to one necessitating rights and law. Custom was not what maintained and guaranteed the rights of landholders who resided outside the hamlet vis-à-vis their land. The universalized law of transcendent political society was required. According to such law, the right to hold land depended on proof documents (*kugen*)—such written deeds were critical to land openers. Thus, the *tennō*-centered polity based on *ritsuryō* law came to have new meaning for the agrarian hamlet. Although it is true that during the Heian Period provincial headquarters (*kokuga*) posed a threat to local land openers and local landlords (*zaichi ryōshu*), the right to hold land was itself guaranteed by these same provincial headquarters. Without the provincial authorities, there would have been no means to certify the rights of land openers regarding newly opened fields.

During the Nara Period (710–784), the integrative and prescriptive aspects of provincial authority were very important. Locals were managed by outsiders, the provincial governors (*kokushi*). But in the Heian Period land-opening landlords feared that provincial headquarters would rob them of their surplus even while they viewed the authorities as guarantors of their legal rights to open and hold land.[9] Both aspects of this relationship must be recognized. In the Heian countryside, political organization and law were no longer something coming from outside. Provincial authority was seen as a force for order by the land openers, something that guaranteed their existence. And when those land openers were eventually given posts as resident provincial officials (*zaichō kanjin*), they implicitly accepted provincial governance in which they themselves had an important role. Still later, the promulgation of the *Judicial Formulary* (*Goseibai shikimoku*) by the Kamakura Bakufu in 1232 furthered this acceptance. So while land openers lived in a world governed by custom, they also came to live in a world governed by classical *ritsuryō* law. Their dual-faceted worldview is evidenced by estate documents wherein both local custom and the more universal practices of the various provinces are cited.

The emergence of land-opening landlords in the countryside therefore affected the advancing trajectory from a world ordered by custom to a world ordered by law. Other factors were at work as well. Although there was a classical system of kinship and fictive kin relations that involved "housemen" (*ke'nin*) and slaves (*nuhi*) in cultivation, the notion of the full authority of the house head (*kachō*, alt. *ie no osa*) over these persons had not fully developed. Those functioning as slaves included both slaves and housemen—in the agricultural village they were considered family members and were closely integrated within the patriarchal family structure. But if they escaped from their masters, the *tennō*-centered state guaranteed the master's right of possession by law. In a sense that very fact obstructed the development of anything other than a system of patriarchal social relations.

In contrast, the proprietary authority exercised by land-opening landlords differed from the earlier kin- and slave-based modes of production. Proprietorship by landlords did not limit itself to direct oversight of cultivators.

In Iga Province, for instance, the rents charged by land-opening landlords were the same as those levied by provincial headquarters, and the two were closely related. The *chinso* tax system of *ritsuryō*, with its 20 percent rent rate levied on public fields let out for cultivation, provided a broad standard for Heian society. Moreover, the local overseer (*shōchō*) on an early estate, who was a forerunner of the later land-opening landlord, paralleled the overseer of state-managed fields known as *kueiden*.[10] These overseers and their descendents, the later land-opening landlords, were more than simply local elites. In the ways they organized cultivators, made payments of food for rice produced, opened and irrigated land, and built needed facilties, these overseers owed much to earlier *ritsuryō* technologies—they were trained in *ritsuryō* administrative practices. Therefore the better we understand the administration of the public provincial domain (*kokugaryō*) in Heian times, the better we can understand the administrative practices of later land-opening landlords.

Although it is generally thought that the provincial domain continued to change its character during the Heian Period, very little has been written on the subject. One even encounters the mistaken notion that the provincial domain became increasingly *shōen*-like. My view is that through the application of law in the provincial domain, local land openers and *ritsuryō* authorities came to enjoy an increasingly reciprocal relationship. Although provincial law was indeed based on Chinese-style *ritsuryō* law, as a notion of customary law developed during the Heian Period, a significant transformation ensued. By the late twelfth century, for instance, the tax rate in Iga Province was three *to* of rice per *tan* (0.294 acres) of public land in addition to subsidiary payments to be made in oil, unthreshed rice, and unhulled rice.[11] Otherwise, specially designated new tenures of land (*beppū*) paid five *to* per *tan*, and fields opened by estate dwellers outside the borders of their estate (*dezukuri*) were assessed at three *to* plus subsidiary payments. While all such levies had their origins in *ritsuryō* taxation practices, changes were made to suit regional conditions. The *ritsuryō sō* tax had been a land-based tax, while *ritsuryō chō* and *yō* taxes were both taxes levied on individuals. However, in the public domain of the Heian-period Kinai region, all three taxes came to be levied on units of land called *myō*. Replacing earlier residential unit registers (*koseki*) or tax account books (*keichō*), *myō* were the taxation units of the Heian provincial domain; and field maps (*denzu*) and field registers (*denseki*) became the primary records on which provincial authorities depended.[12]

In addition to these changes in tax administration, each province saw the development of its own distinct customary law. In Iga, for instance, outsiders who came into the province to open land were exempted from the labor tax, known as *zōyaku*. This was a quite distinctive practice. Also, those who moved their residences to sites within the boundaries of an estate were not charged labor taxes, a clear change from original *ritsuryō* law.[13] In estate records we see such phrases as "according to the custom of this province" or "according to the custom of other provinces," which refer to the customary law of various provinces as distinct from either *ritsuryō* law or estate law. It was precisely this customary provincial law that came to govern agrarian society in Heian times.

In one sense it was part of *ritsuryō* law. But as *myō* emerged and other basic changes occurred, the original *ritsuryō* provisions were no longer appropriate or effective.[14]

Those who were most familiar with this evolving customary provincial law were the hereditary provincial officers who resided in the province and staffed the governors' absentee headquarters (*rusudokoro*) in every province.[15] They occupied the various posts of provincial government as well as those of districts (*gun*) and neighborhoods.[16] They sometimes functioned as tax-collecting *myō* managers (*myōshu*) and held salary fields associated with that post.[17] They were all land openers. And since they worked as field contractors (*tato*) who collected taxes, they were also quite familiar with law at the local level. The provincial office that they staffed was thus the organization through which large and middling land openers dominated cultivators. As the provincial headquarters and district chiefs united against Tōdaiji's interference at Kuroda Estate in Iga (in the tenth and eleventh centuries), so was the provincial domain increasingly "privatized" by the efforts of these land-opener officials.

The emergent customary provincial law (*kokuga hō*) was law by and for local land openers. As the central aristocracy withdrew from provincial politics, *ritsuryō* law ceased to be applicable locally.[18] In Heian times it continued to exist only in formal and prescriptive ways, as centrally promulgated supplementary regulations and protocols known as *kyaku* and *shiki*. The only reason for the survival of the provincial proprietary domain, itself a creation of *ritsuryō* administration, was the support from local elites who functioned as resident provincial officers.

The medieval land-opening stratum therefore emerged in tandem with a system of law that was far from primitive. The unifying political thought of *ritsuryō* law was not transmitted by Heian urban aristocrats. Instead it was passed down by land openers working in the countryside. A notable facet of the mental history of the agrarian hamlet is that its resident landlords grew to political maturity synthesizing *ritsuryō* political thought—the public law and authority of their domains—with their own customary patriarchal kin relations. The transformation from a world of custom to a world of law—the very trajectory that gave birth to the medieval world—resulted from this convergence of the customs of the hamlet and the classical culture of the capital.[19]

Dōri and Medieval Law

The weightiness of custom, representing the traditions of social life formed over a long span of time, is what transforms custom into duty and obligation. Any law for which general assent is sought must be considered rightful by those over whom it rules—it needs a font of legitimacy. And different epochs require different legal principles. The term *dōri* emerged in the *Judicial Formulary* of 1232 as the fundamental "principle of things" in the medieval period. It existed with a variety of meanings in aristocratic and monastic societies and enjoyed a long history in warrior (*buke*) society as well.

The long and distinct history of *dōri* thought in warrior law can be traced through the history of the agrarian hamlet. I have argued that custom reigned when rural life was focused on the hamlet and community life was irrevocably tied to the shrine (*jinja*). The worship of the deities (*jingi*) was the spiritual foundation of hamlet life—the concept of law was closely tied to the concept of deity (*kami*) and law itself was considered the revealed will of the deity. Even after the Taika era in the 640s, agrarian society did not change fundamentally in that regard. According to the Taika edicts of 646, adjudication (*saiban*) remained in the hands of local elites, such as the "allied chieftains" (*tomo no miyatsuko*) and provincial chieftains (*kuni no miyatsuko*) who served concurrently as shrine ritualists. In that capacity, such provincial magnates were well placed to receive the *kami*'s commands, to know the will of the *kami*, and to negotiate human conflicts accordingly. Under the *ritsuryō* system, these chieftains continued to serve as district chieftains (*gunji*), and in later times too regional leaders most likely maintained the adjudicative prerogatives of earlier provincial chieftains.

Classical *ritsuryō* law did not displace the territorial authority of the *kuni no miyatsuko*. Even in the Heian Period the provincial chieftain of Izumo continued to serve as a shrine ritualist—he received oracles from the deity and took young daughters of local notables as tribute maidens (*uneme*).[20] In such circumstances we can see the origin of sacral prerogatives held by provincial chieftains over their subjects. Japan's classical political structure was characterized by *ritsuryō* law "governing the realm" in tandem with and limited by the social hierarchy presided over by such elites in the agrarian countryside.

The inseparability of law from the will of the gods is evidenced by pledges (*kishōmon*) made by villagers while assembled before a shrine. In the customary power relations of village life, adjudication was understood to be the deity's judgment (*shimpan*). For instance, in the late Heian Period when a conflict erupted between Ki Tomonari and Ōmiwa Suesada over property in Bungo Province's Kono Township in Usa District, it was decided that the matter should be settled by the gods. So when Ki proffered clear evidence that several of Ōmiwa's relatives had died and that the latter himself had suffered other misfortunes, it was assumed that the deities of Usa Shrine favored Ki.

In Ōmiwa's case there was already tension between *dōri* and *shimpan* —Ōmiwa had taken over the property in question based on *dōri*.[21] Indeed, in agrarian society the notion of *dōri* emerged in contrast with the notion of judgment based on the gods' will. Heian people frequently used the word *dōri* to insist on their own prerogatives and claims—it is often seen on land documents in such phrases as *sōdenryō dōri*, meaning that one's claims were legitimate, that one possessed the proper proof documents. *Dōri* also came to mean "precedent." So whether by proof documents or by precedent, *dōri* connoted what was appropriate and legal. As land-opening landlords emerged in the eleventh century, the notion of law matured among local cultivators. The concept of *dōri* represented a secularizing vector, a movement away from the world of gods toward that of humans. Law came to be understood not as the will of the gods but rather as a manmade framework for society; and this represented a major transformation in hamlet culture.

By that time local cultivators could neither lodge a complaint with district chieftains nor complain directly to estate proprietors in the capital. In other words, the juridical order over which provincial chieftains had once presided was no longer functioning. And yet in Iga's Nabari District a legacy of the provincial chieftain's authority remained, because the record shows that field contractors there had not yet rejected the social organization underlying the old *ritsuryō* residence unit used for census-taking, the *gōko*.[22] Complete decline of the provincial chieftain system awaited internal stratification within the cultivator order, evidenced by the emergence of resident landlords and their taking over of the district chieftain's post.[23] Diffusion of the term *dōri* at the hamlet level was certainly facilitated by *ritsuryō* structures, but real penetration of hamlet society by *dōri* required the transcendence of old lifeways within hamlet society itself.

Although the concept of *dōri* represented the transformation of law as the will of the deities into an ideal plan for human society, in warrior law it was also seen pragmatically as the result of the real possession and the exercise of might. In this regard the eighth article of Kamakura's *Judicial Formulary* recognized that after the passage of twenty years the right of possession was indisputable. Humans could obstruct both law and ideal. This contrasts with Germanic law, which held that a century of wrong could not make an instant of right—law as the will of the gods was not something humans could manipulate. The *Judicial Formulary* recognized the historical reality of Minamoto Yoritomo's time that was still anchored in customary law: that law was not something instituted by village society in awe of divine authority. As land-opening proprietors emerged to claim proprietary holdings (*chigyō*) of land and cultivators, they advanced a pragmatic conception of law.

Warrior and shrine-ritualist families in medieval times looked to the gods to decide their futures. Take the example of Atsunobu, a ritualist at Shinano Province's Suwa Shrine. During the Jōkyū War (1221) he reportedly trusted in an oracle; and having received the god's command to go out to battle, he raised an army and headed for the capital. In another instance, at the time of the Genkō struggle (1331), the Munakata of Chikuzen Province decided to ally themselves with Ashikaga Takauji because of an oracle's words. In the essentially confined, unpredictable, and extralegal world wherein warrior and shrine families resided, it is hardly surprising that many looked to omens and decisions of the gods. The attitude that a family's fortunes were subject to the gods' will was a characteristic of medieval warrior society.

On the other hand, the pragmatic attitude that one must respond perspicaciously to an outbreak of fighting and then move into action with one's kin after deciding allegiance was also an aspect of medieval life. The warrior's power came from his venturesome spirit, which led him to seek new relationships transcending those of a single kin group or hamlet. Such an attitude was also rooted in the medieval warrior's custom of seeking the gods' judgment. The shrine was certainly an important locus of spiritual life for the local land opener, and I would argue that this was not a case of the medieval rejecting the classical. Rather, we witness how a facet of classical life remained firmly rooted in medieval life. In fact, the medieval warrior believed that *dōri* and the will of the gods were inseparable. When Hōjō Yasutoki went to Kyoto at the time of the Jōkyū fight with Go-Toba's forces, he prayed to the deity Hachiman, "If in proceeding to the capital I am contravening *dōri,* instantly take my life and aid me in the afterworld. Then again, if I am to become an instrument of the realm in pacifying the people and making Buddhism prosper, take pity on me—the fact that I am not acting in self-interest is clear."[24] Shiba Yoshimasa put it another way in his *Chikubashō*: "The appearance of the Buddhas and deities is for the good of people in the world. Even one who fails to serve [them] once, even one who never visits a shrine, if he is honest in his heart and merciful, even the Buddhas and deities will not disdain him as lacking merit."[25]

Hōjō Yasutoki, perhaps the most upright of the Kamakura Bakufu leaders, had a deep belief in *dōri*. In a missive sent to Rokuhara concerning the *Judicial Formulary* on the eleventh day of the ninth month in 1232, he noted: "When you seek the very root of this [law], it is none other than *dōri*."[26] And in another letter on the eighth day of the eighth month he wrote, "Followers should be loyal to their superiors, children should be filial to their parents, and wives should follow their husbands. So will humans reject what is twisted and prize what is straight, and each will work for the peace and prosperity of all the people in the realm."[27]

Dōri was thus the ideal that unified the life of the warrior band. How can we grasp the actual practice of *dōri*? In the third volume of the monk Mujū Ichien's *Collection of Sand and Pebbles* (*Shasekishū*) tale collection, there is a story wherein a senior male heir (*chakushi*) bought back and returned to his father the land that the impoverished parent had once sold away.[28] Still, that senior heir subsequently failed to receive any part of his father's property—instead, the younger brother inherited everything. When a quarrel broke out between the brothers, Hōjō Yasutoki opined, "It is true that the elder brother has official obligations and that what he says is according to *dōri*. But the younger brother holds the testament in his hand and it is difficult to adjudicate the matter." When Yasutoki later referred the matter to a legal scholar, the scholar ruled that it was not possible to go against the father's will because such an act would violate *dōri*. Besides filial relations between fathers and sons, however, there were also responsibilities to the *bakufu* as well as relations within the warrior band to be considered, according to Article 22 of the *Judicial Formulary*. So while for courtier law the primacy of filiality as an ideal was unquestionable, for pragmatic warriors dealing with the problems of everyday life, it was insufficient.

According to the ninth-century *Collected Legal Commentaries on the Administrative Code* (*Ryō no shūge*), *dōri* in "courtier law" (*kuge hō*) connoted decisions based on written *ritsuryō* law. It was quite abstract and proceeded from the ideals of state-builders rather than from real life. In contrast, the *dōri* described in the seventh section of the monk Jien's *Gukanshō* is a transcendent principle that surpasses goings-on in the world.[29] This *dōri* is a historical consciousness—a kind of logic in the early middle ages—that is completely different from the *dōri* of the *ritsuryō* legal specialists. The *dōri* of the *Gukanshō* is based on the author's understanding of the "Latter days of the Buddhist law" (*mappō*). While he had no choice but to accept the reality of the establishment of the warrior government of Kamakura, Jien still considered such an establishment contradictory to the transcendent principle of *dōri*. Jien's primary concern was to understand the vectors of past history, an endeavor in which his aristocratic historical consciousness is unmistakable.

In contrast, the sense of *dōri* expressed by Hōjō Yasutoki as the fundamental principle in the *Judicial Formulary* is a much simpler concept. It does not emerge from the past—it is ahistorical. As he wrote to the Rokuhara deputies, *dōri* represented living practice, the product of the customary law of warriors and the people (*buke no narai, minkan no hō*). This perception that law was not something set by written texts but rather something that lived as practice and as the customary law of warriors and commoners was a significant intellectual breakthrough in Yasutoki's day, and in this transformation medieval law came into existence. I do not mean that the actual practice of various land-opening landlords as local warriors (*zaichi bushi*) itself represents medieval law; but it was from this time that medieval law began to take shape under military men like Yasutoki. As he wrote, "Around the capital, what I have laid out may be laughed at as something ignorant easterners have compiled in writing." Yet his criticism of aristocratic law and his full confidence in the *Judicial Formulary* can be strongly felt all the more becuse he did not fully articulate the critique. For Yasutoki, since *ritsuryō* law was nothing more than a dying system, his goal was to emphasize customary law.

Consider the provisions concerning slaves in the *Judicial Formulary*. According to Article 41, "As for the offspring of slaves and various servants, even though there are detailed specifications in the law, according to the precedents of this honorable reign, let boys go with their fathers and girls with their mothers." Ishii Ryōsuke has pointed out that this stipulation amounts to a revision of *ritsuryō* law. According to the latter, the offspring of slave mothers were all to remain with their mothers. Even after slavery was outlawed in the late Heian Period, the *Hōsōshiyōshō* indicates that legal scholars did not reject earlier practice in this regard.[30] Courtier reliance on earlier written law is obvious. But we see a clear and formal break from such legal practice in the *Judicial Formulary*, which amounted to both critique and continuation of *ritsuryō* law. The idea that slaves are like herds of domesticated animals is rejected. Local warriors had received *ritsuryō* law and developed their own society and law based on it, but by the time of the *Judicial Formulary* they had reached the stage of creating their own law and rejecting the primacy of *ritsuryō*.

This would have been impossible without a new conception of the actual nature of law, and such consciousness did not appear just because warriors gained governing power through the Kamakura Bakufu. Rather, there was a slow process of intellectual development that took place over the long history of land opening and associated local landlordship. In this respect the *Judicial Formulary* was a founding document of Japan's medieval society—in the realm of law, it represented nothing less than the overcoming of the classical by the medieval in the countryside hamlet.

Law based on actual relationships is different from prescription superimposed on real life. *Hō* and *dōri* take their forms from lived life—they are replete with reality and take actual political relations as their premise. This dawning of a new appreciation of the political can be intuited in war-tale literature, the appearance of which signals the dawn of the middle ages. While such war tales constantly refer back to Chinese exemplars, their attitudes toward the merits and defects of politics, however tentative and simplistic, contrast notably with the literature of the earlier Heian age, in which any sense of politics is lacking. The basic concern of the war tales is power relations—by what sort of government should land openers be governed? It was at this stage that the warrior stratum reached a moment of dynamic development and moved toward the establishment of a feudal system. For warriors, political relations were of great moment even if urban aristocrats, whose world was in its final throes, had little political consciousness. That is why it was the warrior Yasutoki who revived the most basic ideal of *ritsuryō* politics, a Buddhist sense of virtuous government. Yasutoki's view was not even necessarily a Confucian one. As he is reported to have said in the *Shasekishū* tale collection, "There is nothing as moving as *dōri*. When a man speaks of *dōri*, listeners are moved to tears!" The demand for universalized justice, law, and morality was complex and multifaceted.

Culture and Politics, from Classical to Medieval

The emergence of the medieval represents the decline of the classical, but this same process of decline was also one of development. While the medieval world amounted to a negation of classical structures, the classical world was the womb of the medieval world—*kodai* and *chūsei* are linked by common substance and contradictions. Both must be analyzed in detail.

From the cultivators who received officially distributed fields (*handen*) in *ritsuryō* times, to the woodcutters (*somaudo*) of Itabae Forest in Iga who came to serve Tōdaiji as "temple slaves," commoners and elites were both participants in the *ritsuryō* system and its obverse, the medieval warrior band.[31] Over time cultivators and woodcutters at Kuroda no shō developed sufficient power to deny both *ritsuryō* authorities and Tōdaiji as estate proprietor, through the historical process whereby systems adapt and change in response to inner contradictions. As a structure that represented the interests of land-opening landlords, the medieval warrior band at Kuroda no shō—one such was led by the district chief of Nabari, Hasetsukabe Chikakuni, and his heirs from the 1080s on—became the agent that brought about this transformation in the classical political system. However, the process by which *chūsei* emerged in the provinces proceeded quite independently from that in the Heian capital. So we dare not overlook the critical relationship between the provinces and capital. Opposition to the classical system arose within capital society just as it did in hamlet society, and failure to recognize these parallel trajectories prevents full comprehension of the contradictions that transformed the classical polity.

To say that the Hōgen and Heiji coups (1156–1159), or the establishment of the Kamakura Bakufu in the 1180s, represent the beginning of the medieval world is appropriate as a periodization of historical events. But when looking at different phenomena, historians cannot avoid the issue of variant periodization schemes. In the realm of literature I think it is persuasive to argue that the middle ages began during the Heian Period, and I cannot help but feel that this view will be widely accepted in the future. That we know so little about the historical meaning of the Heian Period obstructs our reflections on the origins of *chūsei*.

Heian historiography is woefully underdeveloped, and even now the treatment of the Heian Period as cultural history makes its historiography distinctive. There is no doubt that the decades spanning the Engi (901–923) and Tenryaku eras (947–957) represent an epoch. Even early on it was said that governance reached a high point in the early tenth century. This was also the time when the last great monuments of *ritsuryō* government, the *Protocols of the Engi Era* (*Engi shiki*) and the *Nihon sandai jitsuroku*, were compiled. It saw the Northern Fujiwara regents grasp power as Fujiwara Tokihira triumphed over Sugawara Michizane and the earliest of the estate control laws were promulgated.[32] But then the outbreak of the Shōhei (931–938) and Tengyō (938–947) uprisings—Masakado in the east and Sumitomo in the west—signaled the dawn of a new age. All this makes investigating the relationship between early tenth-century developments and the medieval age important.

The most characteristic form of late Heian culture is represented by Amidist thought and prose literature. That Ki Tsurayuki, the initiator of prose literature, and the holy man Kūya, an early representative of Amidist thought, both lived during the Engi era is revealing, as is their centrality to the *mentalité* of the early tenth century. If in the early Heian Period aristocratic society coalesced around two pillars—the *ritsuryō* status hierarchy and a broad alliance of courtier families—the decline of the *ritsuryō* polity in the post-Engi era and resulting Fujiwara autocracy weakened both pillars. The result was a tremendous outpouring of intellectual production by courtiers reflecting on the decline of aristocratic society and seeking liberation from its reality. The Jōdo Amidist faith expressed the spirit of this period most clearly and was intimately related to the unraveling of the courtier alliance.

The basis for the rise of Pure Land (Jōdo) faith was the weakening of courtier solidarity. As the Jōdo faith spread, it transcended the restraints of family temples (*ujidera*) and deities (*ujigami*) whose propitiation had as object a single family's good fortune and prosperity. Worship of elite family deities under the leadership of family chieftains (*uji no chōja*) had been the basis for a potent sense of elite solidarity. Furthermore, the cooperation of elite kin groups entailed more than spiritual matters. Economic and political support, including income from corporate property and political support for *uji* members by the chieftain, who was normally the highest-ranking courtier in an elite family, were both involved.[33] Northern Fujiwara Yoshimi (813–867), for instance, built the Sushin'in on one corner of his palace precincts for needy members of his clan, and he had the Enmeiin hospice constructed in 859 for sick relatives.[34]

Courtier kin groups maintained such familial institutions and were able to assure their relatives' elite status through their leaders' ongoing status as high-ranking courtiers. Northern Fujiwara autocracy, however, upset this aristocratic order because those who were not members of the Regents' Line found it impossible to maintain high courtier status.

The Tachibana family provides an example. It declined in Heian times and ceased producing appointees to the Council of State. Once there was no Tachibana kin placed highly enough at court to help members of their clan gain official posts, Fujiwara Michitaka (of the Northern Fujiwara line) was allowed to assume the Tachibana chieftaincy in the Kanna era (985–987).[35] After that, headship of the family shrine, the Ume no Miya, and the family academy, the Gakkan'in, came into the hands of claimants from Michichika's own Northern Fujiwara family. This is one example of elite families without political power becoming dependents of the Northern Fujiwara. To some extent the Tachibana were able to maintain a degree of solidarity founded on the family shrine and school, but most aristocratic families fell into jealous factionalism in the environment of economic disarray resulting from the decay of clan structures.[36]

Looking at the courtier world in the early eleventh-century era of Northern Fujiwara Michinaga (966–1027), there were but twenty-five senior noble members of the Council of State. Among them were nineteen Fujiwara, and those serving as middle counselors (*chūnagon*) or above were all blood or affinal relatives of Michinaga. Courtier society had become increasingly exclusive, and former aristocrats living in severely reduced circumstances were numerous. The latter could either move out to the provinces or allow themselves to sink to the level of commoner residents of the capital. Considering the huge number of land-sale records from Heian times in the archives of courtier families, it is clear that lower-ranking members were selling residences and fields to gain liquidity, thereby contributing to a substantial lowering of land values. Many aristocrats were impoverished and became commoner urbanites.

The loosening of aristocratic bonds of solidarity and the resulting isolation and powerlessness of many courtiers led to the rapid spread of the Jōdo faith. This faith was characterized by its emphasis on introspection and experience: it stressed the importance of each individual's perception of his or her own evil passions and sinfulness. The harsh reality of life in the Heian capital was a stimulant for such enlightenment. In that regard Jōdo preached the virulence of the five pollutants in the latter days of the Buddhist law, when human society was thought to have devolved to a brutish extreme. Urban Heian was thought to demonstrate the truth of such beliefs.

As the earliest compiler of "biographies of the saved" (*ōjōden*), the courtier Yoshishige Yasutane was also the author of *An Account of My Retreat by a Pond* (*Chiteiki*). In that text we get a unique look at unhappy conditions in the capital at the turn of the eleventh century.[37] Gazing at the towers of the prosperous and the hovels of the poor in the capital of his day led Yoshishige to a conversion experience. For him the decline of urban life meant disasters such as fire, brigands, and flood. A few decades earlier the holy man Kūya (903–972) had spent his life proselytizing among commoners at Fourth Ward (Shijō) crossing and in capital marketplaces. He was called the evangelist of the marketplace (*ichi no hijiri*) and his life's work was inseparable from his urban existence. His spiritual heir, the monk Hōnen (1133–1212), most likely never left the capital, which was the locus of his preaching. Both holy men dwelling in the capital were deeply aware of their own sinfulness and that of all sentient beings.

That Jōdo teachers lacked regard for the *kami*, the old deities for which earlier Buddhists had held great respect, is due in part to the urban character of the Jōdo faith. Urban residents of the capital had lost their faith in *kami* protectors. For instance, the author of the *Sarashina nikki* expressed her limited knowledge about such deities, and she was not alone in her ignorance.[38] Notions that had given rise to great titled family (*uji*) solidarity and upon which both Yamato kingship and *ritsuryō tennō*-centered polity had been founded had dissipated. For urbanites, only individual experience and reflection served as guides. With little faith in the deities, urban dwellers embraced Amida's saving vow. The capital thus also became a place where members of the old aristocracy met to mourn their now-meaningless genealogies and past glory.

Because of the nature of its teachings and the sociopolitical situation of the time, individuals who embraced the Amidist faith became prospective authors of fictional prose narratives. Narrative literature evolved in the midst of aristocratic decline and represented the efforts of introspective individuals to comprehend reality.[39] Such individuals were aristocrats, but we should not see them simply as "aristocratic." For instance, the author of *Kagerō nikki*, the self-identified "Fujiwara Michitsuna's mother," was provoked to write her account by the exile of Daigo Tennō's prince, Minamoto Takaakira (914–982).[40] That she was deeply shocked by Takaakira's fall from power despite her lack of a special bond with him suggests how other intellectuals of the time reacted to such political events. Consider too how in the "Kuniyuzuri" section of the *Tales of the Hollow Tree* (*Utsubo monogatari*) there is a fictional conflict between the Fujiwara and the Minamoto. The Minamoto victory in that section does not reflect the author's true identity as a clan member. Rather it suggests that intellectuals like the *Utsubo* author sympathized with the Minamoto in their struggle against the Fujiwara regents' leadership at court. The emergence of a courtier intelligentsia around this time is closely connected with these developments. Intellectuals came from old *uji* families (*shizoku*) or from families whose members routinely gained the fifth rank. In the late tenth century Sei Shōnagon was representative—although she was born in a family with a long tradition of scholarship, she experienced the disaffection of the provincial governor class that she herself derided in her *Pillow Book* (*Makura no sōshi*).[41] Her consciousness surely stemmed from the experiences of her own father, Motosuke. We cannot separate her enthusiasm for learning, her piercing derision of philistine males, and even her motivation for court service from her own past experience.

What I am arguing here is that literature created by late Heian intellectuals comprises something more complex than "aristocratic literature," because it includes critical reflection on the meaning of membership in the aristocratic world. So were two characteristic features of post-Engi culture—Jōdo thought and narrative literature—intimately connected. Both reflect introspection by individuals negatively affected by the breakdown of the original *ritsuryō* aristocratic order. And Amidist thought transcended critique to deny the efficacy of *uji*-based institutions and the status differences that were the heart of the aristocratic worldview. Given that, it did not take long for the old order to crumble.

Such introspective thinkers were not members of the high nobility. Rather, they emerged from the lower ranks of officialdom and their critiques were varied. One stream represented those who moved out to the provinces and created new livelihoods for themselves. Younger sons of some high-ranking courtiers chose that path—indeed, the martial bands that emerged in the provinces were led by the countrified sons of *ritsuryō* officialdom. Still another stream of critique was articulated in an urban setting, but such authors proved unable to propose an alternative social order. Nonetheless it is worth examining this stream of critical urban culture, since it served as the legacy of Heian culture in the medieval world.

Aristocratic society was urban society for the writers of narrative prose.[42] The late tenth-century *Utsubo monogatari* and eleventh-century *Genji monogatari* represent the apex of the narrative prose genre, while what came later is less impressive. And yet we must remember that such prose narratives represent but a single category of late Heian literature. Another category is occupied by war tales such as the late tenth-century *Chronicle of Masakado* (*Shōmonki*), the eleventh-century *A Tale of Mutsu* (*Mutsuwaki*), together with the twelfth-century *Collection of Tales Old and New* (*Konjaku monogatarishū*).[43] In all three instances the identity of the author remains uncertain, but they were doubtless members of aristocratic society with significant interest in provincial warrior society. Authors of war tales represent a sector of the aristocracy that had discovered the world beyond the capital. In the *Shōmonki*, for instance, we have a depiction of the ambitious heroism of eastern warrior society. In the *Mutsuwaki* we experience the hardships of frontier battles while following the heroic Yoriyoshi in action amid inspiring relationships binding lord and follower in the warrior band.

When we compare the *Utsubo monogatari* to war tales depicting eastern warriors, it is hard to fathom how such different genres emerged from the same aristocratic environment. And yet these varying perspectives originated in the different perceptions of individuals living in Heian times. Given the reality of decline and impoverishment that trapped urban aristocrats, few writers among those aristocrats could but stare in wonder at the heroic figures of great generals in the midst of intense relations in camp and on the battlefield. Like the movement of aristocrats out to the provinces, war-tale literature represents direct criticism of aristocratic society as well as confrontation with a new world. Such an attitude did not stir the author's imagination to the production of fiction. Rather, such writers rejected the fictionality of *monogatari* like the *Sarashina nikki* and focused on real experience. They set out to record the world with the utmost sincerity. Although the forms they chose varied, they had the same objective as did the compiler of war tales in volume 25 of the *Konjaku monogatarishū*.

The *Konjaku* tale concerning the Iga land opener, Fujiwara Kiyokane, is a humorous but faithful portrayal of a land-opening landlord who actually took up residence in the provinces.[44] The desire to record such reality did not arise from an interest in the exotic, as has sometimes been suggested; instead it emerged out of a caustic view of contemporary culture seen to be intoxicated by fiction and emotion (*mono no aware*). Although there were many points of agreement between this "recording" literature as an expression of aristocratic critique through authoring *monogatari* literature, in actuality the two became contrasting genres, each with its own view of reality. The Heian war tales—*Shōmonki* and *Mutsuwaki*—and the *Konjaku monogatarishū* tales all differ from mainstream *monogatari* literature. While some readers may find them lacking in aesthetics and polish, they were the sole avenue of escape and transcendence available to members of the aristocracy as literary expressions of their critique of contemporary circumstances.

The Significance of the *Heike monogatari*

The trajectory initiated by the *Shōmonki* and the *Konjaku monogatarishū* eventually became mainstream literary expression in the medieval age. That is why I consider the *Heike monogatari* a direct heir of late Heian literarature.[45] Specifically, the ability of the *Heike* to dispense with the fragmentary reporting of earlier war tales came from its inheritance of the spirit of Heian prose literature. Although the flourishing literary spirit of the *Tale of Genji* (*Genji monogatari*) quickly declined in imitative works, the creative form of episodic prose narrative continued in the *Heike*. The *Heike* was thus the heir not only of the *Shōmonki* and *Konjaku monogatarishū* but also of older works such as the *Genji* and the *Great Mirror* (*Ōkagami*).

Nonetheless, the *Heike* constructed a world fundamentally different from that of later Heian court literature. Reflection on these relationships is a central concern for those seeking a better understanding of Japan's medieval world. Specifically, the *Heike monogatari* is epic literature describing the destruction of the Taira war band during the Gempei fighting between 1180 and 1185. Generally it is categorized as both warrior and aristocratic literature. The putative author of the ur-*Heike*, the former provincial governor known as Yukinaga, was closely associated with the court leader, Kujō Kanezane (1149-1207), and his brother, the abbot of Enryakuji on Mount Hiei and author of the *Gukanshō*, Jien (1155-1225). Yukinaga was closely associated with Enryakuji, whose worldview he shared after receiving his monastic training there. At the same time, however, he was an intellectual maverick distanced from the courtier elite. Nonetheless literary historians still see his *Heike* as a product of aristocratic culture, however vividly it describes the *bushi*'s world. The fact is, the worldview and hierarchical order of the *Heike* come from earlier Heian literature: just as the *Genji monogatari* represents the high point of narrative prose artistry up to its time, the *Heike* represents the high point of literary style from the later Heian age.

Nonetheless, when elements of the *Heike monogatari* are analyzed and compared with those of earlier literary works, there are many distinctive and original components. To begin with, battle scenes are not depicted in an isolated fashion, nor are greater and lesser heroes set apart from their groups in the midst of the fighting. Unlike the *Shōmonki*, the *Heike* is not the story of a single hero. In its narrative individuals are swept along by the fate of their corporate kin. Episodes are unified by the narrative, but the links are not those of emotion or fancy—the torrent that destroyed the *Heike* war band is described objectively as a product of real historical change based on the Buddhist law of karma. Indeed, the *Heike* is an epic poem about the Gempei War that was initially composed in the pre-Jokyū (1219–22) period when memories of that war remained fresh. It was written under the overarching influence of remembered historical reality. Rather than being an attempt to look back and report what had taken place, the *Heike*'s objective was to extol momentous and tragic events. Such an attitude distinguishes the *Heike* from earlier historical narrative and reporting.

It may go against prevailing wisdom to see the *Heike* as something new and different compared with earlier Heian literature, but a close examination of the work proves my point. Even were we to admit that the author of the *Heike* was himself an intellectual aristocrat, the author's origins are not the only important factor. Whether aristocrat or monk, the author could still produce a piece of written literature that took a perspective different from that of either group. An author certainly can transcend his origins. It is particularly dangerous to overlook this possibility in the case of the ur-*Heike* author, who was a member of the marginalized lower aristocracy facing decline at an epochal divide in history.[46]

Moreover, the *Heike* is permeated with the worldview of Amidism. In addition to the author's putative identity as a courtier, that is why the *Heike* is seen as aristocratic literature. But was the Amidist worldview actually aristocratic? I have argued that Amidism represents a philosophy constructed by urban aristocratic society. Nonetheless, given its ideological insistance that regardless of status, birth, or livelihood one could be saved by faith alone, Amidism was not so much aristocratic as anti-aristocratic. Moreover, that anti-aristocratic character enabled its wide diffusion throughout medieval society.

Common wisdom also has it that the emergence of Amidism represented a sort of religious reformation not unlike that experienced in the Western European early modern era. Despite some superficial parallels, such a comparison is quite mistaken. If there ever was a comparable moment in the West, it was the rise of Christianity in the midst of the decline, rebellion, and superstition rife in late Roman society. As European medieval society could not deny the dominance of the Christian worldview, classical aristocratic literature could not deny the preeminence of the Amidist worldview.[47]

We might ask, of what usefulness are the two categories, aristocratic literature and warrior literature, for characterizing the *Heike monogatari*? The category of warrior literature (*bushi bungaku*) derives from the knightly literature of the West. Proper methodology would have us contextualize a literary production in its historical epoch, which would make the *Heike monogatari* into Heian courtly literature. But we must also take note of the *Heike* as a product of oral storytelling (*katarimono*). The original text of the *Heike* was certainly produced for other purposes than reading, and without its storytelling aspect, there would be no *Heike*. Nor could the *Heike* have been produced without the mixed Sino-Japanese and Japanese literary forms that had developed during Heian times. It is this character of the *Heike* as oral storytelling that distinguishes it as something new compared with earlier works of Heian courtly literature. Moreover, its oral character is internal and organic to the *Heike*, and it is closely tied to the Buddhist thought and proselytizing that were objectives of the epic. The creation of the *Heike* in its present form for a broad audience of readers and listeners during the Kamakura age constituted a decisive moment in literary history. The *Heike* distanced itself from aristocratic literature while constructing a new world of quite a different sort. And yet, the *Heike* should not be characterized as warrior literature: the order of fighting men represented but a single group of the contemporary populace. That is why I argue that we should consider the *Heike monogatari* as popular literature, the world of which was neither aristocratic nor warrior. Rather, it was medieval.[48]

In the classical world there were groups whose livelihoods included oral transmission of lore for both elites and commoners. One such group included the *biwa hosshi*, lute-strumming monk-reciters who appear in Heian-period records.[49] They were entertainers who roamed from place to place reciting stories for a living. We cannot separate the emergence of the *Heike* from the existence of such entertainers. It is not hard to imagine that after the defeat of the Taira forces in 1185, such *biwa*-strumming monks spread stories of Gempei battles to every corner of the realm.

Nonetheless, simply compiling such stories could never have created a work like the *Heike monogatari*. The author of the *Heike* was critically important. As a person familiar with the literary traditions of the Heian court, he drew upon those for his literary project. Since late Heian narrative prose included a critical perspective on the courtier world—it had after all produced the *Shōmonki* and the *Konjaku monogatari* as well as the *Genji monogatari* and later tales—the courtier author of the *Heike*, having experienced the epochal struggle of the Gempei War, took it as his topic. Had he written a work only for courtiers, even had he succeeded in creating a new sort of war-tale literature, the results would never have been the equivalent of the *Heike monogatari*. Instead, the *Heike*'s author had readers and listeners beyond the courtly world in mind as he wrote. He was inspired to create an unprecedented work that was both an heir to late Heian literature and one that rejected aristocratic ways. As a result it became a work of medieval literature.

How was the *Heike* author inspired to compose for a broad audience of readers and listeners beyond the aristocracy? It is not an easy question to answer. The commoner stratum targeted by our *Heike* author was itself just emerging, comprised of commoners recruited into warrior bands by land-opening landlords, who were themselves military specialists (*bushi*). Because of them, hamlet society transcended its classical mode of organization while nurturing these land-opening elites. The latter were the social base for the establishment of the Kamakura Bakufu; and their existence enabled the courtier author of the *Heike* to reject his aristocratic environment, discover a new commoner audience, and fashion his *Heike* as a work of medieval popular literature. All this constituted an epochal historical development. In other words, establishment of such war bands and the emergence of the Kamakura Bakufu represented the climax of the process by which the classical world spawned contradictions within itself and eventually gave birth to the medieval age. The *Heike* represents a conjuncture of popular storytelling from the agrarian hamlet with the prose narrative tradition of urban aristocrats.

The fourteenth-century *Essays in Idleness* (*Tsurezuregusa*) report concerning how Yukinaga's original *Heike* text resulted from collaboration between a recluse, the former Shinano provincial governor, and Shōbutsu, a blind lute-playing monk, is striking. While there are literary historians who regret that Japan lacks the genre of knightly literature and gives pride of place to courtier literature, I would argue that the medieval world is symbolized by the warrior described in war tales. Nor are the contents of such battle narratives insignificant—they represent the meeting of hamlet and city and the transcending of classical ways of life by those of the feudal village.[50] Western researchers have debated two scenarios for the transition from classical to medieval—one stressing continuity and the other stressing discontinuity; but in my view such theoretical debates lack both concepts and methodology. Historians of Japan must overcome this weakness. The *Heike monogatari* emerges from the late Heian age and should be characterized as popular literature.

Liberation from Chinese Culture and Medieval Popular Culture

It is well known that in the early tenth century the court intellectual Sugawara Michizane distinguished Chinese knowledge from "Yamato spirit" (*Yamato damashii*).[51] He and other thinkers of the time were attempting to liberate themselves from the strong influence of classical Chinese culture. The phrase *Yamato damashii* originally denoted the spirit of thirty-one syllable Japanese poetry (*waka*) as distinguished from the ability to read and write Chinese. Gradually, however, its meaning grew broader. In Fujiwara Tokihira's section of the *Ōkagami* and in the Otome chapter of the *Genji monogatari*, *Yamato damashii* denotes a stout-hearted and resolute character. It connotes a spiritual ethic rather than scholarship or talent. Stronger emphasis on *Yamato damashii* paralleled a rising sense that the ways of classical China no longer expressed the feelings and thoughts of aristocrats living in the difficult and complex times of the later Heian Period. Such consciousness was seen to form the distinct culture of the island realm.

The successful revival of *waka* together with the maturing of narrative prose, especially *monogatari*, articulated this spiritual reaction against Chinese ways. Such autonomy from Chinese culture coincided with the process by which a distinctive language for use in literature emerged. This last was one of the greatest legacies left to later periods. Furthermore, development of the Japanese syllabary, or *kana*, which symbolized the independence of a distinct Japanese culture, was part of this process. Being able to express one's own thoughts and emotions in one's own language rapidly liberated people from the conventional way of expressing ideas in Chinese characters, as Sino-Japanese (*kambun*). As a result a surprising number of new literary forms bloomed. Just as the *Ōkagami* imitated forms of Chinese historical writing, it also occasioned a degree of self-consciousness and the author's sense of "Japaneseness." And once a distinctive Japanese culture had emerged, Chinese culture was no longer limiting. Rather it became a stimulus for creativity. Two different literary styles—*wabun*, delicate and replete with chiaroscuro, and *wakan kōkobun*, mixed Chinese and Japanese forms resulting in a powerful and precise medium—represented two modes of late Heian artistocratic consciousness, Chinese knowledge and Japanese spirit. What resulted from this synthesis was the distinctive literature of the island realm of Nihon.

Given the character of the *Heike monogatari* its authors employed the latter of the two literary styles, the mixed Chinese-Japanese form. The *Heike* style is admirably rich and full of drama. The mixed Chinese-Japanese style in which the *Konjaku monogatarishū* and other such works were written was of a rather limited quality; but the distinctive style of the *Heike monogatari*, which made full use of a number of Buddhist and Chinese terms instead of excluding foreign terms as *kana* literary forms had done in the past, radically improved the mixed Chinese-Japanese literary form. The theme of the *Heike* was partially responsible, while at the same time its linguistic variety was nurtured by the wide spectrum of readers and listeners who functioned as the *Heike*'s co-authors. As a work of medieval literature, the *Heike* represents a decisive moment in the climax of the process begun in the Heian age that resulted in autonomy from Chinese culture. There could be no drastic revolution in the language of literature without substantial literary and historical transformation as well. Indeed, I would argue that the greatest historical accomplishment of the medieval age was liberation from Chinese culture.

The classical legal system had derived from the Chinese legal system.[52] This was not simply the result of cultural interchange and diffusion. Rather it was the necessary result of the autocratic organization that characterized both polities. But the same cannot be said of the realm of the liberal arts, which had quite a different character from law. The fact that Nara courtiers produced the *Kojiki*, the *Nihongi*, the *Man'yōshū*, and the *Kaifūsō* demonstrates that a distinct island culture was never completely buried by Chinese culture. What characterized the culture of the Japanese archipelago from Nara into early Heian times was Chinese culture functioning not as a foreign element but rather as an essential component of Japan's classical age. Chinese culture was not merely an imported culture, to be forgotten over time as indigenous examples emerged. It was one thread woven into the fabric that was classical Japan.[53] Contintental culture was developed in Japan by courtiers possessed of an unparalleled questing spirit, and its later rejection was not due to its foreign origins but instead was linked to a rejection of the classical autocratic system itself. The eventual rejection of this despotism led to the rejection of the Chinese culture with which it had earlier been associated. In the later Heian age, the aristocracy reevaluated the influence of Chinese society and allowed a new independent culture—we term it *kokufū bunka*—to emerge.[54] Nevertheless

Chinese customs remained preeminent in later Heian culture as a whole. Japanese culture existed in the unofficial sphere, and just as the Heian aristocracy could never deny the *ritsuryō* system, neither could they deny the Chinese liberal arts. I would argue that the latter remained dominant as long as there was an aristocracy—true independence from Chinese culture was accomplished not by the aristocracy but by new forces outside it. And promulgation of the *Judicial Formulary* in 1232 confirms that. In Hōjō Yasutoki's missive mentioned earlier he explained reasons for the formulary:

> Although there may be some slight variations from the prescriptions of the law in this formulary, *ritsuryō* law was written in Chinese characters only for those who can read formal characters. But for those who understand only *kana*, trying to read Chinese characters is like being blind. This formulary is for those who only know *kana*. And since there are many who can read only *kana*, to bring ease to all people no member of the *bakufu* should flee from its dictates . . . In this way, even those who are illiterate can reflect on the law. This formulary is promulgated so that judgments can be consistent.[55]

Ritsuryō supplementary enactments, the *kyaku* and *shiki*, were understood to be law for those who could read Chinese characters, a minority of the population. The *Judicial Formulary* was law for the majority who could read only *kana*. The idea that law should be understood by the populace forced Yasutoki to consider the issue of the inaccessibility of *ritsuryō* law. Only his new medieval conception of law could effectively deny the earlier triad of *ritsuryō* law, Sino-Japanese characters, and aristocratic society.

In parallel fashion, the literary style of the *Heike monogatari* assumed that it would be read, heard, and experienced by the masses. Meanwhile, leaders of newly emergent religious sects like Shinran (1173–1262) wrote in a mixture of Chinese characters and *kana*, espousing the idea that "those who make a living by fishing on the sea or rivers, those who sustain themselves by hunting wild boar or catching birds in the fields or mountains, and those who trade goods while being skilled cultivators, they are all the same." I submit then that the *Judicial Formulary*, the tales of the *Heike monogatari*, and Shinran's *Tannishō* are the three pillars of the Japanese medieval world. What they have in common is the author's discovery of the masses and a deep, pulsating, and fully conscious bond with them.

This does not mean that the medieval world should be thought of as comprising only "commoners." Just as the *Judicial Formulary* was promulgated in order to allow the illiterate to know the law, what characterized the medieval world was an energetic desire to educate. The *Heike monogatari* was replete with proselytizing ideas, and such motives underlay the flowering of tale (*setsuwa*) literature as well. This strong desire to educate and enlighten stems from a heightened consciousness of commoners and their mental world. Medieval society took form around such consciousness. Commoners became aware of themselves as distinct from the aristocracy by transcending bonds that had restrained them in the classical *tennō*-centered system. The continental culture that supported such classical rulership could never have been rejected without this increasingly self-conscious populace.

It remains to consider the process by which this self-conscious populace emerged. Also, I am aware that there will be some who disagree with my characterization of the medieval world as "popular," by which I mean that various strata constituting "the masses" were struggling against the classical autocratic system. Here I want to elucidate some key elements of medieval culture at the turn of the thirteenth century, from the Gempei War of 1180–1185 into the early Kamakura Period, which I term "the medieval heroic age."

From the Engi era (901–923) onward, members of the Northern Fujiwara regents' lineage certainly exercised a degree of autocratic leadership at court and based their economic wherewithall on landed estates (*shōen*). Estates accumulated by leading Northern Fujiwara courtier households and major temples and shrines—these powerful establishments were termed "gates of power" (*kenmon*) and "powerful houses" (*seika*) at the time—developed quite rapidly due to the commendation of land by local land openers. Small and large land openers were opening land to cultivation, but to assure ongoing legal privileges and private possession, they commended (*kishin*) their new fields to high-ranking nobles and religious institutions. The *ritsuryō* polity had long assumed high rank and post as a qualification for holding property, but in the post-Engi era the *ritsuryō* fiscal system was being transformed from an earlier emphasis on such elements as post and rank fields, biannual salaries, and prebendal residence units into a new economic system based on estates. Lower-ranking aristocrats whose positions were not sufficiently lofty to make them recipients of commended estates faced penury—there are many stories concerning how the inherited property of such lower aristocrats faced take-over or obstruction by locals, and was then commended to nobles or religious institutions. The result was ever greater accumulation of land in the hands of the central nobility.

Whether or not laws to regulate estates from the Engi era onward were consciously designed to increase estate accumulation in the regents' hands, this process of estate formation resulted in a reconfiguration of aristocratic society in mid-Heian times.[56] Turmoil and transformation are associated with this process, and even intellectuals producing literature recognized the political and socioeconomic problems inherent in these developments. However, the change in the economic base of the Heian nobility did not fundamentally transform the character of the nobility. Since the commendation of land by locals was prompted by the desire to protect themselves from provincial authorities, commendation benefited the central nobility, who were capable of levying pressure against those authorities. There was no need for the nobility to deny *ritsuryō*—indeed, without its hierarchical ordering of the realm, they would not have become estate proprietors (*shōen ryōshu*) at all. It is true that the Northern line of the Fujiwara as the Regents' Line (Sekkanke) succeeded in subordinating an older nobility whose fiscal base remained rooted in *ritsuryō* structures. And yet the Northern Fujiwara were not a new nobility that came to power as commended estates increased—they had participated in the highest circles at court since early *ritsuryō* times, and given their preeminence in the *ritsuryō* structure they were able to amass estates all over the realm. They even utilized *shōen* regulatory laws to further concentrate *shōen* in their own hands.

Looking at the historical character of the central nobility and its institutions, including the royal temple Tōdaiji, they were not simply estate proprietors. Nor does their role as estate proprietors signify their transformation into feudal proprietors (*hōkenteki ryōshu*). Rather, noble houses and religious proprietors took responsibility for guaranteeing title to commended land in exchange for part of the produce. Meanwhile, their prerogatives and perquisites vis-à-vis the land and its cultivators were limited. Preeminent and second-level estate proprietors (*honjo* and *ryōshu*) remained basically urban and aristocratic.[57] But since they did not directly manage residents and cultivators, their absentee proprietorship necessitated the existence of resident landlords.

Continuing this same line of reasoning, the circumstances of late Heian courtly culture—characterized by unrest, a darker worldview, and loss of leadership in cultural production—cannot be explained by the fact that nobles became estate proprietors. The special meaning of *shōen* development for culture at this time is related to the breakdown of noble society caused by regental leadership at court and the decline of other noble families. Lower aristocrats facing bankruptcy established themselves as a conscious social stratum and took a critical view of traditional culture. But there were distinct limits to their vision: dependent on estates for their livelihood, aristocrats could not shuck off their old historical character as *ritsuryō* officials, which remained the basis for their contemporary social position. The reason these nobles could peacefully maintain the foundations of their culture was that as estate proprietors they could position themselves to reap the rewards of local land opening. The hierarchy and processes of the *ritsuryō* polity were still strong at the local level, and as long as the political status of local land openers remained low, it was possible for high-ranking central nobles to serve as estate proprietors. Had local openers been able to overcome their low status, the estate system would never have taken shape. On the other hand, as the increasingly complex multitiered proprietorship system took form, it was inevitable that noble society would decline—only nobles who left the city to settle in the countryside were able to resituate themselves as a new productive stratum. But even in decline, the *ritsuryō* polity was capable of feeding large numbers of nobles—those who functioned as provincial governors or tax farmers raked in good incomes. Noble society maintained itself as long the *ritsuryō* polity did—the estate system was but another form of noble society coping with changed circumstances.

That is why we cannot view the late Heian Period as a distinct historical era characterized by a system fundamentally different from that of earlier *ritsuryō* times. Rather, the Heian Period represented the late classical age, when *ritsuryō* institutions and practices were in decline and when noble society exhibited clear signs of ongoing decay. Therein lie the seeds that produced the antecedents of medieval culture and eventually gave form to medieval culture itself. On the one hand, late Heian noble society drew parasitic sustenance from deteriorating *ritsuryō* structures. On the other hand, it depended on commendation of property by local land openers whose status was only developing slowly. In the process, all political relations once enjoyed by *ritsuryō* nobles with local society dissipated. Court nobles increasingly separated themselves from the provinces, exhausted their very source of livelihood, and walked the path to their own penury. Even the new spiritual forces that emerged as antecedents of medieval culture did not escape decay, because the medieval age of the land opener emerging from the hamlet was grasping the thrust of history as its own. We should remember, in this regard, that cultural history is but one aspect of the superstructure—we must not separate out culture and argue about it in a detached fashion.

Although in later Heian times the urban nobility grew increasingly distanced from the provinces, new linkages were nonetheless forged. Through commendation new bonds joined metropole and agrarian countryside even as two groups of elites—one urban and one rural—grew more distinct in their lifestyles. Before the *ritsuryō* era, courtier elites had possessed property in the countryside that provided a base for their power; it was also where their kin (*dōzoku*) resided. Even after the creation of the *ritsuryō tennō*-centered polity, such relations continued. Consider, for instance, the Nara-period *Man'yōshū* poetess Ōtomo Sakanoue Iratsume, who lived on rice-producing properties at Takeda and Atomita, the landscapes of which had enduring influence on her life and poetry.[58] While such ties to the countryside had not completely vanished by the time that the *Ise monogatari* was written in the tenth century, urban nobles of the later era had few connections with provincial elites, save from stops made while making pilgrimages to shrines and temples. They maintained suburban country houses as sites for banquets and relaxation, but their lifestyles were little affected by such rural places. And while nobility in earlier times had actually taken part in the management of their countryside properties, by the later Heian age nobles simply had yearly dues shipped to the capital. For urban nobles, such dues were the sole import of their proprietary holdings. And since there was so little connection between the lifestyles of those in the capital and countryside, it was inevitable that the provinces would become increasingly independent of the capital. Even as land openers in the provinces developed political relations linking themselves with the capital, the consciousness of distance from the countryside by the urban nobility was a clear symptom of its impending decline.[59]

Paradoxically, such a sense of distance was an essential precondition for closer ties between capital and countryside. *Ritsuryō* officialdom had not been conscious of conflict between the worlds of city and agrarian hamlet. More important than the fact that Heian had not yet fully matured as an urban center was that when classical aristocrats like Ōtomo Sakanoue Iratsume held agrarian property, a differentiated urban consciousness did not arise. The *ritsuryō tennō*-centered polity was founded on close ties between city and countryside—city and hamlet were managed in tandem without a sense of differentiation. The law of courtly society—*ritsuryō*—was the universal law for all subjects, and noble culture and ways of life were not limited to the royal metropole and palace.

By mid-Heian times, however, not only were land openers in the provinces closely linked politically with the center; but since those links were parasitic, the urban consciousness of the nobility stimulated a new sense of differentiation, even of conflict, within residents of the countryside. We see evidence of this in literature dating from the early tenth century onward. Therein one occasionally catches a glimpse of antipathy between *miyako,* the capital at Kyoto, and *inaka,* the provinces. From the culturally undeveloped countryside, the capital was seen as a world blessed with traditional culture and luxury. Still, in contrast with the *ritsuryō* ideal that visualized the polity as an integrated unity with its urban metropole, the new consciousness gave equal importance to city and country even as consciousness of conflict increased. Urban aristocrats were unable to divest themselves of their basic character as *ritsuryō* officialdom, but this did not prevent them from becoming partners with provincial land openers as shareholders in newly opened fields. The relationship was not one of urban aristocrats versus rural subjects. Rather, the two sets of elites were partners in exploiting commonly held property. Urban nobles certainly felt superior to countryside elites, a sense of superiority apparent in the literature of the late Heian age. At the same time, we can see in the *Chronicle of Masakado* and the *Tales Old and New* the discovery by some urban elites of a new provincial world.

Heian aristocrats had two faces—they were at once *ritsuryō* leaders and urban nobles. Following the grasp of power by Northern Fujiwara regents, the first of these roles was nullified and only the second remained. Moreoever, this second occasioned neither group solidarity nor a positive sense of state.[60] Parasitic in their reliance on the provinces, later Heian urban aristocrats no longer had a political sense, nor did they develop new political ideals. Their political system was constituted by traces and residues from *ritsuryō* structures and practices, and the emergence of a new age could not but conflict with those traces.

Tōdaiji as Estate Proprietor, a Classical Structure

Relations between the urban nobility and the great Buddhist temples of the southern capital at Nara are also important. Among these temples, Tōdaiji was founded in the eighth century for the purpose of realm protection. It saw its economic strength inalienably linked to the *tennō*-centered polity and it was clearly an institution that could not exist outside the *ritsuryō* organization that built it. But as Heian nobles became urban aristocrats, the positive sense of state that had characterized the *ritsuryō* conception weakened, and the relationship between the nobility and Nara's great temples changed as well. Aristocrats turned increasingly toward family temples (*ujidera*) as objects of faith. Despite Kōfukuji's existence, the Fujiwara embraced Amidism more and more, and as new temples were established, respect for the great Nara temples decreased. Nonetheless, Kōfukuji was something of an exception.[61] As regental leadership at court increased in mid-Heian times, Kōfukuji developed rapidly as a representative of realm-protecting *ritsuryō* Buddhism.[62]

In such an environment Tōdaiji found itself in a dangerous position. Specifically, in the age of the regents relations between Tōdaiji and Kōfukuji changed; and from the early tenth century on, there was ongoing warfare between the two temples. Tōdaiji was increasingly the target of various pressures. For instance, in Iga Province's Nabari District, generations of Iga provincial governors subjected Tōdaiji's interests to strong pressure. This was the result of the alliance between the regents and provincial governors.

Another issue is how *shōen*-limiting regulations, promulgated first by regents and then by retired monarchs, affected temple estates. Estates with proper documentation were exempt from such regulation, but as Regent Fujiwara Yorimichi once remarked to the retired monarch, central institutions and aristocratic households that became the preeminent proprietors of estates (*honke*) usually held no written deeds.[63] Tōdaiji's Kuroda Estate in Iga was comprised of new fields (e.g. *harita, dezukuriden, kanōden*) opened by estate residents (*shōmin*) who lacked the necessary proof documents (*shōken*). They were targets of new laws issued in 1156 by Go-Shirakawa Tennō, who then urged provincial governors to confiscate all fields held by the powerful for which proof documents could not be produced. Provincial governors were also ordered to control all misconduct (*rangyō*) by estate dwellers. The required proof documents were *kanshōfu*, that is, specific orders of the Council of State noting the borders of tax-exempt land. The purpose of estate-limiting regulation was to keep estates within defined boundaries. Residents' newly opened fields abutting original exempted fields were sorely impacted by the new laws, while commended fields suffered less. It is hard to know if this conflict was what estate regulators foresaw, but what cannot be denied are the results of the regulations.[64]

It has been asserted that estate-limiting regulations had little effect, but in fact Iwashimizu Hachiman Shrine lost thirty-four estates to confiscation in the Enkyū era (1069–1074). Tōji too saw its property at Ōyama Estate in Tamba confiscated little by little. Tōdaiji's property at Kuroda Estate in Iga was exempted from confiscation but nonetheless bore the brunt of significant pressure from the provincial headquarters during the Regency era. Furthermore, compared with the estate over which the Northern Fujiwara Michinaga served as proprietor in Iga and Yamada Districts, Tōdaiji's Kuroda no shō residents were able to incorporate additional fields outside estate boundaries (*kanōden*) in Nabari District only through concerted effort and over a long period.[65] Therefore, it would be a serious mistake to overlook the basic conflict between urban nobles and official temples like Tōdaiji. But as the regent-led court ultimately accepted Tōdaiji's "temple slave" logic, urban nobles and official temples both represented the classical polity. Whatever conflict there was between them, that sense of unity won out. In its complaints submitted to the court, Tōdaiji described itself as an institution founded by Shōmu Tennō (r. 724–749) and argued that there was no reason to confiscate estates established to support the temple's realm-protecting rites. This was not just because of custom. The temple described its ongoing work as "restoring" the ideal of reciprocity between the Buddha's law and royal law (*ōhō*, or "the king's law") in the minds of urban nobles on the verge of forgetting *ritsuryō* ideals. Given such logic, Heian nobles found it impossible to refuse to restore temple fields.

Tōdaiji was generally forced into a defensive posture. Unlike the court nobles who transformed their economic base into a parasitic reliance on commended *shōen*, Tōdaiji's properties were fundamentally different. In the case of *shōen* commended to aristocrats, there were close ties with local land openers that preconditioned a recognition of these land developers and their management prerogatives. But early estates belonging to temples like Tōdaiji were premised on direct management of estate residents and the denial of local prerogatives. Since the political circumstances of the Heian Period favored the expansion of local prerogatives, central nobles were able to greatly expand their landed holdings across the realm while old official temples like Tōdaiji found it difficult to strengthen direct management over local land openers. The best that temples could do was to strive to gain the privilege of "non-entry" (*funyū*), by which provincial officials were barred from the temple's property. Temples might also seek unified control of an estate (*ichienteki shihai*) by seeing an estate custodian appointed. In the earlier *ritsuryō* era, Tōdaiji and *ritsuryō* officials had shared the same interests. But in the new environment of expanding perquisites for local land openers—and the central nobles' development of the commended estate system in response to same—the old official temples developed "non-entry" to preserve their prerogatives established according to *ritsuryō* principles.

The central nobility and the old temples were both representatives of the classical age. But the regents, while not yet medieval in terms of their culture, actually exhibited intellectual tendencies prefiguring those of medieval times. Urban nobles fashioning their estates from commended land had no intention of creating any sort of new political structure. Nonetheless, what started out as unofficial management of estates by the Regents' House administrative office (*Sekkanke mandokoro*) turned that office into a locus of realm-wide power. That was not in itself a denial of *ritsuryō*, but the move toward governance of land and cultivators by such a household agency surely reflects progress toward a new and different political system. Meanwhile, members of the monastic communities on Mount Hiei and in Nara bore sacred trees and palanquins to Kyoto for religious protests in later Heian times for a variety of reasons, one of which was to insist on the inalienability of state and religion—a very old political ideal—in the face of regental governance. Monastic and shrine protestors were expressing old values in a new age.

After initiation of the "no entry" policy for provincial authorities on temple estates, we can distinguish the existence of two distinct classical worlds. Their relations were articulated in prohibitions against new religious practices at the old official temples. As I have said, Amidism was the most important religious production of the Heian urban nobility, and its emphasis on individual salvation put it in fundamental conflict with the Buddhism of the great official temples. Given the basic beliefs of Amidism, it could not help but trickle down to countryside hamlets where it began to produce a genuinely medieval religion. As that happened, conflict with the old official temples became unavoidable. What began as a religious confrontation then became a political fight. Specifically, as the new beliefs penetrated into the hamlet, primary converts were generally members of the land-opening class. Confirming that, just as the Amidist Senshuji of Takada was built on the foundation of the old Makabe family residence, so was Nichiren's memorial temple built on the remains of the old Namiki family homestead.[66] Likewise, a Jishu follower who battled prohibitions by Kyoto's Eastern Temple, Tōji, was a wealthy cultivator named Hōami from Yano Estate, of which the official temple Tōji was the proprietor.[67] And at Tōdaiji's Ōbe Estate in Harima the custodian at the local Jōdoji who was a practitioner of *nembutsu* (chanting the name of Amida Buddha) was a local land opener.[68] In short local land openers were the first to accept the new Buddhist ideals and practices prohibited by the official temples.[69]

Shrines had always served as centers of spiritual activity in the hamlet, and shrine worship remained important both for agrarian communities and kin groups. But since land openers were important members of local agrarian communities and were also able to assert themselves outside such communities, the communitarian beliefs and ideals of realm-protection embraced by the old Buddhism seemed wanting in their eyes. Based on individual self-awareness and interior reflection, they converted to the new Buddhism to gain salvation as individuals. They harmonized group and individual beliefs in the everyday reality of hamlet life, but such harmony quickly dissipated when problems moved from the communal life of the hamlet into the political arena. Indeed, fifteenth-century followers of the Ikkō sect in the Hokuriku region went so far as to say that to deny the various deities and Buddhas (*shoshin shobutsu*) was a natural consequence of Shinshu teachings. The monk Rennyo—whose preaching initially inspired Ikkō members—spent extraordinary energy suppressing the sect because he was anxious about the resulting discord with traditional authority. For similar reasons, the Ji sect followers of Ippen amended Hōnen's views and inserted shrine worship into its teachings, making the issue of faith not just a personal one but also a political one. Since a new social class received such teachings, a complex political problem emerged—members of the Ji sect within Tōdaiji's Ōbe Estate formed their solidarity at Jōdoji to resist Tōdaiji. They eventually attacked the estate office and even wounded local shrine officials. This group of *nembutsu* practitioners were local elites, and to resist Tōdaiji they were even willing to ally themselves with the deputy provincial constable (*shugodai*).

Thus, the new Buddhist groups of Kamakura times and later nurtured resistance by local land openers toward Tōdaiji. It is important to note, however, that Harima's Ōbe Estate was actually a holding closely associated with Tōdaiji's Hachiman Shrine—there was naturally some tendency for Ōbe residents to resist Tōdaiji's monks. But to do so they had first to liberate themselves from the authority of the Nara Hachiman Shrine and its attendants (*kambito*). Since that was impossible for a community of estate dwellers whose spiritual life was centered around a shrine, such liberation became possible only for members of the land-opening class as they developed over time.

Resistance to Tōdaiji as estate proprietor and conversion to the "new Buddhism" were therefore two facets of a single historical process for local land openers. The old official temples did not exert pressure on new Buddhist groups as rivals in terms of proselytizating or competition for estates. The competition concerned influence over and control of the land-opening class itself. So do we find prohibitions against both private land openers and *bakufu* housemen entering the properties of the old temples—the two were closely related phenomena. From the late Heian Period into medieval times, by denying and excluding the new, institutions of the classical world, including Tōdaiji, walked on toward their historical demise.

Notes

1. A good overview of this publishing history can be found in an explanatory essay by Nagahara Keiji in Ishimoda's collected works, vol. 5. See Nagahara Keiji 1988.

2. This reminds us of the temple's troubles at the hands of the Mino Genji in the eleventh and twelfth centuries. See chapter 11 by Miyazaki in this volume.

3. For the best English rendering of the Jōei Formulary see Hall 1906.

4. There are several English translations of Kakuichi's *Heike monogatari*, including Kitagawa and Tsuchida 1975, and McCullough 1988. For an English rendering of the *Tannishō*, see Hirota 1982 and Unno 1984. And for a contextual discussion, see Kasahara Kazuo 2001, 193–99.

5. Notably, a recent study of medieval Japan translated from the French uses similar language. See Souryi 2001. Indeed, Souryi's views are very close to those of Ishimoda.

6. See for instance Irumada Nobuo and Murai Shōsuke 1986, Amino Yoshihiko 1986, and Amino Yoshihiko et al. 1988.

7. In addition to the essay by Nagahara Keiji cited above, the final three volumes of Ishimoda's collected works include helpful articles by various historians on Ishimoda's work. Also of interest is a special issue of *Rekishi hyōron* on Ishimoda's oeuvre, "Ishimoda Shō-shi no hito to gakumon," No. 436 (1986).

8. The essay interpreted here is one subsection of Ishimoda Shō 1957, 218–63.

9. Interpreter's note: Ishimoda is referring here to new land-opening laws issued in 723 and 743. They provided that land openers were to seek permission for opening land from provincial governors. Amounts of land that could be opened depended on the rank, or sometimes the post, of the opener. According to the 743 law, openers and their heirs were to be permitted to hold newly opened land in perpetuity when they also opened irrigation facilities to water the new fields.

10. Interpreter's note: Concerning *kueiden*, in 923 the chief administrator of the Kyūshū headquarters (the Dazaifu) proposed that large numbers of public fields be cultivated by conscript farmers who were to be given seed and tools by the government. Members of the local elite were to be employed as overseers. The government would then collect the entire harvest. The purpose was to guarantee increased production. The strategy is seen as a major stage in the reform of the *ritsuryō* tax system moving from poll taxes to land-based taxes. But many aspects of the system as it actually functioned remain unclear.

11. Interpreter's note: The term for unthreshed rice is *kentō*; that for unhulled rice is *ei*. Such subsidiary payments were termed *junmai*, "rice equivalents."

12. Interpreter's note: For a good discussion in English see Batten 1993 and Kiley 1999, esp. 122–23.

13. See Ishimoda Shō 1957, part 2. Interpreter's note: This development can be clearly seen through the documents of Kuroda Estate. See Takeuchi Rizō 1975–1979.

14. Interpreter's note: In English see Batten 1993.

15. Interpreter's note: See Mass 1983, 85–89. Mass usually translates *zaichō kanjin* as "hereditary provincial officer." He describes how a local Fujiwara lineage in Aki Province used their public officerships to gain confirmation of their landholdings through several generations. Holding public office, opening land, and grasping wealth and power locally were closely related in the mid-to-late Heian Period. Mass nonetheless points out the vulnerability of distinguished provincial houses to the forces of central politics—an important house, the Chiba, lost its holdings in the twelfth century. But in Kamakura times, as housemen of the Kamakura Bakufu, provincial elites became more secure.

16. Interpreter's note: One such neighborhood official was the *tone.*

17. These associated salary fields were known as *zaichō myōden* (*myō* fields managed by officials of the provincial office, or *zaichō*), *gunji shikiden* (office fields of *gunji*), and *gōjiden* (fields belonging to township officials, or *gōji*).

18. Interpreter's note: Again, see Batten 1993, who dates this development from the tenth century and beyond.

19. Interpreter's note: Here Ishimoda demonstrates comparativist interests when he draws a parallel with the West. He observes, "The process was not unlike that when Germanic law matured and was synthesized with Roman law."

20. Interpreter's note: For confirming evidence, see an order against the practice archived in the early tenth-century compilation of ad hoc legislation, the *Ruijū sandai kyaku.* The order dates from Enryaku 17 (798): "The Izumo provincial chieftain also serves as shrine head. On the day when he is newly appointed he discards his senior wife and takes daughters of numerous commoners to wife, calling them 'shrine tribute maidens.'" See Shintei zōho kokushi taikei *Ruijū sandai kyaku,* vol. 1, 31.

21. Interpreter's note: According to Ishimoda, resort to the gods continued in Kamakura times, as seen in the *Protocols for Admissable Oaths* (*Kishōmon no jōjō*) dated 1235. These rules were probably established by the Office of Royal Police, the Kebiishichō. Such oaths were an important part of evidentiary statements by the twelfth century. See Satō Shin'ichi and Ikeuchi Yoshisuke 1955-78, vol. 1, 94–95. For a translation see J. Piggott's "On Admissible Oaths, 1235," unpublished manuscript. For examples of oaths from the Heian Period, see Takeuchi Rizō 1973-1980, vol. 6, doc. 2644, and vol. 7, doc. 3155.

22. See Ishimoda Shō 1957, part 3, sec. 2, "Bushidan no seiritsu." Interpreter's note: For a good discussion of the most recent research on the *ritsuryō* residence unit called *gōko*, see Akashi Kazunori 1966. According to Akashi, the *gōko* of the seventh through tenth centuries averaged twenty to thirty individuals and was led by its patriarch, the residence unit head (*koshu*). Members might include both kin and non-kin, including dependents (*yoriguchi*) and slaves (*nuhi*). Unlike the situation in China, however, the census unit consisted of real social units, nuclear households (*ie*) made up of husband, wife, and unmarried children. Such units functioned independently of the larger official census unit. See also Nambu Noboru 1992.

23. Interpreter's note: I suspect that Ishimoda would date this from the age when land opener Hasetsukabe Chikatada took over the district chieftaincy of Nabari District in the late eleventh century.

24. Interpreter's note: This story is told in *Togano-o Myōe Shōnin denki,* a biography of the holy man Myōe that was compiled sometime before 1250. In English see Lieteau 1975.

25. Interpreter's note: The *Chikubashō* is a set of rules for his heirs authored by the Ashikaga Bakufu prime minister (*kanrei*), Shiba Yoshimasa (1350–1410). For an English translation see Wilson 1982, 46–55.

26. Interpreter's note: See Takeuchi Rizō 1984–1995, vol. 6, doc. 4373. *Kamakura ibun* compiles the extant documents of the Kamakura Period. Hereafter *Kamakura ibun* will be cited as *KI.*

27. Interpreter's note: See *KI,* vol 6, 391, doc. 4357.

28. Interpreter's note: Mujū Ichien (1226–1312) was a Buddhist monk who compiled an eclectic collection of didactic tales, *Shasekishū,* in Kamakura times, beginning around 1283.

29. Interpreter's note: The *Gukanshō* is a history of Japan composed by the then-abbot of Enryakuji, Jien, early in the thirteenth century. Unlike earlier official histories, Jien's project was to diagnose current wrongs in society and to determine what might be done to correct them.

30. Interpreter's note: The *Hōsōshiyōshō* is a legal commentary dating from the late Heian or early Kamakura Period. It demonstrates key concerns and issues of legal scholars late in the classical era. For a good discussion on the history of slavery in Japan, see Nelson 2004.

31. Interpreter's note: Prior to the twelfth century, Tōdaiji documents often referred to its estate residents as *somaudo,* meaning woodsmen. It was only in the twelfth century that the term "temple slaves" (*tera no nuhi, jinu*) became common. For instance see Takeuchi Rizō 1975–1979, vol. 1, doc. 196, dated 1124.

32. Interpreter's note: On laws regulating estates (*shōen seiri rei*) see Satō 1979.

33. Ishimoda directs readers to documents in the twelfth-century *Chōya gunsai,* that demonstrate the role of heads (*chōja*) of the Kyōke and Shikike Fujiwara in securing appointment for Fujiwara *uji* members.

34. Interpreter's note: Yoshimi was the fifth son of Fujiwara Fuyutsugu. He was also Fujiwara Yoshifusa's full brother and a maternal uncle of Montoku Tennō. Several of his daughters served as royal consorts. In 834 the scholarly Yoshimi left the university to serve as a royal secretary (*kurōdo*), and later he served as a royal bodyguard and attendant. He was appointed to the Council of State as an advisor (*sangi*) after the Jōwa Disturbance of 842. Yoshifusa's clique was empowered by the latter, which excluded the Ōtomo-Tachibana clique from court. This disturbance in 842 prepared the way for a routinized Fujiwara regency, giving the Northern Fujiwara leadership at court. In 857 Yoshimi became minister of the right. He was involved in all the scholarly projects of the day, including compilation of the annal *Shoku nihon kōki,* the legal compendium *Jōgan kyaku,* and the procedural handbook *Jōgan shiki.*

35. Interpreter's note: Michitaka (953–995) was the eldest son of Northern Fujiwara Kaneie and a brother of the famous Michinaga. He achieved the junior third rank in 984. In 990 his daughter became Ichijō Tennō's consort, after which he served as regent. Although he hoped that his son would succeed him, his dream was dashed by a brother, Michikane, who became chancellor after Michitaka's death.

36. Interpreter's note: In this regard Ishimoda cites the example of the provincial governor of Mikawa, Minamoto Tsunemi. See the entry in the courtier journal *Shunki* dated Chōryaku 3 (1039) 11/01, for which a French rendering is available: Herail 2001- , vol. 1, 366–67. Ishimoda notes that divisiveness caused by diverging economic interests was also demonstrated by the Sugawara *uji* when its chieftainship was distanced from other members of the kin group after the chieftain was appointed director (*bettō*) of the family temple, Anrakuji. See the entry in the records of the Kamakura Bakufu, *Azuma kagami*, for Bunji 2 (1186) 06/05.

37. Interpreter's note: See the English rendering by Peter M. Wetzler in Wetzler 1977. Yoshishige's birth date is unknown but he died in 1002.

38. Interpreter's note: The *Sarashina nikki* was compiled in the mid-eleventh century by the daughter of a provincial governor, Sugawara Takasue, who accompanied her father out to the eastern province of Kazusa during his tour of duty. It covers some forty years of her life, in the provinces and in the capital, and it is therefore an important document for the mid-eleventh century.

39. Interpreter's note: Ishimoda notes that his study of the *Utsubo monogatari* led him to these conclusions. See Ishomoda Shō 1943.

40. Interpreter's note: Minamoto Takaakira was one of Daigo Tennō's princes. In 920 he was made a commoner and he took the daughter of (Northern) Fujiwara Morosuke as wife. But when his own daughter became the senior consort (*kisaki*) of the crown prince, he earned the enmity of the Regents' Line and was implicated in the Anna Coup of 969, for which he was exiled to the Dazaifu in Kyūshū. He was the author of the important handbook of court ritual and protocol, the *Saikyūki*. For an English translation of *Kagerō nikki*, see Arntzen 1997.

41. Interpreter's note: Sei Shōnagon was the daughter of a provincial governor who served at the court of Ichijō Tennō's senior consort, Fujiwara Teishi, in the early 990s. Besides penning her well-known *Pillow Book* (*Makura no sōshi*), Sei is remembered for her poetry collection, the *Sei Shōnagon shū*.

42. Interpreter's note: This is a theme that Japanese historians are taking up in greater detail recently. See for instance Hotate Michihisa 1996, in which Hotate specifically refers to the Heian monarchy as an "urban kingship." For an English translation of *Utsubo monogatari*, see Uraki 1984; and for *Genji monogatari*, see the translations by Arthur Waley, Edward Seidensticker, and Royall Tyler.

43. Interpreter's note: The *Shōmonki* narrates events of the rebellion of Taira Masakado in the late 930s. It is thought to have been written not long after those events by someone in the capital. The *Mutsuwaki* describes events of the Former Nine Years War in mid-eleventh century Mutsu. It is thought to have been compiled not long after the events it chronicles. The extensive tale collection known as the *Konjaku monogatarishū* dates from the late Heian Period.

44. Interpreter's note: The tale is entitled, "How the Fifth-Ranker of the Ministry of Finance Was Afraid of Cats." See *Konjaku monogatarishū*, vol. 28, tale 31.

45. Interpreter's note: While recent scholarship in both Japanese and English has become increasingly mindful of the fact that Kakuichi's *Heike monogatari* is but one part of a broader corpus, it seems that Ishimoda's sense of the *Heike monogatari* was mostly fixed on Kakuichi's text, compiled in the mid-fourteenth century. He mentions the ur-*Heike* text thought to have been composed by Fujiwara Yukinaga, which is not extant; but he does not mention the many other variants, which include performed and read versions. In English on the broader Heike corpus see Bialock 2000, Hasegawa 1967, as well as analysis in Butler 1966, Butler 1967, and Butler 1969.

46. Interpreter's note: This makes it clear that even if the establishment of the Kamakura Bakufu did not represent the beginning of the medieval world for Ishimoda, in his estimation the Gempei War still amounted to a major historical divide.

47. Interpreter's note: Ishimoda adds an important thought here, although it seems somewhat misplaced in the body of the argument. He opines, "There is an accord, a unity, between the epic tale and Amidist soteriology, and therein is found the distinctiveness of the *Heike monogatari* and its special character as a medieval epic . . . The most important reason that the *Heike* is seen to be aristocratic literature is that it did not emerge among warriors. It is true that the *Heike* as a whole does not articulate a distinct consciousness or emotions and lifestyles of warriors. It was not, therefore, warrior literature. But this does not mean that it was aristocratic literature either, or that it was in any way distanced from the warriors' [world]." For an argument in English against viewing the new religious trends of Kamakura as a "reformation," see Foard 1980.

48. Interpreter's note: In other words, Ishimoda's conceptualization is in agreement with that of Barbara Ruch. See Ruch 1990.

49. An early reference can be found in the *Chūyūki*, the journal of the courtier Fujiwara Munetada, in an entry dated 1114 02/18. See Zōho shiryō taisei kankōkai 1974, vol. 4, 266.

50. Interpreter's note: Ishimoda stresses the tension between two concurrent modes of production underway in Heian times, that of the more despotic and bureaucratic *tennō*'s court in the capital versus a feudal (*hōkenteki*) lordship by which local elites dominated cultivators in the countryside as land openers and landlords. Ishimoda's fundamental historical paradigm is Marxist. How the two modes related one to the other is a major theme in Ishimoda's study of Kuroda Estate.

51. Interpreter's note: In English on Sugawara see Borgen 1986.

52. For a more detailed account of this argument see Ishimoda Shō 1957, chapter two.

53. Interpreter's note: In light of Ishimoda's thoughts here, readers may want to reconsider the meaningful concept of the *wakan* (Japanese-Chinese) dialectic proposed by David Pollock. See Pollack 1986, esp. 27.

54. Interpreter's note: On the debate concerning *kokufū bunka*, see the relatively recent overview in Enomoto Jun'ichi 1992.

55. Satō Shin'ichi and Ikeuchi Yoshisuke 1955-78, vol. 1, 56–57.

56. Tōma Seita argued that the Fujiwara designed *shōen*-limiting regulations (*shōen seiri rei*) quite consciously to result in commendation, which led to accumulation of estates in the regents' own hands. See Tōma Seita 1942.

57. Interpreter's note: A *honjo* was the preeminent estate proprietor with very high status at court; the *ryōshu* was the secondary proprietor in the later Heian estate hierarchy.

58. The daughter of Ōtomo Yasumarō, Iratsume, was considered by many the best female poet of her era, in the mid-Nara Period. She had close relations with a number of important courtiers, including Fujiwara Maro and her half-brother, Ōtomo Naramaro. Her poetry is said to have been influenced by that of her famous poet kinsman, Ōtomo Yakamochi.

59. Interpreter's note: For other views, see essays by Toda and Hotate in this volume. Both would probably argue that Ishimoda is overemphasizing the isolation of the high court nobility here.

60. Interpreter's note: Here I am using an expression from Bruce Batten's work, which fits Ishimoda's own articulation quite well. See Batten 1989.

61. Interpreter's note: Kōfukuji in Nara was the Fujiwara family temple. For more on this temple's development and role, see Motoki's essay in this collection. In English see Adolphson 2000.

62. Interpreter's note: A somewhat different view comes through Motoki's essay in this volume: he notes that the regents may have been less supportive of Kōfukuji than of Enryakuji. Motoki's view, based on detailed research, indicates a new perspective against which Ishimoda's views should be considered.

63. Interpreter's note: The source is Jien's *Gukanshō*.

64. Interpreter's note: It is generally said that a tremendous amount of new land was opened during the tenures of Shirakawa, Toba, and Go-Shirakawa as retired monarchs. Much of this land was commended to temples associated with the retired monarchs. See Hurst 1976, esp. 125–278.

65. Interpreter's note: In fact beginning in the 1050s, over 150 years Tōdaiji waged its long battle to get fields to the east of the Nabari River recognized as part of Kuroda Estate. By 1121, 100 temple-associated settlers had built homes east of the river and provincial officials bemoaned their inability to collect taxes from them. Nonetheless, in the Yagawa area the provincial officials enlisted the district chieftain to serve on their side and he became the enemy of Tōdaiji settlers in that vicinity. See, for example, Takeuchi Rizō 1975–1979, vol. 1, docs. 86, 95, 148, 292, 321, and 335.

66. Interpreter's note: On Nichiren and Senshuji in English, see Rodd 1978 and Kasahara Kazuo 2001, 255–84.

67. Interpreter's note: The Jishu, or Time Sect, was the corporate body of Ippen's followers. In English see Thornton 1999 and Kasahara Kazuo 2001, 211–26.

68. Interpreter's note: Here Ishimoda may be overlooking the fact that the rebuilder of Tōdaiji in the early Kamakura age was himself an Amidist proselytizer, Chōgen. In other words, within Tōdaiji itself there were monks who practiced Amidism. On these proselytizers, known as *hijiri*, see Goodwin 1994, especially 67–106 on Chōgen specifically.

69. Interpreter's note: An example that Ishimoda did not include here is Kumagai Naozane's conversion to Hōnen's following. In English see Miyazaki Fumiko 1992.

14

East and West in the Late Classical Age

KOYAMA YASUNORI

Introduction by Bruce L. Batten

ONE IMPORTANT MEASURE OF PROGRESS in historical research in Japan has been the publication of multivolume essay collections designed to summarize the current "state of the field" for educated lay readers. Among the best of these collective efforts, at least in the subfield of Japanese history, is the *Iwanami kōza nihon rekishi* (*Iwanami Lectures on Japanese History*).[1] This series has gone through several incarnations since its original conception, the essay here being taken from the twenty-seven volumes published between 1975 and 1977. Four of those volumes were devoted to ancient and classical history, and of the thirty-six articles they contain, Koyama Yasunori's study of "East and West in the Late Classical Age" is my personal favorite.

According to the author, "East and West in the Late Classical Age" was written "to clarify the historical and regional differences between eastern Japan [Tōgoku] and western Japan [Saigoku] that developed in the Heian Period, during the transition from classical *ritsuryō*-based society to medieval *shōen*-based society." The article is composed of four main sections followed by a conclusion. Although each of these sections contains a wealth of historical detail, the main points are fairly easy to summarize. I would like to discuss each section briefly before assessing the overall significance of Koyama's work.

The first section represents the author's attempt to define his chosen analytical terms. Here Koyama examines historical usage of the terms "Tōgoku" and "Saigoku" from the Nara through the Kamakura periods. The author finds that Saigoku was not a distinct concept during the *ritsuryō* period, presumably because the political elite "did not see much of a qualitative difference between the Kinai and western Japan as a whole." The term "Tōgoku," by contrast, was fairly common. It was used in three different senses, but most commonly it referred to the area east of and including Tōtōmi in the Tōkaidō circuit and Shinano in the Tōsandō circuit. According to Koyama, this region, unlike western Japan, had an independent existence in the mind of the Kyoto aristocracy because of its historical subordination to the Yamato state. Later, in the Kamakura Period, Saigoku came into its own as an autonomous concept, most commonly referring to western Honshū, Shikoku, and Kyūshū. Tōgoku also remained in common use, although it then sometimes referred to a larger region than before—the entire eastern half of Japan. Koyama thinks that the emergence of Tōgoku and Saigoku as "equal and competing regional concepts" reflected the Kamakura warrior government's attempt to place eastern Japan on equal ideological footing with the west.

Next, Koyama provides an excellent summary of political events in western Japan during the Nara and Heian periods. The author describes in considerable detail Japan's diplomatic relations with China and Korea during the eighth and ninth centuries, the growth of maritime trade with the continent after the ninth century, and the emergence of "pirate-type warriors" along the Inland Sea during the middle and late Heian Period. The main points to be gleaned from this section are that western Japan had deep and continuous ties with the Asian continent, that most transportation and communication within the region was by sea rather than by land, and that western warrior bands tended to be composed of sea-based pirates rather than land-based cavalry units.

The third section provides a similar survey of events in eastern Japan. Koyama first describes state relations with the "barbarian" Emishi, including the establishment of districts and provinces in northeast Honshū, the role of Fort Taga and other Nara-period fortifications, the shift to a policy of outright military conquest in the late Nara and early Heian periods, and the government's attempt to integrate the original residents of this region into the larger Japanese polity. Much of the discussion here is based on the work of Takahashi Tomio, whose essay "The Classical Polity and Its Frontier" is also in this volume (see chapter 5). An important and original point made by Koyama is that state policies vis-à-vis the Emishi were organically linked with the defense of the western periphery in Kyūshū. The author then turns his attention to the emergence of mounted warriors in the Tōgoku. The main point here is that elite warriors in the east were not pirates, as in the west, but mounted fighters skilled in archery. The emphasis on horse-riding, according to Koyama, was due to the prevalence of overland (as opposed to maritime) routes of communication and to the widespread existence of pasture land. Archery, he contends, was a skill learned from the Emishi.

In the next section, Koyama looks at patterns of landholding in the late Heian Period. Basing most of his discussion around the estate holdings of a "royally constituted vow temple," Hōshōgon'in, he compares and contrasts the characteristics of estates (*shōen*) in the Tōgoku, Saigoku, and Kinai regions. Here Koyama makes a number of important points, including: (1) estates tended to be small in central Japan and large along the periphery; (2) estates in central and western Japan paid dues to central proprietors in the form of grain and other "heavy freight," whereas those in eastern Japan sent mostly "light freight" such as cloth, a difference Koyama relates to the fact that maritime transportation was most developed in the west; (3) estates in the former Emishi territories in northeast Honshū paid dues in the form of gold, furs, and other "primitive luxury products"; (4) estates in northern Kyūshū served as bases for international maritime trade and paid dues in the form of high-quality textiles, drugs, fragrances, and other imported luxury items; (5) militarized "resident proprietors" (*zaichi ryōshu*), that is to say, local landlords, were able to exert more control over agricultural villages in the east than in central Japan or the west, where village communities had greater autonomy. Koyama seems to ascribe this difference to the greater opportunity for land reclamation —requiring strong leadership—in the eastern part of the country.

The concluding section examines the role of the Taira and Minamoto families in the late Heian Period. After tracing the history of the two families, Koyama attempts to relate several well-known differences between these families to regional characteristics discussed in previous sections. For example, the ultimate failure by the Taira to achieve a stable, autonomous power base is ascribed to the "volatile" nature of the western pirate bands. The success of the Minamoto family in creating a new form of government, by contrast, is said to lie in the "autonomous" nature of eastern society, which facilitated the formation of strong new organizational forms.

For the Western reader, "East and West in the Late Classical Age" is important for two main reasons. First, and most obvious, it presents much historical information not otherwise available in English. Second, and more important, the theme of regional diversity provides a new way of looking at premodern Japanese history. In terms of information content, the article easily accomplishes Koyama's self-imposed task of clarifying differences between eastern and western Japan during the Heian Period. In fact, the article goes well beyond its relatively limited agenda, both chronologically and geographically. Koyama discusses the broader sweep of Japanese history from Nara to Kamakura times. And while the eastern and western peripheries receive the lion's share of attention, developments in central Japan, particularly with regard to land tenure, are also discussed at length.

While a good deal of the specific information in the article is available elsewhere in Japanese, less has found its way into the English literature. To be sure, the determined reader can discover information on diplomacy in the Nara Period, maritime trade in the Heian Period, the emergence of mounted warriors in the Tōgoku, and characteristics of the Taira and Minamoto families.[2] But many other topics, including the conceptual aspects of political geography in classical Japan, the role of "pirate-type" warriors in the Inland Sea, and the regional characteristics of estates all receive their first detailed English-language treatment in the present essay.

Koyama's article also breaks new conceptual ground in its focus on regionalism in early Japanese history. To be sure, local history is of great interest to both professional and amateur historians in Japan, and there is a voluminous literature, both academic and popular, on the history of any given region. But few if any of the works in this genre go beyond their primary geographic focus to make interregional comparisons. And while books and articles on specific historical topics like the estate system or the emergence of warrior bands sometimes make comparisons between different geographic areas, there is little that transcends these specific topics to give a comprehensive overview of regionalism in early Japan. Aside from the present article, in fact, I know of only one other major statement on this topic—Amino Yoshihiko's *Higashi to nishi no kataru nihon no rekishi* (*Telling Japanese History, East and West*), published in 1982.[3]

While the general paucity of English-language works on early Japan explains the lack of published material on regionalism, the gap in Japanese-language historiography is more puzzling. The most likely explanation, as noted by Amino in his book, is that Japanese historians, like their countrymen at large, tend to see Japan as a *tan'itsu minzoku*—a single, homogeneous nation. Of course, there is an element of truth in this concept. Japan does have its ethnic minorities (the Ainu people, the Korean population, etc.) and its social outcasts, the *burakumin*. But these groups add up to only a small percentage of the country's 125 million permanent residents. And while regional variations in social customs, food preferences, and speech patterns are widespread, most of the differences are relatively minor. Whether a man speaks with the accent of Osaka or that of far-eastern Honshū (Tōhoku), the underlying language is still fundamentally the same.

But the fact that Japanese society is relatively homogeneous today does not guarantee that things were always that way. After all, the ancestors of today's Japanese are known to have come to the archipelago from different places at different times. Although it was previously believed that most differences between these immigrant populations disappeared quite early in Japan's history—the Yayoi and Kofun periods are often cited—recent studies have shown that Japanese society retained its "multiethnic" character until the early Heian Period.[4] Questions of ethnicity aside, regionalism of all kinds undoubtedly played an important role in Japanese history until at least the 1900s. Much of contemporary Japan's cultural homogeneity, one suspects, is the product of modern communications and transportation and of a centralized educational system. None of this existed before the Meiji Period, but the image of a homogeneous Japan has nonetheless had a strong influence on how modern historians see their nation's past.

Koyama's article does not answer all these questions. Limited in chronological scope, it can trace neither the origins of regionalism nor its ultimate fate in the modern period. Nor does it discuss, except briefly with reference to the Emishi, the question of ethnic or racial diversity in the Japanese archipelago. Both of these problems are dealt with at greater length in Amino's stimulating book, to which the interested reader is referred. But for a short yet solid introduction to the important topic of regional diversity in early Japan, readers can do no better than the article presented here.[5]

KOYAMA YASUNORI

East and West in the Late Classical Age

Interpreted by Bruce L. Batten

My task in the present essay is to clarify the historical and regional differences between Tōgoku and Saigoku that developed in Japan in the Heian Period, during the transition from the classical *ritsuryō*-based society to the medieval *shōen*-based society.[6] Although regional variation has been the focus of much previous research in the fields of classical and medieval history, such studies tend to compare and contrast regions on the basis of whether they were "advanced" or "peripheral" or somewhere in between. The use of differences in economic development as a criterion for analysis is a fundamental research tool which has produced many significant results worthy of further development. The weak point of this method, however, is that it reduces the richly varied social characteristics of different regions to simple differences in economic, and in particular agricultural, productivity. Accordingly, it is necessary to introduce more varied analytical tools in order to achieve a correct understanding of the characteristics of the regional structure. In the present chapter I will first discuss the highly political nature of regional concepts such as Tōgoku and Saigoku in the classical and medieval periods, and then proceed to show how the political structure of local society changed over time. To put it another way, I hope to demonstrate the potential for a new kind of political history, one that takes account of regional social structure during the transition from classical to medieval in Japan.[7]

If the problem is formulated this way, obvious candidates for analysis include (1) the Masakado and Sumitomo rebellions, which broke out in eastern and western Japan at almost the same time in the tenth century; and (2) the local power bases of the Minamoto and Taira families. But these issues have received excellent treatment in recent articles by Fukuda Toyohiko and Tanaka Minoru.[8] I will therefore limit my discussion to the specific regional characteristics of these conflicts.

A question that I have consciously attempted to answer in this article is how the Tōgoku and Saigoku interacted with the so-called East Asian world. Because the Saigoku functioned as Japan's gateway to Asia, it always had deep political and commercial ties with the outside world. For that reason, interaction with the East Asian world is an issue that must be confronted in order to understand the special characteristics of the Saigoku. In comparison, the Tōgoku's relationship with East Asia was at best indirect. When we consider, however, that gold from Mutsu and Dewa Provinces (known as the Ōshū region) was an important export item in the Japan-Sung trade, and that the Ōshū Fujiwara family of these provinces maintained an immense hoard of imported luxury goods (*karamono*), it is clear that even the Tōgoku was linked to the East Asian world through the medium of trade.[9]

Above and beyond fundamental foreign relations, characteristics of the "East Country" (Tōgoku) and the "West Country" (Saigoku) were also influenced by the political ideology that resulted from the interaction of the domestic political order with the international, China-centered political order known as the "tribute system," of which the *ritsuryō*-based state was itself a part. This is because the political role of the Tōgoku was in part defined by the "Emishi problem" and, as previous scholars have noted, the *ritsuryō* state's control of the Emishi had much in common with its policies vis-à-vis Silla and Parhae, whose inhabitants were also treated as "people outside the fold" (*kagai'nin*). An important objective of the present chapter, therefore, is to contribute to the theory of international relations in classical East Asia.[10]

East Japan and West Japan in Classical and Medieval Times

"Tōgoku" and "Saigoku" referred to specific regions in the classical and medieval periods. However, the geographical extent of these terms is not entirely clear—different authors understand them in different ways, and usage is often loose. In part, this stems from the multifaceted nature of the terms themselves, but such vagueness cannot be tolerated here. We must begin with an examination of how these terms were used in order to make their meaning, and particularly their geographic scope, as precise as possible. This is not simply an exercise in semantics. By doing so and building whenever possible on previous research, we should also be able to cast some light on the politico-geographic perceptions of the ruling class—that is, how they viewed the Tōgoku and the Saigoku under the classical *ritsuryō* system and during the medieval Kamakura Period.[11]

Under the *ritsuryō* system, Japan's political geography took the form of a series of concentric circles. At the center was the capital and the Kinai, the five-province hub in the capital region. Further out were the ordinary provinces, which were linked to the Kinai by the seven circuit highways (*shichidō*) [see Map 0.1, frontis].[12] Beyond these were regions "outside the fold" (*kagai*), to which the sovereign's authority did not extend. This classification, which was based on the "middle kingdom" ideology of ancient China, presumed that the sovereign's authority became progressively weaker as one moved outward from the capital. Chinese rulers therefore employed various policies aimed at enlarging the scope of their authority, to bring new areas "within the fold." A similar kind of regional division is seen in the Popular Affairs (Minbu) section of the early tenth-century *Protocols of the Engi Era* (*Engi shiki*), which distinguishes among the Kinai, "near provinces," "middle provinces," and "far provinces" on the basis of the number of days required for tax shipments to reach the capital.

The concepts of Tōgoku and Saigoku, by contrast, are derivative. They are not defined in the *ritsuryō* codes and reflect a somewhat different conception of political geography. Moreover, the terms themselves have a completely different historical origin. Whereas Tōgoku and related regional appellations such as "Kantō" and "Bandō" occur with some frequency in historical sources from the *ritsuryō* era, there are almost no clear references to Saigoku.[13] My reading is, the lack of references to Saigoku means that aristocrat-officials of the *ritsuryō* period did not see much of a qualitative difference between the Kinai and western Japan as a whole.

The next problem is the meaning of Tōgoku and related regional appellations such as "Kantō" and "Bandō." The latter two terms are defined in the *ritsuryō* codes and had precise administrative meanings. "Kantō" designated various provinces east of the three barriers—Suzuka in Ise Province, Fuwa in Mino Province, and Arachi in Echizen Province—which are described in the Law on Military Defense (Gumbōryō) in the *ritsuryō* codes. Since all three barriers bordered Ōmi Province, the Kantō region encompassed the Tōkaidō, Tōsandō, and Hokurikudō circuits minus the provinces of Ōmi, Iga, and Wakasa. "Bandō" meant "east of the passes" of Ashigara and Usui, namely, all provinces from Sagami Province eastward in the Tōkaidō circuit and from Kōzuke Province eastward in the Tōsandō circuit[14] (see Map 6.1, p. 148). Judging from the fact that the Bandō is mentioned repeatedly in connection with punitive expeditions against the Emishi as well as from the existence of frequent references to the "eight Bandō provinces," its territory would seem to have been more or less equivalent to that of the modern Kantō region. The *ritsuryō* polity thus treated the Kantō and Bandō as more or less distinct regions.

The Tōgoku, by contrast, was never clearly defined—the term is used vaguely in historical sources. By induction, however, we can identify three main types of usage. First, "Tōgoku" is sometimes used as a synonym for Kantō, that is, as a label for the area east of the three barriers. We know this because in the Jinshin War of 672 the troops of Prince Ōama (later, Great King Temmu) are said to have entered the Tōgoku after passing through Ōmi's Fuwa Barrier (see Map 7.3, p. 188); and because during the so-called Kusuko Coup in 810, the retired Heizei Tennō fled from the Kawaguchi Road into the Tōgoku. Second, "Tōgoku" is sometimes used as a synonym for the Bandō. While uncommon, clear examples are provided by the late-Heian *Honchō seiki* annal, which uses "Tōgoku" and "Bandō" to describe the area of Taira Masakado's rebellion in the early tenth century. The third sense of "Tōgoku" appears in passages such as "many border guards [*sakimori*] from the Tōgoku remain in Kyūshū" and "men from the Tōgoku were deployed as border guards."[15] Since Tōgoku stands on its own in these sources, we can assume that it denotes the area from Tōtōmi Province eastward in the Tōkaidō circuit, and from Shinano Province eastward in the Tōsandō circuit. This, as we know from the poems by border guards in the *Man'yōshū*, was where these soldiers were conscripted. Although border guards were not recruited from Mutsu and Dewa, these provinces may also have sometimes been included within this third definition of "Tōgoku," given the fact that some of the "songs of the east country" (*azumauta*, wherein Azuma denoted the Tōgoku) in the eighth-century *Man'yōshū* originated in Mutsu. Another well-known characteristic of this Tōgoku region is that many of its provinces were required to send horses to the capital as tribute.

Although "Tōgoku" was thus used in these three ways during the *ritsuryō* period, we should also note that these regional concepts were interrelated and evolved over time. The first meaning of "Tōgoku," as a synonym for "Kantō," is thought to be the oldest, while the second, in which it serves as a synonym for

"Bandō," appears later. The most common sense of the word would seem to have been the third, where "Tōgoku" referred to the provinces of Tōtōmi and Shinano and parts further east in the Tōkaidō and Tōsandō circuits.[16] Although there was no real concept of Saigoku under the *ritsuryō* system, aristocrat-officials perceived the Tōgoku, whether broadly or narrowly defined, as a qualitatively different world that was subordinate to the Kinai and the western provinces. Such subordination was rooted in the historical eastward advance of Yamato kingship, and it was institutionalized in special obligations such as the conscription of border guards and the rendering of horses as tribute.

In contrast with these Nara usages, next I would like to examine the usage of "Tōgoku" and "Saigoku" in the Kamakura Period (1185–1333), when a medieval sense of the concepts was established. In contrast with the situation in the classical period, "Saigoku" was the more common term in Kamakura times. According to legal pronouncements issued by the Kamakura Bakufu, "Matters in the Saigoku are to be adjudicated by Rokuhara" and "Rokuhara is the office which polices the capital [Kyoto] and exercises judicial authority in the Saigoku."[17] The "Saigoku" was thus legally defined as the area under the jurisdiction of the Bakufu's deputies (*tandai*) stationed at the Rokuhara headquarters in Kyoto—the central provinces of Owari (later Mikawa), Hida, Kaga, and all parts further west. Nonetheless, the same legal sources sometimes make a distinction between the region around the Kinai and the Saigoku, as in one statute "concerning boundary disputes in the area around the Kinai and in the Saigoku."[18] We can therefore postulate the existence of a second, narrow concept of "Saigoku" denoting only part of the area supervised by Kamakura's representatives at Rokuhara in the capital. An examination of standard Kamakura-period sources such as the *Azuma kagami*, *Gukanshō*, and *Heike monogatari* confirms that the term "Saigoku" was also used to refer to the sphere of Taira (alt. Heike) power during the period of civil war.[19] In concrete terms, it refers to those areas of the San'yōdō, Nankaidō, and Saikaidō circuits that bordered the Inland Sea. Broad and narrow definitions of the Saigoku thus coexisted in the Kamakura Period, but the narrow sense would seem to have had more currency in society at large than the broader legal definition.

Since there are relatively few references to Tōgoku in Kamakura times, its usage then is somewhat problematic, but it would seem that it too was used in three ways. First, "Tōgoku" was used in contradistinction to the area under Rokuhara jurisdiction. In concrete terms this meant Mikawa (and, later, Tōtōmi) in the Tōkaidō circuit, Shinano in the Tōsandō circuit, Etchū and Noto in the Hokurikudō circuit, and all parts further east. This represented the broadest sense and that defined by law. The term was also used as a synonym for the so-called Kantō allotment provinces (*Kantō onbun kuniguni*), which corresponded to the fifteen provinces from Tōtōmi and Shinano in the west to Mutsu and Dewa in the east. The Bakufu exercised special rights and privileges in this region through its control of provincial headquarters.[20] If we ignore Mutsu and Dewa, this conception of the Tōgoku is identical to the most common meaning of the term under the *ritsuryō* system. Finally, Tōgoku also referred to the eight Bandō provinces.[21] Of these three usages, the most representative is the second, whereby "Tōgoku" refers to the area from Tōtōmi and Shinano on east. The third use of the term probably reflects the fact that the Bandō served consistently as the core of this larger region. "Tōgoku" in the first and broadest sense—where it referred to half of the entire realm—was most likely an ideological extension of the original *ritsuryō* conception.[22] The concept of "Tōgoku" was thus enlarged during the Kamakura Period; but in contrast to the *ritsuryō* period, it was a subjective, autonomous expansion spearheaded by the Kamakura Bakufu and intended as an ideological assertion of equality between "east" and "west" Japan. It was during the Kamakura Period that "Tōgoku" and "Saigoku" first came to be used as equal and competing regional concepts.

The West Country and the East Asian World Order

Foreign Relations in the Late Nara and Early Heian Periods

From the Chinese perspective the international order in East Asia, which from Ch'in and Han dynasty times was based on Chinese suzerainty over surrounding kingdoms, is generally represented as "the tribute system." The T'ang Dynasty, like its predecessors, was a universal empire, meaning that the neighboring kingdoms of Silla, Parhae, and Japan were all subsumed within its sphere in one way or another. This type of international order is characterized by a type of feedback in which the external stimulus of presenting tribute and receiving gifts produces changes in a country's domestic politics, while at the same time domestic politics serve to define the nature of foreign relations.[23] Nevertheless, the relationships between T'ang China and surrounding states were not homogeneous, and the impact of external stimuli naturally differed from state to state.[24]

Japan presented tribute to T'ang monarchs from the seventh century onward by dispatching envoys called *kentōshi*. But unlike rulers of Silla and Parhae, Japan's kings were never formally recognized by T'ang Sons of Heaven, and relations between Japan and China remained fairly distant. Japan attempted to establish an equal relationship with T'ang China, referring to it as a "neighboring state" (*rinkoku*, meaning an equal), even while the T'ang authorities viewed Japan as an uncivilized country that had not been formally invested as a tributary realm by the Chinese ruler. The main reason why Japan attempted to maintain equal relations with T'ang (if only fictive ones) was because of Japan's treatment of Silla as a vassal state. Japan has been called a "universal empire in microcosm" because, despite its sense of subordination to T'ang, it attempted to establish suzerainty over its own tributaries, Silla and Parhae.[25] This was also a product of efforts by Silla and Parhae to maintain a certain distance from T'ang. But because Silla was a much more advanced state than Japan, attempts to subordinate it into a tribute-rendering realm had a strong fictive component, and relations between the two countries soon began to deteriorate.[26] Repercussions of these Japanese foreign relations led to domestic problems.

Indeed, Japanese relations with Silla began to worsen in the Tempyō era in the mid-eighth century, and a large-scale invasion of Korea was even planned by the court leader Fujiwara Nakamaro in 762. Relations between the two countries deteriorated because Silla wanted to end subordinate relations and to exchange envoys on an equal basis. Japan, meanwhile, wanted to maintain the old relationship. Each side frequently expelled the other's envoys on grounds of "disrespectful behavior," but official relations between Japan and Silla were somehow maintained until 779. After that Silla stopped sending official envoys, but visits to Japan by private individuals, far from coming to a stop, actually increased in frequency. The reason for this is said to be ceaseless peasant insurgency within Silla, which caused merchants and homeless farmers to venture overseas. The *ritsuryō* polity, following ancient custom, carried out trade with the merchants under the supervision of the Kyūshū headquarters at the Dazaifu, and foreign immigrants were also welcomed as "men from 'outside the fold' who have thrown themselves upon the *tennō*'s mercy" (that is, as *kikajin* or "ones who have been civilized"). Despite the break in public contact, therefore, we can detect no exclusionary sentiment in Japanese dealings with Silla through the early ninth century.

Beginning in the Jōwa era (834–848), however, there was a tendency to view Koreans as a source of danger. In the eighth month of 842, Dazaifu Senior Assistant Governor-General Fujiwara Mamoru sent a memorial to the court requesting prohibition of trade on grounds that "from the distant past, men from Silla have come to present tribute. But since the reign of Shōmu Tennō (r. 724–749) they have failed to observe the old precedents, always harboring evil intentions. They offer no gifts as tribute and spy on state affairs under the guise of commerce."[27] Despite this proposal private trade was not prohibited, but from around this time the government began to deny Koreans permission to immigrate and enforced a policy of rejection and deportation.[28] Such exclusionary sentiment grew in strength toward the middle of the ninth century.

By the Jōgan era (859–877) fears of an invasion from Silla had created a pervasive sense of crisis. Instances of conspiracy involving Japanese nationals and Koreans were exposed and military reforms—use of a new kind of bow which had proved effective in the anti-Emishi campaigns, and deployment of subjugated Emishi—were carried out along the western periphery, particularly in the vicinity of the Kyūshū headquarters at the Dazaifu. And yet only one actual attack by Silla pirates is recorded for this period, a raid on Hakata Bay that resulted in the loss of one year's tax shipment (made up of silk and silk floss) from Buzen Province. We must conclude, therefore, that the sense of crisis appeared before any real threat. In fact attacks by Korean pirates only became conspicuous in the Kampyō era (889–898), near the end of the ninth century. That era saw a number of battles at the Dazaifu and on the island of Tsushima, and exclusionary sentiment centering on notions of the Korean enemy also reached a peak. The abolition of diplomatic exchanges with T'ang China in 894 was directly linked to this sentiment.

Japanese relations with Silla thus deteriorated continuously during the late eighth and ninth centuries. Let us now explore the significance of this trend in more detail. During the Nara Period, the government used a combination of appeasement and military strength—as seen in the case of Fujiwara Nakamaro's planned invasion—to relegate Silla to the status of a "barbarian" tributary. After the move to the Heian capital in 794, however, this policy was gradually rejected. Silla came to be viewed as an enemy and the court adopted a defensive posture centered on staving off invasion. It would seem that this changing perception of Silla was closely tied to the progressive crisis which began to afflict the *ritsuryō* system in the Tempyō era (729-767). As that crisis deepened, the court became more willing to adopt hard-line policies, even those that might lead to a break in diplomatic relations. In this sense, the court's policy toward Silla had much in common with its policy toward the Emishi, another group "outside the fold" on the frontiers of the Japanese state. The direct connection between the two is illustrated most clearly by military reforms at the Dazaifu in the Heian Jōgan era. Here we should note that many of the practical measures adopted to rebuild the *ritsuryō* system during the late Nara and early Heian periods were based, at least in part, on such thinking.

As mentioned previously, official relations between Japan and Silla essentially ceased after Silla's final embassy of 779. True, envoys sent by Japan to Silla can be confirmed sporadically until 836. The purpose of most of these missions, however, was to ask for aid in rescuing or repatriating embassies shipwrecked in the course of visits to T'ang China. In this sense they were far removed from earlier diplomatic missions whose purpose had been to pay respects to the Sillan court in return for the latter's dispatch of envoys to Japan.

As formal relations with Silla came to an end, how did Japan's relations with T'ang change? As is well known, the dispatch of embassies to T'ang China was abandoned in 894 at the suggestion of the scholarly official, Sugawara Michizane. However, the seventeenth and last embassy returned to Japan in 839 or 840, so as a practical matter diplomatic relations with T'ang ceased in the early ninth century. Although relations with Parhae, which had begun in the early Nara Period, continued through the early 900s, it is fair to say that Japan abandoned formal relations with its neighbors in the ninth century. Although this might be construed to mean that Japan became isolated from the East Asian world and entered a "closed country" (*sakoku*) condition, such was not really the case. Certainly official relations with Silla, T'ang China, and finally Parhae ceased in and around the ninth century, and no effort was made to establish official relations with either Koryô on the Korean peninsula or Sung China in the tenth century. However, trade was carried out with peninsular merchants, even when official relations between Japan and Silla reached their nadir. Moreover, merchants from T'ang also began to arrive in the Jōwa era (834–848), when Japan for all practical purposes had stopped sending embassies. One can hardly say, in other words, that Japan became isolated from the East Asian world.[29]

Development of Private Trade and Transformation of the Dazaifu

Under the *ritsuryō* system, official envoys from tribute-rendering realms who carried a diplomatic missive from their monarch—they were officially known as *bankyaku*—could carry out trade in the capital after entering Japan via the

Dazaifu. By contrast, *shōkyaku,* that is, merchants who arrived for the sole purpose of private trade, conducted trade in Kyūshū under the supervision of the Dazaifu authorities. Envoys from Parhae alone continued to be received as official envoys until the beginning of the tenth century, but the many Chinese and Korean merchants who began to arrive in the mid-ninth century were all foreign merchants. In response to their appearance, the *ritsuryō* state imposed various legal restrictions on private trade, of which three, all dating from the Engi era in the early tenth century, will be discussed here:[30]

(1) An ordinance of 903 specified that merchant ships arriving from China were to be inspected by government officials. As for the cargo, the officials had first pick of certain designated items, and the remainder was placed on sale at government-fixed prices.[31]

(2) An ordinance issued in 909 abolished government purchasing agents (*kōeki karamono tsukai*) who had previously been sent from the capital to carry out trade with Chinese visitors. After that, authority to designate which goods were subject to government monopoly purchase came to be vested in the Dazaifu.[32]

(3) An ordinance of 911 stipulated a minimum interval of two years to be observed between visits by foreign ships. Merchant vessels which came before the stated interval had elapsed were immediately deported by order of the Council of State, which issued a directive to this effect to the Dazaifu.[33]

The control mechanisms defined by these tenth-century laws were not all completely new, since clear precedents exist for the ordinances of 903 and 909. The former, in which first pick of foreign goods was reserved for government-dispatched agents and a price schedule was applied even to trade with private citizens, was based on *ritsuryō* protocols for conducting trade with *bankyaku* in the capital. The only major difference was that the site of trade had now shifted to the Dazaifu. The 909 ordinance, which abolished the use of government purchasing agents, was simply an extension to another country (China) of the system used by the Dazaifu for trade with peninsular *shōkyaku,* which had never merited the dispatch of purchasing agents from the capital. According to a Council of State directive (*daijōkampu*) dated the ninth day of the seventh month of 831, strict adherence to the government's (in this case, the Dazaifu's) monopoly rights and price schedules was prescribed in the case of peninsular merchants as well.[34] The ordinances of 903 and 909 thus contained nothing new in terms of form; but when the cessation of relations with Parhae put an end to trade in the Heian capital, the Dazaifu became the sole site for trade, providing so-called wealthy provincials from the city wards (*kakunai fugō no tomogara*) there with the opportunity to gain effective control over commercial relations. Nonetheless, it would be rash to conclude that authority to supervise trade suddenly shifted to the Dazaifu at the beginning of the tenth century. For example, a government purchasing agent was again dispatched to the Dazaifu in 919, suggesting that the ordinance of 909 was not intended to have permanent effect.[35] The distinction between public trade and private trade became uncertain, and trade was transformed into a means for Dazaifu officials to accumulate private wealth.

Next, let us consider the ordinance of 911, which fixed a minimum interval (*nenki*) between the arrival of merchant vessels. According to two later courtier journals, this law was established in the Engi era (901–923).[36] Its stipulations are also known from later fragmentary sources. Unlike the other two laws reviewed above, the *nenki* has no clear precedent. Moreover, the law seems to have been applied quite rigorously through the middle of the tenth century. As a result, relatively few foreign merchant vessels entered Japan during this interval, which corresponded to a period of violent dynastic change in both Korea and China.

By the end of the tenth century, however, foreign vessels, especially from Sung China, began to arrive in great numbers, and the year limit for merchant ships was abandoned for all practical purposes. The government thus maintained some degree of control over trade in the ninth and tenth centuries; but from the late tenth and particularly the eleventh centuries, this control became almost completely nominal. The result was the emergence of a private trade network centered on the Dazaifu, which had been given supervisory authority over foreign trade. Moreover, during the first half of the eleventh century, the Dazaifu itself began to undergo change. Actual control of the organization fell into the hands of third- and fourth-level officials, who functioned as secretaries and recorders and were resident at the Dazaifu.[37] For instance, it is known that most of the defenders who repelled the Jurchen invasion of 1019 were such officials, and this group became the driving force in private trade.

Another point of interest concerns the actual structure of trade around the Dazaifu and demand for imported goods. Let me draw on the results of archaeological research concerning ceramics imported from China during the T'ang, Five Dynasties, and Sung periods.[38]

Aside from a very small amount of tricolor ware (in Japanese, *sansai;* in Chinese, *sants'ai*) and white porcelain, most Chinese ceramics unearthed in sites from the mid-Heian (early eleventh century) age or earlier consist of Late T'ang, Five Dynasties, and early Sung celadon known collectively as Yueh Ware. Yueh Ware celadon, which was produced in Chechiang, is thought to have been brought to Japan by *shōkyaku* from the trading ports of Mingchou and Hangchou. These late T'ang and early Sung ceramics have been found at some forty sites in Japan, all of them in western Japan—none have been found further east than Ōmi Province. With the exception of some sites in northern Kyūshū, most of the finds are at the location of temples or government offices. The overwhelming majority of finds, amounting to some 2,500 pieces of celadon, come from a single site, the Kōrokan, an official lodge for foreign visitors at the Dazaifu. The fact that sites possessing these ceramics are restricted tallies with the fact that trade at the Dazaifu remained under fairly strict government control in this period. Accordingly, the extent of private trade is thought to have been relatively limited prior to the beginning of the eleventh century.

By contrast, sites containing imported ceramics from the mid-Heian Period—particularly from the beginning of the eleventh century—through the Kamakura Period are distributed nationwide, although admittedly the greatest concentration remains in western Japan. Furthermore, the number of artifacts is also of an order of magnitude larger than before. In this period, the earlier Yueh Ware is largely replaced by white or grey-white porcelain from Ch'uanchou. This tallies with the fact that from around the eleventh century most *shōkyaku* came from Fuchien rather than Chechiang.

We must next consider what sort of domestic demand was responsible for the rapid expansion of private Sino-Japanese trade in the early eleventh century. Although government control of trade, and therefore government demand, slackened in the eleventh century, the desire of individual aristocrat-officials for imported goods—including not only ceramics but also high-quality Chinese textiles, fragrances, drugs, precious woods, exotic animals and birds, books, and other luxury products—actually increased. A classic example is Minister of the Right Fujiwara Sanesuke (957-1046). His *Shōyūki* journal records reception of rare Chinese luxury goods in the form of annual dues and gifts from the Munakata family, whose members administered his estate, Takada no Maki in Chikuzen Province. Another instance is Fujiwara Korenori, who was criticized for his improper acquisition of "countless riches" (i.e., Chinese goods) during his tenure as senior assistant governor-general of the Dazaifu.[39] Apart from demand from the aristocratic class, the nationwide distribution of white Ch'uanchou porcelain, by no means a luxury product, probably reflects demand by regional landholders, provincial notables, and even wealthy farmers. In particular in western Japan there have been many finds from village sites indicating that porcelain could be acquired by a fairly broad stratum of society. Some scholars even cite this as a reason for the failure of an indigenous pottery industry to develop in western Japan during the medieval period.[40]

Not only did foreign trading ships begin to arrive at a brisk pace in the eleventh century, but Japanese merchants also started to venture abroad. These merchants, who are thought to have been pirate-like landlord-elites from northwest Kyūshū, began to visit the kingdom of Koryô on the Korean peninsula in the middle of the eleventh century as well as Sung China in the twelfth century. Also, in the twelfth century Sung merchants did not always disembark at the Dazaifu near Hakata Bay. Instead they went directly to other harbors along the northwest Kyūshū coast, where various estate ports served as bases for trade. As is well known, the Japan-Sung trade provided an important source of revenue for the late twelfth-century regime of Taira Kiyomori.[41] This was only possible due to the rapid growth of private trade, especially with China, as described above. While the Taira made a positive effort to organize the pirate-like warrior-merchants of western Japan, it is difficult to imagine that they embarked on any sudden change in foreign policy per se. Accordingly, it is not correct to postulate a change from "isolationism" in the ninth and tenth centuries to a more "open" foreign policy in the eleventh and twelfth centuries. On the contrary, the ninth and tenth centuries should be seen in a much more positive light, since they represent a transitional period when strict control of trade under the *ritsuryō* system began to give way to private, nongovernmental trade. Although Japan certainly did become isolated from the East Asian diplomatic world with the crumbling of state-to-state tribute relations, it came to have even deeper connections with a new East Asian world centering on distribution and trade.[42]

Transportation in the Inland Sea and Emergence of Pirate-Warriors

The Inland Sea region had always been viewed as an important route linking the capital with the Dazaifu in Kyūshū. Under the *ritsuryō* system, official highways (i.e., the "seven circuits") were classified as "great," "medium," or "small" according to their importance and frequency of usage by government envoys. The only highways classified as "great" were the San'yōdō and the short road in Kyūshū which connected the San'yōdō to the Dazaifu. This fact shows how tremendously important the Dazaifu was to the classical Japanese state, which itself developed as part of the larger international order in East Asia. This is also why the Dazaifu was referred to as a "distant capital," or as "the heartland of the western periphery and the core of the inner lands."[43] However, during the Heian Period, the San'yōdō rapidly declined in importance.

In 806 provincial officials newly appointed to the San'yōdō provinces were authorized by the Council of State to travel to their posts by sea. The directive in question contains the phrase, "following the precedent of the Saikaidō circuit," which suggests that provincial officials in Kyūshū were already traveling to their posts by sea. The Popular Affairs section of the *Engi shiki* also stipulates that officials newly appointed to the San'yōdō, Nankaidō, and Saikaidō provinces should take the sea route to their posts. Tax goods were transported by boat even before this—in 756, for example, the sea route was adopted for annual shipments of polished tax rice (*nenryō shōmai*) from the San'yōdō and Nankaidō provinces to the capital. Even earlier, officials, peasants, and traveling merchants were censured for transporting "provincial goods" from Kayano Harbor in Buzen and the harbors of Kunisaki and Sakata in Bungo to Naniwa without first passing through the Dazaifu in 746. Beginning in 796, direct travel between these three ports and Naniwa was authorized to individuals holding a travel pass (*kasho*) issued by the Dazaifu.[44] In this way the Inland Sea route underwent rapid development during the late Nara Period and completely supplanted the San'yōdō in importance during the following Heian Period.[45]

As the sea route became the main link between Kyūshū and the capital, the Inland Sea region gave birth to a new class of professional shippers. At the same time, the waterways became infested with pirates, some of whom were virtually indistinguishable from the transport workers themselves. In the second half of the ninth century, the court repeatedly authorized pursuit and capture of pirates who were ravaging the San'yōdō and Nankaidō provinces by "forming gangs, killing traveling merchants, and seizing public and private goods."[46] Since the pirates were fleet of foot and ranged over a wide geographic area, pursuit-and-capture (*tsuibu*) orders were typically issued to all San'yōdō and Nankaidō provinces, rather than to any particular region or office. The actual nature of the pirates is not entirely clear, but like the officials, peasants, and traveling merchants in the above-mentioned edict of 746, they were probably a heterogeneous group of coastal residents engaged in trade, transport, and fishing, supplemented by retired local officials and vagrant peasants. We can guess that most of their attacks were aimed at official and private goods being transported to the capital region through the Inland Sea. These would have included tax shipments as well as property acquired by government officials who served in the provinces.[47]

The most significant pirate uprising was the "rebellion" of Fujiwara Sumitomo, which took place over a two-year period beginning in 939. Sumitomo, whose father Nagara reportedly served as Dazaifu senior assistant governor-general, was originally a third-level official (*jō*) at the provincial headquarters in Iyo. As such, it was his responsibility to suppress piracy; but at some point he set himself up as an outlaw leader. The Sumitomo rebellion is often compared to the rebellion of Taira Masakado, which broke out nearly simultaneously in the Bandō region. But in terms of impact on central political circles, the Sumitomo affair was much more important. This was partly because some of Sumitomo's adherents were active quite close to the capital. More important, however, was the fact that the Tōgoku was perceived as a world apart from Kyoto, whereas the Saigoku—like the capital region itself—was part of the aristocrat-officials' traditional base of power. Any rebellion there threatened to cut off the flow of commodities from this core region to the capital. This accounts for the relative speed of the court's response to the two rebellions. In the case of Taira Masakado, it took over two months from first reports of the rebellion until the court dispatched a general, Fujiwara Tadafumi, to "pacify the east." In the case of Fujiwara Sumitomo, by contrast, an order to pursue and capture was issued immediately after information on the rebellion was received, and soon afterward an "envoy to pursue and capture" (*tsuibushi*), Ono Yoshifuru, was dispatched.[48] The two rebellions also differed in terms of length. If, for the sake of argument, we define the beginning of each rebellion as the point in time when reports from the provinces were first processed at court—that is, when aristocrat-officials became aware of the rebellions—then the Masakado incident was suppressed in only a month and a half while the rebellion of Sumitomo lasted for a full year and seven months. This also helps to account for the tremendous impact of Sumitomo's rebellion upon the central aristocracy.

Unlike the Tōgoku, which was the scene of frequent later uprisings, the Saigoku saw no further rebellions to compare with that of Sumitomo. This would seem to reflect differing government policies toward the two regions. As previous scholars have noted, appointments of "envoys to subdue the territory" (*ōryōshi*) and "envoys to pursue and capture" increased after the Masakado and Sumitomo rebellions, just as the militarization of provincial officials also proceeded rapidly.[49] In the Saigoku, a special type of *ōryōshi* known as a "capital tax rice transport agent and envoy to subdue the territory" (*kyōjō kanmai ōryōshi*) or "rice transport agent and envoy to subdue the territory" (*unmai ōryōshi*) came to be appointed by provincial offices around this time—as their title suggests, these agents were responsible for guarding shipments of tax rice from the provinces to the capital.[50] With the exception of some small shipments from the Tōkaidō, most tax rice destined for Kyoto originated in the Saigoku and the

Hokuriku regions. It is probably safe to say, then, that most of these special *ōryōshi* were appointed in western Japan. Similar appointments were also made at the Dazaifu. According to Fujiwara Sukefusa's *Shunki* journal, Higo resident Taira Masataka, who served as a private retainer (*rōtō*) to the Dazaifu Provisional Governor-General Fujiwara Takaie, was sent to Kyoto in the fourth month of 1040 as a rice transporter and enforcer (*unjōmotsu no ōryōshi*). It is worth noting too that provincial appointments of this type were generally given to men described as warriors (*musha*) or commanders (*shōgun*). These early warriors achieved their posts and status by guaranteeing the safe arrival of tax shipments and thus played an important role in commodity distribution.

The strengthening of government surveillance over the Inland Sea region was one reason why pirate uprisings were kept under control. But it is also likely that the pirates themselves were transformed by the changing nature of foreign relations. When private trade between Japan and Sung began to flourish at the end of the tenth century, many of the pirates could have moved into the new field of foreign commerce. This was because they were not just plunderers but also primitive merchant capitalists; and since their participation in the regional division of labor was limited to commodity distribution, they found it more profitable to focus on rare luxury goods from overseas than on cheap domestic products. Pirate-warriors from northwest Kyūshū were involved in the Sung trade as well as trade with Koryô from an early date—well-known medieval warriors of this type include members of the Munakata family of Chikuzen and the Matsura League of Hizen. These pirate-warriors even maintained marital ties with Sung Chinese, as Japan's national boundary in this period was permeable to trade and other links with foreign residents. This was the type of warrior that the Taira family managed to organize so skillfully in the later twelfth century. Indeed, most of the medieval warrior bands (or "fleets") in the Saigoku had "pirate" blood in their veins.

The Emishi Problem and the East Country

Development of the Subordinated Emishi Problem

"Emishi" is a term of derision that the classical state applied, following Chinese precedent, to "barbarian" tribes in the northeast that were not yet under the authority of the *tennō*. Under the *ritsuryō* system, ethnic groups and tribes "outside the fold" of the *tennō*'s control were divided into three categories: (1) *rinkoku*, or "neighboring states" (in practice, meaning T'ang); (2) *shoban*, or "vassal states" (i.e., Silla and Parhae); and (3) *iteki*, or "barbarians" (i.e., the Emishi and Hayato).[51] Just as relations with T'ang China and Silla had a strong ideological component, relations with the Emishi and Hayato were deeply colored by ideology. Although the Emishi lived in Mutsu and Dewa during the Nara Period, they had formerly ranged as far as Echigo Province and Sado Island. Most of them were of the same racial stock as the Japanese and, indeed, the concept of "Emishi" had nothing to do with racial distinctions.[52] As is clear from recent archaeological finds, it is also wrong to take the legends in the *Kojiki* and *Nihongi* at face value and conclude that the Emishi were simply primitive hunters unfamiliar with agriculture. Nonetheless, the Emishi did comprise an autonomous pastoral-agrarian tribal society that retained certain primitive forms of production such as hunting.[53] The deep north was even called Michinoku, the "end of the road" (see Map 5.1, p. 132). This "backwardness" was one reason why the classical state treated the Emishi as outsiders. However, the Emishi were not unique in this respect—hunters and fisherfolk lived in all parts of the country during the *ritsuryō* period. The reason only those people in the deep north were treated as "people outside the fold" was related to the *ritsuryō* state's political ideology, according to which Nihon—Japan—was seen as a "little universal empire" modeled after T'ang China.

Takahashi Tomio divides the "subjugation of the Emishi" into three successive stages: (1) an "age of establishing provinces and districts," from the mid-seventh century through the early Nara Period (710-784); (2) an "age of armed colonization" during the Nara Period; and (3) an "age of military subjugation," from the end of the Nara Period until the beginning of the Heian Period.[54] Although this periodization is basically correct, it is not the final word on the matter. An investigation of how districts were established in the two provinces of Mutsu and Dewa shows that many administrative units were in fact established during the "age of armed colonization."[55] Of course, the number of districts in Mutsu and Dewa under the *ritsuryō* system is not entirely clear, since different figures are given by the *Engi shiki* and the encyclopedic *Wamyōruijūshō* compiled in the 930s (hereafter *Wamyōshō*).[56] The existence of special "provisional districts" (*gongun*) must also be taken into account. For the sake of argument, however, let us follow the *Engi shiki*, which lists thirty-five districts in Mutsu and eleven in Dewa, for a grand total of forty-six. Of these districts, twenty had already been established by the beginning of the Nara Period. In other words, nearly half of the districts in these two provinces were established during Takahashi's "age of establishing provinces and districts." On the other hand, at least seventeen districts were also established during the stage of "armed colonization," meaning that district establishment and armed colonization were proceeding contemporaneously.[57]

In the next stage, that of military subjugation, there was a rapid decrease in the number of newly established districts—nine districts were established during this period. However, five of these resulted from the division or reorganization of preexisting districts. The only new administrative units were four districts established in the middle reaches of the Kitakami River system, which was the primary focus for military activity during this period. From this we may conclude that although the state did embark upon a drastic policy of "military subjugation" in the Hōki era (770–780), the original *ritsuryō* policy of establishing districts as a means of asserting control over new territory had already reached a more or less successful conclusion before the start of the third stage identified by Takahashi. The real significance of the "age of military subjugation" must be found elsewhere.

The nucleus of state control over Mutsu and Dewa was the Pacification Headquarters (Chinjufu) at Fort Taga, where the Mutsu provincial headquarters (*kokufu*) was also located (see Map 5.1). Fort Taga is generally thought to have been constructed in 724, but a slightly later date is also possible. In the Tempyō era, state policy toward Mutsu and Dewa emphasized the construction of forts (*jōsaku*) and the resettlement of colonists (*sakko*) from further west. For instance, in 733 Fort Dewa (Dewa no ki) was moved from its original location at the mouth of the Mogami River all the way to Akita. Four years later, in 737, construction began on a new road directly linking Mutsu Province with the new fort. Two more fortresses, Okachi and Monō, were built in 758. This spate of fort construction, which involved mobilization of large numbers of soldiers, was preliminary to resettlement of peasant-colonists from Mutsu, Dewa, and other provinces in the Bandō region. In other words, military support was now required for the establishment of districts.[58]

This could be taken as evidence that the Emishi had become hostile to the *ritsuryō* authorities. Still, as no large-scale Emishi resistance is recorded for this period, we must conclude that the state's perception of crisis outpaced reality. We should recall here that relations with Silla began to deteriorate during this same Tempyō era. The first crisis of the *ritsuryō* system, which was symbolized by promulgation of the "Law Concerning Permanent Possession of Reclaimed Land" (*Konden einen shizaihō*, 743) and the reduction of peasant corvée obligations, was therefore accompanied by problems with people "outside the fold" in both the east and west. In other words, just as the *ritsuryō* polity began to adopt more practical policies vis-à-vis commoners (*kōmin*) in the interior, it adopted an even more faithful imitation of the T'ang political order for external objectives, attempting to strengthen control over people "outside the fold." This trend is exemplified by Fujiwara Nakamaro, famous for his "T'ang-style politics" and the introduction of hard-line policies toward the Emishi and Silla. That the latter two groups were seen as elements of the same problem is clear from the fact that most of the senior and junior military commissioners deployed in conjunction with the projected invasion of Silla were men with experience in the Emishi campaigns.[59]

The "age of military subjugation" began with the 774 attack on Fort Monō, the 780 rebellion of Iji Azamaro, and the subsequent abolishment of Emishi tribute missions to the Kinai court. One reason for the ceaseless military campaigns in this period was certainly the Emishi's tenacious resistance.[60] The abnormal scale of military mobilization also reflects the *ritsuryō* state's perception of crisis, expressed by phrases such as, "the fate of the Bandō depends on this single effort."[61] This crisis consciousness also seems organically linked to the rupture in official relations with Silla at the end of the Nara Period.

It is well known that large-scale Emishi resistance disappeared during the reign of Kammu Tennō (781–806), when the Emishi were more or less subjugated by the great armies of Sakaue Tamuramaro and Fun'ya Watamaro, and when the Chinjufu was moved north to Fort Izawa.[62] It would be wrong, however, to conclude that the conquest of the Emishi resulted solely from the military prowess of the *ritsuryō* state. Government conscript soldiers (*heishi*) from the Bandō and other areas lacked fighting spirit. They reportedly carried out trade with the Emishi in collusion with members of the central nobility, and they were frequently defeated in individual battles with the enemy, who excelled as archers. The most important reasons for the *ritsuryō* state's victory were probably its successful mobilization of Emishi turncoats—known as *fushū*, or "Emishi who surrendered"—and the progressive development of schisms within the Emishi leadership.

After Kammu Tennō's reign, the Emishi seem to have more or less submitted to the *ritsuryō* state. Whether or not they were forcibly relocated to other provinces, they were treated as subjugated people, and through state-sponsored indoctrination efforts they were subjected to even more ideological control than before. Ono Minemori, a well-known example of the so-called new officials who appeared in the ninth century, expressed the following sentiments in two Chinese poems composed when he left the capital to become governor of Mutsu in 815: "Your servant has received his orders to carry the battle standard afar. Through myriad leagues of desert: I will regret my departure. At the frontier pavilion, birds and flowers of the season will differ. I expect to hear the oriole's song only when I play it on my flute!"[63] Considering that Fun'ya Watamaro's campaign took place only three years before this poem was written, it is natural that Minemori describes Mutsu as a place where one would carry a battle standard. The phrase "myriad leagues of desert" (*banri no sunaba*) calls to mind the inhospitable desert region inhabited by the Western Xiong-nu during China's Han dynasty. In ninth-century Chinese-style poems, such as those in the *Collection of Literary Masterpieces* (*Bunka shūreishū*) and *Anthology Ordering the State* (*Keikokushū*), Chinese imagery is often used to describe the Japanese landscape—the frontier region is depicted as a "desert" or a "barbarian land" (*kokoku*) in contrast with the Heian capital. On the other hand, authors of these poems, including Ono Minemori, are the same men who were praised for giving new life to *ritsuryō* governance through their pragmatic reforms of local administration.[64] There appears to be a contradiction between the Sinophilic ideological tendencies of these men and their pragmatic administrative policies, which found expression in new laws being issued as supplemental regulations (*kyaku*) and protocols (*shiki*). Actually their revisionist policies, which addressed actual problems faced by local administrators, were informed and complemented by the classical Chinese ideal of benevolent government. This helps to explain how various reforms in the ninth and early tenth centuries, while objectively paving the way for a new system of control—what contemporary historians term "court-centered polity" (*ōchō kokka*)—were at the same time subjectively seen as "restoring" *ritsuryō* ideals.

After serving as governor of Mutsu, Ono Minemori went on to provincial posts in Awa and Ōmi and finally became senior assistant governor-general of the Dazaifu in 822. There he proposed a system of state-managed public fields (*kueiden*) as well as various military reforms, including a system of elite professional troops (*senshi*), all based on his experience in Mutsu. There are many other cases of men transferred to official positions at the Dazaifu or nearby provincial offices on the basis of experience gained from tenures in Mutsu or Dewa, which again illustrates how relations with the Emishi and defense of the western periphery were viewed as parallel problems.

The state also began to deploy subjugated Emishi in Kyūshū when relations with Silla deteriorated in the mid-ninth-century Jōgan era. One reason for this was the continued belief among central aristocrat-officials in the old Chinese principle of "using barbarians to quell barbarians." A more important reason, however, was that the court was aware of the military skills—especially in mounted archery—of these "semi-domesticated" Emishi. Although indoctrination or assimilation was the ostensible reason for resettling *fushū* throughout the interior, in practice the policy was aimed at supplementing the military and police-related powers of provincial offices. That is no doubt why the *Engi shiki* mentions thirty-five provinces where Emishi were settled, mostly in the Bandō and along the Inland Sea. After the middle of the ninth century, however, *fushū* rebellions occurred in many areas, and it was also feared that ordinary peasants might join these armed uprisings in open warfare against the *ritsuryō* state. Meanwhile, in the mid-Heian Period, "eastern barbarian chiefs"—like those described in the eleventh-century martial account, *Mutsuwaki*—used their authority over the "six marcher districts" (*oku rokugun*) in Mutsu and Dewa for territorial organization, a process that eventually culminated in the rise of the Abe and Kiyowara families.[65]

Emergence of Mounted Warriors in the East Country

Under *ritsuryō* governance the Tōkaidō and Tōsandō in the east were classified as highways of secondary importance in comparison with the San'yōdō in the west. This reflected the different roles of the various roads—the San'yōdō connected the capital with the Dazaifu, while the Tōkaidō and Tōsandō were merely routes leading to Emishi territory. Of the two, the latter was apparently considered more important. Mutsu and Dewa, for example, were included within the Tōsandō, and Musashi was also on that circuit until 771, when it was reassigned to the Tōkaidō. The Tōkaidō crossed the lower reaches of many large rivers, making it quite risky as a transportation route in the classical period. By contrast, the Tōsandō was seen as relatively safe, despite the fact that it passed through a number of precipitous mountainous regions. From the middle of the Heian Period, however, the Tōkaidō increased in relative importance. From the tenth century onward, government envoys and provincial governors began to ask the court's permission to use the Tōkaidō. Nevertheless, in 914 this practice was prohibited on grounds that it caused hardship to districts and post stations located along the way.[66] Next, in 971, provincial officials traveling to their posts in Dewa began to go by way of the Tōkaidō.[67] Thus, from the middle of the Heian Period advances in transportation technology caused the Tōkaidō to eclipse the Tōsandō in status. However, it was not until at least the Kamakura Period that the Tōsandō became a "back road" to the Tōkaidō.

Goods transported to the capital from the various provinces of the Tōkaidō and Tōsandō consisted mostly of light freight such as cloth, silk fabric, and silk floss. They included no grain or other heavy freight. This suggests that travel from the Tōgoku to the capital was largely by horse, and that boats were hardly ever used, in contrast to the case in the Saigoku. Along the Tōkaidō and Tōsandō, a horse-based transport industry emerged at an early date. In 899 there was violence by the so-called Packhorse Gang, which consisted of "rich men [*fugō no tomogara*] from the various Bandō provinces," mostly drawn from the ranks of the transport industry.[68] The Tōgoku, and particularly the provinces of Kai, Shinano, Musashi, and Kōzuke, contained many pastures and thus provided tribute horses to the court. People's livelihoods there depended on the horse, which was not only the primary means of transportation but also a tribute product and a means of production. In other words, a strong social foundation for the emergence of the ubiquitous mounted warriors of the medieval period already existed there.

Within the Tōgoku it was the eight Bandō provinces where these social characteristics were manifested most typically, and it was also the Bandō that was most directly connected with the problem of *fushū*. The various Bandō provinces served as a rear base for the subjugation of the Emishi, and they were thus the focus of countless requests for soldiers and materiel. Medieval mounted warriors were effective primarily because of their skill at archery, which was honed through battles with the Emishi. It was said, for example, that "fighting with bows and horses is a custom of the barbarian hunters; one of them is a match for even ten ordinary men."[69] These mounted archers became a universal feature of Tōgoku society after the early tenth-century rebellion of Taira Masakado.

Taira Masakado's kin, descendents of Kammu Tennō and thus known as the Kammu Heishi, first achieved a presence in the Bandō when their ancestor, Prince Takamochi, took up office as vice-governor of Kazusa at the end of the ninth century.[70] In the second half of the same century, there were numerous *fushū* uprisings in the Bandō, which led to attacks on provincial offices by ordinary local residents including that of the Packhorse Gang.[71] The dispatch of the royally descended Kammu Heishi to the Tōgoku was above all intended to suppress uprisings by this kind of gang.[72] In fact, during the tenth century, gang activity disappears almost entirely from the historical sources. The Kammu Heishi not only repeatedly worked in the various Bandō provinces as provincial governors (*zuryō*) but they also played an active role in managing Mutsu and Dewa as pacification commanders (*chinjufu shōgun*). As a result, they established a role for themselves as regional military aristocrats. Even while not serving as governors or in other provincial offices, they came to oversee a regional power bloc with sufficient status to receive official communiques, called *ichō*, which marked them as equals vis-à-vis the provincial headquarters.[73] This was not only because they were mercenaries possessing superior military force, but also because in their role as "private landlords" (*shiryōshu*) they could contract to collect taxes for the provincial office. However it would be wrong to see them as identical to later medieval warriors who were local landlords, because private landlords of the tenth and eleventh centuries did not have a strong hold over cultivator communities. Rather, they exploited farmers from a position outside those communities and made no effort to guarantee villagers' long-term survival. For this reason they were looked on with contempt by both the central aristocrats and the general farming population.

Accordingly, the so-called feuding—"private fighting" (*shitō*)—that characterized the first half of Masakado's rebellion contains no recognizable element of a people's war. Later, however, after Masakado gave his support to Fujiwara Haruaki (an enemy of the Hitachi provincial office who, like Masakado, was a regional military aristocrat of sufficient status to receive horizontal missives from local officials), Masakado's rebellion began to take on the antigovernment characteristics associated with earlier uprisings like that of the Packhorse Gang.[74] Still, Masakado never thought in terms of toppling the *ritsuryō* state itself. After he gained mastery of the Bandō and began calling himself a "new monarch" (*shintei*), he compared his own position to that of the founder of Eastern Khitan, who had overrun Parhae on the continent.[75] What this meant was that he had established a small state, the Bandō, which was subordinate to the *ritsuryō* state in the same way that Khitan was a tributary of T'ang China.[76] In the context of East Asian history, Masakado's political ideology made perfect sense. The fact that the Bandō was never intended to be an autonomous, miniature version of the *ritsuryō* state explains why Masakado repeatedly stressed to Regent Fujiwara Tadahira that he had no rebellious intent. The central government, however, did not see it this way. It branded Masakado as a rebel on the theory that "nothing under the sky can be outside the sovereign's territory; no one in the nine states can not be his subject."[77] Moreover the existence of a political ideology is the decisive difference between Masakado and his counterpart in the west, Fujiwara Sumitomo. Although Sumitomo attacked the Dazaifu, he simply abandoned it after an orgy of plunder and arson. The Masakado rebellion did not give the aristocrat class as much of a shock as the Sumitomo rebellion, but it left an important heritage for the future by expressing the potential for a state in the Bandō.

From the time of Taira Tadatsune's rebellion in 1028, the Tōgoku (and especially the Bandō) was frequently termed a "devastated land" by officials.[78] "Devastated" was an expression used to argue for limited tax amnesties, on the basis of the undependable revenue flow from the various Tōgoku provinces.[79] Although the Tōgoku, where rice productivity was especially low, was often said to be "devastated," the word was applied to other areas as well. Iga, for example, was called a "devastated, unpopulated province."[80] Such devastation was probably related to widespread abandonment of public land in the eleventh century. The tendency for farmers to abandon public fields was not solely the result of unpredictable natural disasters. Rather, we should see it as a product of peasant resistance against private proprietors. References to "devastation" in this period actually reflect the ruin of private landlords and their replacement by new, medieval-type cultivator communities.[81] As a result, the image of "devastation" disappears in the twelfth century with the appearance of local landlords who resided within medieval communities. In the Tōgoku, where rice agriculture was very low in productivity, the role played by these local landlords was much greater than in other regions.

West Country and East Country under the Estate System

Regional Classification of Shōen and the Transport System

The fundamental characteristic of medieval estates was their enclosed, territorial nature, which resulted from the organic integration of agricultural land (wet and upland fields), villages, mountains, fields, rivers, and coastal areas. *Shōen* of this type began to appear in the middle of the eleventh century and became universal during the twelfth, especially during the era when the retired Toba Tennō (alt. Toba In) led the court from 1129 to 1156. As the *ritsuryō* system broke down and during the subsequent court-centered polity, *shōen* comprised rights over tax-exempt agricultural land (*mendenpata*) in addition to rights for use of mountains, fields, rivers, and coastal territory that was either slated for development as paddyland or utilized in the form of timberland (*soma*), pastures (*maki*), hunting preserves, or sacred ground.[82] But prior to the middle of the eleventh century, each type of land was exploited distinctly, *shōen* were not based around local settlements, and the territory comprising an estate was not linked in any organic, unified fashion.[83]

At this early stage the expansion and development of *shōen* was politically suppressed—as a form of landholding, estates did not yet determine the structure of society, nor did they exhibit significant regional variations. By contrast, medieval *shōen* were generally territorial entities centered on a specific settlement and they displayed marked regional variation, excepting estates in some parts of the Kinai. To put it abstractly, territorial rule over *shōen* was achieved on the basis of the medieval cultivator community through the mediation of local landlords, with a further component of ideological manipulation (e.g., the idea of the unity of gods and Buddhas, known as the *honji suijaku* concept) and the Buddhist prohibition against killing living things.[84] *Shōen* and territory under the control of the provincial office underwent a process of structural homogenization, while at the same time individual *shōen* came to achieve separate identities based on regional peculiarities or differences in the ideology of their proprietors.

Previous research on the regional characteristics of medieval *shōen* has tended to contrast the advanced regions of central Honshū with the peripheral regions of the Tōgoku or Kyūshū in terms of the relative size of estates, the presence or absence of local landlords, and differences in the pattern of exploitation. Using this method based on differences in productivity as a starting point, I would like to propose a regional classification of *shōen* that emphasizes the political characteristics of distinct regions such as the Tōgoku, Saigoku, and the Kinai.

A paucity of sources makes it difficult to obtain a nationwide overview of the size, management, and exploitation of estates from the period when retired *tennō* led the court through the early Kamakura Period. Some important clues, however, are provided by the 1159 "Record of *Shōen* Possessed by Hōshōgon'in."[85] The Hōshōgon'in was a royal vow temple (*goganji*) established by Toba In. The document in question shows, albeit imperfectly, the classic form taken by *shōen* established in the twelfth century. From almost all of its estates, Hōshōgon'in collected not just the so-called preeminent proprietor's share (*honke tokubun*) but also the basic annual land-tax levy known as *nengu*.

As shown in Table 14.1, six of Hōshōgon'in's twelve *shōen* were located in central Honshū, in the provinces of Ōmi, Tamba, and Tango; four were located in the Saigoku, in the provinces of Bitchū, Bingo, Awa, and Chikugo; and two were located in the Tōgoku, in the provinces of Tōtōmi and Kai. A problem is that none of Hōshōgon'in's estates were located in the Kinai, Hokuriku or the Bandō. But for these regions, supplemental information can be gathered from other sources. Let us begin our analysis by looking at the size of the various *shōen*.

We cannot know the precise size of Hōshōgon'in's landholdings because the document does not list the total areas of cultivated land. But it is possible to make a general estimate by considering the origins of estate names and trying to identify them with actual geographic locations. With three exceptions, all of the estates in central Honshū and the Saigoku seem to derive from *ritsuryō*-period townships (*gō*) that were previously recorded in the tenth-century *Wamyōshō*.[86] It seems likely, therefore, that these *shōen* were no larger (and in many cases, probably smaller) than the original townships. Estates on the periphery, by contrast, were of much grander size: Minuma Estate in Kyūshū was as big as an entire district, while Hatsukura Estate and Amari Estate in the Tōgoku were also quite large. In fact, estates as big or bigger than these three were the norm in the Bandō region. Meanwhile, at the opposite end of the spectrum, Mimura Estate and Kō Estate in Ōmi were hamlet-sized *shōen* similar to the numerous small-scale estates in the Kinai. *Shōen* were thus smaller as one approached the advanced areas of the Kinai and central Honshū, and larger toward the periphery in both the Tōgoku and Saigoku. In terms of size alone, therefore, there is little difference between estates in eastern and western Japan. But when we look at the types of revenue these *shōen* supplied, marked regional differences begin to appear.

Here too it is useful to think in terms of three regions: central Honshū, the Saigoku, and the Tōgoku. *Shōen* from central Honshū produced mostly "heavy freight" such as rice and oil, together with miscellaneous dues (*zōkuji*) in the form of reed mats, perfume, rice cakes, and sundry utensils. These are roughly the same items that were collected from estates in the Kinai. By contrast, goods from the Saigoku were limited to rice, oil, and floss silk, without any similar miscellaneous tax items named above. Estates in the Tōgoku rendered annual dues in cloth and other "light freight."[87] Of course, this might simply have been a carryover from classical times, and for that reason I would like to refer briefly to the Popular Affairs section of the tenth-century *Engi shiki*, which gives a list of the provinces responsible for making shipments of polished grain (*shōmai*) to the court. These provinces are probably the same ones that sent grain to the capital under the earlier *ritsuryō* system.

TABLE 14.1.

Shōen Belonging to Hōshōgon'in

REGION	PROVINCE	NAME OF *SHŌEN*	TAX OBLIGATIONS	NAME MATCHES *WAMYŌ-SHŌ* TOWNSHIP?	PROPRIETOR (*RYŌKE*) OR CUSTODIAN (*AZUKARI-DOKORO*)
CENTRAL HONSHU	Ōmi	Mimura no shō	rice (300 *koku*) oil (1.6 *koku*) reed mats (300)	no	Jōza Hōgen Seiken
	"	Kō no misono	perfume (5 *koku*)	no	Masanori ason
	"	Hayami no shō	rice-cakes (380)	yes	Ajari Jinshin (Hōshōji ryō)
	Tamba	Kadono no maki	rice (100 *koku*) oil (1.1 *koku*)	yes	Tomotaka-Kyō
	"	Anka no shō	sundry utensils	yes	Udaijin Nyūdō
	Tango	Shiraku no shō	rice (250 *koku*) hachijō silk (50 *hiki*)	yes	Daini Kiyomori ason
SAIGOKU	Bitchū	Take no hō	soldiers (2 per month)	yes	Hyoe no suke tsubone (Sonshōji binpo)
	Bingo	Tsukuchi no shō	rice (300 *koku*) oil (4.3 *koku*)	yes	widow of Tadayoshi-Kyō
	Awa	Ōno no shō	rice (256.43 *koku*) oil (4.249 *koku*)	yes	Sueyuki-Kyō
	Chikugo	Minuma no shō	rice (600 *koku*) floss silk (41 *ryō*)	no	Takasue-Kyō
TŌGOKU	Tōtōmi	Hatsukura no shō	rokujō fine cloth (13.2 *tan*) yonjō white cloth (300 *tan*)	no	Tomotaka-Kyō
	Kai	Amari no shō	yonjō white cloth (50 *tan*)	no	Saki no ryō no kami Tadafusa

Note: 1 *koku* = c. 180 liters
1 *hiki* = 1 *ryō* = a bolt of fabric measuring c. 20 meters in length
1 *tan* = a bolt measuring c. 10 meters in length
1 *jō* = a bolt measuring c. 3.5 meters in length

In the Saigoku, according to the *Engi shiki*, grain taxes were collected from the San'yōdō as far as Aki Province, from the San'indō as far as Inaba Province, and from all parts of the Nankaidō. In the Tōgoku, by contrast, grain was collected from as far away as Kaga in the Hokurikudō, but only as far as Tōtōmi and Mino in the Tōkaidō and Tōsandō. This is because grain was considered "heavy freight," which was usually carried by ship. Most parts of the Tōgoku, as we have seen, were only accessible overland, which meant that grain transport was only feasible from regions relatively near the capital. With that established, which regions sent grain to the capital under the later *shōen* system? In the case of estates belonging to the Hōshōgon'in, grain was sent only from properties located in central Honshū and the Saigoku. However, if we look at other individual examples, it is clear that grain was sent from a somewhat broader region. In the Saigoku, grain shipments were made from all of the San'yōdō and Nankaidō provinces and from all of Kyūshū except for the southern provinces of Hyūga, Satsuma, and Ōsumi. In the Tōgoku, by contrast, grain was sent from as far away as Echigo Province in the Hokurikudō but from a much more restricted region in the Tōkaidō and Tōsandō. For a time, estates in Owari, Tōtōmi, and Kazusa in the Tōkaidō sent rice to the capital, but these shipments were soon converted into "light freight," leaving only Iga and Ise to supply rice to the court. In the Tōgoku, rice shipments were made from Ōmi, but no examples are known from Mino or points further east.[88] In sum, rice shipments from the Tōkaidō and Tōsandō became more restricted geographically, while those from the Saigoku and Hokurikudō underwent expansion, producing regional differences even more pronounced than they had been in the classical period.

What was responsible for these marked regional variations in the content of annual dues and taxes? One obvious reason is the high level of productivity for rice agriculture in central Honshū and the Saigoku, as compared to the relatively low level in the Tōgoku. Even more important, however, is the role played by different means of transportation. To get from the Tōgoku to the capital region, it was necessary to negotiate the Kumano Sea, where shipwrecks were common. Levies of grain thus became restricted to the Saigoku and Hokurikudō regions, where transportation was less of a problem.

A description of some special characteristics of *shōen* in Mutsu and Dewa provinces, as well as in northwest Kyūshū, is also needed. In the former, the Northern Fujiwara family of Hiraizumi assumed power after the end of the eleventh century through control of the pacification headquarters organization, and much public land evolved into medieval-type landholdings without being converted into *shōen*.[89] Especially in Mutsu, many so-called new townships (*hō*) were established.[90] But this region also contained special types of *shōen*. For instance, in 1148 five estates (Takakura no shō and Motoyoshi no shō in Mutsu; and Ōsone no shō, Yashiro no shō, and Yusa no shō in Dewa), were transferred from Fujiwara Tadazane to his second son, Yorinaga, who began to negotiate with the lord of Hiraizumi, Fujiwara Motohira, for increased annual dues.[91] These dues consisted mainly of gold, horses, and cloth; but they also included lacquer, eagle feathers, and sealskins. These items differed significantly from those collected from *shōen* in the Tōgoku as discussed above. In other words, *shōen* proprietors attempted to obtain special primitive luxury products in the form of annual dues from their estates in Mutsu and Dewa. Gold, in particular, was at the time valued as a means of payment in the Japan-Sung trade, and the thirty *ryō* of gold given by Fujiwara Yorinaga in 1185 to the Sung trader Liu Wen-ch'ung in exchange for Chinese books is thought to have come from these *shōen* in Mutsu and Dewa.[92]

A special characteristic of *shōen* in northwest Kyūshū was their service as bases for the Japan-Sung trade. Merchant vessels that arrived at places other than Hakata Bay were supposed to be brought to the Dazaifu via Hakata Bay. But from the early eleventh century this regulation was ignored and merchant ships began to use various harbors in northwest Kyūshū. The island of Tsushima and the estates of Kanzaki and Uno in Hizen are well known as bases for trade in this period, but even along Hakata Bay powerful central temples and shrines established *shōen* to gain a foothold in foreign trade. Takada Pasture (Takada no maki), for example, belonged to the courtier Ononomiya (Fujiwara) family; Hakozaki Hachiman Shrine and Kashii Shrine were converted into branch shrines of Iwashimizu Hachiman Shrine; and Daisenji became a branch temple of Mount Hiei's Enryakuji. In this way, Hakata Bay itself came to be shared by central estate proprietors for the common purpose of trade.[93] Not only did *shōen* proprietors use revenue from their estates to purchase high-quality textiles, drugs, fragrances, ceramics, books, and other items not produced in Japan, but the trade became structurally intertwined with the *shōen* system to the point that Chinese merchants could and did participate in local shrine organizations.[94] As foreign trade became more dependant on *shōen* (and particularly on their local administrative organs) in the twelfth century, local proprietors and other direct participants in the trade became more aware of the outside world. But at the same time, the international consciousness of the central nobility, who merely wished to obtain luxury products, underwent a sharp decline. This accounts for the upper aristocracy's conservatism with regard to foreign relations at the end of the Heian Period.

Regional Variations—Shōen Cultivator Communities and Resident Landlords

Early medieval cultivator communities and local landlords varied from region to region in much the same way as did estates. Regional variations in the medieval district-township system began to appear around the middle of the eleventh century.[95] In some cases, *ritsuryō* township names recorded in the *Wamyōshō* continued to exist into the medieval period, while in others they fell into disuse. The problem is to identify the special conditions that were responsible for such regional results.

Dissolution and disappearance of *Wamyōshō* township names is particularly pronounced in the Bandō and other parts of the Tōgoku. Hitachi is the only province where this can be systematically checked using Kamakura-period land registers (*ōtabumi*), but individual examples from *shōen*-related documents in other provinces help to confirm the point that most townships listed in the tenth-century *Wamyōshō* did not survive the transition to the medieval period.

On the other hand, in the Saigoku and particularly in the Inland Sea region, the percentage of *Wamyōshō* township names that remained in use during the medieval period is extremely high. In Awa Province, for example, almost all of the old *Wamyōshō* township names survived as designations for estates or new townships. And although full information is lacking for other provinces, a great many also survived into the medieval period in Sanuki, Aki, and Bingo as well. Still, this is a relative phenomenon. In provinces like Iga or Owari, where the overall rate of survival was about 50 percent, the rate of survival was highest in the area around the provincial office and lowest at the peripheries of the province. Nonetheless, the overall rate of survival of township names was so low in the Tōgoku and so high in the Saigoku that internal variations can be put aside.[96]

Wamyōshō township names are thought to date from the late ninth century and reflect the final distribution of townships under *ritsuryō* governance. Moreover, since *ritsuryō* townships were organized around land cultivated under the *jōri* grid system, their rate of survival correlates positively with how continuously the land was cultivated across the classical-to-medieval boundary. This relationship is best demonstrated by the strong tendency for the *jōri* system and the *Wamyōshō* township names to survive near the provincial office and to disappear along the periphery of each province. We might posit then that in the Tōgoku, where almost no *Wamyōshō* township names survive into the medieval period, the cultivated land base was unstable. Conversely, in the Saigoku, where such names were retained by medieval landholdings, the cultivated land base was relatively stable.

To be sure, in the Tōgoku there were many large rivers such as the Tonegawa that were difficult to control in classical and medieval times. There were also many low moist floodplains where it was difficult to drain rice paddies. This is suggested by the eighth-century *Hitachi Gazeteer* (*Hitachi fudoki*), which states, "in years of much rain, one hears laments about unripened seedlings; in years of drought one merely sees the joy occasioned by a bountiful harvest of grain."[97] Even after these low moist areas were converted into agricultural land, they frequently reverted to wasteland. In the Saigoku and the Kinai, by contrast, there were few large rivers: in both the classical and medieval periods usable, small to medium-sized rivers were the norm. Moreover, many areas in the Inland Sea climatic zone were prone to drought, making irrigated fields relatively easy to maintain.[98] Nonetheless we must not ignore the fact that in the Tōgoku there were more upland fields and plains than in the Saigoku, making it possible to compensate for the low productivity of rice paddies by producing silk or cloth or by carrying out animal husbandry. These natural differences between the Tōgoku and the Saigoku affected village communities and local landlords within the *shōen* system.

Given the fact that medieval *bushi* bands have frequently been linked to the activities of "land-opening landlords" (*kaihotsu ryōshu*), land reclamation was an indispensable component in the system of local landlordship associated with such bands. Homesteads (*horinouchi*, lit. "within the ditch") used as a base for development or reclamation by local openers were located on natural dikes or highlands at the tip of alluvial deltas, and they were surrounded by large expanses of moist, unstable cultivated land. The method of reclamation favored by opener *bushi* lords was to enclose small to medium-sized rivers and springs within the boundaries of their homestead, where proprietary rights were strongest. Thus they converted unstable cultivated land into more-or-less usable fields around which they organized villages and achieved a new degree of control over local cultivators. In this way reclamation by local proprietors was always oriented toward moist lowlands. Even after these were converted to cultivated land, however, it was a constant battle to keep the paddies from going to waste. A warrior's success in maintaining them on a permanent basis was what defined his status and the overall scope of his control.[99]

Keeping these general conditions for the emergence of local proprietors in mind, how did landholding compare in the Tōgoku and the Saigoku? In the Tōgoku, the large scale of holdings is notable because of the wide distribution of moist lowlands and fields which land openers occupied for the purpose of development. They managed their holdings by stationing family members throughout the land in question, planning development and subsequent village organization under the general supervision of the family head, eventually termed the *sōryō*. This type of large-scale, extensive proprietorship progressed rapidly in the twelfth century, probably due to the "miscellaneous" tax exemption (*zōyakumen*) given by the court to developers of abandoned public land, much of which had been "devastated" for years, making it virtually indistinguishable from uncultivated land. In most cases development was carried out by provincial officials or descendants of local military aristocrats, who were able to requisition labor by asserting their public authority.

In the Saigoku, by contrast, there were relatively few moist lowlands to serve as a base for the activities of local proprietors, and most cultivated land was already in use by ordinary farmers. But construction and effective use of irrigation works such as ponds and ditches was particularly important in areas subject to drought. As is clear from the case of Koinumaru New Township (Koinumaru no hō) in Harima Province, such works were heavily dependent on the communal labor of locals, and it was extremely difficult for landlords to monopolize water rights. This circumstance would explain why land openers in the Tōgoku seem to have had control over all communal functions, while in the Saigoku their presence was much less obvious. Nonetheless, the situation was not really that simple, as can be seen by attempting a regional classification of *shōen* communities.

There were basically two types of *shōen* communities: those where local landlords were present and those where they were not. The latter type is frequently seen in Kinai *shōen*, particularly those belonging to temples and shrines. This type of community emerged when absentee *shōen* proprietors tried to rule their estates directly by negating or co-opting the control mechanisms of private or local landlords. In such cases, a classic early-medieval community composed of a relatively well-to-do tax manager (*myōshu*) class and ordinary or small peasants organized in the form of a shrine-based unit (*za*) was directly exposed to the power of the absentee *shōen* proprietor, leading to a state of permanent rivalry or confrontation.[100] However, such villages were relatively few. The other type of village, where local landlords continued to play some role, was more common. Even here, however, we find some variations characterizing the Tōgoku and Saigoku. In the Tōgoku, the reproductive capacity of paddyland was commonly maintained through the efforts of local landlords, who built their homesteads within the community and promoted agricultural production. For this reason, a strong sense of community among the cultivators themselves rarely developed. At the same time, however, peasants in the Tōgoku did not get their entire livelihood from rice agriculture. There were many broad plains, pastures, and upland fields; and these areas, as well as the labor involved in cultivating them, were largely outside the control of the landlord. That farmers in the Tōgoku were generally controlled as homesteads (*zaike*) was a result of this type of lifestyle. This, in conjunction with the tendency of *shōen* proprietors to collect "light freight" (silk and cloth), restricted the ability of local landlords to exert control over their holdings. Accordingly, village communities in the Tōgoku retained a certain primeval quality.

In the Saigoku, however, farmers exhibited a strong degree of leadership in paddy agriculture and the power of local landholders was greatly restricted by the village community. For example, the Kumagai family at Miru Estate in Aki Province had unquestioned authority within the *shōen* itself but participated in village religious ceremonies as members of the community. This was a region where shrine worship was inextricably bound up with rice paddy agriculture, as seen in the later emergence of the shrine guild organizations called *miyaza*.[101] In the Saigoku, accordingly, control exerted by local landlords over village communities is thought to have owed much to the specialized role they played in commodity distribution. A more concrete statement of this point must await future study.

The Ōshū Fujiwara family of Mutsu Province represented a special type of "marcher" (frontier) local landholder.[102] They were related to the Kiyowara family, which came to power during the Former Nine-Years War of the 1050s and the Latter Three-Years War (1083–1087). Apart from their actual ancestry, they were called "chieftains of the eastern barbarians" and "leaders of the *fushū*." They oversaw a regional power bloc that owed its existence to the *shōen* system and shared many similarities with the local landholders in the Tōgoku. Family founder Kiyohira, for example, who was criticized for establishing a new township enclosing 700 *chō* around the turn of the twelfth century, created vast private holdings within the public domain in collusion with authorities at the Mutsu provincial office.[103] His son Motohira, who held local offices in five *shōen* in Mutsu and Dewa, then argued with the estate proprietor (*ryōke*) Fujiwara Yorinaga over annual dues from these estates. These facts demonstrate clearly that the Ōshū Fujiwara functioned as local landlords. But they were also tribal chieftains who retained strong control over the primitive forms of production symbolized by gold, horses, and other items sent to court as tribute. In this regard they were qualitatively different from the local landlords of the Tōgoku. Their claim to be "chieftains of the eastern barbarians" and "leaders of the *fushū*" was perhaps an ideological necessity for them to gain and maintain control over all of Mutsu and Dewa through the provincial organization there.

Conclusion: The Regional Foundations of Military Hegemony

Powerful military leaders who managed to organize local landlords into medieval warrior bands in various regions through vassalage ties are usually called "military hegemons" (*buke no tōryō*). Hegemons whose power extended throughout a single province—for instance, the Ōshū Fujiwara family—emerged here and there; but lineages from only two families, the Kammu Heishi and the Seiwa Genji, were able to become true military hegemons in the sense of subordinating warrior bands from multiple provinces. I would like to conclude this essay with an investigation of the regional power bases of the Heishi and Genji in order to survey regional characteristics inherited by the Taira polity and the Minamoto-led Kamakura Bakufu.

Although we frequently speak of the "western Heishi" and the "eastern Genji," this distribution only holds true during the era when retired *tennō* were active as court leaders. Prior to that, during the mid-Heian Period, the positions of the two families were reversed: the Heishi held sway in the Tōgoku, while the Genji were most active in and around the Kinai.

As we have seen, local entrenchment of the Kammu Heishi in the Tōgoku began with Prince Takamochi at the end of the ninth century; and it is clear from Masakado's rebellion that Takamochi's descendants thrived in Kazusa, Shimōsa, Hitachi, and other eastern provinces. There is no doubt that through the middle of the tenth century the Kammu Heishi were primarily active as regional military-aristocrats in the Bandō. In the late tenth and early eleventh centuries, however, there was an armed dispute in Ise Province between Korehira, whose father Sadamori had defeated Masakado; and Muneyori, whose grandfather Yoshikane had also fought Masakado. The dispute seems to have resulted in Yoshikane's victory, and his family, which later came to be known as the "Ise Heishi," became the principal Heishi line.[104] We can thus confirm that one branch of the Taira family shifted its base of operations to central Honshū in the early eleventh century, but most of the Kammu Heishi remained ensconced in the Bandō, as we know from the outbreak of Taira Tadatsune's rebellion in the Bōsō area of modern Chiba Prefecture around this same time. Nonetheless, the structure of Heishi holdings in the Bandō seems to have undergone a qualitative change in the two or three generations after Tadatsune, and only those branches which succeeded in making the transition from private to local landlords managed to survive.[105] Among these powerful lineages were the Chiba and Kazusa families, who as resident provincial officials (*zaichō kanjin*) managed to achieve hegemon status within a single province. But they nevertheless lacked the ability to establish control over warrior bands from other parts of the Bandō. To organize warrior bands on a supraprovincial basis, noble status (*kishu*) was an indispensable condition. Furthermore, noble status was something that was acquired politically—it was not simply the result of having an aristocratic pedigree.

It was not until the time of Taira Masamori, Korehira's great-grandson, that the Ise Heishi were noticed by central elites. In 1097 Masamori gained the attention of Shirakawa In by commending twenty *chō* of privately held paddy and upland fields in the two villages of Tomoda and Yamada in Abe District, Iga Province (but bordering Ise), to Shirakawa's daughter, Rokujōin. Afterward, Masamori and his son Tadamori achieved military distinction by capturing pirates and rebels in the Saigoku, and they also received a number of provincial governorships in the west as a reward for financial contributions to the court. Throughout they served as powerful mercenaries of the retired monarchs' regime. The Taira thus came to have deep ties with the Saigoku in the first half of the twelfth century during the time when Shirakawa In and Toba In presided over courtly society.

The Seiwa Genji, for their part, were descended from Tsunemoto, otherwise known as Prince Rokuson, who helped to suppress both the Masakado and Sumitomo rebellions. His son Mitsunaka emerged as an informant in the Anna Incident in 969, at which time he was already a mercenary in the service of the Northern Fujiwara Regent's House.[106] Mitsunaka's sons Yorimitsu, Yorichika, and Yorinobu (founders, respectively, of the Settsu Genji, Yamato Genji, and Kawachi Genji), established power bases in various parts of the Kinai and central Honshū. Members of the family also settled in distant provinces like Shinano and Kai, but the main line of the Seiwa Genji was most active in and around the Kinai.

The Genji first gained ties with the Tōgoku when Yorinobu of the Kawachi Genji, serving as the governor of Kai, quelled Tadatsune's rebellion in 1028. Then, in the late eleventh century, his descendants Yoriyoshi and Yoshiie intervened in internal disputes between aspiring local proprietors among the Ōshū chieftains, and thereby gained distinction in the Former Nine-Years War and the Latter Three-Years War. It is often said that the Genji established lord-vassal ties with the Tōgoku *bushi* from the time of Yoriyoshi and Yoshiie, but this has little basis in fact. Specifically, medieval *bushi* bands had not yet emerged in the Tōgoku at the end of the eleventh century, and while it is true that Yoriyoshi and Yoshiie mobilized troops from the Tōgoku, the latter had not yet evolved into true local landlords. Other reasons for denying the existence of any deep ties between the Genji and the Tōgoku at this time are the facts that Yoshiie's heir, Yoshichika, served as the governor of Tsushima at the beginning of the twelfth century; and furthermore, Tameyoshi, who became heir after Yoshichika's death, was active mainly in Kyoto. Only from the time of Tameyoshi's son, Yoshitomo, do we have clear evidence of a Genji leading medieval *bushi* bands in the Tōgoku. Many of the troops mobilized by Yoshitomo in the mid-twelfth century Hōgen Coup (1156) were from Tōgoku-based medieval *bushi* bands.[107] The Genji's power base in the Tōgoku dated from no earlier than the time of Yoshitomo in the first half of the twelfth century.[108]

The main reason why the principal Heishi and Genji lines became true military hegemons in the twelfth century is to be found in their successive appointments as provincial governors and their roles as mercenaries for the court in pacifying rebellions and disturbances. Notably, however, while the

Heishi had many *zuryō* appointments concentrated in the Saigoku, the Genji had relatively few in the east or west.[109] Heishi family members made use of their positions as provincial governors and their role in pacifying disputes to organize pirate-like warriors in the Inland Sea region and in northern Kyūshū to benefit from the profits of the Japan-Sung trade. The vast profits that resulted provided a material basis for buying their way into additional provincial governorships, while at the same time their status as governors allowed them to maintain an active role in the Japan-Sung trade in spite of criticism from the conservative upper nobility. The Genji, by contrast, retained the character of powerful military aristocrats based in the periphery (i.e., the Bandō), as is seen from their invasion of Sagami Province's Ōba Estate in the Tenyō era (1144–1145). They consciously intervened in various disputes between members of the local landlord class both within estates and in the public domain. Through a repeated process of suppression and mediation—by exercising police and judicial rights derived from their military power—they succeeded in organizing Tōgoku warriors as vassals. So were they able to acquire property rights within both estates and the public domain. But it should also be said that the Genji tendency to intervene in disputes frequently led to the expansion rather than suppression of hostilities.

In my view differences between the Genji and Heishi in the organization of their warrior bands—how they established lord-vassal relationships—were ordained by regional differences. Nevertheless, it is unlikely that strong lord-vassal ties were in existence as early as the mid-eleventh century. This is because hegemons who were to serve as organizers were still mercenaries of the court, and in their quest for noble status they were primarily interested in obtaining offices in the capital.[110] As a result, the hegemons had no choice but to put up with frequent defections from local warriors. This inherent weakness was not fundamentally overcome even by the Taira polity. Indeed, the Taira polity had its principal power base in an extremely volatile group of Saigoku pirate-warriors, and it was highly dependent on trade capital. It could eat away at the court's authority from within but was incapable of effecting radical change. By contrast, the Kamakura warrior government was based on the relatively autonomous society of the Tōgoku, which permitted an independent organization of *bushi* bands to revolutionize the existing polity and achieve leadership in the *shōen*-based society that characterized medieval society.

Notes

1. The series *Iwanami kōza nihon rekishi* was published by Iwanami shoten between 1975 and 1977. For the article, see vol. 4 (Kodai 4), 231-70.

2. In English see Wang Zhenping 1989, Batten 1989, Mori Katsumi 1972, Batten 1999, Rabinovitch 1986, Friday 1992, and the work of Jeffrey P. Mass, particularly Mass 1990.

3. Amino Yoshihiko 1982.

4. See, particularly, Ishigami Eiichi 1987.

5. Batten himself has just published a new book in English on these issues. See Batten 2003.

6. Koyama Yasunori 1976.

7. Linguistic structure (accents), blood types, and patterns of family organization (matrilineal or patrilineal) all divide along lines of east and west around the Great Fault (Fossa Magna). This phenomenon is of great importance in studying the differences between Tōgoku and Saigoku, but since research in these areas is generally supra-historical and based on cultural critiques and comparisons, I was not able to make use of it in the present study.

8. Interpreter's note: Koyama refers here to Fukuda Toyohiko 1976 and Tanaka Minoru 1976, both of which originally appeared together with this translated essay in Asao Naohiro et al. 1976.

9. Interpreter's note: On the Fujiwara of Mutsu ("the Ōshū Fujiwara" or the "Northern Fujiwara" of Hiraizumi), see Yiengpruksawan 1999. In recent years there has been extensive excavation at their headquarters at Hiraizumi, confirming this point and greatly increasing what we know about it.

10. See, among others, Nishijima Sadao 1962, Hatada Takashi 1962, Tōma Seita 1966, Ishimoda Shō 1973a, Ishimoda Shō 1973b, Hori Toshikazu 1963a, and Hori Toshikazu 1963b.

11. Interpreter's note: On the classical period, see Ishii Ryōsuke 1958a and Yagi Atsuru 1963. On the medieval period, see Ishii Ryōsuke 1958b and Uwayokote Masataka 1963.

12. On the seven circuit roads, see chapter 6 by Takeda Sachiko in this volume.

13. Ishii Ryōsuke 1958a, makes the *a priori* asumption that originally Tōgoku referred to the Tōkaidō circuit and Saigoku to the Saikaidō circuit, a position with which I cannot agree. An exception to this rule comes from the tenth century when the annal *Honchō seiki* makes scattered use of the term Saigoku to describe the locale of Fujiwara Sumitomo's rebellion. See *Honchō Seiki*, entries for Tengyō 2–4 (939–941).

14. However, the Law on Official Communications and Protocols (Kushikiryō) in the codes reserves the term Bandō for the Tōkai provinces, using the term Sandō, "east of the mountains," for the area falling within the Tōsandō circuit.

15. *Shoku nihongi* entry of Tempyō Jingo 2/4/8; and *Ruijū sandai kyaku, daijōkampu* dated Ten'an 3/3/13.

16. A problem related to the first and second usages is the jurisdictional scope of the "eight Tōgoku governors" reportedly established in the Taika era According to Inoue Mitsusada, this region extended from Mikawa on east in the Tōkaidō and from Shinano on west in the Tōsandō (Inoue Mitsusada 1965). By contrast, Harashima Reiji 1960 and Seki Akira 1962 exclude Mikawa and add the Koshi region instead. Here I would like to reserve judgment, waiting for the results of future research.

17. Interpreter's note: My rendering here is based on that of Steenstrup 1980, 417. The *Sata mirensho* was written to explain the Kamakura Bakufu suit process between 1319 and 1323. Rokuhara was the office of the Kamakura Bakufu in the capital, established after the Jōkyū War in 1221.

18. Kamakura Bakufu *Tsuikahō* 42. See Satō Shin'ichi and Ikeuchi Yoshisuke 1955-78, vol. 1, 81. Interpreter's note: After the *Judicial Formulary* was issued in 1232, additional protocols and regulations, termed *tsuikahō*, were also issued.

19. Interpreter's note: On the nature of these sources, see the primary source list at the end of the volume.

20. Ishii Susumu 1970, 224–242.

21. This is relatively uncommon, but one example is found in the *Azuma kagami,* which states that after Minamoto Yoritomo moved to his new residence in Ōkura-gō, Kamakura, in the twelfth month of 1180, "everyone in the Tōgoku . . . recognized him as the Lord of Kamakura." In this case, Tōgoku probably corresponds to the Bandō.

22. The relationship between the first two usages and two passages in the *Azuma kagami* is problematic. In the entry for 4/15 of 1185, "Tōgoku samurai" appointed without Yoritomo's permission are prohibited from taking up office east of Sunomata (in Owari); while in the entry for 6/21 of 1186, the area where "provincial *jitō*" were not to be cancelled is defined as Mikawa, Shinano, Echigo, and points east. Although the Tōkaido and Hokurikudō were in turmoil at this time, these examples seem most closely related to the first meaning of "Tōgoku."

23. See Nishijima Sadao 1962 and Ishimoda Shō 1973b.

24. See Hatada Takashi 1962.

25. Ishimoda Shō 1973b. Interpreter's note: In English on Japanese diplomacy within the tribute system see Wang Zhenping 1989 and Wang Zhenping 1994.

26. Suzuki Yasutami 1969.

27. *Shoku nihon kōki* 842 08/15.

28. Saeki Arikiyo 1970.

29. This position was advanced by Shimada Jirō 1974. The present study is intended to further advance this perspective. Interpreter's note: For a particularly useful discussion of trade between Japan and the continent see Verschuer 1988. It has been translated into English and will soon be published by the Cornell East Asia Series.

30. Regarding the trends in foreign relations, particularly trade, in this period, I owe much to Mori Katsumi 1975. On Japan-Koryô relations, also see Aoyama Kōryō 1955.

31. *Ruijū sandai kyaku* Engi 3 (903).

32. *Fusō ryakki* 909.

33. Conjectured on the basis of the entry for Tengyō 8 (945) 7/29 in Fujiwara Tadahira's abstracted journal, *Teishinkōkishō.*

34. *Ruijū sandai kyaku* 831 09/07.

35. Interpreter's note: By the eleventh century, when the necessity of dispatching purchasing agents came to be debated at court, the system evidently existed in name only. See *Midō kampakuki,* the journal of Fujiwara Michinaga (966-1027), entry for Kankō 9 (1012) 9/22.

36. See *Shōyūki* Chōgen 1 (1028) 11/29; and *Sochiki* Chiryaku 4 (1068) 10/23.

37. On the organization of the Dazaifu and its transformation, see Takeuchi Rizō 1956; Takeuchi Rizō 1973; and Ishii Susumu 1970, 40-117.

38. Kamei Meitoku 1975, with accompanying explanation by Hasebe Gakuji. Interpreter's note: See also the later Kamei Meitoku 1986 and Hasebe Gakuji 1995.

39. *Shōyūki* Chōgen 2 (1029) 9/5.

40. Kamei Meitoku 1975. For details in English, see relevant sections of Batten 1989, Batten 1993, and Batten 2003.

41. Interpreter's note: Taira Kiyomori (1118-1181), son of Tadamori (1096-1153) of the "Ise Taira," was posted to several provincial governorships in western Japan from the 1130s onward. There he was charged with controlling pirates in the Inland Sea, which gave him a vital interest in, and ability to profit from, marine trade and transport. Eventually Kiyomori became head of the Dazaifu and also developed the port at Owada, today's Kobe. He became Taira family head in 1153, a warrior supporter of Go-Shirakawa Tennō in the Hōgen Disturbance of 1156, paramount warrior in the realm in 1159, a member of the Council of State in 1160, and prime minister (*daijōdaijin*) at court in 1167.

Eventually, however, he and the retired Go-Shirakawa had a parting of the ways and by 1179 Kiyomori had locked Go-Shirakawa up and taken martial control over the capital city of Kyoto. His grandson took the throne as Antoku Tennō in 1180. For discussions of the Taira epoch and Kiyomori's leadership in English, see Mass 1999, esp. 13-36; and Farris 1992, esp. 241-89.

42. Interpreter's note: This point is made very clear in a recent essay by Arano Yasunori. See Arano Yasunori 1993. Arano's fourth stage, dating from the later eighth to the tenth centuries, is characterized by the fall of the T'ang Dynasty and the rise of private marine trade (*kōeki*). It was followed by a fifth stage, with a trading system of private traders linking Japan, Sung China, and Koguryô on the Korean peninsula during the later tenth to thirteenth centuries.

43. See *Nihon Montoku Tennō jitsuroku*, entry for Ninju 2 (852) 2/8.

44. *Ruijū sandai kyaku* Enryaku 15 (796) 11/21.

45. Interpreter's note: On this issue, see chapter 6 by Takeda Sachiko in this volume.

46. *Nihon sandai jitsuroku* Jōgan 4 (862) 5/20.

47. These tax shipments were variously termed *nenryō shōmai, chō, yō,* and *kōeki zōmotsu*.

48. Interpreter's note: On *tsuibushi* see Friday 1992, 148–59.

49. Takeuchi Rizō 1958, Inoue Mitsuo 1968, and Inoue Mitsuo 1969. Interpreter's note: In English, on *ōryōshi* see Friday 1992, esp. 141-48; and Farris 1992, 120-49.

50. The information for *ōryōshi* is based on the mid-Heian *Old Primer* (*Ko ōrai*) from Kōzanji. Interpreter's note: See chapter 10 by Toda Yoshimi in this volume, for which it was also an important source. The *Old Primer* has been published in Kōzanji tenseki monjo sōgō chōsadan 1972.

51. Ishimoda Shō 1973b.

52. According to Tanaami Hiroshi 1956, the Chinese characters originally read as "Emishi" came to be read as "Ezo" at the end of the Heian Period, by which time the term came to be used specifically for the Ainu. The first such usage is a poem by Owari governor Chikataka in the *Kyūan rokunen gohyakushū* of 1150, in *Gunsho ruijū* (Wakabu). Interpreter's note: For other takes on the terms "Emishi" and "Hayato" in English, see Hudson 1999 and Batten 2003.

53. Takahashi Tomio 1963, 267–273.

54. Takahashi Tomio 1963, 51–167.

55. See Hattori Masayuki 1963.

56. Interpreter's note: In the *Wamyōshō* by Minamoto Shitagō, pronounciation of characters is glossed in *man'yōgana*. See the published facsimile edition, Kyōto daigaku bungakubu kokugogaku kokubungaku kenkyūshitsu 1968.

57. It appears that districts established in this period succeeded in bringing the Senboku plain in the lower reaches of the Kawakami River drainage system as well as the Yokote basin and the Akita plain, both in the drainage system of the Omono River, under the control of the *ritsuryō* authorities.

58. Based on the results of recent excavations, some scholars argue that these facilities were more administrative than military in nature. See Kudō Masaki 1973 and Hirakawa Minami 1975. Regarding this point I would like to await the results of further research.

59. Kishi Toshio 1969, 261–292.

60. Kadowaki Teiji 1953; Sekiguchi Akira 1972.

61. *Shoku nihongi* Enryaku 7 (788) 12/7.

62. Interpreter's note: For a detailed discussion in English see Friday 1997.

63. Interpreter's note: Grateful acknowledgment is made to Robert Borgen for his help in translating this poem.

64. Satō Sōjun 1964; Satō Sōjun 1967.

65. Interpreter's note: For the Heian military context see Farris 1992, 223–33.

66. *Ruijū fusenshō* Engi 14 (914). Interpreter's note: Unfortunately the translator has been unable to locate the cited passage, which was not specified by the author.

67. *Chōya gunsai* Tenryaku 2 (971). Interpreter's note: Unfortunately the translator has been unable to locate the cited passage, which was not specified by the author.

68. Interpreter's note: A full translation of the source follows. "A recent report from the Kōzuke provincial headquarters states, 'Of late, robberies take place frequently and danger is rife in the province. When we quietly inquire into it, we hear of packhorse bands. Rich men of the Bandō use packhorses to transport goods. Where do these packhorses come from? They are all stolen. They steal them from the Mountain Route and use them on the Sea Route. And they steal horses on the Sea Route to use them on the Mountain Route. [Stealing] a single horse results in the death of a cultivator. Over time they have formed bands to commit such crimes. But when provincial officials from nearby provinces join together to hunt them down, they disperse and head for the borders.'" See *Ruijū sandai kyaku* Shōtai 2 (899) 09/19, *daijōkampu,* in Shintei zōho kokushi taikei version, vol. 2, 565.

69. *Shoku nihon kōki* 839 2/8.

70. Interpreter's note: Princes who were not eligible for succession to the throne were dropped from the rolls of the royal family and given commoner names, such as Taira (also known as the Heishi) or Minamoto (also known as the Genji). Kammu Tennō gave his princes the family name of Taira, and so were they known as the Kammu Heishi.

71. Toda Yoshimi 1968.

72. Takada Minoru 1970, Toda Yoshimi 1970, and Takahashi Masaaki 1971.

73. Toda Yoshimi 1968 (later published as Toda Yoshimi 1991), Toda Yoshimi 1970, and Ishii Susumu 1969.

74. Miyake Chōbei 1954.

75. The source is the *Shōmonki* (alt. *Masakadoki*).

76. Uwayokote Masataka 1976. An emissary of Khitan came to Japan in 930 (Enchō 8, in *Fusō ryakki*), so the overthrow of Parhae was known prior to Masakado's rebellion.

77. *Honchō monzui,* vol. 2, Tengyō 3 (940) 01/11 *kampu* (order of the Council of State). Interpreter's note: For a modern gloss and annotated edition of the above order see Fukuda Toyohiko 1997, 129–30.

78. Interpreter's note: On the rebellion of Taira Tadatsune, see Farris 1992, esp. 192–200.

79. *Heian ibun,* vol. 1, doc. 1351 (p. 1311), *daijōkampu* Kaho 2 (1095). The provincial governor of Kōzuke, a "devastated province," was unable to pay tax levies.

80. Interpreter's note: As examples see *Heian ibun,* vol. 3, 834, doc. 701; and vol. 3, 857–59, doc. 732.

81. Interpreter's note: Ishimoda Shō makes a similar argument with regard to changes at Kuroda Estate from Fujiwara Saneto's day in the early eleventh century to the later eleventh century, when Hasetsube Chikakuni emerged as a local land opener and made his alliance with the provincial governor. See chapter 13 by Ishimoda in this volume.

82. Interpreter's note: On the court-centered polity see Sasaki's article in this volume.

83. Interpreter's note: Two recent studies of general estate history in Japanese that shine light on periodizing the *shōen* system are Nagahara Keiji 1998 and Amino Yoshihiko

et al. 1989–. To date, seven volumes of the latter series have been published. Particularly helpful for their overviews are the first four volumes. Archaeology is also adding depth to *shōen* studies. See Uno Takao 2001.

84. See Koyama Yasunori 1974. Interpreter's note: To be more specific, the *honji suijaku* philosophy taught that Shintō deities were manifestations of Buddhas or bodhisattvas.

85. *Heian ibun*, vol. 6, 2454–55, doc. 2986. A similar pattern has been detected in the estates of Anrakujuin, as analyzed in Nagahara Keiji 1961. But as noted in Fukuda Ikuo 1975, the Anrakujuin document collection must be used with caution.

86. The three exceptions are Mimura no shō, Kō no misono (a royal property where vegetables were raised), and Minuma no shō.

87. Although not apparent from the Hōshōgon'in document, silk fabric and floss were also levied as annual dues on many Tōgoku estates.

88. Shinjō Tsunezō 1967, 36–58.

89. Interpreter's note: Earlier, Koyama defined the "medieval-type *shōen*" as a territorial unit centered around a settlement of cultivators.

90. Interpreter's note: A *hō* was an administrative unit that emerged within the public sector, both in the countryside and in the capital, in the mid-to-later Heian Period.

91. *Taiki* Nimpyō 3 (1153) 9/14.

92. Mori Katsumi 1965.

93. Miura Keiichi 1970.

94. *Hie sanō rishōki*. Interpreter's note: This is a history of Hie Shrine.

95. See Sakamoto Shōzō 1972, 241–323.

96. I have not examined the Kinai in this context since most holdings there were small in scale.

97. Interpreter's note: On the *Hitachi fudoki* see chapter 4 by Inoue Tatsuo in this volume.

98. Koide Haku 1975, 24–87.

99. Koyama Yasunori 1968.

100. Kuroda Toshio 1975. Interpreter's note: As Ishimoda Shō has noted, Kuroda Estate in Iga was an example, as demonstrated by Tōdaiji's appointment of the prelate Kakunin as administrator around 1157. See chapter 13 by Ishimoda in this volume.

101. Interpreter's note: For insights on the beliefs underlying shrine worship in the medieval period, in English see Miyazaki Fumiko 1992.

102. See Takahashi Tomio 1958 and Itabashi Gen 1961. Interpreter's note: On the Northern Fujiwara in English see Yiengpruksawan 1999.

103. Regarding this 700 *chō* and the wealth of the Kiyowara, see the *Chūyūki* journal of Fujiwara Munetada, entry for Daiji 2 (1127) 12/15 in Zōho shiryō taisei kankōkai 1974, 350.

104. Takahashi Masaaki 1975.

105. Private proprietors (*shiryōshu*) were *tsuwamono*-type warriors while the later local landlords (*zaichi ryōshu*) were medieval *bushi*.

106. Interpreter's note: In the Anna Coup of 969, Minister of the Left Minamoto Takaakira was accused of plotting against the throne and he was subsequently exiled to the Dazaifu, just as Sugawara Michizane had been at the turn of the tenth century. Most historians consider the incident to have been a plot by which members of the Northern Fujiwara regents' line and their supporters excluded other powerful voices at court.

107. Yasuda Motohisa 1960.

108. Interpreter's note: For more information and a different view, see Mass 1993.

109. Gomi Fumihiko 1975.

110. Interpreter's note: G. Cameron Hurst has made this argument elegantly in the case of Minamoto Yoritomo. See Hurst 1982. So has Jeffrey P. Mass reiterated it more recently in Mass 1999, esp. 13–64.

Primary Sources and Documentary Collections Cited in the Volume

Azuma kagami 吾妻鏡 Mirror of the East is an annal compiled for and by the Kamakura Bakufu. Compilation began in the late thirteenth century, and entries cover years from 1180 to 1266. Several published editions in Japanese include that in the Shintei zōho kokushi taikei as well as the modern glossed edition by Kishi Shozō and Nagahara Keiji 1976–1979. In English, partial translations of various sections include Shinoda 1960 and McCullough 1968.

Bunka shūreishū 文華秀麗集 Collection of Literary Masterpieces is an official anthology of poetry written in Chinese. It was compiled by a team led by the courtier Fujiwara Fuyutsugu (775-826), following an order from Saga Tennō (r. 809-23); and it was completed in 818. For the text, see Kojima Noriyuki 1964. In English concerning the collection see Konishi Jin'ichi 198, and Webb 2004. For translations of selected poems in English, see Watson 1975, vol. 1.

Chikubashō 竹馬抄 Handbook for Youth is a compendium of precepts for his heirs written by the shogunal chancellor (*kanrei*) Shiba Yoshimasa (1350-1410). It was written in the mid-1380s. For the text see Gunsho ruijū (Zatsubu). For an English translation see Wilson 1982, 46–55.

Chiteiki 池亭記 Notes from an Arbor by the Pond is an essay composed by Yoshishige Yasutane (?-1002) in 982. A courtier and scholar who had held a post in the Ministry of Royal Affairs (Nakatsukasashō) before his retirement, Yoshishige was critical of contemporary government and after retirement devoted himself to scholarly and devotional activities at his Arbor by the Pond. For the text in Japanese see Ōsone Shōsuke 1992, 335-37. For an English translation, see Wetzler 1977.

Chōshūki 長秋記 is the journal of the courtier Minamoto Morotoki (1077–1136), who reached the high post of provisional middle counselor (*gonchūnagon*) on the Council of State. Its entries originally covered the years from 1087 to 1136, but many sections are no longer extant. See Zōho shiryō taisei 1965.

Chōya gunsai 朝野群載 Compendium of Exemplary Writing from Court and Provinces is a compendium of records and literary works in Sino-Japanese (*kambun*) and dating from the Heian Period. It was compiled primarily by Miyoshi Tameyasu (1049–1139) in 1116, but some materials were added later. See Shintei zōho kokushi taikei.

Chūyūki 中右記 is the journal of Minister of the Right Fujiwara Munetada (1062–1141). It covers years from 1087 to 1138 and is one of the most important sources for court history during that time. See Zōho shiryō taisei and Dai nihon kokiroku 1993- (five volumes have now been published).

Denryaku 殿暦 is the journal of Fujiwara Tadazane (1078–1162), who rose to the high post of viceroy (*kampaku*) in 1105. Extant sections cover the years from 1098 to 1118. See Dai nihon kokiroku 1960-1970.

Engi shiki 延喜式 Protocols of the Engi Era is a massive compilation of procedures to be followed by various offices and officials of court government. It was completed in 927 under the direction of Senior Counselor Fujiwara Tadahira (880-949) and Right Senior Controller Tachibana Sumikiyo (859-925). In Japanese see Kōten kōkyūsho zenkoku shinshokukai 1993 and Miyagi Eishō 1975. Partial English translations include Bock 1972 and Bock 1985.

Fudoki 風土記 Gazeteers are provincial records that describe topography, customs, and other pertinent local lore. Compilation was first ordered by all provinces in 713 but only five gazeteers are fully extant today. However there are extant fragments from others. See Akimoto Kichirō 1958. For a full English translation of extant texts and fragments, see Aoki 1997.

Fusō ryakki 扶桑略記 Abbreviated Chronicle of Japan is a Buddhist history of Japan (Fusō) up to 1024. It was compiled by a Tendai scholar-monk named Kōen (?-?) late in the Heian Period. See Shintei zōho kokushi taikei.

Gishi Wajinden 魏志倭人伝 Accounts of the Wa People in the Wei History comprises a section of the History of the Wei Dynasty (*Gishi*), compiled about 297 C.E. The accounts describe eastern barbarians known as the Wa, who maintained relations with the Chinese. For a Japanese annotated and glossed text, see Mizuno Yū 1987. For an English translation, see Goodrich 1951, 8-16.

Gōdanshō 江談抄 Selections from Ōe's Anecdotes include accounts of court life, events, and personalities compiled by Ōe Masafusa (1041–1111), an outstanding administrator and literatus of his time. See Gotō Akio 1997. For selections translated into English see Ury 1993.

Gonijō Moromichiki 後二条師通記 is the journal of the viceroy (*kampaku*) Fujiwara Moromichi (1062-99). Extant entries cover the period from 1083 to 1095, with some gaps. See Dai nihon kokiroku 1956-1958.

Goseibai shikimoku (alt. *Jōei shikimoku*) 御成敗式目 Judicial Formulary is the list of judicial norms promulgated for its courts and housemen by the Kamakura Bakufu in 1232, during the Jōei era (1232-33). Its purpose was to inform Kamakura's clients of legal norms to be enforced in Kamakura's courts. In Japanese see Satō Shin'ichi 1955, vol. 1, 3-60; and in English, see Hall 1906.

Gukanshō 愚管抄 Notes on My Foolish Views is a history of Japan from the mythical age of the gods through the early thirteenth century. It was authored by the abbot of Enryakuji, Jien (1155–1225), around 1220. Jien's brother, Kujō Kanezane (1149-1207), served as regent at the court from 1191 to 1196. See Shintei zōho kokushi taikei 1930, and Nakajima Etsuji 1969. In English see Brown and Ishida 1979.

Gumaiki 愚昧記 is the journal of Sanjō Sanefusa (1147–1225), who rose to the post of minister of the left. Extant entries cover the period from 1166 to 1195, but with frequent gaps. Sanefusa was known as an expert on court protocol.

Heian ibun 平安遺文 Documents Extant from Heian Times is a modern compendium of Heian-period materials that was conceived and edited by the late Takeuchi Rizō (1907-97). There are 11 volumes, including sources originally written on paper (*komonjo*), a volume of inscriptions found on metal or stone (*kinsekibun*), a volume of prefatory (*dai*) and postscriptive (*hatsu*) texts, and two volumes of indexes (*sakuin*). Publication began in 1947, but a later printing is Takeuchi Rizō 1973-1980 (Tōkyōdō).

Heihanki 兵範記 is the journal of Taira Nobunori (1112–87), a houseman of the Northern Fujiwara regental house (*sekkanke*). The extant manuscript, written in his own hand, covers affairs at court from 1132 to 1184, but with portions of the text missing. See Zōho shiryō taisei 1965-1974.

Heike monogatari 平家物語 Tale of the Heike is a long narrative focusing on political and military struggles between the forces of Taira Kiyomori and those of various Minamoto commanders at court and in the provinces from the 1150s to 1180s. Since there are many variant texts, researchers now refer to the "Heike corpus" rather than to a single text. The version that has been translated into English is that created by the monk-chanter (*biwa hosshi*) Kakuichi (1357–1425) in the later fourteenth century. In Japanese there are many editions, including Ichiko Teiji 1973-1975. For English translations see McCullough 1988 and Kitagawa 1975. On the history of the text in English, see Hasegawa 1967; Bialock 2000; and Watson 2003.

Hie san'ō risshôki 日吉山王利生記 Records of the Origins of the Hie Mountain Deity is a chronicle detailing the origins and historical development of the Hiyoshi (Hie) Shrine on Mount Hiei. See Zoku gunsho ruijū (Jingibu 4).

Hōgen monogatari 保元物語 Tales of Hōgen is an account of events surrounding and during the unsuccessful coup to dethrone Go-Shirakawa Tennō (r. 1155-58) in 1156, during the Hōgen era (1156-59). The text is written in Sino-Japanese and the Japanese syllabary, a style called *wakan konkōbun;* and it is generally thought to have been composed in the fourteenth century. In Japanese see Tochigi Yoshitada 1992. In English see Wilson 2002.

Honchō monzui 本朝文粋 Literary Essentials of Our Realm is an anthology of essays, documentary materials, and verse composed in Sino-Japanese up to the mid-eleventh century. It was compiled by the scholar-official Fujiwara Akihira (?-1066), probably between 1037 and 1045. See Shintei zōhō kokushi taikei; and for annotated texts see Kojima Noriyuki 1964, Kakimura Shigematsu 1968, and Tsuchii Yoichi 2000.

Honchō seiki 本朝世紀 Annals of Our Realm was compiled by Fujiwara Michinori (alt. Shinzei, 1106-59) in the late Heian Period by order of the retired monarch, Toba (r. 1107-1111). It follows the historiographical tradition of the earlier six official histories (*rikkokushi*) by recording events from the reigns of Uda (r. 887-97) through Konoe (r. 1141-55). Extant sections cover the years from 935 to 1153 with some gaps. See Shintei zōho kokushi taikei.

Hōsōshiyōshō 法曹至要抄 Essentials of Law is a legal compendium dating from the late Heian or early Kamakura age, and it was probably compiled by a courtier from the Sakanoue family of legal scholars. It includes sixty-two sections concerning crimes and criminals, fourteen sections of prohibitions, eight sections on trade, one section on debt, six sections on rice lending (*suiko*), three sections on other types of lending, four sections on pawning, one section on taking or giving things in trust, three sections on fallow land, seventeen sections on inheritance testaments (*shobunjō*), five sections on mourning, twenty-three sections on dress, and thirteen sections on "various pollutions." For the text see Zoku gunsho ruijū (Ritsuryōbu).

Hyakurenshō 百練抄 Exquisitely Polished Mirror is an annal recording court affairs that originally included entries covering the years from 968 to 1259, but early sections are not extant. Compilation probably began during the reign of Kameyama (1259-74). Sources included many courtier journals now lost. See Shintei zōho kokushi taikei.

Ishimpō 医心方 Essentials of Medicine is a compendium of medical lore authored by Tamba Yasuyori (912–95) in the late tenth century. The work was ordered by Enyū Tennō (r. 969-84) in 982, and it was presented to the throne two years later. See Masamune Atsuo 1988; and in English, see the translation by Emil Hsia et al., 1986.

Jōgan kyaku 貞観格 Supplementary Legislation of the Jōgan Era is an official compendium of legislation—royal orders and directives of the Council of State issued between 820 and 869—compiled by Fujiwara Yoshimi and Fujiwara Ujimune. It was promulgated in 869 and continued the process of compilation begun by the earlier *Kōnin kyaku*. While the *Jōgan kyaku* is no longer extant, fragments can be found in the early tenth-century *Sandai kyakushiki* 三代格式 and in the early eleventh-century *Seiji yōryaku* 政事要略. Both are published in the Shintei zōho kokushi taikei.

Jōgan shiki 貞観式 Procedures of the Jōgan Era is an official compilation of ritual and administrative procedures compiled by order of the monarch and promulgated in 871. Its organization follows the pattern of the earlier *Kōnin shiki* (*Procedures of the Kōnin Era)* 弘仁式. The text is no longer extant, but for a reconstruction of some sections see Torao Toshiya 1993.

Kagerō nikki 蜻蛉日記 The Gossamer Years is the memoir of the mother of Fujiwara Michitsuna (955-1020), who was also a consort of Fujiwara Kaneie (929-990). It records events from the author's life between 954 and 974. See Kimura Masanaka 1995. English translations include Arntzen 1997, and Seidensticker 1964.

Kaifūsō 懷風藻 Fond Recollections of Poetry is an anthology of poetry written in Chinese by Japanese courtiers from the later seventh through the mid-eighth century. Compilation began in 751 by an anonymous compiler. The assemblage contains 118 poems—although different manuscripts contain slightly different numbers of verses—written by 64 poets. See Kojima Noriyuki 1964. In English concerning the anthology see Konishi Jin'ichi 1984, vol. 1, 315-23; and Webb 2004, 62-127.

Kamakura ibun 鎌倉遺文 Documents Extant from Kamakura Times is a modern compendium of extant records (*komonjo*) of the Kamakura Period assembled, transcribed, and edited by the late Takeuchi Rizō (1907-1997). Forty-two volumes were published with supplements, including indices. See Takeuchi Rizō 1984–1995 (Tōkyōdō).

Kanshoku hishō 官職秘抄 Essentials concerning Official Posts is a treatise concerning official posts of the *ritsuryō* bureaucratic system. It was compiled by Taira Motochika (1151– ?) for the princely monk Shūkaku of Ninnaji around 1200. The text describes qualifications (status, house, and other criteria) required for appointment to each post. See Gunsho ruijū (Kanshokubu).

Kasuga kannushi Sukekata ki 春日神主祐賢記 is one of many journals kept by the Nakatomi chief ritualists (*kannushi*) of Kasuga Shrine in Nara. Entries cover the late twelfth and the thirteenth century. See Zōho shiryō taisei 1955-1959.

Keikokushū 経国集 Anthology Ordering the State is an official collection of verse in Chinese (*kanshi*). The compendium was made by the royal order of Saga Tennō (r. 809-23) and it was prepared by a committee led by Yoshimune Yasuyo (785-830). It was completed in 827. See Kojima Noriyuki 1978, vols. 3.1-3.3. For translations of selected poems see Watson 1975, vol. 1.

Keizu san'yō 系図纂要 Essental Compilation of Genealogies is a genealogical compendium of royal and noble lineages assembled in the Tokugawa Period, probably by Iida Tadahiko (1799-1861).

Kojidan 古事談 Talks Concerning Past Matters is a compilation of anecdotes and lore from Heian courtly society assembled by the courtier Minamoto Akikane (1160-1215). It was created in the early 1200s but contains materials thought to date from as early as the eighth century. Researchers consider it an important source for tale (*setsuwa*) literature. See Shintei zōho kokushi taikei 1942; and for annotated editions, see Nihon koten bungakkai 1978 and Kobayashi Yasuharu 1981.

Kōfukuji bettō shidai 興福寺別当次第 Chronology of Kōfukuji Monastic Directors is a chronological register of heads of the Fujiwara clan temple, Kōfukuji, in Nara. Entries also include key events from many directors' tenures. See Dai nihon bukkyō zensho 1965.

Kōfukuji ryakunendaiki 興福寺略年代記 Abbreviated Chronicle of Kōfukuji traces the history of the Fujiwara clan temple, Kōfukuji of Nara. It was compiled using thirteenth- and fourteenth-century sources by the monk Shōen in the 1720s. See Zoku gunsho ruijū (Zatsubu 2).

Kogo shūi 古語拾遺 Gleanings in Old Words is a treatise authored by Imbe Hironari in 807 for presentation at court during the reign of Heizei Tennō (r. 806–809). It argues that Imbe forebears once held positions as shrine ritualists equal to those of the Nakatomi in stature. But by early Heian times, the Nakatomi had become the preeminent ritualists at court and at official shrines all over the realm. See Akimoto Yoshinori 1977; and in English, see Bentley 2002, 67-92.

Kojiki 古事記 Record of Ancient Matters includes myths from the Age of the Gods, legendary accounts of the establishment of the Yamato polity, and later materials tracing the history of the Yamato court and its monarchs through the reign of Great King Suiko (~592–628). Completed in 712, it was written in Chinese characters used to represent the sounds of Japanese, a form of writing called *man'yōgana*. See Kurano Kenji 1958; and for an English translation, see Philippi 1968.

Konjaku monogatarishū 今昔物語集 Anthology of Tales Old and New is an extensive compendium of tales (extant versions contain up to 1040 stories) thought to have been compiled in the twelfth century. One count yields 663 Buddhist stories and 377 secular tales said to derive from India, China and Japan. But tales from Japan comprise 65% of the collection. See Mabuchi Kazuo 1971-1976; and in English, see Ury 1979; Brower 1952; and Tyler 1987.

Ko ōrai 古往来 Old Primer comprises 56 letters probably dating from the eleventh century assembled to serve as a handbook of letter-writing. It is thought to postdate another such manual, the *Unshū ōrai* (Collected Letters from Izumo Province) by Fujiwara Akihira (989-1066). See Kōzanji tenseki monjo sōgō chōsadan 1972.

Kōtai jingū nenjūgyōji (alt. *Kenkyū san'nen Daijingū nenjūgyōji*) 皇太神宮年中行事 Annual Ritual Calendar of the Royal Shrine at Ise describes the annual calendar of rites at the royal ancestral shrine. It was authored by Arakita Tadanaka in 1292. See Zoku gunsho ruijū (Jingibu).

Kōzanji shiryō sōsho 高山寺資料叢書 Documentary Archives of Kōzanji are the modern published archives of Kōzanji, a temple in Kyoto Prefecture said to have been founded by the monk Son'i (866-940) in mid-Heian times. Selected materials from the temple's extensive library have been published in this 21-volume series.

Kugyō bunin 公卿補任 Appointment Register of Senior Nobles records appointees to the Council of State, whose members were called senior nobles (*kugyō*) in Heian times and beyond. The record begins in the eighth century, but the register itself was compiled beginning in early Heian times and continuing through 1868. See Shintei zōho kokushi taikei.

Kyūan rokunen gohyakushū (alt. *Kyūan hyakushū*) 久安六年御百首 Anthology of the Hundred Verses of 1150 is a excerpted record (*buruiki*) of verses written in response to the command of the retired monarch Sutoku (r. 1123-1141), who commanded that 14 noted poets each compose 100 verses in 1150. See Gunsho ruijū (Wakabu).

Makura no sōshi 枕草子 The Pillow Book is a miscellany by the eleventh-century court lady Sei Shōnagon (?-?), in which she describes many aspects of court life from her personal point of view. There are many editions in Japanese including Watanabe Minoru 1991. In English see Morris 1967.

Man'yōshū 万葉集 The Anthology of Ten Thousand Leaves is the oldest extant anthology of court poetry in Japanese, but written in Chinese, using Chinese characters (*kanji*) for their sounds, as *man'yōgana*. It was completed in 759. There are many editions in Japanese including Kojima Noriyuki 1971-1975. For an English translation of 1000 selected poems (out of 4500), see Nihon gakujutsu shinkōkai 1965. Ian Levy has translated the first five (of twenty) books in Levy 1981.

Midō kampakuki 御堂関白記 is the journal of the court leader and minister of the left (*sadaijin*) Fujiwara Michinaga (966-1027). Entries cover the years from 998 to 1021. See the Dai nihon kokiroku edition, 1952-1954; and for a modern gloss, see Yamanaka Yutaka 1985-. For a French translation, see Herail 1987-88.

Mutsuwaki 陸奥話記 A Tale of Mutsu describes events in the Former Nine Years War of the 1050s, between Minamoto Yoriyoshi (988-1075) and the provincial-magnate family in Mutsu Province known as the Abe. The latter were accused of not paying taxes and obstructing provincial government. The tale was probably compiled not long after the events it chronicles. See Zoku gunsho ruijū (Kassenbu). In English see McCullough 1964–1965.

Nanto taishu jūrakki 南都大衆入洛記 A Record of Monks from the Southern Capital Protesting in the Capital is a short record of events surrounding several demonstrations by the monastic community (*taishu*) of Kōfukuji in Nara, the "southern capital" (*nanto*), against the court situated in the "northern capital" of Heiankyō, today's Kyoto. See Zoku gunsho ruijū (Zatsubu 2).

Nara ibun 寧楽遺文 Documents Extant from Nara Times is a modern compendium of Nara-period (710-784) documents in three volumes compiled by the late Takeuchi Rizō (1907-1997). See Takeuchi Rizō 1962 (Tōkyōdō).

Nihongi (alt. *Nihon shoki*) 日本紀 The Chronicle of Japan is the first of six official court histories. It was presented to the reigning monarch, Genshō Tennō (r. 715-24), in 720. Written in Chinese, it chronicles the mythical age of the gods, the protohistorical reigns of Yamato rulers, and the early historical reigns of Temmu and his wife-successor Jitō through the late seventh century. There are many editions including the annotated Sakamoto Tarō 1967; and the annotated and glossed Sakamoto Tarō 1994. In English see Aston 1972.

Nihon kōki 日本後紀 The Later Chronicle of Japan is the third of six official court annals. It was compiled in 840, with the courtier Fujiwara Ōtsugu as editor; and it covers the years from 792 to 833. See Shintei zōho kokushi taikei 1980; and for an annotated edition, see Kurosaka Nobuo 2003.

Nihon kiryaku 日本紀略 The Abbreviated History of Japan is a late Heian-period compilation spanning the age of the gods and the early eleventh-century reign of Go-Ichijō (r. 1016–36). Its compiler is unknown. Early sections abstract entries from the six official court annals (*rikkokushi*) while later sections drew on both official and unofficial records, including courtier journals. See Shintei zōho kokushi taikei.

Nihon Montoku Tennō jitsuroku 日本文徳天皇実録 The Veritable Records of Japan's Montoku Tennō is the fifth of the six official court annals. Its compilation began in 879, and it covers the years from 850 to 858, with some sections missing. See Shintei zōho kokushi taikei 1979. In English see Shimizu 1951.

Nihon ryōiki 日本霊異記 Miraculous Stories from Japan is a collection of didactic tales (*setsuwa*) on Buddhist themes compiled by the monk Keikai (?-?) in the early ninth century. Many tales focus on the concept of karma—the law of cause and effect—and on the miraculous powers of the Buddha. See Nakada Norio 1975. In English see Nakamura 1973.

Nihon sandai jitsuroku 日本三代実録 Veritable Records of Three Reigns is the last of Japan's six official court annals (*rikkokushi*) and the most extensive in its coverage of court affairs. It was ordered compiled by Uda Tennō (r. 887–97) in 892, to record key events from the reigns of his predecessors (Seiwa, r. 858-76; Yōzei, r. 876-84; and Kōkō, r. 884-87). Fujiwara Tokihira (871-909), court leader during the 890s, was one of its editors, along with his rival, Sugawara Michizane (845-903). The text was completed in 901. See Shintei zōho kokushi taikei 1979-1981; and the annotated and glossed Takeda Yūkichi 1986.

Ōkagami 大鏡 The Great Mirror is a historical narrative likely authored by a late Heian-period aristocrat who was not a member of the leading Northern Fujiwara regents' lineage. Its narrative takes the form of a dialogue between persons who engage in a sometimes sarcastic discussion of Northern Fujiwara regency leadership at court, especially that of Fujiwara Michinaga (966-1027). There are many editions in Japanese, including Tachibana Kenji 1974. In English see McCullough 1980; and for a recent discussion of its historiography see Bialock 1997.

Owari no kuni no gebumi 尾張国解文 The Owari Petition is a complaint filed at court by local elites from the province of Owari concerning illegal acts by their governor. It was submitted in 988 and included thirty-one accusations against Fujiwara Motonaga, who had "collected unwarranted taxes and (let his ruffians) run amok" for three years. It was signed by "the district chieftains (*gunji*) and yeoman cultivators (*hyakushō*) of Owari Province." In Japanese, see Takeuchi Rizō's *Heian ibun*, vol. 2, 473-85 (doc. 339); and Abe Takeshi 1971. In

English see the essay by Charlotte von Verschuer in Mikael Adolphson and Stacie Matsumoto, eds. *Centers and Peripheries in Heian Japan* (forthcoming, University of Hawaii Press).

Ruijū kokushi 類従国史 The History of the Realm Topically Arranged is a compendium of information from the six official annals (*rikkokushi*) arranged topically. The extant text is, however, incomplete. It may have been compiled by Sugawara Michizane (845-903), probably in 892. Topics are eighteen in number and include such categories as the deities, the monarch, the back palace, music, and Buddhism. See Shintei zōho kokushi taikei.

Ruijū fusenshō 類従符宣抄 Royal Commands and Orders of the Council of State Topically Arranged is a compendium of directives issued by the Council between 737 and 1093 that are arranged topically. It was completed in the late eleventh or early twelfth century, but it was probably begun in the early eleventh century by a royal prince, Minamoto Tsuneyori (985-1039), who served long years as a member of the Controllers' Office (Benkankyoku) under the court leaders Fujiwara Michinaga (966-1027) and Fujiwara Yorimichi (992-1074). Our extant text is not complete. See Shintei zōho kokushi taikei.

Ruijū sandai kyaku 類従三代格 Supplementary Legislation of Three Reigns Topically Arranged is an eleventh-century compendium of approximately 1000 supplementary laws (*kyaku*) issued during the eighth, ninth, and early tenth centuries. Assembled by an unknown hand, the extant text is incomplete. Entries are arranged by government office and various topics, following the system initiated by earlier compendia of legislation and protocols. See Shintei zōho kokushi taikei.

Ryō no gige 令義解 Commentary on the Administrative Code is an official commentary on the Yōrō administrative code (*ryō* 令) composed in 838 by Kakuda Imatari for the purpose of systematizing legal thought of the time. It contains extensive citations from the *Ryō no shaku*, the earliest known legal commentary likely composed by Iyobe Iemori, who had visited T'ang China as a Japanese ambassador in 777. See Shintei zōho kokushi taikei.

Ryō no shūge 令集解 Collected Commentaries on the Administrative Code is a treatise on the administrative code (*ryō*) in which the Yōrō Code itself, sections of the Taihō Code, and many different commentaries (ex. *Koki, Ryō no shaku, Atoki, Anaki*) are quoted. The compendium has therefore played a key role in efforts to reconstruct the earlier codes. The text was compiled between 859 and 868 by Koremune Naomoto of the Hata-no-kimi family from Sanuki Province. Hata was a doctor of law (*myōhō hakase*) trained in the royal university, the Daigakuryō. See Shintei zōho kokushi taikei.

Ryōunshū 凌雲集 Cloud-borne Anthology is an official collection of poetry composed by courtiers in Chinese (*kanshi*). The collection was ordered prepared by Saga Tennō (r. 809-23) and it was completed in 814, with Ono Minemori (778-830) as the lead editor. For an annotated edition see Kojima Noriyuki 1978, vol. 2.2. In English, on *kanshi* at the early Heian court see Webb 2004 and Denecke 2004. And for translations of selected poems, see Watson 1975.

Saikyūki 西宮記 Notes of the Western Palace is the oldest of the extant privately assembled handbooks describing procedures for court ritual (*gishiki*) and government processes (*seimu*). It was compiled in the tenth century by the prince Minamoto Takaakira (914-82), a son of Daigo Tennō (r. 897-930). Takaakira reached the high post of minister of the left (*sadaijin*) in 967 but then was accused of plotting in the Anna Coup of 969 and exiled to the Dazaifu in Kyūshū. Eventually, however, he was allowed to return to the capital, where he probably completed the manual at his "western palace," located in the Right Capital (*ukyō*). Some manuscripts include comments and notes thought to have been added by later hands. See Shintei zōho kojitsu sōsho.

Sakeiki 左経記 is the journal of Minamoto Tsuneyori (985-1039), who reached the posts of left senior controller and advisor (*sangi*) on the Council of State under the court leaders Fujiwara Michinaga (966-1027) and Fujiwara Yorimichi (992-1074). Entries covering the years from 1016 to 1036 ae extant. See Zōho shiryō taisei 1965.

Sankaiki 山槐記 is the journal of Nakayama Tadachika (1131–95). Tadachika served long years as a member of the Royal Secretariat (Kurōdo) and became an advisor (*sangi*) on the Council of State. He was close to Taira Tokuko (alt. Kenreimon'in, 1155-1213) and her son, Antoku Tennō (r. 1180-85). Tadachika continued to serve the retired Go-Shirakawa even after the Taira defeat in 1185. The journal covers the years from 1150 to 1194. See Zōho shiryō taisei 1965.

Sanne jōikki 三会定一記 Record of Appointments to the Three Assemblies lists appointments to prestigious monastic offices associated with the three annual official Buddhist rites known as the *sandaie*, which were held in Nara and Kyoto during Heian times. See Dai nihon bukkyō zensho 1965 (Kōfukuji sōsho 1).

Sarashina nikki 更級日記 Sarashina Diary was compiled in the mid-eleventh century by the daughter of the provincial governor Sugawara Takasue (973-?). She accompanied her father out to his province during his tour of duty. The diary covers some forty years of her life, in the provinces and in the capital. See Hasegawa Masaharu 1989. In English see Morris 1971.

Seiji yōryaku 政事要略 Abstracted Compendium of Government Affairs is a compilation of documents and materials concerning court government gathered by the legal scholar Koremune Tadasuke beginning around 1002. See Shintei zōho kokushi taikei.

Sendai kuji hongi 先代旧事本紀 Original Record of Old Things in Previous Ages comprises materials reportedly compiled during Great King Suiko's reign at the turn of the seventh century. One section is entitled "Records of Provincial Chieftains" (*Kuni no miyatsuko no hongi*). However, many researchers suspect its later compilation during the early Heian Period. See Shintei zōho kokushi taikei, and Shintō taikei (Kotenhen 8).

Shakke kampanki 釈家官班記 Records of Buddhist Appointments is an encyclopedic listing and history of clerical offices that was compiled during the fourteenth century. See Gunsho ruijū (Shakkebu).

Shasekishū 沙石集 Collection of Sand and Pebbles is a compilation of didactive tales by the monk Mujū Ichien (1226-1312) from around 1283. See Watanabe Tsunaya 1966. For a partial English translation see Morrell 1985.

Shingishiki 新儀式 New Ritual Protocols is a handbook of court ritual compiled between 947 and 957, with additional notes added through the 960s. It was assembled by order of Murakami Tennō (r. 946–67). Only parts are extant. See Gunsho ruijū (Kujibu).

Shinsarugakuki 新猿楽記 Record of the New Monkey Music is an account of a night-time festival in the streets of the Heian capital in the mid-eleventh century. While its authorship is unknown, the writer was clearly a literatus of the time. Most scholars agree that he was Fujiwara Akihira (?-1066). Aside from describing the vaudeville-like acts of entertainers, the account includes vignettes of members of the audience, including the extended family of a mid-level Heian official, thereby providing clues to urban society of the eleventh-century capital. For annotated and glossed texts see Yamagishi Tokuhei 1979, Kawaguchi Hisao 1983, and Shigematsu Akihisa 1982.

Shinsen shōjiroku 新撰姓氏録 New Register of Aristicratic Kindreds is a compendium listing elite families resident in the capital region in the early ninth century. Begun in 816, it categorizes 1182 clans as descendents of a monarch (*kōbetsu*) or deity (*shinbetsu*), or as naturalized foreigners (*shoban*). See Saeki Arikiyo 1962.

Shisseishoshō 執政所抄 Notes from the Regents' Chancellery is a compendium of ritual protocol and procedures for use by the Northern Fujiwara regents' household. It was compiled in the early twelfth century, c. 1118-1121. See Zoku Gunsho ruijū (Kanshoku, Ritsuryō, Kujibu).

Shokugenshō 職原抄 Notes on the Origins of Court Offices is a compendium of materials concerning the history of court posts. It was compiled in 1340 by Kitabatake Chikafusa (1293–1354), tutor and minister for Go-Daigo Tennō (r. 1318-39), who by then had established his Southern Court in Yoshino. See Shirayama Yoshitarō 1980.

Shoku nihongi 続日本紀 Chronicle of Japan Continued is the second of six official court annals (*rikkokushi*). Compilation was ordered by Kammu Tennō (r. 781-806), with Fujiwara Tsugutada (727-96) and Sugano Mamichi (741-814) as editors. It covers the years from 697 to 791, and it was completed in 797. There are several annotated and glossed editions in Japanese including Aoki Kazuo 1989-2000.

Shoku nihon kōki 続日本後紀 Later Chronicle of Japan Continued is the third of the six official court annals (*rikkokushi*). It covers the years from 833 to 850 and was completed in 869 by Fujiwara Yoshifusa and others. See Shintei zōho kokushi taikei.

Shōmonki (alt. *Masakadoki*) 将門記 Chronicle of Masakado traces events of the Kantō-based rebellion of Taira Masakado (?-940) against court government in the early tenth century. It is thought to have been composed not long after the fact by someone in the capital. See Fukuda Toyohiko, 1997, 17–106. For an English translation, see Rabinovitch 1986.

Shōyūki 小右記 is the journal of Fujiwara Sanesuke (957–1046). Extant entries cover the period from 982 to 1032 with some sections missing. See Dai nihon kokiroku 1959-1986, and Zōho shiryō taisei.

Shunki 春記 is the journal of Fujiwara Sukefusa (1007-57), which covers the period from 1038 to 1054. See Zōho shiryō taisei; and for a modern gloss see Akaki Shizuko 1981. For a French translation see Herail 2001- .

Sochiki 帥記 is the journal kept by a commander of the Dazaifu, Minamoto Tsunenobu. It covers the years from 1068 to 1088. See Zōho shiryō taisei.

Sōgō bunin 僧綱補任 Appointment Register of Prelates lists appointments to the Prelate's Office (Sōgōsho) which, according to the *ritsuryō* codes, oversaw Buddhist affairs for the monarch. The record begins in Great King Suiko's era, around the turn of the seventh century, and it continues through 1142. See Dai nihon bukkyō zensho (Kōfukuji sōsho, vol. 1), and Minato Toshiro 1995-2002.

Sompi bun'myaku 尊卑分脈 Lineages High and Low is an encyclopaedic compilation of noble genealogies—those of courtier and warrior families—initially completed in the late fourteenth century, with some materials added later. See Shintei zōho kokushi taikei.

Suisaki 水左記 is the journal kept by Minister of the Left Minamoto Toshifusa (1035–1121). Only parts covering the period from 1062 to 1108 are extant. Toshifusa was the eldest son of Minamoto Morofusa and his senior consort, Fujiwara Sonshi, a daughter of Fujiwara Michinaga. He became a senior noble (*kugyō*) in 1057 when he was made a counselor (*sangi*); and he became minister of the left in 1082. See Zōho shiryō taisei.

Taiki 台記 is the journal of Minister of the Left Fujiwara Yorinaga (1120–56). It covers the years from 1136 to 1155, but with frequent lapses. See Zōho shiryō taisei.

Tannishō 歎異鈔 Notes on Lamenting Deviations is in part a statement of the teachings of the Amidist preacher Shinran (1173-1262), which were collected and edited by his disciple Yuien in the thirteenth century. Yuien included comments of his own. See *Teihon Shinran shōnin zenshū* (vol. 5, Genkōhen) 1976-1979. And for English translations, see Hirota 1982 and Unno 1984.

Tamefusakyōki 為房卿記 is the journal of the Council of State advisor (*sangi*) Fujiwara Tamefusa (1049–1115), a member of the Kajūji Fujiwara lineage. He served at the courts of several retired monarchs, and the journal covers the period from 1071 to 1114 with some gaps.

Teiōhennenki 帝王編年記 Royal Annals is a history of the realm from the mythical age of the gods up through the reign of Go-Fushimi Tennō (r. 1298–1301). It was compiled in the later fourteenth century—internal evidence suggests a date between 1364 and 1380, during the reign of Go-Kōgon—by an unknown author. For each reign the text identifies important officials, including the regent, ministers, royal guard commanders, the shogun, shogunal co-signers (*shikken*), Rokuhara deputies (*tandai*), and key temple directors. See Shintei zōho kokushi taikei.

Ten'en ni'nenki 天延二年記 (alt. *Chikanobukyōki*) is the journal of Taira Chikanobu (946-1017), a client of the regent Fujiwara Koremasa and a member of the Royal Chancellery (Kurōdo) of Enyū Tennō (r. 969-84). See Zoku gunsho ruijū (Zatsubu).

Teishinkōki 貞信公記 is the journal of the Northern Fujiwara regent Tadahira (880-949), who served as court leader for Suzaku Tennō (r. 930-46) and Murakami Tennō (r. 946-67). Today it is only known through an abstracted version made by Tadahira's son, Fujiwara Saneyori (900-70), the *Teishinkōkishō*. Entries begin in 907 and end in 948, although sections are missing. Fragments are extant in various ritual handbooks and in courtier journals. See Dai nihon kokiroku 1956.

Tōdaiji monjo 東大寺文書 Archives of Tōdaiji are the extant records of the royal temple, Tōdaiji (The "Great Eastern Temple") in Nara. They are being published by the Historiographical Institute (Shiryō hensanjo) at the University of Tokyo in the Dai nihon komonjo series, beginning in 1944 (18 vols. to date).

Togano'o Myōe Shōnin denki 栂尾明恵上人伝記 Biography of the Togano'o Holy Man Myōe narrates the life of the monk Myōe (1173-1232). It was compiled sometime before 1250. See Hiraizumi Akira 1980; in English, see Lieteau 1975.

Tōji chōja bunin 東寺長者補任 Register of Appointments of Tōji Monastic Directors records names of monastic directors (*chōja*) of Tōji in Kyoto. Entries begin with the appointment of Kūkai (774-835) as the director of construction in 814. Entries frequently include not only details concerning the chief monk but also important events that occurred during a his tenure. These records are therefore an important source for the temple's history. For variant texts see Gunsho ruijū (Buninbu) and Zoku zoku gunsho ruijū (Shidenbu).

Tokinoriki (alt. *Jihanki*) 時範記 is the journal of Taira Tokinori (1054–1109), who served as a senior controller of the right (*udaiben*) and houseman (*keishi*) to various Northern Fujiwara court leaders. Extant portions include entries from 1099, which provide insights into Tokinori's experiences as a new provincial governor in Inaba Province. See Miyazaki 1962-1986.

Tsurezuregusa 徒然草 Essays in Idleness by the courtier Yoshida Kaneyoshi (alt. Kenkō, 1283-1351) is traditionally considered a miscelleny (*zuihitsu*). See Satake Akihiro 1989; and in English see Keene 1967.

Uchigikishū 打聞集 is a Buddhist tale collection comprising twenty-seven stories from the later Heian Period, composition of which is thought to have been completed after 1134. Relatively few of the tales are found in other major *setsuwa* collections such as *Konjaku monogatarishū* and *Uji shūi*. There may have been three scrolls originally, but only one is now extant. See Nakajima Etsuji 1965; and Uchigikishū o yomu kai 1971.

Utsubō monogatari 宇津保物語 Tale of the Hollow Tree is a fictive prose narrative generally attributed to the tenth century. See Kōno Tama 1959.

Wamyōruijūshō (alt. *Wamyōshō*) 和名類聚抄 Japanese Names Topically Arranged is Japan's earliest encyclopedia. The text was compiled between 930 and 937 by Minamoto Shitagō (911-83), a well known poet and scholar. One section included lists of provinces with district and township names, and this part of the text is frequently cited by historians interested in the geographic distribution of population. There are various manuscripts extant, the longest comprising twenty volumes. See Ikebe Wataru 1981.

Yōrō ritsuryō 養老律令 The Yōrō Code supplanted the Taihō Code, which had been promulgated at the turn of the eighth century. The new code was reportedly compiled by the court leader Fujiwara Fuhito around 720 and was later promulgated by his grandson, Fujiwara Nakamaro (706-64) in 757. There were some changes made, but scholars believe that the two codes were much alike. There is no extant text but for efforts at reconstruction see Inoue Mitsusada 1976, and Aida Hanji 1964.

Zoku honchō monzui (alt. *Honchō zoku monzui*) 続本朝文粋 Literary Essentials of Our Realm Continued is a compendium of composition in Chinese—both poetry and prose—gathered by an unknown compiler in the mid-twelfth century and organized according to the earlier model set by categories in Fujiwara Akihira's *Honchō monzui* in the later eleventh century. Selected works number 332, and they date from the reign of Go-Ichijō (r. 1016-1036) to that of Sutoku (r. 1123-1141). See Shintei zōho kokushi taikei.

Selected Glossary

agata 県 a unit of the realm of Yamato paramounts (ōkimi 大王 "Great Kings") from the fifth century onward.

agatanushi 県主 chieftain of an *agata*, and thus a client of the Yamato Great King.

akō 阿衡 a Chinese term denoting a particularly trusted minister. In Japan, in 887 the scholar-official Tachibana Hiromi (837-90), who was closely allied with Uda Tennō, proposed that Fujiwara Mototsune be given the title of *akō*. He thereby initiated debate over the proper role and title for the leading minister at court. Tachibana lost the debate when Fujiwara Mototsune's authority over the Council of State (Daijōkan), as viceroy (*kampaku*) rather than as *akō*, was confirmed.

akusō 悪僧 "evil monk," one who in Buddhist terms does not follow the monastic precepts. However, officials often branded monks who mounted protests against the court "evil monks."

akutō 悪党 "evil band," brigands, often so named by officials whose jurisdiction was being resisted. An early use is found in the eighth-century *Shoku nihongi*, but use of the term became more frequent in Heian times.

anju 案主 an official with record-keeping responsibilities, either in a government office or for an estate.

atai 直 a noble title (*kabane*) granted to regional chieftains by a Yamato Great King.

azechi 按察使 royal inspectors appointed to supervise provincial administration in the provinces of one of the circuits during Nara and Heian times.

azukaridokoro 預所 an estate custodian, generally a courtier of the fifth rank or higher.

azuma'uta 吾妻歌 "songs of the east country" that are archived in the eighth-century *Man'yōshū* poetry anthology. They are thought to have come from what became the province of Mutsu.

bakufu 幕府 "curtained headquarters," denoting a general's field headquarters, which term later came to be associated with warrior governments at Kamakura and beyond.

Bandō 板東 the term means "east of the (Ashigaru and Usui) passes" and thus denotes the ten provinces from Sagami eastward in the Tōkaidō circuit and from Kōzuke eastward in the Tōsandō circuit.

banki 万機 denotes the throne's plenary powers. The expression first appears in the eighth-century *Nihon shoki* to denote the prerogatives enjoyed by Prince

Umayado (ltr. Shōtoku 574-622) during the reign of Great King Suiko at the turn of the seventh century. It was subsequently used to describe the authority of regents (*sesshō*) and viceroys (*kampaku*) in Heian times.

bankoku 蕃国 a subordinate and tribute-rendering realm. According to the Chinese ideal vision of their "middle kingdom," rulers and peoples of peripheral realms recognized the supremacy of the Chinese monarch and paid him both obeissance and tribute. In the same way, peninsular kingdoms such as Silla and Paekche are sometimes depicted in Japanese records as *bankoku* of the *tennō*'s realm.

bankyaku 蕃客 official envoys from tribute-rendering realms.

bantō 番頭 a tax collector within an estate (*shōen*).

be 部 a specialized worker community that served the Yamato Great King, members of the royal family, or a noble family (*uji*) up to *ritsuryō* times. A *be* was typically overseen by a hereditary royal vassal (*tomo no miyatsuko*) who was in turn subject to a courtier possessing the noble title (*kabane*) of *muraji*.

ben 弁 a controller on the staff of the Office of Controllers (Benkankyoku).

Benkankyoku 弁官局 the Office of Controllers, which in the eighth century provided staff support to the Council of State while mediating with the Council, ministries, and provinces. By early Heian times, the office was charged with overseeing the writing out and execution of royal directives.

beppu 別符 a special jurisdictional unit in the public domain (*kokugaryō*) or an estate (*shōen*) during mid-to-late Heian times and beyond.

betsuin 別院 a branch temple, generally associated with one of the great official temples of the capital region. Many examples of *betsuin* appear in sources of the early Heian Period.

betsumyō 別名 a "special named unit," many of which were created due to the reorganization of public fields (*kōden*) up to the eleventh century.

bettō 別当 a director in some offices of the *ritsuryō* bureaucracy; also, the monastic director at some temples.

bettō shiki 別当職 generally, the directorship of an estate.

biwa hosshi 琵琶法師 performers dressed like monks who played the Japanese lute (*biwa*) while reciting and chanting stories in later Heian times.

bōko 房戸 a subdivision of a larger census unit (*ko*, *gōko*) referred to in eighth-century sources. Modern scholars suspect that in the eighth century a *bōko* may have represented the actual commensal unit residing under a single roof.

bokushodoki 墨書土器 inscribed pottery, a great deal of which has been found at eighth-century and later archaeological sites.

buke 武家 a warrior lineage; or, alternatively, by Kamakura times, "warrior government" (in contrast to the Kyoto court, *kuge* 公家).

buke hō 武家法 "the law of warrior government," that is to say, of the *bakufu*.

buke (no) tōryō 武家棟梁 the leading warrior in the realm, a term that appears by mid-to-later Heian times.

bunkajin 文化人 (alt. *bunjin*) literatus, a scholar-official.

bunkan 文官 a civil official (in contrast to a military official, *bukan* 武官).

Buppō 仏法 Buddha's law (in contrast to the monarch's law, *ōhō* 王法).

bushi 武士 (alt. *tsuwamono*) "man of war," a military specialist.

bushidan 武士团 a warrior band.

busshi 仏師 a craftsman who produced Buddhist images.

Buyakuryō 賦役令 the *ritsuryō* Law on Labor Taxes.

buzoku rengō 部族連合 a modern term denoting a tribal alliance.

chakunan 嫡男 the senior male heir designated by a father, alternatively called the *chakushi* 嫡子.

chigyō 知行 a proprietary holding, including land and cultivators, which was frequently associated with an official post (*shiki* 職).

chigyōkoku 知行国 a prebendal province—by late Heian times these were held primarily by senior nobles and retired monarchs.

Chinjufu 鎮守府 the Pacification Headquarters in Mutsu Province, where the Chinjufu commander (*shōgun*) had his office and residence.

chinso 賃租 land rent for public fields let out for cultivation, for which part of the rent was paid in the spring (*chin*) and part in the fall (*so*).

chō 調 a craft or produce tax, one of the forms of tribute-taxation instituted by the *ritsuryō* codes.

chō 町 a unit of land measurement (one *chō* = 2.94 acres).

chō 牒 according to the *ritsuryō* codes, an official form of correspondence to be exchanged horizontally between offices or officers of the same status, or between a temple (which was actually outside the official hierarchy) and a government office.

chōja 長者 an elder, or boss; alternatively, the monastic director at some temples.

chokushi 勅旨 a royal order, often in written form. According to the *ritsuryō* codes, after a royal order was transmitted orally, it was to be put down in writing.

chokushiden 勅旨田 "royal grant fields" bestowed by the monarch on royals and royal favorites; they were especially prominent in the ninth century, but such grants were forbidden beginning in the Engi era (901-23).

chōsei 朝政 the exercise of plenary governing authority by the Heavenly Sovereign (*tennō* 天皇). The original locus for such on a daily basis was the Throne Hall (Daigokuden 大極殿), with the monarch facing representatives of officialdom (*hyakkan* 百官) assembled in the Halls of State (Chōdōin 朝堂院, alt. Hasshōin 八省院). But such assemblies grew less frequent, and by the era of Kammu Tennō (r. 781-806) its locus moved to the Shishiiden (紫宸殿), which was the reception hall of the royal residence. In Heian times a relic of this practice was called *shunsei* 旬政, which was held seasonally either with the *tennō* participating, or by the senior nobles (*kugyō* 公卿) without the royal presence (in the latter case, it was termed "empty seated," *hiraza* 平座).

chōshūshi 朝集使 an agent who carried reports and petitions from provincial headquarters to the capital during Nara and Heian times. There were four categories of provincial messengers, known collectively as the *yodo no tsukai* 四度の使.

chōyō 調庸 produce and labor taxes mandated by the *ritsuryō* codes.

chūgoku 中国 originally, the San'yōdō circuit that bordered the Inland Sea. Later, the designation was used to designate both the San'yōdō and San'indō circuits.

chūjō 中将 a mid-level commander in the Left or Right Inner Palace Guards (Konoefu), who frequently held a concurrent appointment as a commander of yet another guard unit as well. The post of *chūjō* was often held by an advisor (*sangi*) on the Council of State.

chūnagon 中納言 a middle counselor on the Council of State.

chūsei 中世 the middle ages, the medieval world—it is a historiographical term rather than a historical one. Related terms include "medieval relations" (*chūseiteki shokankei* 中世的諸関係) and "medieval feudal relations" (*chūsei hōkenteki shokankei* 封建的諸関係).

Daigaku 大学 the royal university first instituted during the era of Great King Tenji (668-71) to train royal officials. Later, a chapter of the *ritsuryō* codes was devoted to its organization and operation by the Bureau of the Royal University, the Daigakuryō 大学寮.

daigeki 大外記 a senior secretary serving in the Council Secretariat (Gekikyoku) of the Council of State.

daijin 大臣 one of two senior ministers on the Council of State. There was a senior minister of the left (*sadaijin* 左大臣) and a senior minister of the right (*udaijin* 右大臣). When there was no prime minister (*daijōdaijin* 太上大臣), a senior minister—generally that of the left—functioned as Council leader (*ichi no kami* 一上).

daijōdaijin 太上大臣 preeminent minister, or prime minister, of the Council of State. According to the *ritsuryō* codes, it was an extraordinary post that was often to be left vacant except when an extraordinary appointee was available.

Daijōe 大嘗会 (alt. *Daijōsai* 大嘗祭) the Great Festival of Enthronement—rites celebrating a new royal reign, which were generally held in the autumn within a year of a new monarch's accession.

daijōkampu 太政官符 a written directive issued by the Council of State to governmental offices to promulgate a royal command.

Daijōkan 太政官 the Council of State established by the *ritsuryō* codes to advise the monarch and promulgate his orders. It included ministers, counselors, and advisors who by Heian times came to be known as "senior nobles" (*kugyō* 公卿).

daimyō 大名 a prominent person in the provinces. The term first appears in later Heian records to denote prominent land-opening elites. In the later medieval age, it came to refer to warlords who ruled their own territories with significant autonomy.

daini 大弐 the second-in-command (*suke*) or senior assistant governor-general of the Kyūshū headquarters, the Dazaifu 大宰府. After the post of governor-general (*sotsu*) became a sinecure in the early Heian Period, the *daini* (originally of the junior or senior fourth rank, later of junior or senior third rank) frequently served as chief administrator until the early twelfth century, when even the *daini* ceased traveling to Kyūshū.

dairi 内裏 the *tennō*'s residential palace, located within the greater palace precincts (*daidairi* 大内裏).

dairyō 大領 (alt. *tairyō*) a senior district chieftain, administrative head of a district (gun 郡) under the *ritsuryō* provincial system made up of provinces (*kuni*), districts, and townships (*gō*).

Dazaifu 太宰府 the Kyūshū headquarters, in the province of Chikuzen near present-day Hakata. It was charged with oversight of all the provinces of Kyūshū and the two islands of Iki and Tsushima, greeting foreign emissaries, overseeing foreign visitors, and defending the realm against external enemies.

dempō kanjō 伝法灌頂 a Buddhist initiation ceremony used in the esoteric Shingon and Tendai schools.

Denryō 田令 the *ritsuryō* Law on Rice Fields.

denseki 田籍 field registers noting the names of tax-paying cultivators. The *ritsuryō* codes mandated keeping these registers as one process of provincial administration.

denzu 田図 maps kept by provincial authorities that charted the location of cultivated fields as well as the names of those responsible for paying taxes on them. When census-taking ceased in early Heian times, these maps became increasingly important for the provincial tax collection process.

dezukuri 出作 fields cultivated by estate dwellers on public lands outside estate boundaries. Such fields were a source of constant contention between estate dwellers, estate proprietors, and provincial authorities by mid-Heian times.

dōri 道理 the "principle of things," reason, custom.

Eizenryō 営善令 the *ritsuryō* Law on Construction and Repair.

Ejifu 衛士府 the Headquarters of the Royal Palace Guards, whose members guarded the gates of the *tennō*'s residential palace. It was renamed the Headquarters of the Royal Gate Guards (Emonfu 衛門府) after 811.

Emishi 蝦夷 (alt. Ezo) inhabitants of the northeast frontier region, they were also known as "hairy men" or "quail barbarians."

Emonfu 衛門府 Headquarters of the Royal Gate Guards, a new name for the Ejifu after 811.

fudai 譜代 hereditary district chieftains whose post, prerogatives, and perquisites were transmitted through several generations.

fudoki 風土記 a provincial gazetteer.

fugō 富豪 the wealthy, a term found in early Heian sources and denoting wealthy provincials.

fuhito 史 a scribe, many of which served in various *ritsuryō* offices.

fuko 封戸 prebendal units or residence units (ko 戸), taxes of which were assigned to support high ranking officials, temples, and shrines under the *ritsuryō* system. However the system had mostly ceased functioning by mid-Heian times.

fumyō 負名 a "named obligée"—one who contracted to collect and forward taxes on a given unit of land. The term *fumyō* 負名 denoted both the contractor and the land from which taxes were collected.

funyū shōen 不入荘園 an estate for which entry by provincial officials was not permitted, by special order of the Council of State.

fushū 俘囚 "surrendered barbarians," specifically denoting those Emishi who had accepted rule by the *tennō*'s court.

ge 解 (alt. *gebumi* 解文) an offical report or petition submitted upward, from a lower ranking to a higher ranking official or office, in *ritsuryō* officialdom.

gekan 外官 postings outside the capital (in contrast to postings within the capital, *naikan* 内官).

geki 外記 a secretary of the Council of State and member of the Council Secretariat (Gekikyoku 外記局). Originally considered as fourth-rankers (*sakan*) for the Shōnagonkyoku 少納言局, they drafted all sorts of administrative documents.

gekisei 外記政 exercise of governing authority by the Council of State within the Office of the Council Secretariat (Gekichō 外記庁), located within the precincts of the Council of State (Daijōkanchō 太政官庁) near the royal residential palace. The procedure developed by the ninth century. Therein the senior nobles (*kugyō* 公卿) deliberated concerning reports and requests sent to them from official agencies and the provinces by way of the Controllers' Office (Benkankyoku 弁官局).

Gembaryō 玄番寮 the *ritsuryō* Bureau for Alien and Buddhist Affairs, which was overseen by the Ministry of Civil Affairs (Jibushō). Its mandate was to oversee Buddhist affairs as well as matters associated with immigrants and foreign emissaries.

ge'nin 下人 servants, generally considered to have been of mean status.

ge'in 外印 the outer seal, which belonged to the Council of State. According to the codes, both it and the inner seal of the *tennō*, the *nai'in* 内印, were required to seal legislation before promulgation.

geshi 下司 (alt. *gesu*) a local estate manager, frequently an office (*shiki* 職) occupied by a land opener who had commended fields to a noble estate proprietor (*ryōke*). In return, the commender received appointment as *geshi* of the land from that proprietor.

Giseiryō 儀制令 the *ritsuryō* Law on Decorum.

gō 郷 a township, a unit in the *ritsuryō* provincial administrative system. Its chief administrator was the township head (*gōchō* 郷長).

goganji 御願寺 a royal vow temple, many of which were founded during the Heian Period.

goin 後院 a detached palace (*rikyū* 離宮) designated by a monarch for use as his retirement palace.

goinden 後院田 "fields of the royal retirement palace"—often land to be opened to cultivation, the usufruct of which was used to support the retired monarch.

gojisō 護持僧 a protector monk, generally from the Tendai or Shingon schools, who acted as spiritual protector to the *tennō*.

gōko 郷戸 a large residence unit, usually comprised of twenty or more individuals, documented in census records (*koseki*) and tax registers of the eighth through tenth centuries.

gon no bettō 権別当 an extranumerary director of an official agency or Buddhist temple-monastery (*tera* 寺).

gon no jōza 権上座 an extranumerary monk leader (*jōza* 上座) of a Buddhist temple-monastery (*tera*).

gōso 強訴 "forceful" protests by monks directed at court authorities in the Kyoto capital.

gun 郡 (alt. *kohori, kōri*) a district, a subdivision of a province (*kuni* 国).

Gumbōryō 軍防令 the *ritsuryō* Law on Defense.

gunga 郡衙 a district office, where the district chieftain (*gunji*) presided (also *gunke* 郡家).

gungōsei 郡郷制 the "district and township system" by which provinces were administered in the *ritsuryō* era.

gunji 郡司 a district chieftain, who presided over a district office (*gunga*). They were generally hereditary officials (*fudai*), but they were overseen by the provincial governor. During Heian times, provincial governors could and did nominate new candidates for the post.

gunkimono 軍記物 martial narratives, the modern term for a literary genre including narratives about warfare such as the mid-Heian *Masakadoki* and *Mutsuwaki*, as well as the medieval *Heike monogatari* and *Taiheiki*.

Hagatame 歯固め a ceremonial banquet held at the palace during the first three days of a new year.

handen 班田 allotment fields that were officially distributed by the *ritsuryō* government to cultivators as members of residence units (*ko*).

haniwa 埴輪 ceramic jars, sometimes in animal and anthropomorphic shapes, that were placed around mounded tombs (*kofun* 古墳) in the pre-*ritsuryō* Kofun age (~300-600 C.E.).

harita 治田 newly opened fields (also *konden* 墾田).

Hayato no tsukasa 隼人司 an office of the Headquarters of the Royal Gate Guards (Emonfu) that oversaw the Hayato as court tributaries. In 808 it was made part of the Ministry of Defense (Hyōbushō 兵部省).

Hayato 隼人 "falcon men" or "swift ones"—non-Yamato people resident in Kyūshū into *ritsuryō* times.

Heiankyō 平安京 the royal capital from 794 to 1868.

heishi 兵士 conscript soldiers for which provision was made in the *ritsuryō* codes.

hinin 非人 a persons of mean status.

hō 保 (alt. *ho*) a new township, which was a new adminstrative unit in the public domain that emerged during the eleventh and twelfth centuries; alternatively, a policing unit in the capital during Heian times.

Hokke Fujiwara 北家藤原 the Northern Fujiwara, descendants of Fujiwara Fusasaki, some of whom became regents (*sesshō*) and viceroys (*kampaku*).

hokkyō 法橋 a preceptor—an elite monastic title that was sometimes granted to artists, sculptors, and medical specialists in Heian times and later.

honji suijaku 本地乗迹 a religious teaching to the effect that Japan's deities (*kami*) are manifestations (*suijaku*) of Buddhas or bodhisattvas, the latter representing their true forms (*honji*).

honjo 本所 (alt. *honke* 本家) a preeminent estate proprietor in later Heian times and beyond.

horinouchi 堀内 "within the ditch," denoting a homestead that was surrounded by newly opened rice fields.

hyakushō 百姓 wealthy cultivators who also served as local notables and tax collectors.

ichien shihai 一円支配 unified control over an estate (*shōen*), which prerogative was being asserted by great religious proprietors over their properties by later Heian times.

ichi no hijiri 市の聖 "evangelist of the marketplace," one of the appellations given to the proselytizing monk Kūya (903-72).

ichinokami 一の上 the senior member of the Council of State, usually one of the senior ministers.

ichinomiya 一の宮 the premier shrine of a province.

ichō 移牒 an official communiqué between equals in the *ritsuryō* bureaucratic system.

ie 家 a household or, alternatively, a patrilineage. The *ritsuryō* codes provided that high-rankers have household officials (*keishi*) to oversee their household affairs. Thus early use of the term emerged among high-ranking aristocrats.

Ifukuryō 衣服令 the *ritsuryō* Law on Dress.

in 院 a retired monarch, which term probably derived from the term *koin*, meaning the retired monarch's retirement place. From the tenth century there were also royal ladies (*nyōin*) whose status was equivalent to that of a retired monarch.

inaka 田舎 the provinces, in contrast with the capital (*miyako, kyō* 京).

In no chō 院庁 the household office of a senior retired *tennō* in the mid-to-late Heian Period.

inzen 院宣 an order issued by a retired *tennō* through his household office, the *in no chō*.

jijū 侍従 a chamberlain in the monarch's residential palace. According to the *ritsuryō* codes, chamberlains belonged to the Ministry of Central Affairs (Nakatsukasashō 中務省).

jingi 神祇 the deities of heaven and earth, also known as *kami* 神, for which the Heavenly Sovereign (*tennō*) served as chief ritual coordinator and patron.

Jingikan 神祇官 the *ritsuryō* Council of Deity Affairs, which oversaw royal relations with the *kami* and their shrines.

jingūji 神宮寺 a Buddhist temple closely affiliated with a shrine.

jinja 神社 a shrine, the place where a *kami* 神 is worshipped.

jin'nin 神人 (alt. *kambito*) a person closely associated with a shrine—thus, a shrine associate.

jin no mōshibumi 陣の申文 reports and petitions from the provinces discussed by members of the Council of State in the guards' chamber east of the Shishiiden within the residential palace. That chamber was known as the *jin* 陣 in Heian times.

jin no sadame 陣定 a process of discussion and debate by the senior nobles of the Council of State in mid-to-late Heian times. It was conducted when the monarch commanded, and afterward the monarch received a complete record of the proceedings for his reference in deciding a matter of serious consequence.

jin no za 陣座 meetings of the Council of State—called the *Kugyō* Council in Heian times—in the *jin* 陣.

jisha 寺社 Buddhist temples and *kami* shrines.

jisharyō 寺社領 proprietary holdings of temples and shrines.

jishu 寺主 a temple rector, a member of the temple management team (*sangō* 三綱).

jitō 地頭 generally, a military steward appointed by the Kamakura Bakufu in the 1180s and beyond.

jō 判官 a third-level manager in a *ritsuryō* agency.

jō 丈 a measure of length approximately 10 feet (*shaku* 尺) long.

Jōdo 浄土 the "Pure Land," as the Buddha Amida's Western Paradise was called.

jōri 条里 the checkerboard grid system used to divide and map official land-opening projects in pre-*ritsuryō* and *ritsuryō* times.

jōri tsubotsuke 条里坪付 land registers in which the location of fields according to their *jōri* location was recorded.

jōza 上座 the leader of the monastic management team (*sangō* 三綱) at a temple.

kabane 姓 a noble title granted by the Yamato Great King or early *ritsuryō*-era *tennō* to lineages that served the throne.

kachō 家長 (alt. *ie no osa*) the head of a household, a patriarch.

kagai 化外 (alt. *kegai*) "outside the transformed," a place or people not under the civilizing rule of the enlightened Heavenly Monarch, and therefore considered uncivilized. The alternative is *kanai* 化内 "within the transformed," those who are ruled and civilized by the monarch. Such thinking was a basic concept of Chinese-style rulership imported into Japan by the fifth century.

kagura 神楽 ritual singing and dancing at the palace, which is associated with worshiping the deities (*kami*).

kaihotsu ryōshu 開発領主 "land-opening proprietor," an opener and possessor of newly opened rice fields.

kami 神 a deity.

kami no wotoko 神の男 "young man of the deity."

kami no wotome 神の女 "young woman of the deity."

kampaku 関白 viceroy, the royal chief-of-staff. From the later ninth century, members of the Northern Fujiwara family with close affinal connections to the throne held this leading ministerial office. In 887 Uda Tennō described the post thusly: "Without the protection of the prime minister (who was *kampaku*), how could I proclaim the royal will throughout the realm and make straight the way of heavenly governance in the palace? . . . He assembles all officialdom, so let every matter be entrusted to him and let him (then) advise me. Whatever he proposes, it is as if it were already done."

kampu 官符 (alt. *daijōkampu*) a written directive of the Council of State promulgating the monarch's command.

kana 仮名 the Japanese syllabary made up of abstracted Chinese character forms and representing Japanese sounds.

kanai 化内 (alt. *kenai*) "within the transformed," meaning a resident of the civilized realm presided over by the *tennō*.

kambito 神人 attendants, advocates, or associates of a shrine.

kandō 官道 official roads.

kammon 勘文 an opinion issued at court by scholars, envoys, the Council of Shrine Affairs, and legal or *yin-yang* specialists.

kannushi 神主 the head ritualist at a shrine.

kansei 官政 the exercise of governing authority (*matsurigoto* 政) by the Council of State (Daijōkan 太政官).

kansenji 官宣旨 an order from the Council of State issued through the Office of Controllers (Benkankyoku 弁官局).

Kanshiryō 関市令 the *ritsuryō* Law on Barriers and Markets.

kanshi ukeou 官司請負 a modern historiographical term denoting the practice of "contracting out" (請負) official posts to specific families or lineages, which led to increasing hereditization. Many historians see this practice as characteristic of Japan's medieval society and polity, beginning in mid-to-late Heian times.

kanshōfu 官省符 a specific order of the Council of State permitting land tax (*sō*) exemption for an estate—such an estate was termed a *kanshōfu shōen*.

kansō 官奏 a memorial to the throne from the Council of State.

karamono 唐物 imported luxury goods.

kasho 過所 a travel pass used to secure passage through an official barrier (*seki* 関). In classical times officials requested such passes from their superiors (*honshi* 本司), while commoners requested them from their district chieftain (*gunji*). In medieval times, barriers turned into toll booths operated for economic benefit.

katarimono 語り物 oral storytelling.

kawaramono 河原者 a medieval appellation for those who lived along riverbanks, who were generally considered to be of mean status.

kebiishi 検非違使 an agent of the Royal Police Office (Kebiishichō 検非違使庁), which was established as an extracodal agency in early Heian times to police the streets of the Heian capital. Its appointees were generally members of other guard units, such as the Right and Left Palace Guards (Emonfu 衛門府). By the tenth century, provincial police agents were also being appointed.

keichō 計帳 a tax register, preparation of which was mandated by the ritsuryō codes as part of the taxation process. Several such registers are extant from Nara and Heian times.

keishi 家司 an official in a noble's household. Such posts were originally established by the *ritsuryō* codes, but new ones were also added in Heian times.

kenden 検田 a field survey, generally for the purpose of assessing taxes or rent. In the public domain such authority *(kendenken* 検田権*)* was vested in provincial government by mid-Heian times. The results were recorded in provincial maps (*kokuzu* 国図) and field survey registers (*kendenchō* 検田帳) which thus served as key documents for provincial administration. Estate proprietors (*ryōke*) also carried out field surveys within their own proprietary holdings.

ke'nin 家人 a "houseman" or client. The term appears in the *ritsuryō* codes as one category of dependent persons whose status was higher than that of slaves (*nuhi* 奴婢). And while such status could be transmitted through generations, *ke'nin* could not be sold. By Heian times, the term was used to denote the clients of noble households.

kenmon seika 権門勢家 "gates of power and powerful houses," an expression used in later Heian-period sources to denote royal and noble households as well as official temples and shrines. Typically their power translated into influence in the countryside over both land and people.

kentōshi 遣唐使 diplomatic envoys sent by the Yamato court to Tang China, beginning during the reign of Great King Suiko at the turn of the seventh century. The last such mission was ordered sent in 894, but it was subsequently cancelled.

Kenyōryō 假寧令 the *ritsuryō* Law on Official Leave.

kikajin 帰化人 "one who has been civilized" by emigrating to the realm of an enlightened monarch and becoming a subject of that monarch (i.e. the *tennō*). This term was used by the Japanese court in referring to immigrants from the Korean peninsula and other regions on the continent.

Kinai 畿内 "the capital district," the five-province region surrounding the royal capital, whether located at Fujiwara, Nara, Nagaoka, or Heian. It included the provinces of Yamato, Yamashiro, Kawachi, Izumi, and Settsu.

kinohe 柵戸 (alt. *sakko*) residence units of colonists attached to a stockade, outside of which they opened new fields. Such stockades were opened along the eastern and northern frontiers in the late seventh through early ninth centuries as a means of asserting Yamato authority over natives, called Emishi.

kinshin 近臣 an "intimate minister," and thus a high-ranking adviser to the monarch.

kisaki 妃, 后 the "queen-consort," the highest ranking royal consort, of which the *ritsuryō* codes allowed for two. Originally they were to be women of the royal family holding the fourth or higher princely rank. But in Nara times women of the Fujiwara family also came to be named queen-consort.

kishin 寄進 to commend land to a high-ranking noble or influential religious institution that could guarantee the tax-exempt status of the land, and its safety from confiscation by provincial authorities. By the eleventh century many estates (*shōen* 荘園) were established by acts of commendation initiated by local land openers (*zaichi ryōshu*). Modern historians call such estates *kishin shōen* 寄進 荘園.

kishōmon 起請文 a pledge to the deities invoking punishment in the case of perjury or failure to carry out one's promise.

kishu 貴種 descent from a "noble seed," specifically that of a father who held court rank higher than the fifth.

kizoku 貴族 a noble, which from *ritsuryō* times onward meant a courtier of the fifth rank or higher.

kizoku rengō taisei 貴族連合体制 the "aristocratic alliance system"—a historiographical term used by modern researchers to describe the political organization of the early Heian court. Similar terms are *kizoku seiken* 貴族政権, meaning "aristocratic polity;" and *kizoku shakai* 貴族社会, meaning "aristocratic society."

kō 公 official, used in opposition to *shi* 私, meaning unofficial or private.

ko 戸 a residence unit, and the object of the *ritsuryō* census-taking and taxation processes. According to the *ritsuryō*, residence-unit registers (*koseki* 戸籍) charting the familial relations of residents and their tax status were to be maintained by the residence-unit head (*kochō* 戸長) in cooperation with township heads (*gōji* 郷司) and district chieftains (*gunji*). Some such registers from the late seventh through ninth centuries are extant.

kodai 古代 a historiographical term denoting "the classical epoch," which spans the Nara (710-84) and much of the Heian (784-1185) periods.

kōeki karamono tsukai 交易唐物使 a purchasing agent for imported goods in Heian times.

kofun 古墳 a Japanese mounded tomb, a tumulus. They were built as chiefly tombs from Yayoi times onward, but traditionally the Kofun Period has been dated from the later third through the seventh centuries.

kōke 公家 (alt. *kuge*) the public realm, the state. A similar expression is *kokka* (国家), denoting the polity or state.

koku 石 a dry measure used for grain—one *koku* equals 4.895 bushels or 350 pounds. It is said that a *koku* denoted the measure of rice needed to feed a human for one year.

kokubunji 国分寺 a provincial monks' temple, construction of which was mandated in every province during the reign of Shōmu Tennō (r. 724-49). Remains of both monks' temples and provincial nunneries (*kokubunniji* 国分尼寺) have been found in many of the 66 provinces. Some of these establishments continued operating into mid-Heian times.

kokufu 国府 provincial headquarters, the center of provincial administration in a province. Its precincts housed the administrative offices and manufacturing shops overseen by the provincial governor (*kokushi*), his residence and those of his staff from the capital, including those occupied by resident provincial officials (*zaichō kanjin* 在庁官人) from mid-Heian times.

kokufū bunka 国風文化 "Japan's own culture," a modern concept denoting the results of ongoing adaptation of continental culture during Heian times.

kokuga 国衙 the provincial headquarters and its administration. The provincial domain made up of public fields (*kōden* 公田) was called *kokugaryō* 国衙領, in opposition to privately held estates (*shōen*). Provincial law was called *kokugahō* 国衙法.

kokunai meishi 国内名士 provincial notables, a term used in mid-Heian sources.

kokushi 国司 the provincial governing team that comprised a group of up to 7 administrators sent out from the capital to govern each province, as mandated by the *ritsuryō* Law on Personnel (Shikiinryō 職員令). But the term is also used to denote only the head of the team, its director (*kami* 守), who in the ninth century came to be called the "custodial governor" (*zuryō* 受領) because of his fiscal accountability to the court.

kokusho 国書 a state letter, used in diplomatic relations between realms and their monarchs.

kokuzō 国造 (alt. *kuni no miyatsuko*) a provincial chieftain—a regional ruler whose authority predated adoption of the *ritsuryō* codes at the turn of the eighth century.

kōmin 公民 a commoner. In *ritsuryō* terms, a free subject of the *tennō* was termed "a good fellow" (*ryōmin* 良民). But the term *kōmin* eventually replaced *ryōmin* to denote a free subject of the *tennō*'s realm.

Konden einen shizai hō 墾田永年資材法 the Law Concerning Permanent Possession of Reclaimed Land, which was promulgated in 743. It proclaimed that rice fields opened by individuals of certain status who utilized newly developed irrigation facilities and gained the permission of the provincial governor were to be considered perpetual hereditary holdings of the opener and his or her descendents.

kōri (alt. *gun*) 郡 a district, which was a subdivision of a province. These units were established in the later seventh century and they remained important for provincial administration into Heian times.

kōryō 公領 public land that comprised the public domain, which came to be called *kokugaryō* 国衙領 by the later Heian Period.

koseki 戸籍 census registers, the keeping of which was mandated by the *ritsuryō* codes. The registers were to list all members of residence units (*ko* 戸). Field distribution, taxation, and other aspects of *ritsuryō* provincial administration depended upon these records.

koshiro 子代 communities of royal cultivators that worked on land held by members of the Yamato royal family before the mid-seventh century.

koshu 戸主 the head of a residential unit (*ko* 戸) who represented the unit to *ritsuryō* authorities. He was responsible for registration and tax payment.

kubunden 口分田 "mouthfield"—officially opened rice fields that were distributed to registered residence units (represented by the head) based on the number of registered subjects therein. According to the *ritsuryō* codes, cultivators were to use the fields during their lifetimes, gaining livelihood therefrom and paying various forms of tax-tributes (*chō*, *yō*, *sō*) to the *tennō*'s government. After a cultivator died, his fields were to be redistributed by provincial authorities. However, the processes of registration and redistribution on which the system depended ceased early in the ninth century.

kueiden 公営田 "public managed fields"—public fields, the cultivation of which was to be performed by cultivators fulfilling their labor tax (*yōeki*

庸役) obligation under the supervision of local managers. The model for the system was proposed by Ono Minemori (778-830), chief administrator at the Dazaifu, in 823.

kuge hō 公家法 "courtier law," the law of the court and courtiers in contrast to that of warrior government—*bukehō* 武家法—by the late twelfth century.

kugen 公験 proof documents for land holdings, typically evidencing the origins and tax status of the land, including stipulations for tax exemption or other special circumstances. Alternatively, the term denoted certifying papers held by a monk that indicated government permission for his monastic (and tax-exempt) status.

kugonin 供御人 royal provisioners, or alternatively, provisioners for a shrine.

kugyō 公卿 senior nobles, a term denoting members of the Council of State in Heian times, the court's senior nobles.

kuji 公事 a tax or other duty owed to government.

Kumeuta 久米歌 songs of the Kume people, some of which are archived in the sections devoted to the early monarch Jimmu in the eighth-century histories, the *Kojiki* and *Nihon shoki*.

kumonjo 公文所 the "record office" at a provincial headquarters, in a noble household, or on an estate.

kuni 国 a province in the territorial administration system of classical and medieval Japan.

kuni no miyatsuko (alt. *kokuzō*) 国造 a provincial chieftain—a regional leader recognized by the Yamato court and later by the *tennō*'s government

kurōdo 蔵人 a royal secretary in the Royal Secretariat, the Kurōdodokoro 蔵人所.

Kurōdodokoro 蔵人所 the Royal Secretariat was an extracodal office established in the ninth century by Saga Tennō (r. 809-23) to support him in his struggle with his elder brother and predecessor, Heizei Tennō (r. 806-809). Therafter the office took over arranging and provisioning various aspects of royal life in the residential palace, including important liaison duties between the throne and other units of *tennō*-centered government.

Kushikiryō 公式令 the *ritsuryō* Law on Official Communications and Protocols.

kusuiko 公出挙 official mandatory rice loans originally meant to encourage agriculture but which came in the eighth century to be used to support provincial administration. Rice seed stored by provincial authorities was distributed to all cultivators as loans in the spring and recollected with interest varying from thirty to fifty per cent in the fall.

kyaku 格 supplementary legislation issued after the promulgation of the *ritsuryō* codes, from the early eighth century onward. They were periodically compiled in compendia such as those of the Kōnin- and Jōgan eras in the ninth century, and in the encyclopaedic *Supplementary Legislation of Three Eras Categorized* (*Ruijū sandai kyaku* 類聚三代格) of the early tenth century.

kyōdōtai 共同体 a modern term denoting a production community, whose members usually reside in close proximity and cooperate in productive endeavors.

li 礼 (Jap. *rei, rai*) a Chinese ideology of ideal social order, hierarchy, and harmony to be maintained in government and broader society by ceremony, protocol, procedure, and law. As an ideal of Chinese society and government, it was imported to Japan through classical texts and Chinese-style monarchical and legal sysems.

mandokoro 政所 the administrative office of a provincial headquarters, noble household, or official religious establishment.

mappō 末法 "the latter days of the Buddhist law," the idea that at a certain point after the lifetime of the Buddha—for some in Japan, after the year 1052—the world would enter into a period of great lawlessness and violence when the Buddha's teachings would become increasingly difficult to teach and follow.

matsuji 末寺 a branch temple of a large official temple.

matsurigoto 政 decision making and other government duties performed by the *tennō* or his officials.

meishi 名士 provincial notables.

menden 免田 tax-exempt fields. Some researchers describe the increasingly patrimonial land tenure system of mid-Heian times—whereby clients of the powerful gained tax exemptions—as *menden yoriudosei* 免田寄人制 "cultivation of tax-exempt fields by dependents."

meshitsugi 召次 an attendant or low-ranking functionary in a noble household.

michi no oku (alt. Michinoku, Rikuoku, Mutsu 陸奥) "the end of the road," denoting the province of Mutsu in far eastern Honshū.

Minbushō 民部省 the Ministry of Popular Affairs in the *ritsuryō*-based government.

Misaie 御斎会 (alt. Gosaie) a realm-protecting official Buddhist ceremony celebrated at court over seven days at the beginning of the new year.

miyake 宅倉 "honorable granary land," a royal estate in the pre-*ritsuryō* age.

miyako 京 the royal metropole, first at Fujiwara, then at Heijō (Nara), and still later at Heian (present-day Kyoto).

miyako no musha 京武者 (alt. *kyō musha*) warriors of high court rank—the fifth or higher—who resided at least part time in the capital in Heian times. The court often turned to them to organize military forces needed for enforcement and defence as needed.

miyaza 宮座 a shrine organization or "guild."

mokkan 木簡 wooden documents—inscribed pieces of wood frequently found in excavations of *ritsuryō* offices and headquarters, although their use continued into medieval times.

monjo tokugyōsei 文章得業生 an advanced scholar of letters chosen from those studying at the Royal University (Daigaku 大学) who might serve as future faculty after successfully passing examinations. The status was created in 730, when two such posts were instituted.

monogatari 物語 a prose narrative.

monzeki 門跡 a monastic lineage deriving from the founder of a given cloister; or alternatively, a Buddhist cloister presided over by princes or high aristocrats.

muraji 連 a hereditary noble title (*kabane* 姓) bestowed by the Yamato monarch in the pre-*ritsuryō* age especially on prominent provincial elite lineages.

musha (alt. *tsuwamono*) 武者 a professional warrior, especially in early Heian times.

myō 名 "a named holding," a unit for tax assessment and collection in both the public domain and private estates by the mid-Heian period.

myōshu 名主 a tax manager for a *myō* unit and, by extension, a wealthy cultivator.

nai'in 内印 the seal of the *tennō*, as opposed to the seal of the Council of State, the *ge'in* 外印.

nagon 納言 a senior counselor (*dainagon*) or middle counselor (*chūnagon*) who served under the senior ministers (*daijin*) on the Council of State. There were also junior counselors (*shōnagon*) charged with memorializing minor matters to the throne and who were frequently concurrently posted as a chamberlains (*jijū*).

nairan 内覧 the prerogative of the viceroy to view all memorials (*sō* 奏) to the throne as well as royal orders (*sen* 宣) issuing from the throne.

Naizenshi 内膳司 the Office of the Royal Table, one of the agencies within the residential palace created by the *ritsuryō* codes. It was subject to the Royal Household Ministry (Kunaishō 宮内省) and charged with preparing the *tennō*'s meals as well as ritual offerings for use in the residential palace.

nashiro 名代 a community of royal cultivators that worked on royal land before the *ritsuryō* era.

nassho 納所 a warehouse for storage of tax rice (*nengu* 年貢), or alternatively an official charged with oversight of same.

nembutsu 念仏 the practice of chanting the name of Amida Buddha.

nengu 年貢 the annual land tax due the *tennō*'s government, or alternatively, the annual rent due an estate proprietor.

nenki 年期 limits placed on the number and frequency of foreign trading ships to be received by the Heian court during the ninth century.

nuhi 奴婢 slaves, those of unfree status according to the *ritsuryō* codes.

nyōin (alt. *nyoin*) 女院 an honorific title denoting a status equal to that of a retired monarch (*in* 院) that was given to women closely associated with the *tennō*, such as a royal matriarch, queen-consort, or princess. The first such appointment was made in 991, to Fujiwara Senshi (962-1001) as Higashi Sanjō In, Royal Retired Lady of the Eastern Third Ward Palace.

obito 首 one of the noble titles (*kabane* 姓) often given to chieftains allied with the Yamato king and resident in the provinces.

ōchō kokka 王朝国家 "court-centered polity," a historiographical expression used by modern historians to differentiate the government presided over by the tenth-century court from that of the *ritsuryō* "*tennō*-centered" government of Nara and early Heian times.

ōhō 王法 "the king's law," or the law of the *tennō*'s court, in contrast with buddhist law, *buppō* 仏法. Such parlance appears in Heian documents from the tenth century onward.

ōjōden 往生伝 "biographies of the saved," hagiographic accounts of those who have been reborn in the Western Paradise of Amida Buddha, compilers of which included Yoshishige Yasutane (?-1002) and Ōe Masafusa (1041-1111).

ōkimi (alt. *daiō*) 大王 Great King, a style in use by later fifth-century paramounts of Wa (Yamato).

oku rokugun 奥六郡 the "six marcher districts" of Mutsu Province, which were under the rulership of the Abe family by the mid-eleventh century. The territory became the site of the Former Nine Years' War (1051-62). Later the "Ōshū Fujiwara," successors to the Abe as territorial lords of the districts, built their stronghold in Mutsu at Hiraizumi.

ōryōshi 押領使 an "envoy to subdue the territory"—an extracodal enforcer temporarily appointed to lead armed troops to suppress banditry and piracy in the provinces from the ninth century onward.

ōshinke 王臣家 "royal and ministerial households" were the powerful noble households in the capital whose assertion of influence in the provinces—over land and cultivators—became increasingly problematic to the court's exercise of its authority during the ninth and tenth centuries.

ōtabumi 大田文 provincial field registers compiled by provincial authorities (*kokuga*) from later Heian times onward.

Ōtenmon 応天門 the Great Heavenly Gate, which was the main gate of the greater palace precints (*daidairi*) at Heian. It opened on the precincts of the Halls of State (Chōdōin 朝堂院).

rangyō 乱行 misconduct, acts without concern for propriety and protocol.

rinji zōyaku 臨時雑役 extraordinary tax levies that began to appear in the historical record in the tenth century.

ringoku 隣国 a neighboring state and diplomatic equal according to the protocols of the Chinese diplomatic sphere.

ritsuryō 律令 Chinese-style penal and administrative codes promulgated in Japan in the late seventh and eighth centuries, which formed the basis for the *tennō*-centered polity of Nara times and beyond.

ronsō sōji 論奏奏事 according to *ritsuryō* protocols, formal memorials made to the throne by the Council of State to request a royal decision on ordinary matters.

rōtō 郎党 an armed follower.

rusudokoro 留守所 from mid-Heian times onward, a governor's absentee headquarters in his province of appointment when he himself is resident in the capital. Such a headquarters was staffed by resident provincial officials (*zaichōkanjin* 在庁官人).

ryō 領 a landed proprietorship.

ryōke 領家 an estate proprietor.

ryōri 良吏 a virtuous provincial governor, which term often appears in official records of the early Heian Period.

ryōshu 領主 a landed proprietor, often one who opened the land or claimed descent from the land opener.

sadaijin 左大臣 the minister of the left on the Council of State, and generally the senior member attending Council meetings.

Saigoku 西国 the west country, including provinces west of Kyoto.

Saishōe 最勝会 a realm-protecting Buddhist ritual that featured reading of the Konkōmyōsaishōōkyō 金光明最勝王経. It was conducted at the royal palace or at an official temple.

sakimori 防人 a border guard sent from eastern Honshū to Kyūshū in Nara times, and mentioned in poems in the eighth-century *Man'yōshū* poetry anthology.

sakoku 鎖国 "closed country," referring to a realm without diplomatic or trading relations with outsiders.

sakyō 左京 the Left Capital, meaning all the capital east of Suzaku Avenue.

sanbun 散文 writing in prose.

sandaie 三大会 (alt. *san'e* 三会) the three great annual Buddhist assemblies held either in the "southern capital" (Nara) or in the greater palace precincts in the capital during Heian times and beyond. They included Kōfukuji's Yuimae, Yakushiji's Saishōe, and the Misaie held at the palace.

sangi 参議 an advisor on the Council of State. The post was an extracodal one created in the eighth century for appointees of the fourth rank or higher.

sangō 三綱 the three monk administrators who presided over the monastic community of a temple-monastery. They included the *jōza*, *tsuina*, and *jishu*.

sanjo 散所 an area set aside for nonagricultural tax-exempt persons, often craftsmen or other specialists. Some such venues were known to have been located within estates (*shōen*).

sankakubuchi shinjūkyō 三角縁神獣鏡 a triangular-rimmed mirror decorated with images of deities and beasts. Some such mirrors were reportedly sent by the Chinese Wei Dynasty monarch to Queen Himiko of Wa in the third century, and many such mirrors have been found buried in third- and fourth-century round keyhole tombs (*zenpōkōenfun* 前方後円墳).

sanmi 三位 an official with rank but no post—an official without portfolio.

sato 里 (alt. *kozato*) a township, and an administrative unit in the *ritsuryō* provincial administrative hierarchy. A township consisted of fifty residence units (*ko* 戸) overseen by a *richō* 里長 (alt. *sato no osa*). In 715 or 717, the *sato* was replaced by the *gō* 郷, a larger township unit, which change was confirmed in 740.

seiifukushōgun 征夷副将軍 "assistant commander for overcoming eastern barbarians."

seimu 政務 governmental administration, especially decisions rendered in response to requests submitted from lower to higher ranking officials.

seisho 清書 a written draft of a royal command.

Sekkanke 摂関家 the Regents' lineage of the Northern Fujiwara family.

senji 宣旨 a royal order, usually but not always transmitted in writing.

senmin 賤民 persons of mean status, below the status of commoners (*ryōmin* 良民).

sesshō 摂政 regent.

setsuwa 説話 a modern literary genre including informal narratives and tales.

shaku 勺 a dry measure of about .0018 liters, used to measure salt and other precious goods.

shi 史 a controller-secretary in the Controllers' Office (Benkankyoku). Such secretaries received reports from offices and provincial headquarters and transmitted them upwards to the controllers (*ben* 弁).

shichidō 七道 the seven circuit highways that connected the provinces to the capital district (Kinai).

shijin 資人 low-ranking staff in princely and noble households during the Nara and Heian periods, they were often used as guards or for general service.

shiki 式 a rule or protocol. From the eighth century onward, various offices developed rules and procedures for carrying out their responsibilities. Major compilations of such rules for all *ritsuryō* agencies include the Protocols of the Jōgan Era (*Jōgan shiki*), finished in 871; and the Protocols of the Engi Era (*Engi shiki*), finished in 927.

Shikibushō 式部省 the *ritsuryō* Ministry of Personnel.

shikiji benkan 職事弁官 by the tenth century, a member of the Controllers' Office (Benkankyoku) who served concurrently in the Royal Secretariat (Kurōdodokoro). Such a controller functioned as an important liaison among the royal residential palace, the Controllers' Office, and the Council of State.

shimboku 神木 a sacred tree in the precincts of a shrine considered to have a special relationship with the shrine's deity.

shingū 新宮 a "new shrine," established by beckoning the deity from an original enshrinement site (*hongū* 本宮) to a new venue.

shinnō shiden 親王賜田 land for field opening granted to princes.

shimpan 神判 a deity's judgement, or a sign thereof.

shinsei 親政 independent rule by the *tennō*—royal rule without a regent (*sesshō*) or viceroy (*kampaku*).

shizoku 氏族 old noble families possessing *kabane* 姓 titles.

shoban 諸蕃 vassal states, according to the Chinese diplomatic system.

shōben 少弁 a junior controller in the Controllers' Office (Benkankyoku).

shōchō 正長 a local overseer for public managed fields (*kueiden* 公営田); or the manager of an early estate (*shoki shōen* 初期荘園) comprising newly opened fields as permitted by the New Fields Law of 743.

shōen 荘園 a private estate.

shōen-kōryōsei 荘園公領制 the "estate-and-public-land tenurial system" of late Heian times. The term is a modern historiographical one for the system comprised of estates and the public domain. An alternative appellation is the *shōen kokugaryōsei* 荘園国衙領制.

shōen seiri rei 荘園 整理令 estate-limiting regulations, the first of which were issued in 902, during the Engi era. Subsequent regulations were issued many times during the Heian Period, with those of 1040, 1045, and 1156 considered most important.

shōgun 将軍 a commander of troops.

shōkan 荘官 local managerial personnel on a private estate (*shōen*).

shōkei 上卿 the noble-in-charge—the member of the Council of State, always holding the seat of middle counselor (*chūnagon* 中納言) or above, charged with overseeing a given activity or affair. This system of divided Council responsibility seems to have developed by the early tenth century.

shoki shōen 初期荘園 early estates, which property was generally based on newly opened fields (*konden*).

shokunin 職人 a craftsman, peddler, transport worker, or other non-agricultural specialist.

shōmai 舂米 polished rice sent annually to the capital from the provinces to feed officials.

shōmin 荘民 dwellers on an estate.

shōryō 少領 a junior district chieftain.

shoshin shobutsu 諸神諸仏 various gods and Buddhas.

shōzeichō 正税帳 an annual tax register sent by a province to court to report taxes collected. It was carried by the *shōzeichōshi* 正税帳使, and was one of four key documents (*shido kumon* 四度公文) sent by provincial authorities to the capital every year during Nara and early Heian times. Several examples are extant in the Shōsōin archives (*Shōsōin monjo*), including some registers from the eighth century.

shuchō 首長 a chieftain in the prehistoric and protohistorical epochs.

shugo 守護 a provincial constable under the Kamakura and Muromachi warrior governments.

shuku 宿 a lodging place, especially for itinerants including non-agricultural specialists, either in the capital or in the provinces.

so 租 a *ritsuryō* tax based on the amount of land cultivated (at a rate of approx. 1 *soku* 束 5 *ha* 把 per *tan* 反, amounting to approx. 3% of the harvest) and paid in kind. The proceeds were stored in the province and lent out in the obligatory public lending program (*suiko* 出挙).

sō 奏 a memorial—whether a report, proposal, or request—to the *tennō;* alternatively, *sōji* 奏事.

Sōgō 僧綱 the Office of Monastic Affairs, established prior to the *ritsuryō* codes but confirmed therein as the agency charged with overseeing monastic affairs under the Bureau for Alien and Buddhist Affairs (Genbaryō), the Ministry of Civil Affairs (Jibushō), and the Council of State. Its prelates—initially at the three ranks of *sōjō*, *sōzu*, and *risshi*, but other ranks were added later—were appointed by the *tennō* from among the best known scholar-monks at official temples. By Heian times its responsibilities became more ritual in nature. Its prelates might also serve as monastic directors (*bettō*) at official temples.

sōjō 僧正 the senior prelate in the Office of Monastic Affairs (Sōgō).

soma 杣 timberland, often belonging to an official temple under construction.

somaudo 杣人 (alt. somabito) a woodcutter residing within a timber-producing area (*soma*).

sōryō 惣領 the family head—the main heir who by later Kamakura times was inheriting a substantial portion of the patriarch's holdings and wealth, and to whom other, lesser heirs were held accountable.

sōzu 僧都 the second-ranking prelate in the Office of Monastic Affairs (Sōgō).

suiko 出挙 rice-seed lending, both official (*kusuiko* 公出挙) and unofficial (*shisuiko* 私出挙).

suke 次官 the second-in-command of a *ritsuryō* agency or office.

Taka no tsukasa 鷹司 originally the Falconry Office of the *ritsuryō* Ministry of Defense, but records show it as having been abolished in 860.

taifu 大夫 an official of the fifth-rank.

taikō 太后 the *ritsuryō* style for the queen-mother.

taishu 大衆 the monastic body of a temple-monastery, which met to decide matters of common interest such as electing the temple's administrative cabinet (*sangō*).

tan 反 a unit of land equal to approx. 0.3 acres.

tato 田堵 a "plowman" whose wealth and agricultural talents made him a provincial governor's choice as a field contractor, charged with guaranteeing tax payment on a given unit of land (*fumyō* 負名).

tenjōbito 殿上人 royal intimates, specifically designated by each *tennō*. From Uda Tennō's reign (887-97) onward, they were given special permission to enter the royal presence, a prerogative known as *shōden* 昇殿.

tennō 天皇 the Heavenly Sovereign, one of several royal styles for the monarch empowered by the *ritsuryō* codes. The title seems to have come into use in the late seventh century—wooden documents on which it is used have been excavated and are thought to date from the 670s, from either the reign of Temmu (673-86) or shortly after.

tō 党 a band, usually considered hostile to government authority.

tomo no miyatsuko 伴造 an "allied chieftain," who was often employed as a manager of an occupational group (*be*) that served the Yamato Great King into the seventh century.

tone 刀禰 a local official in early to mid-Heian times, either in the capital or in the countryside—they often held some sort of official post in *ritsuryō* government.

toneri 舎人 an attendant at court or in a princely or noble household. But in the ninth century, the royal guards' headquarters also recruited followers in the countryside who were called *toneri*.

Tsuchigumo 土蜘蛛 "earth-spider people" who appear in Yamato folklore as frontier people unsubordinated by court forces.

tsuchō 津長 harbor master.

tsuibu kampu 追捕官符 a Council of State order to pursue and destroy a criminal.

tsuibushi 追捕使 "envoy to pursue and capture" a criminal.

tsuina 都維那 a monastic superintendent—a member of a temple's monastic administrative cabinet (*sangō*), following the *jōza* and *jishu* in hierarchy.

tsuitō senji 追討宣旨 a royal order empowering an enforcing agent to pursue and strike down criminals.

tsuwamono 武者 a professional military man.

udaijin 右大臣 minister of the right, and generally the second in rank on the Council of State.

uji 氏 a royally recognized noble kin that, under the influence of *ritsuryō* practices, fissured into lineages (*ie* 家). A frequently used translation is "conical clan."

ujidera 氏寺 a temple built and maintained by a noble kin group (*uji*), usually as a site of memorial services for deceased members.

ujigami 氏神 the patron deity of a noble kin (*uji* 氏).

uji no chōja 氏長者 the chieftain of a noble kin group—generally in Nara and early Heian times, he was the highest ranker of the family.

ukesaku 請作 contractual cultivation of fields within an estate (*shōen*), by permission of the absentee proprietor. The cultivator was termed a "contractual cultivator" (*ukesakunin*).

umaya 駅 an official post station, many of which were established in *ritsuryō* times along the seven circuit highways (*shichidō*). Such post stations were to be used by officials travelling to and from the capital—the stations provided horses and other needed provisions.

uneme 采女 tribute maidens presented to the Yamato Great King, and later to the *tennō*, by provincial and district elites. According to the *ritsuryō* codes, those holding the post of junior district chieftain (*shōryō*) and higher could send women to serve the *tennō* in his backpalace, where their services were overseen by the Office of Tribute Maidens (Uneme no tsukasa).

unkyaku 運脚 porters charged by the *ritsuryō* codes with transporting *chō* and *yō* tax goods from their townships (*gō*) to the capital.

unmai ōryōshi 運米押領使 "rice transport agent and envoy to subdue the territory."

uramonjo 裏文書 a document written on the reverse-side of a previously written document.

wabun 和文 writing in the Japanese syllabary (*kana* 仮名), in contrast with writing in Chinese (*kambun* 漢文) or mixed Chinese and Japanese (*wakankonkōbun* 和漢混淆文).

waka 和歌 a thirty-one-syllable poem written in Japanese.

Yamato damashii 大和魂 "Yamato spirit," a sense of pragmatism beyond book-learning, per the locus classicus in the eleventh-century *Genji monogatari*.

yashiki 屋敷 a homestead in the provinces. In the Heian Period the term is often associated with a warrior's residence.

yasoshima 八十島 a multitude of islands or sandbars.

Yayoi 弥生 a style of pottery and its associated historical epoch, dating from the third century B.C.E. to the third century C.E.

yō 庸 a tax levied on individuals by the *ritsuryō* codes that was payable in cloth and other goods. Proceeds from it plus proceeds from the *chō* produce tax were to be sent to the capital to support government there.

yoribito (alt. *yoriudo*) 寄人 a dependent, one who served a noble house or estate proprietor in Heian times and beyond.

Yuimae 維摩会 the Yuima Assembly, an officially patronized Buddhist ceremony celebrated annually at Kōfukuji in Nara during the tenth lunar month. The rite celebrated the Vimalakirti Sutra (Yuimakyō) and also memorialized the ancestor of the Fujiwara, Fujiwara Kamatari (614-69), who reportedly initiated the event.

za 座 an association of tradespeople or craftsmen often likened to a guild. Such organizations first appeared in Heian times as groups of specialists who gained monopolist prerogatives for their services or products through the patronage of a prominent religious institution which they served, often as provisioners.

zaichi ryōshu 在地領主 a resident local landlord, often a local land opener or his descendent from later Heian times onward.

zaichō 在庁 the provincial governor's office in his province, rather than his office at his residence in the capital.

zaichō kanjin 在庁官人 resident provincial officials—provincial officials who resided permanently in a given province.

zaike 在家 a homestead, upon which taxes or rents were inceasingly imposed by mid-Heian times.

zasu 座主 the monastic director (abbot) at Enryakuji on Mount Hiei; and sometimes the monastic director for temples of the Shingon school, such as the Kongōbuji temple-monastery complex on Mount Kōya in Kii Province.

zenpōkōenfun 前方後円墳 a mounded tomb with a round head and rectangular body, thus often termed a "round keyhole tomb." Their construction began in Yamato during the later third century and continued to diffuse across the archipelago through the fifth century. Their spread is seen to have represented the expanding cultural influence of the Yamato Great King.

zokubettō 俗別当 a secular administrator of a temple in Heian times, often a high ranking courtier on the Council of State (Daijōkan) or in the Royal Secretariat (Kurōdodokoro).

zōkuji 雑公事 miscellaneous taxes levied on provincial cultivators and their land holdings by the mid-Heian Period.

Zōryō 雑令 the chapter of Miscellaneous Laws in the *ritsuryō* codes.

Zō-Tōdaijishi 造東大寺司 the Todaiji Construction Agency, which built and maintained the official temple called Todaiji in Nara during the mid-eighth century.

zuryō 受領 a custodial governor, the first- (*kami*) or second-in-charge (*suke*) on the provincial governor team who was responsible for fiscal aspects of provincial administration by the later ninth century.

Bibliography

Abe Takeshi. 1971. *Owari no kuni no gebumi no kenkyū*. Tokyo: Ōhara shinseisha.

Adolphson, Mikael et al. Forthcoming. *Centers and Peripheries in Heian Japan*. Honolulu: University of Hawaii Press.

Adolphson, Mikael. 2000. *Gates of Power: Monks, Courtiers and Warriors in Premodern Japan*. Honolulu: University of Hawaii Press.

Aida Hanji. 1964. *Chūkai Yōrōryō*. Tokyo: Yushindō.

Aida Nirō. 1962. *Nihon no komonjo*. 2 vols. Tokyo: Iwanami shoten.

Akashi Kazunori. 1966. "Gōko," in *Jiten kazoku*, ed. Hikaku kazokushi gakkai. Tokyo: Kōbundō: 313.

Akashi Mariko. 1976-1977. "Hitachi fudoki." *Traditions* 1 (2, 3): 23–47, 55–78.

Akatsuka Jirō. 1988. "Tōkai no zenpōkōhōfun." *Kodai* (86): 84-109.

Akimoto Kichirō. 1958. *Fudoki*, Nihon koten bungaku taikei. Tokyo: Iwanami shoten.

Akimoto Kichirō. 1963. "Hitachi oyobi Kyūshū fudoki no henjutsu to Fujiwara Umakai," in *Fudoki no kenkyū*. Osaka: Osaka keizai daigaku kōenkai: 76–223.

Akimoto Yoshinori, ed. 1977. *Kogo shūi*, Shinsen nihon koten bunkō. Tokyo: Gendai shirosha.

Amakasu Ken. 1964. "Zenpōkōenfun no seikaku ni kansuru ichi kōsatsu," in *Nihon kōkogaku no shomondai*, ed. Kondō Yoshirō. Okayama: Kōkogaku kenkyūkai: 173-202.

Amino Yoshihiko. 1972. "Chūsei ni okeru tennō shihaiken no ichi kōsai." *Shigaku zasshi* 81 (8): 1–60.

Amino Yoshihiko. 1982. *Higashi to nishi no kataru nihon no rekishi*. Tokyo: Soshiete.

Amino Yoshihiko. 1986. *Chūsei saikō: Rettō no chiiki to shakai*. Tokyo: Nihon edeita- suku-ru shuppanbu.

Amino Yoshihiko et al. 1988. *Nihon chūseishizō no saikentō*. Tokyo: Yamakawa shuppansha.

Amino Yoshihiko et al. 1989–. *Kōza nihon shōenshi*. 10 vols. Tokyo: Yoshikawa kōbunkan.

Anazawa Wakou and Manome Jun'ichi. 1986. "Two Inscribed Swords," in *Windows on the Japanese Past*, ed. R. Pearson et al. Ann Arbor: University of Michigan Center for Japanese Studies: 375-94.

Anazawa Wakō. 1994. "Kobayashi Yukio Hakase no kiseki: kansei no kōkogakusha no hyōden," in *Kōkogaku Kyoto gakuha*, ed. Tsunoda Bun'ei. Tokyo: Yūzankaku: 178-210.

Aoki Kazuo et al. 1989-2000. *Shoku nihongi*. 6 vols, Shin nihon koten bungaku taikei. Tokyo: Iwanami shoten.

Aoki, Michiko. 1971. *Izumo Fudoki*. Tokyo: Sophia University.

Aoki, Michiko. 1991. "Empress Jito," in *Heroic with Grace: Legendary Women of Japan*, ed. C. I. Mulhern. Armonk, N.Y.: M.E. Sharpe: 40–76.

Aoki, Michiko. 1997. *Records of Wind and Earth*. Ann Arbor: Association for Asian Studies.

Aoki, Michiko Y. 1974. *Ancient Myths and Early History of Japan*. New York: Exposition Press.

Aoyama Kōryō. 1955. "Nichirai kōshōshi no kenkyū." *Meiji daigaku bungakubu kenkyū hōkoku, Tōyōshi 3*: 10–32.

Araki Toshio. 1974. "Hachi, kyū seiki no zaichi shakai no kōzō to jinmin." *Rekishigaku kenkyū* 406: 34-35.

Arano Yasunori. 1993. "Jiki kubun," in *Ajia no naka no nihonshi*. Tokyo: Tōkyō daigaku shuppankai: 1-57.

Aritomi Yukiko. 1989. "Nihon kodai no shoki chihō jiin no kenkyū: Hakuhō jidai o chūshin ni." *Shiron* (42): 23-48.

Arntzen, Sonja. 1997. *Kagero Nikki*. Ann Arbor: Center for Japanese Studies, University of Michigan.

Asaka Toshiki. 1971. *Kodai no shukōgyōshi no kenkyū*. Tokyo: Hōsei University Press.

Asao Naohiro et al., eds. 1976. *Iwanami kōza nihon rekishi 4, Kodai 4*. Tokyo: Iwanami shoten.

Aston, W. G. 1972. *Nihongi*. 2 vols. Rutland: Charles Tuttle.

Aung-thwin, Michael. 1995. "The "Classical" in Southeast Asia: The Present in the Past." *Journal of SE Asian Studies* 26: 75-91.

Ayusawa Hisashi. 1968. *Minamoto no Yorimitsu*. Tokyo: Yoshikawa kōbunkan.

Azuma Ushio. 1987. "Tettei no kisoteki kenkyū." *Kashihara kōkogaku kenkyūjo kiyō: kōkogaku ronkō* 1 (2): 70-188.

Barnes, Gina. 1982. "Toro," in *Atlas of Archaeology*, ed. K. Branigan. London: Book Club Association; MacDonald: 198–201.

Barnes, Gina. 1988. *Protohistoric Yamato*. Ann Arbor: University of Michigan Center for Japanese Studies.

Barnes, Gina, ed. 1990. *Bibliographic Reviews of Far Eastern Archaeology: Hoabinhian, Jomon, Yayoi and Early Korean States*. Oxford: Oxbow Books.

Batten, Bruce. 1989. "State and Frontier in Early Japan," (Ph.D. diss., Stanford University).

Batten, Bruce. 1993. "Provincial Administration in Early Japan: From *Ritsuryō kokka* to *Ōchō kokka*." *Harvard Journal of Asiatic Studies* 53 (1): 103-34.

Batten, Bruce. 1999. "Frontiers & Boundaries of Premodern Japan." *Journal of Historical Geography* 25 (2): 166-82.

Batten, Bruce. 2003. *To the Ends of Japan*. Honolulu: University of Hawaii Press.

Bentley, John R. 2002. *Historiographical Trends in Early Japan*. Lewiston, Queenston, Lampeter: Edwin Mellen Press.

Bialock, David. 1997. "Peripheries of power: voice, history, and the construction of imperial and sacred space in the tale of the Heike and other medieval and Heian historical texts." Ph.D. diss. Columbia University, New York.

Bialock, David T. 2000. "Nation and Epic: *The Tale of the Heike* as Modern Classic," in *Inventing the Classics: Modernity, National Identity, and Japanese Literature*, ed. H. Shirane and T. Suzuki. Stanford: Stanford University Press: 151–78.

Bloch, Marc. 1953. *The Historian's Craft*. New York: Vintage.

Bock, Felicia. 1972. *Engi Shiki: Procedures of Engi Era*. 2 vols. Tokyo: Sophia University.

Bock, Felicia. 1985. *Classical Learning and Taoist Practices in Early Japan: Books XVI and XX of the Engi Shiki*, Occasional Paper 17. Tucson: Center for Asian Studies Arizona State University.

Bol, Peter. 1992. *This Culture of Ours*. Stanford: Stanford University Press.

Borgen, Robert. 1986. *Sugawara no Michizane and the Early Heian Court*. Cambridge: Council on East Asian Studies, Harvard University.

Brower, Robert Hopkins. 1952. "The Konzyaku Monogatarisyu." Ph. D. diss. Stanford University, Palo Alto.

Brown, Delmer and Ichirō Ishida. 1979. *The Future and the Past: A Translation and Study of the Gukanshō, and Interpretative History of Japan*. Berkeley: University of California Press.

Dai nihon bukkyō zensho. 1915. *Kōfukuji bettō shidai*.In Kōfukuji sōsho, pt. 2. Ed. Bussho kankōkai. Tokyo: Bussho kankōkai.

Dai nihon bukkyō zensho. 1915. *Sanne jōikki*. In Kōfukuji sōsho, pt.1. Ed. Bussho kankōkai. Tokyo: Bussho kankōkai.

Dai nihon bukkyō zensho. 1915. *Sōgō bunin*. In Kōfukuji sōsho, pt. 1. Ed. Bussho kankōkai. Tokyo: Bussho kankōkai.

Butler, Kenneth. 1969. "Heike monogatari and the Japanese Warrior Ethic." *Harvard Journal of Asiatic Studies* 29: 93-108.

Butler, Kenneth Dean. 1966. "Textual Evolution of the Heike monogatari." *Harvard Journal of Asiatic Studies* 26: 5-51.

Butler, Kenneth D. 1967. "Heike Monogatari and theories of Oral Epic Literature." *Seikei daigaku Bungakubu kiyō* 2: 37-54.

Childe, V. Gordon. 1950. "The Urban Revolution." *Town Planning Review* (21): 3-17.

Claessen, Henri. 1978. "The Early State: A Structural Approach," in *The Early State*, ed. H. Claessen and P. Skalnik. The Hague: Mouton: 533-96.

Claessen, Henri and Peter Skalnik. 1981. *The Study of the State*. The Hague: Mouton.

Conlan, Thomas. 1997. "Largesse and the Limits of Loyalty in the Fourteenth Century," in *The Origins of Japan's Medieval World*, ed. J. P. Mass. Stanford: Stanford University Press: 39–64.

Dai nihon kokiroku. 1956-58. *Gonijō Moromichiki*. Ed. Tōkyō daigaku shiryō hensanjo. 3 vols. Tokyo: Iwanami shoten.

Dai nihon kokiroku. 1993– . *Chūyūki*. Ed. Tōkyō daigaku shiryō hensanjo. 5 vols. to date. Tokyo: Iwanami shoten.

Dai nihon kokiroku. 1960–70. *Denryaku*. Ed. Tōkyō daigaku shiryō hensanjo. 5 vols. Tokyo: Iwanami shoten.

Dai nihon kokiroku. 1952-54. *Midō kampakuki*. Ed. Tōkyō daigaku shiryō hensanjo. 3 vols. Tokyo: Iwanami shoten.

De Bary, William Theodore. 2001. *Sources of Japanese Tradition*. 2nd ed. New York: Columbia University Press.

Denecke, Wiebke. "Chinese Antiquity and Court Spectacle in Early Kanshi." *Journal of Japanese Studies* 30 (1): 97-122.

Dobbins, James C., ed. 1996. *Kuroda Toshio and his Scholarship, Journal of Japanese Religious Studies 26, 3-4 (Special Issue).*

Edwards, Walter. 1983. "Event and Process in the Founding of Japan." *Journal of Japanese Studies* 9 (2): 265-95.

Edwards, Walter. 1991. "Buried Discourse: The Toro Archaeological Site and Japanese National Identity in the Early Postwar Period." *Journal of Japanese Studies* 17 (1): 1-23.

Edwards, Walter. 1995. "Kobayashi Yukio's 'Treatise on Duplicate Mirrors,' An Annotated Translation." *Tenri daigaku gakuhō* (178): 179-205.

Edwards, Walter. 1996. "In Pursuit of Himiko." *Monumenta Nipponica* 51 (1): 53-80.

Edwards, Walter. 1999. "Mirrors on Ancient Yamato." *Monumenta Nipponica* 54 (1): 75-110.

Endō Keita. 2000. "'Shoku nihon kōki' to Jōwa no hen." *Kodai bunka* 52 (4): 238-46.

Engels, Frederick. 1965. *Kazoku, shiyū zaisan, kokka no kigen*. Translated by Tohara Shirō. Tokyo: Iwanami shoten.

Engels, Frederick. 1972 ed. *Origin of the Family, Private Property, and the State*. New York: New World Publications.

Enomoto Jun'ichi. 1992. "'Kokufū bunka' to chūgoku bunka," in *Kodai o kangaeru Kara to nihon*. Tokyo: Yoshikawa kōbunkan: 154-78.

Farris, William Wayne. 1985. *Population, Disease and Land in Early Japan, 645-900*. Cambridge: Harvard University Press.

Farris, William Wayne. 1992. *Heavenly Warriors: The Evolution of Japan's Military, 500-1300*. Cambridge: Harvard East Asia Monographs.

Farris, William Wayne. 1998. *Sacred Texts and Buried Treasures: Issues in the Historical Archaeology of Ancient Japan*. Honolulu: University of Hawaii Press.

Foard, James. 1980. "In Search of a Lost Reformation: A Reconsideration of Kamakura Buddhism." *Japanese Journal of Religious Studies* 7 (4): 261-87.

Friday, Karl. 1992. *Hired Swords: The Rise of Private Warrior Power in Early Japan*. Palo Alto: Stanford University Press.

Friday, Karl. 1997. "Pushing Beyond the Pale: The Yamato Conquest of the Emishi and Northern Japan." *Journal of Japanese Studies* 23 (1): 1-24.

Fukuda Ikuo. 1975. "Anrakujuinryō shōen ni tsuite." *Komonjo kenkyū* (9): 11–42.

Fukuda Toyohiko. 1974a. "'Chūsei kokka' no shudō," in *Shimpojiumu nihon rekishi, vol. 7, Chūsei kokka ron*. Tokyo: Gakuseisha: 50–52.

Fukuda Toyohiko. 1974b. "Ōchō kokka o megutte," in *Shimpojiumu nihon rekishi, vol. 7, Chūsei kokka ron*. Tokyo: Gakuseisha: 13–82.

Fukuda Toyohiko. 1976. "Ōchō gunji kikō to nairan," in *Iwanami kōza nihon rekishi 4, Kodai 4*. Tokyo: Iwanami shoten: 81–120.

Fukuda Toyohiko, ed. 1997. *Taira Masakado shiryōshū*. Tokyo: Shinjimbutsu ōraisha.

Fukui-kenritsu toshokan, 1963. Wakasa gyoson shirō. Fukui-shi.

Fukunaga Shin'ya. 1989. "Kofun jidai no kyōdō bochi: misshūkei dokōbo no hyōka ni tsuite." *Machikaneyama ronsō (Shigakuhen)* 23: 83-103.

Furuse Natsuko. 1986. "Heian jidai no 'gishiki' to tennō." *Rekishigaku kenkyū* (560): 36-45.

Furuse Natsuko. 1998. *Nihon kodai ōken to gishiki*. Tokyo: Yoshikawa kōbunkan.

Gomi Fumihiko. 1975. "In shihaiken no ichi kōsatsu." *Nihonshi kenkyū* (158): 1–22.

Gomi Fumihiko. 1979. "Heishi gunsei no shodankai." *Shigaku zasshi* 88 (8): 1–36.

Gomi Fumihiko. 1984a. "Inseiki chigyōkoku no hensen to bumpu," in *Inseiki shakai no kenkyū*. Tokyo: Yamakawa shuppansha: 123–69.

Gomi Fumihiko. 1984b. "Zenki-insei to shōen seiri no jidai," in *Inseiki shakai no kenkyū*. Tokyo: Yamakawa shuppansha: 41–69.

Goodrich, L. Carrington, ed. 1951. *Japan in the Chinese Dynastic Histories*. South Pasadena: D. and Ione Perkins.

Goodwin, Janet R. 1994. *Alms and Vagabonds*. Honolulu: University of Hawaii Press.

Gorman, Robert A., ed. 1986. *Biographical Dictionary of Marxism*. Westport, Conn.: Greenwood Press.

Gotō Akio et al. 1997. *Gōdanshō, Chūgaishō, Fukego*, Shin nihon koten bungaku taikei. Tokyo: Iwanami shoten.

Groner, Paul. 1984. *Saichō*. Honolulu: University of Hawaii Press.

Groner, Paul. 2002. *Ryōgen and Mount Hiei: Japanese Tendai in the Tenth Century*. Honolulu: University of Hawaii Press.

Gunsho ruijū. Zatsubu. 1901. *Chikubasho*. Ed. Hanawa Hokiichi and Ōta Fujishirō. Tokyo: Keizai zasshisha.

Gunsho ruijū. Ritsuryōbu. 1932. *Hōsōshiryōshō*. Ed. Hanawa Hokiichi and Ōta Fujishirō. Tokyo: Zoku gunsho ruijū kanseikai: 71-136.

Gunsho ruijū. Kanshokubu. 1932. *Kanshoku hishō*. Ed. Hanawa Hokiichi and Ōta Fujishirō. Tokyo: Keizai zasshisha.

Gunsho ruijū. Jingibu. 1932. *Kōtaijingū gishikichō*. Tokyo: Zoku gunsho ruijū kanseikai: 1-43.

Gunsho ruijū. Wakabu. 1932. *Kyūan rokunen gohyakushū*. Ed. Hanawa Hokiichi and Ōta Fujishirō. Tokyo: Keizai zasshisha.

Gunsho ruijū. Kassenbu. 1929. *Mutsuwaki*. Ed. Hanawa Hokiichi and Ōta Fujishirō. Tokyo: Zoku gunsho ruijū kanseikai: 22-32.

Gunsho ruijū. Shakkebu. 1901. *Shakke kampanki*. Ed. Hanawa Hokiichi and Ōta Fujishirō. Tokyo: Keizai zasshisha.

Gunsho ruijū. Kujibu. 1932. *Shingishiki*. Ed. Hanawa Hokiichi and Ōta Fujishirō. Tokyo: Zoku gunsho ruijū kanseikai: 219-57.

Gunsho ruijū. Zatsubu. 1932. *Taikai hisshō*. Ed. Hanawa Hokiichi and Ōta Fujishirō. Tokyo: Zoku gunsho ruijū kanseikai.

Hall, John Carey. 1906. "Institutes of Judicature (Goseibai shikimoku)." *Transactions of the Asiatic Society of Japan* First Series 34: 17–44.

Hall, John Whitney. 1966. *Government and Local Power in Japan 500 to 1700.* Princeton: Princeton University Press.

Hanada Katsuhiro. 1989. "Yamato seiken to kaji kōbō: Kinai no kaji sengyō shūdan o chūshin ni." *Kōkogaku kenkyū* 36 (3): 67-97.

Hara Hidesaburō. 1971. "Engerusu 'Kazoku, shiyūzaisan, kokka no kigen'," in *Rekishi no meichō,* ed. Rekishi kagaku kyōgikai. Tokyo: Azekura shobō.

Hara Hidesaburō. 1984. "Nihon rettō no mikai to bummei," in *Kōza nihon rekishi,* ed. Rekishgaku kenkyūkai & Nihonshi kenkyūkai. vol. 1: Genshi/kodai 1. Tokyo: Tōkyō daigaku shuppankai: 1-38.

Hara Hidesaburō. 1986. "Iwatahara kofungun no kentō." *Kodai o kangaeru* 41: 29-69.

Harashima Reiji. 1960. "Kodai tōgoku to Yamato seiken." *Shoku nihongi kenkyū* (7.6, 7.7, 7.8): 1–14, 12–25, 16–22.

Harunari Hideji. 1997. "Kōkogaku to kiki no sōkoku: Kobayashi Yukio no denseikyōron." *Kokuritsu Rekishi Minzoku Hakubutsukan kenkyū hōkoku* (70): 59-95.

Hasebe Gakuji. 1995. *Nihon shutsudo no chūgoku tōjiki.* Tokyo: Heibonsha.

Hasegawa Masaharu, ed. 1989. *Tosa nikki, Kagerō nikki, Murasaki Shikibu nikki, Sarashina nikki,* Shin nihon koten bungaku taikei. Tokyo: Iwanami shoten.

Hasegawa, Tadashi. 1967. "The Early Stages of the Heike monogatari." *Monumenta Nipponica* 22 (1-2): 65-81.

Hashimoto Yoshihiko. 1976. "Kizoku seiken no seiji kōzō," in *Iwanami kōza nihon rekishi 4, Kodai 4.* Tokyo: Iwanami shoten: 1–42.

Hashimoto Yoshinori. 1981. "Gekishi no seiritsu, tojō to gishiki." *Shirin* 64 (6): 25-61.

Hatada Takashi. 1962. "Jū jūni seiki no Higashi Ajia to nihon," in *Iwanami kōza nihon rekishi 4, Kodai 4.* Tokyo: Iwanami shoten:

Hattori Masayuki. 1963. "Tōhoku chihō ni okeru gun no seiritsu." *Shirin* 46 (2): 138–65.

Hayashi Rokurō. 1969. "Sagami no kuni no chōtei." *Shōnan shigaku* (1): 2-12.

Hayashiya Tatsusaburō. 1955. "Sanjo," in *Kodai kokka no kaitai.* Tokyo: Tōkyō daigaku shuppankai: 285–315.

Hayashiya Tatsusaburō, ed. 1970. *Kyōto no rekishi.* Tokyo: Gakugei shorin.

Heibonsha chihō shiryō senta-, ed. 2000. *Shizuoka-ken no chimei.* vol. 22, Nihon rekishi chimei taikei. Tokyo: Heibonsha.

Herail, Francine. 1987-88. *Notes Journalières de Fujiwara no Michinaga.* 2 vols. Geneva and Paris: Librairie Droz.

Herail, Francine. 2001-. *Notes Journalieres de Fujiwara no Sukefusa.* Geneva: Droz.

Hirakawa Minami. 1975. "Taga-jō ato no hakkutsu chōsa no genjō to kadai." *Nihonshi kenkyū* (153): 1–17.

Hirano Kunio. 1975. "Yamato ōken to chōsen," in *Iwanami kōza nihon rekishi 1, Genshi oyobi kodai 1,* ed. Asao Naohiro et al. Tokyo: Iwanami shoten: 227-72.

Hirano Kunio. 1977. "The Yamato State and Korea in the Fourth and Fifth Centuries." *Acta Asiatica* 31: 51-82.

Hirano Kunio. 1983a. "Be," in *Kodansha Encyclopedia of Japan*. vol. 1. Tokyo: Kodansha: 147.

Hirano Kunio. 1983b. "Uji," in *Kodansha Encyclopedia of Japan*. vol. 8. Tokyo: Kodansha: 131.

Hirano Takuji. 1988. "San'yōdō to bankaku." *Kokushigaku* (135): 25-50.

Hiraoka Jōkai. 1981a. "Fujiwara-shi no ujidera no seiritsu ni tsuite," in *Nihon jiinshi no kenkyū*. vol. 1. Tokyo: Yoshikawa kōbunkan: 581-99.

Hiraoka Jōkai. 1981b. "Rikushōji no seiritsu ni tsuite," in *Nihon jiinshi no kenkyū*. Tokyo: Yoshikawa kōbunkan: 600-675.

Hirata Toshiharu. 1986. "Nanto hokurei no akusō ni tsuite," in *Ronshū nihon bukkyōshi: Heian jidai*, ed. Hiraoka Jōkai. Tokyo: Yūzankaku shuppan: 261-96.

Hirose Kazuo. 1983. "Kawachi Furuichi Ōmizo no nendai to sono igi." *Kōkogaku kenkyū* 29 (4): 53-69.

Hirose Kazuo. 1994. "Kōkogaku kara mita kodai no sonraku," in *Iwanami kōza nihon tsūshi*, ed. Asao Naohiro et al. vol. 3 (Kodai 2): 129-62.

Hirose Kazuo et al. 1976. "Ōzono Iseki hakkutsu chōsa gaihō, no. 3. Ōsaka-fu: Ōsaka-fu kyōiku iinkai.

Hirota, Dennis. 1982. *Tannishō, a primer*. Kyoto: Ryukoku University.

Hisano Nobuyoshi. 1980. "Kakunin kō: Heian makki no Tōdaiji to akusō." *Nihonshi kenkyū* (219): 1–39.

Hōgetsu Keigo and Tokoro Mitsuo. 1971. Gifu-kenshi Shiryōhen 3. Kodai-chūsei. Gifu-shi: Gifu-ken.

Hōjō Yoshitaka. 1986. "Funkyū ni hyōji sareta zenpōkōenfun no teishiki to sono hyōka: seiritsu tōsho no Kinai to Kibi to no taihi kara." *Kōkogaku kenkyū* 32 (4): 42-66.

Hori Toshikazu. 1963a. "Higashi Ajia no rekishizō o dō kōsei suru ka." *Rekishigaku kenkyū* (276): 64–69.

Hori Toshikazu. 1963b. "Kindai izen no Higashi Ajia sekai." *Rekishigaku kenkyū* (281): 14–18.

Hotate Michihisa. 1978. "Shōensei shihai to toshi nōson kankei." *Rekishigaku kenkyū* (Bessatsu): 65-74.

Hotate Michihisa. 1979. "Ritsuryōsei shihai to tohi kōtsū." *Rekishigaku kenkyū* (468): 1-48.

Hotate Michihisa. 1996. *Heian ōchō*. Tokyo: Iwanami shinsho.

Hsia, Emil C. H. et al. 1986. Tamba Yasuyori's *Ishimpō (Essentials of Medicine in ancient China and Japan)*. 2 vols. Leiden: Brill.

Hudson, Mark. 1999. *Ruins of Identity*. Honolulu: University of Hawaii Press.

Hurst, G. Cameron. 1972. "The Reign of Go-sanjō." *Monumenta Nipponica* 27 (1): 65-83.

Hurst, G. Cameron. 1974. "Structure of the Heian Court," in *Medieval Japan: Essays in Institutional History*, ed. J. W. Hall and J. P. Mass. New Haven & London: Yale University Press: 39-59.

Hurst, G. Cameron. 1976; Reprint Stanford, 1995. *Insei*. New York: Columbia University Press.

Hurst, G. Cameron. 1982. "The Kōbu Polity," in *Court and Bakufu in Japan: Essays in Kamakura History*, ed. J. P. Mass. New Haven, CT: Yale University Press. Repr. Stanford University Press, 1995: 3–28.

Hurst, G. Cameron. 1999. "Insei," in *The Cambridge History of Japan, vol. 2, Heian*, ed. D. Shively and W. H. McCullough. Cambridge: Cambridge University Press: 576–643.

Ichihara-shi kyōiku iinkai. 1988. Ōshimei tekken gaihō: Chiba-ken Ichihara-shi Inaridai Ichigōfun shutsudo. Tokyo: Yoshikawa kōbunkan.

Ichiko Teiji, ed. 1973-75. *Heike monogatari*. 2 vols, Nihon koten bungaku zenshū. Tokyo: Shōgakukan.

Ikebe Wataru. 1981. *Wamyōruijūshō gun go sato umaya mei kōshō*. Tokyo: Yoshikawa kōbunkan.

Inoue Mitsuo. 1968. "Ōryōshi no kenkyū." *Nihonshi kenkyū* (101): 1-26.

Inoue Mitsuo. 1969. "Heian jidai no tsuibushi." *Komonjo kenkyū* (2): 28–59.

Inoue Mitsusada. 1949. "Bemin no kenkyū," in *Nihon kodaishi no shomondai*. Tokyo: Shisakusha: 18–97.

Inoue Mitsusada. 1956. "Mutsu no zokuchō Michishima no Sukune ni tsuite," in *Emishi*, ed. Kodaishi danwakai. Tokyo: Asakura shoten.

Inoue Mitsusada. 1965a. *Nihon kodai kokka no kenkyū*. Tokyo: Iwanami shoten.

Inoue Mitsusada. 1965b. *Shinwa kara rekishi e*. vol. 1, Nihon no rekishi. Tokyo: Chūō koronsha.

Inoue Mitsusada. 1965c. "Taika kaishin to tōgoku," in *Nihon kodai kokka no kenkyū*. Tokyo: Iwanami shoten: 351–381.

Inoue Mitsusada. 1985. *Nihon jōdōkyō seiritsushi no kenkyū*. Tokyo: Iwanami shoten.

Inoue Mitsusada et al. 1976. *Ritsuryō*, Nihon shisō taikei. Tokyo: Iwanami shoten.

Inoue Mitsusada et al. 1984. *Nihon rekishi taikei*. vol. 1. Tokyo: Yamakawa shuppan.

Inoue Tadao et al. 1988. "Mitsudera I iseki. Gumma-ken: Gumma-ken maizō bunkazai jigyōdan.

Inoue Tatsuo. 1978. "Hekibe kō," in *Kodaishi ronsō* 1, ed. Inoue Mitsusada Hakushi kanreki kinenkai, 3 vols. Tokyo: Yoshikawa kōbunkan: 381-431.

Inoue Tatsuo. 1980a. *Kodai ōken to shukyōteki bemin*. Tokyo: Kashiwa shobō.

Inoue Tatsuo. 1980b. "Taika zendai no Nakatomi-shi," in *Kodai ōken to shukyōteki bemin*. Tokyo: Kashiwa shobō: 189–255.

Inoue Tatsuo. 1989a. *Hitachi fudoki ni miru kodai*. Tokyo: Gakuseisha.

Inoue Tatsuo. 1989b. "Kusakabe o meguru ni, san no kōsatsu." *Nihon rekishi* (488): 1-22.

Irumada Nobuo and Murai Shōsuke. 1986. "Atarashii chūsei kokkazō o saguru." *Rekishi hyōron* (437): 11-33.

Ishibe Masashi. 1975. "Kofun bunkaron," in *Nihonshi o manabu, vol. 1: Genshi jidai*, ed. Yoshida Akira et al. Tokyo: Yūzankaku: 46–62.

Ishigami Eiichi. 1987. "Kodai Higashi Ajia chiiki to nihon," in *Nihon no shakaishi 1: Rettō naigai no kōtsū to kokka*. Tokyo: Iwanami shoten: 55–96.

Ishigami Eiichi. 1991. "Tsude Hiroshi's 'Nihon kodai no kokka keisei, zenpōkōenfun taisei no teishō' ni tsuite no oboegaki." *Nihonshi kenkyū* (343): 43-54.

Ishii Ryōsuke. 1958a. "Tōgoku to saigoku—jōdai oyobi jōsei ni okeru," in *Taika kaishin to Kamakura bakufu no seiritsu*. Tokyo: Sōbunsha: 52-86.

Ishii Ryōsuke. 1958b. "Tōgoku to saigoku—Kamakura jidai ni okeru," in *Taika kaishin to Kamakura bakufu no seiritsu*. Tokyo: Sōbunsha: 205-224.

Ishii Susumu. 1969. "Chūsei seiritsuki gunsei kenkyū no ichi shiten." *Shigaku zasshi* 78 (12): 1–32.

Ishii Susumu. 1970. *Nihon chūsei kokkashi no kenkyū*. Tokyo: Iwanami shoten.

Ishii Susumu. 1985. "Formation of Bushi Bands." *Acta Asiatica* (49): 1–14.

Ishii Susumu. 1991. "Shōen no ryōyū taikei," in *Kōza nihon shōenshi*, ed. Amino Yoshihiko et al. vol. 2. Tokyo: Yoshikawa kōbunkan: 84-103.

Ishikawa Noboru. 1989. *Zenpōkōenfun chikuzō no kenkyū*. Tokyo: Rokkō shuppan.

Ishimoda Shō. 1956a. *Kodai makki seijishi josetsu*. Tokyo: Miraisha.

Ishimoda Shō. 1956b. "Kodai no tenkanki toshite no jū seiki," in *Kodai makki seijishi josetsu*. Tokyo: Miraisha: 13–100.

Ishimoda Shō. 1957. *Chūseiteki sekai no keisei*. Tokyo: Tōkyō daigaku shuppankai.

Ishimoda Shō. 1962. "Kodaishi gaisetsu," in *Iwanami kōza Nihon rekishi 1*. Tokyo: Iwanami shoten: 1–76.

Ishimoda Shō. 1971. "Kokka seiritsushi ni okeru kokusaiteki keiki," in *Nihon no kodai kokka*. Tokyo: Iwanami shoten: 1-92.

Ishimoda Shō. 1973a. *Nihon kodai kokka ron*. Tokyo: Iwanami shoten.

Ishimoda Shō. 1973b. "Nihon kodai ni okeru kokusai ishiki ni tsuite," in *Nihon kodai kokka ron*. Tokyo: Iwanami shoten: 249–309.

Ishimoda Shō. 1973c. "Tennō to shoban," in *Nihon kodai kokka ron*. Tokyo: Iwanami shoten: 329–359.

Ishimoda Shō. 1943. "Utsubo monogatari ni tsuite no oboegaki." *Rekishigaku kenkyū* (115-116): 1-38.

Itabashi Gen. 1961. *Ōshū Hiraizumi*. Tokyo: Shibundō.

Itō Hiroyuki. 1987. "Shichi, hachi seiki Emishi shakai no kiso kōzō." *Iwate shigaku kenkyū* (70): 27–62.

Itō Nobuo. 1955. "Kōkogaku kara mita tōgoku kodai bunka," in *Tōgokushi no shinkenkyū*, ed. Furuta Ryōichi Hakase kanreki kinenkai. Tokyo: Bunri tōsho.

Iwamoto Jirō. 1983. "Ikaruga chiiki ni okeru jiwari no saikentō," in *Bunkazai ronsō: Nara Kokuritsu Bunkazai Kenkyūjo sōritsu sanjūshūnen ronbunshū*. Kyoto: Dōbōsha shuppan: 217-41.

Izumi Seiichi. 1952. "Saru Ainu no chien shūdan ni okeru iwor." *Minzokugaku kenkyū* 16 (3-4): 29-45.

Izumiya Yasuo. 1959. "Koden kensen no ichi kōsatsu." *Rekishi hyōron* (106): 15–27.

Izumiya Yasuo. 1970. "Kinai no shōen to nōmin," in *Kodai no nihon, vol. 5: Kinki*, ed. Tsuboi Kiyotari and Kishi Toshio. Tokyo: Kadokawa shoten: 319–336.

Izumiya Yasuo. 1972. *Ritsuryō seido hōkai katei no kenkyū*. Tokyo: Meibōsha.

Kadowaki Teiji. 1953. "Emishi no hanran." *Ritsumeikan bungaku* (96): 41-57.

Kadowaki Teiji. 1971. *Nihon kodai kyōdōtai no kenkyū*. Tokyo: Tōkyō daigaku shuppankai.
Kadowaki Teiji. 1975. "Kodai shakairon," in *Iwanami kōza nihon rekishi 2, Kodai 2*, ed. Asao Naohiro et al. Tokyo: Iwanami shoten: 331–377.
Kadowaki Teiji. 2000. *Kodai nihon no chiiki kokka to Yamato ōkoku*. 2 vols. Tokyo: Gakuseisha.
Kageyama Tsuyoshi. 1984. *Chūgoku kodai no shōkōgyō to senbaisei*. Tokyo: Tōkyō daigaku shuppankai.
Kajihara Masaaki, ed. 1976. *Shōmonki*. Tokyo: Heibonsha.
Kakimura Shigematsu, ed. 1968. *Honchō monzui chūshaku*. 2 vols. Tokyo: Fuzanbō.
Kamei Meitoku. 1975. "Chūgoku tōjiki shutsudo iseki ichiran hyō," in *Nihon shutsudo no chūgoku tōjiki*. Tokyo: Tōkyō kokuritsu hakubutsukan.
Kamei Meitoku. 1986. *Nihon bōeki tōjikishi no kenkyū*. Tokyo: Dōbōsha.
Kanaizuka Yoshikazu et al. 1982. *Kodai tōgoku to Yamato seiken*. Tokyo: Jimbutsu ōraisha.
Kasahara Kazuo. 2001. *A History of Japanese Religion*. Tokyo: Kosei.
Kasai Shin'ya. 1981. "Himiko no chōbo to Hashihaka," in *Yamataikoku kihon ronbunshū*, ed. Saeki Arikiyo. vol. 1. Osaka: Sōgensha: 427–438.
Katō Tomoyasu. 1979. "Nihon kodai ni okeru unsō ni kansuru ichi shiron." *Genshi kodai shakai kenkyū* 5: 219-95.
Katō Yoshinari. 1987. *Izumo no kuni fudoki sankyū*. Matsue: Imai shoten.
Katsuno Ryūshin. 1955. *Sōhei*. Tokyo: Shibundō.
Katsuura Noriko. 1976. "Harima no kuni Sakoshi, Kambe ryōgō ge (Hoi)," in *Shigaku ronsō*, ed. Kodaishi kenkyūkai. vol. 6.
Katsuura Noriko. 1977. "Ritsuryōseika nie kōnō no hensen." *Nihon rekishi* (352): 19–42.
Katsuyama Seiji. 1995. "Benzaishi no seiritsu ni tsuite." *Nihonshi kenkyū* (150–51): 111–119.
Kawaguchi Hisao, ed. 1983. *Shinsarugakuki*, Tōyō bunko. Tokyo: Heibonsha.
Kawakami Tasuke. 1946. "Ōchō jidai no rōnin ni tsuite," in *Nihon kodai shakaishi no kenkyū*.
Kawane Yoshiyasu. 1971. *Chūsei hōkensei seiritsu shiron*. Tokyo: Tōkyō daigaku shuppankai.
Kawane Yoshiyasu. 1964. "Chūsei shakai seiritsuki no nōmin mondai." *Nihonshi kenkyū* (71): 14-27.
Keirstead, Thomas. 1992. *Geography of Power in Medieval Japan*. Princeton: Princeton University Press.
Kiley, Cornelius. 1974. "Estate and Property in the Late Heian Period," in *Medieval Japan*, ed. J. W. Hall and J. P. Mass. New Haven: Yale University Press. Repr. Stanford University Press, 1988: 109–26.
Kiley, Cornelius. 1999. "Provincial Administration and Land Tenure in Early Heian," in *Cambridge History of Japan, vol. 2, Heian*, ed. D. Shively and W. H. McCullough. Cambridge: Cambridge University Press: 236–240.
Kiley, Cornelius J. 1973. "State and Dynasty in Archaic Yamato." *Journal of Asian Studies* 33 (1): 25-49.

Kimoto Masayasu. 2000. *Kodai no dōro jijō*. Tokyo: Yoshikawa kōbunkan.

Kimura Masanaka and Imuta Tsunehisa, eds. 1995. *Tosa nikki, Kagero nikki,* Shinpen nihon koten bungaku zenshū. Tokyo: Shōgakukan.

Kinda Akihiro. 1990. "Kokuzu no jōri puran to shōen no jōri puran." *Nihonshi kenkyū* (332): 1–35.

Kinoshita Ryō. 1996. "Kodai dōro kenkyū no kinnen no seika," in *Kodai o kangaeru*. Tokyo: Yoshikawa kōbunkan: 1-26.

Kirchoff, Paul. 1959. "The Principles of Clanship in Human Society," in *Readings in Anthropology*, ed. M. Fried. New York: Thomas Crowell: 370-81.

Kishi Shozō and Nagahara Keiji, eds. 1976–1979. *Zen'yaku Azuma kagami*. 6 vols. Tokyo: Shinjinbutsu ōraisha.

Kishi Toshio. 1966. "Gōrisei haishi no zengo," in *Nihon kodaishi kenkyū*. Tokyo: Hanawa shobō: 257–88.

Kishi Toshio. 1969. *Fujiwara no Nakamaro*. Tokyo: Yoshikawa kōbunkan.

Kishi Toshio. 1985. "Jōrisei ni kansuru jakkan no teisetsu." *Jōrisei kenkyū* (1): 4–12.

Kishimoto Naofumi. 1989. "Yoro Hisagozuka Kofun sokuryō chōsa hōkoku." *Shirin* 71 (6): 154-75.

Kita Sadakichi. 1928. "Keitai Tennō ika san tennō kōi denshō ni kansuru gimon." *Rekishi chiri* 52 (1): 1–29.

Kita Sadakichi. 1929–1930. *Hyūga kokushi*. Tokyo: Shishi shuppansha.

Kitagawa, Hiroshi and Bruce T. Tsuchida. 1975. *The Tale of the Heike*. 2 vols. Tokyo: University of Tokyo Press.

Kitayama Shigeo. 1970. *Ōchō seijishi ron*. Tokyo: Iwanami shoten.

Kitayama Shigeo. 1976. "Nara zenki ni okeru futan taikei no kaitai," in *Rekishi kagaku taikei 3: Kodai kokka to doreisei*, ed. Yoshida Akira. Tokyo: Azekura shobō: 171-220.

Kitō Kiyoaki. 1985. "Higashi Ajia ni okeru kokka keiseishi no rironteki shomondai: nihon no kodai kokka no keisei o sozai ni." *Rekishigaku kenkyū* (540): 14-23.

Kitō Kiyoaki. 1990. Review of Tsude Hiroshi's *Nihon nōkō shakai no seiritsu katei. Nihonshi kenkyū* (330): 115-23.

Kitō Kiyoaki. 1995. "Some Questions Concerning Ancient Japanese History: With Reference to State Theory." *Acta Asiatica* 69: 1-13.

Kitō Kiyoaki. n. d. "The Formation of the States in Ancient Asia and their Mutual Contacts." *Rapports entre l'Est et L'Ouest*.

Kobayashi Shōji. 2001. "Zenkindai no sekikokasen kōtsū to iseki tachi no chiikishiteki kenkyū. Niigata: Kagaku kenkyūhi hojokin kiban kenkyū A-2.

Kobayashi Yasuharu, ed. 1981. *Kojidan*. 2 vols, Koten bunko. Tokyo: Gendai shichōsha.

Kobayashi Yukio. 1952. "Kofun jidai bunka no seiin ni tsuite," in *Nihon minzoku*, ed. Nihon jinrui gakkai. Tokyo: Iwanami shoten: 113-29.

Kobayashi Yukio. 1961a. "Dohankyō kō," in *Kofun jidai no kenkyū*. Tokyo: Aoki shoten: 95-133.

Kobayashi Yukio. 1961b. *Kofun jidai no kenkyū*. Tokyo: Aoki shoten.

Kobayashi Yukio. 1961c. "Kofun no hassei no rekishiteki igi," in *Kofun jidai no kenkyū*. Tokyo: Aoki shoten: 135-59.

Kobayashi Yukio. 1961d. "Shoki Yamato seiken no seiryokuken," in *Kofun jidai no kenkyū*. Tokyo: Aoki shoten: 191-223.

Kobayashi Yukio. 1961e. "Zenki kofun no fukusōhin ni arawareta bunka no nisō," in *Kofun jidai no kenkyū*. Tokyo: Aoki shoten: 161-90.

Kodai kōtsū kenkyūkai, eds. 2004. *Nihon kodai dōro jiten. Tokyo: Yagi shoten.*

Koide Haku. 1975. *Tonegawa to Yodogawa*. Tokyo: Chūō kōronsha.

Kojima Noriyuki. 1962. *Jōdai nihon bungaku to chūgoku bungaku*. 3 vols. Tokyo: Hanawa shobō.

Kojima Noriyuki, ed. 1964. *Kaifūsō, Bunkashūreishū, Honchōmonzui*, Nihon koten bungaku taikei. Tokyo: Iwanami shoten.

Kojima Noriyuki et al., eds. 1971-75. *Manyōshū*. 4 vols, Nihon koten bungaku zenshū. Tokyo: Shōgakukan.

Kojima Noriyuki. 1978. *Kokufū ankoku jidai no bungaku*. 11 vols. Tokyo: Hanawa shobō.

Kokuritsu rekishi minzoku hakubutsukan. 1994. *Nihon shutsudo kagami de—ta shūsei*. Sakura: Kokuritsu rekishi minzoku hakubutsukan.

Kokuritsu rekishi minzoku hakubutsukan, ed. 1997. *Nihon shōen shiryō*. Tokyo: Yoshikawa kōbunkan.

Kometani Toyonosuke. 1975. "In mushadokoro kō: Shirakawa, Toba ryō, Inseiki o chūshin toshite," in *Nihonshi ronshū*, ed. Toki-noya Masaru Kyōju taikan kinen jigyōkai. Osaka: Seibundō.

Kondō Yoshirō. 1983. *Zenpōkōenfun no jidai*. Tokyo: Iwanami shoten.

Kondō Yoshirō. 1984. *Doki seien no kenkyū*. Tokyo: Aoki shoten.

Kondō Yoshirō et al. 1986. "Zenpōkōenfun no tanjō," in *Iwanami kōza nihon kōkogaku 6: Henka to kakki*. Tokyo: Iwanami shoten: 189-202.

Konishi Jin'ichi. 1984. *A History of Japanese Literature*. 4 vols. Princeton: Princeton University Press.

Konishi Tōru. 1970. "Kodai un'yū seidō no ichi kōsatsu." *Kansei gakuin shigaku* (12).

Kōzanji tenseki monjo sōgō chōsadan, ed. 1972. *Kōzanji-bon Ko ōrai*, Kōzanji shiryō sōsho, vol. 2. Tokyo: Tōkyō daigaku shupppansha.

Koten isan no kai, ed. 1963. *Shōmonki*. 2 vols. Tokyo: Shin dokushosha.

Kōten kōkyūsho zenkoku shinshokukai, ed. 1993. *Kōchō Engi shiki*. 3 vols. Kyoto: Rinsen shoten.

Koyama Yasunori. 1968. "Kamakura jidai no tōgoku nōson to zaichi ryōshusei." *Nihonshi kenkyū* (99): 1-27.

Koyama Yasunori. 1974. "Shōenseiteki ryōiki shihai o meguru kenryoku to sonraku." *Nihonshi kenkyū* (139–140): 103–119.

Koyama Yasunori. 1976. "Kodai makki no tōgoku to saigoku," in *Iwanami kōza nihon rekishi 4* (*Kodai 4*). Tokyo: Iwanami shoten: 231-70.

Kōzanji tenseki monjo sōgō chōsadan, ed. 1972. *Kōzanji-bon Ko ōrai*, Kōzanji shiryō sōsho, vol. 2. Tokyo: Tōkyō daigaku shupppansha.

Kubota Kurao. 1973. "Uwanabe ryōbo sankōchi baichō takazuka." *Shoryōbu kiyō* (25): 63-73.
Kudō Keiichi. 1960. "Nihon chūsei no tochi shoyū no rikai ni tsuite." *Rekishigaku kenkyū* (242): 36–43.
Kudō Keiichi. 1974. "Kyūshū ni okeru ōke-ryō shōen no sonzai keitai," in *Kyūshū chūsei shakai no kenkyū*, ed. Watanabe Nobuo Sensei kokikinen jigyōkai. Tokyo: Gakuseisha: 403–26.
Kudō Keiichi. 1983. "Shōen." *Acta Asiatica* (44): 1-27.
Kudō Masaki. 1973. "*Tōhoku* kodaishi to jōsaku." *Nihonshi kenkyū* (136): 17–33.
Kudō Masaki. 1989. *Jōsaku to emishi*, Kōkogaku raiburarii 51. Tokyo: Nyū saiensusha.
Kūnaichō shoryōbu, ed. 1981–82. *Kōshitsu seido shiryō: Sesshō*. 2 vols. Tokyo: Yoshikawa kōbunkan.
Kurahayashi Shōji, ed. 1983. *Nihon matsuri to nenjūgyōji jiten*. Kyōto: Ōfūsha.
Kuramoto Kazuhiro. 1987. "Ichijō-chō ni okeru jin no sadame ni tsuite." *Kodai bunka* 39 (6).
Kurano Kenji and Takeda Yukichi. 1958. *Kojiki, Norito,* Nihon koten bungaku taikei. Tokyo: Iwanami shoten.
Kurihara Hiromu. 1999. "Fujiwara Yoshifusa, Mototsune no yoshi kankei no seiritsu jiki ni tsuite." *Kodai bunka* 43 (12): 1-13.
Kuroda Toshio. 1963. "Chūsei kokka to tennō," in *Iwanami kōza nihon rekishi 6, Chūsei 2*, ed. Ienaga Saburo et al. Tokyo: Iwanami shoten: 261-301.
Kuroda Toshio. 1975a. "Chūsei jisha seiryoku ron," in *Iwanami kōza nihon rekishi 6, Chūsei 2*, ed. Asao Naohiro et al. Tokyo: Iwanami shoten: 245–95.
Kuroda Toshio. 1975b. "Chūsei no sonraku to za," in *Nihon chūsei hōkenseiron*. Tokyo: Tōkyō daigaku shuppankai: 57-79.
Kuroda Toshio. 1976. *Nihon chūsei no kokka to shūkyō*. Tokyo: Iwanami shoten.
Kuroda Toshio. 1980. *Jisha seiryoku: mō hitotsu chūsei no sekai*. Tokyo: Iwanami shoten.
Kuroda Toshio. 1996. "The Buddhist Law and the Imperial Law." *Japanese Journal of Religious Studies* 23 (3–4): 271-277.
Kurokawa Harumura, ed. 1989–90. *Rekidai zanketsu nikki*. 35 vols. Kyoto: Rinsen shoten.
Kurosaka Nobuo and Morita Tei, eds. 2003. *Nihon kōki*, Yakuchū Nihon shiryō. Tokyo: Shūeisha.
Kushiki Yoshinori. 1996. *Nihon kodai rōdōryoku hensei no kenkyū*. Tokyo: Hanawa shobō.
Kyōkai. 1972. *Nihon ryōiki (Miraculous Stories from the Japanese Buddhist Tradition)*. Translted by Nakamura, Kyoko Motomichi. Cambridge, MA: Harvard University Press.
Kyōto daigaku bungakubu kōkogaku kenkyūshitsu. 1992. *Tsubai Ōtsukayama Kofun to sankakubuchi shinjūkyō*. Kyoto: Kyōto daigaku bungakubu.
Kyōto daigaku bungakubu kokugogaku kokubungaku kenkyūshitsu, ed. 1968. *Wamyōshō*. 3 vols. Kyoto: rinsen shoten.
Levy, Ian Hideo. 1981. *The Ten Thousand Leaves*. Princeton: Princeton University Press.

Lieteau, Haruyo. 1975. "The Yasutoki-Myōe Discussion." *Monumenta Nipponica* 30 (2): 203–10.

Mabuchi Kazuo et al., ed. 1971-76. *Konjaku monogatarishū*. 4 vols, Nihon koten bungaku zenshū. Tokyo: Shōgakukan.

Maezawa Terumasa. 1989. "Sōshutsuki kofun no funkei to kibo no kikakusei ni tsuite." *Kodai* (88): 108-25.

Maizō bunkazai kenkyūkai. 1994. "Wajin to kagami, sono 2: san, yon seiki no kagami to funbo." Paper read at the Thirty-sixth Maizō Bunkazai Kenkyūkai, August, 1994, Osaka.

Marx, Karl (trans. Jack Cohen). 1964. *Pre-Capitalist Economic Formations*. New York: International Publishers.

Masamune Atsuo, ed. 1988. *Ishimpō*. 7 vols, Nihon koten zenshū. Tokyo: Gendai shichōsha.

Mass, Jeffrey. 1983. "Patterns of Provincial Inheritance in Late Heian Japan." *Journal of Japanese Studies* 9 (1): 67–95.

Mass, Jeffrey P. 1990. "The Kamakura Bakufu," in *The Cambridge History of Japan, vol. 3, Medieval Japan*. Cambridge: Cambride University Press: 46–88.

Mass, Jeffrey P. 1993. "The Missing Minamoto in the Twelfth-century Kantō." *Journal of Japanese Studies* 19 (1): 121–45.

Mass, Jeffrey P., ed. 1997. *Origins of Japan's Medieval World: Courtiers, Clerics, Warriors, and Peasants in the Fourteenth Century*. Stanford: Stanford University Press.

Mass, Jeffrey P. 1999. *Yoritomo and the Founding of the First Bakufu: Origins of Dual Government in Japan*. Stanford: Stanford University Press.

Masuda Yoshirō. 1969. "Seiji shakai no shokeitai: Toku ni shuchōsei shakai/chii shakai no gainen ni tsuite." *Shisō* (535): 80-92.

Matsubara Hironobu. 1976. "Kodai ni okeru tsu no seikaku to kinō," in *Kodai kokka no keisei to tenkai*, ed. Ōsaka rekishi gakkai. Tokyo: Yoshikawa kōbunkan: 465–504.

Matsubara Hironobu. 1985. *Nara kodai suijō kōtsū no kenkyū*. Tokyo: Yoshikawa kōbunkan.

Matsubara Hironobu. 1994. "Kodai suijō kōtsū kenkyū no genjō to kadai: Setonaikai kōtsū o chūshin ni." *Kodai kōtsū kenkyū* (3): 1–20.

McCullough, Helen. 1964–65. "Mutsuwaki (Tales of Mutsu)." *Harvard Journal of Asiatic Studies* (25): 178–211.

McCullough, Helen. 1980. *Okagami*. Princeton: Princeton University Press.

McCullough, Helen Craig. 1988. *The Tale of the Heike*. Stanford: Stanford University Press.

McCullough, William H. 1968. "The Azuma kagami Account of the Shōkyū War." *Monumenta Nipponica* 23: 102-55.

Mikawa Kei. 1996. "Jisha mondai kara miru insei no seiritsu," in *Insei no kenkyū*. Tokyo: Rinsen shoten: 107–32.

Mills, D. E. 1970. *A Collection of Tales from Uji*. Cambridge: Cambridge University Press.

Minami Hideo. 1989. "Naniwanomiya de mitsukatta kofun jidai no ōgata tatemono gun ni tsuite." *Hisutoria* (124): 31–43.

Miura Keiichi. 1970. "Nissō kōshō no rekishiteki igi," in *Kokushi ronshū*, ed. Kobata Atsushi Kyōju taikan kinenkai. Kyoto: Kobata Atsushi Kyōju taikan kinen jigyōkai: 327–340.

Miyake Chōbei. 1954. "Masakado no ran no shiteki zentei." *Ritsumeikan bungaku* (112): 57-73.

Miyagi Eishō. 1975. *Engi shiki no kenkyū*. 2 vols. Kyoto: Taishūkan.

Miyamoto Tasuku. 1973. "Ritsuryōteki tochi seido," in *Tochi seidoshi*, ed. Takeuchi Rizō. vol. 1. Tokyo: Yamakawa shuppansha: 49-83.

Miyazaki Fumiko. 1992. "Religious Life of the Kamakura Bushi." *Monumenta Nipponica* 47 (4): 435–67.

Miyazaki Yasumitsu. 1978. "Kodai makki ni okeru Mino Genji no dōkō." *Shoryōbu kiyō* (30): 22–36.

Miyazaki Yasumitsu, ed. 1990. *Kokushi bunin*. 6 vols. Tokyo: Zoku gunso ruijū kanseikai.

Mizuno Masayoshi. 1969. "Kikajin no funbo: Shiga-gun ni okeru kanjinkei kika shizoku o megutte." *Gekkan bunkazai* (73): 23-33.

Mizuno Masayoshi. 1973. *Ōsaka-fu bunkazai chōsa gaiyō 1972*. vol. 4, Furuichi daikōkyo hakkutsu chōsa gaiyō. Osaka: Ōsaka-fu kyōiku iinkai.

Mizuno Masayoshi. 1985. "Yamato gaien chiiki no kofun jidai shūraku," in *Kōza kōkochirigaku, vol. 4: Sonraku to kaihatsu*, ed. Fujioka Kenjirō. Tokyo: Gakuseisha: 102-10.

Mizuno Ryūtarō. 1964. "Suiko kankei bunken mokuroku." *Shoku nihongi kenkyū* (124): 33-35.

Mizuno Shōji. 1988. "Futatsu no chūsei sonraku." *Nihonshi kenkyū* (310): 110–141.

Mizuno Yū. 1987. *Hyōshaku Gishi Wajinden*. Tokyo: Yūzankaku shuppan.

Mogi Masahiro. 1974. *Zenpōkōhōfun*. Tokyo: Yūzankaku.

Morgan, Lewis Henry. 1877. *Ancient Society: Researches in the Lines of Human Progress from Savagery through Barbarism*. New York: Henry Holt.

Mori Katsumi. 1965. "Nissō bōeki to Ōshū no kōtsū," in *Chūō daigaku hachijū shūnen kinen ronbunshū (Bungakubu)*. Tokyo: Chūō daigaku: 329-259.

Mori Katsumi. 1972. "The Beginning of Overseas Advance of Japanese Merchant Ships." *Acta Asiatica* (23): 1–24.

Mori Katsumi. 1975. *Shintei Nissō bōeki no kenkyū*. vol. 1, Mori Katsumi chosaku senshū. Tokyo: Kokusho kankōkai.

Morimoto Jikichi. 1942. *Takahashi Mushimaro*. Tokyo: Seigōdō.

Morita Tei. 1973. "Kodai chihō gyōsei kikō ni tsuite no ichi kōsai." *Rekishigaku kenkyū* (401): 15–27.

Morita Tei. 1980. *Kenkyūshi ōchō kokka*. Tokyo: Yoshikawa kōbunkan.

Morita Tei. 1991. "Sekkan seiji e no michi," in *Kodai o kangaeru: Heian no miyako*, ed. Sasayama Haruo. Tokyo: Yoshikawa kōbunkan: 221-240.

Morohashi Tetsuji. 1955. *Dai kanwa jiten*. 13 vols. Tokyo: Taishukan shoten.

Morrell, Robert. 1985. *Collection of Sand and Pebbles*. Albany: State University of New York Press.

Morris, Dana. 1980. "Peasant Economy in Early Japan," (Ph.D. diss., University of California at Berkeley).

Morris, Ivan. 1967. *Pillow Book of Sei Shonagon*. 2 vols. New York: Columbia University Press.
Morris, Ivan. 1971. *As I Crossed a Bridge of Dreams (Sarashina Nikki)*. New York: Dial Press.
Motoki Yasuo. 1993. "Miyako no hen'yō: seiiki to bōryoku." *Kodai bunka* 45 (9): 13-21.
Motoki Yasuo. 1996. *Inseiki seijishi kenkyū*. Tokyo: Shibunkan shuppan.
Murai Shōsuke. 1995. "Ōdo ōmin shisō to kyūseiki no tenkan." *Shisō* (847): 23-45.
Murai Yasuhiko. 1958. "Shōen to yorisakunin," in *Chūsei shakai no kihon kōzō*, ed. Nihonshi kenkyūkai shiryōbukai. Tokyo: Ōchanomizu shobō: 43–80.
Murai Yasuhiko. 1965. "Kō suikosei no henshitsu katei," in *Kodai kokka kaitai katei no kenkyū*. Tokyo: Iwanami shoten: 11–60.
Murai Yasuhiko. 1968. *Kodai kokka kaitai katei no kenkyū*. tokyo: Iwanami shoten.
Murai Yasuhiko. 1974. *Ōchō kizoku*. Tokyo: Shōgakukan.
Murakami Einosuke. 1977. "Tettei no honshitsu to sono hennen josetsu." *Kōkogaku kenkyū* 24 (2): 33-51.
Murakami Hiromichi. 1988. "Higashi Ajia no nishu no chūzō teppu o megutte." *Tatara kenkyū* (29): 1-20.
Murao Jirō. 1953. "Izumo no kuni fudoki no kanzō to setsudoshi," in *Izumo no kuni fudoki no kenkyū*, ed. Hiraizumi Kiyoshi. Kyoto: Kōgakkan daigaku shuppanbu: 516–20.
Nagahara Keiji. 1961. "Shōensei no rekishiteki ichi," in *Nihon hōkensei seiritsu katei no kenkyū*. Tokyo: Iwanami shoten: 65–70.
Nagahara Keiji. 1968. *Nihon no chūsei shakai*. Tokyo: Iwanami shoten.
Nagahara Keiji. 1988. "Kaisetsu," in *Chūseiteki sekai no keisei*, ed. Nagahara Keiji, vol. 5 Ishimoda Shō chōsakushū. Tokyo: Iwanami shoten: 349–63.
Nagahara Keiji. 1998. *Shōen*. Tokyo: Yoshikawa kōbunkan.
Naganuma Kenkai. 1956. *Nihon no kaizoku*. Tokyo: Shibundō.
Nagashima Fukutarō. 1960. "Kodai makki ni okeru bushi no ichi kōsatsu — Yorichikaryū Yamato no Uno-shi no baai." *Jimbun ronkyū* 11 (2): 22-.
Nagayama Yasutaka. 1970. "Zōyōsei no seiritsu." *Hisutoria* (54): 1–17.
Nagayama Yasutaka. 1981. "Marukusu shugi kodai kokka riron ni kansuru ni, san no gimon." *Atarashii rekishigaku no tame ni* (162): 1–17.
Nagayama Yasutaka. 1984. "Zenki Yamato seiken no shihai taisei." *Nihon rekishi* 432: 17-39.
Nakada Norio, ed. 1975. *Nihon ryōiki*, Nihon koten bungaku zenshū. Tokyo: Shōgakukan.
Nakajima Etsuji, ed. 1969. *Gukanshō zenchūkai*. Tokyo: Yūseidō.
Nakamura, Kyoko Motomochi. 1973. *Miraculous Stories from the Japanese Buddhist Tradition*. Cambridge: Harvard-Yenching Institute Monograph Series.
Nakazawa Teiji et al. 1988. "Gennojō iseki hakkutsu chōsa hōkokusho. Isesaki-shi: Isesaki-shi kyōiku iinkai.
Nambu Noboru. 1992. *Nihon kodai koseki no kenkyū*. Tokyo: Yoshikawa kōbunkan.
Naoki Kōjirō. 1958. *Nihon kodai kokka no kōzō*. Tokyo: Aoki shoten.

Naoki Kōjirō. 1965. "Kodai kokka to sonraku: keikaku sonraku no shikaku kara." *Hisutoria* (42): 14-26.
Naoki Kōjirō. 1968. *Nihon kodai heiseishi no kenkyū*. Tokyo: Yoshikawa kōbunkan.
Nara kokuritsu hakubutsukan. 1989. *Hakkutsu sareta kodai no zaimei ihō*. Nara: Nara kokuritsu hakubutsukan.
Nemoto Akira. 1974. *Kōyaku Hitachi fudoki*. Tokyo: Ronshobō.
Nihon gakujutsu shinkōkai. 1965. *The Man'yōshū: One Thousand Poems*. New York: Columbia University Press.
Nihon koten bungakkai. 1978. *Kojidanshō*. Tokyo: Nihon koten bungakukai.
Nihon rekishi gakkai. 1999. *Nihonshi kenkyūsha jiten*. Tokyo: Yoshikawa kōbunkan.
Nishiguchi Junko. 1986. "Shirakawa goganji shōron," in *Ronshū nihon bukkyōshi: Heian jidai*, ed. Hiraoka Jōkai. vol. 3. Tokyo: Yūzankaku shuppan: 239-60.
Nishijima Sadao. 1961. "Kofun to Yamato seiken." *Okayama shigaku* 10: 154–207.
Nishijima Sadao. 1962. "Roku-hachi seiki no Higashi Ajia," in *Iwanami kōza nihon rekishi 2, Kodai 2*. Tokyo: Iwanami shoten: 229–278.
Nishijima Sadao. 1981. *Chūgoku kodai no shakai to keizai*. Tokyo: Tōkyō daigaku shuppankai.
Nishioka Toranosuke. 1953. "Shōen ni okeru sōko no keiei to kōwan no hattatsu to no kankei," in *Shōenshi no kenkyū*. vol. 1.1. Tokyo: Iwanami shoten: 111–300.
Nishioka Toranosuke. 1956–1957. *Shōenshi no kenkyū*. Tokyo: Iwanami shoten.
Nishiyama Ryōhei. 1978. "Ritsuryōsei shūdatsu kikō no seikaku to sono kiban." *Nihonshi kenkyū* (187): 42–67.
Niunoya Tetsuichi. 1975. "Fuzen no tomogara ni kansuru hito kōsai." *Hisutoria* (68).
Niunoya Tetsuichi. 1976. "Zaichi tone no keisei to rekishiteki ichi," in *Chūsei shakai no seiritsu to tenkai*, ed. Ōsaka rekishi gakkai. Tokyo: Yoshikawa kōbunkan: 141-224.
Nogami Jōsuke. 1970. "Setsukasen ni okeru kofungun no keisei to sono tokushitsu." *Kōkogaku kenkyū* 16 (3, 4): 43-72; 69-84.
Noto Takeshi. 1990. "Mitsudera I Iseki no seiritsu to sono haikei: goseikidai ni okeru kasen idō o tomonau suiden kōchi no kakudai ni tsuite." *Kodai bunka* 42 (2): 3-15.
Ōbayashigumi purojekuto chi-mu. 1985. "Ōryō." *Kikan Ōbayashi* (20): 1-51.
Oboroya Hisashi. 1968. *Minamoto Yorimitsu*. Tokyo: Yoshikawa kōbunkan.
Okada Seiji. 1970. *Kodai ōken no saishi to shinwa*. Tokyo: Hanawa shobō.
Okada Seiji. 1970. "Kodai ni okeru shūkyō tōsei to jingi kanshi." *Rekishigaku kenkyū* (Bessatsu).
Okada Seiji. 1987. "Development of State Ritual in Ancient Japan." *Acta Asiatica* 51: 22-41.
Okami Masao and Akamatsu Toshihide, eds. 1967. *Gukanshō*, Nihon koten bungaku taikei. Tokyo: Iwanami shoten.
Okamura Hidenori. 1989. "Tsubai Ōtsukayama Kofun no igi," in *Tsubai Ōtsukayama Kofun to sankakubuchi shinjūkyō*, ed.

Kyoto daigaku kōkogaku kenkyūshitsu. Kyoto: Kyoto daigaku bungakubu: 68-73.

Okuda Isao. 1972. "Kōzanji-bon Ko ōrai o megutte," in *Kōzanji-bon Ko ōrai*, ed. Kōzanji tenseki monjo sōgō chōsadan, Kōzanji shiryō sōsho. Tokyo: Tōkyō daigaku shuppansha: 726-52.

Okuno Takahiro. 1943. *Kōshitsu gokeizaishi no kenkyū*. vol. 2. Tokyo: Unebi shobō.

Ōmachi Ken. 1978. "Ritsuryō kokka no furō, tōbō seisaku no tokushitsu." *Genshi kodai shakai kenkyū* 4: 107-31.

Origuchi Shinobu. 1955. *Origuchi Shinobu chosakushū*. vol. 8. Tokyo: Chūō kōronsha.

Ōsone Shōsuke, ed. 1992. *Honchō monzui*, Shin nihon koten bungaku taikei. Tokyo: Iwanami shoten.

Ōsumi Kiyoaki. 1991. "Benkan no henshitsu to ritsuryō daijōkansei." *Shigaku zasshi* 100 (11): 1–42.

Ōtsuka Hatsushige. 1962. "Zenpōkōhōfun josetsu." *Meiji daigaku jinbun kagaku kenkyū kiyō* 1: 1-59.

Ōtsuka Hatsushige et al. 1989. *Nihon kofun daijiten*. Tokyo: Tōkyōdō.

Ōyama Kyōhei. 1974. "Shōenseiteki ryōiki shihai o meguru kenryoku to sonraku." *Nihonshi kenkyū* (139–140): 103–119.

Ōyama Kyōhei. 1976. "Chūsei no mibunsei to kokka," in *Iwanami kōza nihon rekishi 8*. Tokyo: Iwanami shoten: 261–314.

Ōyama Kyōhei. 1985. "Konoe-ke to Nanto Ichijōin: *Kan'yō ruijū shōkō*," in *Nihon seiji shakai kenkyū*, ed. Kishi Toshio Kyōju taikan kinenkai. Tokyo: Hanawa shobō: 9-48.

Ōyama Kyōhei. 1990. "Medieval *Shōen*," in *Cambridge History of Japan, vol. 3, Medieval japan*, ed. K. Yamamura. Cambridge: Cambridge University Press: 89–127.

Oyamada Yoshio. 1967. "Ise Jingū yakubukumai seido ni tsuite, Inseiki o chūshin ni." *Ryūtsū keizai ronshū* 2 (2): 14-.

Philippi, Donald. 1968. *Kojiki*. Tokyo: University of Tokyo Press.

Philippi, Donald. 1990. *Norito*. Princeton: Princeton University Press.

Piggott, Joan. 1987. "Tōdaiji and the Nara Imperium," (Ph.D. diss., Stanford University).

Piggott, Joan. 1989. "Sacral Kingship and Confederacy in Early Izumo." *Monumenta Nipponica* 44 (1): 45-74.

Piggott, Joan R. 1997. *The Emergence of Japanese Kingship*. Stanford: Stanford University Press.

Piggott, Joan. 1999. "Chieftain Pairs and Corulers," in *History and Gender in Japan*, ed. H. Tonomura et al. Ann Arbor: University of Michigan Center for Japanese Studies: 17-52.

Piggott, Joan R. 2001. "Trouble With Naming," in *Japan Memory Project Conference Proceedings Academic Year 2000-2001*. Tokyo: Shiryō Hensanjo, Tokyo University: 186-216.

Piggott, Joan. 2005. "On 'The New Monkey Music,' an extract and introduction to Fujiwara Akihira's Shinsarugakuki." In Haruo Shirane ed. *An Anthology of Premodern Japanese Literature*. Columbia University Press.

Pollack, David. 1986. *The Fracture of Meaning*. Princeton: Princeton University Press.

Rabinovitch, Judith. 1986. *Shōmonki: The Story of Masakado's Rebellion*. Tokyo: Sophia University.

Reischauer, Jean and Robert Reischauer. 1967. *Early Japanese History*. 2 vols. Gloucester, Mass.: Peter Smith.

Rodd, Laurel Raspica. 1978. *Nichiren: A Biography*. vol. 11, Occasional Papers. Tuscon: Arizona State University.

Ruch, Barbara. 1990. "The Other Side of Culture in Medieval Japan," in *Cambridge History of Japan*, ed. K. Yamamura. vol. 3. Cambridge: Cambridge University Press: 500–43.

Saeki Arikiyo. 1962. *Shinsen shōjiroku no kenkyū*. 9 vols. Tokyo: Yoshikawa kōbunkan.

Saeki Arikiyo. 1970. "Kyū seiki no nihon to chōsen," in *Nihon kodai no seiji to shakai*. Tokyo: Yoshikawa kōbunkan: 289–308.

Saeki Ariyoshi, ed. 1940. *Shoku nihongi*. 2 vols, Rikkokushi. Tokyo: Asahi shimbunsha.

Saga-ken kyōiku iinkai. 1990. "Kanjō shūraku Yoshinogari iseki gaihō." Tokyo: Yoshikawa kōbunkan.

Sahlins, Marshall D. 1968. *Tribesmen*. Englewoods Cliffs, NJ: Prentice Hall.

Saitō Tadashi. 1966. *Kofun bunka to kodai kokka*. Tokyo: Shibundō.

Sakaehara Towao. 1972. "Nara jidai no ryūtsū keizai." *Shirin* 55 (4): 18-60.

Sakaehara Towao. 1975. "Wadō kaichin no tanjō." *Rekishigaku kenkyū* (416): 1–15.

Sakaehara Towao. 1976. "Nihon kodai no enkyori kōeki ni tsuite," in *Kodai kokka no keisei to tenkai*, ed. Ōsaka rekishi gakkai. Tokyo: Yoshikawa kōbunkan: 435–64.

Sakaguchi Tsutomu. 1963. "Fugōsō ni tsuite." *Rekishigaku kenkyū* (276): 18–23.

Sakamoto Shōzō. 1972a. "Gungōsei no kaihen to bechimyō no sōsetsu," in *Nihon ōchō kokka taisei ron*. Tokyo: Tōkyō daigaku shuppankai: 241–323.

Sakamoto Shōzō. 1972b. *Nihon ōchō kokka taiseiron*. Tokyo: Tōkyō daigaku shuppankai.

Sakamoto Taro. 1956. "Nihon shoki to emishi," in *Emishi*, ed. Kotenshi danwakai. Tokyo: Asakura shoten.

Sakamoto Tarō. 1928. *Jōdai ekisei no kenkyū*. Tokyo: Shibundō.

Sakamoto Tarō. 1960. *Nihon zenshi: kodai 1*. Tokyo: Tōkyō daigaku shuppankai.

Sakamoto Tarō et al., eds. 1967. *Nihon shoki*. 2 vols, Nihon koten bungaku taikei. Tokyo: Iwanami shoten.

Sakamoto Tarō et al. 1994. *Nihon shoki*. 5 vols, Iwanami bunko. Tokyo: Iwanami shoten.

Sansom, George. 1931. *Japan: A Short Cultural History*. New York: Appleton.

Sasaki Ken'ichi. 1975. "Ritsuryōsei seiritsuki no zaichi no dōkō to zaichi shuchōsei." *Rekishigaku kenkyū* 58 (Bessatsu): 52-60.

Sasaki Muneo. 1994. *Nihon ōchō kokka ron*. Tokyo: Meichō shuppan.

Sasaki Muneo. 1999. "Sesshōsei, kampakusei no seiritsu." *Nihon rekishi* (610): 1-18.

Sasayama Haruo. 1975. *Kodai kokka to guntai*. Tokyo: Chūō shinsho.

Satake Akira. 1988. "Fujiwarakyū no chōtei to shayū girei." *Nihon rekishi* (478): 1-19.

Satō, Elizabeth. 1979. "Ōyama Estate and Insei Land Policies." *Monumenta Nipponica* 34 (1): 73-99.

Satō Ken'ichi. 1964. "Hōkenteki shūjūsei no genryū ni kansuru ichi shiron: Sekkanke keishi ni tsuite," in *Shoki hōkensei no kenkyū*, ed. Yasuda Motohisa. Tokyo: Yoshikawa kōbunkan: 228–280.

Satō Makoto. 1991. "Sekkansei seiritsuki no ōken ni tsuite no oboegaki," in *Sekkan jidai to kokiroku*, ed. Yamanaka Yutaka. Tokyo: Yoshikawa kōbunkan: 440-55.

Satō Shin'ichi. 1983. *Nihon no chūsei kokka*. Tokyo: Iwanami shoten.

Satō Shin'ichi. 1997. *Shimpan komonjogaku nyūmon*. Tokyo: Hōsei daigaku shuppankyoku.

Satō Shin'ichi and Ikeuchi Yoshisuke, eds. 1955-78. *Chūsei hōsei shiryōshū*. 5 vols. Tokyo: Iwanami shoten.

Satō Sōjun. 1964. "Heian shoki no kanjin to ritsuryō seiji no henshitsu." *Shirin* 47 (5): 1–35.

Satō Sōjun. 1967. "Emishi no hanran to risturyō kokka no hōkai." *Shirin* 50 (3): 1-32.

Satō Sōjun. 1977. *Heian zenki seijishi josetsu*. Tokyo: Tōkyō daigaku shuppankai.

Sawada Goichi. 1972. *Narachō jidai minsei keizai no sūteki kenkyū*. Tokyo: Kashiwa shobō.

Seidensticker, Edward. 1964. *Gossamer Years*. Rutland: Tuttle.

Seidensticker, Edward. 1976. *The Tale of Genji*. New York: Alfred Knopf.

Seki Akira. 1962. "Taika kaishin no tōgoku kokushi ni tsuite." *Bunka* 26 (2): 1-23.

Seki Akira. 1989. "Nashiro koshiro," in *Kokushi daijiten*. vol. 10. Tokyo: Yoshikawa kōbunkan: 699-700.

Sekiguchi Hiroko. 1972. "Kodai jinmin no ideorogi tōsō no shodankai." *Rekishigaku kenkyū* (Bessatsu): 35-49.

Sekiguchi Kōichi. 1986. "Kaburagawa ryūiki no jōrisei jiwari: jōri jiwari no settei to jizoku ni kansuru ichi jirei." *Jōrisei kenkyū* (2): 81-98.

Sekiyama Hiroshi. 1989. "Kofun jidai chūki no ōgata sōkogun: Naniwa no kura to Ki no kura o meguru ichi shiron." *Ōsaka no rekishi* (30): 37-66.

Service, Elman R. 1971. *Primitive Social Organization: An Evolutionary Perspective*. 2nd ed. New York: Random House.

Service, Elman R. 1975. *Origins of the State and Civilization: The Process of Cultural Evolution*. New York: W. W. Norton.

Shida Jun'ichi. 1974. *Hitachi fudoki to sono shakai*. Tokyo: Yūzankaku.

Shigematsu Akihisa, ed. 1982. *Shinsarugakuki, Unshū shōsoku*, Koten bunko. Tokyo: Gendai shichōsha.

Shimada Jirō. 1974. "Heishi seiken no tai-Sō bōeki no rekishiteki zentei to sono tenkai," in *Rekishi kenkyū to kokusaiteki keiki*, ed. Chūō daigaku keizai kenkyūjo. Tokyo: Chūō daigaku shuppanbu.

Shimizu Masatake. 1965. *Shōen shiryō*. Tokyo: Kadokawa shoten.

Shimizu, Osamu. 1951. "Nihon Montoku Jitsuroku: An Annotated Translation." Ph. D. diss. University of Toronto.

Shimomukai Tatsuhiko. 1981. "Ōchō kokka kokuga gunsei no kōzō to tenkai." *Shigaku kenkyū* (151): 44-67.

Shimomukai Tatsuhiko. 1987. "Ōchō kokka gunsei kenkyū no kihon shikaku," in *Ōchō kokka kokuseishi no kenkyū*, ed. Sakamoto Shōzō. Tokyo: Yoshikawa kōbunkan: 285-345.

Shimonaka Kunihiko/Heibonsha chihō shiryō senta-, ed. 1979-81. *Nihon reikishi chimei taikei, vols. 26-27: Kyōto-shi*. Tokyo: Heibonsha.

Shinjō Tsunezō. 1967. *Kamakura jidai no kōtsū*. Tokyo: Yoshikawa kōbunkan.

Shinjō Tsunezō. 1970. "Chūsei no kōtsū," in *Kōtsū shi*, ed. Toyota Takeshi et al. Tokyo: Yamakawa shuppansha: 39–69.

Shin nihon koten bungaku taikei. 1997. *Gōdanshō*. Tokyo: Iwanami shoten.

Shinoda, Minoru. 1960. *The Founding of the Kamakura Shogunate*. New York: Columbia University Press.

Shintei zōho kojitsu sōsho.1953. *Saikyūki*. 2 vols. Ed. Kojitsu sōsho henshūbu. Tokyo: Meiji tosho shuppan kabushiki kaisha.

Shintei zōho kokushi taikei. 1932. *Azuma kagami*. Ed. Kuroita Katsumi. Tokyo: Yoshikawa kōbunkan.

Shintei zōho kokushi taikei, 1938. *Chōya gunsai*. Ed. Kuroita Katsumi and Kokushi taikei henshūkai. Tokyo: Yoshikawa kōbunkan.

Shintei zōho kokushi taikei. 1979a. *Engi shiki*. 3 vols. Ed. Kuroita Katsumi and Kokushi taikei henshūkai. Tokyo: Yoshikawa kōbunkan.

Shintei zōho kokushi taikei. 1932. *Fusō ryakki. Ed.* Kuroita Katsumi and Kokushi taikei henshūkai. Tokyo: Yoshikawa kōbunkan.

Shintei zōho kokushi taikei. 1930. *Gukanshō. Ed.* Kuroita Katsumi and Kokushi taikei henshūkai. Tokyo: Yoshikawa kōbunkan.

Shintei zōho kokushi taikei 1941. *Honchō monzui, Zoku Honchō monzui*. Ed. Kuroita Katsumi. Tokyo: Yoshikawa kōbunkan.

Shintei zōho kokushi taikei. 1964. *Honchō seiki. Ed.* Kuroita Katsumi and Kokushi taikei henshūkai. Tokyo: Yōshikawa kōbunkan.

Shintei zōho kokushi taikei.1981. *Hyakurenshō*. Ed. Kuroita Katsumi and Kokushi taikei henshūkai. Tokyo: Yoshikawa kōbunkan.

Shintei zōho kokushi taikei. 1942. *Kojidan*. Ed. Kuroita Katsumi and Kokushi taikei henshūkai. Tokyo: Yoshikawa kōbunkan.

Shintei zōho kokushi taikei.1936. *Kojiki, Sendai kyūji hongi, Shintō gobusho*. vol. 7. Ed. Kuroita Katsumi. Tokyo: Yoshikawa Kōbunkan.

Shintei zōho kokushi taikei.1986. *Kugyō bunin*. 6 vols. Ed. Kuroita Katsumi and Kokushi taikei henshūkai. Tokyo: Yoshikawa kōbunkan.

Shintei zōho kokushi taikei.1984-85. *Nihon kiryaku*. 3 vols. Ed. Kuroita Katsumi and Kokushi taikei henshūkai. Tokyo: Yoshikawa kōbunkan.

Shintei zōho kokushi taikei.1980. *Nihon kōki*. Ed. Kuroita Katsumi and Kokushi taikei henshūkai. Tokyo: Yoshikawa kōbunkan.

Shintei zōho kokushi taikei. 1979. *Nihon Montoku Tennō jitsuroku*. Ed. Kuroita Katsumi and Kokushi taikei henshūkai. Tokyo: Yoshikawa kōbunkan.

Shintei zōho kokushi taikei. 1979-1981. *Nihon sandai jitsuroku*. 2 vols. Ed. Kuroita Katsumi and Kokushi taikei henshūkai. Tokyo: Yoshikawa kōbunkan.

Shintei zōho kokushi taikei.1985. *Nihon shoki*. Ed. Kuroita Katsumi and Kokushi taikei henshūkai. Tokyo: Yoshikawa kōbunkan.

Shintei zōho kokushi taikei.1933. *Ruijū fusenshō*. Ed. Kuroita Katsumi and Kokushi taikei henshūkai, Tokyo: Yoshikawa kōbunkan.

Shintei zōho kokushi taikei. 1979. *Ruijū kokushi*. Ed. Kuroita Katsumi and Kokushi taikei henshūkai. Tokyo: Yoshikawa kōbunkan.

Shintei zōho kokushi taikei.1979-81. *Ruijū sandai kyaku*. 2 vols. Ed. Kuroita Katsumi and Kokushi taikei henshūkai. Tokyo: Yoshikawa kōbunkan.

Shintei zōho kokushi taikei.1983. *Ryō no gige*. Ed. Kuroita Katsumi and Kokushi taikei henshūkai. Tokyo: Yoshikawa kōbunkan.

Shintei zōho kokushi taikei.1978-80. *Ryō no shūge*. 3 vols. Ed. Kuroita Katsumi and Kokushi taikei henshūkai. Tokyo: Yoshikawa kōbunkan.

Shintei zōho kokushi taikei.1980. *Seiji yōryaku*. 3 vols. Ed. Kuroita Katsumi and Kokushi taikei henshūkai. Tokyo: Yoshikawa kōbunkan.

Shintei zōho kokushi taikei. 1981. *Shoku nihongi*. 2 vols. Ed. Kuroita Katsumi and Kokushi taikei henshūkai. Tokyo: Yoshikawa kōbunkan.

Shintō taikei hensankai. 1980. *Sendai kyūji hongi*. Shintō taikei. Kotenhen 8. Tokyo: Shintō taikei hensankai: 3-195.

Shiraishi Taichirō. 1969. "Kinai ni okeru ōgata kofungun no shōchō." *Kōkogaku kenkyū* 16 (1): 8-26.

Shiraishi Taichirō. 1984. "Nihon kofun bunka ron," in *Kōza Nihon rekishi, vol. 1: Genshi/Kodai*, ed. Rekishigaku kenkyūkai and Nihonshi kenkyūkai. vol. 1. Tokyo: Tōkyō daigaku shuppankai: 159-91.

Shiraishi Taichirō. 1985. "Nendai ketteiron (2): Yayoi jidai ikō no nendai kettei," in *Iwanami kōza nihon kōkogaku 1: kenkyū no hōhō*, ed. Kondō Yoshirō et al. Tokyo: Iwanami shoten: 218-42.

Shirayama Yoshitarō. 1980. *Shokugenshō no kisoteki kenkyū*. Shintōshi kenkyū sōsho 12 ed. Kyōto: Shintōshi gakkai.

Shiryō hensanjo, ed. 1955. *Dai nihon komonjo Tōdaiji monjo*. 18 vols. to date. Tokyo: Tōkyō daigaku shuppankai.

Shizuoka-ken hensan senmon iinkai. 1994. *Shizuoka-ken shi*. Shizuoka: Shizuoka-ken.

Shōji Hiroshi. 1977. *Henkyō no sōran*. Tokyo: Kyōikusha.

Souryi, Pierre Francois. 2001. *The World Turned Upside Down: Medieval Japanese Society*. New York: Columbia University.

Steenstrup, Carl. 1980. "*Sata Mirensho*: a Fourteenth-century Law Primer." *Monumenta Nipponica* 35 (4): 405-35.

Suga Masatomo. 1907. "Hitachi fudoki no koto," in *Suga Masatomo zenshū*. Tokyo: Kokusho kankokai: 629–32.

Suzuki Yasutami. 1969. "Nara jidai ni okeru taigai ishiki," in *Nihon shiseki ronshū*, ed. Iwahashi Koyata Hakase shōju kinenkai. vol. 1. Tokyo: Yoshikawa kōbunkan: 145–193.

Suzuki Yasutami. 1996. "Nihon kodai no shuchōsei shakai to taigai kankei: kokka keisei no shodankai no saikentō." *Rekishi hyōron* (551): 17-32.

Suzuki Yasutami. rev. ed. 1983. *Kodai kokkashi kenkyū no ayumi*. Tokyo: Shinjimbutsu ōraisha.

Tachibana Kenji. 1974. *Okagami*, Nihon koten bungaku zenshū. Tokyo: Shōgakukan.

Taira Masayuki. 1992a. "Chūsei kōki no kokka to bukkyō," in *Nihon chūsei no shakai to bukkyō*. Tokyo: Kōshobō: 75–109.

Taira Masayuki. 1992b. *Nihon chūsei no shakai to bukkyō*. Tokyo: Kōshobō.

Takada Minoru. 1966. "Nihon hōken shakai seiritsuki no ni, san no mondai." *Atarashii rekishigaku no tame ni*.

Takada Minoru. 1970. "Jūseiki no shakai henkaku," in *Kōza nihonshi*, ed. Rekishigaku kenkyūkai & Nihonshi kenkyūkai. vol. 2. Tokyo: Tōkyō daigaku shuppankai: 17-46.

Takahashi Kazuo. 1979. "Keikaku sonraku ni tsuite." *Kodai o kangaeru* (20): 1-24.

Takahashi Masaaki. 1971. "Masakado no ran no hyōka o megutte." *Bunka shigaku* (26).

Takahashi Masaaki. 1975. "Ise Heishi no seiritsu to tenkai." *Nihonshi kenkyū* (157, 158): 1–23, 23–47.

Takahashi Masaaki. 1984. *Kiyomori izen: Ise Heishi no kōryū*. Tokyo: Heibonsha.

Takahashi Mikuni. 1991. "Kinai no kōtsū," in *Shimpan kodai no nihon* 6. Tokyo: Kadokawa shoten: 327-46.

Takahashi Takahiro. 1972. "Kodai yusō kō." *Shisen* (44, 45): 1-27, 34-58.

Takahashi Takashi. 1972. "Mutsu, Dewa no gunsei." *Shigen* (15): 22–30.

Takahashi Tomio. 1958. *Fujiwara-shi yondai*. Tokyo: Yoshikawa kōbunkan.

Takahashi Tomio. 1962a. "Kodai kokka to henkyō," in *Iwanami kōza nihonshi 3: Kodai 3*. Tokyo: Iwanami shoten: 229-59.

Takahashi Tomio. 1962b. "Tōgoku kodaishijō no sakuko to chinpei." *Nihon rekishi* (90): 36–41.

Takahashi Tomio. 1963. *Emishi*. Tokyo: Yoshikawa kōbunkan.

Takahashi Tomio. 1984. *Hiraizumi no sekai: Fujiwara Kiyohira*. Tokyo: Shimizu shinsho.

Takashima Masato. 1997. *Fujiwara Fuhito*. Tokyo: Yoshikawa kōbunkan.

Takeda Sachiko. 1984. "Nihon ifukuryō no seiritsu," in *Kodai kokka no keisei to ifukusei*. Tokyo: Yoshikawa kōbunkan: 283–303.

Takeda Sachiko. 1988a. "Kodai ni okeru minzoku to ifuku," in *Nihon no shakaishi*, ed. Asao Naohiro et al. vol. 8. Tokyo: Iwanami shoten: 11–48.

Takeda Sachiko. 1988b. "Michi to kodai kokka." *Hyōrin* (15): 69-88.

Takeda Sachiko. 1989. "Kodai ni okeru michi to kokka." *Hisutoria* (125): 116-33.

Takeda Yūkichi and Satō Kenzō. 1986. *Kundoku Nihon sandai jitsuroku*. Kyoto: Rinsen shoten.

Takeuchi Masato and Doi Takayuki. 1983. *Wakayama-shi Zemmyōji shozai Narutaki iseki bakkutsu chōsa gaihō*. Wakayama-ken: Wakayama-ken kyōiku iinkai.

Takeuchi Rizō. 1956. "Dazaifu mandokoro kō." *Shien* (71): 25-54.

Takeuchi Rizō. 1958a. "Jiin no hōkenka," in *Ritsuryōsei to kizoku seiken: Kizoku seiken no kōzō, pt. 2*. Tokyo: Ochanomizu shōbō: ??

Takeuchi Rizō. 1958b. "Zaichōkanjin no bushika," in *Ritsuryōsei to kizoku seiken, part II*. Tokyo: Ochanomizu shōbō.

Takeuchi Rizō, ed. 1962. *Nara ibun*. 3 vols. Tokyo: Tōkyōdō shuppan.

Takeuchi Rizō. 1973a. "Dazaifu to tairiku," in *Kodai Ajia to Kyūshū (Kyūshū bunka ronshū 1)*, ed. Fukuoka UNESCO Kyōkai. Tokyo: Heibonsha. Reprint in Takeuchi Rizō. *Chosakushū* vol. 4. Kadokawa shoten: 514-65.

Takeuchi Rizō, ed. 1973b. *Taikei nihonshi sōshō Tochi seidoshi*. Tokyo: Yoshikawa kōbunkan.

Takeuchi Rizō, ed. 1973-1980. *Heian ibun*. 15 vols. Tokyo: Tōkyōdō.

Takeuchi Rizō. 1975. *Shōen bumpuzu*. Tokyo: Yoshikawa kōbunkan.

Takeuchi Rizō. 1975–1979. *Iga no kuni Kuroda no shō shiryō*. 2 vols. Tokyo: Yoshikawa kōbunkan.

Takeuchi Rizō, ed. 1984–1995. *Kamakura ibun*. 46 vols. Tokyo: Tōkyōdō.

Takeuchi Rizō. 1999. "The Rise of the Warriors," in *Cambridge History of Japan, vol. 2, Heian*, ed. D. Shively and W. H. McCullough. Cambridge: Cambridge University Press: 664–70.

Tanaami Hiroshi. 1956. "Kodai Emishi to Ainu," in *Emishi*, ed. Kodaishi danwakai. Tokyo: Asakura shoten.

Tanaami Hiroshi. 1960. "Suikosei no kigen." *Nihon rekishi* (146): 2-9.

Tanaami Hiroshi. 1969. *Kodai no kōtsū*. Tokyo: Yoshikawa kōbunkan.

Tanabe Shōzō. 1981. *Sueki taisei*. Tokyo: Kadokawa shoten.

Tanaka Fumihide. 1994. "Go-Shirakawa inseiki no seiji kenryoku to kenmon jiin," in *Heishi seiken no kenkyū*. Kyoto: Shibunkaku shuppan: 165–217.

Tanaka Kiyomi. 1989. "Goseiki ni okeru Settsu, Kawachi no kaihatsu to toraijin." *Hisutoria* (125): 1-25.

Tanaka Minoru. 1976. "Insei to Jishō, Juei no ran," in *Iwanami kōza nihon rekishi 4, Kodai 4*. Tokyo: Iwanami shoten: 193-230.

Tateno Kazumi. 1998. *Nihon kodai no kōtsū to shakai*. Tokyo: Hanawa shobō.

Terasawa Kaoru. 1990. "Yayoi jidai no enpunkyū." *Kodaigaku kenkyū* (123): 150-60.

Thornton, Sybil. 1999. *Charisma and Community Formation in Medieval Japan: The Case of the Yugyōha (1300–1700)*. Ithaca, N.Y.: East Asia Program, Cornell University.

Tochigi Yoshitada, ed. 1992. *Hōgen monogatari*, Shin nihon koten bungaku taikei. Tokyo: Iwanami shoten.

Toda Yoshimi. 1958. "Kokugaryō no myō to zaike ni tsuite," in *Chūsei shakai no kihon kōzō*, ed. Nihonshi kenkyūkai shiryō kenkyūbukai. Tokyo: Ochanomizu shobō: 183–210.

Toda Yoshimi. 1967a. "Heimin hyakushō chii ni tsuite." *Hisutoria* (47): 17–22.

Toda Yoshimi. 1967b. *Nihon ryōshūsei seiritsushi no kenkyū*. Tokyo: Iwanami shoten.

Toda Yoshimi. 1967c. "Ritsuryōseika no yake no hendō," in *Nihon ryōshusei seiritsushi no kenkyū*. Tokyo: Iwanami shoten: 74-115.

Toda Yoshimi. 1967d. "Ryōshūteki tochi shoyū no senku keitai," in *Nihon ryōshūsei seiritsushi no kenkyū*. Tokyo: Iwanami shoten: 116-67.

Toda Yoshimi. 1968. "Chūsei seiritsuki no kokka to nōmin." *Nihonshi kenkyū* (97): 193–230.

Toda Yoshimi. 1970. "Kokuga gunsei no keisei katei," in *Chūsei no kenryoku to minshū*, ed. Nihonshi kenkyūkai. Osaka: Sōgensha: 5–45.

Toda Yoshimi. 1972. "Chūsei shakai seiritsuki no kokka," in *Shimpojiumu nihon rekishi, vol. 5, Chūsei shakai no keisei*. Tokyo: Gakuseisha: 212–276.

Toda Yoshimi. 1974–1975. "Bushidan no seichō," in *Nihon seikatsu bunkashi 3*, ed. Kadowaki Teiji et al. 10 vols. Tokyo: Kawade shobō shinsha: 49-66.

Toda Yoshimi. 1975a. "Kyū seiki tōgoku shōen to sono kōtsu keitai — Kazusa no kuni Mohara no shō o megutte." *Seiji keizai shigaku* (110): 1-10.

Toda Yoshimi. 1975b. "Teikō shi hanran suru hitobito," in *Tsuchi ikki to nairan (Nihon minshū no rekishi 2)*. Tokyo: Sanseidō: 21–44.

Toda Yoshimi. 1976. "Ōchō toshi to shōen taisei," in *Iwanami kōza Nihon rekishi 4 (*Kodai 4*)*, ed. Asao Naohiro et al. Tokyo: Iwanami shoten: 159-92.

Toda Yoshimi. 1991a. "Chūsei to wa dō iu jidai ka — chūsei zenki," in *Shoki chūsei shakaishi no kenkyū*. Tokyo: Tōkyō daigaku shuppansha: 1–11.

Toda Yoshimi. 1991b. "Ōchō toshiron no mondaiten," in *Shōki chūsei shakaishi no kenkyū*. Tokyo: Tōkyō daigaku shuppankai: 175–86.

Tokoro Isao. 1970. *Miyoshi Kiyoyuki*. Tokyo: Yoshikawa kōbunkan.

Tōkyō daigaku shiryō hensanjo, ed. 1901-. *Dai nihon shiryō*. Tokyo: Tōkyō daigaku shuppankai.

Tōkyō daigaku shiryō hensanjo. 1902-43. *Dai nihon komonjo: Shōsōin hen'nen monjo*. 25 vols. Tokyo: Tōkyō daigaku shuppankai.

Tōma Seita. 1942. "Shōen funyūsei seiritsu no ichi kōsatsu." *Rekishigaku kenkyū* (100): 1-34.

Tōma Seita. 1947a. *Nihon kodai kokka*. Tokyo: Itō shoten.

Tōma Seita. 1947b. *Nihon shōen shi: kodai yori chūsei ni itaru henkaku no keizaiteki kiso kōzō no kenkyū*. Tokyo: Kondō shoten.

Tōma Seita. 1966. *Higashi Ajia sekai no keisei*. Tokyo: Shunjūsha.

Tonegawa Akihiko. 1999. "Nihon no kofun jidai wa, shoki kokka de yoi ka? Zenpōkōenfun taiseiron o megutte." *Kodaigaku* 16: 1-8.

Torao Toshiya. 1993. *Kōninshiki, Jōganshiki ibun shūsei*. Tokyo: Yoshikawa kōbunkan.

Tsuchida Naoshige. 1965. *Ōchō no kizoku*. Tokyo: Chūō koronsha.

Tsuchii Yoichi and Nakao Maki, eds. 2000. *Honchō monzui no kenkyū*. 3 vols. Tokyo: Benseisha.

Tsuda Sōkichi. 1930a. "Koshiro, nashiro no be," in *Nihon jōdaishi no kenkyū*. Tokyo: Iwanami shoten: 519–75.

Tsuda Sōkichi. 1930b. "Tomo no miyatsuko no seiryoku no hensen," in *Nihon jōdaishi no kenkyū*. Tokyo: Iwanami shoten: 648–77.

Tsuda Sōkichi. 1948a. "Kumaso seitō no monogatari," in *Nihon koten no kenkyū*. Tokyo: Iwanami shoten: 138–178.

Tsuda Sōkichi. 1948b. *Nihon koten no kenkyū*. Tokyo: Iwanami shoten.

Tsude, Hiroshi. 1996. "Homogeneity and Regional Variability in Cultures of the Kofun Period." Paper read at Interdisciplinary Perspectives on the Origins of the Japanese, September 25-28, 1996, at International Research Center for Japanese Studies, Kyoto.

Tsude Hiroshi. 1974. "Kofun shutsugen zenya no shūdan kankei." *Kōkogaku kenkyū* 20 (4): 37-45.

Tsude Hiroshi. 1988. "Kofun jidai shuchō keifu no keizoku to danzetsu." *Machikaneyama ronsō* 22: 1-26.

Tsude Hiroshi. 1989a. "Kofun jidai no hōkaku sekkei." *Jōrisei kenkyū* 5: 1-14.

Tsude Hiroshi. 1989b. *Kofun jidai no ō to minshū*. Tokyo: Kōdansha.

Tsude Hiroshi. 1989c. *Nihon nōkō shakai no seiritsu katei*. Tokyo: Iwanami shoten.

Tsude Hiroshi. 1989d. "Zempōkōenfun no tanjō," in *Kodai o kangaeru: kofun*, ed. Shiraishi Taichirō. Tokyo: Yoshikawa kōbunkan: 1-35.

Tsude Hiroshi. 1990. "Chiefly Lineages in Kofun-period Japan." *Antiquity* 64: 923-31.

Tsude Hiroshi. 1991. "Nihon kodai no kokka keisei josetsu: zenpōkōenfun taisei no teishō." *Nihonshi kenkyū* (343): 5-38.

Tsude Hiroshi. 1992. "The Kofun Period and State Formation." *Acta Asiatica* 63: 64-86.

Tsude Hiroshi. 1996. "Kokka keisei no shodankai: Shuchōsei, shoki kokka, seijuku kokka." *Rekishi hyōron* (551): 3-16.

Tsude Hiroshi. 1998. "Toshi keisei to kokkaron," in *Nihon kodai kokka to sonraku*, ed. Yoshida Akira. Tokyo: Hanawa shobō: 35-54.

Tsunoda Bun'ei. 1966. "Fujiwara Tadahira no eitatsu," in *Murasaki Shikibu to sono jidai*. Tokyo: Kadokawa shoten: 215-378.

Tsunoda Bun'ei. 1977. "Shōmu Tennō ryō to Kōfukuji akusō Shinjitsu," in *Ōchō no meian*. Tokyo: Tōkyōdō shuppan: 337–54.

Turner, Frederick Jackson. 1921. *The Frontier in American History*. New York: Henry Holt.

Tyler, Royall. 2001. *The Tale of Genji*. Viking Press.

Tyler, Royall. 1987. *Japanese Tales*. New York: Pantheon Books.

Ueda Masaaki. 1964. "Saikansei seiritsu no igi," in *Nihon shoki kenkyū*, ed. Mishina Shōei. vol. 1. Tokyo: Hanawa shobō: 91-114.

Ueda Masaaki. 1967. *Yamato chōtei*. Tokyo: Kadokawa shoten.

Ueda Masaaki. 1979. "Agatanushi," in *Kokushi daijiten*, 15 vols. Tokyo: Yoshikawa kōbunkan: vol. 1, 61.

Uejima Susumu. 1990. "Ikkoku heikinyaku no kakuritsu katei." *Shirin* 73 (1): 41–72.

Ueki Hisashi. 1989. "Ōsaka-shi Chūō-ku Hōenzaka chiku de hakken sareta kenchiku ikō." *Hisutoria* (124): 55-65.

Umehara Sueji. 1922. *Samida oyobi Shin'yama kofun kenkyū*. Tokyo: Iwanami shoten.

Umehara Sueji. 1955. "Ōjin, Nintoku, Ritchū no san tennō ryō no kibo to chikuzō." *Shoryōbu kiyō* (5): 1-15.

Unno, Taitetsu. 1984. *Tannishō: a Shin Buddhist Classic*. Honolulu: Buddhist Study Center Press.

Uno Takao. 2001. *Shōen no kōkogaku*. Tokyo: Aoki shoten.

Uraki, Zirō. 1984. *Tale of the Cavern (Utsubo monogatari)*. Kyoto: Shinozaki shorin.

Ury, Marian. 1979. *Tales Old and New*. Berkeley and Los Angeles: University of California Press.

Ury, Marion. 1993. "The Ōe Conversations." *Monumenta Nipponica* 48: 359-80.

Uwayokote Masataka. 1963. "Chūsei nihon no higashi to nishi." *Kokubungaku no kaishaku to kanshō* 28 (5): 53-59.
Uwayokote Masataka. 1976. "Masakado biiki ni tsuite." *Rekishi to jimbutsu* (February): 100–167.
Uwayokote Masataka. 1981. "Inseiki no Genji," in *Goke'nin sei no kenkyū*, ed. Goke'ninsei kenkyūkai. Tokyo: Yoshikawa kōbunkan:
Uwayokote Masataka et al., eds. 1994. *Kodai, chūsei no seiji to bunka*. Kyoto: Shibunkaku shuppan.
Vargo, Lars. 1979. "The *Bemin* System in Early Japan," in *European Studies on Japan*, ed. I. Nish and C. Dunn. Tenterden, Kent: Paul Norbury Public: 10-15.
Verschuer, Charlotte von. 1988. *Le Commerce Extérieur du Japon des Origines au XVI Siècle*. Paris: Éditions Maisonneuve & Larose.
Wada Atsumu. 1985. "Sekisen to dōkyōsai—chimata ni okeru matsuri to saigi." *Kikan nihongaku* 6.
Wada Atsumu. 1995. "The Origins of Ise Shrine." *Acta Asiatica* 69: 63-83.
Wada Seigo. 1981. "Mukō-shi Itsukahara kofun no sokuryō chōsa yori," in *Ōryō no hikaku kenkyū*, ed. Onoyama Setsu. Kyoto: Kyoto daigaku kōkogaku kenkyūshitsu: 49-63.
Wakita Haruko. 1969. "Shōen ryōshu keizai to shōkōgyō," in *Nihon chūsei shōgyō hattatsushi no kenkyū*. Tokyo: Ochanomizu shobō: 127–234.
Wakita Haruko. 1983. "Cities in Medieval Japan." *Acta Asiatica* (44): 28–52.
Waley, Arthur. 1956-57. *The Tale of Genji*. Doubleday.
Wang Zhenping. 1989. "Sino-Japanese Relations before the Eleventh Century," (Ph.D. diss., East Asian Studies, Princeton University).
Wang Zhenping. 1994. "Speaking with a Forked Tongue: Diplomatic Correspondence between China and Japan, 238-608 A.D." *Journal of the American Oriental Society* 114 (1): 23-32.
Watanabe Minoru, ed. 1991. *Makura no sōshi*, Shin nihon koten bungaku taikei. Tokyo: Iwanami shoten.
Watanabe Shin'ichirō. 1989. "Kandai no zaisei un'ei to kokkateki butsuryū." *Kyōto furitsu daigaku gakujutsu hōkoku: jimbun* 41: 1-20.
Watanabe Tsunaya. 1966. *Shasekishū*. Nihon koten bungaku taikei. Tokyo: Iwanami shoten.
Watanabe Yoshimichi. 1948. *Kodai shakai no kōzō*. Tokyo: Itō shoten.
Watson, Burton. 1975. *Japanese Literature in Chinese*. 2 vols. New York: Columbia University Press.
Watson, Michael Geoffrey. 2003. "A Narrative Study of the Kakuichi-bon Heike monogatari." Ph.D. diss. Queen's College, University of Oxford, Oxford.
Webb, Jason. 2004. "In Good Order." Ph.D. diss. Princeton University, Princeton, N.J.
Weber, Max. 1909. "Agrarverhaltnisse im Altertum," in *Handworterbuch der staatswissenschaften*. 3rd ed: 55-74.
Wechsler, Howard J. 1985. *Offerings of Jade and Silk*. New Haven: Yale University Press.

Wetzler, Peter M. 1977. "Yoshishige no Yasutane," Ph.D. diss., University of California, Berkeley.

Wilson, William. 1982. *Ideals of the Samurai*. Tokyo: Ohara Publications.

Wilson, William. 1971. *Hōgen monogatari*. Tokyo: Sophia University. Reprint 2002, Cornell East Asia Series.

Wilson, William Ritchie. 1979. "The Way of the Bow and Arrow, the Japanese Warrior in *Konjaku monogatarishū*." *Monumenta Nipponica* 28 (2): 177-233.

Wittfogel, Karl. 1939. *Die Theorie der Orientalischen Gesellshaft (Tōyōteki shakai no riron)*. Translated by Moriya Katsumi and Hirano Yoshitarō. Tokyo: Nihon hyōronsha.

Wittfogel, Karl. 1961. *Oriental Despotism (Tōyōteki sensei shugi: zentaishugi ken-ryoku no hikaku kenkyū)*. Translated by Ajia keizai kenkyūjo. Tokyo: Ron-sōsha.

Yagi Atsuru. 1963. "Jōdai nihon no higashi to nishi." *Kokubungaku kaishaku to kanshō* 28 (5): 45-52.

Yamagishi Tokuhei et al., eds. 1979. *Shinsarugakuki*, Nihon shisō taikei: *Kodai seiji shakai shisō*. Tokyo: Iwanami shoten.

Yamamura, Kozo, ed. 1990. *Cambridge History of Japan, vol. 3, Medieval Japan*. Cambridge and New York: Cambridge University Press.

Yamanaka Yutaka, ed. 1985- . *Midō kampakuki zenchūyaku*. Tokyo: Kokusho kan-gyōkai/ Takashina shoten.

Yamao Yukihisa. 1972. *Gishi Wajinden: Tōyōshijō no kodai nihon*. Tokyo: Kōdan-sha.

Yamao Yukihisa. 1983. *Nihon kodai ōken keisei shiron*. Tokyo: Iwanami shoten.

Yasuda Motohisa. 1960. "Kodai makki ni okeru Kantō bushidan," in *Nihon hōkensei seiritsu no shozentei*. Tokyo: Yoshikawa kōbunkan: 1–111.

Yasuda Motohisa. 1976. "'Genji naifun,' no seijiteki haikei," in *Nihon shoki hoken-sei no kiso kenkyū*. Tokyo: Yamakawa shuppansha: 73-97.

Yasuda Motohisa. 1984. *Senran*. Tokyo: Kintō shuppansha.

Yiengpruksawan, Mimi. 1994. "What's in a Name: Fujiwara Fixation in Japanese Cultural History." *Monumenta Nipponica* 49 (4): 423-453.

Yiengpruksawan, Mimi. 1999. *Hiraizumi: Buddhist Art and Regional Politics in Twelfth-century Japan*. Cambridge: Harvard University Asia Center.

Yoneda Yūsuke. 1970. "Ritsuryōseika no gōzoku," in *Kōza nihonshi 1*, ed. Reki-shigaku kenkyūkai. Tokyo: Tōkyō daigaku shuppankai: 241-64.

Komeya Toyonosuke. 1975. "In mushadokoro kō." In *Nihonshi ronshū*, ed. Toki-noya Masaru Kyōju taikan kinen jigyōkai. Osaka: Seibundō.

Yoshida Akira. 1958. "Nassho shōron." *Shirin* 41 (3): 22-38.

Yoshida Akira. 1973. *Nihon kodai kokka seiritsu shiron: kokuzōsei o chūshin toshite*. Tokyo: Tōkyō daigaku shuppankai.

Yoshida Akira. 1998. "Nihon kodai kokka no keisei katei ni kansuru oboegaki: shoki kokkaron o chūshin toshite," in *Nihon kodai no kokka to sonraku*, ed. Yoshida Akira. Tokyo: Hanawa shobō: 3-34.

Yoshida Takashi. 1976. "Ritsuryōsei to sonraku," in *Iwanami kōza nihon rekishi 3*. Tokyo: Iwanami shoten: 141-200.

Yoshida Takashi. 1983. *Ritsuryō kokka to kodai shakai*. Tokyo: Iwanami shoten.

Yoshida Tōgo. 1922–23. *Dai nihon chimei jisho*. 7 vols. Tokyo: Fuzanbō.

Yoshie Akio. 1970. "Chūsei ikōki ni okeru shihai ideorogi to jinmin tōsō." *Rekishigaku kenkyū* (Bessatsu): 30-44.

Yoshie Akio. 1973. "Hō no keisei to sono tokushitsu." *Hokkaidō daigaku bungakubu kiyō* 22 (2): 121-250.

Yoshie Akio. 1986. "Sekkan-Inseiki chōtei no keibatsu saitei taikei," in *Chūsei, kinsei no kokka to shakai*. Tokyo: Tōkyō daigaku shuppankai: 2–69.

Yoshikawa Shinji. 1989. "Ritsuryō kanjin no saihen." *Nihonshi kenkyū* (320): 1-27.

Yoshikawa Shinji. 1998. "Sekkan seiji no tensei," in *Ritsuryō kanryōsei no kenkyū*. Tokyo: Yoshikawa kōbunkan: 401-26.

Yoshimura Takehiko. 1973. "Nihon kodai ni okeru ritsuryōseiteki nōmin shihai no tokushitsu." *Rekishigaku kenkyū* (Bessatsu): 34-44.

Yoshioka Masayuki. 1993. "Heian jidai no seimu o megutte," in *Shinshiten nihon rekishi 3: Kodai*, ed. Yoshimura Takehiko. Tokyo: Shinjimbutsu ōraisha: 96–103.

Zōho shiryō taisei kankōkai, ed. 1965. *Chōshūki*. 2 vols, Zōho shiryō taisei. Kyoto: Rinsen shoten.

Zōho shiryō taisei kankōkai, ed. 1974. *Chūyūki*. 7 vols, Zōho shiryō taisei. Kyoto: Rinsen shoten.

Zōho shiryō taisei kankōkai, ed. 1965-74. *Heihanki*. 4 vols, Zōho shiryō taisei. Kyoto: Rinsen shoten.

Zōho shiryō taisei kankōkai, ed. 1955-59. *Kasuga kannushi Suketaka ki*, Zōho zoku shiryō taisei. Kyoto: Rinsen shoten.

Zōho shiryō taisei kankōkai, ed. 1965. *Sakeiki*, Zōho shiryō taisei. Kyoto: Rinsen shoten.

Zōho shiryō taisei kankōkai, ed. 1965. *Sankaiki*, Zōho shiryō taisei. Kyoto: Rinsen shoten.

Zoku gunsho ruijū. Kanshoku, ritsuryō, kujibu. 1926. *Shisseishoshō*. Ed. Hanawa Hokiichi and Ōta Fujishirō. Tokyo: Zoku gunsho ruijū kanseikai: 420-27.

Zoku gunsho ruijū. Jingibu. 1975. *Kōtai jingū nenjūgyōji*. Ed. Hanawa Hokiichi and Ōta Fujishirō. Tokyo: Zoku gunsho ruijū kanseikai: 354-476.

Zoku gunsho ruijū. Jingibu. 1925. Ed. Hanawa Hokiichi & Ōta Fujishirō. *Hie sannō risshōki*. Tokyo: Zoku gunsho ruijū kanseikai: 654–702.

Zoku gunsho ruijū. Zatsubu. 1975. *Nanto taishu jūrakuki*. Ed. Hanawa Hokiichi and Ōta Fujishirō. Tokyo: Zoku gunsho ruijū kanseikai.

Zoku gunsho ruijū. Zatsubu. 1926. *Kōfukuji ryakunendaiki*. Ed. Hanawa Hokiichi and Ōta Fujishirō. Tokyo: Zoku gunsho ruijū kanseikai: 107–205.

Zoku zoku gunsho ruijū. Shidenbu. 1969. *Tōji chōja bunin*. Ed. Kokusho kankōkai. Tokyo: Zoku gunsho ruijū kanseikai.

INDEX

Page numbers in italic denote illustrations, glossary entries, and primary source listings.

CORNELL EAST ASIA SERIES

4 F. Teiwes, *Provincial Leadership in China: The Cultural Revolution and Its Aftermath*
8 C. C. Kubler, *Vocabulary and Notes to Ba Jin's Jia: An Aid for Reading the Novel*
16 M. Bethe & K. Brazell, *Nō as Performance: An Analysis of the Kuse Scene of Yamamba*
17 Royall Tyler, tr.: *Pining Wind: A Cycle of Nō Plays;* 18 *Granny Mountains* (2nd cycle)
23 Knight Biggerstaff, *Nanking Letters, 1949*
28 Perushek, ed., *The Griffis Collection of Japanese Books: An Annotated Bibliography*
37 JV Koschmann et al, eds., *International Perspectives on Yanagita Kunio & Japanese Folklore Studies*
38 James O'Brien, tr., *Murō Saisei: Three Works*
40 Kubo Sakae, *Land of Volcanic Ash: A Play in Two Parts,* revised ed., tr. D. G. Goodman
44 Susan Orpett Long, *Family Change and the Life Course in Japan*
48 McCullough, *Bungo Manual: Selected Reference Materials for Students of Classical Japanese*
49 Klein, *Ankoku Butō: The Premodern & Postmodern Influences on the Dance of Utter Darkness*
50 Karen Brazell, ed., *Twelve Plays of the Noh and Kyōgen Theaters*
51 David G. Goodman, ed., *Five Plays by Kishida Kunio*
52 Shirō Hara, *Ode to Stone,* tr. James Morita
53 P. J. Katzenstein & Yutaka Tsujinaka, *Defending the Japanese State: Structures, Norms & the Political Responses to Terrorism and Violent Social Protest in the 1970s & 1980s*
54 Su Xiaokang & Wang Luxiang, *Deathsong of the River: A Reader's Guide to the Chinese TV Series* Heshang, trs. Richard Bodman & Pin P. Wan
55 Jingyuan Zhang, *Psychoanalysis in China: Literary Transformations, 1919-1949*
56 Jane Kate Leonard & John R. Watt, eds., *To Achieve Security and Wealth: The Qing Imperial State and the Economy, 1644-1911*
57 A. F. Jones, *Like a Knife: Ideology & Genre in Contemporary Chinese Popular Music*
58 Peter J. Katzenstein & Nobuo Okawara, *Japan's National Security: Structures, Norms and Policy Responses in a Changing World*
59 Carsten Holz, *The Role of Central Banking in China's Economic Reforms*
60 C. Shimazaki, *Warrior Ghost Plays from the Japanese Noh Theater*
61 E. G. Ooms, *Women & Millenarian Protest in Meiji Japan: Deguchi Nao & Ōmotokyō*
62 C. Morley, *Transformation, Miracles, & Mischief: The Mountain Priest Plays of Kōygen*
63 David R. McCann & Hyunjae Yee Sallee, tr., *Selected Poems of Kim Namjo*
64 Hua Qingzhao, *From Yalta to Panmunjom: Truman's Diplomacy & the Four Powers, 1945-1953*
65 Margaret Benton Fukasawa, *Kitahara Hakushū: His Life and Poetry*
66 Kam Louie, ed., *Strange Tales from Strange Lands: Stories by Zheng Wanlong*
67 Wang Wen-hsing, *Backed Against the Sea,* tr. Edward Gunn
69 B. Myers, *Han Sōrya & North Korean Literature: The Failure of Socialist Realism in the DPRK*
70 Thomas P. Lyons & Victor Nee, eds., *The Economic Transformation of South China*
71 D. G. Goodman, tr., *After Apocalypse: Four Japanese Plays of Hiroshima & Nagasaki*
72 Thomas P. Lyons, *Poverty & Growth in a South China County: Anxi, Fujian, 1949-1992*
74 M. Atkins, *Informal Empire in Crisis: British Diplomacy & the Chinese Customs Succession, 1927-1929*
76 Chifumi Shimazaki, *Restless Spirits from Japanese Noh Plays of the Fourth Group*
77 Br, Anthony of Taizé & Young-Moo Kim, trs., *Back to Heaven: Selected Poems of Ch'ŏn Sang Pyŏng*
78 K. O'Rourke, tr., *Singing Like a Cricket, Hooting Like an Owl: Selected Poems by Yi Kyu-bo*
79 I. Averbuch, *The Gods Come Dancing: A Study of the Japanese Ritual Dance of Yamabushi Kagura*
80 Mark Peterson, *Korean Adoption and Inheritance*
81 Yenna Wu, tr., *The Lioness Roars: Shrew Stories from Late Imperial China*
82 Thomas Lyons, *The Economic Geography of Fujian: A Sourcebook,* Vol. 1
83 Pak Wan-so, *The Naked Tree,* tr. Yu Young-nan
84 C.T. Hsia, *The Classic Chinese Novel: A Critical Introduction*
85 Cho Chong-Rae, *Playing With Fire,* tr. Chun Kyung-Ja

86 Hayashi Fumiko, *I Saw a Pale Horse & Selections fm Diary of a Vagabond,* tr. Janice Brown
87 Motoori Norinaga, *Kojiki-den, Book 1,* tr. Ann Wehmeyer
88 Chang Soo Ko, tr., *Sending the Ship Out to the Stars: Poems of Park Je-chun*
89 Thomas Lyons, *The Economic Geography of Fujian: A Sourcebook,* Vol. 2
90 Brother Anthony of Taizé, tr., Midang: *Early Lyrics of So Chong-Ju*
92 J. Matsumura, *More Than a Momentary Nightmare: The Yokohama Incident & Wartime Japan*
93 Kim Jong-Gil tr., *The Snow Falling on Chagall's Village: Selected Poems of Kim Ch'un-Su*
94 Wolhee Choe & Peter Fusco, trs., *Day-Shine: Poetry by Hyon-jong Chong*
95 Chifumi Shimazaki, *Troubled Souls from Japanese Noh Plays of the Fourth Group*
96 Hagiwara Sakutarō, *Principles of Poetry (Shi no Genri),* tr. Chester Wang
97 Mae J. Smethurst, *Dramatic Representations of Filial Piety: Five Noh in Translation*
98 Ross King, ed., *Description and Explanation in Korean Linguistics*
99 William Wilson, *Hōgen Monogatari: Tale of the Disorder in Hōgen*
100 Yasushi Yamanouchi, J. V. Koschmann & Ryūichi Narita, eds., *Total War & 'Modernization'*
101 Yi Ch'ŏng-jun, *The Prophet and Other Stories,* tr. Julie Pickering
102 S.A. Thornton, *Charisma & Community Formation in Medieval Japan*
103 S. Cochran, ed., *Inventing Nanjing Road: Commercial Culture in Shanghai, 1900-1945*
104 H. Tanner, *Strike Hard! Anti-Crime Campaigns & Chinese Criminal Justice, 1979-1985*
105 Br. Anthony of Taizé & Young-Moo Kim, trs., *Farmers' Dance: Poems by Shin Kyŏng-nim*
106 S. O. Long, ed., *Lives in Motion: Composing Circles of Self & Community in Japan*
107 P. J. Katzenstein, Natasha Hamilton-Hart, Kozo Kato, & Ming Yue, *Asian Regionalism*
108 K. A. Grossberg, *Japan's Renaissance: The Politics of the Muromachi Bakufu*
109 John W. Hall & Toyoda Takeshi, eds., *Japan in the Muromachi Age*
110 Kim Su-Young, Shin Kyong-Nim, Lee Si-Young; *Variations: Three Korean Poets*
111 Samuel Leiter, *Frozen Moments: Writings on* Kabuki, *1966-2001*
112 Wang & Wang, *Early One Spring: A Learning Guide to Accompany the Film Video* February
113 T. Conlan, *In Little Need of Divine Intervention: Scrolls of the Mongol Invasions of Japan*
114 Jane Kate Leonard & Robert Antony, eds., *Dragons, Tigers, and Dogs: Qing Crisis Management and the Boundaries of State Power in Late Imperial China*
115 Shu-ning Sciban & F. Edwards, eds., *Dragonflies: Fiction by Chinese Women in the 20th Century*
116 D. G. Goodman, ed., *The Return of the Gods: Japanese Drama and Culture in the 1960s*
117 Yang Hi Choe-Wall, *Vision of a Phoenix: The Poems of Hŏ Nansŏrhŏn*
118 M. Smethurst & C. Laffin, eds., *The Noh* Ominameshi*: A Flower Viewed from Many Directions*
119 J. Murphy, *Metaphorical Circuit: Negotiations Between Literature & Science in 20th Century Japan*
120 Richard F. Calichman, *Takeuchi Yoshimi: Displacing the West*
121 *Visions for the Masses: Chinese Shadow Plays from Shaanxi & Shanxi,* by Fan Pen Li Chen
122 S. Yumiko Hulvey, *Sacred Rites in Moonlight: Ben no Naishi Nikki*
123 Tetsuo Najita & JV Koschmann, *Conflict in Modern Japanese History: The Neglected Tradition*
124 Naoki Sakai, Brett de Bary, & Iyotani Toshio, eds., *Deconstructing Nationality*
125 J. Rabinovitch & T. Bradstock, *Dance of the Butterflies: Chinese Poetry fm the Japanese Court Tradition*
126 Yang Gui-ja, *Contradictions,* trs. Stephen Epstein and Kim Mi-Young
127 Ann Sung-hi Lee, *Yi Kwang-su and Modern Korean Literature:* Mujŏng
128 Pang Kie-chung & M. D. Shin, eds., *Landlords, Peasants, & Intellectuals in Modern Korea*
129 Joan R. Piggott, ed., *Capital and Countryside in Japan, 300-1180: Japanese Historians Interpreted in English*
130 Kyoko Selden & Jolisa Gracewood, eds., *Annotated Japanese Literatary Texts* Vol. 1 Stories by Tawada Yōko, Nakagami Kenji, and Hayashi Kyōko

Order online: www.einaudi.cornell.edu/eastasia/CEASbooks, or contact Cornell East Asia Series Distribution Center, 95 Brown Road, Box 1004, Ithaca, NY 14850, USA; toll-free: 1-877-865-2432, fax 607-255-7534, ceas@cornell.edu

SB/4-06/0.5M pb/.2M hc

www.ingramcontent.com/pod-product-compliance
Ingram Content Group UK Ltd.
Pitfield, Milton Keynes, MK11 3LW, UK
UKHW041905060225
454777UK00001B/75

9 781885 445292